Cano

Introductory Statistics
for the Behavioral Sciences

Introductory Statistics for the Behavioral Sciences

Seventh Edition

Joan Welkowitz, Barry H. Cohen, R. Brooke Lea

JOHN WILEY & SONS, INC.

Library of Congress Cataloging-in-Publication Data:
Welkowitz, Joan.
   Introductory statistics for the behavioral sciences / Joan Welkowitz, Barry H. Cohen, R. Brooke Lea. — 7th ed.
     p. cm.
    Includes bibliographical references and index.
    ISBNs 978-0-470-90776-4; 978-1-118-14972-0; 978-1-118-14973-7; 978-1-118-14971-3
   1. Social sciences—Statistical methods. 2. Psychometrics. 3. Sociology—Statistical methods. 4. Educational statistics.
I. Cohen, Barry H. II. Lea, R. Brooke. III. Title.
   HA29.W445 2012
   519.5024′3—dc23

                                                2011029117

Printed in the United States of America
10 9 8 7 6 5 4 3 2 1

*This book is dedicated
to Lori, Michael, and Melissa;
to Emily and Jackson;
and to the memory of Joan Welkowitz,
our mentor and brilliant, much-loved friend.*

Contents

Preface   xv
Acknowledgments   xix
Glossary of Symbols   xxi

Part I   **Descriptive Statistics   1**

Chapter 1   **Introduction   3**
Why Study Statistics?   4
Descriptive and Inferential Statistics   5
Populations, Samples, Parameters, and Statistics   6
Measurement Scales   7
Independent and Dependent Variables   10
Summation Notation   12
Ihno's Study   16
Summary   18
Exercises   19
Thought Questions   23
Computer Exercises   23
Bridge to SPSS   24

Chapter 2   **Frequency Distributions and Graphs   26**
The Purpose of Descriptive Statistics   27
Regular Frequency Distributions   28
Cumulative Frequency Distributions   30
Grouped Frequency Distributions   31
Real and Apparent Limits   33
Interpreting a Raw Score   34
Definition of Percentile Rank and Percentile   34
Computational Procedures   35
Deciles, Quartiles, and the Median   38
Graphic Representations   39
Shapes of Frequency Distributions   43
Summary   45

Exercises   47
Thought Questions   49
Computer Exercises   49
Bridge to SPSS   50

Chapter 3   **Measures of Central Tendency and Variability   53**

Introduction   54
The Mode   56
The Median   56
The Mean   58
The Concept of Variability   62
The Range   65
The Standard Deviation and Variance   66
Summary   73
Exercises   75
Thought Questions   76
Computer Exercises   77
Bridge to SPSS   78

Chapter 4   **Standardized Scores and the Normal Distribution   81**

Interpreting a Raw Score Revisited   82
Rules for Changing μ and σ 84
Standard Scores (z Scores)   85
T Scores, SAT Scores, and IQ Scores   88
The Normal Distribution   90
Table of the Standard Normal Distribution   93
Illustrative Examples   95
Summary   101
Exercises   103
Thought Questions   105
Computer Exercises   106
Bridge to SPSS   106

Part II   **Basic Inferential Statistics   109**

Chapter 5   **Introduction to Statistical Inference   111**

Introduction   113
The Goals of Inferential Statistics   114
Sampling Distributions   114

The Standard Error of the Mean 119

The *z* Score for Sample Means 122

Null Hypothesis Testing 124

Assumptions Required by the Statistical Test for the Mean
    of a Single Population 132

Summary 133

Exercises 135

Thought Questions 137

Computer Exercises 138

Bridge to SPSS 138

Appendix: The Null Hypothesis Testing Controversy 139

Chapter 6 **The One-Sample *t* Test and Interval Estimation 142**

Introduction 143

The Statistical Test for the Mean of a Single Population When σ Is
    Not Known: The *t* Distributions 144

Interval Estimation 148

The Standard Error of a Proportion 152

Summary 155

Exercises 156

Thought Questions 157

Computer Exercises 158

Bridge to SPSS 158

Chapter 7 **Testing Hypotheses About the Difference Between
    the Means of Two Populations 160**

The Standard Error of the Difference 162

Estimating the Standard Error of the Difference 166

The *t* Test for Two Sample Means 167

Confidence Intervals for $\mu_1 - \mu_2$ 172

The Assumptions Underlying the Proper Use of the *t* Test for Two
    Sample Means 175

Measuring the Size of an Effect 176

The *t* Test for Matched Samples 178

Summary 185

Exercises 187

Thought Questions 190

Computer Exercises 191

Bridge to SPSS 191

Chapter 8   **Nonparametric Tests for the Difference Between Two Means 194**

Introduction 195

The Difference Between the Locations of Two Independent Samples: The Rank-Sum Test 199

The Difference Between the Locations of Two Matched Samples: The Wilcoxon Test 205

Summary 210

Exercises 212

Thought Questions 215

Computer Exercises 216

Bridge to SPSS 216

Chapter 9   **Linear Correlation 218**

Introduction 219

Describing the Linear Relationship Between Two Variables 222

Interpreting the Magnitude of a Pearson r 229

When Is It Important That Pearson's r Be Large? 234

Testing the Significance of the Correlation Coefficient 236

The Relationship Between Two Ranked Variables: The Spearman Rank-Order Correlation Coefficient 239

Summary 242

Exercises 244

Thought Questions 247

Computer Exercises 248

Bridge to SPSS 248

Appendix: Equivalence of the Various Formulas for r 251

Chapter 10   **Prediction and Linear Regression 253**

Introduction 254

Using Linear Regression to Make Predictions 254

Measuring Prediction Error: The Standard Error of Estimate 263

The Connection Between Correlation and the t Test 265

Estimating the Proportion of Variance Accounted for in the Population 271

Summary 273

Exercises 275

Thought Questions 277

Computer Exercises 277

Bridge to SPSS 278

Chapter 11   **Introduction to Power Analysis 281**

Introduction 282

Concepts of Power Analysis 283

The Significance Test of the Mean of a Single Population 285

The Significance Test of the Proportion of a Single Population 290

The Significance Test of a Pearson r 292

Testing the Difference Between Independent Means 293

Testing the Difference Between the Means of Two Matched Populations 297

Choosing a Value for **d** for a Power Analysis Involving Independent Means 299

Using Power Analysis Concepts to Interpret the Results of Null Hypothesis Tests 301

Summary 304

Exercises 306

Thought Questions 308

Computer Exercises 309

Bridge to SPSS 310

Part III   **Analysis of Variance Methods 313**

Chapter 12   **One-Way Analysis of Variance 315**

Introduction 317

The General Logic of ANOVA 318

Computational Procedures 321

Testing the F Ratio for Statistical Significance 326

Calculating the One-Way ANOVA From Means and Standard Deviations 328

Comparing the One-Way ANOVA With the t Test 329

A Simplified ANOVA Formula for Equal Sample Sizes 330

Effect Size for the One-Way ANOVA 331

Some Comments on the Use of ANOVA 333

A Nonparametric Alternative to the One-Way ANOVA: The Kruskal-Wallis H Test 336

Summary 339

Exercises 343

Thought Questions 346

Computer Exercises 346

Bridge to SPSS 346

Appendix: Proof That the Total Sum of Squares Is Equal to the Sum of the Between-Group and the Within-Group Sum of Squares 348

Chapter 13   **Multiple Comparisons 349**

Introduction 350

Fisher's Protected *t* Tests and the Least Significant Difference (LSD) 351

Tukey's Honestly Significant Difference (HSD) 355

Other Multiple Comparison Procedures 360

Planned and Complex Comparisons 362

Nonparametric Multiple Comparisons: The Protected Rank-Sum Test 365

Summary 366

Exercises 368

Thought Questions 369

Computer Exercises 370

Bridge to SPSS 370

Chapter 14   **Introduction to Factorial Design: Two-Way Analysis of Variance 372**

Introduction 373

Computational Procedures 374

The Meaning of Interaction 384

Following Up a Significant Interaction 387

Measuring Effect Size in a Factorial ANOVA 390

Summary 392

Exercises 395

Thought Questions 398

Computer Exercises 399

Bridge to SPSS 399

Chapter 15   **Repeated-Measures ANOVA 402**

Introduction 403

Calculating the One-Way RM ANOVA 403

Rationale for the RM ANOVA Error Term 408

Assumptions and Other Considerations Involving the RM ANOVA 408

The RM Versus RB Design: An Introduction to the Issues of Experimental Design 411

The Two-Way Mixed Design 415

Summary 423

Exercises 428

Thought Questions 430

Computer Exercises 430

Bridge to SPSS 431

Part IV — Nonparametric Statistics for Categorical Data 435

Chapter 16 — Probability of Discrete Events and the Binomial Distribution 437

Introduction 438
Probability 439
The Binomial Distribution 442
The Sign Test for Matched Samples 448
Summary 450
Exercises 451
Thought Questions 453
Computer Exercises 453
Bridge to SPSS 454

Chapter 17 — Chi-Square Tests 457

Chi Square and the Goodness of Fit: One-Variable Problems 458
Chi Square as a Test of Independence: Two-Variable Problems 464
Measures of Strength of Association in Two-Variable Tables 470
Summary 472
Exercises 474
Thought Questions 476
Computer Exercises 477
Bridge to SPSS 478

Appendix 481

Statistical Tables 483
Answers to Odd-Numbered Exercises 499
Data From Ihno's Experiment 511

Glossary of Terms 515
References 525
Index 527

Preface

It has been both a joy and a privilege to create this seventh edition of one of the longest-running statistics texts in the behavioral sciences. (This title has been in print continuously since 1971.) In doing so, we tried to maintain the original purpose of this text, as expressed in the preface to the second edition: to introduce and explain statistical concepts and principles clearly and in a highly readable fashion, assuming minimal mathematical sophistication, but avoiding a "cookbook" approach to methodology.

At the same time that we have endeavored to stay true to the original mission of this classic text, we have added a new co-author, Brooke Lea of Macalester College, and have revised and improved nearly all of our chapters, which included updating many of the examples and exercises. Naturally, we took this opportunity to correct any mistakes we and others had noticed from previous editions, and to add some explanatory sentences for the concepts that we know our students have struggled with in the past.

As with the sixth edition of this text, the supplementary materials of this edition will overlap with those for the third edition of Barry Cohen's graduate-level statistics text, *Explaining Psychological Statistics,* also published by John Wiley & Sons. In addition to visiting the Wiley Web site for this text, students and instructors are encouraged to explore the supplemental materials available on Barry Cohen's statistics Web page: www.psych.nyu.edu/cohen/statstext.html.

There are several structural changes in this edition that are worth noting, as described next.

1. Numbering of Key Formulas

All of the important formulas in the text have been given unique numbers (for example, the formulas in Chapter 3 are numbered 3.1, 3.2, etc.), making it much easier to refer to formulas earlier in the same chapter, as well as to formulas in previous chapters. This feature greatly facilitates one of our chief strategies for making statistics understandable—that is, to point out the connections between formulas that look quite different superficially, but nonetheless perform strikingly similar functions.

2. Consolidation of the Early Chapters

To reduce redundancy and to make room for some slightly more advanced material in later chapters, we consolidated the first eight chapters of the previous edition (i.e., Part I, Descriptive Statistics) into just four. We have dropped a few rarely used procedures (e.g., "mean-on-spoke" representations; linear interpolation formulas for percentiles), but retained all of the main computational examples from the previous edition. The added material for which we made room deals mostly with confidence intervals, measures of effect size, and follow-up tests for complex analyses. We also address, rather directly, the basis of the controversy over the nearly universal use of null hypothesis testing in the behavioral sciences.

3. Moving Ordinal Tests From the Last Chapter to the Middle of the Text

We became aware that a significant number of statistics instructors prefer to teach nonparametric alternative tests directly after the parametric tests to which they correspond. To facilitate this approach, we moved the bulk of the chapter on tests for ordinal data so that it now appears immediately after the chapter on two-group t tests. The ordinal tests corresponding to procedures described in later chapters were incorporated at the ends of those chapters. However, we feel that tests for categorical data do not have the close correspondence to parametric tests that ordinal tests do, so the chapter on the binomial distribution, and the chapter on chi-square tests remain at the end of the text.

4. Creation of Separate Correlation and Regression Chapters

The previous edition presented linear correlation and prediction in one large chapter and then followed it with a chapter about the connection between correlation and the t test. We have now given correlation and regression their own chapters and folded into the latter the connection these procedures have with the t test. (In line with the previous point, Spearman rank-order correlation has been added to the end of the correlation chapter.) The result is that we have been able to expand our coverage of important issues (e.g., when can a statistical correlation be used to infer a causal link?). We have also infused these chapters with new examples that help motivate the concepts.

5. Updating the Computer Exercises and SPSS Sections

We expanded Sarah's data set somewhat from the previous edition to create Ihno's data set for this edition and added computer exercises to many of the chapters. We also took this opportunity to update our Bridge to SPSS sections to reflect changes in the most recent versions of SPSS for Windows. (The version current during the writing of this edition is 19.0.)

In several chapters we have now included screen shots to illustrate the main SPSS dialog boxes commonly used by researchers to perform the analyses described in this text. In some cases we have also included results boxes from the output that SPSS produces for particular analyses, in order to draw connections between the terms used by SPSS to label its output and the corresponding (sometimes different) terms used in this text.

6. Advanced Chapter (18) on the Web

A number of reviewers of the previous edition of this text requested that we include at least one chapter devoted to more advanced statistical methods, such as ANCOVA, MANOVA, and factor analysis. They did not want to see detailed computations of these advanced procedures, but rather a series of consumer-friendly descriptions of these techniques that could help students to gain a clearer understanding of the results of such methods, as published in the empirical journals they are likely to encounter in advanced psychology courses, when engaged in literature reviews, or when assisting professors with their research. In answer to these requests, we will be posting Chapter 18 of this edition on the Web. Please see www.psych.nyu.edu/cohen/statstext.html for further details.

7. New Ancillaries

We have added a companion site on the Wiley Web site just for students, which can be found at: www.wiley.com/go/welkowitz
  The student Web site includes the following items:

- **Basic Math Review:** A review of all the basic math operations you will need to know to perform the statistical exercises in this text. Includes numerous exercises and quizzes with answers.
- **Study Guide:** A lively chapter-by-chapter review of the text with additional exercises and answers. Created by graduate students who recently served as teaching assistants for statistics, it provides another perspective on the material presented in this text.

We have also completely updated the Wiley instructor companion site for the seventh edition, which can also be found at: www.wiley.com/go/welkowitz
  The instructor Web site includes the following items:

- **Instructor's Manual:** Step-by-step answers to all of the computational exercises in the text.
- **Test Bank:** Multiple choice questions, both conceptual and computational, that can be used to create quizzes to assess the students' mastery of each chapter in the seventh edition.

- **Power Point Slides:** Expanded and updated for this new edition, these slides provide convenient summaries of the important points of each chapter, and can help instructors to organize their lectures around the key concepts for each statistical topic.

Barry H. Cohen
R. Brooke Lea

Acknowledgments

Thanks are due to our many encouraging friends and relatives, to all of the colleagues and reviewers who made many useful comments on previous editions, and especially to five new reviewers, all of whom gave us helpful reviews of the sixth edition and suggestions for this latest edition: Danica Hays, PhD, Old Dominion University; Faith-Anne Dohm, PhD, Fairfield University; James Sexton, PhD, Argosy University, Washington DC; Litze Hu, PhD, University of Santa Cruz; and Tai Chang, PhD, California School of Professional Psychology. Once again, we want to take this opportunity to thank our many students who, throughout the years, have provided invaluable feedback on our teaching of statistics, as well as on earlier editions of this text and its accompanying workbook. Special thanks go to recent survivors of the "RIP" sequence at Macalester College for their trenchant suggestions for improving the text.

This latest edition surely owes its very existence to Patricia Rossi (Executive Editor) at John Wiley & Sons, whose constant support and prodding have ensured that this text will now begin its 40th year in continuous print. Along the way, Ms. Rossi's efforts on our behalf have been ably aided by several highly competent editorial assistants, as well as more senior staff at Wiley; most recently, Kara Borbely (Editorial Program Coordinator) and Kate Lindsay (Senior Production Editor) have been enormously helpful in getting this edition into print and its ancillaries on the Web. We are also grateful to those responsible for the attractive look and design of this text—especially, Rose Sullivan, Senior Production Manager.

Finally, we are happy to acknowledge a debt of gratitude to Ihno Lee for revising the data set (now named after her) that we use for the computer exercises, as well as for correcting several errors in the previous edition, and to Grace Jackson and Samantha Gaies, who created a lively and engaging new study guide (available on the Student Companion Web site for this text), which we feel certain will be much appreciated by both the adopters and readers of this text. We also appreciate the careful and accurate help provided by Emily Haselby and Melissa Lazarus in preparing the Instructor's Manual.

Barry H. Cohen
R. Brooke Lea

Postscript

I cannot close this Acknowledgments section without sadly paying homage to the two departed professors, who, along with a colleague now living in Florida, wrote and edited the original text and kept it fresh and alive over the course of several decades. I had the pleasure of working closely with the senior author, Dr. Joan Welkowitz, on the previous edition of this text, and it is not possible to overestimate the continued influence of both her and her former co-author and friend, Jacob Cohen, on this text and on my approach to the teaching of statistics. (No, to my knowledge, I am not genetically related to Jack Cohen.) The one living author of the original text, Robert Ewen, wrote nearly all of the exercises and thought questions you see in this edition. Though many of the exercises and examples in the text have been updated, Dr. Ewen's careful craftsmanship and editorial skills are still visible in this edition.

Finally, I was delighted to keep the close connection between this text and New York University alive by adding Dr. Brooke Lea as a co-author of the present edition. Brooke received his doctorate in experimental psychology at NYU while Joan Welkowitz and Jack Cohen were still teaching there. Brooke was a student in one of the first statistics classes I taught at NYU, was later my teaching assistant for the same course, and turned out to be instrumental in getting me to write my first text, *Explaining Psychological Statistics*. Moreover, Brooke and I co-authored a statistics manuscript at NYU (playfully titled "The Joy of Stats"), which was later reworked and published in 2004 by John Wiley & Sons as *Essentials of Statistics for the Social and Behavioral Sciences*. The joy is still there. Thanks, Brooke!

Barry H. Cohen

Glossary of Symbols

Numbers in parentheses indicate the chapter in which the symbol first appears.

a_{YX}	Y-intercept of linear regression line for predicting Y from X (10)
α	criterion (or level) of significance; probability of Type I error (5)
α_{EW}	experiment-wise alpha (13)
α_{FW}	family-wise alpha (14)
α_{pc}	alpha per comparison (13)
b_{YX}	slope of the linear regression line for predicting Y from X (10)
β	probability of Type II error (5)
$1 - \beta$	power (11)
cf	cumulative frequency (2)
χ^2	statistic following the chi square distribution (12)
D	difference between two scores (7)
$\overline{D}$	mean of the Ds (7)
$\mathbf{d}$	effect size involving two populations (11)
df	degrees of freedom (6)
df_{Bet}	degrees of freedom between groups (12)
df_{W}	degrees of freedom within groups (12)
df_1	degrees of freedom for factor 1 (14)
df_2	degrees of freedom for factor 2 (14)
$df_{1 \times 2}$	degrees of freedom for interaction (14)
δ	delta (11)
η^2	eta squared; effect size in multiple samples (12)
$\mathbf{f}$	effect size involving multiple populations (12)
f	frequency (2)
f_{e}	expected frequency (17)
f_{o}	observed frequency (17)
F	statistic following the F distribution (12)
g	effect size involving two samples (7)
H	statistic for the Kruskal–Wallis test (12)
H_0	null hypothesis (5)
H_A	alternative hypothesis (5)
HSD	Tukey's Honestly Significant Difference (13)

i	case number (1)
k	a constant (1)
k	number of groups (12)
LSD	Fisher's Least Significant Difference (13)
Mdn	median (3)
MS	mean square (12)
MS_{Bet}	mean square between groups (12)
MS_W	mean square within groups (12)
MS_1	mean square for factor 1 (14)
MS_2	mean square for factor 2 (14)
$MS_{1\times2}$	mean square for interaction (14)
μ	population mean (3)
n	number of observations in one of two or more equal-sized samples (7)
N_T	total number of subjects or observations (1)
N_i	number of observations or subjects in group i (12)
ω^2	omega squared; proportion of variance accounted for in a population (10)
π	hypothetical population proportion (6)
p	probability of attaining results as extreme as yours when the null hypothesis is true (5)
P	observed sample proportion (6)
$P(A)$	probability of event A (16)
PR	percentile rank (2)
ϕ	phi coefficient (17)
ϕ_C	Cramér's ϕ (17)
q	studentized range statistic (13)
r_C	matched pairs rank biserial correlation coefficient (8)
r_G	Glass rank biserial correlation coefficient (8)
r_{pb}	point-biserial correlation coefficient (10)
r_s	Spearman rank-order correlation coefficient (9)
r_{XY}	sample Pearson correlation coefficient between X and Y (9)
$\overline{R}$	mean of a set of ranks (8)
ρ_{XY}	population correlation coefficient between X and Y (9)
s	sample standard deviation (5)
s^2	population variance estimate (5)
s_D^2	variance of the Ds (7)
s_{pooled}^2	pooled variance (7)
$s_{\overline{X}}$	standard error of the mean (6)

$s_{\overline{X}_1-\overline{X}_2}$	standard error of the difference (7)
s_{est}	estimate of σ_y' obtained from a sample (10)
SIQR	semi-interquartile range (3)
SS	sum of squares (3)
SS_T	total sum of squares (12)
SS_{Bet}	sum of squares between groups (12)
SS_W	sum of squares within groups (12)
SS_1	sum of squares for factor 1 (14)
SS_2	sum of squares for factor 2 (14)
$SS_{1\times2}$	sum of squares for interaction (14)
$\sum$	summation sign (1)
σ	population standard deviation (3)
σ^2	population variance (3)
σ_p	standard error of a sample proportion (6)
σ_T	standard error of the ranks of independent samples (8)
σ_{T_M}	standard error of the ranks of matched samples (8)
$\sigma_{\overline{X}}$	standard error of the mean when σ is known (5)
σ_{est}	standard error of estimate for predicting Y (10)
t	statistic following the t distribution (6)
T	T score (4)
T_E	expected sum of the ranks (8)
T_i	sum of ranks in group i (8)
X'	predicted X score (10)
$\overline{X}$	sample mean (3)
$\overline{X}_i$	mean of group i (12)
$\overline{X}_G$	grand mean (12)
Y'	predicted Y score (10)
z	standard score (4)

Introductory Statistics
for the Behavioral Sciences

Part I
Descriptive Statistics

Chapter 1   Introduction

Chapter 2   Frequency Distributions and Graphs

Chapter 3   Measures of Central Tendency and Variability

Chapter 4   Standardized Scores and the Normal Distribution

Chapter 1
Introduction

PREVIEW

Why Study Statistics?

What are four important reasons why knowledge of statistics is essential for anyone majoring in psychology, sociology, or education?

Descriptive and Inferential Statistics

What is the difference between descriptive and inferential statistics?

Why must behavioral science researchers use inferential statistics?

Populations, Samples, Parameters, and Statistics

What is the difference between a population and a sample?

Why is it important to specify clearly the population from which a sample is drawn?

What is the difference between a parameter and a statistic?

Measurement Scales

What types of scales are used to measure variables in the behavioral sciences?

Independent and Dependent Variables

What is the difference between observational and experimental studies?

Summation Notation

Why is summation notation used by statisticians?

What are the eight rules involving summation notation?

Ihno's Study

An example that provides a common thread tying together all of the subsequent chapters

Summary

Exercises

Thought Questions

(continued)

PREVIEW (*continued*)

Computer Exercises

Bridge to SPSS

Why Study Statistics?

This book is written primarily for undergraduates majoring in psychology, or one of the other behavioral sciences. There are four reasons why a knowledge of statistics is essential for those who wish to conduct or consume behavioral science research:

1. *To understand the professional literature.* Most professional literature in the behavioral sciences includes results that are based on statistical analyses. Therefore, you will be unable to understand important articles in scientific journals and books unless you understand statistics. It is possible to seek out secondhand reports that are designed for the statistically uninformed, but those who prefer this alternative to obtaining firsthand information probably should not be majoring in the fields of behavioral science.

2. *To understand and evaluate statistical claims made in the popular media.* This is a relatively new reason to acquire quantitative reasoning skills: The "Information Age" of the early 21st century has ushered in an explosion of quantitative claims in newspapers, television, and the Internet. Unfortunately, the difference between claims that are statistically sound and those that merely appear that way can be difficult to detect without some formal training. You will make many important life decisions over the next decade that will require weighing probabilities under conditions of uncertainty. A competence with basic statistics will empower you to make maximal use of the available information and help protect you from those who may wish to mislead you with pretty graphs and numbers.

3. *To understand the rationale underlying research in the behavioral sciences.* Statistics is not just a catalog of procedures and formulas. It offers the rationale on which much of behavioral science research is based—namely, drawing inferences about a population based on data obtained from a sample. Those familiar with statistics understand that research consists of a series of educated guesses and fallible decisions, not right or wrong answers. Those without a knowledge of statistics, by contrast, cannot understand the strengths and weaknesses of the techniques used by behavioral scientists to collect information and draw conclusions.

4. *To carry out behavioral science research.* In order to contribute competent research to the behavioral sciences, it is necessary to design

the statistical analysis *before* the data are collected. Otherwise, the research procedures may be so poorly planned that not even an expert statistician can make any sense out of the results. To be sure, it is possible (and often advisable) to consult someone more experienced in statistics for assistance. Without some statistical knowledge of your own, however, you will find it difficult or impossible to convey your needs to someone else and to understand the replies.

Save for these introductory remarks, we do not regard it as our task to persuade you that statistics is important in psychology and other behavioral sciences. If you are seriously interested in any of these fields, you will find this out for yourself. Accordingly, this book does not rely on documented examples selected from the professional literature to prove to you that statistics really is used in these fields. Instead, we have devised several artificial, but realistic, examples with numerical values that reveal the processes and issues involved in statistical analyses as clearly as possible.

One example we use throughout this text is based on a hypothetical study performed by a new student named Carrie on the relative friendliness of four dormitory halls on her campus. We present the data for this study in the first exercise at the end of this chapter and return to it in many of the subsequent chapters.

We have tried to avoid a "cookbook" approach that places excessive emphasis on computational recipes. Instead, the various statistical procedures and the essential underlying concepts have been explained at length, and insofar as possible in standard English, so that you will know not only what to do but *why* you are doing it. Do not, however, expect to learn the material in this book from a single reading; the concepts involved in statistics, especially inferential statistics, are sufficiently challenging that it is often said that the only way to completely understand the material is to teach it (or write a book about it). Having said that, however, there is no reason to approach statistics with fear and trembling. You certainly do not need any advanced understanding of mathematics to obtain a good working knowledge of basic statistics. What *is* needed is mathematical comprehension sufficient to cope with beginning high school algebra and a willingness to work at new concepts until they are understood, which requires, in turn, a willingness to spend some time working through at least half of the exercises at the end of each chapter (and, perhaps, some additional exercises from the online Study Guide).

Descriptive and Inferential Statistics

One purpose of statistics is to summarize or describe the characteristics of a set of data in a clear and convenient fashion. This is accomplished by what are called **descriptive statistics**. For example, your grade point average serves as a convenient summary of all of the grades that you have received in college. Part I of this book is devoted to descriptive statistics.

A second function of statistics is to make possible the solution of an extremely important problem. Behavioral scientists can never measure *all* of the cases in which they are interested. For example, a clinical psychologist studying the effects of various kinds of therapies cannot obtain data on every single mental health patient in the world; a social psychologist studying gender differences in attitudes cannot measure all of the millions of men and women in the United States; a cognitive psychologist cannot observe the reading behavior of all literate adults. Behavioral scientists want to know what is happening in a given **population**—a large group (theoretically an infinitely large group) of people, animals, objects, or responses that are alike in at least one respect (e.g., all women in the United States). They cannot measure the entire population, however, because it is so large that it would be much too time-consuming and expensive to do so. What to do?

Turns out there's a reasonably simple solution: Measure just a relatively small number of cases drawn from the population (i.e., a **sample**), and use inferential statistics to make educated guesses about the population. **Inferential statistics** makes it possible to draw inferences about what is happening in the population based on what is observed in a sample from that population. (This point is discussed at greater length in Chapter 5.) The subsequent parts of this book are devoted to inferential statistics, which makes frequent use of some of the descriptive statistics discussed in Part I.

Populations, Samples, Parameters, and Statistics

As the above discussion indicates, the term **population** as used in statistics does not necessarily refer to people. For example, the population of interest may be that of all white rats of a given genetic strain or all responses of a single subject's eyelid in a conditioning experiment.

Whereas the population consists of all of the cases of interest, a **sample** consists of any subgroup drawn from the specified population. It is important that the population be clearly specified. For example, a group of 100 Macalester College freshmen might be a well-drawn sample from the population of all Macalester freshmen or a poorly drawn sample from the population of all undergraduates in the United States (poorly drawn because it probably will not be representative of all U.S. undergraduates). It is strictly proper to apply (i.e., *generalize*) the research results only to the specified population from which the sample was drawn. (A researcher *may* justifiably argue that her results are more widely generalizable, but she is on her own if she does so, because the rules of statistical inference do not justify this.)

A **statistic** is a numerical quantity (such as an average) that summarizes some characteristic of a sample. A **parameter** is the corresponding value of that characteristic in the population. For example, if the average studying time of a sample of 100 New York University freshmen is 7.4 hours per week, then 7.4 is a statistic. If the average studying time of the population of all NYU freshmen is 9.6 hours per week, then 9.6 is the corresponding population parameter. Usually the values of population parameters are unknown because the population is too large to measure in its entirety, and appropriate techniques of inferential statistics are therefore used to estimate the values of population parameters from sample statistics. If the sample is properly selected, the sample statistics will often give good estimates of the parameters of the population from which the sample was drawn; if the sample is poorly chosen, erroneous conclusions are likely to occur. Whether you are doing your own research or reading about that of someone else, you should always check to be sure that the population to which the results are generalized is proper in light of the sample from which the results were obtained.

Measurement Scales

- nominal scales
- ordinal
- interval / ratio

You may have noticed that we have used the term *data* several times without talking about where the data come from. It should come as no surprise that in the behavioral sciences, the data generally come from measuring some aspect of the behavior of a human or animal. Unlike physics, in which there are quite a few important **constants** (values that are always the same, such as the speed of light or the mass of an electron), the behavioral sciences deal mainly with the measurement of **variables**, which can take on a range of different values. An additional complication faced by the behavioral scientist is that some of the variables of most interest are difficult to measure (e.g., anxiety). In this section we discuss the measurement scales most commonly used in the behavioral sciences. It is important to know which scale you are using because that choice often determines which statistical technique is appropriate. The scales differ with respect to how finely they can distinguish differences among instances. For example, the nominal scale can only distinguish whether an item is in one category or another, but the categories have no inherent order (e.g., the color of your iPhone). The ordinal scale involves measurements that can distinguish order on a set of values (e.g., bigger, smaller). Interval scales add the capability to measure quantities on a scale that have equal intervals between units (e.g., inches; temperature), and ratio scales are interval scales for which a value of zero means that *absolutely none* of the variable being measured is present. We describe them below in order of complexity.

Nominal Scales

The crudest form of measurement is to classify items by assigning names to them (categorization), which does not involve any numerical precision at all. Such a scale is called a **nominal scale**. For example, a person's occupation can only be "measured" on a nominal scale (e.g., accountant, lawyer, carpenter, sales clerk). We can count the number of people who fall into each category, but (unlike ordinal, interval, or ratio scales) there is no obvious order to the categories, and certainly no regular intervals between them. We refer to such categorical data as being **qualitative**, as distinguished from data measured on one of the **quantitative** scales described next.

Ordinal Scales

Sometimes it is possible to order your categories, even though the intervals are not precise. The most common example of this in psychological research is called a Likert scale (after its creator, Rensis Likert), on which respondents rate their agreement with some statement by choosing, for instance, among "strongly agree," "agree," "uncertain," "disagree," and "strongly disagree." The order of the categories is clear, but because there is no way to be sure that they are equally spaced (is the psychological distance between "strongly agree" and "agree" the same as between "agree" and "uncertain"?), this type of scale lacks the interval property and is therefore called an **ordinal scale**. Although it is a somewhat controversial practice, many behavioral researchers simply assign numbers to the categories (e.g., strongly agree is 1, agree is 2, etc.) and then treat the data as though they came from an interval scale.

Another, less common, way that an ordinal scale can be created is by rank ordering. It may not be possible to measure, in a precise way, the creativity of paintings produced by students in an art class, but a panel of judges could rank them from most to least creative, with perhaps a few paintings tied at the same rank.

It is important to distinguish between the *characteristics of the variable* we are measuring, on one hand, and the particular *scale with which we choose to measure that variable*, on the other. For example, suppose a teacher wishes to measure how often middle school students raise their hands in class. Hand-raising frequency is a variable that can be measured quantitatively by just counting how often each student raises a hand. However, when the teacher uses these data to understand hand-raising behavior in his class, his purposes may be best served by organizing the students into three broad, but ordinal, groups: (1) those who never raised their hand (most of the group); (2) those who did so just a few times; and (3) those who did so many times. In that case, he will want to create an ordinal scale to present data that was originally measured on an interval scale (described next). In other words, just because you are using a variable that has the *potential* to be measured on a particular scale does not necessarily mean that the data you collect will possess or display the characteristics of that scale. Sometimes researchers have quantitative measurements that vary in such an odd way that it becomes more useful just to rank them all and use the ranks in place of the original measurements. We explain this somewhat unusual practice when we describe statistical tests based on ordinal data in Chapter 8.

Interval/Ratio Scales

The most precise scales are the kinds that are used for physical measurement. For instance, the temperature of the skin at your fingertips can be related to the amount of stress that you experience (high stress can cause the constriction of peripheral blood vessels, resulting in a decrease in skin temperature). Using either the Fahrenheit or Celsius temperature scale allows a precise measurement of skin temperature. Because degrees on either scale are fixed units that are always the same size, you can be sure that the interval between, say, 32 and 33 degrees Celsius is exactly the same as the interval between 18 and 19 degrees Celsius. These two temperature scales are therefore called *interval scales*. Another desirable property that scales may have is the ratio property, which requires that the scale have a true zero point, that is, a measurement of zero on the scale indicates that there is really nothing left of what is being measured. For example, a measurement of zero pounds indicates the total absence of weight. If the scale has a true zero point in addition to the interval property, a measurement of 6 units, for instance, will actually indicate twice as much of what is being measured as compared to only 3 units. Thus, it is appropriate to call these scales *ratio scales*. A measurement of zero degrees on the Kelvin temperature scale means that there is no temperature at all (i.e., absolute zero), which is not the case for the Fahrenheit or Celsius scales. Therefore, Kelvin is a ratio scale, whereas the other two are just interval scales (zero degrees Celsius, e.g., does not indicate the complete absence of temperature—it just means that water will freeze into ice).

It is only the interval property that is needed for precise measurement, so for our purposes it is common to make no distinction between interval and ratio scales, referring instead to interval/ratio data, or simply *quantitative data*, as opposed to qualitative data. It's worth noting that the quantitative/qualitative distinction may best be thought of as a dimension on which the clearest cases are at the extremes, with fuzzier cases falling toward the middle. For example, when members of one category can be distinguished from members of another based only on *qualitative features of the items* (e.g., shape or color), not on the quantity of such features, then you have categorical (nominal) data; it makes sense that data of this sort are called *qualitative.* By contrast, variables that assign values based on the *quantity of the variable measured* (e.g., weight, length), rather than the type measured, are reasonably called *quantitative.* But what if you have ranked paintings on the basis of creativity, as in the example from the section on ordinal variables above? Is the difference in creativity between the #1 ranked painting and the #2 ranked painting only qualitative (one painting is in a different category of creativity from the other), or quantitative (one exhibits more creativity than the other)? It may not be clear. Arguably both qualitative *and* quantitative differences create the separation between the two paintings. What about survey data based on participants' answers to questions on a 10-point scale? As we stated earlier, social scientists often behave as though these data possess interval-scale properties and therefore analyze them quantitatively. So, are ordinal data qualitative, quantitative, or both? As our examples illustrate, the quantitative/qualitative distinction may not be as useful for characterizing ordinal data as it is for categorical and interval/ratio data. In any case, in this text, we describe specific methods for dealing with ordinal data, and at some point you can decide for yourself when to treat your ordinal data as though it came from an interval or ratio scale (looking, of course, at what your colleagues are doing with similar data).

Independent and Dependent Variables

Most behavioral research can be classified into one of two categories: **observational** or **experimental**.

In the simplest experiment, a researcher creates two conditions. The participants assigned to one of the conditions get some form of treatment, such as a pill intended to reduce depression. Those assigned to the other condition get something that superficially resembles the treatment, such as a pill that is totally ineffective (i.e., a placebo); they are part of a control group. These two conditions are the two different levels of an **independent variable**, or one that is created by the experimenter. Commonly, an independent variable is one whose levels are qualitative (e.g., a pill that contains medicine versus a placebo that does not). The **dependent variable**, or the variable that is measured by the experimenter and is expected to change from one level of the independent variable to another, is usually quantitative (such as a self-rating of depression). We will begin to describe such experiments in Part II of this text, when we turn to inferential statistics.

True independent variables are under the control of the experimenter, as in the example above. **Quasi-independent variables** are those that are *not* under the control of the experimenter. Quasi-independent variables are also referred to as subject variables, selected variables, or grouping variables. An obvious example is gender. An experimenter cannot (ethically) randomly assign some participants to be in the "male" group and others to be in the "female" group. The experimenter just *selects* participants who have already identified themselves as male or female to be in her study. Other examples of quasi-independent variables are religion, marital status, and age. In these cases, the experimenter cannot decide whether you will be Lutheran or Jewish or whether you will be single or married; participants' group memberships have already been determined before they arrive at the study.

Why does it matter whether an independent variable is "true" or "quasi"? Inferences concerning causality depend on this distinction. True independent variables allow experimenters to draw a causal link between the independent variable and the dependent variable (assuming the rest of the experiment was conducted properly). Establishing causality is important to progress in science. In the hypothetical antidepressant experiment described previously, the researcher can establish whether the active ingredient in the pill really *caused* people to become less depressed. With a quasi-independent variable, such causal conclusions cannot be made (e.g., if married people are less depressed, is it because being married is causing a reduction in depression, or because those who are less depressed are more likely to get married?).

Some independent variables can be truly experimental or quasi-experimental depending on the design of the study. For example, suppose you wanted to know whether exercising leads to better health (as measured by number of sick days taken at work). You could ask a sample of workers about their exercise habits and number of sick days over a 6-month period. If the data reveal that those who exercise the most have the fewest sick days, the researcher is *not* entitled to draw a causal relationship between the two. In this example, exercise habit is a subject variable; the experimenter did not manipulate how many hours per week each person spends in the gym. That lack of control leaves open other possible explanations. Maybe the causal arrow points the other way and people who are healthy tend to (and are able to) work out more. Perhaps some third variable like optimism drives both health and exercise. You just cannot be sure which conclusion is correct.

Now imagine that the researcher had assigned people at random to work out 0, 5, 10, or 15 hours per week at a gym and that after 6 months she got the same inverse association between hours spent exercising and number of sick days. In this situation, the researcher *can* claim that exercise causes fewer sick days. Other possibilities such as those mentioned earlier have been controlled for. Optimism cannot explain the results because random assignment would have distributed the optimistic people evenly among the four workout groups. Note also that true experiments are usually more difficult to conduct compared to quasi-experimental versions of the same studies. Therefore, a trade-off often exists between effort and expense, on one hand, and the sort of conclusions that can be drawn, on the other. In fact, behavioral researchers often study the relationships among variables that are not convenient, or even possible, to ever manipulate. If one simply measures the relationship between two dependent variables (e.g., self-esteem in teenagers and their family's annual income to see if those from more affluent families tend to have higher—or lower—self-esteem), this is an observational (i.e., quasi-experimental) study.

Methods for dealing with studies in which both the independent and dependent variables (or two dependent variables) are quantitative will be presented in Chapter 9. Research in which both variables being related are qualitative will be discussed in the last chapter of this text. Simple studies, in which one variable has only one or two qualitative levels, while the other is continuous and therefore has many (theoretically, infinite) possible levels, will be analyzed in Chapters 6 and 7. For now, it is important to begin developing the tools you will need to work with quantitative data. One of the most basic of such tools is the summation procedure, to which we turn next.

Summation Notation

Mathematical formulas and symbols can appear forbidding, if you're not used to working with them. Once you get to know them, however, you see that they actually simplify matters. They are just convenient ways to clearly and concisely convey information that would be much more awkward to express in words, much in the same way that "LOL" and "OMG" simplify expression in email and text messages. In statistics, a particularly important symbol is the one used to represent the *sum* of a set of numbers—that is, the value obtained by adding up all of the numbers.

To illustrate the use of summation notation, let us suppose that eight students take a 10-point quiz. Letting X stand for the variables in question (quiz scores), let us further suppose that the results are as follows:

$$X_1 = 7 \quad X_2 = 9 \quad X_3 = 6 \quad X_4 = 10$$
$$X_5 = 6 \quad X_6 = 5 \quad X_7 = 3 \quad X_8 = X_N = 4$$

Notice that X_1 represents the score of the first student on X; X_2 stands for the score of the second student; and so on. Also, the *number of scores* is denoted by N; in this example, $N = 8$. The last score may be represented by either X_8 or X_N. The *sum of all the X scores* is represented by

$$\sum_{i=1}^{N} X_i$$

where $\sum$, the Greek capital letter sigma, stands for "the sum of" and is called the *summation sign*. The subscript below the summation sign indicates that the sum begins with the first score (X_i where $i = 1$), and the superscript above the summation sign indicates that the sum continues up to and including the last score (X_i where $i = N$ or, in this example, 8). Thus,

$$\sum_{i=1}^{N} X_i = X_1 + X_2 + X_3 + X_4 + X_5 + X_6 + X_7 + X_8$$
$$= 7 + 9 + 6 + 10 + 6 + 5 + 3 + 4$$
$$= 50$$

Most of the time, however, the sum of *all* the scores is needed in the statistical analysis. In such situations it is customary to omit the indices i and N from the notation, as follows:

$$\sum X = \text{sum of all the } X \text{ scores}$$

The absence of written indication as to where to begin and end the summation is taken to mean that all the X scores are to be summed.

Summation Rules

Certain rules involving summation notation will prove useful in subsequent chapters. But first, we'd like to flash back to junior high when you learned the order in which mathematical operations should be computed. Do you recall learning the order of operations, PEMDAS, together with a phrase to help you remember it like "Please Excuse My Dear Aunt Sally"? Or perhaps "Pandas Eat: Mustard on Dumplings, and Apples with Spice"? "PEMDAS" stands for "Parentheses, Exponents, Multiplication and Division, and Addition and Subtraction." It describes the order in which you should perform mathematical operations: Parentheses are taken care of before exponents, followed by multiplication and division (which are at the same rank), followed by addition and subtraction (also at the same rank). As you will see, these summation rules often involve operations beyond addition, so Please Excuse My Dear Aunt Sally. Let us suppose that the eight students previously mentioned take a second quiz, denoted by Y. The results of both quizzes can be summarized conveniently as follows:

Students (S)	Quiz 1 (X)	Quiz 2 (Y)
1	7	8
2	9	6
3	6	4
4	10	10
5	6	5
6	5	10
7	3	9
8	4	8

We have already seen that $\sum X = 50$. The sum of the scores on the second quiz is equal to

$$\sum Y = Y_1 + Y_2 + Y_3 + Y_4 + Y_5 + Y_6 + Y_7 + Y_8$$
$$= 8 + 6 + 4 + 10 + 5 + 10 + 9 + 8$$
$$= 60$$

The following rules are illustrated using the small set of data just shown, and you should verify each one carefully.

Rule 1. $\sum(X + Y) = \sum X + \sum Y$

Illustration	S	X	Y	$X + Y$
	1	7	8	15
	2	9	6	15
	3	6	4	10
	4	10	10	20
	5	6	5	11
	6	5	10	15
	7	3	9	12
	8	4	8	12
		$\sum X = 50$	$\sum Y = 60$	$\sum(X + Y) = 110$
			$\sum X + \sum Y = 110$	

If you remember your Aunt Sally, this rule should be intuitively obvious; the same total should be reached regardless of the order in which the scores are added.

Rule 2. $\sum(X - Y) = \sum X - \sum Y$

Illustration	S	X	Y	X − Y
	1	7	8	−1
	2	9	6	3
	3	6	4	2
	4	10	10	0
	5	6	5	1
	6	5	10	−5
	7	3	9	−6
	8	4	8	−4
		$\sum X = 50$	$\sum Y = 60$	$\sum(X - Y) = -10$
		$\sum X - \sum Y = -10$		

As with the first rule, it makes no difference whether you subtract first and then sum $\left[\sum(X - Y)\right]$ or obtain the sums of X and Y first and then subtract $\left(\sum X - \sum Y\right)$.

Unfortunately, matters are not so simple when multiplication and squaring are involved.

Rule 3. $\sum XY \neq \sum X \sum Y$

That is, first multiplying each X score by the corresponding Y score and then summing $\left(\sum XY\right)$ is *not* equal to summing the X scores $\left(\sum X\right)$ and summing the Y scores $\left(\sum Y\right)$ first and then multiplying once $\left(\sum X \sum Y\right)$.

Illustration	S	X	Y	XY
	1	7	8	56
	2	9	6	54
	3	6	4	24
	4	10	10	100
	5	6	5	30
	6	5	10	50
	7	3	9	27
	8	4	8	32
		$\sum X = 50$	$\sum Y = 60$	$\sum XY = 373$
		$\sum X \sum Y = (50)(60) = 3,000$		

Observe that $\sum XY = 373$, while $\sum X \sum Y = 3,000$.

Rule 4. $\sum X^2 \neq \left(\sum X\right)^2$

That is, first squaring all of the X values and then summing $\left(\sum X^2\right)$ is *not* equal to summing first and then squaring that single quantity, $\left[\left(\sum X\right)^2\right]$.

Illustration	S	X	X^2
	1	7	49
	2	9	81
	3	6	36
	4	10	100
	5	6	36
	6	5	25
	7	3	9
	8	4	16
		$\sum X = 50$	$\sum X^2 = 352$

$$\left(\sum X\right)^2 = (50)^2 = 2{,}500$$

Here, $\sum X^2 = 352$, while $\left(\sum X\right)^2 = 2{,}500$.

Rule 5. If k is a *constant* (a fixed numerical value), then

$$\sum k = Nk$$

Suppose that $k = 3$. Then,

Illustration	S	k
	1	3
	2	3
	3	3
	4	3
	5	3
	6	3
	7	3
	8	3
		$\sum k = 24$

$$Nk = (8)(3) = 24$$

Rule 6. If k is a constant,

$$\sum (X + k) = \sum X + Nk$$

Suppose that $k = 5$. Then,

Illustration	S	X	k	$X + k$
	1	7	5	12
	2	9	5	14
	3	6	5	11
	4	10	5	15
	5	6	5	11
	6	5	5	10
	7	3	5	8
	8	4	5	9
		$\sum X = 50$	$\sum k = Nk = 40$	$\sum (X + k) = 90$

$$\sum X + Nk = 50 + (8)(5) = 90$$

This rule follows directly from Rules 1 and 5.

Rule 7. If k is a constant,

$$\sum(X - k) = \sum X - Nk$$

The illustration of this rule is similar to that of Rule 6 and is left to the reader as an exercise.

Rule 8. If k is a constant,

$$\sum kX = k\sum X$$

Illustration	Suppose that $k = 2$. Then,			
	S	X	k	kX
	1	7	2	14
	2	9	2	18
	3	6	2	12
	4	10	2	20
	5	6	2	12
	6	5	2	10
	7	3	2	6
	8	4	2	8
		$\sum X = 50$		$\sum kX = 100$
		$k\sum X = (2)(50) = 100$		

Ihno's Study

The process of summation can be considered the "workhorse" of statistics; you will see it used in one form or another in all of the statistical procedures described later in this text. Specifically, the summation sign is an important part of most statistical formulas, and we think it is vital that you understand how statistical formulas work. Although we expect, and certainly hope, that all statistics students will eventually become proficient at performing statistical analyses by computer, we believe that there is important educational value in asking students to apply basic statistical formulas directly to small sets of numbers to see how the formulas work and to thus gain a greater conceptual understanding of the statistical results being generated by computer programs. At the same time, we want to help you become familiar with the use of statistical software, especially the statistical package known as SPSS, so to that end, we created a fairly large data set (100 participants and more than a dozen variables), which is included in a table in the appendix of this book and is also available in several electronic formats online. In addition to exercises at the end of each chapter, which ask the reader to apply the formulas of that chapter to small sets of data, we have also included a set of computer exercises in each chapter, and each of those exercises refers to the same large data set in the Appendix, which is described next.

The data in the Appendix comes from a hypothetical study performed by Ihno (pronounced "Eee-know"), an advanced doctoral student, who is the teaching assistant for several sections of a statistics course. The 100 participants are the students who were enrolled in Ihno's sections and who attended one of two review classes that she conducted each week as the teaching assistant (TA) for the course. (Of course, all of her students voluntarily signed proper informed consent forms, and her study was approved by the appropriate review board at her hypothetical school.) Her data were collected on two different days. On the first day of classes, the students who came to either Ihno's morning or afternoon review session filled in a brief background questionnaire on which they provided contact information, some qualitative data (gender, undergrad major, why they had enrolled in statistics, and whether they regularly drink coffee) and some quantitative data (number of math courses already completed, the score they received on a diagnostic math background quiz they were all required to take before registering for statistics, and a rating of their math phobia on a scale from 0 to 10).

The rest of Ihno's data were collected as part of an experiment that she conducted on one day in the middle of the semester. The combined results of the two class sessions on that day add up to a total of 100 students who participated in the experiment. (Due to late registration and other factors, not all of Ihno's students took the diagnostic math background quiz.) At the beginning of the experiment, Ihno explained how each student could take his or her own pulse. She then provided a one-minute interval during which they counted the number of beats and wrote down that number as their (baseline) heart rate in beats per minute (bpm). Then each student reported how many cups of coffee they had drunk since waking up that morning and filled out an anxiety questionnaire consisting of 10 items, each rated (0 to 4) on a 5-point Likert scale. The questionnaire items inquired about anxiety and how the student was feeling at the present time (e.g., "Would you say that you are now feeling tense and restless? Circle one: Not at all; Somewhat; Moderately; Quite a bit; Extremely"). Total scores could range from 0 to 40, and provided a measure of baseline anxiety.

Next, Ihno announced a pop quiz. She handed out a page containing 11 multiple-choice statistics questions on material covered during the preceding two weeks, and asked the students to keep this page face-down while taking and recording their (prequiz) pulse and filling out an anxiety questionnaire for a second time (i.e., prequiz). Then Ihno told the students they had 15 minutes to take the fairly difficult quiz. She also told them that the first 10 questions were worth 1 point each but that the 11th question was worth 3 points of extra credit. Ihno's experimental manipulation consisted of varying the difficulty of the 11th question. Twenty-five quizzes were distributed at each level of difficulty of the final question: easy, moderate, difficult, and impossible to solve. After the quizzes were collected at the end of the 15 minutes, Ihno asked the students to provide heart rate and anxiety data (postquiz) one more time. Finally, Ihno explained the experiment, adding that the 11th quiz question would not be scored and that, although the students would get back their quizzes with their score for the first 10 items, that score would not influence their grade for the statistics course. All of the data from Ihno's experiment is printed out in the Appendix at the end of this book.

The computer exercises in this text can be solved by any major statistical package, and because the data for Ihno's study is also available on the Web as both a tab-delimited text file and an Excel 2007 file (go to www.psych.nyu.edu/cohen/statstext.html), most packages will be able to read in the data directly from the electronic file. However, because SPSS is currently the most popular statistical package among behavioral researchers, we have also included Ihno's data as an SPSS file. More-over, Bridge to SPSS sections at the end of each chapter can give you further assistance with computer analysis, unless, of course, your statistics instructor has assigned different statistical software. However, note that our Bridge to SPSS sections are not meant to replace a basic guide to the SPSS program (one advantage of using such a popular package is that there are many good guides available at a variety of different levels and prices); they are designed to help you bridge the gaps between the labels SPSS uses to present results in its output files and the statistical terms and notation used in this text. The Bridge to SPSS sections also help to ensure that you will know how to use SPSS to solve the computer exercises in the corresponding chapters.

Summary

Descriptive statistics are used to summarize and make large quantities of data understandable. *Inferential statistics* are used to draw inferences about numerical quantities (called *parameters*) concerning *populations* based on numerical quantities (called *statistics*) obtained from *samples.* Some behavioral variables cannot be measured quantitatively (e.g., choice of religion) but can only be measured qualitatively using categories (e.g., Catholic, Jewish, Buddhist), which comprise a *nominal* scale. If the categories can be placed in order (e.g., the belts awarded for different levels of skill in the martial arts—black belt, brown belt, etc.), an *ordinal* scale has been created. If the scale involves precise measurement resulting in units of equal size, the data are considered to be *quantitative*, whether the scale has a true zero point (*ratio* scale) or not (*interval* scale). (Ordinal scales are often treated as quantitative in behavioral research; nominal scales always produce *qualitative* data.) Experiments involve measuring dependent variables that are expected to vary somewhat as a function of the different levels of one or more independent variables created by the researcher. *Observational* research involves comparing dependent variables to each other because no variables are being manipulated, nor are participants being assigned to experimental conditions.

The summation sign, $\sum$, is used to indicate "the sum of" and occurs frequently in statistical work. Remember that $\sum X$ is a shorthand version of

$$\sum_{i=1}^{N} X_i$$

(where N = number of subjects or cases).

Summation Rules:

1. $\sum(X + Y) = \sum X + \sum Y$
2. $\sum(X - Y) = \sum X - \sum Y$
3. $\sum XY$ (multiply first, then add) $\neq \sum X \sum Y$ (add first, then multiply)
4. $\sum X^2$ (square first, then add) $\neq (\sum X)^2$ (add first, then square)
5. If k is a constant, $\sum k = Nk$
6. $\sum(X + k) = \sum X + Nk$
7. $\sum(X - k) = \sum X - Nk$
8. $\sum kX = k \sum X$

Exercises

A first-year student from Oklahoma named Carrie is trying to decide which of four dormitories to list as her first choice. She wants to live in the dorm with the friendliest students, so she makes up a friendliness questionnaire, on which a score of 20 indicates the friendliest a student can be and zero, the least friendly. She manages to get 15 students each from two of the dorms to fill out her questionnaire, 10 from a third dorm, and 5 from a fourth. The individual friendliness scores are shown in Table 1.1. Exercise 1 in this chapter refers to the set of data just described. We will return to this data set several times in later chapters.

Table 1.1 **Hypothetical Scores on a 20-Point Friendliness Measure for Students From Four Different Dormitories at One Midwestern College**

Turck Hall ($N = 15$)	17	18	6	13	9
	17	11	16	5	15
	11	13	10	20	14
Kirk Hall ($N = 15$)	17	8	12	12	3
	12	7	14	1	11
	9	8	6	11	7
Dupre Hall ($N = 10$)	9	11	6	5	4
	9	10	4	5	7
Doty Hall ($N = 5$)	14	8	17	6	10

1. Compute the following (these values will not by themselves help Carrie to make a decision about the dormitories, but we will use these values as steps in future exercises to answer Carrie's concern):

    (a) For Turck Hall:

    $$\sum X = \underline{\quad} \quad \sum X^2 = \underline{\quad} \quad \left(\sum X\right)^2 = \underline{\quad}$$

    (b) For Kirk Hall:

    $$\sum X = \underline{\quad} \quad \sum X^2 = \underline{\quad} \quad \left(\sum X\right)^2 = \underline{\quad}$$

    (c) For Dupre Hall:

    $$\sum X = \underline{\quad} \quad \sum X^2 = \underline{\quad} \quad \left(\sum X\right)^2 = \underline{\quad}$$

    (d) For Doty Hall:

    $$\sum X = \underline{\quad} \quad \sum X^2 = \underline{\quad} \quad \left(\sum X\right)^2 = \underline{\quad}$$

2. Express the following words in symbols.

    (a) Add up all the scores on test X, then add up all the scores on test Y, and then add the two sums together.

    (b) Add up all the scores on test G. To this, add the following: the sum obtained by squaring all the scores on test P and then adding them up.

    (c) Square all the scores on test X. Add them up. From this, subtract 6 times the sum you get when you multiply each score on X by the corresponding score on Y and add them up. To this, add 4 times the quantity obtained by adding up all the scores on test X and squaring the result. To this, add twice the sum obtained by squaring each Y score and then adding them up. (Compare the amount of space needed to express this equation in words with the amount of space needed to express it in symbols. Do you see why summation notation is necessary?)

3. Five students are enrolled in an advanced course in psychology. Two quizzes are given early in the semester, each worth a total of 10 points. The results are as follows:

Student	Quiz 1 (X)	Quiz 2 (Y)
1	0	2
2	2	6
3	1	7
4	3	6
5	4	9

(a) Compute each of the following:

$$\sum X = \underline{\qquad}$$ $$(\sum X)^2 = \underline{\qquad}$$ $$\sum (X - Y) = \underline{\qquad}$$

$$\sum Y = \underline{\qquad}$$ $$(\sum Y)^2 = \underline{\qquad}$$ $$\sum X - \sum Y = \underline{\qquad}$$

$$\sum X^2 = \underline{\qquad}$$ $$\sum (X + Y) = \underline{\qquad}$$ $$\sum XY = \underline{\qquad}$$

$$\sum Y^2 = \underline{\qquad}$$ $$\sum X + \sum Y = \underline{\qquad}$$ $$\sum X \sum Y = \underline{\qquad}$$

(b) Using the results of part (a), show that each of the following rules listed in this chapter is true:

Rule 1: $\underline{\qquad} = \underline{\qquad}$

Rule 2: $\underline{\qquad} = \underline{\qquad}$

Rule 3: $\underline{\qquad} \neq \underline{\qquad}$

Rule 4: $\underline{\qquad} \neq \underline{\qquad}$ (X data)

$\underline{\qquad} \neq \underline{\qquad}$ (Y data)

(c) After some consideration, the instructor decides that Quiz 1 was excessively difficult and decides to add 4 points to each student's score. This can be represented in symbols by using k to stand for the constant amount in question, 4 points.

Using Rule 6, compute $\sum (X + k) = \underline{\qquad} + \underline{\qquad} = \underline{\qquad}$.
Compute $\sum X + k = \underline{\qquad} + \underline{\qquad} = \underline{\qquad}$. (Note that this result is different from the preceding one.)
Now add 4 points to each student's score on Quiz 1 and obtain the sum of these new scores.

(d) Had the instructor been particularly uncharitable, he might have decided that Quiz 2 was too easy and subtracted 3 points from each student's score on that quiz. Although this is a new problem, the letter k can again be used to represent the constant; here, $k = 3$.

Using Rule 7, compute $\sum (Y - k) = \underline{\qquad} - \underline{\qquad} = \underline{\qquad}$.
Compute $\sum Y - k = \underline{\qquad} - \underline{\qquad} = \underline{\qquad}$. (Note that this result is different from the preceding one.)
Now subtract 3 points from each student's score on Quiz 2 and obtain the sum of these new scores.

(e) Suppose that the instructor decides to double all of the original scores on Quiz 1.

Using Rule 8, compute $\sum kX = \underline{\qquad} \times \underline{\qquad} = \underline{\qquad}$.
Now double each student's score on Quiz 1 and obtain the sum of these new scores.

4. For each of the following (separate) sets of data, compute the values needed in order to fill in the answer spaces. Then answer the additional questions that follow.

Data set 1:

S	X	Y
1	1	2
2	3	5
3	1	0
4	0	1
5	2	3

$N = \underline{\qquad}$

$\sum X = \underline{\qquad}$

$\sum X^2 = \underline{\qquad}$

$(\sum X)^2 = \underline{\qquad}$

$\sum XY = \underline{\qquad}$

$\sum (X + Y) = \underline{\qquad}$

$\sum Y = \underline{\qquad}$

$\sum Y^2 = \underline{\qquad}$

$(\sum Y)^2 = \underline{\qquad}$

$\sum X \sum Y = \underline{\qquad}$

$\sum (X - Y) = \underline{\qquad}$

Data set 2:

S	X	Y
1	7.14	0
2	8.00	2.60
3	0	4.32
4	4.00	2.00
5	4.00	6.00
6	1.00	1.15
7	2.25	1.00
8	10.00	3.00

$N = \underline{\qquad}$

$\sum X = \underline{\qquad}$

$\sum X^2 = \underline{\qquad}$

$(\sum X)^2 = \underline{\qquad}$

$\sum XY = \underline{\qquad}$

$\sum (X + Y) = \underline{\qquad}$

$\sum Y = \underline{\qquad}$

$\sum Y^2 = \underline{\qquad}$

$(\sum Y)^2 = \underline{\qquad}$

$\sum X \sum Y = \underline{\qquad}$

$\sum (X - Y) = \underline{\qquad}$

	set 1	set 2
If every X score is multiplied by 3.2, what is the new $\sum X$ in each set?	_____	_____
If 7 is subtracted from every Y score, what is the new $\sum Y$ in each set?	_____	_____
If 1.8 is added to every X score, what is the new $\sum X$ in each set?	_____	_____
If every Y score is divided by 4, what is the new $\sum Y$ in each set?	_____	_____

(Hint: Use the appropriate summation rule in each case so as to make the calculations easier.)

5. Compute the values needed to fill in the blanks.

Data set 3:

S	X	Y
1	97	89
2	68	57
3	85	87
4	74	76
5	92	97
6	92	79
7	100	91
8	63	50
9	85	85
10	87	84
11	81	91
12	93	91
13	77	75
14	82	77

$N = \underline{\qquad}$

$\sum X = \underline{\qquad}$

$\sum X^2 = \underline{\qquad}$

$(\sum X)^2 = \underline{\qquad}$

$\sum XY = \underline{\qquad}$

$\sum (X + Y) = \underline{\qquad}$

$\sum Y = \underline{\qquad}$

$\sum Y^2 = \underline{\qquad}$

$(\sum Y)^2 = \underline{\qquad}$

$\sum X \sum Y = \underline{\qquad}$

$\sum (X - Y) = \underline{\qquad}$

Thought Questions

1. What is the difference between (a) a population and a sample? (b) a parameter and a statistic? (c) descriptive statistics and inferential statistics?

2. What is the difference between a constant and a variable?

3. What is the difference between a ratio scale and an interval scale?

4. What important property do interval scales have that ordinal and nominal scales do *not* have?

5. If we are classifying psychiatric patients as having one or another of five different psychological disorders—Major Depressive Disorder, Bipolar Disorder, Generalized Anxiety Disorder, Obsessive-Compulsive Disorder, and Phobic Disorder—what kind of measurement scale are we using?

6. A poll of sportswriters ranks the 25 best college football teams in the country, where #1 is the best team, #2 is the second best team, and so on. What kind of measurement scale is this?

7. What kind of measurement scales are used for each of the following variables in Ihno's study? (a) The gender of each student. (b) The undergraduate major of each student. (c) The number of math courses each student has already completed. (d) Score on math background quiz.

8. What is the difference between an independent variable and a dependent variable?

Computer Exercises

1. Read Ihno's data into your statistical software package. For those not using the Statistical Package for the Social Sciences (SPSS), we have provided the data in two convenient formats: a tab-delimited text file and an Excel spreadsheet (Microsoft Office 2007). For the convenience of SPSS users, we have also included the data as an SPSS.sav file, though your instructor may want you to know how to read text or Excel files into SPSS.

2. Label the values of the categorical (i.e., qualitative) variables according to the following codes: For gender, 1 = Female and 2 = Male; for undergrad major, 1 = Psychology, 2 = Pre-med, 3 = Biology, 4 = Sociology, and 5 = Economics. Your instructor may ask you to fill in missing-value codes for any data that are missing (e.g., blank cell in the Excel spreadsheet).

3. A good many statistical functions can be performed in Excel. As a first step, use the Sum function to add up the scores for each of the quantitative variables in the Excel file of Ihno's data.

4. Create a new variable that adds 10 points to everyone's math background quiz score. How does the sum of this variable compare to the

sum of the original variable? What general rule is being illustrated by this comparison?

5. Create a new variable that is 10 times the statistics quiz score. How does the sum of this variable compare to the sum of the original variable? What general rule is being illustrated by this comparison?

Bridge to SPSS

SPSS is certainly not the only statpack available, and your instructor may prefer to teach you how to use SAS, Minitab, *R*, or another statistical program. However, because SPSS is the most popular statistical software package in the social and behavioral sciences, and is particularly easy to learn for introductory statistics students, we provide this section after the computer exercises in each chapter. (This should help students translate the terminology used by SPSS into the language that we are using to describe the same topics in this text.) We also show you briefly how to obtain from SPSS the statistics discussed in the chapter, along with a few tricks and shortcuts. However, we understand that even though you may be using SPSS in your statistics course, you may not be using the latest version, which will probably be 20.0 by the time this text is printed. Therefore, we only describe aspects of SPSS that have not changed between version 14 and the latest version.

The rightmost column in SPSS's Variable View spreadsheet is labeled **Measure**, and it allows you to classify each of your variables as being measured by one of the following three types of scales: nominal, ordinal, or scale. The first two terms are used the same way by SPSS that we have defined them in this chapter. *Scale* is SPSS's term for interval/ratio data. In general, numerical data are set to **scale** by default, whereas string data—which contain letters instead of, or in addition to, numbers—are set to **nominal**. In practice, these scale designations are not important, because SPSS uses them only to determine the way some charts are displayed.

For simplicity, Ihno's data set is presented entirely in terms of numbers, even for the categorical variables of gender and undergrad major. To assign meaningful labels to the arbitrary numbers we have used to represent the different levels of the categorical variables, go down the Values column of Variable View until you reach the row for a categorical variable. Then click in the right side of that cell to open the Value Labels box. For gender, you would type **1** for Value, and then tab to Value Label, where you can type **female**. Click the **Add** button, and provide a label (male) for value **2**, then **Add** again, and **OK**. The process is similar for undergrad major. Note that if you use the Missing column to define a particular value of a variable, say 99, as meaning that the value is missing, rather than just leaving the cell blank (e.g., you could use 99 to mean "missing" for the math background quiz, because none of the real values can be that high), you can then attach a value label to that value, such as "never took the math quiz."

To create new variables that are based on ones already in your spreadsheet, which some of our computer exercises will ask you to do, click on the **Transform** menu, then **Compute**. In the Compute Variable box that opens up, Target Variable is a name that you make up (and type into that box) for the new variable (but no more than eight characters and no embedded spaces); when you have filled in a Numeric Expression and then click **OK**, the new variable will suddenly appear in the rightmost column of your Data View spreadsheet. We will leave it to your instructor, or an SPSS guidebook, to teach you various ways to create numeric expressions that transform your existing variables into new ones.

Chapter 2
Frequency Distributions and Graphs

PREVIEW

The Purpose of Descriptive Statistics

What is the primary purpose of descriptive statistics?

What are the most useful types of descriptive statistics?

Regular Frequency Distributions

What is a regular frequency distribution, how is it constructed, and why is it useful?

Cumulative Frequency Distributions

How does a cumulative frequency distribution differ from a regular frequency distribution, and how is it constructed?

Grouped Frequency Distributions

How does a grouped frequency distribution differ from a regular frequency distribution, and how is it constructed?

What is gained by using a grouped frequency distribution?

What is lost by using a grouped frequency distribution, and why are such distributions usually not used when computing means and other statistics?

Real and Apparent Limits

How do real limits differ from apparent limits, and how does that difference influence how data are assigned to groups?

Interpreting a Raw Score

What is a raw score?

Why is it often necessary to compare a raw score to the specific group of scores in which it appears?

What is a transformed score?

Definition of Percentile Rank and Percentile

What are percentile ranks and percentiles?

What is the primary purpose of percentile ranks and percentiles?

Why must we take careful note of the reference group to interpret a percentile rank correctly?

PREVIEW (*continued*)

Computational Procedures

How is a raw score transformed into a percentile rank?

Given a percentile, how do we determine the corresponding raw score?

How can percentile ranks be determined more easily when a stem-and-leaf display has been prepared?

Deciles, Quartiles, and the Median

What is a decile? What is a quartile? What is the median?

Graphic Representations

What are bar charts, histograms, and stem-and-leaf displays?

When is a bar chart preferable to a histogram?

Shapes of Frequency Distributions

What is meant when we say that a distribution is symmetric? Skewed? Unimodal? Bimodal? Normal? Rectangular? A J-curve?

Summary

Exercises

Thought Questions

Computer Exercises

Bridge to SPSS

The Purpose of Descriptive Statistics

The primary goal of descriptive statistics is to bring order out of chaos. For example, consider the plight of a professor who has given an examination to a class of 85 students and has recorded the score for each student's exam. In order to decide what represents relatively good and poor performance on the examination, the professor must find a way to comprehend and interpret 85 numbers. Or consider a researcher who runs 60 participants in a memory experiment for 20 faces and records a rating of familiarity for each face for each participant during the recall phase. This scientist must contend with the problem of interpreting a total of 1,200 (i.e., 60×20) numbers!

In addition to causing problems for the professor or researcher, the large quantity of numbers also creates difficulties for the audience they intend to inform. The students in the first example are likely to request information about the distribution of test scores so they can interpret their

Descriptive stats

own performance; otherwise, they will have trouble trying to grasp the meaning of 85 unorganized numbers. The readers of the scientific paper on face recognition will have an even harder time trying to interpret a table with more than 1,000 numbers in it.

Descriptive statistics help to resolve problems such as these by allowing us to *summarize and describe large quantities of data.* Among the various techniques that you will find particularly useful are the following, which are described in this and the next two chapters:

Frequency distributions and graphs—Procedures for describing all (or nearly all) of the data in a convenient way.

Measures of "central tendency"—Single numbers that describe the location of a distribution of scores: where the "center of gravity" of the scores generally falls within the infinite range of possible values.

Measures of variability—Single numbers that describe how "spread out" a set of scores is: whether the numbers are similar to each other and vary very little, as opposed to whether they tend to be very different from one another and vary a lot.

Transformed scores—New scores that replace each original number and show at a glance where any particular score is in comparison to the other scores in the group.

Areas under the normal curve—Proportions that tell you the probability of randomly selecting a score smaller or larger than yours from a particular normal distribution.

Each of these procedures serves a different (and important) function. Our discussion of descriptive statistics begins with frequency distributions and graphs; the other topics are treated in subsequent chapters.

Regular Frequency Distributions

One way of making a set of data more comprehensible is to write down every possible score value in numerical order and record next to each score value the number of times that the score occurs. For example, imagine that you are interested in the psychology of social networking sites such as Facebook and MySpace. In particular, you have a theory about the rate at which people are friended on opening a Facebook account. You randomly sample 80 eighth graders who are about to open a Facebook account and measure how many friend requests they receive in the first 24 hours. The scores (i.e., number of friend requests) of the 80 students are shown in Table 2.1.

As you can see, the table of 80 numbers is difficult to interpret. A *regular frequency distribution*, however, will present a clearer picture. The first step in constructing such a distribution is to list every *possible score value* (typically denoted by the symbol X) in the first column of a table,

Table 2.1 Number of Friend Requests Within 24 Hours of Opening a Facebook Account by 80 Eighth Graders

5	8	3	6	5	6	3	7
6	8	7	4	6	5	8	7
5	3	6	1	8	6	8	5
8	9	6	9	6	5	9	9
8	5	8	4	8	6	7	4
8	7	6	8	5	7	6	9
4	8	6	8	6	5	4	7
7	4	5	5	9	6	6	7
10	3	5	7	9	10	6	7
6	9	8	7	8	5	7	4

with the highest score at the top. The *frequency* (denoted by the symbol f) of each score, or the number of times a particular score was obtained, is listed to the right of the score in the second column of the table. To arrive at the figures in the "Frequency" column, you could go through the data and count all the 10s, go through the data again and count all the 9s, and so forth, until all frequencies were tabulated. A more efficient plan is to go through the data just once and make a tally mark next to the appropriate score in the score column for each score, and add up the tally marks at the end.

The complete regular frequency distribution is shown in Table 2.2 (ignore the "Cumulative Frequency" column for the moment; it will be discussed in the next section). The table reveals at a glance how often each score was obtained. For example, eight of the students were friended 9 times each, and only four were friended 3 times each. This method of

Table 2.2 Regular and Cumulative Frequency Distributions for Data in Table 2.1

Score (X)	Frequency (f)	Cumulative frequency (cf)
10	2	80
9	8	78
8	15	70
7	13	55
6	17	42
5	13	25
4	7	12
3	4	5
2	0	1
1	1	1
0	0	0

organizing the data makes it easier to interpret the friending behavior, because you can conveniently ascertain (among other things) that 6 was the most frequently obtained score, scores distant from 6 tended to occur less frequently than scores close to 6, and that the majority of people received at least five friend requests.

Cumulative Frequency Distributions

The primary value of *cumulative frequency distributions* does not become apparent until later in this chapter, when they prove to be of assistance in the computation of certain statistics (such as the median and percentiles). To construct a cumulative frequency distribution, first form a regular frequency distribution. Then start with the *lowest* score in the distribution and form a new column of *cumulative frequencies* by adding up the frequencies as you go along. For example, the following diagram shows how the cumulative frequencies (denoted by the symbol *cf*) in the right-hand column of the bottom half of Table 2.2 were obtained.

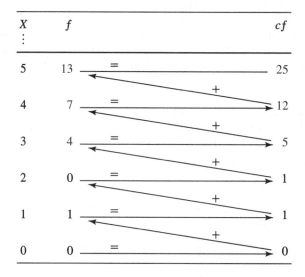

The *cf* for the score of 4 is equal to 12. This value was obtained by adding the frequency (*f*) of that score, namely 7, to the *cf* of the next lower score (i.e., 3), which is 5. The other *cf*s were obtained in a similar fashion.

The *cf* distribution is interpreted as follows: The *cf* of 12 for the score of 4 means that 12 people obtained a score of 4 *or less*. This can be readily verified by looking at the frequencies (*f*): seven people scored 4, four people scored 3, and one person scored 1, for a total of 12 people with scores at or below 4:

X	f	cf
⋮		
5	13	25
4	7	12 scores of 4 or less
3	4	5
2	0	1
1	1	1
0	0	0

scores of 4, scores of 3, scores of 2, scores of 1, score of 0, score of 0

The *cf* for the score of 7 in Table 2.2 is 55, which means that 55 people obtained a score of *7 or less.* Everyone obtained a score of *10 or less,* so the *cf* for a score of 10 equals 80, the total number of people counted in this distribution. (The *cf* for the *highest* score should always equal *N.*) Now, can you tell how many people obtained a score of *6 or more?* The *cf* distribution reveals that 25 people obtained scores of 5 or less, so there must be 55 people who scored 6 or more. This can be checked by using the frequencies; there were *17* scores of 6 + *13* scores of 7 + *15* scores of 8 + *8* scores of 9 + *2* scores of 10. Although no unique information is presented by the *cf* distribution, it allows you to arrive at certain needed information more quickly and conveniently than is possible using the regular *f* distribution.

Grouped Frequency Distributions

When the number of *different scores* to be listed in the score (*X*) column is not too large, regular frequency distributions are an excellent way to summarize a set of data. If, however, there are more than 15 or 20 values of *X* to be written, interpreting a regular frequency distribution is likely to prove tedious. One way of avoiding a summary that does not summarize enough, is to use a *grouped frequency distribution.* Instead of listing single scores in the score column (e.g., 0, 1, 2, 3, 4, 5, 6, 7,...), several score values are grouped together into a *class interval* (e.g., 0–4, 5–9, 10–14, 15–19,...), and frequencies are tallied for each interval.

The data in Table 2.3 represent the scores of 85 students on a quiz that range from zero to 50. Inspection of the data, however, shows that the actual scores range from a low of 9 to a high of 49. Even so, if a regular frequency distribution were to be used, some 41 separate scores and corresponding frequencies would have to be listed. To avoid such a cumbersome table, a grouped frequency distribution has been formed in Table 2.4. An *interval size* of 3 has been chosen, meaning that there are three score values in each class interval; successive intervals of size 3 are formed until the entire range of scores has been covered. Next,

Table 2.3 Scores of 85 Students on a 50-Point Math Background Quiz

39	42	30	11	35	25	18	26	37	15
29	22	33	32	21	43	11	11	32	29
44	26	30	49	13	38	26	30	45	21
31	28	14	35	10	41	15	39	33	34
46	21	38	26	26	37	37	14	26	24
32	15	22	28	33	47	9	22	31	20
37	40	20	39	30	18	29	35	41	21
26	25	29	33	23	30	43	28	32	32
34	28	38	32	31					

Table 2.4 Grouped and Cumulative Frequency Distributions for Data in Table 2.3

Class interval	Frequency (f)	Cumulative frequency (cf)
48–50	1	85
45–47	3	84
42–44	4	81
39–41	6	77
36–38	7	71
33–35	9	64
30–32	14	55
27–29	8	41
24–26	10	33
21–23	8	23
18–20	4	15
15–17	3	11
12–14	3	8
9–11	5	5

frequencies are tabulated, with all scores falling in the same interval being treated equally. For example, a score of 39, 40, or 41 would be entered by registering a tally mark next to the class interval 39–41. When the tabulation is completed, the frequency opposite a given class interval indicates the number of cases with scores in that interval.

Note that grouped frequency distributions lose information, because they do not provide the exact value of each score. They are very convenient for purposes of summarizing a set of data but generally should not be used when computing means and other statistics.

In the illustrative problem, the interval size of 3 was specified. In your own work, it will be up to you to construct the proper intervals. The conventional procedure is to select the intervals according to the following three guidelines:

1. Have a total of approximately 8 to 15 class intervals.
2. Use an interval size of 2, 3, 5, or a multiple of 5, selecting the smallest size that will satisfy the first rule. (All intervals should be the same size.)
3. Make the lowest score in each interval a multiple of the interval size.

Notice how Table 2.4 follows these guidelines: 14 intervals; an interval size of 3; and the lowest scores of the intervals (9, 12, 15, etc.) are all multiples of the interval size, 3. However, we could also have satisfied these guidelines by using the following set of intervals: 5–9; 10–14; 15–19; 20–24; 25–29; 30–34; 35–39; 40–44; 45–49. The best way to decide between these two possible sets of intervals is usually to create the table in both formats and then see which seems to better convey the information in the data. (For further information on the construction of grouped frequency distributions, see B. H. Cohen, 2008.)

Real and Apparent Limits

So far, the scores we have been dealing with, such as number of friends or points on an exam, come only as whole numbers (teachers can give half points, but that has not been the case yet for our examples). However, when measuring physical quantities, like height or weight, we can round off to whole numbers, or we can keep more accurate measures that include decimal points. For example, imagine that the scores in Table 2.3 represent the amounts of time taken by 85 participants, all of whom solved the same puzzle. In that case it could be that the data have been rounded off to the nearest minute, though the original scores included one digit past the decimal point. In fact, it is important to understand that Table 2.4 could have been constructed in the same way even if the scores in Table 2.3 were all presented to the nearest 10th of a minute (e.g., 37.2, 17.8).

At first glance, it may appear that some fractional scores would fall between the cracks in Table 2.4. For instance, in which interval would you place a score of 38.7? It seems that this score is too large to be in the 36–38 interval but too small to be in the 39–41 interval. But that is because the intervals in Table 2.4 are described in terms of their *apparent limits*. When dealing with continuous data, the apparent limits provide a convenient way to express the intervals, but they are not the *real limits* of the intervals. For continuous data, the real limits of the 36–38 interval are 35.5 to 38.5, and the real limits of the next higher interval (39–41) are 38.5 to 41.5. Note that there are no gaps between the real limits of the intervals, so there is no ambiguity about where to place a score of 38.7; this score falls clearly in the interval with the apparent limits of 39 to 41, because it is between 38.5 and 41.5. Any score between 38.5 and 39.0 belongs in the 39–41 interval, and any score between 38.0 and 38.5 belongs in the 36–38 interval. Of course, there is potential ambiguity for a score of exactly 38.5. For such borderline cases, it would be acceptable to decide between the two possible intervals at random, separately for each case, or to adopt a consistent rule, such as always rounding up (e.g., 38.5 would always be placed in the 39–41 interval).

Interpreting a Raw Score

Most raw scores are difficult to interpret in isolation. For example, consider the raw scores of 28, 950, and 8. The first score represents the number of words you were able to remember from a list of 50 words, the second is your reaction time in milliseconds to decide that the letter string TUBTER is not an English word, and the third is the number of people who friended you in the first 24 hours of your Facebook account. Are these "good" scores? Without knowing anything about other scores, it is difficult to know. "Good compared to what?" you might ask. Twenty-eight out of 50 words does not sound too impressive. But what if you found out that 28 was the highest score and that most participants recalled fewer than 14 words? A reaction time of 950ms sounds pretty fast—less than a second! If most people responded within 500ms, however, then your response starts to look leisurely. You can probably see where we are going with this: scores often lack meaning—they are difficult to interpret—out of context. Without additional information it is hard to know whether 8 friend requests in 24 hours is a lot of requests, relatively few, or about average.

Alternatively, you might know what part of the distribution you are interested in and want to know which score falls there. For example, which raw score falls in the exact middle of the distribution? Which score cuts off the bottom 25%? (Or the top 75%?) One way to obtain this additional information is to transform the original score (called the *raw score*) into a new score that will show at a glance where the score fits in with others. There are several different kinds of transformed scores. We discuss one of them in this chapter—percentiles—and defer discussion of others (which depend on concepts we have not covered yet) until Chapter 4.

Definition of Percentile Rank and Percentile

The *percentile rank* of a score is a single number that gives the *percent of cases in the specific reference group scoring at or below* that score. If your raw score of 8 (friends) corresponds to a percentile rank of 87.5, this means that 87.5% of your classmates obtained scores equal to or lower than yours, while 12.5% (the remainder) of the class received higher scores. If instead your raw score of 8 corresponded to a percentile rank of 55, this would signify that your score was slightly above average; 55% of the class received equal or lower scores, while 45% obtained higher scores.

Conversely, a *percentile* is the score at or below which a given percent of the cases lie. A score that would place you at the 5th percentile on an exam, for example, might be a cause for concern, because 95% of the class did better and only 5% did as poorly or worse. Stated another way, the 5th percentile is the score in a distribution whose percentile rank is 5.

As these examples illustrate, percentile ranks and percentiles show directly how an individual score compares to the scores of a specific group. In order to interpret a percentile rank correctly, however, you must take careful note of the reference group in question. A college senior who obtains a test score with a percentile rank of 90 would seem to have done well, because his score places him just within the top 10% of some reference group. But if the reference group consists of *high school* seniors, then perhaps the student should not feel so proud of his performance! A score at the 12th percentile is usually considered poor, because only 12% of the reference group did as badly or worse. But if the score was obtained by a high school ninth grader and the reference group consists of college graduates, the score may actually represent good performance relative to other high school freshmen.

Indeed, there are many practical situations where misleading conclusions can easily be drawn. Scoring at the 85th percentile on the Graduate Record Examination, where the reference group consists of college graduates, is superior to scoring at the 85th percentile on a test of general ability, where the reference group consists of the whole population (including those people without the benefits of a college education). Conversely, if you score at the 60th percentile on a midterm examination in statistics and a friend in a different class scores at the 90th percentile on his statistics midterm, he is not necessarily superior. The students in his class might have a relatively weak aptitude for statistics, which could make it easier for him to obtain a high standing in comparison to his reference group. Remembering that a percentile *compares* a score to a *specific group of scores* will help you to avoid pitfalls such as these.

Computational Procedures

In this section, we describe how to use cumulative frequencies to translate raw scores into percentile ranks, and percentiles into raw scores, for both regular and grouped frequency distributions. However, our emphasis is not on precise calculations, but rather on the process of obtaining good approximations and understanding the purpose of these measures.

Case 1: Given a Raw Score, Compute the Corresponding Percentile Rank

To illustrate the computation of percentile ranks (PRs), let us consider the case of a student who received a score of 8 (friend requests) in the Facebook study whose scores were initially displayed in Table 2.1 and then tallied and presented as both frequency and cumulative frequency distributions in Table 2.2.

To find the PR corresponding to any particular raw score, do the following: First locate the raw score (8 in our example) in the Score column of your distribution table. Then take the *cf* for this score, which is 70 (see Table 2.2), and divide it by the sample size, N (80, in this example). Finally, multiply that quotient by 100. Presented as a formula, it looks like this:

$$PR = (cf \text{ of critical score}/N) \times 100 \hspace{2cm} \text{Formula 2.1}$$

For our example, the PR of 8 is: $(70/80) \times 100 = .875 \times 100 = 87.5$.

The above calculation also answers the question: What score is at the 87.5th percentile? Unfortunately, as in this case, scores in the table rarely correspond to the nice round percentiles in which we are usually interested.

For some extra practice, imagine that our Facebook data came from a sample size (N) of 160 students, instead of 80 students. What would be the PR of someone who got 8 friend invitations in this case? Assuming the cf stayed the same (i.e., that 70 of the 160 scores were at or below the score of 8), should the PR be larger or smaller than the one we just calculated? Before you do the math, think about this conceptually: Have you exceeded a *greater proportion* of the sample if you beat 70 out of 80 people or if you have beaten 70 out of 160 people? For 160 people, the PR would be:

$$PR = (70/160) \times 100 = .4375 = 43.75\%$$

Can you see why it makes sense that the PR was cut in half when the sample size was doubled? It can be useful to estimate your answer before using the formula to do the calculation. Try thinking of it this way: If 80 of 160 eighth graders had gotten 8 invitations or fewer, then the score of 8 would have divided the scores exactly in half, with 50% getting 8 or fewer invitations and the other 50% getting more than 8. But if only 70 students had scored 8 or below, the PR should be somewhat smaller than 50% (43.75%, to be exact). If you equaled or exceeded 70 out of only 80 people, however, then your PR should be bigger—twice as big in this example because the proportion of people you bested is twice the size.

Case 2: Given a Percentile, Compute the Corresponding Raw Score

In the previous problem, we focused on a raw score (8) and wished to find the corresponding percentile rank. It is also useful to know how to apply the percentile procedure in reverse—to find the raw score that corresponds to a specified percentile value. For example, suppose that you're interested in studying eighth graders at the low end of the Facebook friending scale, say the bottom 25%. What raw score would be at the borderline (i.e., the 25th percentile)? In this example, the percentile (25th) is specified first, and it is the corresponding raw score that we wish to find, so the steps are as follows: First, convert the desired percentile to a proportion by dividing by $100(25/100 = .25)$. Then find the corresponding cumulative frequency by multiplying the proportion by N. In the present example, this is equal to $.25 \times 80 = 20$. Finally, find the raw score that corresponds to the cf you calculated. The formula for finding the cf is as follows:

$$\text{Desired } cf = (\text{Percentile}/100) \times N \qquad \text{Formula 2.2}$$

For our example: $cf = (25/100) \times 80 = 20$

Unfortunately, the cf you calculate will not often appear as an entry in the table for your cumulative distribution, making the final step of finding the desired percentile somewhat tricky. More commonly, your calculated cf will fall somewhere between two entries in your table. Such is the case for the present example; looking at Table 2.2, you will see that 20 does not appear in the cf column. A cf of 20 falls between the cfs of 12 and 25 in that table; therefore, the 25th percentile falls somewhere between the raw scores that correspond to 4 and 5, respectively. Moreover, the 25th percentile is closer to 5 than to 4, because 20 is closer to 25 than to 12. As a rough approximation, you could say that the 25th percentile is about 4.6 friends, though a fractional answer does not make much sense when dealing with discrete rather than continuous measurement. When a fractional value for a percentile is useful (or when dealing with grouped rather than regular distributions, as we will show shortly), you can use a mathematical approximation known as *linear interpolation* to obtain a more accurate answer. However, given the availability of computer software to summarize and describe data, we will not take the space to cover linear interpolation in detail. Instead, we will cover the concept in a very approximate way for the grouped distribution (next section) and use our SPSS section to show you how to obtain percentiles by letting the computer do the work.

Case 3: Finding Percentile Ranks and Percentiles for Grouped Frequency Distributions

Calculating a percentile rank for a score in a grouped frequency distribution is a bit more complicated than in the case of a regular frequency distribution. PRs are easy to find only for the real limits of the intervals in a grouped distribution. For example, the PR for a score of 38.5 is easy to find for Table 2.4, because it is at the top of the 36–38 interval, for which the cf is 71. Using Formula 2.1, we can calculate that the PR for 38.5 is $71/N \times 100 = 71/85 \times 100 = .835 \times 100 = 83.5$. But what about the PR for a score of 40.0? Because that score is at the exact midpoint of the 39–41 interval, it is also easy to find, if you make the assumption that underlies linear interpolation, which is that the scores in the 39–41 interval are spread evenly across the interval. With that assumption in mind, we can say that the cumulative frequency for 40.0 is exactly halfway between the cfs corresponding to the real limits of 38.5 and 41.5. We already found from Table 2.4 that the cf for 38.5 is 71, and, similarly, the cf for 41.5 is 77, because 41.5 is at the top of the 39–41 interval. Therefore, the linear interpolation approximation tells us that the *cf* for 40.0 is halfway between 71 and 77, which is 74. Then we apply Formula 2.1 again to find that the PR for 40.0 is $74/85 \times 100 = .871 \times 100 = 87.1$.

For a score that is a quarter of the way from 38.5 to 41.5 (i.e., 39.25), the *cf* would be assumed to be a quarter of the way from 71 to 77 (i.e., 73.5), and so on. The exact calculations for a score like 38.7 get rather tedious, so we prefer to let our computers do the work. Also, note that if Table 2.4 were constructed differently, say with an interval of 5 instead of 3, the exact PR of each score would change considerably (though remaining in the same ballpark), so it seems pointless to be concerned about extreme accuracy for PRs derived from a grouped frequency distribution.

As described for regular frequency distributions, the procedure for finding percentiles is the reverse of the procedure for PRs. For a given percentile, say the 75th, we start by using Formula 2.2 to find the desired *cf*, which for Table 2.4 is $75/100 \times 85 = .75 \times 85 = 63.75$. This *cf* is just slightly lower than the *cf* for the 33–35 interval (64), so we can say that the 75th percentile is a score of about 35.4 or 35.3. As in the case of finding PRs, if the desired *cf* were midway between two *cf*s in our table, then the corresponding percentile would be midway between the upper real limits of the two intervals corresponding to those two *cf*s. Again, we will let the computer do the heavy lifting for us.

Deciles, Quartiles, and the Median

Certain percentile values have specific names, as follows:

Percentile		Decile		Quartile		
90th	=	9th				
80th	=	8th				
75th	=			3rd		
70th	=	7th				
60th	=	6th				
50th	=	5th	=	2nd	=	MEDIAN
40th	=	4th				
30th	=	3rd				
25th	=			1st		
20th	=	2nd				
10th	=	1st				

Whereas the percentile divides the total number of cases into 100 equal parts, the *decile* divides the number of cases into 10 equal parts and the *quartile* divides the number of cases into four equal parts. The score corresponding to the 50th percentile has the unique property that exactly half the scores in the group are higher and exactly half the scores in the group are equal or lower. It is called the *median*, and it is one of the measures of central tendency that is discussed in the next chapter. By the way, if you happened to be interested in the exact value for the 15th percentile in the Facebook example just discussed, you would be in luck because: $cf = (15/100) \times 80 = 12$, and 12 appears as a cf in Table 2.2. The raw score that corresponds to a cf of 12, and therefore the exact value for the 15th percentile, is 4—that is, exactly 15% of the students received 4 friend invitations, or less, in the first 24 hours.

Graphic Representations

It is often effective to express frequency distributions pictorially as well as in tables. Four procedures for accomplishing this are discussed next.

Bar Charts

Suppose that Ihno tabulated the number of math courses that each of the 25 pre-med students in her class had taken prior to enrolling in statistics, and the results were as follows:

Number of math courses (X)	f
7 or more	0
6	1
5	0
4	3
3	4
2	8
1	5
0	4

A **bar chart** (or *bar graph*) of these data is shown in Figure 2.1. To construct a bar chart, the Y-axis (vertical axis) is marked off in terms of *frequencies,* and the X-axis (horizontal axis) is marked off in terms of *score values.* The frequency of any value is expressed by the height of the bar above that value. For example, to show that a score of 3 (courses) occurred 4 times, a bar 4 units in height is drawn above this score.

Bar charts can be used for any kind of data, but they are particularly appropriate for *discrete* data, where results between the score values shown *cannot* occur. In the present example, it is impossible for a student to have taken 2.4 courses, and this fact is well expressed in the bar chart by the separate and distinct bars above each score value. Categorical data (e.g., each student's undergraduate major) are always discrete and are therefore good candidates for being displayed as bar charts.

Histograms

A **histogram** is similar to a bar chart except that adjacent bars are allowed to touch, because the data being graphed are considered *continuous.* When

Figure 2.1

Bar Chart Expressing Number of Prior Math Courses Taken by 25 Pre-Med Students

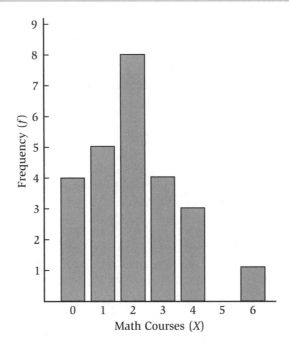

dealing with continuous data, results between whole score values can occur, or could if it were possible to measure with sufficient refinement. Interval and ratio data are often treated as continuous, regardless of whether fractions can occur. Ordinal data (somewhat agree, strongly agree, etc.) are sometimes graphed as a histogram but are usually more appropriately displayed in a bar chart.

Treating the scores in Table 2.3 as numbers of minutes to solve a problem, and therefore as measures that are continuous, the frequencies in Table 2.4 are presented as a histogram in Figure 2.2. As in the bar chart, the Y-axis is marked off in terms of frequencies, and the frequency corresponding to a score (or class interval, as found in Table 2.4) is expressed by the height of the bar above the X-axis. However, because the scale being marked off on the X-axis is treated as continuous, it is marked off in terms of the *real limits* of each class interval, rather than its *apparent limits*. For instance, whereas the apparent limits of the two lowest class intervals in Table 2.4, 9–11 and 12–14, do not appear to touch, if the scale is considered continuous, the real limits of those intervals are 8.5–11.5 and 11.5–14.5; these intervals *do* touch, and therefore do not allow any fractional scores to fall between the intervals.

Frequency Polygons

In some cases, line graphs are easier to interpret than a series of bars. Line graphs can be used to represent various kinds of frequency distributions, as described next.

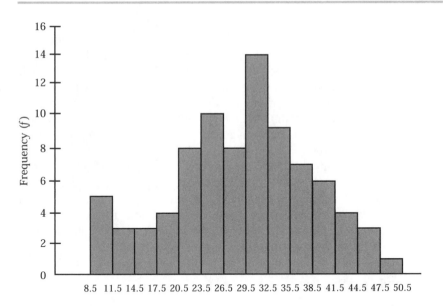

Figure 2.2

**Histogram
Representing the
Grouped Data in
Table 2.4**

Regular Frequency Polygons

An alternative to the histogram that is also appropriate only for continuous
data is the **frequency polygon**. The frequency data in Table 2.4, which
were graphed in Figure 2.2, are presented again as a *regular frequency
polygon* in Figure 2.3. The strategy is the same as in the case of the
histogram: the frequency of a score (or score interval) is expressed by
the height of the graph vertically above the X-axis (as measured along
the Y-axis), and the scores are measured horizontally along the X-axis.

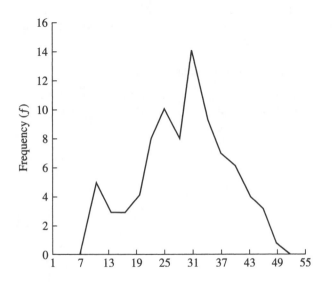

Figure 2.3

**Regular Frequency
Polygon for Data in
Table 2.4**

The difference is that points, rather than bars, are used for each entry. Thus, the frequency of 5 for the class interval of 9–11 is shown by a dot 5 units up on the Y-axis above the score of 10 (the midpoint of the 9–11 interval); with a regular frequency distribution, as in Table 2.2, each score would be entered on the X-axis. All dots are connected with straight lines, and the leftmost and rightmost dots are connected to the X-axis at the midpoints of the next intervals to the left and right, respectively (see Figure 2.3). Regular frequency polygons are particularly appropriate when many different scores (or intervals) are being represented on the X-axis, because a histogram with many very narrow bars is particularly tedious to look at. Also, it is relatively easy to draw two frequency polygons on the same graph if, for example, you wanted to compare the quiz distribution for this semester with the corresponding distribution from the previous semester. Imagine how hard it would be to look at and compare two histograms drawn on the same set of axes.

Stem-and-Leaf Displays

A simple and useful technique for summarizing a set of data, the **stem-and-leaf display** is a hybrid that combines features of the frequency distribution and the histogram (see Tukey, 1977). The "stems" consist of class intervals, while the "leaves" are strings of specific values within each interval.

To illustrate, consider once again the scores of the 85 eighth graders shown in Table 2.3. Let us choose an interval size of 5 for the stem-and-leaf display, and order the stems (intervals) from small to large going down the page (see Table 2.5). Each leaf is made up of the scores within a given interval, with each score represented solely by its unit's digit, and the scores in each leaf are ordered from low to high. Because each observation takes up one space, the stem-and-leaf display provides the same graphic representation as the histogram (after the stem-and-leaf display has been rotated 90° counterclockwise), while at the same time

Table 2.5 Stem-and-Leaf Display for Data in Table 2.3

Stems (intervals)	Leaves (observations)	Frequency (f)	Cumulative frequency (cf)
5–9	9	1	1
10–14	0 1 1 1 3 4 4	7	8
15–19	5 5 5 8 8	5	13
20–24	0 0 1 1 1 1 2 2 2 3 4	11	24
25–29	5 5 6 6 6 6 6 6 8 8 8 8 9 9 9 9	17	41
30–34	0 0 0 0 0 1 1 1 2 2 2 2 2 2 3 3 3 3 4 4	20	61
35–39	5 5 5 7 7 7 7 8 8 8 9 9 9	13	74
40–44	0 1 1 2 3 3 4	7	81
45–49	5 6 7 9	4	85

explicitly displaying the value of each score. Thus you can see both the overall shape of the distribution and such particulars as the largest and smallest observations. The stem-and-leaf display may be supplemented by the frequency distribution and/or the cumulative frequency distribution, as needed.

Since the stem-and-leaf display is used primarily to help understand a set of data, you may use or invent whatever variations best accomplish this purpose. For data that cover a wide range of values, you can use the last two digits to represent each score in the leaf (e.g., 460–479 | 63, 68, 74, 74, 78). Or, if there are a great many observations, you might choose to let each leaf entry represent not one but two or more cases.

Shapes of Frequency Distributions

It is often useful to talk about the general shape of a frequency distribution. Some important definitions commonly used in this regard are as follows.

Symmetry Versus Skewness

A distribution is *symmetric* if and only if it can be divided into two halves, each the mirror image of the other. For example, Distributions A, B, C, and G in Figure 2.4 are symmetric. Distributions D, E, F, and H are *not* symmetric, however, since they cannot be divided into two similar parts.

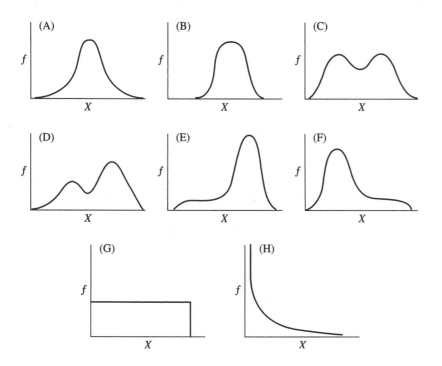

Figure 2.4

Shapes of Frequency Distributions.
(A) Normal curve (symmetric, unimodal).
(B) Symmetric, unimodal.
(C) Symmetric, bimodal.
(D) Asymmetric, bimodal.
(E) Unimodal, skewed to the left.
(F) Unimodal, skewed to the right.
(G) Rectangular.
(H) J-curve.

A markedly asymmetric distribution with a pronounced "tail" is described as *skewed* in the direction of the tail. Distribution E is *skewed to the left* (or negatively skewed), because the long tail is to the left of the distribution. Such a distribution indicates that most people obtained high scores but some (indicated by the tail) received quite low scores, as might happen if an instructor gave an exam that proved easy for all but a few students. Distribution F, however, is *skewed to the right* (or positively skewed), as is indicated by the position of the tail. This distribution indicates many low scores and some quite high scores, as could occur if an instructor gave a difficult examination on which only relatively few students excelled. If you were to inspect the distribution of baseline anxiety scores for all of Ihno's students, you would see a positive skew. Most of the students have fairly low anxiety scores when not facing a threat (like a statistics quiz!), but a few of the students are chronically anxious.

Modality

Modality refers to the number of clearly distinguishable high points, or peaks, in a distribution. In Figure 2.4, Distributions A, B, E, and F are described as **unimodal** because there is one peak; Distributions C and D are **bimodal** because there are two clearly pronounced peaks; and Distribution G has no modes at all. Be careful, however, not to be influenced by minor fluctuations when deciding whether to consider a distribution unimodal or bimodal.

Special Distributions

Certain frequency distributions have names of their own. A particular bell-shaped, symmetric, and unimodal distribution shown in Example A of Figure 2.4 is called the **normal distribution**, about which much more will be said in subsequent chapters. In this distribution, frequencies are greatest at the center, and more extreme scores (both lower and higher) are less frequent. Many variables of interest to the behavioral scientist, such as spatial ability, are approximately normally distributed. The distribution of math quiz scores, as shown in Figure 2.4, may look more like Example B than Example A in Figure 2.4, but it is similar enough to the normal distribution for most statistical purposes. This will be made clear in later chapters.

Example G illustrates a *rectangular* distribution, in which each score occurs with the same frequency. A distribution approximately like this would occur if one fair die were rolled a large number of times and the number of 1s, 2s, and so on were recorded.

Example H is an illustration of a *J-curve,* wherein the lowest score is most frequent and the frequencies decrease as the scores become larger. An example of such a distribution would be the number of industrial accidents per worker over a 2-month period: The majority of workers would have no accidents at all, some would have one accident, a few would have two accidents, and very few unfortunate souls would have a larger number of accidents. The mirror image of this distribution, which is shaped almost exactly like a J, is also called a *J-curve*.

Summary

In *regular frequency distributions,* all score values are listed in the first column and the frequency corresponding to each score is listed to the right of the score in the second column. *Grouped frequency distributions* sacrifice some information for convenience by combining several score values in a single *class interval* so that fewer intervals and corresponding frequencies need to be listed. *Cumulative frequency distributions* are obtained by starting with the frequency corresponding to the lowest score and adding up the frequencies as you go along. Cumulative frequencies can be easily converted into percentages that help us find the *percentile rank* of any one score—that is, the percentage of the scores that are at or below that particular score. *Percentiles* are scores in the distribution with particular percentile ranks, the most useful of which are *deciles* and *quartiles*. For instance, the fifth decile, which is also the second quartile and is best known as the median, is the score whose percentile rank is 50. *Bar charts* and *histograms* are two similar methods for graphing frequency distributions, but bar charts are particularly appropriate for discrete data and histograms are preferred for continuous data. *Frequency polygons* are a useful alternative to histograms when you want to compare the shapes of two distributions. The *stem-and-leaf display* combines features of the frequency distribution and histogram and facilitates the comprehension of a data set by allowing the reader to see it all at once and with as much detail as is needed.

Regular Frequency Distributions

List every score value in the first column, with the highest score at the top. List the *frequency* (symbolized by *f*) of each score to the right of the score in the second column.

Grouped Frequency Distributions

List the *class intervals* in the first column and the frequencies in the second column. It is usually desirable to do the following:

- Have a total of about 8 to 15 class intervals.
- Use an interval size of 2, 3, 5, or a multiple of 5, selecting the smallest size that will satisfy the first rule. (All intervals should be the same size.)

- Make the lowest score in each interval (or, perhaps, the highest) a multiple of the interval size.

Do not use grouped frequency distributions if all scores can be quickly and conveniently reported, because grouped frequency distributions lose information.

Cumulative Frequency Distributions

To the right of the frequency column, form a column of cumulative frequencies (symbolized by *cf*) by starting with the frequency for the lowest score and adding up the frequencies as you go along.

The *percentile rank* corresponding to a given score refers to the percent of cases in a given reference group *at or below* that score. A specified raw score may be converted to the corresponding percentile rank to express its standing relative to the reference group, or the raw score corresponding to a specified percentile may be determined, as shown in the following three cases.

Finding Percentiles and Percentile Ranks

Cumulative frequencies (*cf*) can be used to translate raw scores into percentile ranks and percentiles into raw scores, using the following approximate procedures.

Case 1: Given a Score, Find the Corresponding Percentile Rank (PR)
To find the percentile rank (PR) corresponding to a raw score in a regular frequency distribution, you can use the following formula (this also works if the score of interest happens to correspond to the upper limit of one of the intervals in a grouped frequency distribution):

$$PR = (cf \text{ of critical score}/N) \times 100 \qquad \text{Formula 2.1}$$

If you are trying to find the PR for a raw score that is between the limits of an interval in a grouped distribution, you will need to use *linear interpolation* (or computer software) to estimate the PR. For example, if a raw score is exactly in the middle of an interval, the best estimate of its PR is midway between the PR for the upper limit of the interval and the PR for the lower limit (calculate these two PRs using Formula 2.1). If the raw score is about a third of the way from the lower to the upper limit of an interval, then its PR would be estimated to be a third of the way from the PR for the lower limit to the PR for the upper limit of that interval.

Case 2: Given a Percentile, Find the Corresponding Raw Score
Convert the desired percentile to a proportion by dividing it by 100 and then find the corresponding *cf* by multiplying that proportion by *N*, as

shown in the following formula:

$$\text{Desired } cf = (\text{Percentile}/100) \times N \qquad \text{Formula 2.2}$$

Because the desired *cf* is not likely to appear in your distribution table (if it does, the percentile is the raw score that corresponds to that *cf*), you may need to use linear interpolation to estimate the desired percentile, especially when dealing with a grouped distribution.

Case 3: Finding Percentile Ranks and Percentiles for Grouped Frequency Distributions

Calculating a percentile rank for a score in a grouped frequency distribution is more complicated than it is for regular frequency distributions. If an estimate will suffice, you can use the linear-interpolation approximation techniques described in this chapter. If a precise result is needed, we recommend using statistical software to derive the answer (see SPSS section further on).

Graphic Representations

Bar charts, in which the frequency of any score is expressed by the height of the bar above that score, and the bars do not touch, are particularly appropriate for discrete data (where results between the score values shown cannot occur). *Histograms* are similar to bar charts except that adjacent bars are allowed to touch, so these types of graphs are particularly appropriate for continuous data (in which results between the score values shown can occur, or could if it were possible to measure with sufficient refinement). *Frequency polygons* are a good alternative to histograms, especially when the frequencies of many scores (or class intervals) are being represented on the *X*-axis and you want to see the shape of the distribution at a glance, or you want to compare two distributions on the same graph. *Stem-and-leaf displays* are formed by listing class intervals ("stems") in a column at the left, with specific values within each interval ("leaves") on a horizontal line next to that interval (often represented solely by the units digit).

Exercises

1. Create regular and cumulative frequency distributions for the data from the Turck, Kirk, and Dupre dormitories (see first exercise of Chapter 1).

2. Create grouped and cumulative grouped frequency distributions for Turck and Kirk Halls.

3. Plot a histogram corresponding to the grouped frequency distribution that you created for Turck Hall in the previous exercise. What kind of distribution shape do you see?

4. Using the grouped frequency distributions you created for Turck and Kirk Halls in Exercise 2, plot the two corresponding frequency polygons on the same set of axes (i.e., in one graph).

5. Create a stem-and-leaf plot for the data from Turck Hall, using an interval size of 3.

6. For each of the frequency distributions shown in the following table, state whether it is

   (a) (approximately) normal
   (b) unimodal, skewed to the right
   (c) unimodal, skewed to the left
   (d) bimodal, approximately symmetric
   (e) bimodal, skewed to the right
   (f) bimodal, skewed to the left
   (g) (approximately) rectangular
   (h) J-curve

(1)		(2)		(3)		(4)		(5)		(6)	
X	f	X	f	X	f	X	f	X	f	X	f
10	0	45–49	2	27–29	2	55–59	0	10	3	80–89	5
9	0	40–44	3	24–26	8	50–54	1	9	4	70–79	4
8	1	35–39	1	21–23	17	45–49	3	8	10	60–69	4
7	0	30–34	4	18–20	24	40–44	3	7	6	50–59	3
6	1	25–29	2	15–17	16	35–39	8	6	2	40–49	5
5	3	20–24	5	12–14	6	30–34	13	5	5	30–39	6
4	0	15–19	12	9–11	8	25–29	19	4	11	20–29	5
3	2	10–14	9	6–8	2	20–24	12	3	6	10–19	4
2	6	5–9	3	3–5	3	15–19	10	2	2	0–9	4
1	14	0–4	0	0–2	1	10–14	4	1	1		
0	21					5–9	2	0	0		
						0–4	0				

7. Use the regular (ungrouped) frequency distribution that you created for Turck Hall in Exercise 1 to solve this exercise. (a) Estimate the percentile rank corresponding to a score of 8. (b) Estimate the percentile rank corresponding to a score of 12.

8. Use the grouped frequency distribution that you created for Kirk Hall in Exercise 2 to solve this exercise.

   (a) Estimate the percentile rank corresponding to a score of 16.
   (b) Estimate the percentile rank corresponding to a score of 7.

9. Use the same distribution for this exercise that you used for Exercise 7.

   (a) Approximately what score corresponds to the 25th percentile?
   (b) Approximately what score corresponds to the 75th percentile?

10. Use the same grouped distribution for this exercise that you used for Exercise 8.

(a) Estimate the score that corresponds to the second decile.

(b) Estimate the score that corresponds to the 50th percentile.

(c) Estimate the score that corresponds to the 68th percentile.

Thought Questions

1. Why would it be a bad idea to create a *grouped* frequency distribution for the Doty Hall data from Chapter 1?

2. For which of the following should you use a bar chart, and for which should you use a histogram? Why? (a) Scores on a midterm examination in psychology taken by 50 students. (b) The number of children in each of the families of the 50 students taking the psychology course.

3. What is a symmetric distribution?

4. In a *positively* skewed distribution, are the unusual scores extremely large or extremely small? At what end of the graph is the "tail"?

5. In a *negatively* skewed distribution, are the unusual scores extremely large or extremely small? At what end of the graph is the "tail"?

6. What is a bimodal distribution? If a distribution of grades in a college course is bimodal, what does this imply about the students who took the course?

7. Why might you want to convert a raw score into a percentile rank?

8. What is the difference between a percentile rank and a percentile?

9. For each of the following, state which one represents better performance or if they are the same: (a) The 3rd quartile and the 70th percentile. (b) The 1st quartile and the 3rd decile. (c) The median and the 50th percentile. (d) The median and the 2nd quartile. (e) The 6th decile and the 80th percentile.

10. Rachel's percentile rank on a psychology test is 93. Darcy's percentile rank on a physics test is 80. Why is it potentially incorrect to conclude that Rachel did better than Darcy?

Computer Exercises

1. Request a frequency distribution and a bar chart for the variable Undergraduate Major across all 100 of Ihno's students.

2. Repeat Exercise 1 for the variables Math Courses and Math Phobia. Would it make sense to request a histogram instead of a bar chart for Math Phobia? Discuss.

3. Request a frequency distribution and a histogram for the variable Quiz Score across all students. Describe the shape of this distribution.

4. Request a frequency distribution and a histogram for the variables Baseline Anxiety and Baseline Heart Rate for all students.

Comment on your statistical software's choice of class intervals for each histogram.

5. Repeat Exercise 4 separately for male and female students. Describe the shapes of all four of the resulting distributions.

6. Request a stem-and-leaf plot for the variables Baseline Anxiety and Baseline Heart Rate for all students. Did your statistical package use the stem-and-leaf arrangement that you would have used for maximum clarity? Explain.

7. Request the deciles for the variable Quiz Score across all students.

8. Request the quartiles for the variables Baseline Anxiety and Prequiz Anxiety for all students. Describe the shift in anxiety scores between these two measurement points.

9. Repeat Exercise 8 separately for male and female students.

10. Request the following percentiles for the variables Baseline Heart Rate and Prequiz Heart Rate for all students: 15, 30, 42.5, 81, and 96.

Bridge to SPSS

Frequency distributions can be obtained from SPSS by clicking on **Analyze/ Descriptive Statistics**, and **Frequencies . . . .** For whichever dependent variable (DV) you move into the Variable(s) box, you get a table with five columns, the first of which contains every different score on that DV. That is, SPSS gives you a regular frequency distribution and does not create a grouped frequency distribution no matter how many different scores you have. The second column is Frequency (the number of times each different score occurs). Note that at the bottom of this table there is a row for Total, followed by a row for (the number of) Missing Values, and then another Total (which includes the number of missing values). If your DV has missing values for any of your participants, as is the case for the Math Background Quiz in Ihno's data set, the two totals will differ, and the values in the three bottom rows become critical for understanding the remaining columns.

The third column from the left is called Percent; each of its entries is the Frequency divided by the Total number of cases (i.e., rows) in your spreadsheet—the bottom-row total that includes any missing values—multiplied by 100. The fourth column is Valid Percent, which differs from the third column in that each frequency is divided by the total number of actual scores in your data (i.e., the total that does not include the missing values—we will call this the Valid Total). This is the percentage you are more likely to be interested in. Finally, the last column contains the cumulative values of the Valid Percents. If you want the cumulative frequency distribution, you will just have to multiply each of these entries by the Valid Total, divide by 100, and round off to the nearest whole number.

Along the bottom of the Frequencies dialog box are three buttons. We will discuss the results that can be obtained by clicking on the **Statistics ...** button in the next chapter. For now, let's consider your choices if you click on the **Charts ...** button. The two choices that are relevant to this chapter are Bar Charts and Histograms. If you select Bar Charts, SPSS will create a graph based on a regular frequency distribution of your variable; class intervals will not be created, no matter how many different score values your data contain. Moreover, a bar chart will treat your data not only as discrete (inserting slim spaces between adjacent bars), but as though it were measured on a nominal or ordinal scale. For instance, no place is held for a value within your variable's range that has zero frequency (e.g., if three students each took one, two, and four prior math courses but no student took three math courses, you would see three equally high and equally spaced bars, with no extra gap to represent the zero frequency for three prior math courses taken). Selecting Bar Charts gives you two choices with respect to the scaling of the vertical axis: frequencies (the default choice) and percentages. The relative heights of the bars will look the same, but if you choose percentages, the *Y*-axis will be marked off to correspond with the fact that the frequencies are being divided by the valid *N* and multiplied by 100.

If your variable has been measured on a scale that can be considered quantitative (especially interval or ratio rather than just ordinal), you will most likely want to choose Histograms, instead of Bar Charts, in the **Frequencies** dialog box on the next page. If you choose Histograms for your selected variables, each variable will be treated as though measured on an interval/ratio scale: Adjacent bars will touch, and if there are many different values, they will be grouped into convenient class intervals (a full bar width will be left for each empty class interval within your range of scores). However, the bars are labeled in terms of the midpoints of the intervals; the real limits of the intervals are not shown (we put them in Figure 2.2 for educational rather than descriptive purposes). If you would like to see stem-and-leaf plots for any of your dependent variables, you cannot request them from the Frequencies dialog box. Instead, after clicking **Analyze** and **Descriptive Statistics,** click on **Explore ....** If you click on **Plots ...** in the **Explore** dialog box, you will have the choice of selecting Stem-and-Leaf as well as Histogram.

Percentiles can be obtained from SPSS by opening the **Frequencies ...** dialog box just described and moving the dependent variables for which you want to find percentiles into the Variable(s) box. Then click on the **Statistics ...** button along the bottom of the dialog box. The upper-left quadrant of the Frequencies: Statistics box that opens presents three choices for obtaining percentiles (see following figure). The topmost choice, **Quartiles,** will give you, of course, the 25th, 50th, and 75th percentiles. The second choice, **Cut points** for ... , will give you the deciles, if you use the default number of 10. If you change that number to 5, for instance, you will obtain the 20th, 40th, 60th, and 80th percentiles. The third choice, **Percentile(s)**, allows you to specify any number of particular

Source: Reprint courtesy of International Business Machines Corporation, © SPSS, Inc., an IBM company. SPSS was acquired by IBM in October 2009.

percentiles that you would like to see—just click **Add** after typing in each one. Click **Continue** to return to the main **Frequencies** dialog box and then click **OK.** You will get a table of all of the percentiles you requested in numerical order (e.g., if you requested quartiles as well as the particular percentiles 35 and 60, the table will list the scores corresponding to the 25th, 35th, 50th, 60th, and 75th percentiles, in that order). Following the table of requested percentiles, SPSS will print the regular frequency distribution that we described earlier in this section, unless you uncheck the little box labeled **Display frequency tables** under the list of all your variables on the left side of the Frequencies dialog box.

Chapter 3
Measures of Central Tendency and Variability

PREVIEW

Introduction

What is a measure of central tendency?

What do we gain by using a measure of central tendency instead of a regular frequency distribution?

What important information is not conveyed by a measure of central tendency?

The Mode

What is the mode?

Why is the mode usually not used as the measure of central tendency?

When is the mode your only choice as a measure of central tendency?

The Median

What is the median, and how is it computed?

How do very large or very small scores affect the median?

In what kind of distribution is the median larger than the mean?

In what kind of distribution is the mean larger than the median?

When should the median be used as the measure of central tendency?

The Mean

How do we compute the mean of a set of scores?

Is the population mean computed any differently from the sample mean?

How is the mean computed from a regular frequency distribution?

How is a weighted mean calculated?

What must the sum of the deviations of all scores from the mean be equal to?

What does this imply about the way in which very large or very small scores affect the mean?

When should the mean be used as the measure of central tendency?

The Concept of Variability

What is meant by the variability of a set of scores?

(continued)

PREVIEW (*continued*)

Why is it usually essential to know about the variability of a set of scores rather than just the central tendency? For example, how might your letter grade on a midterm exam be strongly affected by the variability of the examination scores?

The Range

What is the range, and how is it computed?

Why is the range usually not used as the measure of variability?

What are the interquartile and semi-interquartile ranges?

How are these measures computed, and when should they be used?

The Standard Deviation and Variance

Why can't we use the average of the deviation scores as a measure of variability? How does squaring all of the deviations solve this problem?

What is the sum of squares of a set of scores?

What is the variance of a set of scores?

What is the standard deviation of a set of scores?

What advantage does the standard deviation have over the variance as a measure of variability?

When computing the variance or standard deviation, when should the sum of the squared deviations be divided by N? When should you divide instead by $N - 1$?

What was the original purpose behind the creation of computing formulas, and why are they less needed now?

What are some of the useful mathematical properties of the standard deviation?

Summary

Exercises

Thought Questions

Computer Exercises

Bridge to SPSS

Introduction

The techniques presented in Chapter 2 are useful when you wish to provide a detailed summary of all of the data in a convenient format. Often, however, your primary objective will be to highlight certain important characteristics of a group of data. For example, suppose that an inquisitive friend wants to know how well you are doing in college. You might hastily

Table 3.1 **Grade Distribution for 20 Courses Taken by One Hypothetical Student**

Grade	f
A	4
B	9
C	6
D	1
F	0

collect all of your semester grade reports and compile a regular frequency distribution such as the one in Table 3.1.

This would show that you received four grades of A, nine grades of B, and so forth. But all this detail is not essential in order to answer the question, and it would undoubtedly prove tiresome both for you and for your audience. In addition, presenting the data in this form would make it awkward for your friend to compare your performance to his own college grades, if he wished. A better plan would be to select one or two important attributes of this set of data and summarize them so that they could be reported quickly and conveniently.

One item of information that you would want to convey is the general *location* of the distribution of grades. You could simply state that your college work was slightly below the B level. If you wished to be precise, you would report your numerical grade point average—a single number that describes the general location of this set of scores. In either case, you would sum up your performance by referring to a central point of the distribution. It would be misleading to describe your overall performance as being at the A or D level, even though you did receive some such grades.

This is one of many situations that benefit from the use of a measure of **central tendency**—*a single number that describes the general location of a set of scores.* Other examples include the average income of families in the United States, the number of dollars and cents gained or lost by an average share of stock on the New York Stock Exchange in a single day, and the number of minutes taken by the average 6-year-old child to complete a particular jigsaw puzzle.

It should be stressed, however, that the *overall magnitude of a set of data* (i.e., the size of the scores) is *not* its only important attribute. Suppose that the average score on a statistics quiz that you have just taken is 5.0. This average provides information as to the general location of these scores along the possible range of quiz scores, but it does not tell you how many high and low scores were obtained. Consequently, you cannot determine what score will be needed to ensure an A (or to just pass with a D!). In a distribution such as the following one, a score of 7 would rank very highly:

$$7 \quad 7 \quad 6 \quad 5 \quad 4 \quad 4 \quad 4 \quad 3$$

However, a score of 7 is not so impressive in a distribution like this:

10   10   9   7   5   4   3   2   0   0

In both examples, however, the average, measured as the arithmetic mean (i.e., the sum of the scores divided by the number of scores), is equal to 5.0. This indicates that there are important aspects of a set of data that are *not* conveyed by a measure of central tendency; a second vital characteristic, called *variability*, is considered later in this chapter.

The Mode

The simplest measure of central tendency is the **mode**. The mode is the score that occurs most often. For example, the mode of the data in Table 3.1 is B because this score was obtained more often (9 times) than any of the others. In a bar chart or histogram (e.g., Figure 2.1 or 2.2), the mode is the score on the *X*-axis that has the highest bar over it. A distribution can have two or more modes, because two or more scores can have exactly the same frequency (e.g., Figure 2.4C). The mode can also be viewed in a less exact, relative sense, as when a distribution is referred to as bimodal even though its two peaks are not equally high (e.g., Figure 2.4D). If one were to examine the relationship between traffic accident occurrence in a metropolitan area and time of day, a bimodal frequency distribution is likely to result. Note that accidents most commonly occur during the morning and the evening rush hours, with relatively few accidents occurring at other times. It would be misleading to pick a single time of day during which most accidents occur; the distribution is bimodal. This manner of describing the shape of a distribution is one advantage that the mode has over the median and mean (which represent distributions with a single number). Distributions can have more than two modes, in which case they can be described as multimodal. Of course, when a distribution has more than five or six modes, it is usually best to simply say that it has no mode.

The mode is a crude descriptive measure of location that ignores a substantial part of the data. Therefore, it is not often used in research in the behavioral sciences. However, when the variable you are dealing with has only categorical levels, the mode is the only measure of central tendency available. For instance, a marketing researcher may allow the children in a study to take home only one toy each but may offer that toy in a choice of five bright colors. If a manufacturer wants to produce the toy in only one color, it would make sense to use the "modal" (i.e., most frequently chosen) color from the research study, especially if there were many children participating in the study.

The Median

The **median** (Mdn) is defined as the score corresponding to the 50th percentile (see Chapter 2). Half of the scores in a distribution are larger than the median, and half are smaller. The median is the *middle* score in the distribution when scores are put in order of size. For example, there are an odd number of scores in Table 2.3, so when they are placed in numerical order, there is a single middle score (the 43rd score from the lowest) with 42 scores below it and 42 scores above it. For those data, the median is 30. If there is an even number of scores (so that there is no single middle score), the median is computed by averaging the two middle scores.

Properties

When the distribution of scores is symmetric, the mean and the median will be equal. In a *positively skewed* distribution, where there are extreme values at the higher end, the mean will be pulled upward by the extreme high scores and will therefore be larger than the median:

$$3 \quad 4 \quad 4 \quad 4 \quad 5 \quad 6 \quad 7 \quad 39$$

The *mean* of these data is 9.0. The *median* is only 4.5, however; it is *not* affected by the size of any extremely large (or extremely small) values. In fact, the median will remain 4.5 even if the value of 39 is changed to a huge number, such as 39,000. (The median will also remain 4.5 if the value of 3 is changed to an extremely small number, such as $-1,000,000$. But the median *will* change somewhat if the value of 39 is reduced to a small number like 3, for there will no longer be 4 cases above it and 4 cases below it.)

In a *negatively skewed* distribution where the extreme values are at the lower end, the mean will be pulled downward by the extreme low scores and will therefore be smaller than the median:

$$3 \quad 6 \quad 25 \quad 26 \quad 27 \quad 27 \quad 27 \quad 29$$

Here the mean is equal to 21.25, while the median is equal to 26.5.

In some cases, the actual size of the extreme scores may be unknown. For example, suppose that a few participants in a learning experiment do not learn the task even after a great many trials. You might have to terminate the experiment for anyone failing to learn after, say, 75 trials. Such participants would therefore have learning scores of "at least 75 trials." They would be the slowest learners (and should not be discarded from the experiment, as the results would then be biased); but their exact scores would be unknown, so you could not compute a sample mean. Undetermined scores also occur in surveys when the highest point on a scale includes a phrase such as "or above." The scale for annual household income, for example, might include the category "$500,000 or above"; the psychologist may not be interested in income distinctions among people making more than half a million dollars per year. But if she wanted to compute the mean income reported, what number should she use for those who chose the $500k + category? This is not a problem for the median because it does *not* take the exact value of extreme scores into account. As long as undetermined scores can be located with respect to other scores in the data set (e.g., "at least 75 trials" is definitely more trials than a score of "74 trials"), then the median can be computed.

Usage

For descriptive purposes, use the median when either (1) the data are highly skewed or (2) there are inexact data at the extremes of the distribution. This will enable you to profit from the fact that the median is not affected by the size of extreme values. In almost all other cases, use the mean so as to benefit from its numerous advantages. Except for a few infrequent situations that require the median (e.g., summarizing data based on ranks), the mean is the measure of location that is usually used in inferential statistics, with the median reserved for situations where the objectives are purely descriptive.

The Mean

When people use the word *average* in everyday language, they are usually referring to what statisticians call the **arithmetic mean**. There are other types of means in statistics (e.g., the *harmonic mean*, which will be introduced in Chapter 7), but in this text the term *mean* by itself will always refer to the arithmetic mean. In the case of populations, the Greek letter mu (μ) is used to represent the *population mean*. Nevertheless, the computational procedure is the same—sum all scores and divide by N.

Computation

The mean of a set of scores is computed by adding up all the scores and dividing the result by the number of scores added. In symbols,

$$\mu = \frac{\sum X}{N},$$

Formula 3.1

where

μ = population mean (it is pronounced "myoo")

$\sum X$ = sum of the X scores (see Chapter 1)

N = total number of scores

In the case of the first set of quiz scores given in the introduction to this chapter, the mean is equal to 5.0:

$$\frac{7 + 7 + 6 + 5 + 4 + 4 + 4 + 3}{8} = \frac{40}{8} = 5.0$$

Note that simply computing $\sum X$ is not sufficient to identify the location of these scores. What is further required is to divide by N (the number of scores). This step ensures that the means of two different samples will be comparable, even if they are based on different numbers of scores. The mean of the second set of quiz scores presented in the introductory section is equal to 50/10 or 5.0; $\sum X$ is different, but the mean correctly shows that the overall location is the same.

The Weighted Mean

The mean can be viewed as a **weighted mean** (also called "weighted average") of the different possible scores in a distribution, each weighted by its frequency. For example, a student's *grade point average* (GPA) is usually found by first assigning a numerical value or score to each possible letter grade (commonly A = 4, B = 3, C = 2, and so on, and sometimes with intermediate grades, such as B+ = 3.3), and then weighting each possible grade by the number of courses that received that grade. (We are assuming that all courses carry the same number of credits. Otherwise you would have to use the numbers of credits for your weights.) The weighted mean will become important in Chapter 7 when we deal with two unequal sample sizes and need to decide how to arrive at the best overall average (solution: use the weighted mean!).

Properties of the Mean

One important property of the mean is that if you add a *constant* (i.e., a fixed number) to every score in a distribution, the mean of the new distribution will be the original μ plus that constant, which we will call k (as we did in Chapter 1). It is easy to prove that this is true by expressing each new score as $(X + k)$ and then following these steps:

$$\mu_{new} = \frac{\sum (X + k)}{N}$$

$$= \frac{\sum X + Nk}{N} \qquad \text{(Rule 6, Chapter 1)}$$

$$= \frac{\sum X}{N} + \frac{Nk}{N}$$

$$= \mu_{old} + k$$

Similarly, we could use Summation Rule 7 from Chapter 1 to show that if we subtract k from every score, $\mu_{new} = \mu_{old} - k$. A related property of the mean follows from Summation Rule 8. If every score is multiplied by k, then the mean of the new scores (i.e., the mean of kX) can be shown to be k times the old mean by the following steps:

$$\mu_{new} = \frac{\sum kX}{N}$$

$$= k\frac{\sum X}{N} \qquad \text{(Rule 8, Chapter 1)}$$

$$= k\mu_{old}$$

Because dividing by k is the same as multiplying by $1/k$, it is just as easy to show that when all of the scores are divided by k, $\mu_{new} = \mu_{old}/k$. We make use of these properties in Chapter 4.

Another important property of the mean is that the sum of the distances (or *deviations*) of all scores from the mean is zero. That is,

$$\sum (X - \mu) = 0$$

It can readily be proved that this must always be true.[1] As an illustration, consider once again the small set of quiz scores discussed previously.

Score	Deviation from mean $(X - \mu)$
7	+2
7	+2
6	+1
5	0
4	−1
4	−1
4	−1
3	−2
$\mu = 5$	

The mean balances or equates the sums of the positive and negative deviations. It is in this sense that it gives the location of the distribution. This implies that the mean will be sensitive to extreme values on one side that are not balanced by extreme values on the other side, as the following example shows:

Score	$X - \mu$
39	+30
7	−2
6	−3
5	−4
4	−5
4	−5
4	−5
3	−6
$\mu = 9$	

As a result of the change in one score from 7 to 39, the mean shows a substantial 4-point increase. Given that change, all of the other seven scores now fall below the mean and, of course, balance the effects of the

---

[1] $\sum (X - \mu) = \sum X - N\mu$ (Rule 7, Chapter 1) but $\sum X = N\mu$ because $\mu = (\sum X)/N$. Therefore, $\sum (X - \mu) = N\mu - N\mu = 0$.

large positive deviation introduced by the 39. One might well question the use of the mean to describe the location of a set of data in a situation where it is so influenced by one extreme score!

As another example of the sensitivity of the mean to unbalanced extreme values, consider the case of an unethical manufacturing company in which the president earns $20 million per year and the 99 assembly-line workers each earn only $36,500 per year. The president might attempt to refute criticism of the company's miserly tactics by arguing that the mean annual income of all 100 people in the company (the 99 workers plus himself) is $236,135. The workers would undoubtedly object to the appropriateness of this figure, which is more than 6 times their actual salaries! Here again, the use of the mean as the index of location is questionable. It almost always is with income data, since almost all income distributions are positively skewed. (The workers would prefer, of course, to use the median to describe the central tendency of the salaries in this case.)

Usage

The mean has many advantageous properties: (a) It takes all of the scores into account, so it makes the most of the information provided by the data; (b) the mean is also the most stable of the measures of central tendency for most distributions encountered in practice: It is the most consistent across different samples drawn from the same population. For these and other reasons, many of the procedures of inferential statistics make use of the mean. Thus, a third major advantage of the mean is that it is usable as a datum in further statistical analyses, while other measures of central tendency usually are not. For these reasons, the mean is very often the most suitable measure of central tendency.

At times, however, the first of the advantages just mentioned becomes a liability instead of an asset. As we have seen, extreme scores at one end of a distribution exert a strong influence on the mean and cause it to give a misleading picture of the location of the distribution. Therefore, when a distribution is highly skewed and when you do not intend to use the measure of central tendency in subsequent statistical analyses, you should consider an alternative to the mean that will not be affected by unbalanced extreme scores, such as the median.

As discussed in the section on the median, the actual size of extreme scores is sometimes undetermined. Scores such as "at least 75 trials" or "$500,000 or above" are difficult to use with the mean because they do not represent discrete values. In such cases, the median is a more reasonable measure of central tendency because it is based on the number of scores (ordered by value), not the specific values of the scores.

In addition to general location, there is a second important attribute of a distribution of scores—its *variability*. Measures of variability are used extensively in the behavioral sciences, so it is essential to understand the meaning of this concept as well as the relevant computational procedures.

The Concept of Variability

Variability refers to how *spread out or scattered* the scores in a distribution are (or how like or unlike each other they are). If an average is thought of as representing the typical score in a distribution, a good measure of variability might be thought of as representing the typical distance the scores fall from the average. As an illustration, six different distributions, each involving a small number of scores, are shown in Table 3.2.

The minimum possible variability is zero. This will occur only if all of the scores are exactly the same, as in Distribution 1, and there is no variation at all.

In Distribution 2, there is a small amount of variability. The scores are somewhat spread out, but only to a slight extent.

Distribution 3 is equal in variability to Distribution 2. The locations of these two distributions differ, but variability is not dependent on location. The distance between each score and any other, and hence the amount of spread, is identical.

Each of the remaining three distributions is more variable than the ones that precede it. At the opposite extreme of Distribution 1 would be a distribution with scores spread out over the entire range from −1,000,000 to +1,000,000 (or more). Such extreme variabilities, however, are rarely encountered in practice.

Variability is important in many areas, although frequently it is not reported (or is described vaguely in words) because it is less familiar to nontechnical audiences than is central tendency. We list a few examples next.

Testing

Suppose that you score 75 on a statistics midterm examination and that the mean of the class is 65; the maximum possible score is 100. Although your

Table 3.2 Six Distributions

Distribution					
1	2	3	4	5	6
7.0	7.2	40.2	7.0	10.0	97.8
7.0	7.1	40.1	7.0	10.0	88.5
7.0	7.1	40.1	6.0	9.0	83.4
7.0	7.1	40.1	5.0	7.0	76.2
7.0	7.1	40.1	4.0	5.0	69.9
7.0	7.0	40.0	4.0	4.0	67.3
			4.0	3.0	58.4
			3.0	2.0	44.7
				0.0	
				0.0	

score cannot be poor because it is above average, its worth in comparison to the rest of the class will be strongly influenced by the variability of the distribution of examination scores.

If most scores are clustered tightly around the mean of 65, your score of 10 points above average will stand out as one of the highest (and may well merit a grade of A). But if the scores are widely scattered, and values in the 80s and 90s (and 40s and 50s) are frequently obtained, being 10 points above average will not be exceptional because many will have done better. In this case, your score may be worth no more than a B– or C+. A mean of 65 together with low variability would indicate that you did very well, whereas a mean of 65 together with high variability would imply that your performance was less than outstanding compared to the group that took the test. These two possibilities are illustrated graphically in Figure 3.1. (Note that the spread of a frequency polygon indicates the variability of the distribution.)

Consider Distributions 4 and 5 in Table 3.2, which happen to be the two sets of scores discussed at the end of the introduction to this chapter (to illustrate how impressive—or not—a score of 7 can be). The mean of both distributions is 5.0. Yet a score of 7 ranks higher in Distribution 4, where the scores are less variable, than in Distribution 5, where the scores are more variable. Looking at the lower end of these distributions, a score of 3 is poorer in comparison to the group in Distribution 4. Being two points above or below average stands out more in a distribution in which there is less spread.

Sports

Suppose that two professional basketball players average 20.3 points per game. Although their mean performance is the same, they may be different in other respects. One player may be consistent (low variability) and always score close to 20 points in every game, rarely scoring as high as 25

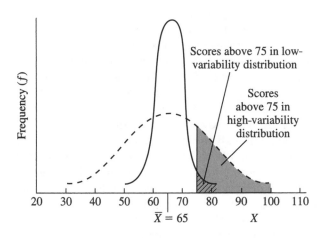

Scores above 75 in low-variability distribution

Scores above 75 in high-variability distribution

Figure 3.1

Frequency Polygons of Two Distributions With the Same Mean but Different Variability

but also rarely falling to 15 or less. The second player may be "streaky" (high variability); he scores more than 30 points in some games but drops to below 10 in others. The second player is likely to be a greater source of frustration to his coach and to the fans. Here again, a measure of variability would provide useful additional information to that given by the mean.

Psychology

Modern psychology is based on the idea that behavior differs. The psychologist's goal is to understand and explain this variability with theories or models. Some psychological research focuses on person-to-person variability. On any trait of interest—musical ability, throwing a baseball, introversion, height, mathematical ability, resilience—people are distributed over the entire range from low to high. Most psychological science, however, is not so much interested in why one particular individual differs from another; instead it is primarily concerned with how various manipulations affect behavior. For example, does imagery improve memory for words? Does a new antidepressant drug decrease negative thoughts? Does conformity vary depending on the social status of the experimenter? Are children able to conserve volume (e.g., realize that the amount of liquid does not change when poured from a short, wide beaker into a tall, skinny one) better depending on how the question is posed to them? In each of these cases, the variability of interest is between groups of individuals who were randomly assigned to participate in different conditions of the study. Were the people asked to visualize words able to remember more, on average, than the group that was asked to think of rhymes for the words? Was the antidepressant group less depressed, on average, than the group that received a placebo instead of the drug? Did people in the lab-coat-experimenter group conform more than those in the Hawaiian-shirt-experimenter group? Were the children in the new-wording group more likely to conserve volume than those in the old-wording group? In all of these examples, the researcher is interested in how a group of people randomly assigned to be treated one way is systematically different (or not) from a group of people treated a different way. Now, of course, individual differences do exist for all of these variables—people do differ with respect to how good their memory is—but those individual differences are usually not the chief object of study in this sort of research. In fact, person-to-person variability is sometimes thought of as error or "unexplained" variance. The goal of much research is to maximize "explained" variability. The more variance a model or theory can explain, the better it can predict behavior. As you may be learning in your psychology classes, we are far from explaining all variability in behavior. As you will learn later in this book, you do not need to understand all or even most variability in order to contribute importantly to science or to help people and society. For now, we simply want you to appreciate how central the concept of variability—and our ability to measure it—is to the behavioral sciences.

Statistical Inference

Another reason for the importance of variability will become evident when statistical inference is discussed beginning in Chapter 5. Other things being equal, the more variable a phenomenon is, the less precise is the estimate you can get of the population's location (e.g., mean) from sample information.

Rather than describe variability in ambiguous terms such as *small* or *large*, it is preferable to summarize the variability of a distribution of scores in a single number. Techniques for accomplishing this are discussed next. As with measures of central tendency, we will start with the simplest measures.

The Range

One possible way of summarizing the variability of a distribution is to look at the distance between the smallest and largest scores. The *range* of a distribution is defined as the largest score minus the smallest score. For example, the range of Distribution 4 in Table 3.2 is $(7.0 - 3.0)$ or 4.0.

Although this procedure makes intuitive sense, it is likely to give misleading results on many occasions because frequently the extreme values are atypical of the rest of the distribution. Consider the following two distributions:

```
DISTRIBUTION A:   10   10   10   9   7   6   5   4   4   3   2   0   0
DISTRIBUTION B:   10    6    6   5   5   5   5   5   5   5   4   4   0
```

In both of these examples, the range is equal to 10. Yet Distribution A, with scores spread out over the entire 10-point range, is more variable than Distribution B, where all but two scores are concentrated near the middle of the distribution. The range is a poor measure of the variability of Distribution B because the extreme values are not typical of the total variation in the distribution; if the two extreme scores are excluded, the range drops to 2. Because this type of distortion occurs fairly often, the range (like the mode) is best regarded as a crude measure that generally should not be used in behavioral science research. However, it is always a good idea to take note of the minimum and maximum values obtained for each of your variables, especially to check for errors and anomalous findings.

The Semi-Interquartile Range

You may recall that a major advantage of the median as a measure of central tendency is that it is not affected by making an extreme score even more extreme. In fact, the median is still valid if there are some scores on either end of the distribution that are undetermined. For example, on a survey question about how many different jobs the respondent has held, several participants may have checked "10 or more." Obviously, the ordinary range is much affected by extreme scores and cannot be used with open-ended responses.

There is a type of range measure, called the *interquartile range*, which has advantages similar to those of the median. It is found by subtracting the score at the 25th percentile (the 1st quartile) from the score at the 75th percentile (the 3rd quartile). The median, of course, is the score at the 2nd quartile. This range measure tells you the total spread for the middle 50% of the scores, and it is clearly not affected by extreme or indeterminate scores (unless the latter comprise as much as 25% of the scores on either end of the distribution). For example, in Chapter 2 we calculated the 25th percentile for the math quiz and found it to be a score of 22.8. Using the same method, the 75th percentile turns out to be 35.4. Thus, the interquartile range for those quiz scores is 35.4 − 22.8, which equals 12.6.

Dividing the value for the interquartile range by 2 results in a useful variability measure called the *semi-interquartile range* (SIQR). The main advantage of the SIQR is that it gives you an immediate idea of the distance of the typical score from the median. (About half the scores in the distribution are farther from the median than the SIQR and about half are closer than the SIQR.) For the math quiz scores, the SIQR is $12.6/2 = 6.3$. This means that if you need to come up with a single number that characterizes how much the scores tend to vary from the median of that distribution, 6.3 points would serve the purpose. Although the SIQR is a good descriptive measure of variability, it does not play a role in more advanced statistical methods, so it will not be discussed further in this text. A more sophisticated way of determining how much the "typical" score differs from the center of the distribution is described in detail next.

The Standard Deviation and Variance

As we have mentioned, the mean, an average that takes all of the scores into account, is usually the best measure of central tendency for inferential purposes. Similarly, an "average" variability that is based on all the scores will usually provide the most useful information for purposes to be described in later chapters. Before an *average* variability can be computed, however, this concept must be defined in terms of an individual score.

Variability actually refers to the difference between each score and every other score, but it would be quite tedious to compute this in practice (especially if N is large). If there are 100 scores, you would have to compute the difference between the first score and each of the 99 other scores, compute the difference between the second score and each of the 98 remaining scores, and so on—4,950 differences in all.

A more reasonable plan, which will serve the purpose equally well, is to define the "differentness" or *deviation* of a single score in terms of how far it is from the center of the distribution. In a distribution of scores that is closely packed together, most scores are close to each other and hence close to their center. Conversely, in a highly variable distribution, some scores are quite a distance from each other and hence far from their center. Since the mean is the most frequently used measure of central tendency, a reasonable procedure is to define the deviation of a single score as its *distance from the mean*:[2]

$$\text{Deviation score} = X - \mu$$

Extremely deviant scores (ones very far from the mean) will have numerically large deviation scores, while scores close to the mean will have numerically small deviation scores.

The next step is to derive a measure of variability that will take into account the deviations of all of the scores. There are several possible ways to do this. If we were to average the deviation scores by the usual procedure of summing and dividing by N, we would get

$$\frac{\sum (X - \mu)}{N}$$

It will prove extremely frustrating to try to use this as the measure of variability because $\sum(X - \mu)$ is *always* equal to zero. As a result, this "measure" cannot provide any information as to the variability of any distribution.

This problem could be overcome if we were to focus on the *size* of the deviations and ignore whether they are positive or negative. We might therefore first take the *absolute value* of each deviation, its numerical value ignoring the sign, and then compute the average variability. That is, we might compute

$$\frac{\sum |X - \mu|}{N}$$

where $|X - \mu|$ is the absolute value of the deviation from the mean. This is not an unreasonable procedure, and in fact yields a good descriptive measure called the *mean* or *average deviation* (often symbolized as MD, or MAD, for the mean absolute deviation). But, unfortunately, measures based on absolute values are unsuitable for use in further statistical analyses (one awkward property of the mean deviation is that it is smaller when deviations are calculated from the *median*, rather than from the mean). The measure that is most frequently used circumvents this difficulty by *squaring* each of the deviations prior to taking the average. The sum of the

---

[2]A reference point other than the mean could be used, but the choice of the mean has certain statistical advantages as well as making good intuitive sense. For example, it can be proved that the mean is the value of c about which $\sum(X - c)^2$, the sum of squared deviations, is a minimum (the importance of which will become apparent in the following discussion).

squared deviations from the mean, $\sum(X - \mu)^2$, is symbolized by SS and is called the **sum of squares**. The measure of variability produced by taking the average, instead of the sum, of the "squares" is called the **variance** and is symbolized by σ^2:

$$\sigma^2 = \frac{\sum (X - \mu)^2}{N} = \frac{SS}{N} \qquad \text{Formula 3.2}$$

This is a basic measure of the variability of any set of data. However, when the data of a sample are used to estimate the variance of the population from which the sample was drawn, the *population variance estimate*, or **sample variance** (symbolized by s^2), is computed instead:

$$s^2 = \frac{\sum (X - \overline{X})^2}{N - 1} = \frac{SS}{N - 1} \qquad \text{Formula 3.3}$$

Note that in Formula 3.3, the mean is symbolized as $\overline{X}$, instead of μ. Even though $\overline{X}$ is always calculated in exactly the same way as μ, we will use the symbol $\overline{X}$ whenever the mean has been calculated for a group of scores that are being viewed as a sample of a population, rather than as an entire population in themselves. This is an important distinction, because sometimes both symbols for the mean will appear in the same formula. In general, you will see that $\overline{X}$, calculated for a sample, is usually used as an estimate of μ for the entire population from which that sample was drawn. Because s^2 is the symbol we will be using whenever the variance is calculated for a sample, and not a population, the mean that you will see represented in formulas for s^2 will be the sample mean ($\overline{X}$), rather than the population mean (μ).

In each of the preceding variance formulas, the order of operations is as follows: (1) subtract the mean from each score; (2) square each result; (3) sum; (4) divide. The sample estimate of the population variance, s^2, is computed just a little differently from σ^2; the sum of squared deviations is divided by $N - 1$ instead of N. This is to enable s^2 to be an *unbiased* estimate of the population variance—that is, an estimate that on the average will be too large no more often than it is too small. Hence, it is common to refer to s^2 simply as the *unbiased variance* and to σ^2 as the *biased variance*.

There is one remaining difficulty. Having squared the deviations to eliminate the negative numbers that otherwise would have led to a total of zero with annoying regularity, the variance is expressed in terms of the original units *squared*. For example, if you are measuring height, the variance indexes variability in terms of square inches. Especially for descriptive purposes, it is preferable to have a measure of variability that is in the same units as the original measure, and this can be accomplished by taking the positive square root of the variance. This yields a very commonly used measure of variability called the **standard deviation**, symbolized by σ or s, depending on whether it is based on the biased or unbiased version of the variance:

$$\sigma = +\sqrt{\sigma^2} = \sqrt{\frac{\sum (X - \mu)^2}{N}} = \sqrt{\frac{SS}{N}} \qquad \text{Formula 3.4}$$

$$s = +\sqrt{s^2} = \sqrt{\frac{\sum (X - \overline{X})^2}{N - 1}} = \sqrt{\frac{SS}{N - 1}} \qquad \text{Formula 3.5}$$

Following the shorthand-naming convention applied to σ^2 and s^2, σ is often called the *biased standard deviation*, and s is called the *unbiased standard deviation*. Of course, $\overline{X}$ appears in the formula for s, which is always based on a sample, whereas μ appears in the formula for σ, the standard deviation of a population.

Whereas the mean represents the "average score," the standard deviation represents a kind of "average variability"—similar to the average of the deviations of each score from the mean $(X - \mu)$—with two minor complications: (1) squaring the deviations before averaging, and then taking the positive square root, to return to the original unit of measurement; and (2) dividing by $N - 1$ instead of N when estimates of the population are involved. Although the standard deviation is not literally the average deviation, it can be thought of, less precisely, as a typical deviation. The formulas we have given are called the *definitional* formulas for σ and s because their primary function is to define the meaning of these terms; they are not necessarily the formulas by which σ and s are most easily computed.

Illustrative examples of the computation of σ^2 and σ and of s^2 and s using the definitional formulas are shown on the left-hand side of Table 3.3. If the eight scores in Table 3.3 represent the entire population, σ is computed; however, if these eight scores are a sample from a larger population, s is computed. Note that a partial check on the calculations is possible in that $\sum (X - \mu)$ should always equal zero. As expected from the previous discussion concerning these distributions, Distribution 5 (from Table 3.2) has a larger standard deviation (is more variable) than Distribution 4. The typical deviation from the mean is 3.66 points in Distribution 5, but only 1.5 points in Distribution 4.

Computing Formulas

Using the definitional formulas to calculate σ and s can be awkward for several reasons. First, if the mean is not a whole number, subtracting it from each score will yield a deviation score with decimal places, which when squared will produce still more decimal places. This can make the computations quite tedious. Second, the mean must be calculated before the formula can be used, which necessitates two steps in the computation of the standard deviation (although normally the mean will be desired anyway). Therefore, before the advent of handheld statistical

Table 3.3   Computation of σ^2 and σ and of s^2 and s, for Two Small Samples Using the Definition and Computing Formulas

Example 1. Distribution 4 (where $\mu = 5.0$)					
X	$X - \mu$	$(X - \mu)^2$		X	X^2
7	$7 - 5 = 2$	4		7	49
7	$7 - 5 = 2$	4		7	49
6	$6 - 5 = 1$	1		6	36
5	$5 - 5 = 0$	0		5	25
4	$4 - 5 = -1$	1		4	16
4	$4 - 5 = -1$	1		4	16
4	$4 - 5 = -1$	1		4	16
3	$3 - 5 = -2$	4		3	9
		$\sum (X - \mu)^2 = 16$		$\sum X = 40$	$\sum X^2 = 216$

A. Definition formulas

$$\sigma^2 = \frac{\sum (X - \mu)^2}{N} = \frac{16}{8} = 2.00$$

$$\sigma = \sqrt{2.00} = 1.41$$

$$MD = \frac{\sum |X - \mu|}{N}$$

$$= \frac{2 + 2 + 1 + 0 + 1 + 1 + 1 + 2}{8}$$

$$= \frac{10}{8}$$

$$= 1.25$$

$$s^2 = \frac{\sum (X - \overline{X})^2}{N - 1}$$

$$= \frac{16}{7}$$

$$= 2.29$$

$$s = \sqrt{2.29} = 1.51$$

B. Computing formulas

$$\sigma^2 = \frac{1}{N}\left[\sum X^2 - \frac{\left(\sum X\right)^2}{N} \right]$$

$$= \frac{1}{8}\left[216 - \frac{(40)^2}{8} \right]$$

$$= \frac{1}{8}(216 - 200)$$

$$= \frac{1}{8}(16) = 2.00$$

$$\sigma = \sqrt{2.00} = 1.41$$

$$s^2 = \frac{1}{N - 1}\left[\sum X^2 - \frac{\left(\sum X\right)^2}{N} \right]$$

$$= \frac{1}{7}\left[216 - \frac{(40)^2}{8} \right]$$

$$= \frac{1}{7}(216 - 200) = \frac{1}{7}(16) = 2.29$$

$$s = \sqrt{2.29} = 1.51$$

(continued)

Table 3.3 (continued)

Example 2. Distribution 5 (where $\mu = 5.0$)				
X	$X - \mu$	$(X - \mu)^2$	X	X^2
10	$10 - 5 = 5$	25	10	100
10	$10 - 5 = 5$	25	10	100
9	$9 - 5 = 4$	16	9	81
7	$7 - 5 = 2$	4	7	49
5	$5 - 5 = 0$	0	5	25
4	$4 - 5 = -1$	1	4	16
3	$3 - 5 = -2$	4	3	9
2	$2 - 5 = -3$	9	2	4
0	$0 - 5 = -5$	25	0	0
0	$0 - 5 = -5$	25	0	0
		$\sum(X - \mu)^2 = 134$	$\sum X = 50$	$\sum X^2 = 384$

A. Definition formulas

$$\sigma^2 = \frac{\sum(X - \mu)^2}{N} = \frac{134}{10} = 13.40$$

$$\sigma = \sqrt{13.40} = 3.66$$

$$MD = \frac{\sum|X - \mu|}{N}$$

$$= \frac{5 + 5 + 4 + 2 + 0 + 1 + 2 + 3 + 5 + 5}{10}$$

$$= \frac{32}{10} = 3.2$$

$$s^2 = \frac{\sum(X - \bar{X})^2}{N - 1}$$

$$= \frac{134}{9}$$

$$= 14.89$$

$$s = \sqrt{14.89} = 3.86$$

B. Computing formulas

$$\sigma^2 = \frac{1}{N}\left[\sum X^2 - \frac{\left(\sum X\right)^2}{N}\right]$$

$$= \frac{1}{10}\left[384 - \frac{(50)^2}{10}\right]$$

$$= \frac{1}{10}(384 - 250)$$

$$= \frac{1}{10}(134) = 13.40$$

$$\sigma = \sqrt{13.40} = 3.66$$

$$s^2 = \frac{1}{N - 1}\left[\sum X^2 - \frac{\left(\sum X\right)^2}{N}\right]$$

$$= \frac{1}{9}\left[384 - \frac{(50)^2}{10}\right]$$

$$= \frac{1}{9}(384 - 250) = 14.89$$

$$s = \sqrt{14.89} = 3.86$$

calculators and personal computers made these calculations so easy to perform, *computing formulas* for σ and s were derived by manipulating the definitional formulas algebraically. Because the computing and definition formulas are algebraically equivalent to each other, they always yield identical results. Although there is no longer much need for them, for historical purposes, as well as to facilitate comparison with the many texts that still present them, the computing formulas for both the biased and unbiased versions of the standard deviation and variance are shown next.

$$\sigma^2 = \frac{1}{N}\left[\sum X^2 - \frac{\left(\sum X\right)^2}{N}\right], \quad \sigma = \sqrt{\frac{1}{N}\left[\sum X^2 - \frac{\left(\sum X\right)^2}{N}\right]}$$

Formula 3.6A&B

$$s^2 = \frac{1}{N-1}\left[\sum X^2 - \frac{\left(\sum X\right)^2}{N}\right], \quad s = \sqrt{\frac{1}{N-1}\left[\sum X^2 - \frac{\left(\sum X\right)^2}{N}\right]}$$

Formula 3.7A&B

Examples of the use of the computing formulas for σ^2 and σ and for s^2 and s are shown on the right-hand side of Table 3.3. For comparison purposes, we have included the calculation of the mean deviation, which is often similar to, but can never be larger than, the standard deviation.

Properties of the Standard Deviation

The properties we discuss here for σ also hold for its unbiased cousin, s. Although σ shares several important properties with the mean, one property it does *not* share is its response to adding a constant to all of the scores in the distribution. (The properties that are associated with addition also hold for subtraction, which can be viewed as the adding of a negative constant.) We demonstrated earlier in this chapter that if the same constant (k) is added to all of the scores, $\mu_{new} = \mu_{old} + k$. However, it is easy to show that adding (or subtracting) a constant to all of the scores has no effect on σ. Consider any one deviation score: $X - \mu$. If you add k to all of the scores, each new deviation score will look like this: $(X + k) - (\mu + k)$. (Remember that the mean is also increased by k.) So the new deviation score equals $X + k - \mu - k = X - \mu$, which is exactly the same as the old deviation score.

Because all of the deviation scores remain the same, σ, which is based on these deviation scores, also remains unchanged. It is as though everyone in a large crowd were to move exactly 12 inches in exactly the same direction. After the move, the people are standing in exactly the same way in relation to each other; only the overall location of the crowd (like the mean of the distribution) has changed. Yet, multiplying by a constant *does* have the same effect on σ as it does on the mean: $\sigma_{new} = k\sigma_{old}$.

(The same properties hold for division.) Again, we look at what happens to any one deviation score when all of the scores are multiplied by k. The new deviation equals $kX - k\mu = k(X - \mu) = k$ times the old deviation. Because the size of each deviation score is multiplied by k, σ is multiplied by k as well.

Like the mean, the standard deviation has the statistically desirable property of being based on *all* of the scores in the distribution. This implies, however, that σ also has the often *un*desirable property that it can be strongly influenced by one very extreme score. It can therefore produce a value for variability that gives a misleading picture of the entire distribution. Unlike the case of the mean, equally extreme scores on both sides of the distribution will not cancel each other out (because their deviations are squared before being added), so σ can be misleading even with symmetrical distributions. Extreme scores have less of an impact on the mean deviation (MD) than they do on σ, because large deviations are not squared in the process of calculating the MD as they are in finding σ. Therefore, the MD could be a useful measure of variability for purely descriptive purposes. However, because it is not suitable for further statistical analyses, it is rarely used at all. In cases where you want to use the median instead of the mean to describe the central tendency of your distribution, it would make sense to use the SIQR as your measure of variability rather than the standard deviation.

As we mentioned earlier, σ has an undesirable property (i.e., bias) that can be corrected by calculating s instead when we wish to estimate the variability in the population from which a sample was drawn. It is the latter measure, the unbiased standard deviation (and its square, the unbiased variance), that is used most frequently as the basis for the more advanced statistical procedures that we begin to describe in Chapter 5.

Summary

Central Tendency

One important attribute of a set of scores is its *location* — that is, where in the possible range between minus infinity and plus infinity the scores tend to fall. This can be described in a single number by using either the *mean*, the best measure in most instances, or the *median* (the score corresponding to the 50th percentile), which is preferable when data are highly skewed or there are extreme data whose exact values are unknown, and when the objectives are purely descriptive. When a variable is not associated with scores at all, but rather distinct categories, a cruder measure, the *mode*, is the only measure that can be used to summarize the frequencies of that variable's various values.

1. The Mode
This is the most frequently obtained score. The mode is at best a rough measure and is usually inappropriate when dealing with quantitative data.

However, it is the only measure of central tendency that can be used with qualitative levels of a variable (e.g., different colors, different diagnoses for mental illness).

2. The Median

For either grouped or ungrouped data, the median is the score that corresponds to the 50th percentile.

3. The Population Mean

$$\mu = \frac{\sum X}{N}$$

Formula 3.1

Variability

A second important attribute of a set of scores is its *variability*, or how much the scores *differ from one another*. In the behavioral sciences, this is customarily summarized in a single number by computing the *variance* or its positive square root, the *standard deviation*. The larger the variance or standard deviation, the more different the numbers are from one another. The concept of variability has many practical applications and is particularly important in statistical work.

1. The Range

The simplest (and crudest) measure of variability encountered in the behavioral sciences is the range, which is equal to the highest score minus the lowest score. Although it is sometimes useful to know the maximum separation of your scores, as a measure of variability, the range is rather unreliable and is therefore generally less useful than the other available variability measures.

2. The Interquartile and Semi-Interquartile (SIQ) Ranges

The interquartile range (IQR) is the distance from the 1st to the 3rd quartile of the distribution, calculated as the 75th percentile minus the 25th percentile. The SIQR is half of that distance (i.e., IQR/2). These measures are useful for descriptive purposes, especially when your distribution contains extreme or indeterminate scores, but are not used for inferential statistics.

3. The Mean Deviation

This is the average of the absolute values of all the deviations from the mean. It is less susceptible to extreme scores (called *outliers*) than the standard deviation, and it makes intuitive sense, but it is not used for drawing inferences about populations. The formula for the MD is:

$$\mathrm{MD} = \frac{\sum |X - \mu|}{N} \qquad \text{where } |X - \mu| = \text{the absolute value of the deviation from the mean}$$

4. The Biased Variance and Standard Deviation

Variance (definitional formula):

$$\sigma^2 = \frac{\sum (X - \mu)^2}{N} \qquad \text{Formula 3.2}$$

Variance (computing formula):

$$\sigma^2 = \frac{1}{N} \left[\sum X^2 - \frac{\left(\sum X\right)^2}{N} \right] \qquad \text{Formula 3.6A}$$

Standard deviation formula (in terms of variance):

$$\sigma = +\sqrt{\sigma^2}$$

When calculated for samples, σ^2 and σ tend to underestimate their corresponding values in the population. Therefore, these measures are acceptable only for descriptive purposes; they are not used to make estimates of, or draw inferences about, population parameters.

5. The (Unbiased) Population Variance Estimate and the Unbiased Standard Deviation

When the data of a sample are to be used to estimate the variance of the population from which the sample was drawn, compute the *population variance estimate.*

Unbiased variance (definitional formula):

$$s^2 = \frac{\sum (X - \overline{X})^2}{N - 1} \qquad \text{Formula 3.3}$$

Unbiased variance (computing formula):

$$s^2 = \frac{1}{N - 1} \left[\sum X^2 - \frac{\left(\sum X\right)^2}{N} \right] \qquad \text{Formula 3.7A}$$

Unbiased standard deviation formula:

$$s = +\sqrt{s^2}$$

Exercises

1. Calculate the friendliness means of Turck, Kirk, Dupre, and Doty Halls (see first exercise of Chapter 1).

2. Compute the median of Turck Hall from the regular frequency distribution you created for that dorm when solving the first exercise of Chapter 2.

3. Find the mode of Kirk Hall by inspecting the regular frequency distribution you created for that dorm when solving the first exercise of Chapter 2.

4. Compute the median of Turck Hall from the *grouped* frequency distribution you created for that dorm when solving the second exercise of Chapter 2.

5. Using the raw data for Dupre Hall, demonstrate that the sum of the deviations from the mean equals zero.

6. Compute the median and mean for Distribution 6 in Table 3.2. Why can't you find the mode of this distribution?

7. Insert the sums you found for Exercise 3 of Chapter 1 into the *computing* formulas given in this chapter to find σ^2, σ, s^2, and s for the four dorms. (We highly recommend that you also learn to obtain these results directly with a handheld calculator.)

8. Recalculate σ^2, σ, s^2, and s for Dupre Hall using the *definitional* formulas, and compare them to the corresponding results from the previous exercise. Which type of formula (computing or definitional) usually leads to greater error due to rounding off before the final result?

9. The mean of an exam is 57.3 and the standard deviation is 9.6. What will happen to the standard deviation of these scores if the instructor (a) adds 5 points to each score? (b) subtracts 4 points from each score? (c) multiplies each score by 2? (d) divides each score by 3?

10. Compute the range for each of the four dorms.

11. Using the results you found for Exercise 9 in Chapter 2, compute the interquartile range and SIQR for Turck Hall. Using the same methods, calculate these measures for Kirk Hall, as well.

12. Using the definitional formula, calculate the (biased) "variance" of Doty Hall in terms of deviations from the median, rather than the mean, of that distribution (just put the five scores in numerical order, and use the middle one as the median). (a) How does this "variance" compare to the σ^2 that you calculated in Exercise 7? (b) What property of the variance from the mean is illustrated by this exercise?

13. Calculate the mean deviation for Doty Hall, and compare it to σ (as calculated in Exercise 7). What do you think would happen to the difference of these two measures if you were to add an extreme score to the data of Doty?

14. Compute the biased and unbiased standard deviations for Distribution 6 in Table 3.2.

Thought Questions

1. For each of the following problems, which measure of central tendency should be computed? (a) An experimental psychologist wants a measure of central tendency for the number of trials taken to learn

a task by 45 eight-year-old children. The maximum number of trials allowed is 30. Most of the children took between 14 trials and 30 trials to learn the task, but five children did not learn the task at all even after 30 trials. (b) A student who has taken 25 college courses, each of which is worth 3 credits, wants to compute her grade point average. (c) A student who has taken 25 college courses, some of which are worth 3 credits and some 4 credits, wants to compute his grade point average. (d) A researcher wants a measure of central tendency for the income of a sample of 100 people that includes Bill Gates and Tiger Woods. (e) The editor of a college student yearbook wants to decide the color of the cover and asks the 30 students working on the yearbook to vote for orange, blue, green, or black.

2. (a) In a *positively* skewed distribution, which is larger, the mean or the median? (b) In a *negatively* skewed distribution, which is larger, the mean or the median? (c) In a *symmetric* distribution (such as the normal distribution), which is larger, the mean or the median?

3. Consider the following set of data, which represents 15 scores on a 10-point quiz: 0, 1, 3, 3, 4, 4, 4, 5, 5, 5, 7, 8, 9, 9, 10. (a) If the score of 10 is changed to 225,000,000, but the other numbers remain the same, what is the general effect on the mean and the median? (b) If the score of 10 is changed to 0, what is the general effect on the mean and the median? Why does the median change in this example, but not in the preceding example?

4. Why is the range much less informative (and much less useful) as a measure of variability than the standard deviation? Give an example of when the range could really be useful.

5. The mean of a statistics examination is 77.0. (a) If your score is 85, would you prefer the standard deviation to be large or small for purposes of getting a better grade? Why? (b) If your score is 69, would you prefer the standard deviation to be large or small? Why?

6. (a) When computing the standard deviation of a set of scores, when do we divide by N, and when do we divide by $N - 1$? (b) What is the difference between σ and s?

7. If the standard deviation of a set of scores is zero, what does this imply about the scores? Can a standard deviation be negative? Why or why not?

8. (a) When is it desirable to use the SIQR as the measure of variability? (b) When is it desirable to use the mean deviation (MD) as the measure of variability?

Computer Exercises

1. Use your statistical package to find the mode, median, and mean for each of the quantitative variables in Ihno's data set.

2. Use your statistical package to find the mode for each of the categorical (i.e., qualitative variables) in Ihno's data set.

3. Use your statistical package to find the range, semi-interquartile range, unbiased variance, and unbiased standard deviation for each of the quantitative variables in Ihno's data set. (Does your statistical package offer you the option of obtaining the biased versions of the variance and standard deviation?)

4. Use your statistical package to create a new variable that is equal to 2 times the diagnostic quiz score, so that the new variable is measured on a 0 to 100 scale. How do the measures of variability found in the previous exercise compare between the new variable and the original math quiz score? What general principle is being illustrated with respect to the standard deviation?

5. Use your statistical package to create a new variable that adds 50 points to the math quiz score. How have the measures of variability changed for this new variable as compared to the same measures calculated for the original math quiz score? What general principle is being illustrated with respect to the standard deviation?

Bridge to SPSS

The three measures of central tendency discussed in this chapter can be obtained from SPSS by opening the Frequencies: Statistics box described in the previous chapter (click on **Analyze**, **Descriptive Statistics**, and **Frequencies...**, and then click on the **Statistics** button). The upper-right quadrant of this box (see Figure 3.2) is labeled "Central Tendency" and allows you to select any number of the following choices: Mean, Median, Mode, and Sum (we do not know why SPSS includes the sum of the scores under the heading of Central Tendency). The mean of a distribution can actually be obtained from quite a few of the choices under **Analyze**; we point out a number of these options in later chapters.

There are three choices on the **Analyze/Descriptive Statistics** menu that will give you measures of variability (along with measures of central tendency). The one that is labeled **Descriptives...** is intended for use with continuous, quantitative data only. For measures of variability (SPSS refers to variability as *dispersion*), its **Options...** box offers only the standard deviation, variance, and range. Note that with respect to the first two measures just mentioned, only the "unbiased" versions are given. In response to how infrequently the biased versions are used in the social sciences, it appears that SPSS does not offer the biased variance or biased standard deviation from any of its menus. (It could be computed, however, by multiplying the unbiased value by $(N-1)/N$.)

The **Frequencies** dialog box is intended to accommodate a broader range of data types, including ordinal data and open-ended distributions. After clicking on the **Statistics** button, you can select **Quartiles** (see upper-left quadrant of Figure 3.2), and then calculate the interquartile and SIQ ranges from those results.

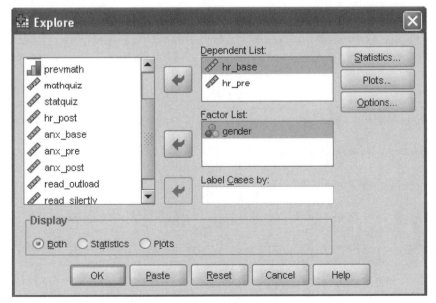

Figure 3.2

**The Frequencies:
Statistics Dialog Box**

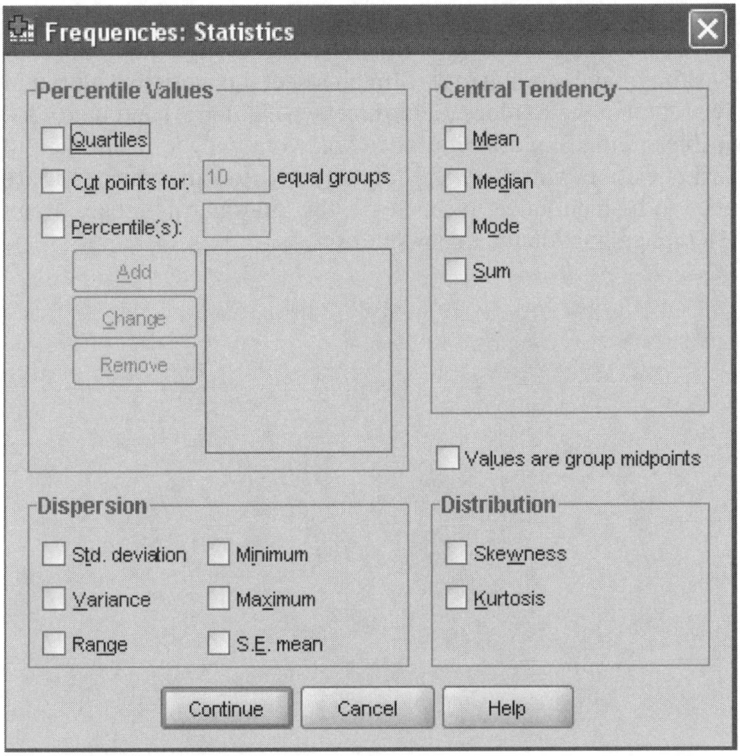

Figure 3.3

**The Explore
Dialog Box**

The third relevant choice on the Analyze/Descriptive Statistics menu is **Explore...**; this selection is intended for the thorough exploration of distributions that may be problematic. If you select the **Statistics** button in the Display section of the **Explore** dialog box (see Figure 3.3) and then click on **Descriptives** in the **Explore: Statistics** box, you will get, in addition to the standard deviation, variance, and range (and a few measures that are too advanced to be mentioned in this text), the interquartile range. If you want the SIQ range, just divide this result by 2.

Chapter 4
Standardized Scores and the Normal Distribution

PREVIEW

Interpreting a Raw Score Revisited

What is the advantage of using a transformed score, such as a percentile rank?

When comparing two (or more) scores from different distributions, why is it useful to refer each score to its mean and standard deviation?

How are we likely to be misled if we look only at the raw scores?

Rules for Changing μ and σ

What will happen to the mean and standard deviation of a set of scores if we do the following: Add or subtract a constant to every score? Multiply or divide every score by a constant?

How can these rules be used to obtain transformed scores with any desired mean and standard deviation?

Standard Scores (z Scores)

What is the mean and standard deviation of a set of z scores? Why are these particular values desirable?

How are z scores computed?

When raw scores are transformed into z scores, what happens to the shape of the distribution?

T Scores, SAT Scores, and IQ Scores

Why might we prefer to use T scores or SAT scores instead of z scores?

How are T scores and SAT scores computed?

What is the mean and standard deviation of a set of T scores or a set of SAT scores?

What is the mean and standard deviation of a set of IQ scores, and how are these scores computed?

The Normal Distribution

What is meant by saying that the normal distribution is a theoretical distribution?

How can the normal curve model be useful when dealing with real data?

(continued)

PREVIEW (*continued*)

What is the shape of the normal curve? Is it unimodal? Is it symmetric?

What is the relationship between the proportion of area within a section of a population distribution, and the probability of randomly selecting a score from that section?

What are the two parameters of the normal distribution?

Table of the Standard Normal Distribution

How is the normal curve table used?

How do we find the percent of the area under the normal curve that falls between the mean and any particular *z* score?

Where in the normal curve are values more likely to occur?

What percent of the area under the normal curve falls between the mean and one standard deviation unit? Between the mean and two standard deviation units?

Illustrative Examples

How do we calculate the proportion of the population that can be expected to have scores between two specified values, or above or below one specified value?

How do we calculate the score that is required to be within a specified proportion of the population (e.g., the top 10% or the middle 60%)?

Summary

Exercises

Thought Questions

Computer Exercises

Bridge to SPSS

Interpreting a Raw Score Revisited

In Chapter 2, we saw that it can be helpful to transform a raw score into a percentile rank. The percentile rank shows at a glance how the score stands in comparison to a specific reference group.

In Chapter 3, we identified two important characteristics of a population of scores: its location, usually summarized by the mean (μ), and its variability, for which the standard deviation (σ) is most often used. It is possible to deduce how well a given score compares to the group of which it is a part by using the mean and standard deviation of that group. As was the case with percentiles, we can build this information into the score itself. Specifically, we can derive a transformed (standardized) score that shows at a glance where the original raw score lies with respect to the mean, using the standard deviation of the reference group as the unit of measurement.

To illustrate, let us suppose that a college student takes three midterm examinations in three different courses and obtains the following raw scores:

	English	Mathematics	Psychology
X	80	65	75
___	___	___	___
___	___	___	___

On the surface, it might seem as though the student's best score is in English and his poorest score is in mathematics. It would be unwise to jump to such a conclusion, however, because there are several reasons why the raw scores may not be directly comparable. For example, the English examination may have been easy and resulted in many high scores, while the mathematics examination may have been extremely difficult. Or the English examination may have been based on a total of 100 points and the mathematics examination on a total of only 70 points. The raw scores provide information about the absolute number of points earned, but they give no clear indication as to how good the performance is and certainly no indication of how good the performance is compared to others.

Suppose that we find out that the mean and standard deviation of each test is as follows:

	English	Mathematics	Psychology
X	80	65	75
μ	85	55	60
σ	10	5	15

This additional information changes the picture considerably. Looking at the means, we can see that the class scores on the English examination were high, so much so that the score of 80 is below average. However, our student's midterm scores in both mathematics and psychology are above average. Therefore, the student's poorest relative result is in English.

The unwary observer might now conclude that the student's best score is in psychology, because that score is 15 points above average while the mathematics score is only 10 points above average. But as we pointed out in Chapter 3, the variability of a distribution of scores also influences the relative standing of a given score. The standard deviation (SD) indicates that a "typical" deviation on the psychology test was 15 points from the mean; so the student's psychology score of 75, which is 15 points (or 1 SD) above average, was certainly exceeded by a number of better scores[1] (though it surpassed quite a few, as well). The average variability on the mathematics examination, however, was only 5 points from the mean. Hence the student's mathematics score of 65 is 10 points (or 2 SDs) above average. That makes the math score unusually far above the mean, and it is therefore likely to be one of the best scores in that class.[2]

The picture presented by the raw scores was quite misleading in this instance. It turns out that the student's best score is in mathematics, the next best score is in psychology, and the poorest score is in English, relative, that is, to the other students in each course.

The raw scores of 80, 65, and 75 cannot be compared directly to each other because they come from distributions with different means and different standard deviations (and maybe even different shapes). That is, the units in which the raw scores are measured are not comparable from test to test. This difficulty can be overcome by transforming the scores on each test to a common scale with a specified mean and standard deviation. This new scale will then serve as a "common denominator," enabling us to compare directly the transformed scores of different tests.

Two questions remain: How do we change the scores so that they will have the desired common mean and SD? And what values of the mean and SD are useful choices for the "common denominator"?

Rules for Changing μ and σ

Suppose that the mathematics instructor in the previous example suffers a pang of conscience about the low mean and decides to add 5 points to everyone's score. She has added a *constant* amount to each score (one that is exactly the same for all the scores), so she does not have to recompute a new mean via the usual formula; we already showed in Chapter 3 that adding 5 points to everyone's score increases the mean by 5 points. Thus, the mean of the transformed scores (symbolized by μ_{new}) will be 60.

We also know from the properties of the mean described in Chapter 3 that if the English instructor subtracts 7.5 points from every score, the new mean will be 77.5. If he multiplies every score by 4, the new mean will be 340. And if he divides every score by 2, the new mean will be 42.5. Recall that these rules for conveniently determining the new mean work only if every original score is altered by exactly the same amount.

Insofar as the variability of the distribution is concerned, we saw in Chapter 3 that adding a constant to every score or subtracting a constant

---

[1]The exact number depends on the shape of the distribution of scores. For example, if the scores are normally distributed, approximately 16% of the scores are more than 1 standard deviation above the mean (as is shown in Chapter 8).

[2]If the distribution is normal, less than $2\frac{1}{2}$% of the scores are more than 2 SDs above the mean.

from every score does *not* change the standard deviation or variance. However, we also showed the following:

If every score is *multiplied* by a positive constant k,

$$\sigma_{new} = k\sigma_{old}$$

and if every score is *divided* by a positive constant k,

$$\sigma_{new} = \sigma_{old}/k$$

Therefore, if the English instructor adds 10 points or subtracts 6 points from every score, the SD remains 10 (and the variance remains 10^2 or 100), but if he multiplies every score by 4, the new SD equals 4×10 or 40 (and the new variance equals $4^2 \times 100$ or 1,600). If he divides every score by 2, the new SD equals 10/2 or 5 (and the new variance equals $100/2^2$ or 25).

These rules make it possible to obtain transformed scores with any desired mean and SD. For example, scores on the English test can be transformed to scores comparable to those on the mathematics test in two steps:

Procedure	New μ	New σ
1. Divide every score on the English examination by 2.0.	$85/2 = 42.5$	$10/2 = 5$
2. Add 12.5 to each of the scores obtained in Step 1.	$42.5 + 12.5 = 55$	5 (no change)

The first step is to change the SD to the desired value by multiplying or dividing each score by the appropriate constant, which affects the value of both μ and σ. Then the desired mean is obtained by adding or subtracting the appropriate constant, which does not cause any further change in σ. When the student's English score of 80 is subjected to these transformations, it becomes $(80/2) + 12.5$ or 52.5, and it is evident that this score is not nearly as good as the student's mathematics score. Note that both the original and the transformed English scores are half a SD below the means of their respective distributions.

Standard Scores (*z* Scores)

The techniques discussed in the preceding section make it possible to switch to any new mean and standard deviation. Therefore, the next logical step is to choose values of μ_{new} and σ_{new} that facilitate comparisons among the scores. One useful procedure is to convert the original scores to new scores with a mean of 0 and a SD of 1; these new scores are called **z scores** or *standard scores*.

Standard scores have two major advantages. Since the mean is zero, you can tell at a glance whether a given score is above or below average;

an above-average score is positive and a below-average score is negative. Also, because the SD is 1, the numerical size of a standard score indicates *how many SDs* above or below average the score is. We saw at the beginning of this chapter that this information offers a valuable clue as to how good the score is; a score 1 SD above average (i.e., a standard score of 1) would demarcate approximately the top 16% in a normal distribution (ND), while a score 2 SDs above average (a standard score of 2) would demarcate approximately the top $2\frac{1}{2}$% in a ND.

To convert a set of scores to standard scores, the first step is to subtract the original mean from every score. According to the rules given in the previous section, the new mean is equal to:

$$\mu_{new} = \mu_{old} - \mu_{old} = 0$$

while the SD is unchanged. Next, each score obtained from the first step is divided by the original SD. As a result:

$$\mu_{new} = \frac{0}{\sigma_{old}} = 0$$

$$\sigma_{new} = \frac{\sigma_{old}}{\sigma_{old}} = 1$$

That is, the mean remains zero, while the SD becomes 1. Summarizing these steps in a single formula yields:

$$z = \frac{X - \mu}{\sigma} \qquad \qquad \text{Formula 4.1}$$

where z is the symbol for a standard score.

Converting each of the original examination scores given at the beginning of this chapter to z scores yields the following:

	English	Mathematics	Psychology
X	80	65	75
μ	85	55	60
σ	10	5	15
z	$\frac{80 - 85}{10} = -0.50$	$\frac{65 - 55}{5} = +2.00$	$\frac{75 - 60}{1.5} = +1.00$

The standard scores show at a glance that the student was half a SD below the mean in English, two SDs above the mean in mathematics, and one SD above the mean in psychology.

It is important to remember that when raw scores are transformed into z scores, *the shape of the distribution remains exactly the same*. We are just measuring all the scores with reference to a new point (the

Table 4.1 **Distribution of 20 Baseline Heart Rate Scores Expressed in Beats per Minute (bpm), z Scores, and Beats per Second (bps)**

Low-phobic male	Heart rate (bpm)	Heart rate z score	Heart rate (bps)
1	72	+2.36	1.200
2	70	+1.24	1.167
3	70	+1.24	1.167
4	70	+1.24	1.167
5	69	+0.67	1.150
6	69	+0.67	1.150
7	68	+0.11	1.133
8	68	+0.11	1.133
9	68	+0.11	1.133
10	68	+0.11	1.133
11	67	−0.45	1.117
12	67	−0.45	1.117
13	67	−0.45	1.117
14	67	−0.45	1.117
15	67	−0.45	1.117
16	67	−0.45	1.117
17	66	−1.01	1.100
18	66	−1.01	1.100
19	66	−1.01	1.100
20	64	−2.14	1.067
μ	67.80	0.00	1.13
σ	1.78	1.00	0.0296

mean instead of zero), and with a new unit size (the SD instead of the original units). To illustrate this point, the baseline heart rates for the 20 low-phobic men from Ihno's statistics class are presented in Table 4.1 along with the corresponding z scores; we will be treating these 20 scores as a population. The scores have been arranged in decreasing order for clarity.

The mean of the baseline heart rate (HR) scores is 67.80 beats per minute (bpm) and the SD is 1.78 bpm; the z scores were obtained using Formula 4.1. For example, the z score corresponding to 72 bpm is equal to

$$z = \frac{72 - 67.80}{1.78} = +2.36$$

In accordance with the previous discussion, the mean of the z scores is 0.00 and the SD is 1.00. The raw score and z score distributions are plotted in Figure 4.1; note that a single graph suffices because the shape of the distribution is the same for both sets of scores. Thus, the relationship of the scores to one another is *not* changed by transforming them to standard scores. The only things changing are the location (i.e., central tendency) and the scaling (i.e., spread) of the distribution.

Figure 4.1

Frequency Distribution of Raw HR Scores and Their z Scores From Table 4.1

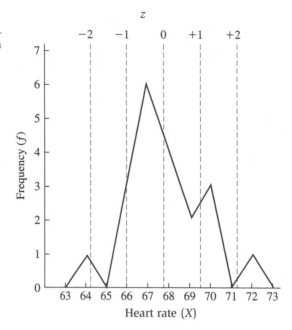

Although the HR scores are measured in beats per minute, identical z scores would be obtained (within rounding-off error) for each individual if HR were measured in beats per *second*, as is shown in the rightmost column of Table 4.1. For example,

HR in beats per minute	z score	HR in beats per second
$\dfrac{70 - 67.80}{1.78} =$	$+1.24$	$= \dfrac{1.167 - 1.13}{.0296}$

This indicates that z scores give an accurate picture of the standing of each score relative to the reference group even after the original scores have been divided by a constant (60, in this case). In fact, the properties of the mean and SD are such that the original scores can be subjected to any combination of addition, subtraction, multiplication, or division by constants without affecting the corresponding z scores.

Standard scores are used extensively in the behavioral sciences. They also play an important role in statistical inference, as we will see in subsequent chapters.

T Scores, SAT Scores, and IQ Scores

Standard scores have their disadvantages. For example, they can be difficult to explain to someone who is not well versed in statistics. A college professor once decided to report the results of an examination as z scores. He was quickly besieged by anxious students who did not understand that a *z* score of 0 represents average performance (and not zero correct!), not to mention the agitated ones who received negative scores and wondered how they could ever make up the negative points.

T Scores

One task of behavioral scientists is to report test scores to people who are not statistically sophisticated, so several alternatives to *z* scores have been developed. The mean and standard deviation of each alternative described next have been chosen so that all of the scores will be positive and so that the mean and SD will be easy to remember. One such alternative, called *T scores,* is defined as a set of scores with a mean of 50 and a SD of 10. The *T* scores are obtained from *z* scores using the following formula:

$$T = 10z + 50 \qquad\qquad \text{Formula 4.2}$$

Each raw score is first converted to a *z* score, then each *z* score is multiplied by 10, and 50 is added to each resulting score. For example, a heart rate of 69 in Table 4.1 is converted to a *z* score of 0.67 by the usual formula. Then *T* is equal to $(10)(0.67) + 50$ or 56.70. It is easy to prove that Formula 4.2 does produce the desired mean and SD:

Procedure	New μ	New σ
1. Convert raw scores to *z* scores.	0	1
2. Multiply each *z* score by 10.	$10 \times 0 = 0$	$10 \times 1 = 10$
3. Add 50 to each score obtained in Step 2.	$0 + 50 = 50$	10 (no change)

Common physical measurements (including heart rates) are rarely transformed to *T* scores, because they are already expressed in units that are familiar. However, a *T* score would still provide additional information in locating a particular individual within a distribution. (You may know that a man who is 6 feet tall is taller than average, but a *T* score of 60 for height would tell you immediately that he is 1 SD above the mean.) But *T* scores are even more helpful when dealing with psychological tests that are measured in arbitrary units. For example, scores on the anxiety scale that Ihno used can range from 10 to 50. Whereas it may be clear that 10 represents very little or no anxiety and 50 a great deal of anxiety, it is certainly not obvious just how to interpret a score of, say, 20 or 30. However, once you become familiar with *T* scores, you can tell at a glance that a student whose baseline anxiety *T* score is 45 is below average in anxiety and, more specifically, that he or she is exactly one half of a SD below average. (A *z* score of −.5 yields the same information but requires dealing with a minus sign and a decimal point.) Although a negative *T* score is mathematically possible, it is very unlikely. It would require that a person be more than 5 SDs below average, and scores more than 3 SDs above or below the mean rarely occur with real data.

SAT Scores

Scores on some nationally administered examinations, such as the Scholastic Aptitude Test (SAT), the College Entrance Examination Boards, and the Graduate Record Examination, are transformed to a scale with a mean of 500 and a standard deviation of 100. These scores, which we will refer to as SAT scores (based on their best-known application), are obtained as follows:

$$SAT = 100z + 500 \qquad \text{Formula 4.3}$$

As in the case of T scores, the raw scores are first converted to z scores; each z score is then multiplied by 100, and 500 is added to each resulting score. A comparison with the T score formula should make it obvious that an SAT score is just 10 times a T score. This explains the apparent mystery of how you can obtain a score of 642 on a test with only 30 or 40 items. And you may well be pleased if you obtain a score of 642, because it is 142 points or 1.42 SDs above the mean (and therefore corresponds to a z score of 1.42 and a T score of 64.2).

IQ Scores

Another common score that is based on transforming z scores to a more convenient form is the *IQ score.* The well-known Stanford-Binet (S-B) test creates its intelligence quotient (i.e., IQ) scores by transforming its z scores according to the following formula:

$$\text{S-B IQ} = 16z + 100 \qquad \text{Formula 4.4A}$$

It is because of this formula, rather than some convenient coincidence, that the average IQ of the population happens to be about 100. You can also see why IQ scores above 148 or below 52 are very unusual: They differ from the mean by 3 SDs. The newer Wechsler Adult Intelligence Scale (WAIS) uses a slightly different formula to create IQ scores. The WAIS is also based on a mean of 100, but unlike the Stanford-Binet test, it uses a standard deviation of 15 instead of 16:

$$\text{WAIS IQ} = 15z + 100 \qquad \text{Formula 4.4B}$$

The Normal Distribution

So far we have shown that a standard score can be more informative than a raw score—for example, when trying to interpret an individual's performance on a difficult exam for which the average could be as low as 40 points out of 100. A z score of 1.0 has to be relatively good no matter what the mean is. However, precisely how good that z score is depends on the *shape* of the distribution you are dealing with.

Suppose that the scores on an exam have an extremely positive skew: The bulk of the scores are a bit below 40, but some scores are over 80, and there are even a few in the 90s. In this case, a z score of 1.0 is not nearly as impressive as it would be in a very negatively skewed distribution because there will be some scores whose z scores are quite a bit larger than 1.0. Conversely, suppose that the scores are clustered slightly above 40 with a "tail" that narrows down as you get near a score of zero, but there are no really high scores. Here, a z score of 1.0 is likely to be one of the highest scores in the class and therefore much more impressive than in the preceding case. Two z scores, each from a different distribution, can be more easily compared if we know that the two distributions have similar shapes.

Whereas z scores are almost always more informative than raw scores, they become especially informative when you are dealing with a well-known distribution called the **normal distribution** (less formally referred to as the *normal curve*). Any distribution of real data will never match the ND exactly. The ND is a *theoretical* distribution—a mathematical abstraction like a perfect circle, or a line that has length but no width. The normal curve is unimodal and symmetric (as was illustrated in Chapter 2) and is most often described as a bell-shape curve because it is high in the middle and low at both ends, or *tails.* However, the ND is not just any bell-shape curve; its shape is defined by a particular mathematical equation.[3] As a theoretical distribution, the ND contains an infinite number of scores. Its tails on either side keep falling closer to the X-axis but do not actually touch it until you go an infinite distance in either direction. (Mathematicians say that the curve approaches the X-axis asymptotically.)

Despite its abstract definition, the ND is a distribution that tends to arise, at least approximately, rather frequently in nature. For example, if you look at the heights of all people of one gender in a large population, their distribution will look rather similar to the ND. However, you can tell immediately that your empirical height distribution cannot match the ND exactly. Your distribution will end abruptly on either side, when you get to the shortest and tallest people in the population. Nonetheless, for many purposes, the ND will be an acceptable approximation for the variable you are dealing with, and it is much easier to work with mathematically than any finite distribution of real data. SAT scores, for which a large number of data points are available, are used later in this chapter as our example of a population that has a distribution similar to the ND.

The statistical procedures described in this chapter may seem relevant only when measuring dependent variables that have approximately normal

---

[3]The formula for the normal curve is fairly complicated:

$$f(x) = \frac{1}{\sigma\sqrt{2\pi}} e^{-(X-\mu)^2/2\sigma^2}$$

where $\pi = 3.1416$ and $e = 2.7183$, both approximately.

distributions in a population. However, we show in the next chapter that the ND has a much broader use as a statistical model when used with groups of scores rather than individuals, even when the variable being measured has a very skewed distribution in the population (e.g., annual income).

As with any frequency distribution, the horizontal axis of the normal distribution in Figure 4.2 represents score values and the vertical axis is related to the relative frequencies of the scores. Also, all values in Figure 4.2 are located *under* the curve. So the *total population* is expressed in the graph as the *total area under the normal curve,* and we can arbitrarily define this area as 100% without bothering about the exact number of cases in the population. Alternatively, we may move the decimal point two places to the left and define the total area under the normal curve as 1.00. This definition is useful when we wish to answer questions that deal with probability, since the sum of all the specific probability values in any distribution is 1.00.

Now suppose that you are asked to find the proportion of the population with values between points X_1 and X_2 in Figure 4.2. Graphically, the answer is given by the percent *area between* these two points. This is equivalent to the percent frequency of all these values and/or to the probability of occurrence of these values.

If you have taken an elementary calculus course, you know that the numerical value of the area between any two X values may be found by integrating the normal curve equation. However, you also know how tedious it would be to carry out an integration every time you wished to use the normal curve model. Fortunately, all necessary integrations have been performed and summarized in a convenient table, which shows the percent frequency of values within any distance (in terms of standard deviations) from the population mean. We explain the use of the normal curve table next.

Figure 4.2

The Normal Curve: A Theoretical Distribution

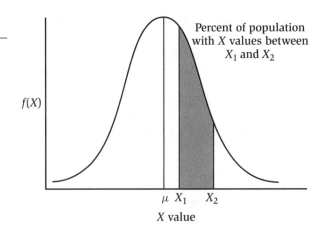

Percent of population with X values between X_1 and X_2

$f(X)$

μ X_1 X_2

X value

Parameters of the Normal Distribution

Normal distributions can differ from each other in just two ways: their locations (represented by their central point, μ) and their variability or spreads (as measured by σ). Just as any rectangle can be specified by giving both its length and width, any ND can be completely determined by giving its μ and σ. These two quantities are referred to as the *parameters* of the ND. (This usage is consistent with the meaning of a parameter as a population value as defined in Chapter 1.) Note that these two parameters appear in the equation for the ND (see footnote on page 91) and must be specified before that equation can be solved for any value of X. Because Parts II and III of this text deal with statistical procedures whose purpose is to estimate or make inferences about the parameters of some ND of interest, procedures in those chapters are referred to collectively as *parametric statistics*.

Table of the Standard Normal Distribution

Although integral calculus could be used *in theory* to create a table of areas for every possible normal distribution, *in practice* this would require an infinite number of tables—one table for each possible combination of μ and σ. Instead, a convenient table has been created for just one special ND, the one whose parameters are $\mu = 0$ and $\sigma = 1$. This ND is called the **standard normal distribution**, and it arises whenever you transform all the scores in any ND into z scores. It is important to recall that transforming raw scores into z scores does *not* change the shape of a distribution at all. Only if a population of raw scores follows a ND will its z scores also form a normal distribution—specifically, the standard ND.

In order to use the table for the standard ND (presented as Table A in the Appendix) to solve problems about *any* ND, it is necessary to convert the scores you are interested in to z scores. Fortunately, as you have seen in the previous chapter, this is easy to do. To illustrate the way areas can be looked up in terms of z scores in Table A, a portion of that table is reproduced next.

Percents calculated from area under the normal curve					
z	.00	.01	.02	.03	...	.09
0.0					
⋮					
1.0	34.13	34.38	34.61	34.85		
1.1	36.43	36.65	36.86	37.08		
1.2	38.49	38.69	38.88	39.07		
1.3	40.32	40.49	40.66	40.82		
⋮					
∞					

The column on the left represents *z* values expressed to one decimal place, while the top row gives the second decimal place. The values within the table represent the *percent area between the mean and the z value,* expressed to two decimal places. For example, to find the percent of cases between the mean and 1.03 SDs from the mean, select the 1.0 row and go across to the .03 column; the answer is read as 34.85%.

The table gives percents on one side of the mean only, so that the maximum percent given in the table is 50.00 (representing half of the area). However, the normal curve is *symmetric,* which implies that the height of the curve at any positive *z* value (such as 1) is exactly the same as the height at the corresponding negative value (−1). Therefore, the percent between the mean and a *z* of 1 is exactly the same as the percent between the mean and a *z* of −1, and presentation of a second half of the table to deal with negative scores is unnecessary. It is up to you to remember whether you are working in the half of the curve above the mean (positive *z*) or the half of the curve below the mean (negative *z*). Also, do not expect the value obtained from the table to be the answer to your statistical problem in every instance. The table only provides values between the mean and a given *z* score, so some additional calculations will be necessary whenever you are interested in the area between two *z* scores (neither of which falls at the mean) or the area between one end of the curve and a *z* score. These calculations are illustrated in the following sections.

Characteristics of the Normal Curve

In Figure 4.3, the normal curve is presented with the *X*-axis marked off to illustrate specified *z* distances from the mean. The percent areas between the mean and those *z* values have been determined from Table A. For example, notice that the percent of the total area between μ (the

Figure 4.3

Normal Curve: Percent Areas From the Mean to Specified *z* Distances

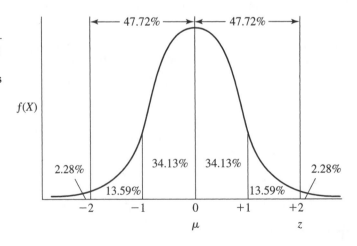

population mean where $z = 0$) and a z of $+1.00$ is 34.13%, and the area between μ and $z = -1.00$ is also 34.13%. Thus, 68.26% of the total area under the normal curve lies between $z = -1.00$ and $z = +1.00$.

Looking at the shape of the normal distribution, you should expect z values between 0 and $+1$ to occur more frequently than z values between $+1$ and $+2$. Even though the score distance between the mean and $z = +1$ is the same as the score distance between $z = +1$ and $z = +2$, the *area* between the mean and $z = +1$ is much greater than the area between $z = +1$ and $z = +2$. As you can see from Figure 4.2, the area between a z of $+1$ and a z of $+2$ is only about 13.6%.

Adding up the areas in Figure 4.3, you can see that about 95% of the normal curve lies within approximately two standard deviation units of μ (more exactly, between $z = -1.96$ and $z = +1.96$). For example, if the heights of U.S. adult males were assumed to be normally distributed with the mean at 5 foot 8 inches and the standard deviation equal to 3 inches, you would expect close to 95% of these males to have heights within 5 foot 8 inches ±6 inches, or between 5 foot 2 inches and 6 foot 2 inches. Table A can be used to answer more complex questions about areas of the normal curve, as we see next.

Illustrative Examples

The exam known familiarly as the SAT is administered each year to many thousands of high school seniors, and the obtained scores are known to have an approximately normal distribution. Therefore, it is reasonable to use the normal curve table (Table A) in the Appendix to answer questions about SAT scores.

However, because scores are given separately for different parts of the SAT, it is simpler for our examples to deal with the score from just one part of the SAT. We chose to express our examples in terms of the math SAT only. Because we know both the μ (500) and σ (100) for the math SAT, we can convert any score on that test to a z score and that can be found in to Table A in the Appendix, using Formula 4.1:

$$z = \frac{X - \mu}{\sigma} = \frac{X - 500}{100}$$

In situations where μ and σ are not known, they can be estimated from the sample $\overline{X}$ and s provided that the sample size is large; we will demonstrate this in the next chapter. There are many problems that can be solved by the use of this model:

1. What percent of high school seniors in the population can be expected to have math SAT scores between 500 and 670?

    The first step in any normal curve problem is to draw a rough diagram and find the part of the curve needed to solve the problem;

Figure 4.4

**Percent of Population
With Math SAT Scores
Between 500 and 670**

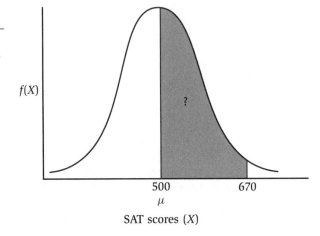

SAT scores (X)

this will prevent careless errors. The desired percent is expressed as the shaded area in Figure 4.4.

To obtain the percent area between the mean (500) and a raw score of 670, convert the raw score to a z score:

$$z = \frac{670 - 500}{100} = +1.70$$

Table A reveals that the percent area between the mean and a z score of 1.70 is equal to 45.54%. Therefore, nearly 46% of the population is expected to have scores between 500 and 670. By using the normal curve model as an approximation, you can reach this conclusion even though you cannot measure the entire population.

The area we just found can be used to determine the percentile rank (PR) for a score of 670. For any raw score, the PR is just the percentage of the area in the distribution below (i.e., to the left of) that score. For scores above the mean, you would need to add 50% (the area below the mean) to the area between the mean and the score of interest (45.54% in this example). Therefore, the PR for a score of 670 is 50 + 45.54, which equals 95.54—that is, a score of 670 is higher than 95.54% of the entire distribution.

2. What percent of the population can be expected to have scores between 450 and 500?

The diagram for this problem is shown in Figure 4.5. Converting the raw score of 450 to a z score yields

$$z = \frac{450 - 500}{100} = -0.50$$

Table A does not include any negative z values, but entering the table at the z score of +.50 will produce the right answer because

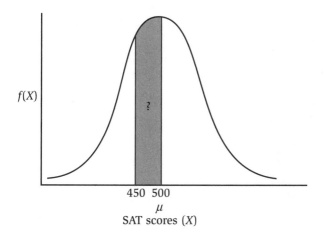

Figure 4.5

**Percent of Population
With Math SAT Scores
Between 450 and 500**

of the symmetry of the normal curve. The solution is that 19.15%, or about 19% of the population, is expected to have scores between 450 and 500.

To find the PR for a score that is less than the mean, such as 450, we need to find the percentage of the distribution that is below that score, and that amount is not given in Table A. However, we can see from Figure 4.5 that together the percentage below the score and the percentage between the score and the mean must add up to 50% (i.e., the total amount of the normal distribution below its mean), so the percentage below the mean can be found by subtracting the area between the score and the mean from 50%. In this example, we can find the PR of 450 by subtracting 19.15% from 50%: thus, the PR for 450 equals $50 - 19.15$, or about 31.

3. What percent of the population can be expected to have scores between 360 and 540?

This problem is likely to produce some confusion unless you use the diagram in Figure 4.6 as a guide. Table A gives values only between the mean and a given z score, so two steps are required. First obtain the percent between 360 and the mean (500); then obtain the percent between the mean and 540. Then *add* the two percentages together to get the desired area. The z values are as follows:

$$z = \frac{360 - 500}{100} = -1.40; z = \frac{540 - 500}{100} + 0.40$$

Table A indicates that 41.92% of the total area falls between the mean and a z of -1.40, and 15.54% falls between the mean and a z of $+0.40$. So the percent of the population expected to have scores between 360 and 540 is equal to $41.92\% + 15.54\%$, or 57.46%.

4. What percent of the population can be expected to have scores between 630 and 700?

Figure 4.6

Percent of Population With Math SAT Scores Between 360 and 540

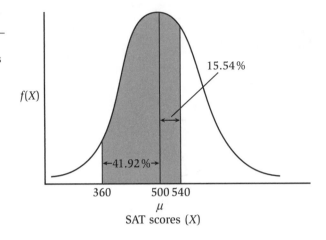

Figure 4.7

Percent of Population With Math SAT Scores Between 630 and 700

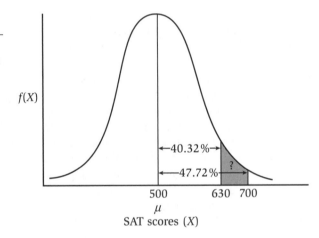

Once again, you are likely to encounter some difficulty unless you draw a diagram such as the one shown in Figure 4.7. The z score corresponding to a raw score of 630 is equal to $(630 - 500)/100$ or $+1.30$, and the z score corresponding to a raw score of 700 is equal to $(700 - 500)/100$ or $+2.00$. According to Table A, 40.32% of the curve falls between the mean and $z = +1.30$, and 47.72% of the curve falls between the mean and $z = +2.00$. So the answer is equal to 47.72% *minus* 40.32%, or 7.4%. In this example, subtraction (rather than addition) is the route to the correct answer, and drawing the illustrative diagram will help you decide on the proper procedure in each case.

5. What percent of the population can be expected to have scores above 720?

The percent to be calculated is shown in Figure 4.8. The z score corresponding to a raw score of 720 is equal to $(720 - 500)/100$ or $+2.20$, and the area between the mean and this z score as obtained

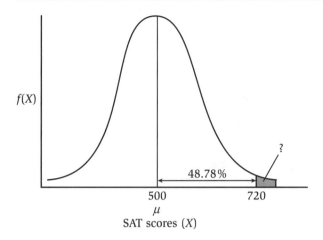

Figure 4.8

Percent of Population With Math SAT Scores Above 720

from Table A is equal to 48.61%. At this point, avoid the incorrect conclusion that the value from the table is the answer to the problem. As the diagram shows, you need to find the percent *above* 720. Since the half of the curve to the right of the mean is equal to 50.00%, the answer is equal to 50.00% − 48.61%, or 1.39%. A score of 720 is close to the 99th percentile, because just a little more than 1% of the population exceeds it.

6. What is the probability that a person drawn at random from the population will have a score of 720 or more?

    This problem is identical to the preceding one, but is expressed in different terminology. As before, convert 720 to a z score, obtain the percent between the mean and 720, and subtract from 50% to obtain the answer of 1.39%. To express this as a probability, move the decimal point two places to the left. The probability that any one individual drawn at random from the population will have a score of 720 or more is .0139, or about .014.

7. A math professor wishes to invite only the top 10% of the student population to join a competitive math team that she is forming. What cutoff math SAT score should she use to accept and reject candidates?

    This problem is the reverse of the ones we have looked at up to this point. Previously, you were given a score and asked to find a percent; this time, the percent is specified and a score value is needed. The problem is illustrated in Figure 4.9.

    The needed value is the raw score value corresponding to the cutoff line in Figure 4.9. The steps are exactly the reverse of the previous procedure:

    (a) If 10% are above the cutoff line, then 40% (50% − 10%) are between the mean and the cutoff line.

    (b) Enter Table A in the *body* of the table (where the percents are given), looking for the value of 40.00 (40%). Read out the z score

Figure 4.9

Math SAT Score That Demarcates the Top 10% of the Population

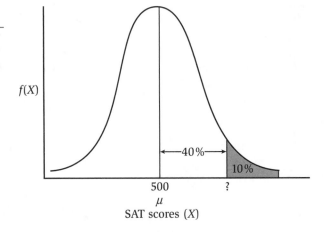

corresponding to the percent nearest in value to 40.00 ($z = 1.28$, which corresponds to 39.97).

(c) Determine the *sign* of the z score. The diagram shows that the desired cutoff score is *above* the mean, so the z score is positive and equals $+1.28$.

(d) Convert the z score to a raw score. Because $z = (X - \mu)/\sigma$, some simple algebraic manipulations yield $X = z\sigma + \mu$. Thus, $X = (+1.28)(100) + 500$, or 628. Any student with a score of 628 or more may try out for the new math team; individuals with scores of 627 or less are not invited. Note that the score that cuts off the top 10% of the distribution is the 90th percentile (or 9th decile). In general, anytime you need to find a percentile greater than the 50th you can follow the procedure above, as long as you realize that the Xth percentile is the score that cuts off the top $(1 - X)$% of the distribution. For percentiles smaller than the 50th, just note that the Xth percentile is the score that cuts off the bottom X% of the distribution, and proceed with the steps listed above, being careful to make your z score negative in Step 3, and then use that negative z to find the raw score in Step 4. The 50th percentile (i.e., the median) is always equal to the mean in a normal distribution.

8. What two cutoff scores enclose the middle 60% of the population?

   Because you are given a percentage and asked to find corresponding raw scores, this is another "reverse" problem; you need to find the two raw scores illustrated in Figure 4.10. Finding the middle X% of a normal distribution is a fairly common task, as you will see when we describe confidence intervals in Chapter 6. The first step in solving this type of problem is to divide X by 2 and then mark off $(X/2)$% on either side of the mean. In the case of the middle 60%, we mark off 30% on each side, as shown in Figure 4.10.

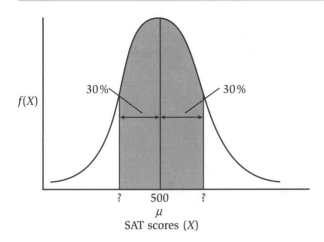

Figure 4.10

Math SAT Scores Enclosing the Middle 60% of the Population

Because the area between the mean and the upper cutoff line is 30%, this is one of the values that must be used to enter Table A. As in the previous problem, look in the body of the table to find the value of interest; in this problem, we want the value in the table that is closest to 30.00, which is 29.95. Then read off the z score corresponding to that value (29.95), which is .84. Next, convert this value to a raw score: $X = (0.84)(100) + (500)$, or 584. Thus, the upper cutoff score is 584. Thanks to the symmetry of the normal curve, we know that the z score for the lower cutoff in Figure 4.10 is $-.84$. Converting this value to a raw score, we obtain: $X = (-0.84)(100) + (500) = 500 - 84 = 416$. So, we can now say that the middle 60% of the scores are contained between 416 and 584. (As a check, add the two boundary values just found, $416 + 584 = 1,000$; the sum should equal twice the value in the middle. This will always be true when the two boundaries are equally distant from the middle.)

As you can see, the normal curve is useful for solving various types of problems involving scores and percentages of distributions. Of even greater importance is its use with certain sampling distributions, such as the sampling distribution of the mean, which is an important topic in the next chapter.

Summary

In order to compare scores based on different means and standard deviations, it is desirable to convert the raw scores to *standardized scores* with a common mean and SD. Some frequently used transformed scores are *z scores* (sometimes called *standard scores*), with a mean of 0 and a SD of 1; *T scores,* with a mean of 50 and a SD of 10; *SAT scores,* with a mean of 500 and a SD of 100; and IQ scores, with a mean of 100 and a SD of

15 or 16 (depending on the test). A transformed score shows at a glance whether a score is above or below average and how far it deviates from the mean in terms of SD units, with respect to a specified reference group.

General Transformations

Operation	Effect on μ	Effect on σ	Effect on σ^2
1. *Add* a constant, k, to every score	New mean = old mean $+ k$	No change	No change
2. *Subtract* a constant, k, from every score	New mean = old mean $- k$	No change	No change
3. *Multiply* every score by a constant, k	New mean = old mean $\times k$	New σ = old $\sigma \times k$	New σ^2 = old $\sigma^2 \times k^2$
4. *Divide* every score by a constant, k	New mean = old mean$/k$	New σ = old σ/k	New σ^2 = old σ^2/k^2

z Scores (Standard Scores)

$$z = \frac{X - \mu}{\sigma}$$

Formula 4.1

T Scores

$$T = 10z + 50$$

Formula 4.2

SAT Scores

$$SAT = 100z + 500 = 10T$$

Formula 4.3

IQ Scores

$$\text{S-B IQ} = 16z + 100$$

Formula 4.4A

$$\text{WAIS IQ} = 15z + 100$$

Formula 4.4B

Normal Distributions

One frequently used theoretical distribution is the *normal curve.* One use of this model is as follows: If it is assumed that raw scores in the population are normally distributed and that we know or can estimate the population mean and standard deviation, we can obtain (a) the percent of the population with raw scores above or below or between specified values and/or (b) the raw score that demarcates specified percentages in the population.

Type 1 Problem: Given a Raw Score, Find the Corresponding Proportion or Percentage of the Normal Curve

(a) Convert the raw score to a z score: $z = (X - \mu)/\sigma$.

(b) Enter the normal curve table in the z column, and read out the percent area from the mean to this z value.

(c) Compute the answer to the problem. Note that Table A gives only the area from the mean to the z value; create an appropriately labeled diagram to make sure your final answer is the one called for by the problem.

Type 2 Problem: Given a Proportion or Percentage of a Normal Curve, Find the Corresponding Raw Score

(a) Compute the appropriate percentage (if a proportion is given) and enter the normal curve table in the body of the table (where the areas are given). Read out the corresponding z score. If the desired raw score is *below* the mean, assign a negative sign to this z score.

(b) Convert the z score to a raw score: $X = z\sigma + \mu$.

Exercises

1. The mean of a set of scores is 8 and the standard deviation is 4. What will the new mean, standard deviation, and variance be if you:

    (a) Add 6.8 to every number?
    (b) Subtract 4 from every number?
    (c) Multiply every number by 3.2?
    (d) Divide every number by 4?
    (e) Add 6 to every number, and then divide each new number by 2?

2. For each of the following, compute the z score; then compute the T score.

    (a) A Turck Hall student with a score of 17.
    (b) A Turck Hall student with a score of 11.
    (c) A Kirk Hall student with a score of 17.
    (d) A Kirk Hall student with a score of 11.
    (e) A Dupre Hall student with a score of 6.
    (f) A Doty Hall student with a score of 6.

3. Consider the following data:

	Psychology test	English test
Student's score	73	67
μ	81.0	77.0
σ	5.0	10.0

This student believes that he has performed better on the psychology test for two reasons: His score is higher, and he is only 8 points below average (as opposed to 10 points below average on the English test). Convert each of his test scores to a z score. Is he right?

4. Which of each pair is better, or are they the same? (You should be able to answer by inspection.)

   (a) A T score of 47 and a z score of $+0.33$
   (b) A T score of 64 and a z score of $+0.88$
   (c) A T score of 42 and a z score of -1.09
   (d) A T score of 60 and a z score of $+1.00$
   (e) A T score of 50 and a raw score of 26 (mean of raw scores $= 26$, $\sigma = 9$)
   (f) A z score of $+0.04$ and a raw score of 1092 (mean of raw scores $= 1113$, $\sigma = 137$)
   (g) A z score of zero and a T score of 50

5. For data set 3 in Chapter 1 (reproduced here), transform each subject's (S) score on X to a z score. Then transform each subject's score on Y to a z score.

S	X	Y	z_X	z_Y
1	97	89	___	___
2	68	57	___	___
3	85	87	___	___
4	74	76	___	___
5	92	97	___	___
6	92	79	___	___
7	100	91	___	___
8	63	50	___	___
9	85	85	___	___
10	87	84	___	___
11	81	91	___	___
12	93	91	___	___
13	77	75	___	___
14	82	77	___	___

6. Find the mean and standard deviation (σ) for the following data set:

   $68.36, 15.31, 77.42, 84.00, 76.59, 68.43, 72.41, 83.05, 91.07, 80.62, 77.83$

   Transform each raw score in the preceding data set into a z score, a T score, and an SAT score.

   The remaining exercises are based on SAT scores, with the assumption that they follow the normal distribution with $\mu = 500$ and $\sigma = 100$.

7. What percent of the population obtains scores of 410 or less?

8. What percent of the population obtains scores between 430 and 530?

9. What percent of the population obtains scores between 275 and 375?

10. How do you explain the fact that the answer to Exercise 9 is smaller than the answer to Exercise 8, even though each problem deals with a 100-point range of scores?

11. What is the minimum score needed to rank in the top 5% of the population?

12. A psychologist wishes to test a new learning strategy on the bottom 15% of those who took the math SAT. What cutoff score should she use to select participants for her study?

13. A single student is drawn at random from the population. What is the probability that this student has a score:

    (a) of 410 or less?
    (b) between 430 and 530?
    (c) between 275 and 375?
    (d) in the top 5% of the population?

    (Hint: Base your answers to this exercise on the percentages you found for the previous exercises.)

14. Between which two SAT scores would you find the middle: (a) 70% of the normal distribution? (b) 90% of the normal distribution?

Thought Questions

1. What are the advantages of having a set of scores that has a mean of zero and a standard deviation of 1 (z scores)?

2. A college student takes two introductory courses for first-year students. On her psychology exam, she scores 73; the mean is 81.0, and the SD is 5.0. On her English exam, she scores 67; the mean is 77, and the SD is 10.0. Both distributions are approximately normal. She concludes that she did better on the psychology exam because her score on that exam is 6 points higher. Is she correct? Why or why not?

3. For the same exams as in the previous question, another student scores 91 on the psychology exam and 93 on the English exam. He concludes that he did better on the English exam because his English score is 16 points above average, while his psychology score is only 10 points above average. Is he correct? Why or why not?

4. Why is Table A given in terms of z scores rather than raw scores?

5. Why is it *not* necessary to know the exact number of cases in the population being studied in order to use the procedures described in this chapter?

6. The distributions of scores on two exams are approximately normal. The mean of the first exam is 80, and the mean of the second exam is 95. The SD of each exam is 15. Draw a figure to show that there *must* be some scores on the first exam that are greater than the mean of the second exam.

7. Suppose that in the previous question, the SD of each exam is changed to 3. How would this affect the likelihood that there are scores on the first exam that are greater than the mean of the second exam? Draw an appropriate figure to help you answer this question.

8. If you know that a distribution of scores is bimodal, or asymmetric, or a J-curve, or any other shape that departs significantly from the normal distribution, would it be correct to use Table A to solve problems, as was done in this chapter? Why or why not?

Computer Exercises

1. Use your statistical package to create new variables consisting of the z scores for the anxiety and heart rate measures both at baseline and prequiz in Ihno's data set. Request means and standard deviations of the z-score variables to demonstrate that the means and SDs are 0 and 1, respectively, in each case. (Note: If, like SPSS, your statistical software computes only s for the standard deviation and not σ, you should calculate your z scores based on s.)

2. Use your statistical package to create a z-score variable corresponding to the math background quiz score, and then transform the z-score variable to a T score, an SAT score, and an IQ score.

3. Repeat Exercise 2 for the statistics quiz score that was part of Ihno's experiment.

   For the remaining exercises, use your statistical package to find the indicated areas under the normal curve (your answer should include six digits past the decimal point):

4. The area below a z score of 3.1.

5. The area above a z score of 3.3.

6. The area below a z score of -3.7.

7. The area between the mean and a z score of .542.

8. The area between the mean and a z score of -1.125.

Bridge to SPSS

After SPSS has calculated the mean and standard deviation for one of the variables in your spreadsheet, you could find the corresponding z scores by creating a new variable in the Compute Variable box available from the Transform menu (just click on the first choice: **Compute ...**). However, an easier way to obtain z scores is available from the Analyze/Descriptive Statistics menu; just choose **Descriptives ....** Then under the list of variables that appears in the Descriptives dialog box, you will see the phrase "Save standardized values as variables" preceded by a small checkbox. Check the box, and move over the variables for which you would like to see the z scores. After you click **OK**, two things will happen. You will get the usual Descriptives output for the variables you moved over, and for each of these variables SPSS will have added a new variable at the end of your spreadsheet, containing the z scores that correspond to the scores of that variable.

We have two warnings for those who create z scores automatically in SPSS. Note that the first of these warnings does not apply to users of SPSS for Windows, version 14.0 or later. SPSS names the new z-score variables by putting the letter z at the beginning of the original name. If the original name consists of the maximum eight characters allowed, the last character will be dropped; for example, if the variable is named anxiety1, the z-score variable will be named zanxiety. However, if you are creating z-score variables for both anxiety1 and anxiety2, the second of these cannot also be called zanxiety, so SPSS will name it zsc001, instead. Choose a shorter original name if you want to ensure that all of your new z-score variable names will have some mnemonic value (or use a version of SPSS that is more recent than 14.0).

Second, because SPSS does not deal at all with the biased variance or standard deviation, it creates z scores by dividing deviations from the mean by the *unbiased* standard deviation. We described z scores in this chapter as based on σ rather than s, because that is the more common method. When you are calculating z scores for individuals, it is usually the case that you are viewing the entire set of individuals as a population instead of just a sample. Because SPSS creates z scores based on s, calculating σ for the set of z scores created will not yield a value of 1.0; it is s that will equal 1.0, in this case. Of course, the mean of the set of z scores will always be zero, even if they were produced by SPSS. To get z scores based on σ instead of s, you would have to multiply all of the z scores created by SPSS by the square root of the ratio of your total N to $N - 1$.

You can use SPSS to obtain areas under the normal distribution with more accuracy (i.e., digits past the decimal point) than is available in Table A and for z scores not found in Table A or most other tables available from books. Start by opening a new (i.e., empty) data sheet and entering the z score of interest in the first cell. For convenience, you can assign the simple variable name "z" to this first column. Then open the Compute Variable box by selecting **Compute . . .** (the first choice) from the Transform menu. In the Target Variable space, type an appropriate variable name like "area." In the Numeric Expression space, type **CDFNORM** and then, in parentheses, the name of the first variable—for example, CDFNORM (z). (*Note:* We are using uppercase letters here for clarity, but SPSS does not distinguish between upper- and lowercase letters in variable or function names.) CDFNORM is a function name that stands for the *Cumulative Density Function* for the *NORMal* distribution; therefore it returns a value equal to all of the area to the left of (i.e., below) the z score you entered. If you multiply this value by 100, you get the percentile rank associated with the z score in question (this works for both positive and negative z scores, as long as you include the minus sign for any negative z score).

If you want the area between the mean and your z value, just subtract .50 from the area obtained by the CDFNORM function (this will work for negative z scores, if you enter them *without* the minus sign). If you want the area above, rather than below, a particular z score, just change the sign in front of the z score (add a minus sign to a positive z score or remove the minus sign from a negative z score); because the normal curve is symmetric around $z = 0$, the area below $-z$ is the same as the area above $+z$. Note that the larger the z score you enter in the first cell of your SPSS datasheet, the more "decimals" you will need to display the answer accurately. The fourth column in Variable View lets you set the number of digits that will be displayed to the right of the decimal point—as long as this number is less than the number in the third column (Width) for that variable. For instance, if you are looking for the area below a z score of 3 or 4, you will want to set the "decimals" number to at least 6.

Part II
Basic Inferential Statistics

Chapter 5   **Introduction to Statistical Inference**

Chapter 6   **The One-Sample *t* Test and Interval Estimation**

Chapter 7   **Testing Hypotheses About the Difference Between the Means of Two Populations**

Chapter 8   **Nonparametric Tests for the Difference Between Two Means**

Chapter 9   **Linear Correlation**

Chapter 10   **Prediction and Linear Regression**

Chapter 11   **Introduction to Power Analysis**

Chapter 5
Introduction to Statistical Inference

PREVIEW

Introduction

The typical population of interest to the behavioral science researcher is extremely large; what serious problem does this create? How does the use of samples help to solve this problem?

What new difficulty is created by the use of samples? What type of statistics helps to solve this problem?

The Goals of Inferential Statistics

What are the most common purposes of inferential statistics?

Sampling Distributions

What is an experimental sampling distribution? Why is this type of statistical model rarely used in inferential statistics?

What is a theoretical sampling distribution? When is it reasonable to use the normal curve as the theoretical distribution (i.e., statistical model)?

The Standard Error of the Mean

We wish to draw inferences about the mean of one population, based on a statistic whose sampling distribution is normal—namely, the sample mean. Why should the standard deviation of the raw scores not be used as the measure of variability? How does the variability of a distribution of sample means differ from that of raw scores?

What is the standard error of the mean? Why can't it be measured directly? How is it estimated?

What does the standard error of the mean tell us about the trustworthiness of a single sample mean as an estimate of the population mean?

The z Score for Sample Means

How is the z score calculated when dealing with sample means instead of individuals?

What is a p value?

(continued)

PREVIEW (*continued*)

Null Hypothesis Testing

What two hypotheses are made prior to conducting the statistical analysis? Which of these hypotheses is assumed to be true?

What is a Type I error?

What is the criterion of significance, and how is it related to a Type I error?

What is the probability of a Type I error?

How does the one-tailed *p* value differ from the two-tailed *p* value?

What are critical values? How are critical values used in null hypothesis testing?

What are the critical values for *z* in a two-tailed significance test using the .05 criterion? What are the critical values using the .01 criterion of significance?

What advantage does the .05 criterion of significance have over the .01 criterion of significance? What is the advantage of the .01 criterion? Which is used more often in behavioral science research?

What is a Type II error?

Why is the probability of a Type II error harder to determine than the probability of a Type I error?

What is the relationship between the probabilities of Type I and Type II errors?

What is a one-tailed test of significance? What are the advantages and disadvantages of this procedure? Why is the two-tailed test more commonly used?

Assumptions Required by the Statistical Test for the Mean of a Single Population

What assumptions underlie the use of the *z* score for sample means in conjunction with the normal distribution?

What can be done when σ is not known?

Summary

Exercises

Thought Questions

Computer Exercises

Bridge to SPSS

Appendix: The Null Hypothesis Testing Controversy

What is controversial about null hypothesis testing? What types of misunderstandings can it lead to?

Introduction

One daunting fact greatly complicates the lives of behavioral scientists: The populations from which they seek to collect data are usually far too large for them to measure every element in the population, or even a sizable portion of the population.

Suppose that a psychologist wishes to test the hypothesis that a new interactive videogame will improve the performance of students in college-level statistics courses. In this study, the population consists of all college students in the United States who are studying statistics. This is enough to frighten off even the most dedicated researcher! No behavioral scientist can afford the time, effort, and money needed to obtain and analyze data from so many thousands of people.

Therefore, the psychologist might decide to limit the study to 100 statistics students selected in some way from the population. This procedure will provide him with a group that can be measured in its entirety, but it creates a serious problem. The data are obtained from only a small part of the population, so there is no assurance that these data will accurately reflect what is happening in that population. If this sample of 100 students is atypical of the population as a whole, the psychologist will suffer some unhappy consequences: The results that he publishes, and his decision concerning the merits of the new video game, may be contradicted subsequently by other researchers who try to verify the psychologist's findings with different samples of students drawn from the same population. If that occurs, the overall effort to advance our scientific knowledge in this area will undergo a setback while researchers try to make sense of the conflicting results. Unfortunately, the only sure way to prevent this confusion would be to measure the entire population—which, as we noted above, is simply not feasible.

In sum: Behavioral scientists need to draw conclusions about populations, but they usually can measure only a small part of those populations. This problem affects all areas of the behavioral sciences. For example, an industrial psychologist studying the effects of pay on job satisfaction cannot measure the entire population of all paid employees in the United States. Even if he were to restrict his attention to one type of job, the population would still be far too large to measure in its entirety. An experimental psychologist studying the performance of rats in a maze under varying conditions cannot run all laboratory rats in the world in her experiment, nor can she obtain all possible runs from any one rat. An anthropologist interested in the effects of different cultures on motivation in children cannot study all of the children from each of the cultures in which she is interested. In fact, this predicament is so common that most behavioral science research would not be possible without some effective resolution. As you may have guessed from the title of this chapter, the answer lies in the use of *inferential statistics*—techniques for drawing inferences about an entire population, based on data obtained from a sample drawn from that population.

The Goals of Inferential Statistics

There are two major kinds of inferences that the behavioral scientist might wish to make about a population. One useful procedure is to estimate the values of population parameters. Given a sample whose mean and variance have been computed, we may wish to estimate the mean and variance of the parent population. Any statistic computed from a single sample (such as $\overline{X}$ or s) that provides an estimate of the corresponding population parameter (such as μ or σ) is called a *point estimate.*

However, for most purposes, a point estimate is not sufficiently informative, because it leaves us with no idea of how far off from the parameter it may be. Such information is supplied by an *interval estimate,* a range of values that has a known probability of including the true value of the parameter. For example, suppose that the cell phone records of a sample of teenagers are gathered for a month, and it is found that they send an average of 60 text messages per day. A point estimate would state that the most reasonable value of μ (per day) is 60. If an estimate in terms of a single number is *not sufficient,* the researcher should use the appropriate techniques of inferential statistics to determine an *interval* that is likely to include the population mean. Suppose she finds this interval to be 54–66, or 60 ± 6. This interval estimate divides all numerically possible values of μ into two sets: "likely" (54–66) and "unlikely" (less than 54 or more than 66), with "likely" and "unlikely" having precise meanings to be discussed in greater detail in the next chapter.

The other major use of inferential statistics is to assess the probability of obtaining certain kinds of sample results under certain population conditions in order to test a specific hypothesis. The aforementioned psychologist might wish to determine the probability that a sample of 100 statistics students, who have been using a new educational videogame that does not help them to learn stats at all, would nonetheless have gained an average of at least 5 points on their exam scores. Why anyone would want to know such a probability will be made clear (we hope!) later in this chapter. First, in order to determine probabilities when dealing with samples instead of individuals, you will need to learn about *sampling distributions.* So, it is to this topic that we turn next.

Sampling Distributions

In the preceding chapter, you learned how to transform a raw score into a new score that shows at a glance how that score stands in comparison to a specific reference group and how to find the proportion of scores above or below that score in a normal distribution. These procedures will be useful in the chapters ahead, but not for the descriptive purposes discussed previously. Behavioral researchers are rarely concerned with the score of any one individual in a distribution. Their studies usually involve a group of individuals, all of whom share some common characteristic (e.g., the same psychopathology diagnosis), or all of whom have been subjected to the same experimental treatment. Therefore, the remainder of this text will focus on the performance of a group as a whole—for instance, on some word-recall task. This is where descriptive statistics becomes immediately useful, as a first step. To describe the performance of an entire group, rather than an individual, we need a measure of central tendency. As we have seen, the arithmetic mean is usually the most suitable of such measures for advanced statistics. Therefore, throughout this part of the text, groups will be dealt with in terms of their means. Also, our interest will not be in the particular groups we are dealing with but in how these groups serve as samples of (and therefore representations of) the entire populations from which they were drawn. Consequently, we will refer to all of the groups that we deal with from now on as *samples,* and we will focus primarily on the means $(\overline{X})$ of these samples.

Before we can introduce statistical inference, we must first apply the descriptive tools you have just learned to entire collections of groups (i.e., samples), rather than to collections of individuals. We begin with a simple (hypothetical) example in which a researcher (let us call her Elsie) is interested in the relationship between diet and physical growth. In particular, Elsie has an interest in—and concern about—growth hormones given to cows to increase their production of milk, and the effect those hormones may or may not have on humans who drink that milk (we will call it GH milk, for short). Before going into the lab to conduct an extensive and expensive randomized trial study, Elsie wants to see if she can find evidence for such an effect in the general population. So, she obtains permission from the ERC (European Research Council) to examine the medical records of Scandinavian women, who are a particularly useful population for this study because of their unusual height. A simple starting hypothesis is that people who were raised drinking GH milk might be slightly taller than those who were not. Elsie begins by finding in the medical records that the height of Scandinavian women is approximately normally distributed with a mean of 68 inches and a standard deviation (SD) of 3.2 inches. If very nearly all Scandinavian women were raised on GH milk, Elsie can use those population parameters as the parameters for all women in the GH milk population.

To test her hypothesis, Elsie will next need to find a random sample of Scandinavian women who were *not* raised on GH milk (perhaps their parents gave them only organic milk or soy milk). She would get the most definitive answer to her research question if she could measure the height of every Scandinavian woman not raised on GH milk, but we will assume that even that specific segment of the population contains tens of thousands of people. The practical strategy for a researcher in Elsie's position, then, is to select as large a sample as she can manage, given her resources, to measure the mean height of her sample and compare it to the population mean she derived from national medical records. Inevitably, Elsie's sample mean will not be exactly equal to the population mean, so she will need to decide how unusual it would be to draw a sample of the same size directly from the GH milk population and obtain a sample mean that deviates in height from the population mean as much as her specially selected sample. When you want to know if the average height of an entire random sample is unusual, rather than a single individual drawn from the population, you will need to discover what the distribution of heights would look like for *groups* of randomly selected people—in Elsie's case, for groups of Scandinavian women. That is, Elsie needs to know what the height distribution would look like if she were to take millions of random samples of Scandinavian women (all samples being the same size), calculate the mean for each sample, and then plot the distribution of the millions of sample means. If she were to do this for an *infinite* number (not merely millions) of sample means, the resulting distribution would be called the **sampling distribution of the mean**. (If, instead, she found the median of each sample and then plotted all of the sample medians, she would be creating the sampling distribution of the *median*; one can create a sampling distribution for any statistic, though we will focus on the mean, as most behavioral researchers do.)

Given that no one is going to draw an infinite number of samples from a population, or even millions of them, we all have to settle for an approximation of the sampling distribution of the mean. There is more than one way to obtain an approximate sampling distribution: (1) directly (i.e., empirically), and (2) indirectly (i.e., theoretically). We'll discuss both, but you'll soon see that the indirect method is *much* easier. To obtain an approximate sampling distribution of the mean directly, you would have to draw a large number of samples, each of the same size, from the defined population, and determine on an empirical basis how often the various alternatives occur. It is important that the samples be *randomly selected*—that is, drawn in such a way as to minimize bias and make the sample typical of the entire population insofar as possible. Technically, a *random sample* is defined as a sample drawn in such a way as to (1) give each element in the population an equal chance of being drawn, *and* (2) make all possible samples of that size equally likely to occur. For example, a random sample for the hormone/height study might be obtained by picking names randomly out of the phone book; an especially problematic nonrandom sample would be selecting women who were hanging around a basketball or volleyball court.

If the mean of each sample is computed and a frequency distribution of the many means is plotted, we will have an idea how often to expect a sample with a particular mean. Such a frequency distribution is called an *experimental sampling distribution* because it is obtained from observed or experimental data.[1] Note that this is not how distributions of sample values are ordinarily determined, but merely how one *could* determine them.

To get concrete about it, suppose that Elsie decides that a sample size of 100 Scandinavian women is the largest she can afford to obtain in terms of both time and funding. She could then create an empirical sampling

---

[1] It is also sometimes called a *Monte Carlo distribution,* and it is usually generated by a computer.

distribution by measuring the height of each woman in her first random sample, computing the mean height of the sample, and then replacing the entire first sample into the population. Then she would have to draw another random sample of 100 Scandinavian women and compute the mean height of *that* sample. If Elsie were to obtain a total of 1,000 samples (each of $N = 100$), the frequency distribution of mean heights of the 1,000 samples might resemble the one in Table 5.1. Figure 5.1 represents the data in Table 5.1 as a frequency polygon.

Of course, anyone who cannot afford to obtain one sample containing more than 100 people would not be able to obtain thousands of samples of 100 each. Fortunately, it is rarely necessary to perform this direct procedure for determining a sampling distribution; we presented it just to make the concept of a sampling distribution more concrete. In practice, you will refer to *theoretical sampling distributions.* But first let us take a look at a reasonable example of an experimental sampling distribution of height that fits Elsie's situation. By inspecting Figure 5.1, you can readily see that most of the sample means cluster around the *grand mean* (i.e., the mean

Table 5.1 Hypothetical Frequency Distribution of Mean Height for 1,000 Samples (Sample $N = 100$)

(A) Mean height (in.)	(B) Number of samples (f)	(C) Proportion of samples ($p = f/N$)
68.55 or more	0	.000
68.50–68.54	1	.001
68.45–68.49	1	.001
68.40–68.44	4	.004
68.35–68.39	11	.011
68.30–68.34	19	0.019
68.25–68.29	31	.031
68.20–68.24	56	.056
68.15–68.19	81	.081
68.10–68.14	112	.112
68.05–68.09	116	.116
68.00–68.04	141	.141
67.95–67.99	131	.131
67.90–67.94	103	.103
67.85–67.89	76	.076
67.80–67.84	57	.057
67.75–67.79	28	.028
67.70–67.74	21	.021
67.65–67.69	7	.007
67.60–67.64	2	.002
67.55–67.59	2	.002
67.54 or less	0	.000
Total	1.000	1.000

Figure 5.1

Hypothetical Distribution of Mean Height for 1,000 Samples (Sample N = 100)

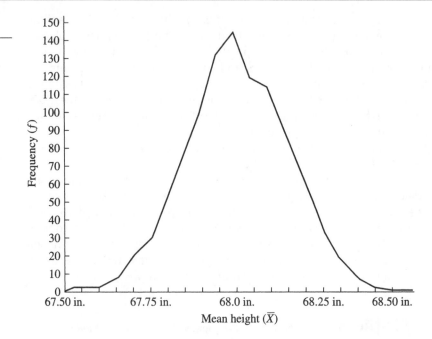

of all of the sample means), which for this example is 68.00; there are fewer and fewer observations as one goes farther away from the grand mean. This distribution closely approximates the theoretical *normal curve*, a statistical model that can describe the sampling distributions of several statistics of interest, including means. Use of the theoretical normal curve model in the proper situations will enable you to avoid the toil and trouble of determining an experimental sampling distribution in order to ascertain the probabilities in which you are interested.

An important law of statistics tells us that when a population of individuals is normally distributed for a particular variable, the corresponding sampling distribution of the mean will also follow the normal distribution (ND). Although actual populations in behavioral research never follow the ND exactly, variables that have a distribution close to the ND (e.g., height) will lead to sampling distributions of the mean that are approximated very well by the ND. Moreover, a statistical law known as the **Central Limit Theorem** states that as the *size* of the samples increases (remember that a sampling distribution assumes an infinite number of samples *all of which are the same size*), the sampling distribution of the mean more closely resembles the ND, regardless of the shape of the original distribution for individual measurements in the population. However, the more the original population distribution departs from the ND, the larger the samples have to be before the sampling distribution of the mean begins to resemble a normal distribution. The implications of this theorem for social and behavioral scientists are enormous, and impossible to overstate. It means that we can study variables that are not normally distributed in nature so long as we study *groups* of individuals. Even variables that are wildly non-normal among individuals produce sampling distributions of the mean that follow the ND fairly well once the sample size grows above 40 or so. For most variables, a sample size of 20 to 30 is all that is required to comfortably assume an ND for your sampling distribution.

It should come as no surprise that the mean height of our 1,000 samples of Scandinavian women (summarized in Table 5.1), 68 inches, is the same as the mean of the population of individual Scandinavian women. As the number of samples becomes infinite, the *mean* of this infinite number of sample means (i.e., the *grand mean*) will always equal the mean of the population (μ), regardless of the size of each sample (N). However, if we want to use z scores to compare the mean of any *one* sample to the whole distribution of sample means, we will also need to know the standard deviation of these sample means (i.e., the SD of the sampling distribution of the mean). It is important to note that the SD of the individual scores, σ (or its estimate s), is *not* the correct measure to use. To see why, consider once again the ND of math SAT scores in the population ($\mu = 500$). Selecting one person at random with a score of 720 is fairly unlikely. But drawing *a whole, totally random, sample of people* with scores so extreme that the sample averages out to a mean of 720 is much less likely, because a greater number of low-probability events must occur simultaneously. This implies that the variability of the distribution of sample means is *smaller* than the variability of the distribution of raw scores. In fact, it decreases as the sample N increases.

If a large number of sample means were actually available (as in Table 5.1), you could measure the variability of the means directly. You would simply calculate the SD *of the sample means,* using the usual formula for computing the SD (see Chapter 3) and treating the sample means just like ordinary numbers. However, behavioral scientists rarely have *many* samples of a given size. They usually have only a few. So instead of measuring the SD of the sampling distribution directly, we will derive it theoretically (much easier!).

The Standard Error of the Mean

Luckily, there is a simple statistical law that relates the standard deviation of the sampling distribution of means to the sample size N and the SD of the population.

$$\sigma_{\bar{x}} = \frac{\sigma}{\sqrt{N}}$$ Formula 5.1

where

σ = the population SD

N = number of observations in each sample

This quantity estimates the variability of means for samples of the given N, so it is a *standard deviation* of *means.* But because it does that,

Figure 5.2

**Distribution
of Observations
of Heights (in Inches)
for a Population
of 5,000,000
Scandinavian Women**

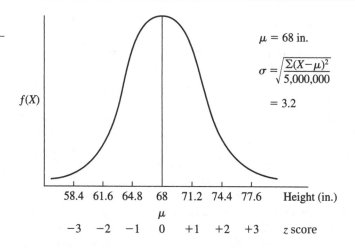

$\mu = 68$ in.

$$\sigma = \sqrt{\frac{\Sigma(X-\mu)^2}{5,000,000}}$$

$$= 3.2$$

$f(X)$

| 58.4 | 61.6 | 64.8 | 68 | 71.2 | 74.4 | 77.6 | Height (in.) |

μ

| -3 | -2 | -1 | 0 | $+1$ | $+2$ | $+3$ | z score |

it also tells you how trustworthy is any single mean that you have. For historical reasons, the SD for means is called the **standard error of the mean**, but conceptually it provides the same information about the distribution it describes as the SD does for a distribution of individual scores: it tells you how far the scores are, on average, from their mean. Only now the scores are means, and the mean of the distribution is the grand mean.

A *small* value of $\sigma_{\overline{X}}$ indicates that if you were to draw several different random samples of the same size from this population, the various values of $\overline{X}$ would be expected to be relatively close to one another (because they would have a small SD). In this situation, therefore, any single value of $\overline{X}$ that you may have is likely to be a rather accurate estimate of μ. But if $\sigma_{\overline{X}}$ is *large,* and you were to draw a bunch of different random samples of the same size from this population, the various values of $\overline{X}$ would likely differ markedly from one another (because they come from a distribution that has a large standard deviation). Therefore, any one value of $\overline{X}$ would be a less trustworthy indication of the true value of μ.

As you can see from Formula 5.1, the standard error of the mean will always be smaller than the SD of the raw scores. It becomes smaller as the sample size grows larger. The term *standard error* implies that the difference between a population mean and the mean of a sample drawn from that population is an "error," caused by the cases that happened by chance to be included in the sample. If *no* error existed (as would happen if the "sample" consisted of the entire population and thus $N = \infty$), all of the sample means would exactly equal each other, and the value of the standard error of the mean would be zero. This situation would be ideal for purposes of statistical inference, because the mean of any one sample would exactly equal the population mean. Of course, this never happens in the real world; real data are always subject to sampling error.

To clarify the preceding discussion, let us return to our example concerning the heights of samples of Scandinavian women and compare

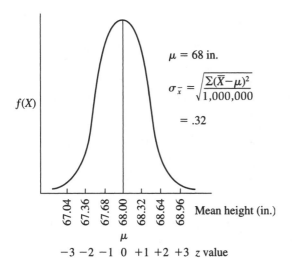

Figure 5.3

Distribution of Mean Heights (in Inches) for 1,000,000 Randomly Selected Samples of N = 100 Height Observations in Each Sample

the distribution of raw scores to the distribution of sample means. A hypothetical distribution of 5 million height observations for Scandinavian women raised on GH milk is shown in Figure 5.2; each X represents one *raw score* (i.e., one individual). Now suppose that one million random samples of $N = 100$ observations each are randomly selected from that population, and the mean of each sample is calculated. The resulting distribution of *sample means* would closely resemble the particular normal curve that is illustrated in Figure 5.3.

Notice that the shape of *both* distributions (the original distribution of raw scores or single observations, and the distribution of sample means) is only approximately normal (all human height distributions have definite endpoints, whereas the normal distribution trails off in each direction indefinitely), and they are both centered around μ (68 inches).[2] However, the distribution of sample means is *less variable* than is the distribution of raw scores. The SD of the raw scores shown in Figure 5.2 would be calculated directly by applying the usual formula for the standard deviation to the 5,000,000 raw scores; let us suppose that σ was found to be equal to 3.2 inches. The SD of the sample means in Figure 5.3 could be calculated directly by applying the usual formula for the SD to the 1,000,000 sample means. More conveniently, we can use the formula to find that the means of the samples, each based on $N = 100$ observations, will have a σ equal to one 10th (i.e., $1/\sqrt{N}$) the σ of the individual observations. As you can see in Figure 5.3, the value of $\sigma_{\overline{X}}$ is $3.2/\sqrt{100}$, or .32.

---

[2]Theoretically, you would need an infinite number of samples before your sampling distribution fit the normal curve perfectly, but a million samples is at least imaginable, and would lead to a very smooth curve.

The z Score for Sample Means

The sampling distribution of the mean for height will closely resemble the normal distribution. Because we know both the mean and standard deviation of this distribution, we can use z scores in conjunction with Table A to answer questions about the proportion of samples that will be shorter or taller than a particular sample. (Why anyone would want to do this will be explained shortly.)

Suppose that Elsie has already measured 100 Scandinavian women chosen at random from among those who were *not* raised drinking GH milk, and their average height turns out to be 67.4 inches. This group is shorter than average for Scandinavian women and therefore in line with the researcher's prediction. But before the researcher yells "eureka!" she must ask herself a question: How unusual is it to randomly select a group of 100 Scandinavian women from the general population with an average height .6 inches shorter than normal? After all, you would expect some samples to be a little taller than 68 inches and others to be a little shorter. If selecting a group of 100 at random with a mean of about 67.4 inches is a fairly likely occurrence, then there is little reason to believe that the group of 100 non-GH-milk drinkers is somehow special (i.e., shorter because of the lack of hormones).

The researcher's task becomes one of figuring out exactly how likely it is to randomly select 100 Scandinavian women with an average height of 67.4 inches, or even less. Fortunately, this is precisely the sort of information a sampling distribution of the mean provides (and why we are learning about them). To get a handle on just how unusually short the women in Elsie's sample are relative to Scandinavian women in general, we can find out just what proportion of all samples ($N = 100$) of Scandinavian women will have an average height less than (or equal to) 67.4 inches. We saw in the previous chapter that this kind of question can be answered by calculating the corresponding z score. However, in this case, we need to calculate a z score for samples rather than individuals, which means that the formula must be based on the *standard error of the mean* as the measure of variability. That is,

$$z = \frac{\overline{X} - \mu}{\sigma_{\overline{X}}}$$

Formula 5.2

where

$\overline{X}$ = the observed value of the sample mean
μ = the hypothesized value of the population mean
$\sigma_{\overline{X}}$ = the standard error of the mean ($= \sigma/\sqrt{N}$)

Given that $\mu = 68$ and $\sigma = 3.2$ for height in the Scandinavian female population,

$$\sigma_{\overline{X}} = \frac{3.2}{\sqrt{100}} = .32,$$

and

$$z = \frac{67.4 - 68}{.32}$$

$$= \frac{-.60}{.32}$$

$$= -1.875$$

To find the proportion of the normal distribution that is below $z = -1.875$, draw a diagram of the normal curve, like the ones in the previous chapter, but label it with vertical lines at two z scores: 0 (at the mean) and -1.875, nearly 2 SDs to the left of the mean. Then shade in the area to the left of the vertical line at -1.875 (a fairly small area). Ignore the negative sign of the z score, and look at the entries for both $= 1.87$ and $z = 1.88$ in Table A in the Appendix. Averaging 46.93 and 46.99, you can determine that the nonshaded area of the left half of your figure (the percent area between the mean and z) contains about 46.96% of the distribution. However, we are interested in the shaded area, so we want to know the percentage of area below -1.875; therefore, we need to subtract the area we just found from 50%. The area below $z = -1.875$ equals $50 - 46.96 = 3.04\%$. As a proportion, this comes to .0304. Stated as a probability, the chance of randomly selecting 100 Scandinavian women whose height averages out to 67.4 inches or less is only .0304, or just a little over 3 out of 100.

We can therefore conclude that the 100 Scandinavian women not raised on GH milk are unusually short as a group when compared to groups of Scandinavian women from the general population even though the group average is only a little more than half an inch less than the population mean. As random samples get larger, their means tend to vary less from the population mean. Therefore, a fairly large random sample does not need to have a mean very different from that of the population to be considered unusual. Probabilities such as the value of .0304 calculated here are called **p values**, and are a valuable tool for a procedure called *null hypothesis testing*, which is discussed next. We introduce this procedure by applying the z score for sample means to another hypothetical study—this one representing a true experiment. (Elsie did not randomly assign Scandinavian babies to different milk-drinking conditions, so her study was a quasi-experiment. Even if her non-GH milk group is very unusually short, there may be reasons other than the milk itself that are responsible—for example, babies raised on GH-milk may have parents who are less educated than average). Note, however, that null hypothesis testing is applied the same way to quasi-experiments as it is to true experiments—it is only the causal conclusions that differ.

College Boards and similar standardized tests are usually taken in a group setting with many other students nearby, and this can be distracting for some students. Let us suppose that you want to test the possibility that taking the math section of the SAT in a comfortable private setting will lead to higher exam scores; although it is possible that taking the test in private might lead to *lower* exam scores (and if that is true you would definitely want to know it), we will begin by expecting that the privacy scores will be higher, not lower, than average. To test this hypothesis, you select 30 names at random from a list of students about to take this test and arrange for these students to take the test individually. After the scores are determined for each of the individually tested students, you calculate the mean math SAT for the group, and find that this average is 534.25. This is a welcome result; it would seem unlikely that a random sample of 30 group-tested students would have such a high mean. But we do not have to rely on our subjective impression of how unlikely this sample mean is; we can use the z score for samples to determine this probability precisely. Recall that for SAT scores, the population mean (μ) is set at 500, and the standard deviation (σ) is 100. Therefore,

$$z = \frac{\overline{X} - \mu}{\frac{\sigma}{\sqrt{N}}} = \frac{534.25 - 500}{\frac{100}{\sqrt{30}}} = \frac{34.25}{18.26} = 1.875$$

Because we are interested in the probability of obtaining a sample mean as high or higher than the one we have observed, we want to look up the area above (i.e., to the right of) a z score of 1.875. However, because of the symmetry of the ND, this area will be the same as the area below $z = -1.875$, which we found for the height example to be .0304. Thus, the probability of selecting 30 students at random from the ordinary population (i.e., the population of students taking the exam in the usual setting), which has a mean of 500, and obtaining a sample whose mean is 534.25 or larger is only .0304. Knowing this probability, which, as we just mentioned, is called a "*p* value," will help us to make a decision about whether we consider our experimental manipulation to have worked—that is, whether we will conclude that individual testing would produce at least some difference in math SAT scores if given to the entire population.

Null Hypothesis Testing

The decision process just alluded to, in which we use a *p* value to decide whether our study found a true effect, is known as **null hypothesis testing** (NHT). In terms of the most recent example, we can say that we will *test the hypothesis* that the mean of the population of individually tested students is equal to 500 on the math SAT. When the testing of a statistical hypothesis is designed to help make a decision about a population parameter (here, μ), the overall method falls under the category of *inferential parametric statistics.*

The Null and Alternative Hypotheses

The first step in NHT is to state the **null hypothesis** (symbolized by H_0), which specifies the hypothesized population parameter. In the present example,

$$H_0: \mu = 500$$

This null hypothesis implies that the sample with mean equal to 534.25 is a random sample from the population with μ equal to 500 (and that the difference between 534.25 and 500 is due to chance factors). The probability of obtaining a sample mean of the observed value (534.25), or even farther above the mean, is calculated under the assumption that H_0 is true (i.e., that $\mu = 500$), as we did above ($p = .0304$).

Next, an **alternative hypothesis** (symbolized by H_A) is formed. It specifies another (usually complementary) value or set of values for the population parameter. In the present study,

$$H_A: \mu \neq 500$$

This alternative hypothesis states simply that the population from which the sample comes does *not* have a μ equal to 500. That is, the difference of 34.25 between the sample mean and the null-hypothesized population mean is due to the fact that the null hypothesis is false—for example, that individual testing leads to a new distribution of scores with a different mean from the group-testing distribution, so that the sample of 30 individually tested students is not actually coming from a population whose mean is 500. (As stated above, the alternative hypothesis is *nondirectional*—no expectation is implied about whether the mean of the tested population will be larger or smaller than the general population. However, in the current example, we actually expect the tested population to have a higher mean. We deal with directional as compared to nondirectional hypotheses a little later.)

The null hypothesis gets its name from the idea that nothing is going on. That is, the null hypothesis states that there is *no* effect or *no* difference of the kind that the experiment is seeking to establish. Usually, the theory that the scientist hopes to support is identified with the *alternative* hypothesis. Rejecting H_0 will cause the scientist to conclude that his theory has been supported, and failing to reject H_0 will cause him to conclude that his theory has not been supported. This is a sensible procedure, because scientific caution dictates that researchers should not jump to conclusions. They should claim success only when there is a strong indication to that effect—that is, when the results are sufficiently striking to cause rejection of H_0.

The Criterion of Significance

Having set up the null and alternative hypotheses, we need to define *how unusual* a sample mean must be to cause you to reject H_0 and accept H_A (by "unusual" we mean unlikely to occur in the null hypothesis distribution). Intuitively, an observed sample mean of 501 would hardly represent persuasive evidence against the null hypothesis that $\mu = 500$, even though it is not exactly equal to the hypothesized population value.

Conversely, an observed sample mean of 700 would do more to suggest that the hypothesized population value was incorrect. Where should the line be drawn? This is where the p value can be helpful.

To simplify our terms, let us refer to an experiment for which the null hypothesis is actually true (e.g., individual testing did *not* affect math SAT scores) as a *null experiment*. The object of null hypothesis testing can then be described as trying to keep under control the number of null experiments for which the null hypothesis is mistakenly rejected; for such experiments, the results can look good solely because of sampling error (e.g., by chance, our sample included a disproportionate number of students who were very good at math). Rejecting the null hypothesis for an experiment in which the null hypothesis is actually true is called a **Type I error**. Although we can never know whether H_0 is true for any particular experiment, and we do not even know how often null experiments are performed by various researchers, we can try to control the rate at which Type I errors are made. We do this by deciding on the proportion of all null experiments we will allow to be declared **statistically significant** (i.e., the null hypothesis has been rejected). This is not something that an individual researcher decides; this is something that a research community decides as a whole.

The proportion of null experiments that will be considered "significant" is called the **criterion of significance** and is symbolized by the first letter of the Greek alphabet, *alpha* (α). Due in large part to the pioneering work of Sir Ronald Fisher, the default value commonly used in behavioral research for alpha is .05. Note that setting alpha to .05 fixes only the Type I error *rate* and does not determine the *total number* of Type I errors. Although no attempt is made to control how many null experiments are performed, universal adoption of the .05 level ensures that only (about) 5% of null experiments (i.e., experiments for which the null hypothesis is actually true) that *are* performed will lead to a rejection of H_0 and therefore to results that are (mistakenly) regarded as statistically significant (i.e., Type I errors). Routinely setting a lower value for alpha (e.g., .01) is an option that would sometimes result in undesirable consequences that will be discussed shortly, and a larger value for alpha would lead to a rather high rate of Type I errors, so the .05 significance level is considered a reasonable compromise. Now let us see how the p value for a particular experiment can be used to make a decision about the null hypothesis.

Critical Values

The p value for the math SAT experiment was .0304. This means that if individual testing has no effect at all (H_0 is true), about 3% of experiments like ours would nonetheless result in sample means as high as or even higher than ours. It may seem that because .0304 is less than .05, we should reject the null hypothesis using the .05 decision rule. However, .0304 is a *one-tailed* p value, in that it applies only to the upper end of the distribution. If our null and alternative hypotheses were set up for a *two-tailed* test, the implication is that we would also have tested our sample mean for statistical significance if it were *below* the population mean. The two-tailed test is the more cautious option, as we will explain shortly, and the one usually required by the better scientific journals. To perform a two-tailed instead of a one-tailed test, all you have to do is double your one-tailed p value (which you obtained from Table 5.1) and compare it to your alpha level.

Students are often puzzled about why we should double a one-tailed p value to arrive at the comparable two-tailed value. Try thinking about it this way: A two-tailed p is defined as the probability of obtaining a result as *extreme* as the one you got—or more extreme—if the null hypothesis is true. We found a result so extreme (SAT $=$ 534.25) that it left only about 3% of the area of the curve above it. That p value (.0304) means that if the H_0 is true, you might still come across a sample with a mean *as high or higher* than 534.25 (there is about a 3% chance of that). But what about sample means as or more extreme at the other end of the distribution? Well, if the sample mean for our individual testing group had been 465.75 (i.e., 34.25 points *below* the mean), then it would have a z score of -1.875, and .0304 of the curve would fall beyond (lower than) it. Therefore, if you have a two-tailed hypothesis—one for which you would be interested in an extreme result in *either direction* from the mean—then you should add the area beyond one extreme score with the area beyond the opposite extreme score to get the total p value. We have just seen that the p value for sample means 34.25 points *above* the mean is .0304, and the p value for sample means 34.25 *below* the mean is also .0304. Therefore, the two-tailed p value for this experiment is $.0304 + .0304 = .0608$. Thus, you can see how the symmetry of the normal curve allows you to double your one-sided p value to go from a one-tailed to a two-tailed significance test. Note that .0608 is *not* less than .05, so H_0 cannot be rejected at the .05 level for a two-tailed test. We will elaborate on the distinction between one- and two-tailed tests shortly.

There is a simpler way to make decisions about the null hypothesis that does not require finding the p value for your experiment. If you are planning to conduct a two-tailed test with, say, $\alpha = .05$, you can find the minimum z score needed for significance ahead of time and then just check the z score for your sample to see if it is larger than the borderline z score. The z scores that fall right at the borderline between the significant and nonsignificant portions of the null hypothesis distribution are called **critical values** (or, less formally, *cutoff scores*). For a two-tailed test there is a critical value on each side of the distribution, as illustrated in Figure 5.4.

When the normal curve model is appropriate, the two-tailed critical values beyond which H_0 should be rejected are easily ascertained using the normal curve table (Table A). Since 2.5% of the area of the curve is in each tail, $50.0\% - 2.5\%$, or 47.5%, falls between the mean and the cutoff score. If we look in the body of Table A for a value of 47.5%, we can see that the critical z values are found to be equal to -1.96 and 1.96. Once the sample mean has been converted to a z score, the .05 criterion of significance states that H_0 should be rejected if z is less than or equal

Figure 5.4

Areas for Rejecting H_0 in Both Tails of the Normal Sampling Distribution Using the .05 Criterion of Significance When H_0 Actually Is True

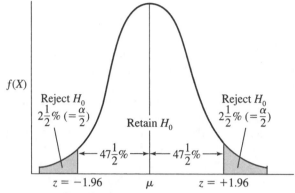

$f(X)$

Reject H_0
$2\frac{1}{2}\% \left(=\frac{\alpha}{2}\right)$

Retain H_0

Reject H_0
$2\frac{1}{2}\% \left(=\frac{\alpha}{2}\right)$

$\leftarrow 47\frac{1}{2}\% \rightarrow \leftarrow 47\frac{1}{2}\% \rightarrow$

$z = -1.96$ μ $z = +1.96$

Sample mean expressed as a z value

to -1.96 or z is greater than or equal to $+1.96$. Conversely, H_0 should be retained if z is between -1.96 and $+1.96$. Note that the area in each rejection region is equal to $\alpha/2$, or $.05/2$ or $.025$, and that the total **area of rejection** (or *critical region*) is equal to the significance criterion (α) or $.05$.

A less common, and more stringent, criterion is the 1% or *.01 criterion of significance.* Using this criterion, two-tailed hypotheses about the population mean are rejected if, when H_0 is true, an obtained sample mean is so unlikely to occur by chance that no more than 1% of sample means would be so extreme. Here again, $\alpha/2$ or $.005$ (or 1/2 of 1%) is in each tail. This criterion is illustrated in Figure 5.5.

When the normal curve model is appropriate, the critical values beyond which H_0 should be rejected using the .01 criterion are ascertained by looking in the body of Table A for the value 49.5%. After rounding off, these cutoff scores, expressed as z scores, are -2.58 and $+2.58$. Once the sample mean has been expressed as a z value, the .01 criterion of significance states that H_0 should be rejected if z is less than or equal to -2.58 or z is greater than or equal to $+2.58$. Conversely, H_0 should be

Figure 5.5

Areas for Rejecting H_0 in Both Tails of the Normal Sampling Distribution Using the .01 Criterion of Significance When H_0 Is True

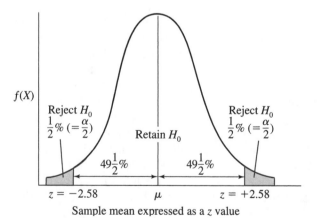

$f(X)$

Reject H_0
$\frac{1}{2}\% \left(=\frac{\alpha}{2}\right)$

Retain H_0

Reject H_0
$\frac{1}{2}\% \left(=\frac{\alpha}{2}\right)$

$49\frac{1}{2}\%$ $49\frac{1}{2}\%$

$z = -2.58$ μ $z = +2.58$

Sample mean expressed as a z value

retained if z is between -2.58 and $+2.58$. Once again, the area of rejection is equal to $\alpha(0.5\% + 0.5\% = 1\%$ or $.01)$, the criterion of significance.

Consequences of Possible Decisions

Admittedly, an event that occurs 1 in 20 times (i.e., that has a probability of occurrence of .05) is not an extremely rare event. Yet when we set alpha to .05, we are saying that whenever our experiment produces a result that is likely to be exceeded by a similar experiment—but one for which H_0 is actually true (a "null" experiment)—no more than 1 in 20 times, we will consider the null hypothesis "sufficiently unlikely" as an explanation for our findings and can therefore reject it.[3] Given that Type I errors are undesirable, why does the behavioral research community not agree to set .01 as the minimum alpha for ordinary circumstances, rather than .05? The short answer is that as you make alpha smaller, the critical value that an experimental result has to exceed to be statistically significant becomes larger. Therefore, more and more experiments for which the null hypothesis is *not* true will nonetheless fail to yield significant results. This is the undesirable consequence of setting a smaller value for alpha that we alluded to earlier.

When the null hypothesis is *not* true but you fail to reject H_0 because your experimental results are not extreme enough, you are making an error that can be thought of as the opposite of a Type I error. It is appropriately called a *Type II error* and its likelihood is symbolized by the second letter of the Greek alphabet, *beta* (β). Whereas alpha is fixed by the researcher, the value for beta associated with any particular experiment depends on a number of factors. Usually it can only be estimated roughly, as we will demonstrate in Chapter 11.

For the math SAT experiment, there are two possibilities with respect to the mean of the theoretical population in which all students are individually tested: Either $\mu = 500$ (H_0 is true), or μ is not equal to 500 (H_0 is false) and individual testing has at least some effect. There are also just two possible decisions you could make based on the results of this experiment: reject H_0, or retain H_0. The four possible combinations of the actual mean of the experimental population and the decision that is made about the experiment can be summarized as follows (see Table 5.2):

1. The population mean for individually tested students is actually 500 (i.e., individual testing would not change the mean of the

---

[3]This is a matter of convention and is not based on any mathematical principle, so common sense is essential in borderline cases. If, for example, $p = .06$, the technically correct procedure is to call the event "not sufficiently unlikely," but .06 is so close to .05 that the best plan is to repeat the experiment and gain additional evidence. The reason that a guide such as the .05 rule is needed is that NHT would quickly become useless if each researcher were free to set alpha to any value he or she found convenient for each result being reported.

Table 5.2   Model for Error Risks in Hypothesis Testing

Outcome of experiment dictates:	State of the population	
	H_0 is actually true	H_0 is actually false
Retain H_0	Correct decision: probability of retaining true H_0 is $1 - \alpha$	Type II error: probability (risk) of retaining false H_0 is β
Reject H_0	Type I error: probability (risk) of rejecting true H_0 is α	Correct decision: probability of rejecting false H_0 (power) is $1 - \beta$

population) and you *incorrectly reject* H_0. You have committed a Type I error.

2. The population mean for individually tested students is actually *not* 500 and you *incorrectly retain* H_0. Failing to reject a *false* null hypothesis is a Type II error.

3. The population mean for individually tested students is actually *not* 500 and you *correctly reject* H_0. The (conditional) probability of reaching this correct decision is called the *power* of the statistical test and is equal to $1 - \beta$.

4. The population mean for individually tested students is actually 500 and you *correctly retain* H_0. The (conditional) probability of making this correct decision is equal to $1 - \alpha$.

One- Versus Two-Tailed Tests of Significance

The statistical tests described thus far in this chapter (see e.g., Figures 5.4 and 5.5) are called two-tailed, or nondirectional, tests of significance. This means that the null hypothesis regarding the population mean, μ, is rejected if a z value is obtained that is either extremely high (far up in the upper tail of the curve) *or* extremely low (far down in the lower tail of the curve). Consequently, there is a rejection area equal to $\alpha/2$ in each tail of the distribution. As we have seen, the corresponding null and alternative hypotheses are:

H_0: $\mu =$ a specific value
H_A: $\mu \neq$ this value (i.e., μ is greater than the value specified by H_0 *or* is less than this value)

Let us suppose, however, that a researcher argues as follows: "My theory predicts that the mean of population X is *less than* 100." (For example, she may predict that children from homes in which there are few books and little emphasis on verbal skills score below average on a

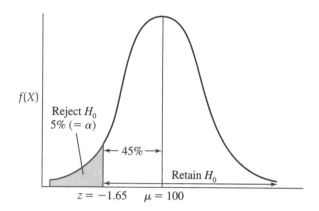

Figure 5.6

One-Tailed Test of the Null Hypothesis That $\mu \geq 100$ Against the Alternative That $\mu < 100$

standardized test of intelligence.) "It's all the same to me whether $\mu_{\overline{X}}$ is equal to 100 or much greater than 100; my theory is disconfirmed in either case. If I use a two-tailed test, I am forced to devote $2\frac{1}{2}\%$ of my rejection region (using $\alpha = .05$) to an outcome that is meaningless insofar as my theory is concerned. Instead, I will place the entire 5% rejection region in the lower tail of the curve." (See Figure 5.6.) "In other words, I will test the following null and alternative hypotheses:

$$H_0: \mu \geq 100$$

$$H_A: \mu < 100$$

$$\alpha = .05$$

"Note that I am being properly conservative by assuming at the outset that my results are due to chance (the null hypothesis). Only if I obtain a result very unlikely to be true if H_0 is true will I conclude that my theory is supported (i.e., switch to the alternative hypothesis). Looking at Table A, I see that a z score of -1.65 encloses about 45% of the normal curve between it and the mean, leaving 5% of the distribution in the lower tail (as shown in Figure 5.6). Therefore, I will use -1.65 as my only critical value. (Actually -1.64 is just as close an approximation to cutting off 5% of the curve, but -1.65 is the more cautious choice with respect to controlling Type I errors.) This means that I will retain H_0 if z is anywhere between -1.65 and $+\infty$ and reject H_0 if z is -1.65 or less. Since a two-tailed test of significance would lead to rejection of H_0 only if z were -1.96 or less (or $+1.96$ or more), the one-tailed value of -1.65 quite properly makes it easier for me to reject H_0 (and conclude that my theory is supported) when the results are in the direction that I have predicted."

Similar reasoning could be applied if the researcher claimed to be interested *only* in the outcome that the population mean was *greater* than 100. The entire rejection region would be placed at the upper end of the curve, and H_0 would be retained if z were between $-\infty$ and $+1.65$ and rejected if z were $+1.65$ or more.

Although behavioral researchers often have a theory that predicts the direction of their results, and could therefore argue for performing a one-tailed test (also called a *directional test*), to be *conservative* (i.e., which in this context means particularly cautious about Type I errors), they usually test their results in terms of two-tailed tests. Consider once again our math SAT example. The z score calculated in that example, 1.875, is larger than the critical value for a one-tailed test at the .05 level, 1.65. Therefore, the null hypothesis would be rejected using a one-tailed test. We might have had good reason to expect the individually tested sample to have a *higher*, rather than lower, average on the math SAT, because such test conditions are usually more conducive to concentration. So it would seem fair to use the one-tailed test in this case and declare statistical significance. However, a one-tailed test implies a promise that we would not have presented our results if our sample mean had been very much *lower* than the mean of the population—even if it were so low as to easily exceed the critical value for a two-tailed test in the other (i.e., lower) direction. If such a promise were routinely made and obeyed, researchers could not ethically report extreme results in the unexpected direction. This could cause serious problems. For example, the individually tested students might feel that they were under close scrutiny and become much more anxious, making them *less* likely to perform well on the test. This could be a finding of interest that deserves to be reported (though it could be argued that the experiment should first be replicated, because it yielded unexpected results).

If you were to lower your critical value by putting your entire alpha in one tail and then put even just half of your alpha in the other tail *after* seeing the results, you would be violating the .05 decision rule. That is, you would really be using an alpha of $.05 + .025 = .075$, which would make the probability of a Type I error greater than .05. Whenever we recognize the significance of a one-tailed test, we are implicitly accepting the promise that the researchers would not have tested and presented their results no matter how extreme their results might have been in the opposite direction. Because the research community does not want to discourage the reporting of paradoxical findings, but also does not want alpha to creep above the .05 level, the two-tailed test is the norm. However, one-tailed tests may be justified if the results would make no sense in the opposite direction and would therefore never be tested in that direction. For example, in a study to test a new analgesic (pain killer), you would not be interested in the distinction between a result in which (a) the experimental drug did not decrease pain and (b) the drug led to significantly *more* pain. Therefore, you would only be interested in testing the lower-pain tail of the distribution with a one-tailed test.

Assumptions Required by the Statistical Test for the Mean of a Single Population

Our use of the z score for sample means, in conjunction with the table of the normal curve, to obtain a p value for our hypothetical math

SAT experiment was based on several assumptions. The most important of these is that the individuals in our sample were selected randomly (and independently) from the population. In the case of the math SAT experiment, it is not hard to imagine that individuals could be selected at random from a list of people registered to take the exam, but the validity of the experiment would then depend critically on the compliance of those who were selected for the new experimental condition. If a considerable number of selected individuals refuse to participate (e.g., the ones who are afraid that the new condition will throw them off or, perhaps, jinx them), the results could easily become biased in one direction or the other (e.g., the worried students might be worse at taking standardized tests in general, so by dropping out, their absence would raise the score of the selected group—even if the new condition does not actually improve performance at all). The usual solution is to randomly divide the sample of individuals willing to comply with the experiment into two groups, one of which gets the new condition, while the other serves as a control group (taking the test in the usual way). Such two-group designs are discussed in Chapter 7, but first we have more groundwork to cover on the one-group case, in the next chapter.

The next most important assumption is that the variable being measured (e.g., math SAT) is normally distributed in the population. The Central Limit Theorem tells us that for fairly large samples, we will get reasonably accurate p values even if the original distribution is not very "normal." However, to use the z-score formula at all, we had to know σ, the standard deviation of the individual scores in the population. Unfortunately, we will know σ only for a few variables that have been studied extensively in the population. More often we will not know σ, and we will have to estimate it from the data we do have. Estimating σ is an additional step that slightly complicates our test of a single population mean. This complication involves a new theoretical distribution that is similar to the normal distribution, and is described in the next chapter.

Summary

Although behavioral researchers are usually interested in what the average response of an entire population would be to some treatment or experimental condition, practical constraints generally lead them to select and study a relatively small, random sample from the population of interest. After the members of the sample have been measured, the following steps can be applied in order to draw some conclusion about the population.

The Standard Error of the Mean

To test null hypotheses about the *mean of one population,* first compute the *standard error of the mean.* This is a measure of how accurate any one sample mean is likely to be as an estimate of the population mean. Then use the standard error of the mean to determine whether the difference between an observed sample mean and the hypothesized value of the population mean is or is not "sufficiently unlikely" to occur if H_0 is true (i.e., if the hypothesized value of the population mean is correct).

The formula for the standard error of the mean is

$$\sigma_{\bar{x}} = \frac{\sigma}{\sqrt{N}}$$ Formula 5.1

where

N = the number of scores in each sample
σ = standard deviation of the population

The z Score for Sample Means

To draw inferences about the population mean, first calculate

$$z = \frac{\bar{X} - \mu}{\sigma_{\bar{X}}}$$ Formula 5.2

Then look in Table A to find the percentage of the normal curve that extends beyond your calculated z. Converted to a proportion, this is the one-tailed p value corresponding to your sample mean. Double this value when you want to obtain a two-tailed p value.

Null Hypothesis Testing: General Considerations

1. State the *null hypothesis* (denoted by the symbol H_0) and the *alternative hypothesis* (denoted by H_A). It is at this point that you should decide whether to perform a one-tailed or two-tailed test. (It is important to understand that you cannot *prove* whether H_0 or H_A is true because you cannot measure the entire population.)

2. Begin with the assumption that H_0 is true. Then obtain the data and test out this assumption. If this assumption leads to unlikely results, you will abandon it and switch your bets to H_A; otherwise, you will retain it.

3. Before you collect any data, it is necessary to define in numerical terms what is meant by "unlikely results." In statistical terminology, this is called selecting a *criterion* (or *level*) *of significance*, represented by the symbol α.

    (a) Using the .05 criterion of significance, "unlikely" is defined as having a probability of .05 or less. In symbols, $\alpha = .05$.

    (b) Using the .01 criterion of significance, "unlikely" is defined as having a probability of .01 or less. In symbols, $\alpha = .01$.

    Other criteria of significance can be used, but these are the most common.

4. Having selected a criterion of significance, and either a one- or two-tailed test, obtain your data and compute the appropriate statistical

test. If the test shows that H_0 is unlikely to be true, reject H_0 in favor of H_A. Otherwise, retain H_0.

5. Though you are siding with the hypothesis indicated by the statistical test (H_0 or H_A), you could be wrong. You could be making either of the following two kinds of error, depending on your decision:

   (a) Type I error: Rejecting H_0 when H_0 is in fact true. This error is less likely when the .01 criterion of significance is used. The Type I error rate is a conditional probability; it is the probability of rejecting H_0 *given* that H_0 is actually true, and it is equal to the chosen criterion of significance, α. p is also a conditional probability. p is the probability of obtaining results as extreme or more extreme as the ones you got, if H_0 is true. It's easy to confuse p with α—try not to.

   (b) Type II error: Retaining H_0 when H_0 is in fact false. This error is less likely when the .05 rather than the .01 criterion of significance is chosen. The probability of this kind of error, denoted by the symbol β, is not conveniently determined, but is discussed in detail in Chapter 11.

   It is the relative importance and consequences of each kind of error that help to determine which criterion of significance to use.

One- Versus Two-Tailed Tests of Significance

The use of one-tailed tests of significance is sometimes justified in behavioral science research. If the results are in the direction predicted by the researcher, it is more likely that statistical significance will be obtained. But if the results are in the opposite direction, the entire experiment should be repeated using a two-tailed design before any conclusions are drawn. Therefore, the two-tailed test is more commonly reported, especially in the more selective psychological journals.

Exercises

1. Assume that the mean height for women at a large American university (to be viewed as a population) is 65 inches with a standard deviation of 3 inches.

   (a) If the women are placed randomly into physical education classes of 36 each, what will be the SD of the class means for height (i.e., the standard error of the mean)?

   (b) Using your answer to part (a), what is the z score for a phys ed class whose average height is 64.2 inches? What are the one- and two-tailed p values for this class?

   (c) If you were testing the null hypothesis (i.e., $\mu = 65$), would you reject H_0 for the class in part b, at the .05 level for a one-tailed test? For a two-tailed test?

(d) Repeat part (b) for a class whose mean height is 67.4 inches. Would you reject the null hypothesis for this class with a two-tailed test at the .05 level? At the .01 level?

2. Assume that the mean IQ for all 10th graders at a large high school (i.e., population) is 100 with $\sigma = 15$ and that the students are assigned at random to classes with an N of 25.

   (a) What is the z score for a class whose IQ averages 104? What is the one-tailed p value for this z score? What is the two-tailed p?
   (b) Repeat part (a) for a class whose mean IQ is 92.
   (c) Perform two-tailed null hypothesis tests for the classes in part (a) and part (b) at both the .05 and .01 levels. In each case explain whether you could be making a Type I or Type II error.

3. Given that for SAT scores, $\mu = 500$ and $\sigma = 100$:

   (a) Test the claim of students at Bigbrain University that they have SAT scores that are statistically significantly higher than the ordinary population, because a random sample of 25 of their students averaged 530 on this test. Make your statistical decision by comparing the z score for the Bigbrain sample with the appropriate critical value for a two-tailed test. Would a one-tailed test be significant in this case? Would it be justified?
   (b) Repeat part (a) for a random sample of 64 students, who also have a mean of 530 on the SAT.

4. Referring to the 20-point friendliness measure used in the first exercise of Chapter 1, assume that the mean score for all American college students is known to be 10, with a SD of 5 points.

   (a) Based on the data in Table 1.1, what is the z score for friendliness for the students sampled from Turck Hall? What are the one- and two-tailed p values for this sample?
   (b) If you were testing the null hypothesis (i.e., $\mu = 10$), would you reject H_0 for the students of Turck Hall at the .05 level for a one-tailed test? For a two-tailed test?

5. Repeat Exercise 4, parts (a) and (b), for the sample from Dupre Hall. What is the same and what is different between your calculations for this exercise, and your calculations for Exercise 4?

6. This exercise is designed to give you a more direct understanding of the standard error of the mean. Create a population as follows: Get 20 identical small slips of paper or file cards. On eight of these slips, write the number 50; on five of the slips, write the number 51; on another five, write the number 49. For the last two slips of paper, write the number 48 on one and 52 on the other. Place all the slips in a bowl and mix thoroughly.

   (a) Draw one slip at random from the bowl and write down its number. Then replace the slip in the bowl, mix thoroughly, and draw at random again (this is called *sampling with replacement*). Keep repeating this process until you have written down the numbers for five random selections. Calculate the average for these five numbers. This is your first sample mean.

(b) Repeat the process described in part (a) until you have calculated a total of six sample means.

(c) Calculate the mean and (unbiased) SD of the six sample means you found in part (b). The latter statistic is the standard error of the mean calculated directly from the sample means rather than estimated from a sample SD divided by N. Is the mean of the sample means about what you expected?

(d) Estimate the standard error of the mean separately from the SD of each of the six samples you drew. How do these six estimates compare to each other, and to the standard error you calculated directly in part (c)?

7. Calculate the mean and (unbiased) SD for the following sample: 5, 10, 15, 20, 25, 30, 35, 40, 45, 50, 50, 55, 60, 65, 70, 75, 80, 85, 90, 95. Assume that the SD of the population from which these data were sampled is the same as the SD that you just calculated for the sample. (a) Are these data consistent with the hypothesis that the mean of the population is 60? Explain. (b) Repeat part (a) for a hypothesized population mean of 36.

Thought Questions

1. What is the difference between descriptive statistics and inferential statistics?

2. (a) Do researchers in the behavioral sciences want to draw conclusions about populations or about samples? Why? (b) Why, then, must researchers use samples? (c) What problems are caused by having to use samples? Include and explain the term *sampling error* in your answer.

3. (a) What is a random sample? (b) Why are random samples desirable in behavioral science research? (c) Why is it often difficult or impossible to obtain a sample that is truly random?

4. Which of the following are random samples from the specified populations and which are not? Why? (a) An experimenter selects every 10th name in the telephone book for her city, starting with one name that is chosen blindly. Population: all those with listed telephone numbers in her city. (b) Teenage American students taking introductory psychology at University X volunteer to participate in an experiment. Population: all American teenagers. (c) The names of all students at one particular college in the United States are written on slips of paper and placed in an extremely large hat. The slips are well shuffled, and 50 names are drawn blindly to serve as participants in an experiment. Population: all students at this college. (d) The

procedure is the same as in part (c) but the population is all college students in the United States.

5. (a) What is the difference between the standard deviation of a set of scores and the standard error of the mean? (b) Do behavioral science researchers want the standard error of the mean to be small or large? Why? (c) What happens to the standard error of the mean as the sample size (N) becomes smaller? Why? What does this imply about the dangers of using samples in behavioral science research that are very small? (d) What happens to the standard error of the mean as the SD of the original scores in the population becomes larger? Why?

6. You are using the .05 criterion of significance. (a) If the two-tailed p value (i.e., the probability of obtaining the results you got if H_0 is true and the hypothesized value of the population mean is correct) is .03, what decision should you make about H_0? Why? (b) If the two-tailed p value is .33, what decision should you make about H_0? Why? (c) Should you treat a result that has a two-tailed p value of .06 the same as a result that has a two-tailed p value of .45? Why or why not?

7. The probability of making a Type I error when using the .01 criterion of significance is lower than when using the .05 criterion of significance. Why, then, don't researchers always use the .01 criterion, instead of the .05 criterion?

8. (a) What is the difference between a one-tailed test of significance and a two-tailed test of significance? (b) What are the disadvantages of using one-tailed tests of significance? Of using two-tailed tests of significance?

Computer Exercises

1. Assuming that a normative study has shown that the mean anxiety level for college students (μ) is 18 ($\sigma = 11$) on the scale that Ihno used, what is the z score for the baseline anxiety scores in Ihno's class? What are the one- and two-tailed p values that correspond to this z score?

2. Assuming that the mean resting heart rate for all college-aged men (μ) is 70 bpm, with $\sigma = 6$, what is the z score for the baseline HR of the men in Ihno's data set? What are the one- and two-tailed p values that correspond to this z score?

3. Repeat Exercise 3 for the women in Ihno's statistics class.

Bridge to SPSS

You can use SPSS to obtain accurate p values from the normal distribution using the CDFNORM function described in the Chapter 4. For a

p value, you will always want the area "beyond" your z score—that is, below a negative z score and above a positive z score. When you enter a negative z score, the area returned by CDFNORM is the one-tailed p value. Just multiply it by 2 if you want a two-tailed p value. If you want the one-tailed p value associated with a positive z score, just enter it with a minus sign in front of it to make it negative. Again, you can obtain the two-tailed p value by doubling the one-tailed p.

Appendix: The Null Hypothesis Testing Controversy

One of the most persistent criticisms of null hypothesis (significance) testing (abbreviated as NHT, or often, NHST) is that the null hypothesis is never actually true in psychological research, or almost never true, so there are very few, if any, Type I errors committed (i.e., 5% of, at most, a tiny number of null experiments actually performed) and a large proportion of Type II errors, because the samples psychologists use are often too small to have much chance of yielding significant results. (For a detailed list of criticisms of NHST, and possible alternative procedures, see Kline, 2004.) These criticisms are likely to be true, given that psychologists are usually building on previously successful research and rarely trying very exploratory conditions, which may not work at all. So, the critics argue, if the null hypothesis is never true, getting significant results is just a matter of using large enough samples. However, those critics are ignoring the important role that NHT plays in preventing *directional* errors.

Returning to our math SAT example, suppose that the effect of individual testing on the entire population would actually be a slight *lowering* of the population mean from 500 to 498. You would not know this, of course, so if your sample of 30 students averaged a 530 on the math SAT, you would be inclined to think you were right about the beneficial effects of privacy on testing and want to publish your results. However, without the necessity to obtain significance, misleading results, like obtaining a sample mean of 530 when the population mean is 498, could too easily be published. With the requirement of NHT in place, the sample mean of 530 (with $N = 30$) would not reach significance (even for a one-tailed test), and that would discourage its publication. It is important to note that, whereas the null hypothesis may never be *exactly* true in psychological research, small effects may be fairly common, and when the effect is small, results in the wrong direction can occur fairly easily (especially when very large samples are not being used).

To be fair, directional errors can still occur with NHT being used, but it is quite rare for a directional error to attain statistical significance. Consider the math SAT example in which the population mean for individual testing is 498. The probability of getting significant results in the *wrong* direction (i.e., above 500) is only about 2%—just slightly less than the chance of getting significance in the correct direction (i.e., below 500). A directional error that attains statistical significance is not a Type I error (because the null hypothesis is *not* true), and it is not a Type II error (because the null hypothesis *is* being rejected), so it is usually called a Type III error (Leventhal & Huynh, 1996). Therefore, even if we do not need NHT to control Type I errors (because the null hypothesis is never true), it can still be useful in controlling directional errors, by keeping the rate of Type III errors to a low level.

The critics are certainly right when they complain that NHT is poorly understood and that its results are often misinterpreted. One source of misunderstanding is the use of the word *significant* when describing a result for which the null hypothesis can be rejected. The criterion (α) usually used for significance is the .05 level, and obtaining a result that can only occur totally by chance a little fewer than 5 times out of 100 (or once in 20 times) is not really such a terribly rare event. A more realistic perspective with which to view NHT is to consider this procedure as a way of casting doubt on any research result, initially. Given all of the variability that exists in the way humans (and other animals) respond to any experimental treatment, we should always be skeptical when first considering the result from a sample. It is possible that the result is due entirely to the chance factors involved in obtaining your samples (e.g., you accidentally assigned most of your strong placebo responders to the treatment rather than the control group) and that the treatment does not work at all (or it works a very tiny bit, or even works a tiny bit *in the wrong direction*). Setting alpha at .05 makes it clear that we are ready to relax our suspicions concerning chance factors fairly easily in the interest of scientific progress. Statistics textbooks usually imply that a *p* value below .05 lets us safely ignore the null hypothesis as a possible explanation for our results, but with all the psychology studies being conducted these days, that is simply not true. A probability of 1 in 20 is not all that low, and a "statistically significant" result is not all that impressive. Note that by declaring a result to be statistical significant we are merely conforming to a standardized and arbitrary convention for deciding when to suspend our skepticism that the result is due entirely to chance. It does not mean that we can now be sure that there would be a noticeable, or even measurable, effect in the population, but it does mean that our scientific community thinks it is acceptable to act that way. Otherwise, we would always be stymied by some sense of doubt about our result being due to chance factors alone.

If psychologists conducted "null" experiments about half the time or more (e.g., performing many studies of paranormal phenomena), an alpha of .05, which screens out 95% of "null" experiments by not letting them reach significance, would probably not be adequate. Making Type I errors on 5% of half or more of the studies you conduct produces quite a few Type I errors overall. It is because null experiments are rarely conducted that we can get away with routinely using an alpha as large as 1 in 20. On the other hand, the large number of Type II errors (i.e., missing a true result) that are normally committed in psychology can be problematic, especially when researchers make the mistake of thinking that failing to reject the null hypothesis means that you have good evidence that there is really no effect in the population. However, if psychologists frequently used very large samples, they would often obtain statistical significance when the population means differed only slightly, and the term *significance* would quickly lose its meaning. We discuss this side of the NHT controversy when we take up the topic of power and the rate of Type II errors, in Chapter 11.

Chapter 6
The One-Sample *t* Test and Interval Estimation

PREVIEW

Introduction

The Statistical Test for the Mean of a Single Population When σ Is Not Known: The *t* Distributions

How do we test hypotheses about the mean of one population when the population standard deviation is not known?

What are degrees of freedom? How many degrees of freedom are associated with this statistical test?

How do the *t* distributions differ from the normal curve model?

Interval Estimation

How do we estimate an interval in which the population mean is likely to fall?

What is gained by using confidence intervals (CIs), as opposed to testing hypotheses about a specific value of the population mean?

What advantage does the 95% CI have over the 99% CI? What is the relative advantage of the 99% CI?

What is the relationship between null hypothesis testing and CIs?

The Standard Error of a Proportion

How do we test hypotheses about the mean of one population when the data are in the form of proportions?

What is the correct standard error term to use in this situation? What is the correct statistical model?

When should these procedures not be used because they are too likely to yield inaccurate results?

Summary

Exercises

Thought Questions

Computer Exercises

Bridge to SPSS

Introduction

In Chapter 5, we described how you could use a z score for sample means to test a null hypothesis concerning the mean of one population. We explained how to find a p value and use it to decide whether it is reasonable to suppose that your sample is just a random selection from the ordinary population (i.e., H_0 is true) or whether your sample mean is so extreme (and therefore p is so small) that the null hypothesis can be rejected on the basis of being "sufficiently unlikely" to account for your results. The latter decision would support the alternative hypothesis that your sample actually represents a population whose mean differs from the null hypothesized value, either because the treatment applied to the participants in the sample had some effect on your dependent variable (as in an experimental study), or because the characteristic for which the participants were selected (e.g., people who exercise regularly) is related to the variable you are measuring (e.g., subjective level of stress). The second case might be called an observational study or quasi-experiment. The statistical procedure for rejecting the null hypothesis is exactly the same for quasi-experiments as it is for true experiments; it is the interpretation of the results following the rejection of the null hypothesis that differs. You cannot draw the same causal conclusions from a quasi-experiment that you can from a true experiment. We return to this point in the context of other statistical procedures in later chapters of this text.

Unfortunately, the z test requires that you know the standard deviation (SD) of your dependent variable in the population (i.e., σ), and this is rarely known for the variables studied by behavioral science researchers. The good news is that you can estimate σ from the data you do have and then use a formula very similar to the z score for sample means, as we demonstrate next.

When you do not know σ, the best that you can do is to estimate it by calculating the value of s for your sample. When divided by the square root of N, the resulting quantity, expressed symbolically as $s_{\overline{X}}$, can be used as an estimate of $\sigma_{\overline{X}}$ in the z-score formula for sample means. The new formula looks like this:

$$\text{est. } \sigma_{\overline{x}} = s_{\overline{x}} = \frac{s}{\sqrt{N}} \qquad \text{Formula 6.1}$$

Notice how similar Formula 6.1 is to Formula 5.1. If we use Formula 6.1 as the denominator of Formula 5.2, we get a z-score formula for groups that can be used when σ is not known.

$$z = \frac{\overline{X} - \mu}{\dfrac{s}{\sqrt{N}}} \qquad \text{Formula 6.2}$$

Note that the use of the symbol z in Formula 6.2 implies that the values from this formula will form a normal distribution (ND). However, this is not strictly true, and is only approximately true when the samples are quite large. That is why Formula 6.2 is sometimes called the *z test for large samples*. It is also why we need to describe a more general-purpose modification of this formula in the next section.

The Statistical Test for the Mean of a Single Population When σ Is Not Known: The *t* Distributions

Although Formula 6.2 looks similar to Formula 5.2, there is a critical difference. As just mentioned, the values obtained from Formula 6.2 are *not* normally distributed; the normal curve will serve as a good approximation for the *z* scores obtained *only* if the sample size is quite large (e.g., more than 100). This is because $s_{\overline{X}}$ is only an estimate of $\sigma_{\overline{X}}$. Using the normal curve procedure will give inaccurate answers, especially when the sample size is small, because as the samples get smaller, *s* becomes less reliable as an estimate of σ. We need a more appropriate statistical model to represent the exact distribution of $(\overline{X} - \mu)/s_{\overline{X}}$, one that is accurate for all sample sizes. This new statistical model is known as the *t distributions*.

In contrast to the normal curve, there is a *different t* distribution for every sample size. The sampling distribution of the mean based on a sample size of 10 has one *t* distribution, while the sampling distribution of the mean based on a sample size of 15 has a different *t* distribution. Fortunately, you do not have to know the exact shape of each of the various *t* distributions. Critical values for the curves corresponding to each sample size have been determined by mathematicians and summarized in statistical tables. All you need do is note the size of your sample and then refer to the appropriate *t* distribution. A table of critical *t* values is presented as Table B in the Appendix. (The assumptions that underlie the use of *t* distributions are discussed in the next chapter.)

Statisticians could have created a table just like Table A (for the normal curve) for each of the *t* distributions, but that would require a large number of tables. Theoretically, an infinite number of tables would be needed (one for each possible sample size), but the *t* distribution begins to resemble the normal distribution rather closely for large sample sizes. In fact, when *N* is about 100 or more, the difference between the corresponding *t* table and the normal curve table becomes small enough to ignore for most purposes. Unfortunately, that would still require a cumbersome number of tables. Providing a *t* table that contains only critical values saves a great deal of space. Unlike Table A, therefore, Table B does not make it possible for you to find the *p* value that corresponds to a particular value for *t*, but you can look up critical values for several commonly used alphas, for both one- and two-tailed tests.

Degrees of Freedom

The *t* table is given in terms of *degrees of freedom* (*df*) rather than sample size. When you are comparing a sample mean to a hypothesized population mean (and σ is not known),

$$df = N - 1$$

That is, the number of df in the present situation is equal to 1 *less* than the sample size. Recall that this is equal to the divisor in the formula for s^2 (Formula 3.3).

Degrees of freedom is a concept that arises at several points in statistical inference; you will encounter it again in connection with other statistical tests in later chapters. The number of df is the number of freely varying quantities in the kind of repeated random sampling that produces sampling distributions. In connection with the test of the mean of a single population, it refers to the fact that each time a sample is drawn and the population variance is estimated, it is based on only $N - 1$ df. That is, there are $N - 1$ freely varying quantities. When you find for each of the N observations its deviation from the sample mean, $X - \overline{X}$, not all of these N quantities are free to vary in a given sample. Because these deviations must sum to zero (as was pointed out in Chapter 3), the Nth value is automatically determined once any $N - 1$ of them are fixed at given observed values. For example, if the sum of $N - 1$ deviations from the mean is −3, the Nth deviation must equal +3 so that the sum of all deviations from the mean will equal zero. So in this situation, there are only $N - 1$ df, and therefore the t distribution is based on $N - 1$ df. The df and not the N is the fundamental consideration, because the df need not be $N - 1$ in other applications of t.

Using the t Distributions to Test Null Hypotheses

The following is an edited section of the t table:

df	$\cdots$	$t_{.05}$	$t_{.01}$	$\cdots$
$\vdots$				
4		2.78	4.60	
$\vdots$				
10		2.23	3.17	
11		2.20	3.11	
12		2.18	3.06	
13		2.16	3.01	
14		2.15	2.98	
15		2.13	2.95	
$\vdots$				
40		2.02	2.70	
$\vdots$				
120		1.98	2.62	
$\vdots$				
∞		1.96	2.58	

Each horizontal row represents a separate distribution that corresponds to the *df* listed in the left column. The row labeled with the symbol for infinity (∞) represents the normal distribution, which is what the *t* distribution becomes when the samples are infinitely large.

To illustrate the use of the *t* distributions, suppose that you wish to test the null hypothesis H_0: $\mu = 17$ against the alternative H_A: $\mu \neq 17$ using the .05 criterion of significance. Perhaps a large-scale survey has shown that among people who engage in text messaging, the average number of messages sent per day is 17. You suspect that the average is higher for young people in high school, so you obtain a sample of $N = 15$ high-school students and find that for them $\overline{X} = 18.80$ and $s = 3.50$. You could try testing the null hypothesis that the average for the entire population of high-schoolers is really just 17 by creating a *z* score with Formula 6.1, but we now know that the mean of a sample size of only 15 is more accurately tested with a *t* distribution. To create a formula for small sample sizes, we need only change the *z* to a *t* in Formula 6.1, like so:

$$t = \frac{\overline{X} - \mu}{s_{\overline{X}}}$$

Formula 6.3

where

$\overline{X}$ = the observed value of the sample mean
μ = the hypothesized value of the population mean
$s_{\overline{X}}$ = the estimated standard error of the mean $(= s/\sqrt{N})$

In the present example, the *t* value would be

$$t = \frac{18.80 - 17}{(3.50/\sqrt{15})} = \frac{1.80}{.90} = 2.00$$

Now you can compare the *t* value that you have computed to a critical value obtained from the *t* table. For 14 *df* (1 less than your *N* of 15), and using the two-tailed .05 criterion of significance, the critical value is 2.145. A *t* value larger than this *in absolute value* (i.e., ignoring the sign) is considered "sufficiently unlikely" (i.e., $p < .05$) to occur if H_0 is true, and would therefore allow you to reject H_0 in favor of H_A. However, the absolute value of the *t* that you computed was *less than* 2.145, so you would have to *retain* H_0. Because the obtained *t* value of 2.00 in our example is not larger in absolute value than 2.145, our data do *not* warrant concluding that the high school population mean differs from 17.

If, instead, your sample size were 121, you would have 120 *df*. The corresponding critical value from the table, again using the .05 criterion of significance, would be 1.98. In this case, calculating a *t* value of 2.00 *would* allow you to reject H_0 in favor of H_A. However, the critical value of *t* using the .01 (two-tailed) criterion of significance with $df = 120$ is 2.617. Therefore, the computed *t* value of 2.0 is statistically significant at the .05 but not the .01 level, when $df = 120$.

The *t* and *z* Distributions Compared

The *t* distribution for 9 degrees of freedom and the normal curve are compared in Figure 6.1. Note the fatter tails in the case of the *t* distribution, so that you have to go farther out on the tails to find points that set off the .05 or .01 areas for rejecting H_0. While 95% of the normal curve lies between the *z* values −1.96 and 1.96, 95% of the *t* distribution for 9 *df* lies between −2.26 and 2.26. So using the two-tailed .05 criterion, 2.26 (and *not* 1.96) must be used as the critical value when σ is not known and *df* = 9.

Notice in the *t* table that the *smaller* the sample size, the *larger t* must be in order to reject H_0 at the same level of significance. Also, when the sample size is very large, *z* and *t* are virtually equivalent. Thus, for 40 *df*, *t* = 2.02 (at the .05 level). For 120 *df*, *t* = 1.98. For sample sizes in the hundreds, the critical *t* values become so close to the *z* value of 1.96 that it makes little practical difference which one you use.

Suppose Ihno suspects that the math aptitude of statistics students at her school is on the rise and that her class in particular is from a population with a higher math aptitude than the population that existed over the previous decade. She finds the means for previous statistics classes on the math background quiz and calculates an average over the previous 10 years. This 10-year average can be viewed as the population mean against which she wishes to test her current class. If this average were equal to 27.31, then the null hypothesis that Ihno would be testing is H_0: μ = 27.31. Because Ihno has only the means from previous classes and not the raw scores, she does not know σ; she will have to estimate the standard error of the mean from the data for her class. We showed in a

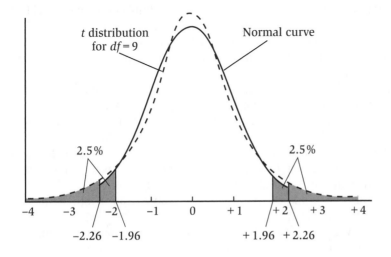

Figure 6.1

A Comparison Between the Normal Curve and the *t* Distribution for *df* = 9

previous chapter that for the 85 students who took the math quiz in Ihno's class, $\overline{X} = 29.07$ and $s = 9.48$. Therefore:

$$s_{\overline{X}} = \frac{s}{\sqrt{N}} = \frac{9.48}{\sqrt{85}} = \frac{9.48}{9.22} = 1.028$$

and

$$t = \frac{\overline{X} - \mu}{s_{\overline{X}}} = \frac{29.07 - 27.31}{1.028} = 1.71$$

Ihno would have to decide to retain H_0 whether she compared 1.71 to the critical t value of 1.99 for $df = 84$ (i.e., $85 - 1$) or to the z value of 1.96. In behavioral science research, it is customary to report the obtained value as a t value even for large samples. The reason is that although z is a good approximation in large samples, it is still an approximation. So you should use the critical t value obtained from the t table, rather than the z value of 1.96 for the .05 criterion or 2.58 for the .01 criterion, unless you happen to know the exact value of σ. *Retain H_0 if your computed t value (ignoring the sign) is smaller than the critical value, and reject H_0* otherwise. (If you used a statistical program to calculate your t value, you have the option of reporting the exact p value provided by your software and comparing that p value directly to alpha.)

Interval Estimation

Null hypothesis testing (NHT) is still surprisingly popular in the behavioral sciences despite the fact that this method has several serious (and much-debated) deficiencies (see Kline, 2004). One drawback to NHT is that when the results are statistically significant, the researcher is entitled to reject *only* the exact value specified by the null hypothesis.

Suppose that the mean math quiz score for Ihno's class were 29.81, instead of 29.07. Then her calculated t would have been $2.5/1.028 = 2.43$, and she would have rejected the null hypothesis in favor of the alternative hypothesis and concluded that the mean for the population of current students in this high school is greater than 27.31.

Although in this latest case, Ihno would be able to reject the null hypothesis that $\mu = 27.31$, she could not, without further testing, reject the hypothesis that $\mu = 28$, that $\mu = 27.4$, or even that $\mu = 27.32$. The research study tested one and only one null hypothesis, namely $\mu = 27.31$, so only this hypothesis can be rejected when the results are statistically significant. To be sure, it is likely that values very close to the null-hypothesized value of 27.31 should also be rejected. But an additional statistical procedure would be required to determine what would count as "very close" numerically.

One good way to increase the information beyond what you could get from NHT alone is to estimate a **confidence interval** (CI) within which the population mean is likely to fall. Rather than specifying a single numerical value (as does H_0), a confidence interval specifies a *range of values* within which a parameter (here, the population mean) is likely to fall. How likely? If you are using the .05 criterion of significance, you can be 95% confident that the population mean falls within the range specified by the CI. The end points of the CI are called *confidence limits*.

Computation

To illustrate the use of confidence intervals, consider the original example involving the math aptitude of Ihno's class. We wish to determine an interval that will include all "not sufficiently unlikely" values of μ (i.e., all values for which H_0 should be retained). Using the .05 criterion of significance and $df = 84$, the farthest that any sample mean can lie from μ and still be retained as "not sufficiently unlikely" is $\pm 1.99\ s_{\overline{X}}$ (where 1.99 is the critical value of t for the specified df, 84). So the upper limit of this confidence interval may be found by solving the following equation for μ:

$$+1.99 = \frac{X - \mu}{s_{\overline{X}}}$$

Similarly, the lower limit of the CI can be found from the following equation:

$$-1.99 = \frac{\overline{X} - \mu}{s_{\overline{X}}}$$

Or we can find both of the CI limits by solving for μ in the following equation:

$$\pm 1.99 = \frac{\overline{X} - \mu}{s_{\overline{X}}}$$

which yields this equation:

$$\mu = \overline{X} \pm 1.99 s_{\overline{X}}$$

which can then be expanded like this:

$$\overline{X} - 1.99 s_{\overline{X}} \le \mu \le \overline{X} + 1.99 s_{\overline{X}}$$

Thus, for our main example,

$$29.07 - 1.99(1.028) \le \mu \le 29.07 + 1.99(1.028)$$

$$29.07 - 2.05 \le \mu \le 29.07 + 2.05$$

$$27.02 \le \mu \le 31.12$$

You should retain any hypothesized value of μ between 27.02 and 31.12, inclusive, using the CI corresponding to the .05 criterion of significance (called the *95% confidence interval*). Conversely, reject any hypothesized value of μ outside this interval.

Note that 27.31 (the hypothesized mean) is in the CI we just calculated, which tells us that it is reasonable to suppose that Ihno's class, with its sample mean of 29.07, comes from a population with a mean of 27.31. This judgment is consistent with *not* rejecting the null hypothesis of 27.31, which was the conclusion reached in the preceding example.

The general formula for computing CIs when σ is not known is:

$$\overline{X} - t_{\text{crit}}s_{\overline{X}} \leq \mu \leq \overline{X} + t_{\text{crit}}s_{\overline{X}} \qquad \text{Formula 6.4}$$

where

$t_{\text{crit}} =$ critical value from the t table for $df = N - 1$
$\overline{X} =$ observed value of the sample mean

The CI corresponding to the .01 criterion of significance is called the *99% confidence interval*. In the math quiz example, the critical value of t is based on $df = 84$, so for the .01 criterion, t_{crit} is 2.62. Thus, the 99% CI is equal to:

$$29.07 - 2.62(1.028) \leq \mu \leq 29.07 + 2.62(1.028)$$

$$29.07 - 2.69 \leq \mu \leq 29.07 + 2.69$$

$$26.38 \leq \mu \leq 31.76$$

Note that the 99% CI is wider than the 95% CI, and contains it completely (i.e., any value in the 95% CI, such as 27.31, will also be in the 99% CI). You can be more sure that the population mean falls in the 99% CI, but you must pay a price for this added confidence: The interval is larger, so μ is less precisely estimated. (You could be absolutely certain that the population mean falls within the "confidence interval" $-\infty \leq \mu \leq \infty$, but such a statement is useless—it tells you nothing that you did not know beforehand.) The trade-off is that by using $\alpha = .05$ to find the critical value in Formula 6.3, you can be only 95% confident that the true population mean falls within the stated interval, but the interval is narrower, and hence more informative, than the 99% CI. By using $\alpha = .01$, instead, you can be 99% confident (more sure) that the true population mean falls within the stated interval, but the interval is now wider and therefore less informative. Note that if σ *is known*, you can use the critical z values (1.96 for the 95% CI; 2.58 for the 99% CI) instead of t_{crit}.

Confidence Intervals and Null Hypothesis Tests

The scientific journals in the behavioral sciences still place a good deal of emphasis on testing null hypotheses, but there is a rapidly growing recognition that interval estimation has important advantages.

Confidence intervals allow you to do everything that null hypothesis testing does, and more. If a value of μ specified by a null hypothesis falls within the CI, that null hypothesis is retained. If a value of μ specified by a null hypothesis falls outside the CI, that null hypothesis is rejected. But confidence intervals have the advantage that they provide a whole range of population means that should be retained. For example, the 95% CI that Ihno found for the mean of the population from which her statistics class was (theoretically) randomly selected is 27.02 to 31.12. Any value for μ that falls within this range should be considered a reasonable possibility for the true value of μ. Because the average math background score for the previous 10 years (27.31) falls inside the 95% CI, it cannot be rejected as a null hypothesis at the .05 level. This is consistent with the conclusion drawn from Ihno's *t* test. Because her *t* (1.71) was less than the .05 two-tailed, critical value for a *t* distribution with 84 degrees of freedom (1.99), the null hypothesis (μ = 27.31) could not be rejected.

As we have just shown, CIs provide an alternative way of interpreting your data that can be more informative than a simple null hypothesis test. To illustrate this point further, let us consider four very different but possible CIs that Ihno's class data could have led to:

1. $28.8 \leq \mu \leq 32.9$
2. $27.2 \leq \mu \leq 31.3$
3. $24.4 \leq \mu \leq 28.5$
4. $22.0 \leq \mu \leq 26.1$

The first set of results supports Ihno's suspicion. She can conclude with 95% confidence that the population mean corresponding to her class is well above 27.31; more specifically, it can be expected to fall between 28.8 and 32.9. The second set of results is much less encouraging. Although the population mean seems likely to be greater than 27.31, Ihno cannot reject the hypothesis that μ is very close to 27.31 or even slightly lower, since the CI extends as low as 27.2. However, because nearly all of the CI is above 27.31, she can be somewhat encouraged that she is on the right track.

The third set of results is downright discouraging. It is unlikely that the population mean is much above 27.31. Therefore, these results provide little support for Ihno's idea that her class comes from a "better" population. Finally, the fourth set of results is completely inconsistent with Ihno's notion about her class. Because 27.31 is well *above* the *upper* confidence limit, these results would lead to the conclusion that, if Ihno's class differs from the previous population at all, it is actually from a population whose mean is *lower* in math aptitude than the population of previous students.

Confidence intervals (CIs) are highly recommended by the American Psychological Association (2010) to supplement null hypothesis testing (NHT) when submitting a study for publication. Many behavioral researchers feel that CIs should be used more widely than they are at present; some have even suggested that the reporting of CIs should replace NHT entirely (Finch & Cumming, 2009). Because CIs provide considerably more information than the results of testing a specific null hypothesis, we feel that it is safe to say that CIs should be used and reported more widely in behavioral science research.

The Standard Error of a Proportion

Suppose that a few weeks before an election, a worried politician takes a poll by drawing a random sample of 400 registered voters. He finds that 53% intend to vote for him, while 47% prefer his opponent.[1] He is pleased to observe that he has the support of more than half of the sample, but he knows that the sample may not be an accurate indicator of the population because an unrepresentative number of his supporters may have been included by chance. What should he conclude about his prospects in the election?

This problem is similar to the preceding ones in this chapter. There is one population in which the politician is interested (registered voters), and he wishes to draw an inference about the mean of this population based on data obtained from a sample. In particular, he would like to know if the percent supporting him at this point in time is greater than 50% (in which case he is likely to win the election). There is one important difference in the present situation, however: His data are in terms of percents or *proportions*.

While the general strategy is the same as in the case of the sampling distribution of the mean, a modified method must be used to deal with proportions. The needed formula is

$$z = \frac{P - \pi}{\sqrt{\pi(1 - \pi)/N}}$$

Formula 6.5

where

$P =$ proportion observed in the sample
$\pi =$ hypothesized value of the *population* proportion
$N =$ number of people in the sample

The denominator of this formula, $\sqrt{\pi(1 - \pi)/N}$, is the *standard error of a proportion*, symbolized by σ_P. It serves a similar purpose to the standard error of the mean, but it is a measure of the variability of *proportions* in samples drawn at random from a population where the

---

[1]For simplicity, we assume that there are no undecided or "won't say" voters in this sample. There will be some such in reality, and in omitting them we make the possibly incorrect assumption that they will break the same way as those who make a choice.

proportion in question is π. (Notice that in this formula π is used to represent the hypothesized value of the population proportion. It does *not* represent the usual mathematical value of approximately 3.14159....)

Since the population π is specified, and the σ of the population in question is considered to be known—it can be proved equal to $\sqrt{\pi(1-\pi)}$—the results are referred to in Table A in the Appendix. In the case of the anxious politician, the critical population value in which he is interested is .50: He wants to know whether the observed sample proportion of .53 is sufficiently different from .50 to enable him to conclude that a majority of the population of voters will vote for him. Thus,

$$\pi = \text{hypothesized population proportion} = .50$$

$$P = \text{proportion observed in sample} = .53$$

The statistical analysis is as follows:

$$H_0: \pi = .50$$

$$H_A: \pi \neq .50$$

$$\alpha = .05$$

$$z = \frac{.53 - .50}{\sqrt{.50(1-.50)/400}} = \frac{.03}{.025} = 1.20$$

The value of 1.20 is smaller than the critical *z* value of 1.96 needed to reject H_0. Therefore, the politician *cannot* conclude that he will win the election. It is "not sufficiently unlikely" for 53% of a sample of 400 voters to support him, even if only 50% of the entire population is willing to vote for him. The politician will therefore have a nervous few weeks until the votes are in, and he may well conclude from the sample results that he should increase his campaigning efforts. The results are illustrated in Figure 6.2.

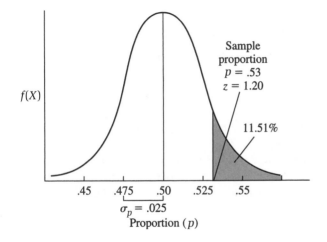

$f(X)$

Sample proportion
$p = .53$
$z = 1.20$

11.51%

.45   .475   .50   .525   .55

$\sigma_p = .025$
Proportion (*p*)

Figure 6.2

Sampling Distribution of *P* When π = .50 and N = 400

There is one important caution regarding the use of the standard error of the proportion. When the hypothesized value of the population proportion (π) is quite large or small (i.e., close to 1.0 or 0) and the sample size is small, computing a z score and referring it to the normal curve table will yield incorrect results. As a rough guide, you should *not* use this procedure when either $N\pi$ or $N(1 - \pi)$ is less than 5. For example, if you wish to test the null hypothesis that $\pi = .85$ with a sample size of 20,

$$N\pi = (20)(.85) = 17 \quad \text{and} \quad N(1 - \pi) = (20)(.15) = 3$$

Because $N(1 - \pi)$ is less than 5, the procedures discussed in this section should *not* be used. For a tested value of π that is as extreme as .85, the proposed sample size of 20 is too small to yield accurate results. You should either use the appropriate nonparametric statistical technique to deal with this situation (the binomial distribution, which will be discussed in Chapter 16), or increase the size of your sample.

Confidence Intervals for π

Suppose you wish to determine all reasonably likely values of the population proportion (π) using the .05 criterion of significance. The formula for the appropriate confidence interval is:

$$(P - 1.96\sigma_P) \leq \mu \leq (P + 1.96\sigma_P) \qquad \text{Formula 6.6}$$

There is one difficulty: σ_P depends on the value of π, which is not known. In the previous section, a value of π was specified by H_0 and used in the calculation of σ_P. However, there is no single hypothesized value of π in interval estimation. One possibility, which yields a fairly good approximation *if the sample size is large,* is to use P as an estimate of π. With a large sample, P is unlikely to be so far from π as to greatly affect σ_p and hence the size of the CI. In the case of the nervous politician in the previous section, $P = .53$; and $\sigma_p = \sqrt{.53(1 - .53)/N} = .025$. Then the 95% CI is equal to:

$$.53 - 1.96(.025) \leq \mu \leq .53 + 1.96(.025)$$

$$.53 - .049 \leq \mu \leq .53 + .049$$

$$.48 \leq \mu \leq .58$$

Since the sample size is large ($N = 400$), the politician can state with 95% confidence that between approximately 48% and 58% of the population will vote for him. Note that the value of .50 *is* within the CI, as would be expected from the fact that the null hypothesis that $\pi = .50$ was retained. To determine the 99% CI, the procedure would be the same except that the z value of 2.58 would be used instead of 1.96.

Summary

The use of the normal distribution to test hypotheses requires that the standard deviation of the population be known. If you have a large sample, its SD can be used in place of σ with negligible error. However, if your sample is small, you will need to use one of the t distributions.

Testing the Mean of a Single Population With the t Distributions

The formula for estimating the standard error of the mean from a single sample is

$$s_{\overline{X}} = \frac{s}{\sqrt{N}} \qquad \text{Formula 6.1}$$

where

$s_{\overline{X}}$ = the estimated standard error of the mean
s = (unbiased) standard deviation of the sample of observations

Then, to draw inferences about a population mean, you can use:

$$t = \frac{\overline{X} - \mu}{s_{\overline{X}}} \qquad \text{Formula 6.3}$$

with $df = N - 1$
Use z (Formula 5.2) instead of t if σ is known. For very large samples, you can use Formula 6.2 (same as Formula 6.3, except with z instead of t on the left side of the equation).

Confidence Intervals

Confidence intervals establish all reasonably likely values of a population parameter, such as a mean or proportion. Confidence intervals provide considerably more information than the results of testing a specific null hypothesis, because they show the decision that should be made for every conceivable null-hypothetical value rather than only one.

   Use $s_{\overline{X}}$ when determining CIs for the mean of one population, if σ is unknown. Obtain a two-tailed critical value of t from the t table $(df = N - 1; \alpha = 1.0 - \text{confidence})$, and compute

$$(\overline{X} - t_{\text{crit}}s_{\overline{X}}) \leq \mu \leq (\overline{X} + t_{\text{crit}}s_{\overline{X}}) \qquad \text{Formula 6.4}$$

where

t_{crit} = critical value from t table

It is reasonable to use a critical z instead of the critical t for very large samples.

Test for a Single Proportion

If the data are in the form of proportions, you can begin by computing the appropriate standard error using this formula (the denominator of Formula 6.5):

$$\sigma_P = \sqrt{\frac{\pi(1-\pi)}{N}}$$

Then compute:

$$z = \frac{P - \pi}{\sigma_P}$$

where

σ_p = the standard error of a proportion
P = proportion observed in the sample
π = hypothesized value of the population proportion

Do *not* use this procedure if $N\pi$ or $N(1-\pi)$ is less than 5. There are more exact tests for such cases (see Chapter 16).

Exercises

1. Answer these problems by calculating a t value and comparing it to the critical value for a two-tailed test at the .05 level. (Note: You can save time by using the means and standard deviations you calculated for the dormitories called Turck and Kirk Halls for previous exercises.)

   (a) Would you retain or reject the null hypothesis that the population mean for Turck Hall is 16?

   (b) Would you retain or reject the null hypothesis that the population mean for Kirk Hall is 11?

2. For Kirk Hall, compute each of the following:

   (a) The 99% CI.

   (b) The 95% CI.

   (c) The 90% CI.

   (d) Explain why the size of the CIs becomes larger as the level of confidence increases.

3. This exercise is based on the following data set: 1, 3, 6, 0, 1, 1, 2, 1, 4.

   (a) Perform a t test in order to decide whether you can reject the null hypothesis of $\mu = 2.5$ at the .05 level (two-tailed) for these data.

   (b) Redo your t test in part (a) for a null hypothesis of $\mu = 6.0$.

   (c) Compute the 95% CI for the population mean from which these data were drawn. Explain how this CI could be used to draw conclusions about the null hypotheses in parts (a) and (b).

4. This exercise is based on the following data set: 68.36, 15.31, 77.42, 84.00, 76.59, 68.43, 72.41, 83.05, 91.07, 80.62, 77.83.

   (a) Perform a *t* test in order to decide whether you can reject the null hypothesis of $\mu = 52.3$ at the .01 level (two-tailed) for these data.
   (b) Redo your *t* test in part (a) for a null hypothesis of $\mu = 85.0$.
   (c) Compute the 99% CI for the population mean from which these data were drawn. Explain how this CI could be used to draw conclusions about the null hypotheses in parts (a) and (b).

5. A politician has staked his political career on whether a new state constitution will pass. To find out which way the wind is blowing, he obtains a random sample of 100 voters a few weeks prior to the election and finds that 60% of the sample says that they will vote for the new constitution. Assuming that the constitution will fail if it receives 50% or less of the vote, should he conclude that the electorate as a whole will support the new constitution? Perform the appropriate statistical test to answer this question.

6. A certain business concern needs to obtain at least 20% of the market in order to make a profit. A random sample of 200 prospective buyers is asked whether they will purchase the product. What should the company conclude if (find the 95% CI in each case, in addition to performing the null hypothesis test):

   (a) 26 of those asked said they would buy the product?
   (b) 46 of those asked said they would buy the product?
   (c) 58 of those asked said they would buy the product?

Thought Questions

1. You are drawing inferences about the mean of one population. (a) When should you use the *t* distributions as the theoretical model rather than the normal curve model? (b) Why is there a different critical *t* value for different degrees of freedom?

2. What advantages do confidence intervals have over testing a specific null hypothesis?

3. (a) What happens to the size of a CI as the standard error of the mean becomes larger? Why? (b) What happens to the size of a CI as the sample size becomes larger? Why? (c) What are the advantages of having a smaller CI?

4. (a) Why does the size of the CI become larger when we change from a 95% CI to a 99% CI? (b) We can be more certain that the unknown population mean falls within the 99% CI than within the 95% CI. Why, then, don't we always use 99% CIs?

5. On a test of scholastic ability administered to college students in the United States, the mean is 500 and the standard deviation is 100.

Each of the following 95% CIs for the mean of one population was computed from a random sample of students from the university in question: University Y, 601.63–642.75; University Z, 502.42–534.68. Both universities claim that their students are superior to the national average of 500. (a) Is this claim correct? (b) How do these results illustrate the advantages that CIs have over testing a specific null hypothesis, such as whether the population mean is equal to 500?

6. A behavioral science researcher wishes to draw inferences about the proportion of one population. (a) Would she prefer that the standard error of a proportion be small or large? Why? (b) Should she use the normal curve model or the t distributions as her theoretical model? Why? (c) When should she *not* use the procedures for drawing inferences about the proportion of one population discussed in this chapter? (d) Why might she prefer to use confidence intervals for the proportion of one population rather than testing a specific null hypothesis?

Computer Exercises

1. Use your statistical package to perform a one-sample t test to determine whether the baseline anxiety of Ihno's students differs significantly ($\alpha = .05$) from the mean ($\mu = 18$) found by a very large study of college students across the country. Find the 95% confidence interval for the population mean represented by Ihno's students.

2. Use your statistical package to perform a one-sample t test to determine whether the average baseline heart rate of Ihno's male students differs significantly from the mean HR ($\mu = 70$) for college-aged men at the .01 level. Find the 99% CI for the population mean represented by Ihno's male students.

3. Use your statistical package to perform a one-sample t test to determine whether the average *postquiz* heart rate of Ihno's *female* students differs significantly ($\alpha = .05$) from the mean resting HR ($\mu = 72$) for college-aged women. Find the 95% CI for the population mean represented by Ihno's female students.

Bridge to SPSS

To perform a one-sample t test in SPSS, select **Compare Means** from the ANALYZE menu, and then choose **One-Sample T Test . . .** . In the dialog box that opens, move the variable you want to test to the Test Variable(s) area, and enter the hypothesized population mean that you want to test against in the space labeled **Test Value.** The **Options . . .** button allows you to select the percentage that will be used to create a confidence interval for the population mean. The other choice you can make in the

Options box applies only when you move more than one variable to the Test Variables area, in order to perform several *t* tests in the same run (all against the same population value, however). The default choice for handling missing values deals with missing values separately for each test variable. However, if you select **Exclude cases listwise**, any case (i.e., row in the data sheet) that is missing a value for *any* of the variables that appeared together in the Test Variables area will be deleted for *all* of the *t* tests in that run (you may want the *t* tests of all your variables to involve exactly the same participants). You will see the **Exclude cases listwise** option presented for a number of other statistical procedures in SPSS, which we describe in subsequent chapters.

Chapter 7

Testing Hypotheses About the Difference Between the Means of Two Populations

PREVIEW

The Standard Error of the Difference

We wish to draw inferences about the difference between the means of two
populations. What is the correct standard error term to use in this situation?
Why can it not usually be measured directly?

What is an experimental group? A control group?

Why is it desirable to use random samples?

How does sampling error affect the difference between the means of the
experimental group and the control group?

What does the standard error of the mean tell us about the trustworthiness of a
single difference between two sample means as an estimate of the difference
between the population means?

Estimating the Standard Error of the Difference

What are the procedures for estimating the value of the standard error
of the difference (SED)?

How is the SED related to the variance of the population? To the sizes of the
samples?

The *t* Test for Two Sample Means

What is the correct statistical model to use in this situation?

How do we test hypotheses about the difference between the means of two
populations based on independent samples?

How are the results of a *t* test usually reported? What are the implications of
retaining the null hypothesis? What are the implications of rejecting the null
hypothesis?

Confidence Intervals for $\mu_1 - \mu_2$

How do we estimate an interval in which the difference between the two
population means is likely to fall?

What is gained by using confidence intervals?

PREVIEW (*continued*)

The Assumptions Underlying the Proper Use of the *t* Test for Two Sample Means

What assumptions underlie the use of this *t* test?

What is the separate-variances *t* test and under what circumstances would its use be considered?

Measuring the Size of an Effect

What is a standardized measure of effect size (g), and when is it particularly useful?

The *t* Test for Matched Samples

How do we test hypotheses about the difference between the means of two matched populations? How does the matched-pairs *t* test compare to the independent-samples *t* test on the same data? What happens to the degrees of freedom (and therefore the critical value) when two sets of scores are matched in pairs?

When is it preferable to measure the same participant twice, and when is it less problematic to match separate participants in pairs? When might you have to give up the idea of conducting a matched-pairs design altogether and use independent samples instead?

Summary

Exercises

Thought Questions

Computer Exercises

Bridge to SPSS

In the preceding two chapters we developed the tools for drawing inferences about the mean of one population. More often, scientists wish to draw inferences about differences between two or more populations. For example, a cognitive psychologist may want to know if the mean of the population of urban Americans on a pencil-and-paper test of spatial abilities is equal to the mean of the population of suburban Americans. Or a behavioral psychologist may wish to find out whether rats perform better on a discrimination learning task to gain a reward or to avoid punishment—that is, whether the mean number of correct responses is greater for the ''reward'' population or for the ''punishment'' population. In both cases, the question of interest begins with a comparison between the means of *two* samples.

In this chapter, we discuss techniques for drawing inferences about the *difference between the means of two populations* ($\mu_1 - \mu_2$) based on the data from two samples. Procedures for drawing inferences about the means of more than two populations, or about other aspects of two or more populations, are considered in later chapters.

The Standard Error of the Difference

Suppose that you wish to conduct a research study to determine whether the use of caffeine improves performance on a college mathematics examination. To test this hypothesis, you could obtain two *random* samples of college students taking mathematics, one to be the *experimental group* and one to be the *control group*. But although random sampling is theoretically the ideal method to avoid obtaining two groups that differ greatly in ability, motivation, or any other variable that might obscure the effects of caffeine, a more common approach is to select one (twice-as-large) convenient sample and then randomly assign the participants to either the experimental or control group. This procedure is called **random assignment**. Unlike random sampling, random assignment is easy to do because it simply involves dividing a sample of participants that you already have into two (or more) groups. For example, you might flip a coin and assign a participant to Group 1 if a "head" comes up and Group 2 if a "tail" comes up (however, we usually constrain the randomness a bit to ensure that the two groups end up as the same size—a variation that can be called "quasi-random").

Once you have formed two groups, you then give all members assigned to the experimental group a small dose of caffeine one hour prior to the test. At the same time, the control group is given a placebo (a pill that, unknown to them, has no biochemical effect whatsoever). This is to control for the possibility that administering *any* pill will affect the students' performance. (For example, they may become more psychologically alert and obtain higher scores, because they are expecting the pill to help them.) Thus, the control group serves as a baseline against which the performance of the experimental group can be evaluated. Finally, the mean test scores of the two groups are compared. Suppose that the mean of the experimental group equals 81, and the mean of the control group equals 78. Should you conclude that caffeine is effective in improving the test scores?

As was shown in the previous chapter, any sample mean is almost never exactly equal to the population mean because of sampling error; the cases that happened, by chance, to be included in the sample may be unusually high or low on the variable being measured. Therefore, the two populations in question (a hypothetically infinite number of test takers given caffeine and a hypothetically infinite number of test takers given a placebo) may have equal means even though the sample means are different. Consequently, you cannot tell what conclusion to reach just by looking at the sample means. You need additional information: namely, whether the 3-point difference between 81 and 78 is likely to be a trustworthy indication that the population means are different (and that caffeine *has* an effect), or whether this difference can be easily attributed solely to which cases happened to fall in each sample (in which case you should not conclude that caffeine has an effect).

How can this additional information be obtained? In the previous chapter we saw that the estimated variability of the sampling distribution of means drawn from one population, $s_{\overline{X}}$, provides information as to how trustworthy is any one $\overline{X}$ as an estimate of μ. The present problem concerns how trustworthy is any one *difference*, $\overline{X}_1 - \overline{X}_2$, as an estimate of the difference between the population means, $\mu_1 - \mu_2$. This problem is also solved by making use of an appropriate sampling distribution: the sampling distribution of the *difference* between *two* sample means.

Suppose that a variable is normally distributed in each of two defined populations and that the populations have equal means and equal variances (i.e., $\mu_1 = \mu_2$ and $\sigma_1^2 = \sigma_2^2$). If many pairs of random samples of equal size were drawn from the two populations, a distribution of differences between the paired means could be established empirically. For each pair, you would subtract the mean of the second sample ($\overline{X}_2$) from the mean of the first sample ($\overline{X}_1$).

Because the means of the two populations are equal, any difference between the sample means must be due solely to sampling error.

Figure 7.1 illustrates the procedure needed to obtain an empirical sampling distribution of 1,000 differences in the case where $\mu_1 = \mu_2 = 80$ and the size of each random sample is 30. The resulting frequency

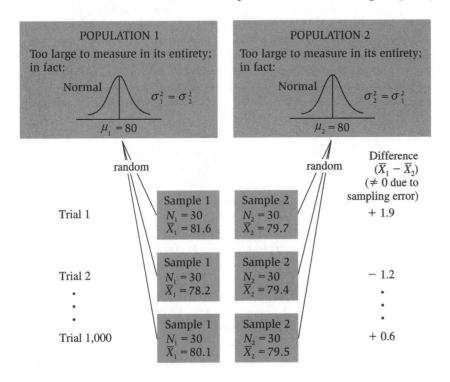

Figure 7.1

Illustration of Procedure for Obtaining the Empirical Sampling Distribution of Differences Between Two Means ($N = 30$)

Figure 7.2

Frequency Polygon of the Data in Table 7.1

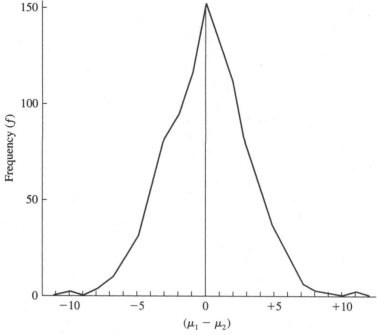

Difference between sample means $(\overline{X}_1 - \overline{X}_2)$

distribution is shown in Table 7.1, and the frequency polygon plotted from this distribution is shown in Figure 7.2. The sample means will rarely be exactly equal to 80, and the differences between pairs of means will almost never be exactly equal to zero, due to sampling fluctuations, though the means will usually be near 80, and the difference will usually be not far from zero. Notice that the distribution is approximately symmetric, which indicates that chance differences are equally likely to occur in either direction—that is, $(\overline{X}_1 - \overline{X}_2) > (\mu_1 - \mu_2)$ or $(\overline{X}_1 - \overline{X}_2) < (\mu_1 - \mu_2)$. Thus, the mean of the distribution of differences tends to be equal to $\mu_1 - \mu_2$, which in this case is zero.

Given the data in Table 7.1, you could calculate the standard deviation (SD) of the distribution of differences for the given sample size by using the usual formula for the SD (see Chapter 3). This SD would tell you how much, on the average, a given $\overline{X}_1 - \overline{X}_2$ is likely to differ from the "true" difference of zero (the central point of the distribution of differences). Consequently, it would indicate how trustworthy is the single difference that you have on hand as an estimate of $\mu_1 - \mu_2$. This SD is therefore called the **standard error of the difference (SED)**.

On one hand, a relatively *large* standard error of the difference indicates that even a moderately sized difference between a pair of sample means must be viewed with grave suspicion. Because a large standard error tells us that large discrepancies between $\overline{X}_1$ *and* $\overline{X}_2$ are likely *even if they come from populations with equal means,* you need quite a large difference before you can safely conclude that μ_1 is not equal to μ_2. If, on the other

Table 7.1   **Empirical Sampling Distribution of 1,000 Differences Between Pairs of Sample Means ($N = 30$) Drawn From Two Populations Where $\mu_1 = \mu_1 = 80$ (Hypothetical Data)**

Difference between sample means $\overline{X}_1 - \overline{X}_2$	Number of samples (f)
Greater than +11.49	0
+10.50 to +11.49	1
+9.50 to +10.49	0
+8.50 to +9.49	1
+7.50 to +8.49	4
+6.50 to +7.49	7
+5.50 to +6.49	21
+4.50 to +5.49	32
+3.50 to +4.49	54
+2.50 to +3.49	77
+1.50 to +2.49	107
+.50 to +1.49	122
−.50 to +.49	153
−1.50 to −.51	114
−2.50 to −1.51	95
−3.50 to −2.51	82
−4.50 to −3.51	60
−5.50 to −4.51	31
−6.50 to −5.51	22
−7.50 to −6.51	10
−8.50 to −7.51	4
−9.50 to −8.51	1
−10.50 to −9.51	2
Smaller than −10.50	0
Total	1,000

hand, the SED is relatively *small,* you can place more confidence in any one sample difference as an estimate of the true population difference. In this case, large discrepancies between $\overline{X}_1$ *and* $\overline{X}_2$ are *not* as likely to occur (and mislead you) if in fact $\mu_1 = \mu_2$, so a fairly large difference between the sample means *is* a trustworthy sign that the population means differ. Of course, we cannot go by our subjective impression of whether a particular difference of sample means is large or not, which is why psychologists depend so heavily (perhaps too heavily at times) on null hypothesis testing (NHT) as a fairly objective, quantitative way to make these judgments. We will show you how to apply NHT to the case of two sample means very shortly.

In practice, behavioral scientists never have many paired random samples of a given size with which to compute the SED empirically. Instead, as in Chapter 6, we must make use of formulas developed by statisticians. In the present situation, before you can apply NHT, you will need a formula that enables you to *estimate* the standard error of the difference based on the *one* pair of samples that you have measured.

Estimating the Standard Error of the Difference

As was the case with $s_{\bar{X}}$, developing the estimation formula for the standard error of the difference by means of a formal proof is beyond the scope of this book. Instead, we will attempt to explain the formula in nonmathematical terms.

If it is assumed that the two population variances are equal, the variances of the two samples may be combined into a single estimate of the common value of σ^2. If the sizes of the two samples are exactly equal, you can obtain this combined or *pooled* estimate by computing the ordinary average of the two sample variances. Often, however, the sample sizes are not equal, in which case greater weight must be given to the larger-size sample. That is, a *weighted* average must be computed. The general formula for the *pooled variance* (symbolized by s^2_{pooled}), which may be used for equal or unequal sample sizes, is

$$s^2_{\text{pooled}} = \frac{(N_1 - 1)s_1^2 + (N_2 - 1)s_2^2}{N_1 + N_2 - 2} \qquad \text{Formula 7.1}$$

where

$s_1^2 =$ population variance estimate of sample 1
$s_2^2 =$ population variance estimate of sample 2
$N_1 =$ number of cases in sample 1
$N_2 =$ number of cases in sample 2

Then the estimation formula for the SED is

$$s_{\bar{X}_1 - \bar{X}_2} = \sqrt{\frac{s^2_{\text{pooled}}}{N_1} + \frac{s^2_{\text{pooled}}}{N_2}} = \sqrt{s^2_{\text{pooled}}\left(\frac{1}{N_1} + \frac{1}{N_2}\right)} \qquad \text{Formula 7.2}$$

where

$s_{\bar{X}_1 - \bar{X}_2} =$ estimated SED

This formula should not look totally unfamiliar. We saw in the previous chapter that the estimate for the standard error of the mean (s_X) is equal to $s/\sqrt{N}$. Consequently, $s^2_{\bar{X}}$ is equal to s^2/N. Here, because a difference is subject to sampling error from *two* means, the sampling error variance reflects both sources of error. In addition, it uses a more stable estimate of the population variance by pooling the variance information from the two samples.

It should be obvious that the larger the variances of the populations (as estimated by s^2_{pooled}), the larger the estimated SED. Only slightly less obvious is the fact that the *larger* the sample sizes, the *smaller* the SED. Differences based on large samples will have smaller sampling errors (and are thus likely to be more accurate estimates of the population difference) than are differences based on small samples, just as is the case for a single mean.

By inserting Formula 7.1 into Formula 7.2, we can create a convenient formula for the SED:

$$s_{\overline{X}_1-\overline{X}_2} = \sqrt{\frac{(N_1-1)s_1^2 + (N_2-1)s_2^2}{N_1 + N_2 - 2} \left(\frac{1}{N_1} + \frac{1}{N_2}\right)} \qquad \text{Formula 7.3}$$

When $N_1 = N_2$, the formula for the SED becomes much simpler:

$$s_{\overline{X}_1-\overline{X}_2} = \sqrt{\frac{(N-1)s_1^2 + (N-1)s_2^2}{2(N-1)} \left(\frac{1}{N} + \frac{1}{N}\right)} = \sqrt{\frac{s_1^2 + s_2^2}{2}\left(\frac{2}{N}\right)}$$

$$= \sqrt{\frac{s_1^2 + s_2^2}{N}} \qquad \text{Formula 7.4}$$

The *t* Test for Two Sample Means

When you test hypotheses about the difference between two population means, and you do not know the standard deviations of the populations (which is virtually always the case), the correct statistical model to use is the *t* distributions. Once the estimated standard error of the difference has been computed, a *t* value (and therefore a probability value) may be found for any given obtained difference, as follows:

$$t = \frac{(\overline{X}_1 - \overline{X}_2) - (\mu_1 - \mu_2)}{s_{\overline{X}_1-\overline{X}_2}} \qquad \text{Formula 7.5A}$$

Notice that the two sample means yield a single difference score, $\overline{X}_1 - \overline{X}_2$, which is compared to the null-hypothesized mean of the difference scores, $\mu_1 - \mu_2$.

It is possible to test any hypothesized difference between the means of two populations. For example, you could test the hypothesis that the mean of the first population is 20 points greater than the mean of the second population by setting $\mu_1 - \mu_2$ equal to 20 in this equation. Much more often than not, however, you will want to test the hypothesis that the means of the two populations are equal (i.e., $\mu_1 = \mu_2$ or $\mu_1 - \mu_2 = 0$). In this situation, the *t* formula can be simplified to:

$$t = \frac{\overline{X}_1 - \overline{X}_2}{s_{\overline{X}_1-\overline{X}_2}} \qquad \text{Formula 7.5B}$$

By inserting Formula 7.2 into Formula 7.5B, we obtain the following useful formula for computing the two-group t test based on the pooled variances:

$$t = \frac{\overline{X}_1 - \overline{X}_2}{\sqrt{s^2_{\text{pooled}}\left(\dfrac{1}{N_1} + \dfrac{1}{N_2}\right)}}$$

Formula 7.6A

for which $df = N_1 + N_2 - 2$.

Although it is painful to look at, it is convenient to insert Formula 7.3 into Formula 7.5B, to obtain a one-step formula for the t test for two (independent) sample means:

$$t = \frac{\overline{X}_1 - \overline{X}_2}{\sqrt{\dfrac{(N_1 - 1)s_1^2 + (N_2 - 1)s_2^2}{N_1 + N_2 - 2}\left(\dfrac{1}{N_1} + \dfrac{1}{N_2}\right)}}$$

Formula 7.6B

Note that by inserting Formula 7.4 instead of Formula 7.3 into Formula 7.5B, you would obtain a (much) simplified t test formula for the case when the two sample sizes are equal (see Formula 7.15 near the end of this chapter). In that case, the degrees of freedom (df) would equal $2N - 2$.

The number of df on which the two-sample t value is based, which is needed to obtain the critical value of t from the t table, is determined from the fact that the population σ^2 is estimated using $N_1 - 1$ df from sample 1 and $N_2 - 1$ df from sample 2. Therefore, the estimate is based on the combined df:

$$(N_1 - 1) + (N_2 - 1) = N_1 + N_2 - 2$$

Recall the problem of caffeine and mathematics test scores posed at the beginning of this chapter. In order to apply null hypothesis testing to the goal of making a statistical decision about the results of such an experiment, it would be convenient to divide the procedure into a series of discrete steps, beginning with a statement of the hypotheses and the selection of a significance criterion.

Step 1: State the Null and Alternative Hypotheses, and the Significance Criterion, α

$$H_0 : \mu_{\text{caf}} = \mu_{\text{con}}$$

$$H_A : \mu_{\text{caf}} \neq \mu_{\text{con}}$$

$$\alpha = .05$$

H_0 states that the caffeine and control samples come from populations with equal means, while H_A states that these two samples come from populations with different means (for the sake of precision, it is customary to state the hypotheses symbolically). The traditional .05 criterion of significance is specified unless there is a special reason to use a different criterion. Because Ihno had good reason to be concerned with the obvious possible effects of caffeine on the heart rates (HRs) of her students, we will reframe the problem in terms of HR rather than test scores.

Wisely, Ihno had asked her students, immediately after they had written down their baseline heart rates, to report their recent consumption of caffeine in terms of the number of cups of coffee they had drunk from the time they woke up that morning until the time they entered the classroom. (Let's assume that Ihno supplied her students with a chart to convert amounts of other caffeinated beverages into the equivalent number of cups of coffee and, of course, did not allow caffeinated beverages in her class on the day of the experiment.) From the variety of responses she received, Ihno selected 22 students who clearly had ingested a good deal of caffeine shortly before class to have their heart rates analyzed as part of her caffeine group[1] and another 20 students who were quite certain they had had no caffeine that day to be in her control group. Suppose that the heart rate results for her two groups were as follows:

Caffeine group	Control group
$N_1 = 22$	$N_2 = 20$
$\overline{X}_1 = 81.0$	$\overline{X}_2 = 68.0$
$s_1 = 12.0$	$s_2 = 16.8$

Step 2: Calculate the Appropriate Test Statistic

For a comparison of the means of two independent samples, the test statistic most commonly calculated is a t value based on pooling the variances of the two samples, in which case this procedure is usually referred to as a **pooled-variances t test**. (The appropriateness of this statistic depends on some assumptions, which are discussed later in this chapter.) Because the Ns for this experiment were not equal, we need to estimate the standard error of the difference using Formula 7.3, as follows:

$$s_{\overline{X}_1 - \overline{X}_2} = \sqrt{\frac{(21)(12^2) + 19(16.8^2)}{22 + 20 - 2}\left(\frac{1}{22} + \frac{1}{20}\right)}$$

$$= \sqrt{(209.664)\left(\frac{1}{22} + \frac{1}{20}\right)}$$

$$= 4.474$$

---

[1]This is not a truly experimental group, as these students decided for themselves to ingest caffeine before class, perhaps because they found statistics to be particularly boring (if you can believe that).

The t value can now be found from Formula 7.5B:

$$t = \frac{81.0 - 68.0}{4.474} = 2.91, \qquad df = 22 + 20 - 2 = 40$$

Step 3: Find the Critical Value and Make a Statistical Decision With Respect to Your Null Hypothesis

For this example, $df = N_1 + N_2 - 2 = 22 + 20 - 2 = 40$. Referring to the t table (i.e., Table B in the Appendix), in the row for $df = 40$ and the column for a two-tailed significance level of .05, we find that the critical t value is 2.021—that is, a calculated t greater in absolute value than (approximately) 2.02 is needed to justify rejection of H_0 at the .05 two-tailed level of significance. (The two rejection regions for this experiment are illustrated in Figure 7.3.)

Because the obtained value of t (2.91) is greater in absolute value than the critical value found in Table B, we can declare that a difference between sample means as large as the one observed by Ihno in this situation arises from sampling error so rarely (i.e., $p < .05$) that she can reject H_0 and therefore conclude that the caffeine and control groups are random samples from populations with *different* means. More specifically, Ihno can declare that caffeine has a statistically significant positive effect on resting heart rates.

Reporting the Results of a t Test

A common way to express the results of a two-sample experiment in a journal article is in the context of a sentence like this one: "The group that reported having ingested caffeine before the session exhibited a higher resting heart rate ($M = 81$ bpm) than the group that had not ingested caffeine that day ($M = 68$ bpm); this difference was statistically

Figure 7.3

Acceptance and Rejection Regions for the Caffeine/Control Comparison in the t Distribution for $df = 40$

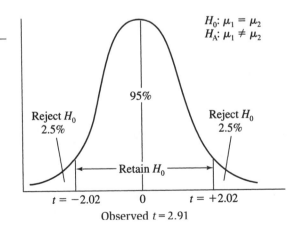

significant, $t(40) = 2.91, p < .01$.[2] (The number in parentheses after t is, of course, the df.) Note that while statisticians prefer to use the symbol $\overline{X}$ to represent the arithmetic mean, the American Psychological Association (2010) dictates that psychologists use an upper case M to represent the mean, when submitting articles for publication. This is a long-standing policy that arose back in the days when printing special characters, like an X with a bar over it, was considerably more costly than printing an ordinary capital letter. Also, note that it is becoming increasingly common to include a measure of effect size, right after the value of t, to aid in the interpretation of the results, so we will return to the format for reporting t test results shortly.

Interpreting the Results of a t Test . . .

Rejecting or retaining the null hypothesis is not the end but rather just a first step in the process of drawing conclusions from your results. Here, and in the next few sections, we describe the next steps in making sense of your two-group comparison.

When Retaining H_0

Suppose that a different caffeine study yielded an obtained t value of 1.14 for $df = 40$. Since 1.14 is smaller than the critical value of t obtained from Table B, you would decide to retain H_0. This does *not* imply that you have shown that the population means are equal. You do not know the probability that your decision to retain H_0 is wrong (i.e., how likely you are to have made a Type II error), so you should limit yourself to a cautious statement such as "There is not sufficient reason to reject the hypothesis that caffeine has no effect." "Retaining" H_0 merely means that we have not refuted it. It does *not* mean that we have shown H_0 to be true, which is why we do not even say that we "accept" the null hypothesis.

When Rejecting H_0

When the results of your statistical analysis indicate that you should *reject* H_0 (i.e., the results are *statistically significant*), you may then conclude that your independent variable (e.g., presence versus absence of caffeine) has some effect. But there is still some chance that you have committed a Type I error and that the population means actually are equal. Therefore, it is usually *not* a good idea to regard any one such statistical finding

---

[2]These days it is common either to report the exact two-tailed p value provided by the computer program that performed the statistical test (e.g., $p = .017$) or to state that p is lower than some potential alpha level that ends in a 1 or a 5, such as $p < .005$ or $p < .001$ (using the lowest alpha that p is less than). The traditionalist sets one alpha level (usually .05) at the outset of a study and then reports p only as less than or greater than that alpha—for example, $p < .05$ or $p > .05$.

as conclusive. You should wait to see if repetitions (*replications*) of your study also indicate similar effects before reaching firm conclusions.

It is also important *not* to confuse statistical significance with practical significance. Depending on your sample sizes, effects too small to be of any consequence can end up statistically significant, and effects that look fairly large can fail to reach statistical significance. To give you some tools with which to judge practical significance, we show you in this chapter how to compute both a confidence interval (CI) for two means, and a standardized measure of effect size. We take up the topic of CIs next.

Although in our example we were able to conclude that caffeine seems to have *some* effect on heart rate,[3] we have just learned that the null hypothesis test (NHT) alone does not allow us to estimate the amount of that effect. For some well-known variables, however, the difference between two sample means does provide a good idea of the size of the effect that we are dealing with. For the present example, $\overline{X}_1 - \overline{X}_2$ equals 13 bpm, which represents a substantial increase in heart rate associated with caffeine. In any case, $\overline{X}_1 - \overline{X}_2$ is the best point estimate for the difference between the two population means $(\mu_1 - \mu_2)$. However, as we pointed out in the previous chapter, a point estimate alone does not tell you how accurate the estimate is. Interval estimation is much more informative, so we now apply this procedure to the two-sample case.

Confidence Intervals for $\mu_1 - \mu_2$

The use of confidence intervals to determine all reasonably likely values of the mean of a *single* population was discussed in the previous chapter. In a similar fashion, all reasonably likely values of the *difference between two population means* can be found by using the following formula for the two-group CI:

$$[(\overline{X}_1 - \overline{X}_2) - t_{crit}s_{\overline{X}_1 - \overline{X}_2}] \leq \mu_1 - \mu_2 \leq [(\overline{X}_1 - \overline{X}_2) + t_{crit}s_{\overline{X}_1 - \overline{X}_2}]$$

Formula 7.7

where

t_{crit} = the critical value obtained from the t table for the specified criterion of significance and the appropriate df

Notice that Formula 7.7 is just Formula 7.5A twisted around algebraically. This CI pertains to the *difference* between two population means, so it is appropriately based on the standard error of the difference $(s_{\overline{X}_1 - \overline{X}_2})$.

---

[3] Strictly speaking, we should not even say that caffeine *affects* heart rate, because we did not assign students to the caffeine group and therefore cannot make causal conclusions. The issue of proving causation is discussed further in Chapter 9.

For the present example, the observed sample means were 81.0 for the caffeine group and 68.0 for the control group; the SED was 4.474, and the critical value of t for $df = 40$ and $\alpha = .05$ (two-tailed) was 2.021. Therefore, the 95% CI interval for the difference between the population means is:

$$[(81.0-68.0)-(2.021)(4.474)] \leq \mu_1-\mu_2 \leq [(81.0-68.0)+(2.021)(4.474)]$$

$$(13.0 - 9.04) \leq \mu_1 - \mu_2 \leq (13.0 + 9.04)$$

$$3.96 \leq \mu_1 - \mu_2 \leq 22.04$$

You can state with 95% confidence that the difference between the means of the caffeine and control populations is included in an interval that runs from 3.96 points to 22.04 points, with the caffeine mean being the larger. Note that zero is *not* in this interval, indicating that we are permitted to treat $\mu_1 = \mu_2$ as an unlikely possibility.

To determine the 99% CI, the procedure would be the same except that the critical value of t for 40 df for $\alpha = .01$, which is 2.704, would be used instead of 2.021. The 99% CI would therefore be:

$$13.0 - (2.704)(4.474) \leq \mu_1 - \mu_2 \leq 13.0 + (2.704)(4.474)$$

$$(13.0 - 12.1) \leq \mu_1 - \mu_2 \leq (13.0 + 12.1)$$

$$.90 \leq \mu_1 - \mu_2 \leq 25.1$$

As always, the 99% CI is wider than the 95% CI. You can be more certain that the true difference between the two population means falls in the 99% CI, but you must pay a price for this added confidence: The interval is larger, so $\mu_1 - \mu_2$ is estimated less precisely.

Here again, CIs allow you to do everything that null hypothesis testing does. If a value of $\mu_1 - \mu_2$ specified by the null hypothesis (such as the frequently used value of zero) falls within the CI, that null hypothesis is retained. If a value of $\mu_1 - \mu_2$ specified by the null hypothesis falls outside the CI, that null hypothesis is rejected. (Note that zero is not included in the 99% CI found above, so the null hypothesis that $\mu_1 = \mu_2$ can be rejected at the .01 level). By specifying a range of population differences that should be retained, CIs provide us with more information.

Admittedly, some CIs are more informative than others. Let us look at two rather extreme examples. Imagine that in the caffeine study, the SED were only 2.97 instead of 4.474. In that case, the 95% CI would extend from 7.0 to 19.0, indicating that the effect of caffeine on resting heart rate is a probable mean increase of at least 7 beats per minute and not more than 13 bpm. However, an SED of 6.2, would lead to a 95% CI of 0.48 to 25.52, which would tell a very different story. In this latter case, caffeine may cause an increase of as much as 25 beats per minute or as little as a half a beat per minute. Since an increase of less than 1 bpm is virtually negligible, the possibility that caffeine has no important practical effect on heart rate would remain a reasonable one. (Such a wide CI suggests the likelihood of substantial sampling error. The best way to improve accuracy is to repeat the experiment with a larger sample.) Yet in both cases, a null hypothesis test will lead to the same simple conclusion: It will tell us only that the null-hypothesized value of zero between the two population means should be rejected.

However, as useful as CIs can be, they are much less meaningful when your dependent variable is measured on a scale that is not commonly used, as when you measure the ability to memorize verbal material in terms of how many words are recalled from a list that you created for your experiment. An increase in HR of 10 bpm is immediately understandable, whereas an increase of 10 correctly recalled words is not. A more universally interpretable measure of the size of an experiment's effect will be discussed shortly. In the meantime, we want to make the point that although we agree with recent efforts toward encouraging the reporting of CI's whenever possible, we also think that all students of statistics should know how to calculate a CI from the results usually given for a null hypothesis test, when a CI is not reported.

For example, suppose you read the following report in a published article: "The caffeine group obtained a higher average score on the motor task ($M = 23.5$) than did the placebo group ($M = 16.1$), and this difference was statistically significant, $t(28) = 3.4, p < .01$." Though it is not obvious, the previous sentence contains all the information you need to use Formula 7.7 to compute a CI for the difference of the caffeine and placebo population means. First, you will need $\overline{X}_1 - \overline{X}_2$, but that is just the difference of the two Ms, which is $23.5 - 16.1 = 7.4$. Next, you will need the critical t, but you can easily look that up in Table B in the Appendix. The df you need is in parentheses following the t (it is 28), and if you want a 95% CI, you should look in the column for a .05, two-tailed test. The critical t equals 2.048. Finally, you need the SED. This is easy to find from Formula 7.5B, which we will rewrite here as: $t = (M_1 - M_2)/\text{SED}$. Remember that you were given the t value in the results (it is 3.4), and we just found the difference of the means to be 7.4, so we know that $3.4 = 7.4/\text{SED}$. Therefore, SED $= 7.4/3.4$, which equals 2.18. Sometimes the SED is reported right after the t value, and that would save you a step, but as long as you have the two means along with the t value, you can easily find the SED for yourself. Now let us insert these values into Formula 7.7:

$$7.4 - (2.048)(2.18) \leq \mu_1 - \mu_2 \leq 7.4 + (2.048)(2.18)$$

$$(7.4 - 4.46) \leq \mu_1 - \mu_2 \leq (7.4 + 4.46)$$

$$2.94 \leq \mu_1 - \mu_2 \leq 11.86$$

The Assumptions Underlying the Proper Use of the t Test for Two Sample Means

It is easy to perform and report two-sample t tests, but some care must be taken in deciding when such a test is appropriate and when an alternative should be considered. The following points should help you to decide when to use the two-group t test.

In theory, the use of the independent-samples t test, as well as the two-group confidence interval just described, is justified only if the first two of these assumptions are met:

1. *Independent random sampling.* The observations within each group have been randomly sampled independently of each other, and all of the observations in one group are independent of all of the observations in the other group. (For true experiments, this assumption is usually accommodated by randomly assigning the members of one convenient sample to two different groups.)

2. *Normal distributions.* The dependent variable is normally distributed within each population.

   In practice, however, you should not be automatically deterred from using the t test even if the assumption concerning normality does not seem to be met. The two-group t test is considered *robust* with regard to this assumption—that is, it gives fairly accurate results even if the assumption is not satisfied—as long as the sample sizes are not very small. When dealing with small sample sizes and questionable distributions, a nonparametric alternative to the t test should be considered, such as the one that will be described in detail in the next chapter.

   The pooled-variance version of the two-sample t test, as expressed in Formula 7.6, requires an additional assumption:

3. The variances of the two populations are equal ($\sigma_1^2 = \sigma_2^2$). This is referred to as the *homogeneity of variance* (HOV) assumption.

The assumption concerning the equality of the two population variances can also be ignored in practice *if* the two sample sizes are equal. But if the sample sizes are fairly unequal (say, the larger is more than 1.5 times greater than the smaller) *and* the population variances are markedly unequal, the t test presented in this chapter may well yield erroneous results. So if there is reason to believe that the population variances differ substantially, it is a good idea to obtain approximately equal sample sizes. Then any differences between the population variances will have little ability to bias the results obtained from the t test.

If you are stuck with a combination of rather unequal sample sizes and the variance for one of your samples is more than twice as large as the variance of the other sample, you should consider the possibility of using a different type of t test. As previously mentioned, the test we have been describing thus far is called the *pooled-variances* t test, for reasons that should be obvious from its formula. The other type of t test does *not* assume that the two population variances are equal, so it does *not* pool the two sample variances. A glance at the following formula should make it clear why this procedure is often referred to as the **separate-variances t test**:

$$t = \frac{\overline{X}_1 - \overline{X}_2}{\sqrt{\dfrac{s_1^2}{N_1} + \dfrac{s_1^2}{N_1}}}$$ Formula 7.8

Note that when the two Ns are equal, the denominator of Formula 7.8 becomes identical to Formula 7.4, so whenever $N_1 = N_2$ you will end up calculating exactly the same t value whether you set out to perform a pooled-variances t test (Formula 7.6), or a separate-variances t test (Formula 7.8). When the Ns are not equal, either t value could be larger, depending on whether the larger sample has the larger or smaller variance.

The tricky part of using the separate-variances t test is determining the right t distribution to use to find your critical value. The number of degrees of freedom associated with this test is usually less than the *df* used for the pooled-variances test (i.e., $N_1 + N_2 - 2$) and often involves fractional values, so this form of the t test is best performed by statistical software. (When a separate-variances t test is called for, the two-group confidence interval should be based on the separate-variances standard error of the difference [i.e., the denominator of Formula 7.8] and the critical t for the separate-variances test.) There are also tests to help you decide whether it is reasonable to assume homogeneity of variance and therefore whether it is reasonable to use the pooled-variance t test, but these HOV tests are also best left to be performed by statistical software. Finally, it is worth noting that the separate-variances t test is rarely reported in journal articles; other procedures, such as data transformations and nonparametric statistics, are more often employed to deal with large discrepancies in sample variances and other violations of the t test's assumptions. Therefore, we do not discuss the separate-variance t test further in this text. Instead, we provide a nonparametric alternative to the t test, as mentioned under assumption #2, in the next chapter.

Measuring the Size of an Effect

If the 95% confidence interval for a new 6-month weight-loss program goes from 10 to 30 pounds lost, you can easily decide for yourself whether you are interested. But if a new memory-improvement program announces, with 95% confidence, that you will recall between 10 and 20 more names from a list after 3 weeks of training, should you be impressed? When the scale used to measure the dependent variable is not a familiar one, it can be more informative to standardize the obtained difference in sample means rather than to report that difference in its original units. This standardized measure of effect size in your data is often called d, or Cohen's d, after Jacob Cohen, one of the original authors of this text. Unfortunately, the symbol d has been used for both the sample effect size and the population effect size of which it is an estimate and therefore can lead to confusion. To reduce ambiguity, we will use the symbol g for the effect size of a two-group comparison in *sample* data, as is commonly used in meta-analysis (a procedure that we will describe briefly in Chapter 11). We will reserve the symbol **d** to represent the effect size comparing two population means, and because we are not using a Greek letter for a population value, we will print **d** in boldface to remind you that it is for a population rather than a sample. Because g is a *standardized* measure of effect size, its formula looks like a z score:

$$g = \frac{\overline{X}_1 - \overline{X}_2}{s_p} \qquad \text{Formula 7.9}$$

Note that s_p is the square root of the pooled variance (Formula 7.1) that is calculated as part of a t test.

For the caffeine study, s_p equals $\sqrt{209.664} = 14.48$, so $g = (81 - 68)/14.48 = 13/14.48 = .9$.

This tells us that the two sample means are nearly an entire standard deviation apart, which is considered a rather large effect.

The interpretation of effect sizes, and the possibility of creating CIs for effect sizes, will be discussed in Chapter 11. An alternative measure of effect size, based on the principle of correlation, will be described in Chapter 10. Note that if you have already calculated g, and your two samples are the same size, you can calculate your t value from g and the sample sizes by using the following formula. (When the two samples are the same size, we can use n to represent the size of just one of those samples—i.e., $n = N_1 = N_2$.)

$$t = g\sqrt{\frac{n}{2}} \qquad \text{Formula 7.10A}$$

More usefully, if you know only the t value and the sample sizes, and the two sample sizes are the same, you can compute the effect size by twisting the preceding formula into this one:

$$g = t\sqrt{\frac{2}{n}} \qquad \text{Formula 7.10B}$$

If $N_1 \neq N_2$, you must compute the **harmonic mean** of the two sample sizes in order to use the preceding formula. The harmonic mean of any two numbers can be calculated as follows:

$$\overline{X}_{\text{harmonic}} = \frac{2N_1N_2}{N_1 + N_2} \qquad \text{Formula 7.11}$$

Combining the formula for the harmonic mean with the formula for g in terms of t and n, and applying a bit of algebra, yields the following formula for unequal Ns:

$$g = t\sqrt{\frac{N_1 + N_2}{N_1 N_2}}$$ Formula 7.12

Applying the above formula to the caffeine study yields the same value for g, of course, that we calculated more directly with Formula 7.9:

$$g = 2.91\sqrt{\frac{42}{440}} = 2.91 \times .309 = .90$$

The t Test for Matched Samples

Suppose that you want to test the hypothesis that in families with two children, the firstborn is more introverted than the secondborn. Once again, the question of interest concerns a comparison between the means of two populations, and the null and alternative hypotheses are as follows:

$$H_0: \mu_{firstborn} = \mu_{secondborn}$$

$$H_A: \mu_{firstborn} \neq \mu_{secondborn}$$

To obtain your samples, you randomly select *matched pairs* of children, with each pair consisting of the firstborn child and the secondborn child from a given family. You then administer an appropriate measure of introversion. The general format of the resulting data would be as follows:

Pair	Firstborn (X_1)		Secondborn (X_2)
1	65	matched	61
2	48	matched	42
3	63	matched	66
⋮	⋮		⋮
N	66	matched	69

The firstborn child from Family 1 has an introversion score of 65, and the secondborn child from Family 1 has an introversion score of 61. Similarly, each pair of children is matched by virtue of coming from the same family.

To illustrate a second (and perhaps more common) use of matched samples, let us suppose that you wish to test the effect of a persuasive message on people's attitudes toward gun control. Each subject's attitude is measured *before* receiving the message (X_1) and again *after* receiving the message (X_2). For Pair 1, the score of 65 could represent the attitude of the first subject before hearing the persuasive message, and the score of 61 could represent the *same* subject's attitude after hearing the message. Each subject therefore serves as his or her own control, and each pair of scores is matched by virtue of coming from the same subject. (It would be desirable to have a control group in this study, but this is beyond the present point.)

The statistical analysis described previously in this chapter involved *independent* random samples. That is, there was no connection between any specific individual in Sample 1 and any specific individual in Sample 2. This approach is not suitable for matched samples, as it does not take advantage of the reduction in the error term that can be produced by focusing on the matched pairs of scores. To analyze matched-pair data (of either of the two types described earlier), the procedure that is used is similar to the one we used in Chapter 6. Because each score in Sample 1 has a paired counterpart in Sample 2, you can subtract each X_1 from each X_2 and obtain a difference score (denoted by D). Then you can use the t test for the mean of one population—in this case, the mean of the population of difference scores.

To illustrate this procedure, let us look at the heart rates for 10 students selected at random from Ihno's class; the data for the baseline and prequiz HRs are shown in Table 7.2. To test whether there is a statistically significant difference in HR from the baseline to the prequiz period, we will focus on the difference scores shown in the last column of Table 7.2; note that it is critical to retain the *sign* of each difference score.

As with any statistical test, we can organize our procedure into three discrete steps.

Table 7.2   Heart Rate in bpm Before and After the Announcement of a Pop Statistics Quiz

Student	Baseline HR (X_1)	Prequiz HR (X_2)	$D = (\overline{X}_2 - \overline{X}_1)$
1	70	77	+7
2	66	75	+9
3	73	68	−5
4	62	62	0
5	74	89	+15
6	63	74	+11
7	64	62	−2
8	65	73	+8
9	71	76	+5
10	72	84	+12
Σ	680	740	+60
Mean	68.0	74.0	+6.0
SD	4.472	8.59	6.48

Step 1: State the Null and Alternative Hypotheses, and the Significance Criterion, α

In terms of the difference scores, the null and alternative hypotheses are as follows:

$$H_0: \mu_D = 0$$

$$H_A: \mu_D \neq 0$$

H_0 states that the mean of the population of difference scores is zero, and H_A states that the mean of the population of difference scores is not zero. For alpha, we will use the usual .05 level, with a two-tailed test.

Step 2: Calculate the Appropriate Test Statistic

We begin by computing the mean difference score obtained from the sample, $\overline{D}$:

$$\overline{D} = \frac{\sum D}{N} = \frac{60}{10} = 6.0$$

Note that N is not necessarily the number of different participants but the number of *paired measurements,* which may be the number of *pairs* of subjects. As is shown in Table 7.2, $\overline{D}$ is equal to $\overline{X}_2 - \overline{X}_1$.[4] Thus, testing the hypothesis that $\mu_D = 0$ is equivalent to testing the hypothesis that $\mu_1 - \mu_2 = 0$, or that $\mu_1 = \mu_2$.

To test the hypothesis about the mean of one population, you compare the sample mean to the hypothesized value of the population mean and divide by the standard error of the mean, as follows:

$$t = \frac{\overline{D} - \mu_D}{s_{\overline{D}}}$$

where

$$s_{\overline{D}} = \frac{s_D}{\sqrt{N}} = \sqrt{\frac{s_D^2}{N}}$$

Note the similarity to Formula 6.3; here we are just changing the symbols in Formula 6.3 to represent difference scores. Thus, s_D represents the ordinary unbiased standard deviation of the difference scores.

Because the hypothesized value of μ_D is generally zero, the matched t formula may be simplified to:

$$t = \frac{\overline{D}}{\dfrac{s_D}{\sqrt{N}}} \qquad\qquad \text{Formula 7.13}$$

---

[4]We are subtracting X_1 from X_2 in this example to reduce the number of difference scores that are negative. This changes the sign, but not the magnitude, of the t value that we will calculate. Therefore, the order of subtraction does not affect our chances of attaining statistical significance.

As is normally the case in tests concerning one population mean, the number of degrees of freedom on which t is based is equal to one less than the number of scores, the scores being difference scores, in this case.

$$df = (\text{number of } pairs) - 1$$

where each pair yields one difference score.

If the computed t is smaller in absolute value than the value of the critical t, as obtained from the table for the appropriate df, retain H_0; otherwise reject H_0 in favor of H_A.

Returning to Ihno's heart rate study, the analysis of the data can be completed by inserting into Formula 7.13 the summary statistics found in the lower-right corner of Table 7.2, as follows:

$$N = 10 \quad \overline{D} = 6.0, \quad s_D = 6.48$$

$$t = \frac{6.0}{\dfrac{6.48}{\sqrt{10}}} = \frac{6.0}{\dfrac{6.48}{3.16}} = 2.93$$

Step 3: Find the Critical Value and Make a Statistical Decision With Respect to Your Null Hypothesis

The critical value of t obtained from Table B for $(10 - 1)$ or 9 degrees of freedom is 2.262. Because the obtained t value of 2.93 is larger in absolute value than the critical value, you can reject H_0: There is sufficient reason to believe that the announcement of a surprise quiz would increase the mean heart rate of the population being sampled.

Confidence Interval for the Population Mean of Difference Scores

A confidence interval for the mean difference score can be computed using a slight variation of Formula 7.7, as shown next.

$$\overline{D} - t_{crit}s_{\overline{D}} \leq \mu_D \leq \overline{D} + t_{crit}s_{\overline{D}} \qquad \text{Formula 7.14}$$

Given that the .05 two-tailed critical value of t is 2.262 and that the standard error of the mean of the differences is equal to 2.05 (i.e., 6.48/3.16), the 95% CI is:

$$6 - (2.262)(2.05) \leq \mu_D \leq 6 + (2.262)(2.05)$$

$$1.36 \leq \mu_D \leq 10.64$$

So, the 95% CI goes from +1.36 to +10.64 bpm, suggesting that the increase in heart rate could reasonably be as small as a little over 1 beat per minute, or as large as more than 10 beats per minute. As would be expected from the rejection of the null hypothesis at the .05 level, the value of zero does *not* fall within the 95% CI.

Comparing the t Test for Matched Pairs With the t Test for Independent Samples

To demonstrate more clearly the usual advantage of the matched-pairs design, let us perform an independent-samples t test on the heart rate data. For this demonstration, we will ignore the connection between the two columns of heart rate data in Table 7.2. Instead, we will treat the 10 baseline HR measurements as though they come from one group of students, while the 10 prequiz HR measurements come from another, completely separate, group of students. Because our two "independent" sets of HR data are the same size, we can use the following simplified, equal-N formula for the independent-samples t test (using Formula 7.4 as its denominator):

$$t = \frac{\overline{X}_1 - \overline{X}_2}{\sqrt{\dfrac{s_1^2 + s_2^2}{n}}} \qquad \text{Formula 7.15}$$

where n is the size of *each* sample. The numerator of the t test remains the same whether you apply the matched-pairs t test or the independent-samples t test to a given set of data (in this example the numerator is 6 bpm); it is the denominator that is likely to change. We will now use the standard deviations we included at the bottom of each column of HR data in Table 7.2. They are squared to yield variances and inserted into Formula 7.15 to obtain the following result:

$$t = \frac{74 - 68}{\sqrt{\dfrac{73.8 + 20}{10}}} = \frac{6}{3.063} = 1.96$$

We do gain additional degrees of freedom by treating the two sets of measurements as independent. For the matched-pairs design, the df was one less than the number of *pairs,* or 9. For the independent-samples design, the df would be $10 + 10 - 2 = 18$. This lowers the critical value of the independent test relative to the matched-pairs test from 2.262 to 2.101. However, the t value calculated for the independent-samples t test (1.96) is smaller than even this reduced critical value (2.101), so the independent-samples t test would *not* be statistically significant. In contrast, matching the HR scores in pairs (based on the two measures coming from the same student) resulted in a decrease in the denominator of the t test from 3.063 for the independent t test to 2.05 for the matched-pairs test, and this increased the calculated t value from 1.96 to 2.93. This increase made the results statistically significant, enabling Ihno to conclude that her heart rate study "worked."

The extent to which matching the scores in pairs increases the t value relative to the independent-samples test, and thus makes statistical significance more likely, depends on how highly the two sets of scores are correlated. We will discuss correlation in detail in Chapter 9. For now, we will simply state that when two sets of scores are positively correlated, one score *tends* to increase when the score paired with it increases. (For example, higher baseline HRs *tend* to be associated with higher prequiz HRs, so the two measures are positively correlated.) In general, measuring the same experimental participant twice, called the *repeated-measures* (RM) design, leads to higher correlations than matching separate participants into pairs. However, the latter design can be very helpful when the RM design is not feasible.

The Different Types of Matched-Pairs Designs

The matched-pairs (difference-score) *t* formula we just described can be applied to the results of two very different experimental designs, which are described next.

The Repeated-Measures (RM) Design

The repeated-measures (RM) design works well if your experiment consists of many similar trials of one type that can be randomly mixed with the same number of trials of some other type. Suppose that participants are told to indicate, as soon as they know it, the missing letter of a word presented on a screen (e.g., POLI_E). Before each word is presented, a priming word is flashed subliminally on the same screen. There are two types of trials: Either the priming stimulus is a word that is relevant to one of the solutions (e.g., "crime" for POLICE, or "manners" for POLITE), or it is an irrelevant word (e.g., "basket"). Because the two types of trials are mixed together in a random order, the experimental participant cannot know which type of trial will be presented next. The reaction times can then be averaged separately for the two types of trials for each participant, so each participant ultimately contributes a *pair* of scores that can be used to create a difference score for the matched-pairs *t* test.

The RM design is potentially more problematic when you cannot mix the two conditions together but must present one condition before the other. The simplest type of *successive* RM design is the before-after design. Our heart rate example falls into this category because HR was measured both *before* and *after* the announcement of the quiz. In order to draw conclusions from a before-after design, a separate control group is usually required. We do not discuss this issue further until Chapter 15.

The other type of successive RM design involves two different experimental conditions. Suppose you want to see if more clerical tasks are correctly performed in a given time interval while participants listen to happy, as compared to sad, music. It would not be a fair comparison of the two conditions to present the same type of music first for all of the participants; it is possible, for instance, that the participants will perform better in the second condition because of the practice they received during the first condition. The common solution to this problem is **counterbalancing**: Half of the subjects perform the tasks first with happy music and then with sad music, while the other half of the subjects are assigned to the reverse order (i.e., sad music first). Counterbalancing averages out **simple order effects**, such as those due to practice or fatigue, but it does not help if you have **differential carryover effects**. For example, if you want to compare the effects of two different types of strategies on problem solving, participants may not be able to stop themselves from employing the first strategy they are given when it is time for them to solve similar problems with a second strategy. This is the case when the RM design becomes problematic.

To avoid carryover effects while still gaining at least some of the benefit of correlated sets of scores, you can employ the design described in the next section, which involves matching your participants into pairs based on some relevant similarity. Although the same statistical procedure (which we have been calling the matched-pairs *t* test but could just as correctly be called the RM *t* test) is used for both designs, from now on we will use the term *RM design* when the same participant is measured twice and reserve the term *matched-pairs* (MP) *design* for the case in which two different participants have been matched together based on some relevant similarity.

The Matched-Pairs (MP) Design

As just mentioned, for some types of experiments, the repeated-measures design is not a reasonable option. Suppose you want to compare two methods for teaching children to read. It would make little sense to teach a child to read by one method for 6 months, measure his or her reading ability, and then teach the same child for another 6 months with the other method. The potential for misleading carryover effects rules out the possibility of counterbalancing. However, the RM design can be approximated by testing the children on various pre-reading skills and then matching the children into pairs based on the similarity of their pre-reading scores, as well as their ages and genders. Some random event, like the flip of a coin, should be used to decide which child in each pair is assigned to each reading method. When the experiment is completed, and all the children have had their reading abilities measured, the reading scores of the two children in a pair are treated as though they were two scores from the same child measured twice: The difference is calculated for the two members of each pair, and then these difference scores are subjected to a matched-pairs *t* test as described for the heart rate example.

There are situations in which the RM design is not feasible but there is no relevant information that can be used to match the participants in pairs. For example, you may wish to test the effects of the level of the experimenter's apparent aggressiveness on the willingness of the participants to donate their time for future experiments. When there is no apparent basis for matching participants, you will not have the advantage of correlated sets of scores, and therefore you will need to make sure that your samples are large enough to have a good chance of attaining significance with the effect size you expect. We show how you can estimate the sample size that you will need when we discuss the topic of power in Chapter 11.

Summary

To test null hypotheses about *differences between the means of two populations,* perform one of the following procedures.

For Independent Samples

The generic formula for the t test for two (independent) sample means is:

$$t = \frac{\overline{X}_1 - \overline{X}_2}{s_{\overline{X}_1 - \overline{X}_2}} \qquad \text{Formula 7.5B}$$

where

$s_{\overline{X}_1 - \overline{X}_2}$ = the estimated standard error of the difference

To obtain the denominator of the preceding formula, you can begin by computing the pooled variance:

$$s^2_{\text{pooled}} = \frac{(N_1 - 1)s_1^2 + (N_2 - 1)s_2^2}{N_1 + N_2 - 2} \qquad \text{Formula 7.1}$$

Once you have calculated the pooled-variance from Formula 7.1, you are ready to use the following formula for the two-group t test:

$$t = \frac{\overline{X}_1 - \overline{X}_2}{\sqrt{s^2_{\text{pooled}}\left(\frac{1}{N_1} + \frac{1}{N_2}\right)}} \qquad \text{Formula 7.6A}$$

with

$$df = N_1 + N_2 - 2$$

Reject H_0 if the computed value of t, ignoring the sign, is greater than the critical value of t obtained from the t table. Note that this t formula may well yield misleading results if σ_1^2 and σ_2^2 are markedly unequal *and* N_1 and N_2 are also markedly unequal. In such a case, the separate-variances t test may be preferable (but see an alternative in the next chapter).

When you reject H_0, it is likely that you will want to estimate the true difference between the population means with a confidence interval. The formula for the CI in the two-group case is similar to the CI for a single population:

$$[(\overline{X}_1 - \overline{X}_2) - t_{\text{crit}} s_{\overline{X}_1 - \overline{X}_2}] \le \mu_1 - \mu_2 \le [(\overline{X}_1 - \overline{X}_2) + t_{\text{crit}} s_{\overline{X}_1 - \overline{X}_2}] \quad \text{Formula 7.7}$$

where

t_{crit} = the critical value obtained from the t table for the specified criterion of significance (e.g., .05, two-tailed for a 95% CI) for the appropriate df

Another useful way to describe the size of the effect you found in your data is by calculating a standardized measure of effect size, such as g:

$$g = \frac{\overline{X}_1 - \overline{X}_2}{s_p}$$ Formula 7.9

where s_p is the square root of the pooled variance $\left(s^2_{pooled}\right)$

For Matched Samples

First compute a difference score (symbolized by D) for each pair, where

$$D = X_1 - X_2$$

Next, compute the mean and standard deviation of the D scores, using the usual formulas for the mean and unbiased SD, or by means of a handheld calculator. Then find the matched t value:

$$t = \frac{\overline{D}}{\frac{s_D}{\sqrt{N}}}$$ Formula 7.13

with

$$df = (\text{number of pairs}) - 1$$

where

$\overline{D} = $ mean of the D scores
$s_D = $ standard deviation of the D scores
$N = $ number of pairs

As usual, reject H_0 if the computed value of t (ignoring the sign) is greater than the critical value of t obtained from the t table.

For matched samples, confidence intervals can be computed in the usual way, using the standard error of the mean of the differences. The formula looks like this:

$$\overline{D} - t_{crit}s_{\overline{D}} \leq \mu_D \leq \overline{D} + t_{crit}s_{\overline{D}},$$ Formula 7.14

where

$$s_{\overline{D}} = \frac{s_D}{\sqrt{N}}$$

Note once again that confidence intervals provide considerably more information than do null hypothesis tests.

The formula for the matched-pairs t test can be used whether the same individual is being measured twice (RM design) or participants are being matched in pairs (MP design). The RM design usually leads to the larger t value, but it may produce misleading results if there are strong carryover effects. The MP design provides much of the benefit of the RM design without the possibility of carryover effects. As long as there is a reasonably high, positive correlation between the two sets of scores, the MP design can be counted on to yield higher t values than an independent-samples t test on the same data, due to a reduction in the denominator of the t formula.

Exercises

1. Use the two-sample t test to determine whether the difference in means between Turck and Kirk Halls is significant at the .05 and .01 levels, two-tailed. Given your decision with respect to the null hypothesis, which type of error could you be making: Type I or Type II? Report the results of your t test in a sentence that includes the means of the two dormitories and a measure of the effect size. Compute both the 95% and 99% confidence intervals for the difference of the two population means. Explain how the presence or absence of zero in each of those CIs is consistent with your decision regarding the null hypothesis at the .05 and .01 levels.

2. Repeat the previous exercise, except that this time compare Turck Hall to Dupre Hall. Would the t value based on the separate-variances formula (7.8) be smaller or larger than the pooled-variances t value?

3. Repeat Exercise 2, but this time compare Kirk Hall to Dupre Hall, and conduct only a one-tailed test at the .05 level, assuming that Kirk will have the larger mean.

4. An industrial psychologist obtains scores on a job-selection test from 41 men and 31 women, with the following results: men, $M = 48.75(SD = 9.0)$; women, $M = 46.07(SD = 10.0)$. Test this difference for significance at both the .05 and .01 levels (two-tailed). Determine the effect size for the difference of these two sample means. Does this effect size seem to be large or small?

5. Suppose that the industrial psychologist from the previous exercise is testing the difference in performance on the job-selection test of two different ethnic groups. Given the following data, can the psychologist reject the null hypothesis (alpha = .05) that the population means of these two groups are the same for the job-selection test she is investigating? If these results are statistically significant, compute the 95% CI for the difference of the population means.

Group 1	Group 2
62	46
54	53
59	50
56	52
59	54

6. Repeat Exercise 5 for the following two sets of summary statistics. In each case, determine if the results would be significant for a one-tailed as well as a two-tailed test, but compute the CI only if the two-tailed test is significant. Regardless of statistical significance, compute g, the standardized measure of effect size in sample data, for each data set.

(a)		Group 1	Group 2
	$\overline{X}$	17.34	21.58
	s	5.83	4.42
	N	32	30

(b)		Group 1	Group 2
	$\overline{X}$	76.57	69.72
	s	20.15	22.87
	N	17	15

7. An educational psychologist has developed a new textbook based on programmed instruction techniques and wishes to know if it is superior to the conventional kind of textbook. He therefore obtains participants who have had no prior exposure to the material and forms two groups: an experimental group, which learns via the pro- grammed text, and a control group, which learns via the old-fashioned textbook. The psychologist is afraid, however, that differences among participants in overall intelligence will lead to large error terms. Therefore, he matches his participants on intelligence and forms 10 pairs such that each pair is made up of two people roughly equal in intelligence test scores. After both groups have learned the material, the psychologist measures the amount of learning by means of a 10-item quiz. The results are as follows:

Pair	Experimental group (programmed text)	Control group (standard text)
1	9	7
2	6	4
3	5	6
4	7	3
5	3	5
6	7	3
7	3	2
8	4	5
9	6	7
10	10	8

Test the results for statistical significance at the .05 level. What should the psychologist decide about his or her new programmed text?

8. For the following set of data, assume that the X score represents the participant's performance in the experimental condition and that the Y score represents the same person's performance in the control condition. (Thus, each participant serves as his or her own control.) Compute the *matched t* test for these data. Also compute the 95% CI for the mean of the difference scores.

Data set 3, Chapter 1

S	X	Y
1	97	89
2	68	57
3	85	87
4	74	76
5	92	97
6	92	79
7	100	91
8	63	50
9	85	85
10	87	84
11	81	91
12	93	91
13	77	75
14	82	77

9. Now carry out a matched t test for the same set of data as in Exercise 8, but with the X values rearranged as shown.

S	X	Y
1	92	89
2	82	57
3	85	87
4	81	76
5	87	97
6	93	79
7	68	91
8	85	50
9	63	85
10	100	84
11	74	91
12	77	91
13	92	75
14	97	77

10. Suppose that you have read the following sentence in a psychology journal: "The experimental group obtained a higher score on the recall task $(M = 14.7)$ than did the control group $(M = 11.1)$, and this difference was statistically significant, $t(38) = 2.3, p < .05$."

Assuming that the two samples are the same size: (a) Find the 95% CI for the difference of the means. (b) Find g, the size of the effect in the sample data.

Thought Questions

1. (a) What is the difference between *random sampling* and *random assignment?* (b) What similar purpose do these two procedures have? (c) Which one is usually much easier to do? Why?
2. A behavioral science researcher wishes to test a null hypothesis about the difference between the means of two populations. (a) Would the researcher prefer that the standard error of the difference be relatively small or large? Why? (b) If the size of one or both samples becomes larger, what happens to the standard error of the difference? Why? (c) If the standard deviation of the individual scores in one or both populations becomes larger, what happens to the standard error of the difference? Why?
3. Suppose that the difference between two sample means is statistically significant. (a) What decision should the researcher make about the null hypothesis? (b) Assuming that all of the procedures and calculations in this experiment were done correctly, why might this decision still be incorrect? (c) If this decision is incorrect, which type of error would the researcher be making, Type I or Type II? (d) What are the practical consequences of making this type of error?
4. Suppose that the difference between two sample means is *not* statistically significant. (a) What decision should the researcher make about the null hypothesis? (b) Assuming that all of the procedures and calculations in this experiment were done correctly, why might this decision still be incorrect? (c) Does the criterion of significance give the probability that this decision is incorrect? (d) If this decision is incorrect, which type of error would the researcher be making, Type I or Type II? (e) What are the practical consequences of making this type of error? (f) Should the researcher conclude that the two population means are equal? Why or why not?
5. Students at Rolling Rock University claim that their school is superior to vaunted Bigbrain University with regard to achievement on a national aptitude test, where the mean is 500 and the standard deviation is 100. A random sample of students is obtained from each university, the mean for the Rolling Rock sample is found to be higher than the mean for the Bigbrain sample, and the 95% confidence interval for the difference between two means is computed. What should the Rolling Rock students conclude if this confidence interval is: (a) −7.63 to 13.44? (b) 2.27 to 19.85? (c) 97.22 to 122.44? (d) Compare examples (b) and (c). How does this comparison illustrate the advantages that confidence intervals have over testing a

specific null hypothesis, such as whether the difference between the means of Rolling Rock University and Bigbrain University is zero?

6. (a) What is the difference between the t test for two independent sample means and the matched-pairs t test? (b) What is the difference between the matched-pairs design and the repeated-measures design? What are their relative advantages and disadvantages?

Computer Exercises

1. Use your statistical package to perform a two-sample t test to determine whether there is a statistically significant difference in baseline anxiety between the men and the women of Ihno's class. Find the 95% CI for this gender difference. Report your results as they might appear in a journal article.

2. Repeat Exercise 1 for baseline heart rate.

3. Perform a two-sample t test to determine whether the students in the "impossible to solve" condition exhibited significantly higher postquiz heart rates than the students in the "easy to solve" condition at the .05 level. Is this t test significant at the .01 level? Find the 99% CI for the difference of the two population means and explain its connection to your decision regarding the null hypothesis at the .01 level.

4. Repeat Exercise 3 for the postquiz anxiety scores.

5. Perform a matched-pairs t test to determine whether there is a significant increase in heart rate from baseline to the prequiz measurement. Also, test the difference between the pre- and postquiz measurements. (Advanced exercise: Repeat these paired t tests separately for men and women.)

6. Repeat Exercise 5 for the anxiety measurements.

Bridge to SPSS

Before you perform an independent-samples t test in SPSS, you should have one column for your grouping variable (usually, "1"s and "2"s), and one for your dependent variable. The matched-pairs t test requires instead that you have two columns for your dependent variable; each column represents your dependent variable measured under a different condition. There is no separate column to indicate group or condition.

Independent-Samples t Test

To perform a two-sample t test in SPSS, select Compare Means from the Analyze menu, and then choose **Independent-Samples T Test . . . .** In the dialog box that opens, move the variable that distinguishes your two groups (e.g., gender) to the area labeled **Grouping Variable:**. Doing that activates the **Define Groups . . .** button; click this button and then enter the numeric values of your two groups. If your grouping variable has more than two values (e.g., undergrad major), you can compare any two of them by specifying their values as Group 1 and Group 2. (Note: The grouping variable can be a string variable, rather than a numeric one, but then you have to enter the exact letter strings representing the two groups, and we do not recommend this. We recommend that you recode into numeric values any string variable that you want to use as a grouping variable.)

Move the dependent variable (DV) you want to test to the Test Variable(s) area (the grouping variable is often thought of as the independent variable (IV), but in many cases it is not truly an IV, because it is just selected for, and not created by, the experimenter). Note that you can test many DVs at the same time. The **Options . . .** button allows you to exclude cases listwise (as explained in Chapter 6) and also to select the percentage that will be used to create a confidence interval for the difference of the two population means.

The default output for this test consists of two boxes, the first of which presents descriptive statistics for the two groups. The second box (see example below) contains both the pooled-variances t test (labeled "Equal variances assumed") and the separate-variances t test (labeled "Equal variances not assumed"). To the left of the t values is a test for homogeneity of variance ("Levene's Test for Equality of Variances"); if the "Sig." (the term SPSS uses for p value) for this test is less than .05, reliance on the separate-variances t test is recommended, unless the two samples are the same size. To the right of the "df" (which usually involves a fractional value when dealing with the separate-variances test) is the two-tailed p value for each version of the t test, labeled "Sig. (2-tailed)."

Independent Samples Test

		Levene's Test for Equality of Variances		t-test for Equality of Means						
							Sig.	Mean	Std. Error	95% Confidence Interval of the Difference	
		F	Sig.	t	df	(2-tailed)	Difference	Difference	Lower	Upper
anx_base	Equal variances assumed	.787	.377	2.161	98	.033	1.8560	.8589	.1515	3.5605
	Equal variances not assumed			2.253	97.988	.027	1.8560	.8239	.2210	3.4909

Matched-Pairs t Test

To perform a matched-pairs t test in SPSS, select Compare Means from the Analyze menu, and then choose **Paired-Samples T Test . . . .** In the dialog box that opens, to the right of the list of variables, you will see an area labeled **Paired Variables**, which contains space for "Variable 1" and "Variable 2" (see next figure).

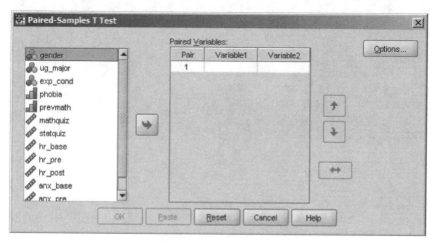

Source: Reprint courtesy of International Business Machines Corporation, © SPSS, Inc., an IBM company. SPSS was acquired by IBM in October 2009.

1. From the list on the left, choose the first of the two variables that you would like to pair together, and click the arrow to move it to the right. This will also open a blank row for Pair 2.

2. Then choose the second variable that you would like in that pair, and click the center arrow again. (Note: These cells will automatically fill in order: Pair 1, right cell, then left cell, then, if you add a second pair, Pair 2, right cell, then left cell. So be sure to watch that the pairs you are intending to put together do in fact end up together on the paired variables side.)

3. The possible Options are the same as for the Independent-Samples test.

The default output for the paired-samples *t* test consists of three boxes, the first of which is the same as the first box for the Independent-Samples test. The second box presents the correlation between the two sets of scores and its corresponding *p* value (labeled "Sig.," as usual); we have more to say about this statistical measure in Chapter 9. The third box contains the *t* value for the matched-pairs test, its *df*, and its two-tailed *p* value. Notice that to the left of these values, the box contains descriptive statistics for the Paired Differences. The first three entries are labeled Mean (the mean of the difference scores, which is the numerator of the *t* formula), Std. Deviation (the unbiased standard deviation of the difference scores), and Std. Error Mean (the standard error of the mean for the difference scores, which is the denominator of the *t* formula).

Chapter 8
Nonparametric Tests for the Difference Between Two Means

PREVIEW

Introduction

What are the main differences between parametric and nonparametric tests?

What are the advantages and disadvantages of using ordinal tests?

What is meant by the power efficiency of a statistical test?

What are some important considerations about significance tests based on ranks?

The Difference Between the Locations of Two Independent Samples: The Rank-Sum Test

What are the procedures for testing the hypothesis that two independent samples of ranked data come from populations with the same location?

When should the rank-sum test be used in place of the t test for two independent sample means?

How should you interpret the results of a rank-sum test? How do we convert a significant result to a measure of strength of relationship?

The Difference Between the Locations of Two Matched Samples: The Wilcoxon Test

What are the procedures for testing the hypothesis that two matched samples of ranked data come from populations with equal values for location?

What is the power efficiency of the Wilcoxon test?

When should the Wilcoxon test be used in place of the matched t test?

How do we convert a significant result to a measure of strength of relationship?

Summary

Exercises

Thought Questions

Computer Exercises

Bridge to SPSS

Introduction

In this chapter, we introduce the topic of nonparametric statistical tests by way of explaining **ordinal tests**. These are statistical tests that are applied to observations that have been ranked relative to one another—that is, the observations have been assigned ranks. In the last two chapters of this text, we will deal with nonparametric tests of categorical (purely qualitative) data. But first, we will make a few points about nonparametric statistics in general.

Parametric Versus Nonparametric Tests

A *parametric* statistical test is so labeled because it involves the estimation of the value of at least one population parameter. For example, the pooled within-group sample variance calculated in most *t* tests is an estimate of the corresponding within-population variance. A *nonparametric* test, on the other hand, does not require such estimation. Also, the mathematical derivations of common parametric tests assume that each population being randomly sampled has a *normal* distribution. A *distribution-free* statistical test, by contrast, requires no assumption about the shape of the distribution in the population. Although the terms *nonparametric* and *distribution-free* have different meanings, most statistical tests that meet one of these conditions also satisfy the other, so the terms tend to be used interchangeably in practice. For convenience, we will use the term *nonparametric* to refer to any statistical test in which none of the variables has been measured on an interval or ratio scale. Sometimes a nonparametric test is used when one or more variables were *originally* measured precisely, but those measurements have been transformed to a less precise ordinal or ranking scale, as we describe in the next section.

Ordinal Tests

There are two main types of situations that give rise to ordinal data and that may therefore call for the tests described in this chapter. First, suppose we can determine if one person has a greater amount of a continuous variable than another person, but we cannot measure this variable with any precision. For example, it may be reasonable to conclude that some junior executives at a given company have strong, moderate, or weak leadership qualities, without being able to quantify leadership much more precisely. To use the ordinal statistical procedures discussed in this chapter, we must at least be able to place all of the junior executives in order (i.e., to *rank* them) according to each one's amount of leadership ability. It is acceptable for some of the executives to be tied at the same rank, but a high percentage of ties would make these procedures inappropriate.

Second, the dependent variable may have already been measured on a precise, quantitative scale, but the distribution of the scores strongly violates the usual assumptions of parametric tests. The advantage of ordinal tests in these situations is that they do not require the population being sampled to be normally distributed. When we discussed the assumption of normality in connection with t tests, we stated that these tests were fairly robust, in that moderate departures from normality in the population did not seriously affect their validity. But it is not at all rare in the behavioral sciences to encounter data that greatly depart from normality. Consider, for example, a typical distribution of reaction times involving a cognitive task: The bulk of the reaction times will be fairly close to zero, but a fair number will be relatively long, and none will be less than zero. Thus the distribution is quite skewed and therefore substantially *non*normal. If our samples are large, the central limit theorem tells us that our sampling distribution will be fairly normal even if the population distributions are not. However, it is not unusual in psychological research to be stuck with rather small samples. So, when we have reason to believe that the population distributions we are sampling from depart greatly from normality, and our sample sizes are not very large, ordinal methods (which require no assumption about population distribution shape) can be desirable. (These methods do generally assume, however, that the population distributions being compared have the *same* shape and variability.)

Of course, it is easy to rank order data that have already been measured precisely, but a good deal of measurement information is lost when scores are transformed to ranks. Whereas the original scores may be at varying distances from each other, their ranks are always one unit apart. For example, suppose that the three lowest IQs of 72, 87, and 89 in a particular sample are converted into ranks of 1, 2, and 3. It is no longer possible to tell that the lowest IQ was well below the other two, or that the IQs ranked second and third were quite close in value. Thus, a considerable loss of the original interval information generally occurs. The ordinal tests discussed in this chapter compensate for this loss of information by being distribution-free, while suffering only a modest loss of power.

The Power Efficiency of Statistical Tests

It may have occurred to you to ask, "Why *ever* use parametric tests, which make normality assumptions about unobservable population distributions, when ordinal tests with nearly as much power are available? After all, one can never *know* that the shape of a population distribution is normal." Good question! The answer is that it can be quite costly to run subjects, and when populations are normally distributed, the sample size required by the parametric test (N_p) is smaller than that required by an alternative distribution-free test (N_d) in order to obtain the same amount of power. The ratio of these sample sizes expressed as a percent, or $(N_p/N_d) \times 100\%$, is called the *power efficiency* of the distribution-free test. Suppose that for a given difference between population means, a given significance criterion, α, and a specified power, a certain ordinal test requires a total sample of $N_d = 80$ cases. Its parametric alternative, however, requires only $N_p = 72$ cases to have the same power. The power efficiency of the ordinal test would be $72/80 = 90\%$, so the parametric test requires only 90% as many cases to have the same probability of rejecting the null hypothesis.

When populations are normally distributed, the power efficiencies of ordinal tests are almost always less than 100%. This means that they require more cases in order to have the same power. Conversely, they have less power for the same number of cases. For this reason, you should *not* rush to use ordinal tests unless substantial non-normality is believed to exist in the population. This is especially true when you are using two-tailed tests and when the sample sizes are *not* very small (say, 20 or more). But if you do have good reason to believe that a population distribution departs substantially from normality, or your data are already in the form of ranks or ordered categories (e.g., very small, small, moderate), an appropriate ordinal test should be performed.

The Basics of Dealing With Data in the Form of Ranks

As previously mentioned, there may be situations for which you will want to convert your interval/ratio data into ranks, so you can perform an ordinal test instead of a *t* test. Although this is not difficult to do, it is important to keep some basic principles in mind. In converting a set of N scores to ranks, it is customary to assign rank 1 to the smallest observation and rank N to the largest. If ties occur, the mean of the ranks in question is assigned to each of the tied scores, in a manner soon to be described.

What makes tests based on ranks work so simply is the fact that the data for any problem involving a total of N cases (where there are no ties) will be the positive integers $1, 2, 3, \ldots, N$. Thus statistical functions of these data are simple functions of N. For example, it can easily be proved that the *sum* of the first N integers (ranks 1 to N) is as follows:

$$\sum R = 1 + 2 + 3 + \cdots + N$$
$$= \frac{N(N+1)}{2}$$

Suppose that there are a total of 22 cases. Whatever their original raw scores may be, the sum of their *ranks* must be $(22)(23)/2 = 253$. And because the mean is equal to the sum divided by N, it therefore follows that the mean of a complete set of ranks (symbolized by R) is equal to:

$$\bar{R} = \frac{\sum R}{N}$$
$$= \frac{N(N+1)}{2N}$$
$$= \frac{N+1}{2}$$

Thus, the mean rank for 22 observations is simply $23/2 = 11.5$. The mean rank can be thought of as the expected rank of a case drawn at random from the N ranks, in the sense that the mean is the best guess as to the value of this case. Therefore, if we draw two cases at random when $N = 22$, the expected sum of the ranks (symbolized by T_E) is $2(11.5) = 23$. For three cases, it is $3(11.5)$ or 34.5, and so on. Generally, if we draw a subset of N_1 cases at random from the total N (symbolized as N_T), their expected sum of ranks is N_1 times the mean rank:

$$T_E = N_1 \overline{R}$$
$$= \frac{N_1(N_T + 1)}{2} \qquad \text{Formula 8.1}$$

It can also be shown that if N_1 cases are randomly and repeatedly drawn from the complete set of N_T ranks, and the sum of the ranks (T) is obtained for each sample, the standard deviation of the resulting sampling distribution of T values (or the *standard error* of T) would be:

$$\sigma_T = \frac{N_1 N_2 (N_T + 1)}{12} \qquad \text{Formula 8.2}$$

where

σ_T = standard error of T
$N_2 = N_T - N_1$

The value of 12 in the denominator is a constant, and is not affected by N_T or any of the N_T values. Regardless of the shape of the population distribution of raw scores, this sampling distribution of a sum of a subset of ranks is approximately normal in form. This is *not* an assumption but a provable mathematical property.

An Example of Ranking Data With Ties

As mentioned previously, there are two situations that can produce ordinal data, and both can lead to tied ranks, which must be dealt with. First, there is direct ranking, in which you combine your two subgroups into one group for the purpose of ranking the individuals relative to each other (but you keep track of the group each one came from). For example, participants A, B, C, D, and E have completed a leadership-training course, while participants W, X, Y, and Z did not. Now you want to rank them from highest to lowest leadership potential based on presentations each of them gave. Suppose that you place them in the following order: B, D, W, C, A, Y, E, X, Z, though you feel that, to be fair, D and W are really tied (i.e., your judges cannot distinguish between them with respect to leadership potential), as are E, X, and Z. (One way this could occur is if you really have just six ordered categories in which to place the participants: very high leadership; high; slightly above average; slightly below average; low; and very low; and B falls into the first category; D and W in the second; C, A, and Y in the third, fourth, and fifth categories, respectively; and E, X, and Z in the lowest category.) In order to preserve the sum of ranks, which is 45 for $N = 9$, you must first assign the ranks from 1 to 9, even when some individuals are tied, like this:

B	D	W	C	A	Y	E	X	Z
9	8	7	6	5	4	3	2	1

Then individuals who are tied are assigned the average of their ranks, so both D and W are assigned the rank of 7.5, and E, X, and Z are each assigned the rank of 2:

B	D	W	C	A	Y	E	X	Z
9	7.5	7.5	6	5	4	2	2	2

Note that these ranks have the same sum (45) as when there are no ties; assigning the ranks as we just did ensured that this would be the case. In this example, I made it particularly easy to keep track of the subgroups by using letters at the beginning or end of the alphabet. The sum of ranks for those who took leadership training is $T = 9 + 7.5 + 6 + 5 + 2 = 29.5$; and for those who did not, $T = 7.5 + 4 + 2 + 2 = 15.5$. (The sum of the ranks of both groups is $29.5 + 15.5 = 45$, as it should be for any nine ranks that are properly assigned.)

The other situation that produces ordinal data occurs when you have precise measurements (e.g., reaction time in milliseconds), but the distribution is so far from normality that you choose to assign ranks to the measurements. For very precise measurements, ties will rarely occur, but for a measurement such as the number of children in a family, ties will be common. In any case, ties are dealt with exactly as in the example just described: Ranks from 1 to N are assigned (arbitrarily in the case of tied measurements), and then tied individuals are each given the average of their ranks.

The Difference Between the Locations of Two Independent Samples: The Rank-Sum Test

Among the most important and useful ordinal tests are those that deal with differences in *location* between populations, based on ranks. We hope you recall from the earlier chapters of this text that the location of a distribution is generally expressed in terms of a measure of its *central tendency*. In parametric statistics, the location of a population or sample is customarily indexed by its arithmetic mean. When we conclude from a *t* test that scores in Population 1 are larger than those in Population 2, we mean literally that $\mu_1 > \mu_2$. But with ordinal tests, the same statement has a different meaning, which is: If we draw at random a case from Population 1 and another from Population 2 and compare them, and do this repeatedly, more than half the time the case from Population 1 will be larger than the case from Population 2. This can be taken for all intents and purposes as an assertion that **median$_1$ > median$_2$**, or written more compactly, **Mdn$_1$ > Mdn$_2$** (the boldface is there to remind you that these are medians of populations, not samples). In this chapter, we describe two tests of location that are parallel to the independent-samples and matched t tests, respectively, but are applied to ordinal data and are considered to be more robust (less dependent on making assumptions) than their corresponding t tests. In fact, both of these tests can be categorized as nonparametric and distribution-free, as we explain shortly, and when they can be used as alternatives to t tests, they are nearly as powerful as their parametric counterparts.

The ordinal test most commonly used as a nonparametric alternative to the t test of two independent sample means is called the **rank-sum** test, or sometimes Wilcoxon's rank-sum test (the Mann-Whitney U test is another version of this test that ultimately yields the same p value). This test requires the type of ranking we just described. We introduce this test in terms of an example for which the use of the ordinary t test would be questionable.

Suppose that at the end of the semester, Ihno decides to use scores on the final exam to compare the performance of her most phobic students (those who rated their math phobia as more than 6) with that of her least phobic students (those who gave a rating of 0). The final exam scores for the 10 least phobic (let us say there were missing data for two of the students who rated their phobia as zero) and the 12 most phobic students are shown in Table 8.1. As you can see, the normality assumption appears to be quite dubious. The samples are also small, so a distribution-free test is appropriate. In particular, we will use the rank-sum test, which allows us to decide whether we can reject the null hypothesis that two independent samples of ranked data come from populations with the *same* location (i.e., central tendency).

From the earlier sections of this chapter, we have all the ingredients we need for hypothesis testing: a sample statistic (T) with a known (in this case, approximately normal) sampling distribution, whose standard deviation is known (σ_T), and a null-hypothetical value to test against (T_E).

Step 1: State the Null and Alternative Hypotheses, and the Significance Criterion, α

The null hypothesis can be stated in terms of the population medians, as follows:

$$H_0: \textbf{Mdn}_1 = \textbf{Mdn}_2$$
$$H_A: \textbf{Mdn}_1 \neq \textbf{Mdn}_2$$

The significance (i.e., alpha) level used for nonparametric tests is no different from that which is typically used for parametric tests, so we will set α to .05.

Step 2: Calculate the Appropriate Test Statistic

First, all 22 observations (ignoring phobia group) are subjected to a single ranking from the lowest ($X = 52$), which is assigned a rank of 1, to the

Table 8.1   The Rank-Sum Test for Two Independent Samples

Least phobic (Group 1)		Most phobic (Group 2)	
X	R	X	R
55	3	52	1
62	7	53	2
69	11	56	4
78	15	58	5
79	16	60	6
84	18	63	8
92	19	64	9
96	20	65	10
98	21	71	12
99	22	74	13
		76	14
		81	17

$$T_1 = 152 \qquad T_2 = 101$$

$$N_1 = 10 \qquad N_2 = 12$$

$$\bar{R}_1 = \frac{152}{10} \qquad \bar{R}_2 = \frac{101}{12}$$

$$= 15.20 \qquad = 8.2$$

$$N_T = N_1 + N_2 = 22$$

$$\sum R = N(N+1)/2 = (22)(23)/2 = 253$$

$$= T_1 + T_2 = 152 + 101 = 253$$

highest $(X = 99)$, which is assigned a rank of 22. The original X scores are ignored from this point on, and the analysis proceeds solely with the ranks. The critical step is to find the sum of the ranks separately for each group, so when ranking observations from both groups together, you do have to keep track of which group each observation came from.

As you can see in Table 8.1, the sum of the 10 ranks in Group 1 (zero phobia), symbolized by T_1, is 152. This sum should be compared to the expected sum of any 10 ranks selected at random from the 22 observations, because that is the sum you would expect if the null hypothesis was true. This is why we needed to derive Formula 8.1:

$$T_E = \frac{N_1(N_T + 1)}{2}$$

$$= \frac{(10)(23)}{2}$$

$$= 115$$

Is the observed T_1 of 152 a statistically significant departure from the null hypothesis (expected) T_E value of 115? Because statisticians have shown that T_1 is normally distributed around a mean of T_E, it is appropriate to use the z score formula for one mean, Formula 5.2, even though our "mean" in this case is actually a sum of ranks. Formula 5.2 can therefore be transformed for our purposes to:

$$z = \frac{T_1 - T_E}{\sigma_T}$$

Like any z score formula, this formula requires knowing not only the mean of the normal distribution of T values but its standard deviation (called a standard error in this case, because we are not dealing with individual observations), as well. Fortunately, that can be estimated quite well, if N is not small, by Formula 8.2. Inserting Formula 8.2 into the preceding formula, we get a convenient z score formula for the rank-sum test:

$$z = \frac{T_1 - T_E}{\sqrt{\dfrac{N_1 N_2 (N_T + 1)}{12}}} \qquad \text{Formula 8.3}$$

Substituting the appropriate values from Table 8.1 for the symbols in Formula 8.3 yields the following value for z:

$$z = \frac{152 - 115}{\sqrt{\dfrac{(10)(12)(23)}{12}}}$$

$$= \frac{37}{15.17}$$

$$= 2.44$$

Step 3: Find the Critical Value and Make a Statistical Decision With Respect to Your Null Hypothesis

Although we would naturally expect the low-phobia group to obtain the larger (i.e., numerically higher) ranks on the final stats exam, it is more conservative, and more widely accepted, to perform a two-tailed test (e.g., suppose the high phobics sought extra help and tutoring and the low phobics turned out to be too complacent?). As you may recall, the critical z values for $\alpha = .05$, two-tailed, are ± 1.96. Because the 37 rank-sum units by which Group 1 exceeds T_E place it 2.44 standard error units above the mean of a normal distribution of rank-sums for the given sample sizes, the observed z score is $+2.44$, which is larger than $+1.96$. Therefore, you can reject the null hypothesis and conclude that the ranks in the zero-phobia group are significantly higher than chance expectation. The symmetry of the normal distribution implies that the ranks in the highly phobic group are significantly *lower* than chance expectation and therefore that the ranks for the least phobic students are generally higher than those for the most phobic.

Interpreting the Results of a Rank-Sum Test

Rejecting the null hypothesis in a rank-sum test allows us to conclude that the location of the two populations from which these samples were randomly drawn differs on X (in this case, performance on the final stats exam), such that the median of the first (zero-phobic) population is greater than the median of the second (highly phobic) population (i.e., their final exam scores are higher).

Note that it makes no difference which of the two sets of ranks you use to compute T (the sum of ranks to be compared in the test) and T_E. For Group 2, $T_2 = 101$, and T_E would now be equal to $(12)(23)/2$, or 138. (Do not forget that T_E depends on the size of the sample associated with the comparison T.) The value of σ_T is unchanged, so z would equal $(101 - 138)/15.17$, or -2.44. And you would reach exactly the same conclusion, with the minus sign indicating that the group being compared (Group 2) is the one with the lower value for location. Although you need compute only T_1 (or only T_2) to carry out this statistical test, it is desirable to calculate both values and then verify that $T_1 + T_2 = N_T(N_T + 1)/2$, as a check against errors in ranking and/or calculating.

The rank-sum test for two samples that we just demonstrated depends on the fact that the sampling distribution of T is well approximated by the normal curve. This will be true provided that the samples are not too small, say at least six to eight cases in each. With smaller samples than that, the normal distribution is not an accurate model for the distribution of the T values. Fortunately, when dealing with small samples, it is not difficult to work out all of the possible arrangements of ranks and to calculate the probabilities that correspond to the various possible values of T. Even more fortunately, statisticians have created convenient tables of critical values for either: (a) the sum of ranks for one of two small groups (Wilcoxon bases his values on the smaller of the two groups, if the two groups are not the same size), or (b) a function derived from the sum of ranks for one of the groups (the test that is credited to both Mann and Whitney is based on a function called the U statistic, so that version of the test is called the "Mann-Whitney U test").

We chose not to include a table of critical values for the rank-sum test in this text, because you are not likely to conduct such a test without statistical software and because, if you do, you should consult a more specialized book devoted to nonparametric statistics, such as the one by Siegel and Castellan (1988). Such books will not only contain the statistical tables you will need but will also cover important refinements to nonparametric procedures with small samples, such as a correction for continuity that is appropriate for two-group comparisons, as well as a procedure for reducing σ_T to take the number of tied ranks into account. (You can also find a table for the rank-sum test and some further explanation in B. H. Cohen, 2008.)

As we pointed out earlier, the parametric analog of the rank-sum test is the well-known t test for two independent sample means. Relative to the t test, the rank-sum test has a power efficiency that tends to range from 92% for small samples to 95% for large samples. Applying the pooled-variance formula to the final exam scores (X) in Table 8.1 yields a t value of 3.14, which, unlike the z for the corresponding rank-sum test, is significant even at the .01 level—but the t and z values are certainly not far apart.

For a given set of conditions, when populations are normally distributed, the same power is obtained using the t test with 92% to 95% of the sample size that would be required by the rank-sum test. Compared to other nonparametric tests, those based on ranks have fairly high power efficiencies, so they should be used whenever the normality assumption is in serious doubt. When this is not the case, however, the behavioral scientist usually cannot afford the luxury of what amounts to throwing away 5% to 8% of the cases.

Measure of Strength of Relationship: The Glass Rank Biserial Correlation

With respect to the two-group t test, we have stressed the general insufficiency of computing only a test of statistical significance, which merely helps us to decide whether or not there is some (nonzero) effect in the population and the desirability of calculating an additional measure to index the *strength* of an observed relationship. In the case of the parametric t test for two independent sample means, we introduced the statistic known as g, as just such a measure in the previous chapter. In Chapter 10, we will describe an alternative measure of effect size for two sample means, which is based on the Pearson correlation coefficient, introduced in the next chapter. The effect-size measure we describe here for the rank-sum test is more closely related to the correlation type of measure but is simple enough to be understood on its own.

A measure of the strength of the relationship between group membership and the *rank* values for two groups is provided by the **Glass rank biserial correlation coefficient**, symbolized by r_G. It is computed using the following formula:

$$r_G = \frac{2(\overline{R}_1 - \overline{R}_2)}{N_T} \qquad \text{Formula 8.4}$$

where

$\overline{R}_1 = $ mean of ranks in Group 1
$\overline{R}_2 = $ mean of ranks in Group 2
$N_T = $ total number of observations

Although the r_G coefficient is *not* a Pearson r, it does conveniently have the same limits: It may take on any value from -1 to 1 (with its sign depending on which group is called Group 1), and its magnitude is interpreted much like that of any correlation coefficient. The maximum value of 1 or −1 occurs when there is no overlap in ranks between the two groups, with one group containing all the highest ranks while the other group contains all the lowest ranks. A value of zero suggests a random mixing of the two groups with respect to ranks, with neither group appearing to be superior to the other. It is important to note that a significant rank-sum test can be associated with a tiny value of r_G (e.g., 0.1) when the sample sizes are very large. In such a case, r_G serves as a useful reminder that statistical significance does not guarantee that there is much separation even in our two samples—only that we are permitted to rule out a *zero* amount of separation in the population.

For the data in Table 8.1, $\bar{R}_1 = 15.20$, $\bar{R}_2 = 8.42$, and $N_T = 22$. Thus,

$$r_G = \frac{2(15.20 - 8.42)}{22}$$

$$= .62$$

This indicates a fairly high degree of relationship between group membership and ranking on X, so it should not be surprising that we obtained significant results even though our samples were rather small.

The Difference Between the Locations of Two Matched Samples: The Wilcoxon Test

The other ordinal test of location we describe in this chapter is the nonparametric alternative to the matched-pairs t test. Like the matched t test, the ordinal test we are about to describe can be used whether the pairs of scores come from matched participants or the same participant measured twice.

Rationale and Computational Procedures

As we saw in the previous chapter, when a comparison is to be made between the means of two matched or dependent samples, the procedure that should be used is different from the case in which the samples are independent. For each of the N matched pairs, the difference (D) between the X_1 and X_2 values is found, and the null hypothesis tested is that the population mean of the D values is zero. Rejection of this null hypothesis necessarily implies that μ_1 and μ_2 are not equal.

The same distinction applies in determining the appropriate rank-based test of the difference in location between two samples. The rank-sum test discussed earlier is used with independent samples, while a different technique, the signed-ranks test (often called the **Wilcoxon matched-pairs signed ranks test**) is used with dependent samples. The Wilcoxon test also begins with $D = X_2 - X_1$ values, but then operates on only the ranks of the absolute values of these difference scores.

Table 8.2   The Wilcoxon Test for Two Matched Samples

Subject	X_A	X_B	$D = X_A - X_B$	R_D	$R(+)$	$R(-)$
1	33	38	−5	7		7
2	45	43	+2	2	2	
3	50	42	+8	10	10	
4	45	44	+1	1	1	
5	46	49	−3	3.5		3.5
6	45	41	+4	5.5	5.5	
7	28	22	+6	8	8	
8	43	46	−3	3.5		3.5
9	32	32	0			
10	40	31	+9	11	11	
11	34	27	+7	9	9	
12	40	44	−4	5.5		5.5

$$\sum R = 66 \qquad T_1 = 46.5 \qquad T_2 = 19.5$$
$$(= T_1 + T_2)$$

$$N = 11 \text{ (deleting subject 9 for whom } D = 0)$$
$$\sum R = N(N + 1)/2 = (11)(12)/2 = 66$$

As an example, let us consider an investigation into the question of whether sensitivity training improves extrasensory perception (ESP) scores. A sample of 12 subjects is tested for ESP before (X_B) and again after (X_A) a series of 10 training sessions, and the results are shown in Table 8.2. In this experiment, therefore, the samples are dependent because the two observations in each pair come from the same subject. (It should be noted, however, that this matched design is obtained whenever there is some connection between the observations making up a pair.)

The first two columns in Table 8.2 give the posttraining (X_A) and pretraining (X_B) ESP scores for the 12 participants. The third column shows each participant's change or difference score, where $D = X_A - X_B$. (You could subtract either score from the other, but it makes sense to subtract the scores in the order that gives you fewer negative scores.) Given the order of subtraction we are using, the D values are positive when the ESP score has increased following sensitivity training and negative when it has decreased. As was the case in the parametric matched t test, all further analyses focus on these D scores.

First, all cases where $D = 0$ are dropped. Case 9 in the table is therefore deleted, and the analysis proceeds on the basis of $N = 11$. (For this test, we will let N stand for the number of *pairs* and not use the symbol N_T.) Then, *ignoring the signs* of the D values, they are rank-ordered from the smallest (rank $= 1$) to the largest (rank $= N$), with ties being resolved as described for the rank-sum test. For example, the differences of $+4$ and -4 are tied with respect to absolute value and initially occupy the ranks of 5 and 6 (the first four ranks go to $+1$, $+2$, and the two -3s); the tie is resolved by assigning the rank of 5.5 to both the $+4$ and the -4

difference. These ranks appear in the column labeled $R_{|D|}$, and they follow the statistical properties associated with any set of ranks from 1 to N; for example, their sum must equal $N(N + 1)/2$, which for $N = 11$ is equal to $(11)(12)/2$, or 66.

If the population locations of X_B and X_A are the same, then (ignoring pairs where $D = 0$) the sum of the ranks of the absolute D values should be approximately equally divided between those that are positive ($R+$) and those that are negative ($R-$). That is, there should be an equal number of cases where $X_B > X_A$ and where $X_B < X_A$. Since the sum of *all* the ranks equals $N(N + 1)/2$, the expectation under the null hypothesis is that the sum of the ranks for the positive Ds and the sum of the ranks for the negative Ds will *each* equal half the sum. That is, the expected result under the null hypothesis is:

$$T_E = \frac{1}{2} \frac{N(N + 1)}{2}$$

$$= \frac{N(N + 1)}{4}$$

For the data in Table 8.2,

$$T_E = \frac{(11)(12)}{4}$$

$$= 33,$$

which is half of 66, the sum of all the ranks.

In the columns headed $R(+)$ and $R(-)$ in Table 8.2, the $R_{|D|}$ values for positive and negative Ds have been segregated. The sum of the ranks of the positive D values, T_1, is equal to 46.5. The sum of the ranks of the negative D values, T_2, is equal to 19.5. Except as a check, only one of these values is needed, so let us choose $T_1 = 46.5$. This value departs 13.5 rank-sum units from the value expected under the null hypothesis, $T_E = 33$. You are then left with the question of whether or not this departure is sufficiently unlikely to reject the null hypothesis, using (say) the $\alpha = .05$ decision rule.

A method for answering this question can be easily derived. In repeated random sampling, T_1 (and also T_2) is approximately normally distributed when the null hypothesis is true. The standard deviation of the sampling distribution of this matched-pairs signed ranks T is called a standard error and is symbolized by σ_{T_M}. The formula for this standard error is as follows:

$$\sigma_{T_M} = \sqrt{\frac{(2N + 1)T_E}{6}} \qquad \text{Formula 8.5}$$

Thus we have a sampling distribution that is approximately normal, whose mean is T_E and whose standard deviation is σ_T, and we have a null hypothesis to test: that the positive and negative rank sums are equal. Once again, we have all the ingredients for a significance test using the normal curve model. Because **Step 1** of our null hypothesis procedure is exactly the same as for the rank-sum test, we will skip to **Step 2**.

Step 2: Calculate the Appropriate Test Statistic

The one-group z test, with the symbols appropriately modified for the Wilcoxon signed-ranks test, looks like this:

$$z = \frac{T_1 - T_E}{\sigma_{T_M}}$$

Inserting Formula 8.5 into the preceding formula yields the following useful z score formula for the signed-ranks test:

$$z = \frac{T_1 - T_E}{\sqrt{\dfrac{(2N+1)T_E}{6}}} \qquad \text{Formula 8.6}$$

For the data in Table 8.2, we found that the null hypothesis leads to an expected value of T_1 (and of T_2) as follows: $T_E = 33$. The observed $T_1 = 46.5$. Therefore,

$$z = \frac{46.5 - 33}{\sqrt{\dfrac{[(2)(11)+1](33)}{6}}}$$

$$= \frac{13.5}{\sqrt{\dfrac{(23)(33)}{6}}}$$

$$= 1.20$$

Step 3: Find the Critical Value and Make a Statistical Decision With Respect to Your Null Hypothesis

Although the investigator would undoubtedly expect the sensitivity training to lead to *higher* ESP scores after training than before, we will again follow the more conservative and widely accepted custom of performing a two-tailed test. Therefore, the critical z values for this problem are ± 1.96. As you can see from the z score just calculated, the observed departure of 13.5 rank-sum units from the null-hypothetical expected value of 33 is only a little more than one standard error and therefore far less than the value of $+1.96$ needed to reject H_0, using the two-tailed .05 criterion of significance. The null hypothesis is retained, though certainly not "accepted."

Interpreting the Results of a Wilcoxon Matched-Pairs Signed-Ranks Test

On one hand, the data do *not* justify the conclusion that 10 sessions of sensitivity training will improve ESP scores in the population from which this sample was randomly drawn. On the other hand, the results do not permit the conclusion that *no* effect exists, of course; in fact, given our small sample, it is likely that the probability of a Type II error is rather high (this issue is discussed in considerable detail in Chapter 11). Only if the population effect were quite large would there be a reasonably good chance of rejecting the null hypothesis with such a small sample.

Relative to the matched t test, the Wilcoxon test has power efficiency ranging from 92% for small samples to 95% for large samples. This means that if the parametric assumptions of the t test for matched samples were valid, our choice of the Wilcoxon test would result in somewhat lower power than the t test would have; our $N = 11$ for the Wilcoxon test is about as powerful as a t test using $N = (.92)(11) = 10$ pairs. (A t test applied to the original [not ranked] 12 D values is also not significant; it equals 1.28, very close to the Wilcoxon z of 1.20.) Note, however, that the Wilcoxon test as presented here should not be used if the sample size is smaller than about 8, because the approximation to normality will then not be sufficiently accurate. As mentioned earlier, statistical tables are available for nonparametric analyses involving small samples (B. H. Cohen, 2008), and it is always a good idea to consult a more specialized text, such as the Siegel and Castellan (1988) book, if you have a large number of zero differences, or tied ranks.

The Sign Test

A considerably cruder alternative to both the Wilcoxon and matched-pairs t test is the *sign* test, presented in Chapter 16 of this text, following a description of the binomial distribution, on which it is based. Because the sign test considers only whether a difference is positive or negative, and therefore ignores virtually all of the quantitative information in the data, it has a power efficiency that is usually below 70% with respect to the matched-pairs t test. The sign test should only be used when the difference of each pair cannot be quantified precisely enough for the differences to be ranked but the directions for most of the differences can be determined. Nonetheless, for dramatic effects, the sign test may be all you need to demonstrate your point.

Measure of Strength of Relationship: The Matched-Pairs Rank Biserial Correlation

The matched-pairs rank biserial correlation, symbolized by r_C, expresses the strength of the relationship between the condition (such as posttest versus pretest) and the dependent variable. Another way to describe r_C is that it indexes the degree of relationship between the sign of D and its rank. It is computed as follows:

$$r_C = \frac{4(T_1 - T_E)}{N(N + 1)}$$ Formula 8.7

The r_C index can take on values from -1 to $+1$. It is equal to zero when T_1 does not differ from the null hypothetical value T_E, and it equals ± 1 when all D values have the same sign. The sign of r_C indicates whether the positive or negative sums of ranks is larger. It is not a Pearson correlation coefficient, as described in the next chapter, but rather it is quite similar to r_G, for the rank-sum test.

When the Wilcoxon test is not statistically significant, there is usually little interest in computing r_C. However, even though the data in Table 8.2 did not yield a significant test, we will demonstrate the calculation of r_C on those data for pedagogical purposes.

$$r_C = \frac{4(46.5 - 33)}{(11)(12)} = .41$$

This value cannot be statistically significant, since the Wilcoxon test for the same data did not yield significance. It may be used to describe the relationship within this particular sample, but there is insufficient reason to conclude that the corresponding population correlation index is different from zero. However, it should be noted that an r_C of .41 indicates a fairly consistent change from before to after, and would be associated with a statistically significant result were the sample size not so small.

Summary

When there is reason to believe that the shape of a population distribution is substantially non-normal and the samples are not very large, nonparametric statistical tests, such as the two ordinal tests described in this chapter, may be desirable.

Basic Considerations

The main advantage of nonparametric and distribution-free statistical tests is that they do *not* require the population(s) being sampled to be normally distributed, so they are applicable when gross non-normality is displayed in your data and therefore suspected in the population. The primary disadvantage of these methods is that when normality does exist, they are less powerful than the corresponding parametric tests (more likely to lead to a Type II error). A numerical measure of the *power efficiency* of a nonparametric test is given by:

$$\frac{N_p}{N_d} \times 100\%$$

where

$N_p =$ sample size required by a parametric test to obtain a specified level of power for a specified criterion of significance and a specified difference between population means

$N_d =$ sample size required by the corresponding nonparametric test to obtain the same power under the same conditions

The power efficiency of a nonparametric test is almost always less than 100%, but the power of the ordinal tests described in this chapter is quite good. Nonetheless, it is wasteful to use these methods when parametric tests are applicable.

The Difference Between the Locations of Two Independent Samples: The Rank-Sum Test

1. Parametric analog: t test for the difference between two independent means (Chapter 7).

    Power efficiency: Approximately 92%–95%

2. Computational procedures: Rank *all* scores from 1 (smallest) to N (largest), regardless of which group they are in. In case of ties, follow the usual procedure of assigning the mean of the ranks in question to each of the tied scores. Then compute a z score using the following formula:

$$z = \frac{T_1 - T_E}{\sqrt{\dfrac{N_1 N_2 (N_T + 1)}{12}}}$$
Formula 8.3

where

T_1 = sum of ranks in group 1

$T_E = N_1(N + 1)/2$

N_1 = number of observations in Group 1

N_2 = number of observations in Group 2

N_T = total number of observations

Do *not* use the preceding formula if there are fewer than six cases in either group. Use an exact table of critical values, such as Table A.15 in B. H. Cohen (2008).

3. Measure of the strength of relationship: If the value of z computed in the rank-sum test is statistically significant, or otherwise interesting, a measure of the strength of the relationship between group membership and the rank values may be found by computing the *Glass rank biserial correlation* (r_G):

$$r_G = \frac{2(\bar{R}_1 - \bar{R}_2)}{N_T}$$
Formula 8.4

where

$\bar{R}_1$ = mean of ranks in Group 1

$\bar{R}_2$ = mean of ranks in Group 2

N_T = total number of observations

The r_G coefficient falls between the limits of -1 and $+1$.

The Difference Between the Locations of Two Matched Samples: The Wilcoxon Test

1. Parametric analog: matched t test (Chapter 7). Power efficiency: Approximately $92\% - 95\%$

2. Computational procedures: First, obtain the D score for each subject by subtracting X_2 from X_1. Next, discard any case where $D = 0$ (and reduce N accordingly). Then, *ignoring the signs* of the Ds, rank them from the smallest (rank $= 1$) to the largest (rank $= N$). Finally, compute a z score using the following formula:

$$z = \frac{T_1 - T_E}{\sqrt{\dfrac{(2N + 1)T_E}{6}}} \qquad \text{Formula 8.6}$$

where

$T_1 =$ sum of ranks for those D values that are positive (note that T_2, the sum of the ranks for those D values that are negative, may be used instead)

$T_E = N(N + 1)/4$

$N =$ number of pairs (excluding cases where $D = 0$)

Do *not* use this procedure if N is less than about 8. Instead, use an exact table of critical values, such as Table A.16 in B. H. Cohen (2008).

3. Measure of the strength of relationship: If the value of z computed in the Wilcoxon test is statistically significant or otherwise interesting, a measure of the strength of the relationship between the independent variable (e.g., condition) and the dependent variable may be found by computing the *matched-pairs rank biserial correlation* (r_C):

$$r_C = \frac{4(T_1 - T_E)}{N(N + 1)} \qquad \text{Formula 8.7}$$

where T_1, T_E, and N have the same meanings as in the Wilcoxon test. The r_C coefficient is very similar to the r_G coefficient, and it also falls between the limits of -1 and $+1$.

Exercises

1. An operator of a certain machine must turn it off quickly if a danger signal occurs. To test the relative effectiveness of two types of signals, a small group of operators is randomly divided into two groups. Those in Group 1 operate machines with a newly designed signal, while those in Group 2 use machines with the standard signal. The signal is flashed unexpectedly, and the reaction time of each operator (time taken to turn off the machine after the signal occurs) is measured in seconds. The actual results (not ranks) are shown here. (a) Use the rank-sum test to determine whether there is a significant difference

between the two groups. (b) Compute the appropriate measure of strength of relationship.

Group 1	Group 2
5	3
3	17
4	13
10	2
1	8
3	16
5	6
2	9
7	11
	8

2. Redo Exercise 5 from Chapter 7 using the rank-sum test instead of a *t* test. Does your statistical conclusion differ from the one you made in the previous chapter? Why would the rank-sum test not be very accurate for the data in that exercise?

3. In Experiment 1 (see the following table), Ihno is comparing scores on a practice final exam between the students who performed most poorly on the midterm (Group 1) and those who got the highest midterm scores (Group 2). Experiment 2 also compares scores on the practice final, but in this case, Group 1 consists of the students who received the highest scores on the first quiz and Group 2 contains the students who received the lowest scores. (a) Perform the rank-sum test for each experiment. Can you reject the null hypothesis in each case? (b) Calculate the appropriate measure for the strength of relationship between the two variables, for each experiment. How strong does the relationship appear to be in each case?

Experiment 1		Experiment 2	
Group 1	Group 2	Group 1	Group 2
43	80	96	43
53	45	78	54
57	62	41	59
41	83	60	70
62	46	53	45
54	87	54	83
63	56	63	57
46	70	46	80
59	75	80	50
50	78	56	87
54	89	75	57
57	96	46	62
57		57	
80		62	
60		89	

4. A psychology professor uses three different methods of instruction in three small classes, with the assignment of students to classes being random, and gives each class the same final examination. The results are in the table that follows. (a) Perform the appropriate test to compare each possible pair of groups and, in each case, state which group had the higher scores and whether the results were statistically significant at the .01 as well as the .05 level. (b) Calculate the appropriate measure of the strength of relationship between method of instruction and examination scores for each pair of groups, and comment briefly on the apparent size of the effect.

Group 1	Group 2	Group 3
94	60	86
97	97	42
100	96	61
72	57	73
99	93	40
96	90	63
98	92	87
97		65
		67

5. For each of the two (separate) experiments that follow, perform the Wilcoxon test. If an experiment yields statistically significant results, also compute r_C.

(a) Experiment 3			(b) Experiment 4		
S	X_1	X_2	S	X_1	X_2
1	12	9	1	15	15
2	13	8	2	25	8
3	23	16	3	9	16
4	17	21	4	13	9
5	19	14	5	11	23
6	20	9	6	19	14
7	15	17	7	10	21
8	14	9	8	12	18
9	22	14	9	15	17
10	18	13	10	14	17
11	25	10	11	9	14
12	11	10	12	11	15
13	20	15	13	20	13
14	15	15	14	10	10
15	10	11	15	20	22

6. Ten subjects participate in a problem-solving experiment. Two judges are asked to rate the solutions with regard to their creativity (1 = most creative, 10 = least creative). The experimenter wishes to know

if the judges were equally lenient in their ratings. Given the ratings in the table, what should the experimenter decide?

Subject	Judge 1	Judge 2
1	8	4
2	7	9
3	2	1
4	9	8
5	2	7
6	5	1
7	10	9
8	5	7
9	6	3
10	8	6

7. A psychology instructor develops a training method that is designed to improve the examination scores of poor students. The performance of a sample of 12 such students on the posttest (X_1) following training, and the pretest (X_2) prior to training, is shown. (a) Test the null hypothesis that the training method has no effect, using the Wilcoxon test. (b) Compute the appropriate measure of the strength of relationship.

S	X_1	X_2
1	77	68
2	64	64
3	56	52
4	56	57
5	71	69
6	54	58
7	76	70
8	57	60
9	63	61
10	68	61
11	71	73
12	66	66

Thought Questions

1. Parametric statistical tests are based on certain assumptions about unobservable population distributions. If these assumptions are incorrect, the parametric tests are likely to yield misleading results (and should therefore not be used). Yet we never know for certain what the population distributions are, so we cannot know for certain if these assumptions are justified. Nonparametric tests do *not* require

such assumptions. Why, then, do psychological researchers often use parametric tests?

2. Give an example of when each of the procedures discussed in this chapter should be used: (a) rank-sum test; (b) Wilcoxon test.

Computer Exercises

1. Separately for each of the five majors in Ihno's data set, use the rank-sum test to determine whether male students differ significantly from female students with respect to (a) statistics quiz scores, (b) prequiz anxiety scores, (c) math phobia ratings.

2. (a) Separately for male and female students, perform the Wilcoxon test to determine whether there is a significant increase in heart rate from baseline to the prequiz measurement. Also, test the difference between the pre- and postquiz measurements. Compare your results to those you obtained in Computer Exercise 5 in the previous chapter, if you did the advanced part of the exercise; otherwise, perform the Wilcoxon test on the entire group (males and females included), and then compare to the previous chapter. (b) Repeat part (a) for the anxiety scores.

Bridge to SPSS

The next to rightmost column in Variable View (rightmost in earlier versions), labeled **Measure**, allows you to define each of your Numeric variables as Scale (i.e., interval or ratio), Ordinal, or Nominal, whereas String variables can only be Ordinal or Nominal. (Numeric or String are the only two types of data we will discuss in this text, and this setting is determined in the second column of Variable View, labeled Type.) This designation can affect the way SPSS displays your output, but in early versions of SPSS, it had no effect on the statistical analyses performed. For the new analysis choices in the latest versions of SPSS, *Measure* matters. Ironically, in the latest versions of SPSS, you cannot request nonparametric tests on variables defined as ordinal. However, to provide continuity for long-term users, SPSS allows you to access its previous analysis modules through its **Legacy Dialogs**. If you are using one of the latest versions of SPSS, we recommend using the Legacy Dialogs for your nonparametric tests. That is the method we will describe in this section.

The Rank-Sum Test

You can perform the rank-sum test in SPSS by selecting **2 Independent Samples** from the Analyze/Nonparametric Tests menu (or from the Analyze/Nonparametric Tests/Legacy Dialogs menu for the newer versions). The first (and default) choice in the dialog box under Test Type is the one that produces the rank-sum test, and it is labeled **Mann-Whitney U**.

Just as in the Independent-Samples *t* test dialog box, you must specify the two levels of the Grouping Variable that you wish to compare (even if there *are* only two levels), as well as the list of Test Variables (DVs) on which you would like the two groups to be compared.

This test produces two boxes of output. The first is descriptive and contains the *N*s, sums, and means of the ranks for each group. The second box contains three Test Statistics: the Mann-Whitney *U* (mentioned only briefly in this chapter), the Wilcoxon *W* (the lower of the two sums of ranks), and *Z*, which is the *z* score we showed you how to calculate for this test. The *p* value associated with *Z* (SPSS uses an uppercase *Z*, to represent the same statistic for which we have been using the lowercase *z*) comes from the normal distribution and is labeled **Asymp. Sig (2-tailed)**. The *U* and *W* statistics are provided so that you can look up their critical values in a statistical table, but that step is not necessary, because the **Exact Sig.** is also provided whenever your sample sizes are small enough to need those tables (i.e., both samples sizes less than 25). [Note that the "exact sig." (i.e., *p* value) is always the same for the *U* and the *W* statistics, as one is just an algebraic transformation of the other.]

The Wilcoxon Test

Any time that your data have been entered in such a way that a paired-samples *t* test can be run, you can perform the *Wilcoxon Signed Ranks test* (as SPSS refers to it) instead. Just select **2 Related Samples** from the Analyze/Nonparametric Tests (/Legacy Dialogs) menu, and make sure that the first choice under Test Type (Wilcoxon) has been checked. Choose *two* variables from the list on the left, and move the pair to the Test Pair(s) List, as you would for a paired-samples *t* test. Repeat this process for each pair of variables that you would like to test.

The Wilcoxon test creates difference scores for each pair of variables to be tested and then ranks these differences by magnitude, temporarily ignoring the signs. SPSS does not show you these difference scores or their actual ranks, but the first output box for the Wilcoxon procedure gives the *N*, sum, and mean rank separately for the positive and negative differences. The number of ties (i.e., differences that are equal to zero—not identical difference scores) is also noted. The second output box contains only the *z* score (labeled **Z**) obtained from the Wilcoxon approximation formula we included earlier in this chapter, along with its two-tailed *p* value.

Chapter 9
Linear Correlation

PREVIEW

Introduction

What is meant by the correlation between two variables?

What is a positive correlation? A negative correlation?

What is a scatter plot?

How is the ability to make predictions related to correlation?

What is a linear relationship?

Describing the Linear Relationship Between Two Variables

What does the z score product formula for r tell us about the meaning of the correlation coefficient?

Why is it easier to determine the numerical value of r by using the computing (or raw score) formula?

Interpreting the Magnitude of a Pearson r

If two variables are significantly correlated, does this mean that one of the variables causes the other?

How can restriction of range lead to misleading conclusions about the correlation between two variables?

How is it possible for two variables to have a Pearson r near zero and yet be closely related? How can the presence of bivariate outliers in a data set lead to misleading conclusions about the correlation between two variables?

When Is It Important That Pearson's r Be Large?

What are the different types of reliability for which the Pearson r is frequently used?

What is the validity of a measure, and why is it important that it be large?

Testing the Significance of the Correlation Coefficient

What are the procedures for testing hypotheses about the population correlation coefficient (usually, that it is equal to zero)?

How much confidence can we have in our conclusion, if we must retain the null hypothesis?

Under what condition can we obtain a statistically significant Pearson r that is too small to be of any practical importance?

PREVIEW (*continued*)

The Relationship Between Two Ranked Variables: The Spearman Rank-Order Correlation Coefficient

What is the procedure for computing the correlation between two variables when both consist of ranked data? When would you want to compute the Spearman correlation instead of the ordinary Pearson *r*?

What is the procedure for testing the significance of the rank-order correlation coefficient? How does this procedure differ from the significance test for the Pearson *r*?

Summary

Exercises

Thought Questions

Computer Exercises

Bridge to SPSS

Appendix: Equivalence of the Various Formulas for *r*

Introduction

The independent-samples *t* test described in Chapter 7 can be viewed as a test of association between two variables: a categorical (i.e., discrete) grouping variable (e.g., gender) and a continuous dependent variable (e.g., height). This two-group example is just a special case of a more general principle: Knowing an individual's value on one variable can help you to predict his or her value on another, related variable (e.g., knowing someone's gender is helpful if you need to guess that individual's height). In this chapter, we show how you can quantify the degree of the relationship between two continuous variables, and in the next chapter, we show how you can use that relationship to make predictions about the values of one variable given values on the other variable.

For example, you learn early in your scholastic career that the amount of time spent in studying is related to grades. True, there are exceptions. Some students may study for many hours and obtain poor grades, while others may achieve high grades despite short study periods. Nevertheless, the general trend holds. In the majority of cases, you can accurately predict that little or no studying will lead to relatively poor grades, while more studying will result in better grades. So if you are dissatisfied with grades that you feel are too low, one likely way to improve this aspect of your environment is by studying more. In statistical terminology, the two variables of ''hours studying'' and ''grades'' are said to be co-related or *correlated*.

Figure 9.1

**Possible Relationship
Between Income
of a Family and Their
Child's IQ**

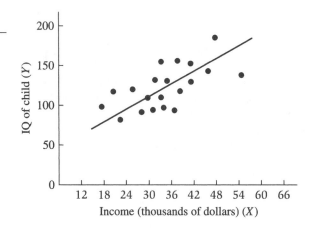

Many pairs of variables are correlated, while many are unrelated or *uncorrelated*. For example, sociologists have found that the incomes of families are positively related to the IQs of the children in the families; the more income, the higher the children's IQs. These variables are said to be **positively correlated**. This relationship is depicted graphically in Figure 9.1, which is called a **scatter plot**. Note that each point on the graph represents two values for one family, income (X variable) and IQ of the child (Y variable). Also, in the case of a positive correlation, the straight line summarizing the points slopes *up* from left to right; as the X values increase in value, so do the Y values. As we discuss later in the chapter, correlation does not imply causation. Therefore, the data presented in Figure 9.1 do not imply that family income directly affects the IQ of children raised in that family.

Golf enthusiasts will readily tell you that the number of years of play is negatively related to their golf score: The more years playing golf, the fewer strokes needed to complete a round of 18 holes. These two variables are said to be **negatively correlated**. (See Figure 9.2.) Notice that in the case of a negative correlation, the straight line summarizing the points slopes *down* from left to right. This "negative slope" indicates that as values on one variable are increasing, values on the other variable are decreasing. Of course, golf scores are getting *better* with more years of play, but *better* golf scores are *lower* golf scores.

This example can also be used to illustrate the importance of choosing your variables carefully. Note that "number of years of play" is a relatively imprecise measure that represents a more specific behavior, perhaps something like experience or practice with golf. Its imprecision can be explored by looking at the two players in our sample who have played about 2.25 years (Figure 9.2). One, we'll call him Dave, is already shooting in the mid-80s—an impressive achievement for such an inexperienced golfer. The other, Sean, is still shooting around 110, much less impressive. You might be tempted, based on this information, to conclude that Dave

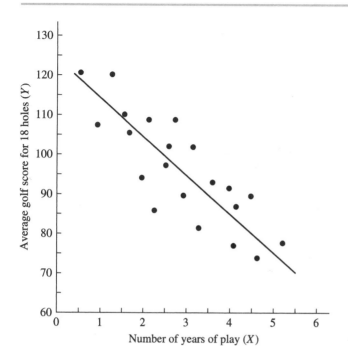

Figure 9.2

Possible Relationship Between Years of Play and Average Golf Score

is a much better athlete than Sean, or perhaps just that he learns sports faster. But if you then discovered that Dave plays 50 rounds of golf each year and Sean plays only 5, then "number of years of play" suddenly seems like a poor proxy for "experience and practice." Dave has played 10 times as much golf as Sean! A more precise version of the predictor variable, such as number of rounds played, would likely tighten the scatter plot around the line and reduce error in prediction. The lesson here is that one should think as precisely as possible about the variables under consideration and choose measures that are as indicative of those variables as possible. Of course, precision can come with a cost; number of shots made (including practice) might be the most precise variable to use in this example. But obtaining number of shots made would be much more tedious than counting the number of rounds played!

A different picture results when two variables are uncorrelated. For example, length of big toes among male adults is uncorrelated with IQ scores, and the corresponding scatter plot is shown in Figure 9.3.

When you can demonstrate that two variables are correlated, you can use the score of an individual on one variable to *predict* or *estimate* her score on the other variable. In Figure 9.2, a fairly accurate prediction of an individual's golf score can be made from the number of years he has played golf. The more closely the two variables are related, the better the prediction is likely to be; if two variables are uncorrelated (as in the case of toe length and IQ), you cannot accurately predict an individual's score on one of them from his score on the other. Thus the concepts of correlation

Figure 9.3

Possible Relationship Between the Length of Big Toe and Male IQ Scores

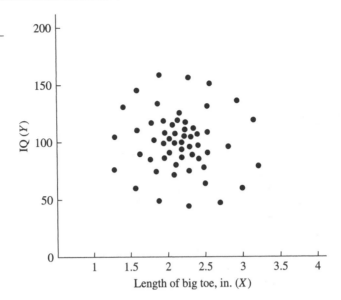

(the topic of this chapter) and the concepts of prediction (the topic of the next chapter) are closely related.

The main topic of this chapter can be divided into two separable aspects: (1) the *description* of the relationship between two variables for a set of observations; (2) making *inferences* about the strength of the relationship between two variables in a population, given the data of a sample. We will deal with one very common kind of relationship between two variables, namely a *linear* or straight-line relationship. That is, if values of one variable are plotted against values of the other variable on a graph, the trend of the plotted points is well represented by a straight line when the relationship is strong. Notice that the data plotted in Figures 9.1 and 9.2 tend to fall near or on the straight line drawn through the scatter plot; this indicates that the two variables in question are highly linearly correlated. The points in Figure 9.3, by contrast, are scattered randomly throughout the graph and cannot be represented well by a straight line. Therefore, these two variables are linearly uncorrelated.

Many pairs of variables that are important to behavioral scientists tend to be linearly related. Although there are many other ways of describing relationships, the linear model is generally the one most frequently used in such fields as psychology, education, and sociology.

Describing the Linear Relationship Between Two Variables

Suppose you want to measure the degree of linear relationship between the scholastic aptitude test (SAT) and college grade point average (GPA). It would be reasonable to expect these two variables to be positively correlated. This means that students with high SAT scores, on average, obtain relatively high GPAs and students with low SAT scores, on average, obtain low GPAs. The phrase "on average" alerts us to the fact that there will be exceptions: Some students with low SAT scores will do very well in college and obtain high GPAs, while some with high SAT scores will do poorly and receive low GPAs. That is, the relationship between SAT scores and GPA is not perfect. Thus the question arises: Just how strong *is* the relationship? How can it be summarized in a single number?

The z Score Product Formula for r

We have seen in Chapter 4 that in order to compare scores on different variables (such as a mathematics test and a psychology test), it is useful to transform the raw scores into standardized scores. These transformed scores allow you to compare paired values directly. For the same reason, to obtain a coefficient of relationship that describes the similarity between paired measures in a single number, it is convenient to transform the raw score into z units.

$$z_X = \frac{X - \mu}{\sigma_X} \quad z_Y = \frac{Y - \mu}{\sigma_Y} \qquad \text{Expressions 9.1A and 9.1B}$$

In Table 9.1, a distribution of SAT scores (X) and GPAs (Y) is presented along with the corresponding descriptive statistics for 25 students at a college in the midwestern United States. (Note that we are using *population* notation with a collection of scores, which could be viewed as either a population or a sample, because our emphasis is on description rather than inference at this point.) The SAT scores were obtained when the students were high school seniors, and the GPAs are those received by the students after 1 year of college. In addition to the raw scores, the z equivalents are also shown in the table. Notice that students with high SAT scores do tend to have high GPAs and consequently both large z_X and z_Y values. Conversely, students with low SAT scores tend to have low GPAs. So the paired z values are similar for most students, and the two variables are therefore highly positively correlated. The *raw scores*, however, need not be numerically similar for any pair, because they are measured in different units for each variable.

If the association between the selected variables was perfect and in a positive direction, each person would have exactly the same z score on both variables (see Figure 9.4A). If the relationship was perfect but in a negative direction, each z_X value would be paired with an identical z_Y value but they would be *opposite in sign* (see Figure 9.4B). These perfect relationships are offered for illustration, but almost never occur in practice.

So, if the pairs of z scores are identical, then we have perfect correlation. But how can we quantify the strength of relationship when correlation is less than perfect? A handy mathematical law states that when you multiply two sets of numbers (say, the z scores for X and Y in Table 9.1), *the sum of the products increases as the similarity of the*

Table 9.1   Raw Scores and z Scores on SAT (X) and GPA (Y) for 25 Students in an Upper Midwestern U.S. College

Student	X	Y	z_X	z_Y
1	650	3.8	1.29	1.67
2	625	3.6	1.08	1.31
3	480	2.8	−.16	−.09
4	440	2.6	−.50	−.44
5	600	3.7	.86	1.49
6	220	1.2	−2.37	−2.89
7	640	2.2	1.21	−1.14
8	725	3.0	1.93	.26
9	520	3.1	.18	.44
10	480	3.0	−.16	.26
11	370	2.8	−1.09	−.09
12	320	2.7	−1.52	−.26
13	425	2.6	−.62	−.44
14	475	2.6	−.20	−.44
15	490	3.1	−.07	.44
16	620	3.8	1.04	1.67
17	340	2.4	−1.35	−.79
18	420	2.9	−.67	.09
19	480	2.8	−.16	−.09
20	530	3.2	.27	.61
21	680	3.2	1.55	.61
22	420	2.4	−.67	−.79
23	490	2.8	−.07	−.09
24	500	1.9	.01	−1.67
25	520	3.0	.18	.26
	$\mu = 498.4$	$\mu = 2.85$	$\sigma_x = 117.3$	$\sigma_y = .57$

items in each pair increases (i.e., large scores on one variable paired with large scores on the other variable, and low scores paired with low scores). The highest sum of products occurs when the numbers in each pair are identical. We can use this law, in light of the fact that higher correlation involves similar z scores, to create a measure of correlation, beginning like this:

$$\sum z_X z_Y \qquad \text{Expression 9.2}$$

The larger this sum, relative to the number of products, the stronger the correlation. We can divide Expression 9.2 by the number of pairs of scores to take into account the number of products. The result is the average of the products of the z scores. That average turns out to be an excellent measure of correlation. It was first devised by Karl Pearson more than 100 years ago, so it is called **Pearson's correlation coefficient**, r:

$$r = \frac{\sum z_X z_Y}{N} \qquad \text{Formula 9.1}$$

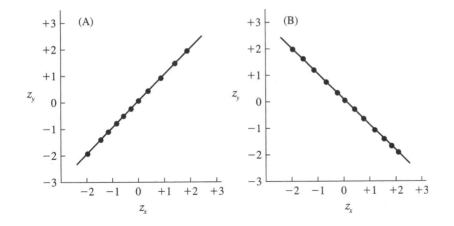

Figure 9.4

**Perfect Linear
Relationship Between
Two Variables:
(A) Perfect Positive
Linear Relationship;
(B) Perfect Negative
Linear Relationship**

As we've seen, when correlation is positive and perfect, z_x and z_y are always identical, so the cross product in every case becomes z-squared:

$$\frac{\sum z_X^2}{N}$$

Expression 9.3

Does this expression look familiar at all? You may not have noticed it, but Expression 9.3 is equivalent to the equation for the *variance of a set of z scores*! Recall the formula for the variance:

$$\sigma^2 = \frac{\sum (X_i - \mu)^2}{N}$$

Formula 3.2

If we express this formula in terms of z scores, then we replace the X scores with z scores, and the mean of the X scores with the mean of the z scores. You may recall from Chapter 4 that the mean of a set of z scores is always zero, so that term is dropped and we end up with Expression 9.4:

$$\sigma_z^2 = \frac{\sum (z_i - \mu_z)^2}{N} = \frac{\sum z^2}{N} = r$$

Expression 9.4

As we saw in Chapter 4, the variance of a set of z scores is always 1.0, so we have shown that when correlation is perfectly positive, Pearson r must also equal +1.0. When correlation is not perfect, some cross products will be negative and others positive; if the negatives balance out the positives perfectly, then r will equal zero. Otherwise, you'll get some value between +1.0 and −1.0.

Computing Formulas for *r*

The preceding procedure for obtaining r, although helpful for understanding the meaning of r, is much too tedious computationally. (Proofs of the equivalence for various formulas for r are given in the appendix at the end of this chapter.) We can avoid the necessity for converting to z values by rewriting Formula 9.1 as:

$$r = \frac{\sum (X - \mu_X)(Y - \mu_Y)}{N\sigma_X\sigma_Y} \qquad \text{Expression 9.5}$$

Expression 9.5 can be rearranged algebraically to produce the following convenient *raw-score formula* for the Pearson correlation coefficient:

$$r = \frac{\dfrac{\sum XY}{N} - \mu_X\mu_Y}{\sigma_X\sigma_Y}, \qquad \text{Formula 9.2}$$

where N is the number of *pairs* of observations (i.e., the number of cases).

The numerator of this formula (the average of the raw-score cross-products minus the cross product of the two averages) is called the *covariance*. When relatively large scores on one variable are paired with relatively large scores on the other, and small scores with small scores, the average of the cross products tends to be larger than the cross product of the averages, producing a positive covariance and therefore a positive correlation. When relatively large scores on one variable are paired with relatively small scores on the other, this relationship is reversed, leading to a negative covariance and therefore a negative correlation. When scores are paired randomly, the two parts of the numerator of r tend to be about the same, leading to a covariance and an r that are near zero.

The calculation of Pearson r for the SAT and GPA data in Table 9.1, using both the raw-score and z product formulas, is shown in Table 9.2. Note that the discrepancy in the results of these two formulas (.64 for raw scores versus .65 for z products) is due to rounding off the means and standard deviations in Table 9.1, which were then used in the calculations in Table 9.2. The raw-score formula is only as accurate as the number of digits you retain for the means and standard deviations (SDs) of the two variables.

An important limitation of Formula 9.2 is that it is based on using the biased SDs in its denominator (it is necessary to use the biased SDs, because the numerator, as calculated in Formula 9.2, is a *biased* estimate of the covariance), and it is more likely that you will have calculated the unbiased SDs if you were thinking of drawing inferences from your data. So, if you want to use s's rather than σ's in the denominator of the raw-score formula, because you have those measures handy, the bias of the covariance in the numerator must be corrected. The resulting formula is not as neat as Formula 9.2, but it always gives the same answer for r (except for any differences in rounding off):

$$r = \frac{\dfrac{1}{N-1}\left[\sum XY - N\overline{X}\,\overline{Y}\right]}{s_X s_Y} \qquad \text{Formula 9.3}$$

Notice that in going from Formula 9.2 to 9.3, we not only changed the σ's to s's, we also changed the μ's to $\overline{X}$ and $\overline{Y}$. Even though μ_X and $\overline{X}$, for

Table 9.2   Calculation of Pearson Correlation Coefficient Between SAT (X) and GPA (Y) by the Raw Score and z Product Methods

Subject	Raw-score method			z product method		
	X	Y	XY	z_x	z_y	$z_x z_y$
1	650	3.8	2470	1.29	1.67	2.1543
2	625	3.6	2250	1.08	1.31	1.4148
3	480	2.8	1344	−.16	−.09	.0144
4	440	2.6	1144	−.50	−.44	.2200
5	600	3.7	2220	.86	1.49	1.2814
6	220	1.2	264	−2.37	−2.89	6.8493
7	640	2.2	1408	1.21	−1.14	−1.3794
8	725	3.0	2175	1.93	.26	.5018
9	520	3.1	1612	.18	.44	.0792
10	480	3.0	1440	−.16	.26	−.0416
11	370	2.8	1036	−1.09	−.09	.0981
12	320	2.7	864	−1.52	−.26	.3952
13	425	2.6	1105	−.62	−.44	.2728
14	475	2.6	1235	−.20	−.44	.0880
15	490	3.1	1519	−.07	.44	−.0308
16	620	3.8	2356	1.04	1.67	1.7368
17	340	2.4	816	−1.35	−.79	1.0665
18	420	2.9	1218	−.67	.09	−.0603
19	480	2.8	1344	−.16	−.09	.0144
20	530	3.2	1696	.27	.61	.1647
21	680	3.2	2176	1.55	.61	.9455
22	420	2.4	1008	−.67	−.79	.5293
23	490	2.8	1372	−.07	−.09	.0063
24	500	1.9	950	.01	−1.67	−.0167
25	520	3.0	1560	.18	−.26	.0468

$$\sum X = 12{,}460 \quad \mu_x = 498.4$$

$$\sum Y = 71.2 \quad \mu_y = 2.85$$

$$\sum z_X z_Y = 16.35$$

$$\sum XY = 36{,}582 \quad N = 25$$

$$N = 25$$

$$r = \frac{\dfrac{\sum XY}{N} - \mu_x \mu_y}{\sigma_X \sigma_Y} = \frac{\dfrac{36{,}582}{25} - (498.4)(2.85)}{(117.33)(.57)}$$

$$r = \frac{\sum z_X z_Y}{N}$$

$$= \frac{1{,}463.28 - 1{,}420.44}{66.8781} = \frac{42.84}{66.8781}$$

$$= \frac{16.35}{25}$$

$$= +.64$$

$$= +.65$$

Figure 9.5

Scatter Plot for Data in Table 9.1 ($r = +.65$)

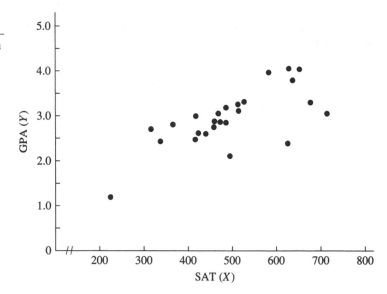

instance, are computed in exactly the same way, we think it is important to use the $\overline{X}$ symbol as a reminder whenever you are treating your data as a sample of a larger population of interest.

The obtained value of .65 indicates that for this group of 25 students, there is a fairly high positive correlation between these two variables. (In fact, this value is higher than most correlations that you would get in the behavioral sciences, unless you are measuring essentially the *same* variable in two different ways.) A scatter plot of the data in Table 9.1 is shown in Figure 9.5.

The Before–After Heart Rate Example

In Chapter 7 we mentioned that the larger the correlation between two sets of scores, the more the denominator of the matched-pairs t formula decreases relative to the denominator of the independent-samples test. As another example of calculating r, let us see just how large the correlation is between the baseline and prequiz heart rates of the 10 students from Ihno's data set, whose data were used in Table 7.2. Because we have already calculated the s's (and not the σ's) for these data in Chapter 7, we will use the Pearson r formula that is based on the unbiased standard deviations.

$$r = \frac{\frac{1}{N-1}\left(\sum XY - N\overline{X}\,\overline{Y}\right)}{s_X s_Y} = \frac{\frac{1}{9}[50{,}553 - 10(68.0)(74.0)]}{(4.472)(8.59)}$$

$$= \frac{\frac{1}{9}(50{,}553 - 50{,}320)}{38.414} = 25.889/38.414 = .674$$

Once you have calculated r for a set of paired scores, you can use an alternative formula for the matched-pairs t test that is based on r. This formula is not really easier to use than the one we introduced in Chapter 7, but it is instructive to see how it uses the Pearson r to obtain its result. This formula, applied to the heart rate data, yields the following value for t:

$$t = \frac{\overline{X}_1 - \overline{X}_2}{\sqrt{\dfrac{s_1^2 + s_2^2}{n} - \dfrac{2rs_1s_2}{n}}} = \frac{74 - 68}{\sqrt{\dfrac{20 + 73.79}{10} - \dfrac{2(.674)(4.472)(8.59)}{10}}}$$

$$= \frac{6}{\sqrt{9.379 - 5.178}} = \frac{6}{2.05} = 2.93$$

Note that this alternative formula always yields the same t value as the formula for difference scores. However, an inspection of the alternative formula reveals an important principle: As Pearson's r increases (all else remaining the same), a larger portion is subtracted from the denominator, making the t value larger. When r is zero, the second term in the denominator drops out and you are left with the equal-N formula for the independent-samples t test. Also note that a Pearson r does not have to be large or statistically significant to be helpful. Moreover, a large, statistically significant r certainly does not guarantee a significant matched-pairs t test. The difference between the two means in the numerator can override either a small or large denominator to determine whether the matched-pairs t test will reach statistical significance.

Interpreting the Magnitude of a Pearson r

A correlation coefficient is a useful way to summarize the relationship between two variables with a single number that falls between -1 and 1. However, any one statistic that is used to summarize a whole set of data is bound to have its limitations, and this is certainly true for Pearson's r. A small value for r, especially one that is much smaller than expected, should never be interpreted without looking at the corresponding scatter plot. We will point out several problems to look for when r is small, but first we must caution you about a potential fallacy that is particularly tempting when the magnitude of r is relatively large.

Correlation and Causation

Several cautions should be noted at this point. You may have heard the expression, "Correlation does not imply causation." We will not disagree with this statement (after all, we made it ourselves just a few pages ago), but we would like to clarify its meaning. People often misunderstand this claim as referring to a characteristic of statistical tests, as in "If you analyze your data using a measure of correlation, you cannot make causal claims about the effects of X on Y." In fact, it is not the statistical methods you use that determine whether you can make causal conclusions from your results, it is your research design that sets the limits on causal inference. In particular, random assignment to groups (or different levels of your independent variable) is the key to a true experimental design that permits causal inferences. If you have randomly assigned your participants to groups, then you can infer causality (assuming that you have done everything else properly); if you have not performed the random assignment, then you cannot.[1]

Most commonly, correlation coefficients are computed between two quantitative dependent variables, both of which are measured on the same randomly (or more often conveniently) selected participants. However, let us consider the case in which you have a truly independent variable with quantitative levels. For example, imagine that you have randomly assigned participants to different amounts of your independent variable (e.g., number of therapy sessions per week, 0, 1, 2, 3, 4, 5) and then measured your participants' improvement on a dependent variable (e.g., level of neurosis) at the end of the experiment. In this case, a significant correlation coefficient computed between your independent variable and your dependent variable *does* allow you to determine that the variance in X *caused* at least some of the variance in Y. (For this example, you could conclude that different amounts of therapy *caused* different amounts of improvement in neurosis.)

By comparison, consider what this study might look like if you did not use random assignment. For instance, you might have created two groups based on how often your participants were already going to therapy ("frequent" and "infrequent") and then performed a t-test to compare the change in levels of neurotic symptoms after a given period of time. In this case, a significant t value *does not* permit you to claim that the frequency of therapy visits is causally related to any changes in neurotic symptoms. Note that the key difference is that in this second version of the study, the participants were not randomly assigned to be in the frequent or infrequent groups; they were already in their "group" based on their own reasons for how often they wanted to go to therapy. The problem, in terms of determining causation, is that maybe it was one of their "own reasons" that was causing the effect. That is, perhaps there is something about people who go to therapy more often (e.g., more disposable income) that is accounting for the difference in improvement in neurosis. If you did not assign your participants to particular amounts of therapy per week anyway, you probably would have been better off just computing the correlation between amounts of therapy and amounts of improvement, rather than arbitrarily classifying

---

[1]There are sophisticated new methods (e.g., Structural Equation Modeling) that can help establish the direction of causality among observed variables without random assignment, but random assignment is always preferable when possible, as it allows more definitive conclusions concerning causation.

your participants into two groups. Your correlation coefficient might have a somewhat better chance of reaching statistical significance than the t test, because it contains more quantitative information, but neither a significant correlation nor a significant t test would allow you to make a causal inference without assigning your participants to different amounts of therapy.

In sum, it is the design of the study that determines whether causality can be inferred, not the statistical methods you use. As we have just shown, you could use random assignment and infer causation with a significant correlation coefficient, or use previously existing groups with a t-test and not be able to make such an inference. Therefore, "correlation" in the expression "Correlation does not imply causation" refers to the correlational (i.e., observational, rather than experimental) design of the study and not to the type of statistics used to analyze the data.

A second point is that, depending on the situation, it can be more or less difficult to resist making causal inferences from large correlations. On one hand, you may have heard well-known examples of bizarre correlations, such as the positive relationship between the volume of ice cream sold and the murder rate in New York City, or a similar relationship between life expectancy and the number of clocks in one's home in medieval Europe. In these cases, it is not particularly tempting to infer that ice cream is setting New Yorkers off on murder sprees or that clocks somehow extended one's time on earth, in addition to measuring it. Instead, it is relatively easy to imagine that in each case a third variable was affecting both of the two variables that exhibited such a surprising relationship (e.g., heat had been affecting both ice cream consumption and the murder rate; wealth affected both longevity and the ownership of clocks).

On the other hand, however, you will encounter correlational results that will be truly difficult to resist. In some cases, the difficulty may be due to the fact that the X variable is indeed causally related to the Y variable, even though the correlational nature of the study does not warrant that conclusion. A classic example of this situation arose with the relationship between cigarette smoking and lung cancer in the 1960s. Mountains of evidence suggested a strong correlational relationship between the two, but because the appropriate experiment could not be conducted (ethically), cigarette companies were able to claim, correctly, that there was no scientific evidence demonstrating a causal connection between cigarette smoking and lung cancer. (Is it not obvious why the critical experiment could not be done ethically?) When researchers finally randomly assigned rats to "smoke" cigarettes, they were able to establish a definitive casual connection between smoking and cancer, but strictly speaking, only for rats. A leap still had to be made to assume that rats are similar enough to humans biologically that the same causal connection between smoking and cancer could be applied to humans.

The relationship between cigarette smoking and lung cancer exemplifies cases in which it is difficult to resist the correlation-causation inference largely because there is such a plausible mechanism connecting the two variables (e.g., various chemicals in the cigarette smoke are making direct contact with the tissue inside a smoker's lungs). But by far the more insidious case, and therefore the one that is of most concern to teachers of research methods and statistics, occurs when the correlation between two variables appears to confirm a previously held belief, theory, stereotype, or prejudice. Once people develop a "rooting interest" in an outcome, it can be astonishingly difficult for them to accept that correlational results only indicate that some relationship exists between the two variables, but that we cannot tell whether X is causing Y, Y is causing X, or some third variable is affecting both. Good scientific education—including basic knowledge of statistics—is our best hope for combating these problematic shortcuts in the thinking process.

Correlation and Restriction of Range

Another important caution has to do with the effect of the variability of the scores on the correlation coefficient. Suppose you calculate the correlation between achievement test scores and elementary school grades for public school children in New York City. You will probably find a strong linear trend when the data are plotted. But what if you were to calculate the correlation between the same two variables for a group of children in a class for the highly gifted? Here, the range of scores on both variables is considerably narrowed, as is shown in Figure 9.6. Because of this, the correlation between the two variables is markedly reduced. (You can see that the points do not line up nicely within the gray box in Figure 9.6.)

It is much harder to make fine discriminations among cases that are nearly equal on the variables in question than it is to make discriminations among cases that differ widely. More specifically, it is difficult to predict whether a gifted child will be an A or A− student. It is much easier to distinguish among a broad range of A to F students. Thus, *when the variability of scores is restricted* on either or both of two variables, the correlation between them usually decreases in absolute value.

Figure 9.6

Effect of Restriction of Range on the Correlation Coefficient

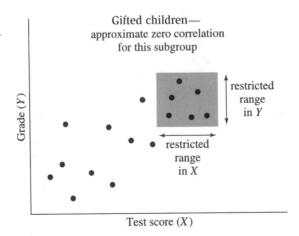

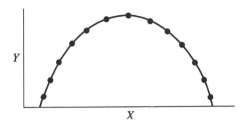

Figure 9.7

Example of Perfect Relationship Between Two Variables Where $r = 0$

Correlation and Nonlinear Relationships

Pearson r detects only linear relationships. Thus, when r turns out to be surprisingly small, the possibility remains that the two variables are related, even closely related, but not in a linear fashion. Indeed, it is possible for two variables to be perfectly related yet to have an r equal to zero. In Figure 9.7, for example, you can predict Y without error given X, but *not* linearly.

The *curvilinear relationship* depicted in Figure 9.7 represents an exception to the usual situation in which restricting the range of either or both of the variables reduces the magnitude of their linear correlation. In this example, restricting the range of X to values that are to the left of the center would result in a fairly high positive correlation, whereas restricting X to values to the right of the center would yield an equally strong negative correlation. When X is not restricted, the correlations for each half of the range of X average out to an r near zero. Looking for evidence of a curvilinear relationship is another good reason for inspecting the scatter plot that corresponds to a correlation in which you are interested, especially if the Pearson r is considerably lower than you expected it to be.

Correlation and Bivariate Outliers

Yet another important caution regarding the interpretation of a Pearson's r concerns the disproportionate effect that a single case can have on r if that case represents a *bivariate outlier*. To illustrate this effect, we have reproduced Figure 9.5 as Figure 9.8 with one important difference: We changed the GPA of the student with the highest SAT score (725) from 3.0 to 1.0. A glance at Figure 9.8 makes it easy to identify this case as a bivariate outlier. A case need not be very extreme on either variable to be a bivariate outlier, as long as that case represents an unusual combination of values (e.g., a 6-foot 4-inch man who weighs 140 pounds). Changing the GPA of this one particular student results in the Pearson r decreasing from .65 to .324. One of the main reasons for creating a scatter plot of your data is to look for such cases.

Bivariate outliers are often, but not always, due to mistakes in recording or entering the data, or to special circumstances involving the participant in question. For example, on further investigation you might discover that the student with the 725 SAT score got a 1.0 GPA because

Figure 9.8

Scatter Plot for Data in Table 9.1 ($r = +.324$) With One Data Point Moved to Create a Bivariate Outlier

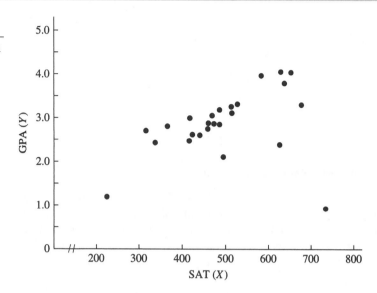

he or she fell ill that semester and decided to "tough it out" instead of taking a medical leave of absence. It is acceptable to remove an outlier from your data when you find an objective reason to do so (e.g., you know that a participant was confused about the experiment's instructions), but it is certainly not acceptable to discard a data point merely because it *is* a bivariate outlier and discarding it would move the statistical results in the direction of your research hypothesis. Note that a single data point can also increase the magnitude of r a great deal; without the student who obtained a 1.2 GPA and scored 220 on his or her SAT, the correlation calculated in Table 9.2 would have been only .25 for the remaining 24 students. Later in this chapter we introduce a version of correlation, called Spearman's rank-order correlation, which is much less influenced by extreme scores. If bivariate outliers are a problem in your data set, you should seriously consider Spearman correlation as a substitute for Pearson's r.

When Is It Important That Pearson's r Be Large?

In the next section, we discuss how to determine whether the r for a sample differs significantly from zero. However, there are a number of important uses for r for which a fairly small r, even if statistically significant at a tiny alpha level (e.g., .001), would be quite disappointing. These include measures of reliability and validity, as discussed in the following paragraphs.

Reliability

The simplest form of reliability involves measuring participants twice with the same scale (often in the form of a self-report questionnaire), always with the (approximately) same time interval between the two measurements. The Pearson r between these two sets of measurements is a measure of **test-retest reliability**. When measuring some trait that is expected to be stable over time (e.g., spatial aptitude, degree of introversion), a scale should have a test-retest reliability that is at least about .7. Otherwise, it would seem that the scale is not measuring the trait in question reliably enough to be trusted. Often, researchers will then modify the scale in an attempt to improve its reliability.

Another commonly used measure of reliability involves the *internal consistency* of the scale. One way to assess this attribute of a scale is to average all of the odd-numbered items together to create an "odd" score and, in an analogous fashion, create an "even" score. The Pearson r between the odd and even scores across all participants is a measure of the scale's **split-half reliability**—an indication of the degree to which the scale is measuring only one distinct trait. However, in the past couple of decades computers have made it easy to calculate more sophisticated measures of a scale's internal consistency (e.g., *Cronbach's alpha*).

Sometimes measurements are necessarily subjective but are not based on self-reports. For instance, the dependent variable in a study could be the creativity exhibited by a child's painting. To be sure that such a quality can be measured reliably, it is necessary that the measurements of two raters—acting without knowledge of each other—be highly correlated. A low correlation would call into question whether this quality can be measured reliably and would likely spur attempts to use better methods of training to increase the **interrater reliability** of the scale. High interrater reliability can also be important when preparing stimuli for an experiment. A common example is rating the attractiveness of yearbook photos so that the attractiveness of the photo can be controlled on any given trial by the experimenter. Without a high degree of interrater reliability, the experimenter cannot trust the attractiveness ratings of the photo stimuli. (If the raters find it too difficult to assign creativity or attractiveness scores but can place the paintings or photos in rank order, a nonparametric measure of correlation can be used, as described in the last part of this chapter.)

Validity

Once the reliability of a measurement scale has been established—that is, we know that the scale measures just *one* quality and does so in a stable, reproducible fashion—our attention would turn to establishing whether our scale is measuring what we think it is measuring. For example, items in a questionnaire are often chosen for their obvious **face** (or content) **validity**, but then it is important to confirm these choices by using some objective criteria. One possible goal for a new scale is to measure some human trait in a way that is quicker, less expensive, or more convenient when compared to some well-established measure. In order to replace a traditional scale, a high Pearson r needs to be found between the new and old scales after both are administered to the same set of participants. We do not expect such a measure of **criterion validity** to be larger than the reliability of the new scale, but it should approach that magnitude.

When trying to measure a quality for which no traditional scale exists, a desirable way to establish criterion validity involves correlating the new scale (after establishing its reliability) with some objective measure of actual behavior, if possible. For example, a new scale for measuring generosity could be validated by asking participants (who had already filled out the generosity questionnaire in some different, unrelated context) to contribute their time to some future experiment or to give back part of the money they were given for their participation so that "additional participants could be recruited after the grant runs out." We would not expect our new scale's correlation with an objective criterion to be larger than .7, as we would expect for a reliability measure. But we would not be satisfied merely to draw conclusions based on a significance test of whether Pearson r is zero or not. By contrast, when investigating the relationship between two variables that are not obviously connected, except on the basis of the researcher's theory, statistical significance can be very encouraging. We turn to this topic next.

Testing the Significance of the Correlation Coefficient

The correlation coefficient of .65 for the group of 25 students whose scores are shown in Table 9.1 conveniently describes the linear relationship between SAT scores and GPA *for this group*. It would be useful to know, however, whether these two variables are correlated in the population of all students. To answer this question, we must draw an inference about likely values of the **population correlation coefficient** (symbolized by rho, ρ). Is it likely that there is actually no correlation in the population and that the correlation in the sample of 25 students was due to sampling error (the cases that happened to wind up in the sample)? Or is the value of .65 large enough for us to conclude that there is some nonzero positive correlation between SAT scores and GPA in the population? The strategy for testing hypotheses about likely values of ρ is similar to that used in previous chapters. The null hypothesis most often tested is that ρ is equal to zero:[2]

$$H_0: \rho = 0$$

$$H_A: \rho \neq 0$$

A criterion of significance, such as the .05 or .01 criterion, is selected. The correct statistical model to use in this situation is the t distribution, so the

---

[2]Other null hypotheses are possible, but a different statistical procedure is required in order to test them. See, for example, B. H. Cohen (2008), pp. 281–282.

critical value for t can be found with degrees of freedom (df) equal to $N - 2$. Then H_0 is retained if the computed t is less than or equal to the critical value of t from the t table. Otherwise, H_0 is rejected in favor of H_A, and r is said to be *significantly different from zero* (or, simply, *statistically significant*).

Fortunately, you do not need to compute the t ratio[3] for testing Pearson's r. This has (in a sense) already been done for you by statisticians who have constructed tables of significant (i.e., *critical*) values of r. Therefore, the procedure for testing a correlation coefficient for statistical significance can be quite simple: You compare your computed value of r to the value of r shown in Table C in the Appendix at the end of the book for $N - 2$ df, where N is equal to the number of pairs. If the absolute value of your computed r is smaller than or equal to the tabled value, retain H_0; otherwise, reject H_0.

As an illustration, suppose that you wish to test the significance of the correlation between SAT scores and GPAs, using $\alpha = .05$. Referring to Table C, you find that for $25 - 2$ or 23 df, the smallest absolute value of r that is statistically significant is .396. Since the obtained r of .65 exceeds this value, you reject H_0 and conclude that there *is* a positive correlation in the population from which the sample of 25 students was randomly selected. Note that a correlation of $-.65$ would indicate a statistically significant negative relationship; due to the symmetry of the t distribution, the sign of r can be ignored when comparing the computed r to the critical value of r. Thus the test described is the usual two-tailed test — it guards against chance departures of r from zero in either the positive or negative direction.

As we observed in Chapters 6 and 7, confidence intervals provide valuable additional information about the probable values of a population parameter. However, the procedures for calculating confidence intervals for correlation coefficients are beyond the scope of this book (see B. H. Cohen, 2008, pp. 280–281).

Implications of Rejecting H$_0$

If a Pearson r is statistically significant, the significance denotes *some* degree of linear relationship between the two variables in the population. It does *not* denote a "significantly high" or "significantly strong" relationship; it just means that the relationship in the population seems unlikely to be zero.

---

[3]The formula for the t ratio to test the significance of a Pearson r is

$$t = \frac{r\sqrt{N - 2}}{\sqrt{1 - r^2}}$$

where $N =$ number of *pairs* of scores.

By inspecting Table C, you can see that the larger the sample size, the smaller the absolute value of the correlation coefficient that is needed for statistical significance. For example, for $N = 12$ ($df = 10$), a correlation larger than .576 is needed for significance using the .05 criterion. For $N = 102$ ($df = 100$), a correlation of only .196 or larger is needed. This implies that the importance of obtaining statistical significance can easily be exaggerated. Suppose that for a very large sample (say, $N = 1,000$), a statistically significant Pearson r of .08 is obtained. This statistical test suggests that ρ is greater than zero. But the obtained r of .08 is so close to zero that the relationship in the population, although not zero and not necessarily equal to .08, is likely to be *very* weak (i.e., likely to be quite close to .08) — too weak, in fact, to allow you to make any accurate statements about one variable based on knowledge of the other. Consequently, such a finding would add little or nothing to our practical knowledge, even though it is statistically significant. (It might conceivably be useful in appraising a theory.) Therefore, you need to have *both* statistical significance *and* a reasonably high absolute value of r before you can conclude that ρ is large enough to be useful in applied work.

Correlation coefficients *cannot* be interpreted as percents. For example, you *cannot* conclude that a correlation of .60 is 60% of a perfect relationship, or that it is twice as much as a correlation of .30. As we will see in the next chapter, however, the *squared* correlation coefficient (r^2) does permit an interpretation, in percentage terms, of the strength of the relationship between the two variables.

As usual, when H_0 is true, the probability of erroneously rejecting it (a Type I error) is equal to the criterion of significance that is selected. Using $\alpha = .05$, when H_0 is true, you will, nonetheless, reject it 5% of the time.

Assumptions Underlying the Use of r

A common assumption underlying the use of the Pearson r is that X and Y are linearly related. If X and Y have a curvilinear relationship (as in Figure 9.7), the Pearson r will not detect it. Pearson's r can be calculated, of course, whether or not the best-fitting function is linear. Ordinarily, however, one would not be interested in the best linear fit when it is known that the relationship is not linear.

Otherwise, no assumptions are made at all in using r to *describe* the degree of linear relationship between two variables for a given set of data. When testing a correlation coefficient for statistical significance, it is, strictly speaking, assumed that the underlying distribution is the so-called bivariate normal — that is, scores on Y are normally distributed for each value of X, and scores on X are normally distributed for each value of Y. However, when the degrees of freedom are greater than 25 or 30, failure to meet this assumption has little consequence for the validity of the test, unless your data contain some extreme bivariate outliers — in which case an even larger sample may be required for an accurate significance test.

The Relationship Between Two Ranked Variables: The Spearman Rank-Order Correlation Coefficient

As we saw with the rank-sum and Wilcoxon matched-pairs tests in the previous chapter, there are times when the assumptions of our parametric tests are not close to being met and we need to consider other options. We now turn our attention to the ordinal alternative to the Pearson r, which is called the **Spearman rank-order correlation coefficient**, symbolized as r_S.[4] As in the case with other ordinal tests, r_S is commonly used when a dependent variable has been measured precisely, but its distribution makes the use of parametric tests questionable, and the sample size is not large. Even if only one of the two variables that you are correlating (e.g., IQ and annual income) seems to violate the distributional assumptions of parametric tests, both variables must be converted to ranks in order to calculate r_S. You *cannot* replace one variable with ranks and correlate it with the raw scores of the other variable, and obtain a meaningful correlation.

Rationale and Computational Procedures

Suppose you wish to determine the relationship between the IQ scores and incomes of 10 entrepreneurs (as in Table 9.3). The income values are extremely skewed, while the IQ scores appear to have a normal distribution. To compute r_S (by hand) you must rank order *both* income *and* IQ. The entrepreneur with the lowest IQ gets a rank of 1 for IQ, the next to lowest is assigned the rank of 2, and so on. These ranks then replace the original IQ scores, which are no longer used. The same procedure is used to determine rank order by income. Finally, r_S is calculated by applying any formula for the Pearson r to the *ranks* rather than to the original scores.

To make sure that your ranks are properly paired, you can start by listing your participants (in any order), along with their scores on both variables. Then list the participants in IQ order separately, and assign ranks. Next to each IQ score in the original table, write the appropriate rank. Again in a separate place, list the participants in order by income and assign ranks, and then write each participant's income rank next to his or her income in the original table (see Table 9.3). You can then apply any Pearson r formula to the two sets of ranks or use a shortcut formula for r_S after calculating the difference for each pair of ranks and then summing the squared differences, as shown in Table 9.3.

---

[4]The Greek letter rho, ρ, is also commonly used to designate the rank-order correlation coefficient. In order to avoid confusion between this statistic and the population parameter for the Pearson correlation coefficient, which is also symbolized by rho, we will use r_S for the Spearman coefficient.

Table 9.3 Ten Entrepreneurs Both Measured and Ranked for IQ and for Annual Income (1 = Least, 10 = Most)

Entrepreneur's first name	IQ score	Ranks for IQ	Annual income (in thousands of dollars)	Ranks for income	D $(X - Y)$	D^2 $(X - Y)^2$
John	108	3	97	4	−1	1
Joseph	107	2	72	1	1	1
Martha	114	5	223	6	−1	1
William	124	9	255	7	2	4
Robert	98	1	88	3	−2	4
Sophia	132	10	974	10	0	0
Donald	120	8	650	9	−1	1
Manuel	113	4	85	2	2	4
Richard	117	7	148	5	2	4
Nancy	115	6	403	8	−2	4
						$\sum D^2 = 24$

The shortcut formula for the Spearman correlation coefficient is:

$$r_s = 1 - \frac{6 \sum D^2}{N(N^2 - 1)} \qquad \text{Formula 9.4}$$

where

D = difference between a pair of ranks
N = number of pairs

If you applied one of the formulas for the Pearson r (as described earlier in this chapter) to rank-order data by simply treating the ranks as raw scores, and if there were no tied ranks, you would get exactly the same value for r_S as you would get from Formula 9.4. (The shortcut formula for r_S takes advantage of certain relationships that hold when the N scores are just the integers from 1 to N.)

Like r, then, r_S varies between −1.0 and 1.0. A high positive value of r_S indicates a strong tendency for the paired ranks to be equal. Conversely, a high negative value of r_S indicates a strong tendency for the paired ranks to be opposite, as would occur if entrepreneurs with the higher ranks for IQ were to have the lower ranks for income. A zero value would indicate no relationship between the two sets of ranks.

In our example, the calculation of ΣD^2 is shown in Table 9.3; r_S is equal to:

$$r_s = 1 - \frac{6(24)}{10(10^2 - 1)}$$

$$= 1 - \frac{144}{990}$$

$$= 1 - .15$$

$$= .85$$

Dealing With Tied Ranks

In the preceding example, if Joseph and John were equal in IQ, both would share second place. This would be expressed numerically by *averaging* the two ranks in question and assigning this average as the rank of each person, just as was done in the ordinal tests described in the previous chapter. The ranks in question are 2 and 3, so the average of these ranks, or 2.5, is the rank that would be given to both John and Joseph, and the next entrepreneur would receive a rank of 4. When there are tied ranks, Formula 9.4 will overestimate the absolute value of r_S. But unless there are many ties, and particularly long ties (i.e., three- or more-way ties), this overestimate is likely to be trivial (less than .01 or .02).

Testing the Significance of the Rank-Order Correlation Coefficient

Although the formula for r_S and the formula for the Pearson r yield the same numerical result in the absence of tied ranks, the significance of the two coefficients *cannot* be tested in the same manner when N is fairly small (especially when it is less than 10). To test the null hypothesis that the ranks are independent in the population from which the sample was drawn, you can use Table I in the Appendix at the end of the book. The minimum values of r_S needed for statistical significance are shown in the table for values of N from 5 to 30. (Note that when using this table, you need only refer to N—the number of pairs of ranks—rather than degrees of freedom.)

To use Table I for the problem involving the data in Table 9.3, you would look up the minimum value necessary for r_S to be statistically significant when $N = 10$. Using the two-tailed .05 criterion, this value is .648. Since the absolute value of the obtained r_S(.85) is greater than the tabled value, you can reject H_0 and conclude that there is a nonzero relationship between the two sets of ranks in the population.

When N is greater than 30, the critical values for testing a Pearson r for statistical significance will give a very good approximation. That is, you can refer the computed Spearman correlation coefficient to Table C in the Appendix with $N - 2$ degrees of freedom.

This test of significance is not, in general, as *powerful* as the test for the Pearson r. That is, it is *not* as likely to detect nonzero relationships. The situation reverses, however, when one of a pair of variables is substantially skewed; transformation into ranks followed by the computation of r_S may well provide a better and more powerful measure of their correlation than the Pearson r computed on the original data. This is the case for the data in Table 9.3. If you calculate the Pearson r for the raw IQ and income scores, you will see that it equals .78, which is less than r_S(.85).

When to Use the Spearman Correlation Coefficient

In some instances the data for both of your variables may be in the form of ranks. Suppose that you wish to determine whether the creativity of abstract paintings can be judged in a reliable way. You ask two art instructors to independently rank the same 10 paintings in order of the creativity they express. The Pearson r for these two sets of ranks *is* a Spearman correlation coefficient (by definition), and therefore its critical value may be found in Table I (unless the number of rank-ordered paintings grows larger than 30). Even if only one of the two variables has been measured ordinally (e.g., you are correlating the creativity ranks from the first art instructor with the price being asked for each painting), it is necessary to compute r_S, so you will have to convert the measurements on the second variable to ranks before computing the correlation.

If both variables have been measured on interval/ratio scales and you are worried about the distribution of both variables in the population—or even just one of them, as in the IQ/income example—both sets of measurements should be converted to ranks and r_S should be computed. Even if each variable follows an approximately normal distribution, if the relationship between them follows a monotonic curve (e.g., the curve begins steeply and then levels off but never reverses its direction) rather than a straight line, the Pearson r of the ranks (i.e., r_S) will be larger than the Pearson r of the raw scores. This is true because r_S measures the degree to which the relationship of two variables is monotonic, whereas the Pearson r applied to the raw scores measures the degree to which the relationship conforms to a single, straight line.

Even when you have interval data that are normally distributed for both variables, Spearman correlation can be a good alternative to Pearson's if you have outliers. For example, imagine that instead of making $974 thousand each year, Sophia (in Table 9.3) made $974 *million*. From the perspective of Pearson correlation (think z score formula), Sophia's z score for income is going to change—a lot! Pearson's r, therefore, will also be affected considerably by the extreme score. But if you are just ranking scores, Sophia's position does not change when you add three zeros to her income. She is still ranked #1. For this reason, Spearman r_S is not affected by the extreme score. Thus Spearman correlation, like the median, the interquartile range, and other *robust* (less quantitatively sensitive) statistics, is not affected by outliers because it does not "know" how extreme the score is. If your data set is being spoiled by one or two outliers, consider using Spearman correlation to minimize their effect.

Summary

Correlation refers to the co-relationship between two variables. The Pearson r coefficient is a useful measure of *linear* correlation.

The Pearson Correlation Coefficient

z score product formula:

$$r = \frac{\sum z_X z_Y}{N}$$

Formula 9.1

raw score formulas:

$$r = \frac{\dfrac{\sum XY}{N} - \mu_X \mu_Y}{\sigma_X \sigma_Y}$$

Formula 9.2

$$r = \frac{\dfrac{1}{N-1}\left[\sum XY - N\overline{X}\,\overline{Y}\right]}{s_X s_Y}$$

Formula 9.3

In the foregoing formulas, N = number of *pairs*.

Points to Remember

1. The numerical value of r indicates the *strength* of the relationship between the two variables in your sample, while the sign indicates the *direction* of the relationship.

2. $-1 \le r \le +1$.

3. The population correlation is symbolized by ρ.

4. r *cannot* be interpreted as a percent, but r^2 can be (see next chapter).

5. r may be tested for statistical significance by referring the obtained value to Table C with $df = N - 2$.

6. r may also be used as a descriptive statistic.

7. r detects only *linear* relationships.

8. Correlation does not imply causation.

9. A restricted range on one or both of your variables, or a single bivariate outlier, can lead to a correlation considerably lower than you were expecting.

10. Even a tiny, inconsequential correlation can become statistically significant with a large enough sample.

11. When using correlation for various practical purposes, especially when measuring the various types of reliability and validity, it is important that the Pearson r be not only statistically significant but large in magnitude as well.

The Spearman Rank-Order Correlation Coefficient

With ranked data, you can compute the Pearson r for the two sets of ranks, or you can use the shortcut formula for the Spearman rank-order correlation coefficient:

$$r_s = 1 - \frac{6 \sum D^2}{N(N^2 - 1)}$$

Formula 9.4

where

D = difference between a pair of ranks
N = number of pairs

When $N < 31$, r_S should be compared to a critical value from Table I in order to determine statistical significance. However, for $N > 30$, the critical values for Pearson r in Table C provide a good approximation.

Exercises

1. A college dean would like to know how well he can predict sopho-more grade point average for first-semester freshmen so that students who are headed for trouble can be given appropriate counseling. After students have been in school for one semester, the dean obtains their numerical final examination average for the first semester (based on a total of 100 points) and the average number of "cuts" per class during the semester. He then waits for a year and a half, and when the students have finished their second year, he obtains their sophomore grade point average. To keep the computations down to a reasonable level, we will assume that the dean has a sample of only seven cases. (Note that in a real study of this kind there would be many more participants, but the same procedures would be used.)

Student	Test score (X)	Cuts (C)	Sophomore average (Y)
1	70	2	2.50
2	90	1	4.00
3	75	2	3.50
4	85	3	3.00
5	80	5	3.00
6	70	3	2.00
7	90	5	3.00
Mean	80	3	3.00
σ	8.02	1.41	.60

(a) Convert the test scores (X) and sophomore averages (Y) to z scores. By inspection of the paired z scores, estimate whether the correlation between these two variables is strong and positive, about zero, or strong and negative. Then verify your estimate by computing r using the z score product formula.

(b) Use (raw-score) Formula 9.2 to compute the Pearson r between the number of cuts (C) and the sophomore average (Y). Can you reject the null hypothesis at the .05 level with a two-tailed test? (Use Table C.)

(c) Repeat part (b) for the correlation between the number of cuts (C) and the test score (X). Is this correlation significant at the .01 level with a one-tailed test?

2. The data from Exercise 7 in Chapter 7 are reproduced in the following table. Calculate the mean and the *unbiased* standard deviations for both the experimental and control groups, and then compute the

Pearson r with the raw-score formula that uses the s's rather than the σ's in its denominator. Is the correlation coefficient significant? Given your decision with respect to the null hypothesis, what type of error could you be making, Type I or Type II? (Advanced exercise: Recompute the matched-pairs t test with the formula that is based on Pearson's r, and compare it to the t value you calculated for these data in the previous chapter.)

Pair	Experimental group (programmed text)	Control group (standard text)
1	9	7
2	6	4
3	5	6
4	7	3
5	3	5
6	7	3
7	3	2
8	4	5
9	6	7
10	10	8

3. The data from Exercises 8 and 9 in Chapter 7 are reproduced in the tables that follow.

(a) Compute the Pearson r for Data Set 3, Chapter 1, and test for significance at the .01 level.

(b) Use the z scores you calculated for these data in the exercises of Chapter 4 to recompute the r with the z-product formula. Is it the same?

(c) Compute the Pearson r for Data Set 3, Chapter 1, *with X rearranged*, and test for significance at the .05 level.

S	X	Y
Data set 3, Chapter 1		
1	97	89
2	68	57
3	85	87
4	74	76
5	92	97
6	92	79
7	100	91
8	63	50
9	85	85
10	87	84
11	81	91
12	93	91
13	77	75
14	82	77

Same data, but with X rearranged

S	X	Y
1	92	89
2	82	57
3	85	87
4	81	76
5	87	97
6	93	79
7	68	91
8	85	50
9	63	85
10	100	84
11	74	91
12	77	91
13	92	75
14	97	77

4. Ten subjects participate in a problem-solving experiment. Two judges are asked to rank order the solutions with regard to their creativity (1 = most creative, 10 = least creative). The experimenter wishes to know if the judges are in substantial agreement. Following are the rankings; what should the experimenter decide?

Subject	Judge 1	Judge 2
1	5	4
2	7	9
3	2	2
4	9	8
5	1	3
6	4	1
7	10	10
8	3	7
9	6	5
10	8	6

5. (a) Convert the data in part (a) of Exercise 3 to ranks, separately for each variable, in order to compute the Spearman rank-order correlation coefficient. Test r_S for statistical significance by using Table I. Compare r_S to the Pearson r that you calculated for Exercise 3, part (a).

(b) Redo part (a) for the data in part (c) of Exercise 3 (i.e., *with X rearranged*).

Thought Questions

1. For each of the following, state whether you would expect the Pearson r correlation between X and Y to be positive, zero, or negative. Assume that each correlation is based on a sample of 50 participants who have scores on both X and Y. (a) $X =$ grades in a high school advanced placement psychology course, $Y =$ scores on the advanced placement psychology test. (b) $X =$ intelligence, $Y =$ size of big toe on right foot. (c) $X =$ number of rounds of golf played, $Y =$ average golf score per 18 holes. (d) $X =$ number of hours spent watching television per week, $Y =$ grades in high school. (e) $X =$ self-esteem (low number indicates low self-esteem), $Y =$ depression (higher number indicates more depressed). (f) $X =$ number of hours spent studying for a test, $Y =$ number of mistakes made on that test.

2. A student obtains scores of 72 on Test X and 72 on Test Y. The student therefore concludes that there is a high correlation between Test X and Test Y. Why is this conclusion incorrect?

3. In a correlational study, X is the number of hours of violent television programs that participants watch, and Y is the number of violent acts committed by the participants in real life. Suppose that there is a moderately high correlation (say, .48) between X and Y for a sample of 100 American males and that this result is statistically significant. Explain why we *cannot* infer causation from a correlational study by showing that each of the following is possible: (a) X could cause Y. (b) Y could cause X. (c) The relationship between X and Y could be caused by a third variable. (Hint: Consider physiological causes of violent behavior.)

4. In a research study using a sample of 30 participants, the Pearson r correlation between X and Y is .09 and is *not* statistically significant. Should the researcher conclude that there is little or no relationship between X and Y? Why or why not?

5. The SAT is used to predict the success of high school students in college. Suppose that the Pearson r correlation between scores on the SAT and grades at University Z during the freshman year, based on a sample of 500 participants, is $+.53$. A student complains that a friend of hers did poorly on the SAT but was admitted to University Z anyway and earned high grades during the first year, while another friend did very well on the SAT but flunked out of University Z in the first year. Should the student conclude from these two results that the SAT is inaccurate and worthless? Why or why not?

6. Using a very large sample of participants, a statistically significant Pearson r correlation of .11 is obtained between X and Y. Does this mean that there is a strong relationship between X and Y? Why or why not?

7. (a) What is the difference between the reliability of a measure and the validity of a measure? (b) What is the difference between test-retest reliability and split-half reliability? (c) What is criterion validity?

8. Describe three situations in which you would consider using Spearman correlation instead of Pearson correlation.

Computer Exercises

1. (a) Use your statistical package to compute the Pearson r between baseline and prequiz heart rates for all students; also, find the Pearson r between the pre- and postquiz heart rate measurements. (b) Recalculate these two r's separately for men and women.

2. Compute the Pearson r between baseline heart rate and baseline anxiety for all students; also, find the Pearson r between prequiz heart rate and prequiz anxiety measurements.

3. Create two new variables: prequiz heart rate minus baseline heart rate and prequiz anxiety minus baseline anxiety. Compute Pearson's r between these two difference scores, and interpret the meaning of this correlation.

4. Use your statistical package to create a scatter plot of the relation between the math background quiz score and the statistics quiz score for the 85 students who have both scores. Describe the pattern that you see. If possible, use your statistical package to add a linear regression line to the scatter plot.

5. In Exercise 7 of the regular (not Computer) exercises in the previous chapter, you were asked to calculate the Wilcoxon matched-pairs test to determine whether a training method improved exam scores for 12 poorly performing students. For this exercise, compute the Spearman correlation between the pre- and posttest scores, and test for significance at the .05 level. How does the magnitude of the Spearman correlation relate to the power of the Wilcoxon test?

6. (a) Separately for male and female students, compute the Spearman correlation coefficient between the baseline and the prequiz heart rates. How do these results relate to those you obtained in part (b) of the first exercise? How do the corresponding p values compare? (b) Compute the Spearman correlations for the corresponding anxiety scores, as well.

Bridge to SPSS

Both the Pearson r and the Spearman r_s can be obtained from the same dialog box in SPSS, as described next.

Linear Correlation

To compute the Pearson r in SPSS, select **Correlate** from the Analyze menu, and then choose **Bivariate....** In the dialog box that opens, move the variables you wish to see correlated to the area labeled "Variables:" to the right of the variable list, and click **OK**. You can select as few as two variables from the list or as many as all of the numeric variables. By default, your output will contain a single matrix with the variables you chose as the labels of the rows, as well as of the columns; the same Pearson r will appear twice for each possible pair of variables from your selected list (the matrix also contains a diagonal, in which each variable is correlated with itself, always yielding a value of 1.000). The two-tailed p value (labeled "Sig.," of course) appears under each Pearson r, with the sample size (i.e., the number of pairs, labeled "N") under that. If "Flag significant correlations" is checked, any Pearson r with a "Sig." less than .05 is marked with an asterisk; if "Sig." is less than .01, that r is marked with two asterisks.

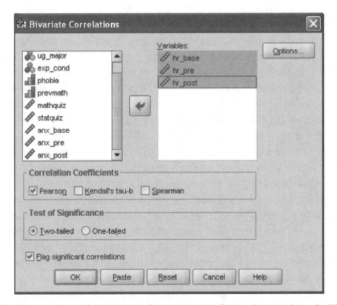

Source: Reprint courtesy of International Business Machines Corporation, © SPSS, Inc., an IBM company. SPSS was incorporated by IBM in October 2009.

The Bivariate Correlations dialog box allows you to select the Kendall's tau-b (not discussed in this text) and the Spearman correlation coefficient instead of, or in addition to, the Pearson r. This dialog box also allows you to select one-tailed rather than two-tailed p values and to suppress (by unchecking) the "flagging" of significant correlations. In addition, the **Options...** button allows you to add some descriptive statistics to your output and to exclude cases listwise instead of pairwise. If you choose to exclude cases *listwise*, *N* will not appear under each

Pearson r. Because N will be the same for each correlation, it appears just once, under the entire matrix. (N will equal the number of cases that do not have a missing value for *any* variable in the selected list.)

The Spearman Rank-Order Correlation Coefficient

The Spearman correlation cannot be obtained from the Analyze/ Nonparametric Tests menu, although it could have easily been included in the procedure for two related samples. Instead, as just mentioned, **Spearman** is one of the choices (the default is **Pearson**) when you open the dialog box for Bivariate Correlations. Unless the data for the two variables to be correlated have already been entered in terms of ranks, the Spearman correlation coefficient (labeled **Spearman's rho** by SPSS) will almost always differ from the Pearson r, as will its "Sig." value. However, either correlation coefficient can be the larger, depending on how the data are distributed for each variable and how the data are distributed bivariately.

Using the Syntax Window

Before there was Windows, one had to type a series of commands to tell SPSS what to do with your data. Now that list of commands is conveniently created for you, behind the scenes, when you make various selections from the pull-down menus and dialog boxes. Depending on the preferences you set, SPSS may or may not show you the command list you created when it displays your output. However, whether you see it or not, SPSS is creating a Syntax file from your command selections, which can be displayed and even modified, in a Syntax Window. This is a third window (along with the Data window and the Output window) that can be saved as a file for future use (the automatic extension given by SPSS is ".sps"). There are two major uses for the Syntax window: saving a long list of complex commands (e.g., computing many new variables) that you may want to repeat in the future (even if you may need to modify them slightly before running them again); and accessing program features that are not included in any of the SPSS menus (obviously, these are features that the SPSS company believes are potentially useful, but not used very often). Because it is relevant to computing correlations, we will describe one of these not-available-by-menu features next.

For many purposes, it is easier not to type a syntax file from scratch but rather to create one by first making selections in the relevant dialog box and then by clicking on **Paste** instead of **OK**. As an example, we will show you how to modify a syntax file for performing correlations so that you do not produce the usual square matrix, with its redundant correlation coefficients. Suppose you want to compute the correlations between one particular criterion variable and each of several potential predictors of that variable, but you are not interested in computing the correlations among the various possible predictors in this run. In the Bivariate Correlations dialog box, move over the criterion variable first, followed by all of the variables you would like to see correlated with the first one. Choose any Options that you want, and then click on the **Paste** button (it is always just beneath or next to the **OK** button). A Syntax file will open automatically, containing the command list needed to perform the analyses you specified in the dialog box.

For instance, if you select one criterion variable and three potential predictors, the syntax file will look something like this:

CORRELATIONS
/VARIABLES s_esteem salary friends body_img
/PRINTTWOTAIL NOSIG
/MISSINGPAIRWISE.

Note that this file consists of just one command, called Correlations, with several (default) subcommands, each of which begins with a slash; the command must be closed by including a period at the end of the last subcommand. Running this command produces the usual square matrix containing 4 × 4 or 16 correlations. However, if you want to compute only three correlations—self-esteem with each of the potential predictors—you can add the keyword **with** after the first variable, so that the Variables subcommand looks like this:

/VARIABLES s_esteem with salary friends body_img

As you would guess, **with** is a "reserved" word in SPSS and therefore cannot be used as the name of a variable. Running the previous syntax file after adding the keyword *with* produces an output box with just a single row containing the three correlation coefficients desired (with Sig. and *N*, as usual). You would get the same output by putting the criterion variable at the *end* of the Variables subcommand, preceded by *with*, except that the Output box will be in the form of a single column instead of a single row.

Appendix: Equivalence of the Various Formulas for *r*

1. $\dfrac{\sum z_X z_Y}{N} = \dfrac{\sum (X - \mu_X)(Y - \mu_Y)}{N \sigma_X \sigma_Y}$

   PROOF: By definition,

   $$z_X = \frac{X - \mu_X}{\sigma_X}, \quad z_Y = \frac{Y - \mu_Y}{\sigma_Y}$$

   Therefore,

   $$r = \frac{\sum \left(\dfrac{X - \mu_X}{\sigma_X} \right) \left(\dfrac{Y - \mu_Y}{\sigma_Y} \right)}{N}$$

   $$= \frac{\sum (X - \mu_X)(Y - \mu_Y)}{N \sigma_X \sigma_Y} \quad \text{(Rule 8, Chapter 1)}$$

2. $\dfrac{\sum (X - \mu_X)(Y - \mu_Y)}{N \sigma_X \sigma_Y} = \dfrac{\dfrac{\sum XY}{N} - \mu_X \mu_Y}{\sigma_X \sigma_Y}$

PROOF: Expanding the numerator yields

$$\sum (X - \mu_X)(Y - \mu_Y) = \sum (XY - X\mu_Y - \mu_X Y + \mu_X \mu_Y)$$
$$= \sum XY - \mu_Y \sum X - \mu_X \sum Y + N\mu_X \mu_Y$$

(Rules 1, 2, 5, and 8, Chapter 1)

Substituting $(\sum X)/N$ for μ_X and $(\sum Y)/N$ for μ_Y yields

$$\sum XY - \dfrac{\left(\sum Y\right)\left(\sum X\right)}{N} - \dfrac{\left(\sum X\right)\left(\sum Y\right)}{N} + \dfrac{N\left(\sum X\right)\left(\sum Y\right)}{(N)(N)}$$
$$= \sum XY - 2\dfrac{\left(\sum X\right)\left(\sum Y\right)}{N} + \dfrac{\left(\sum X\right)\left(\sum Y\right)}{N}$$
$$= \sum XY - \dfrac{\sum X \sum Y}{N}$$

Dividing the numerator by N yields

$$\dfrac{\sum XY}{N} - \dfrac{\sum X \sum Y}{N \times N} = \dfrac{\sum XY}{N} - \left(\dfrac{\sum X}{N}\right)\left(\dfrac{\sum Y}{N}\right) = \dfrac{\sum XY}{N} - \mu_X \mu_Y$$

Now that we have divided the numerator by N, we must do the same to the denominator:

$$\dfrac{N\sigma_X \sigma_Y}{N} = \sigma_X \sigma_Y$$

Put the transformed numerator over the transformed denominator to obtain the raw-score formula used in Table 12.2. This formula is sometimes called a raw-score *definition* formula; the terms in the formula are meaningful, but the format may not be optimal for computation.

Chapter 10
Prediction and Linear Regression

PREVIEW

Introduction

Where does the term *linear regression* come from?

Using Linear Regression to Make Predictions

What are the procedures for computing the regression line for predicting scores on Y from scores on X?

How do we define errors in prediction? Why are some such errors inevitable?

Why is the regression line referred to as the least-squares regression line?

What is the Y-intercept of the regression line? The slope?

What are some important properties of linear regression?

How do we predict scores on X from scores on Y?

Measuring Prediction Error: The Standard Error of Estimate

What is the standard error of estimate? Why is it useful?

What formula should be used when you wish to draw inferences about the standard error of estimate in a population?

The Connection Between Correlation and the *t* Test

What are the procedures for computing the correlation between one continuous and one dichotomous variable (the point-biserial correlation coefficient)?

How is a point-biserial correlation coefficient tested for statistical significance?

When we obtain a statistically significant value of t for the difference between two means, why is it desirable to convert this value to a point-biserial correlation coefficient? How is this done?

What is the relationship between r_{pb} and the effect-size measure known as g?

What does squaring r_{pb} tell you about the proportion of the total variance that is accounted for by the dichotomous variable?

Estimating the Proportion of Variance Accounted for in the Population

How can the formula for r_{pb}^2 be adjusted to create an unbiased estimator of the variance accounted for in the population?

What is ω^2, and how is it related to the population effect-size measure known as d?

(continued)

PREVIEW (*continued*)

Summary

Exercises

Thought Questions

Computer Exercises

Bridge to SPSS

Introduction

Behavioral scientists are indebted to Sir Francis Galton for making explicit some elementary concepts of relationships and prediction. Galton wrote his now-classic paper "Regression toward Mediocrity in Hereditary Stature" in 1885. In it he presented the theory that the physical characteristics of offspring tend to be related to, but are on the average less extreme than, those of their parents. That is, tall parents on the average produce children *less tall* than themselves, and short parents on the average produce children *less short* than themselves. In other words, physical characteristics of offspring tend to "regress" toward the average of the population. If you were to predict the height of a child from a knowledge of the height of the parents, you should predict a less extreme height—one closer to the average of all children.

Plotting data on the stature of many pairs of parents and offspring, Galton calculated the median height of offspring for each height category of parents. For example, he plotted the median height for all offspring whose fathers were 5 foot 7 inches, the median height for all offspring whose fathers were 5 foot 8 inches, and so forth. By connecting the points representing the medians, Galton found not only that there was a positive relationship between parental height and height of the offspring, but also that this relationship was fairly linear. The line connecting each of the medians (and after Pearson, the means) came to be known as the **regression line**. This term has been adopted by statisticians to indicate the straight line used in predicting or estimating values of one variable from a knowledge of values of another variable with which it is paired. The statistical procedure for making such predictions is called **linear regression**.

Using Linear Regression to Make Predictions

Predicting behavior is at the core of the behavioral sciences. A truism in psychology is that people's past behavior is the best predictor of their future behavior. Regression generalizes this logic from individuals to populations and formalizes the process by measuring systematic variation in the environment. In general, the procedure begins by measuring people on two variables (e.g., SAT and college GPA), creating a prediction equation from those data, and then using the equation to predict a future event (e.g., college GPA) from a past event (e.g., SAT score). For example, when colleges select applicants, they do not pick names randomly from a hat (though it may seem that way at times). The admissions department wants to identify which applicants are most likely to succeed and be happy at their institution. To help them make accurate predictions, admission staff collect a set of data from each applicant (e.g., SAT scores, high school GPA, letters of recommendation, personal essay), and, based on the relationship these data have with the success of past students, they make informed guesses about who is likely to be a good fit at their college. Because the relationship between variables such as SAT and college GPA are never perfect, their predictions also will not be perfect. However, to the extent that the correlation between the two variables is greater than zero, the admissions committee can make more accurate predictions than simply selecting randomly. Regression not only provides a systematic way to make these predictions, it also provides specific information about how much better your predictions will be compared to random selection.

Predicting behavior is not just of interest to behavioral scientists. Almost everyone would benefit from being able to predict what people will do, even if just a little better than they are able to now. Here's a simple example: Suppose your summer job is to sell ice cream from a portable freezer cart at the zoo. Each morning you carefully decide how much ice cream to take with you to the zoo. This is an important decision. If you take too much, then you will lose money on the unsold (and melted) ice cream at the end of the day. If you take too little, then you will sell out early and turn away hungry customers and their money. A perfect day would consist in selling all the ice cream you brought without turning away any customers. So what can you do to increase the chances that you will have a perfect day? One thing you may have noticed is that ice cream tends to sell faster on warmer days. So suppose that each day you note the high temperature and how many ice-cream cones you sold that day. After a few weeks you compute Pearson r and discover that there is a $+.47$ correlation between temperature and cone sales—you were right! So now you know to take more ice cream on days that are supposed to be warmer. But how much more ice cream? Using regression, you can plug in the temperature forecast for any particular day, and the prediction equation will produce the number of ice-cream cones you are likely to sell that day! For example, the regression equation might tell you that if the temperature is predicted to reach $85°$, then you should take 127 ice-cream cones. The predictions will not be perfect, but they will be better than if you did not take into account the relationship between temperature and demand for ice cream.

Computational Procedures

Now that we have considered a couple of everyday examples, let us think about regression in a more abstract way. Let us assume that we wish to predict scores on Y from scores on X. Y, the variable being predicted or estimated, is called the *dependent* variable or **criterion**. X, which provides the information on which the predictions are based, is referred to as the *independent* variable (even if it is not manipulated by the experimenter) or **predictor**. In this chapter, we discuss the simplest method of prediction—an equation that produces a *straight line*. One way of writing such an equation is

$$Y' = b_{YX}X + a_{YX} \qquad \text{Formula 10.1}$$

where

$$Y' = predicted \text{ score on } Y$$
$$b_{YX} = slope \text{ of the line, also called the } regression\ coefficient$$
$$\text{for predicting } Y \text{ from } X$$
$$a_{YX} = Y\text{-}intercept, \text{ or the value of } Y' \text{ when } X = 0$$

The value of b_{YX} summarizes the average rate of change in the Y score per unit increase in the X score, while the value of a_{YX} indicates the Y value at which the regression line crosses the Y-axis. For any given set of data, b_{YX} and a_{YX} are constant values in the equation. A straight line has only one slope, and there is only one value of Y' for which X equals zero. We wish to keep our errors in prediction (especially the *squared* errors) to a minimum, and the actual values of b_{YX} and a_{YX} are selected with this objective in mind.

The way in which a regression line is used to obtain a predicted score is illustrated in Figure 10.1. Suppose a person has a score of 20 on X, and you want to predict what her score on Y will be. Given the regression

Figure 10.1

Use of Regression Line to Obtain Predicted Scores on Y

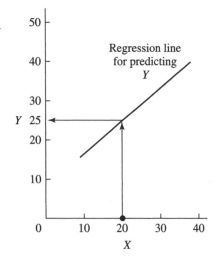

line for predicting Y shown in Figure 10.1, you enter the X-axis at 20 and proceed up to the regression line. You then move left until you reach the Y-axis and read off the predicted Y score; Y' for this subject is equal to 25. In practice, predicted scores are computed according to the regression equation, because eyeball estimates from a graph are likely to be relatively inaccurate.

The **regression** (or prediction) **line** is the straight line that best represents the trend of the dots in a scatter plot. In any real situation, the dots will *not* all fall exactly on a straight line. Therefore, you will make *errors* when you use a regression line to make predictions. The error in predicting a particular Y value is defined as the difference (keeping the sign) between the *actual* Y value and the *predicted* Y value, Y'. That is,

$$\text{error in predicting } Y = Y - Y'$$

A graphic representation of errors in prediction for one set of data is shown in Figure 10.2. For example, the predicted Y value for the individual with an X score of 68 is equal to approximately 159.8. His actual Y value, however, is equal to 148. The difference of approximately -11.8 between the actual and predicted values represents an error in prediction for this individual, and the negative sign indicates that the actual value is smaller than the prediction. These errors are also called **residual scores**, and they always sum to zero (just like deviations from the mean).

In Figure 10.2, vertical lines have been drawn between each observed Y score (actual weight) and the predicted weight score (Y'). This has been done for each value of X (actual height) that occurs in the sample. These vertical distances are the errors in prediction (or residuals). All *predicted*

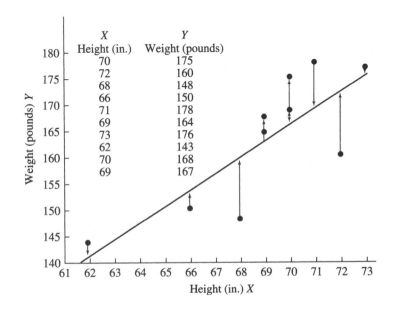

X	Y
Height (in.)	Weight (pounds)
70	175
72	160
68	148
66	150
71	178
69	164
73	176
62	143
70	168
69	167

Figure 10.2

Regression Line of Y on X Showing Extent of Error (Difference Between Actual Weight Score and Predicted Weight Score) scores lie on the (straight) regression line. Since there are two height scores of 70 inches with two different weight scores and two height scores of 69 inches with two different weight scores, the smaller error has been superimposed upon the larger in each of these cases.

The preferred linear regression prediction line is the one that minimizes the sum of *squared* errors in prediction, symbolized as:

$$\sum (Y - Y')^2$$

That is, values are chosen for b_{YX} and a_{YX} that define a particular regression line for predicting Y: the line that makes $\sum(Y - Y')^2$ smaller than you would get using any other prediction line for that set of data. This line is therefore called the **least-squares regression line** of Y on X.

To see why it makes more sense to minimize the sum of *squared* errors rather than the sum of unsquared errors, let us suppose that you wish to predict students' college GPAs from their scores on the SATs. After making your predictions, you wait until the students finish college and see what their actual GPAs turn out to be. The results for two students are as follows:

Student	Actual GPA (Y)	Predicted GPA (Y')	Error ($Y - Y'$)
1	3.8	3.4	+0.4
2	2.1	2.5	−0.4

The actual GPA of the first student is about half a grade point above the prediction, whereas the GPA of the second student is a similar amount below the prediction for that student. Thus, some error in prediction has been made. (This is unavoidable unless $r \pm 1$, which never happens with real data.) Yet if you were to compute the average of the error column, it would always equal zero! The same unhelpful result would be obtained had the predicted Y' values been 2.4 for student 1 and 3.5 for student 2, yielding substantial errors of +1.4 and −1.4.

As this example shows, it is not sufficient to have a prediction line whose errors balance out (have a mean of zero); *all* lines that go through the point $\overline{X}, \overline{Y}$ have this property. In order to obtain a useful measure of the total amount of prediction error, we must find the line about which the variation of the Y values, and hence the *squared* errors, is as small as possible. (As we see later in this chapter, a good measure of the magnitude of prediction error can be computed by averaging these squared errors and taking the square root.)

As we just mentioned, the values of b_{YX} and a_{YX} in the general formula for a straight line are chosen so as to minimize the value of $\sum(Y - Y')^2$. Equations that produce these values have been found (by the laws of statistics) to be:

$$b_{YX} = r_{XY}\frac{\sigma_Y}{\sigma_X} \qquad \text{Formula 10.2A}$$

$$b_{YX} = r_{XY} \frac{s_Y}{s_X}$$ Formula 10.2B

$$a_{YX} = \overline{Y} - b_{YX}\overline{X}$$ Formula 10.3

Formula 10.2A for b_{YX} is used when values of σ_X and σ_Y are available, and the second version of the formula (10.2B) is used when working with the unbiased standard deviations (SDs); the latter is the more common case, but the value for the slope will be the same regardless of which formula is used. For the Y-intercept, this distinction does not arise.

To illustrate finding a "best-fit" regression line, let us return to our example of SAT and GPA from the previous chapter. We have already seen that μ_x (or $\overline{X}$) = 498.4, μ_y (or $\overline{Y}$) = 2.85, σ_X = 117.33, σ_Y = .57, and r_{XY} = +.65, so, by Formula 10.2A:

$$b_{YX} = (+.65)\frac{.57}{117.33}$$
$$= .0032$$

Because b_{YX} is the slope of the line, this result indicates that each unit of increase in X is associated with .0032 units of increase in Y. Then, according to Formula 10.3:

$$a_{YX} = 2.85 - (0.0032)(498.4)$$
$$= 1.26$$

This is the value of Y' when X is equal to zero. Such a value need not be a *logical* possibility for a given set of data. This is the case here, since SAT scores of zero are outside the possible range of scores.

Combining the preceding two results, by using Formula 10.1, yields the linear regression equation for predicting Y (GPA):

$$Y' = b_{YX}X + a_{YX}$$
$$= .0032X + 1.26$$

This equation can now be used to obtain predicted GPAs (Y'), given an SAT score (X). For example, the predicted GPA for a student with an SAT score of 400 is:

$$Y' = (.0032)(400) + 1.26 = 1.28 + 1.26 = 2.54$$

This is the *best* linear prediction you can make, the one that on the average would yield the smallest squared error.

Note that a sample with scores on *both* the X and Y variables is needed in order to compute a linear regression prediction equation. Thus, to predict GPA from SAT, you must first obtain a sample of college students for whom you have both GPAs and scores on the SAT, and then compute such essential values as r_{XY}. Once you have determined the regression line, you can then use it to *make predictions for new cases for which you have data on only the predictor*—that is, to make predictions for graduating high school seniors based on their SAT scores. However, you *must* be careful to ensure that the original sample of college students on whom the regression equation is calculated is representative of the future groups for whom the predictions will be made.

Properties of Linear Regression

The linear regression procedure has numerous important properties. We have already seen that there is precisely one predictor and one criterion, a straight line is used to make predictions, and the line is such that the sum of squared errors in prediction is minimized. Some additional principles of importance include the following.

1. If there is no good information on which to base a prediction, the same estimate—the mean of the criterion—is made for everyone.

Suppose that a group of graduating high school seniors asks you to predict what each one's college GPA will be, but the only information that they give you is the length of each student's right big toe. Since big toe length is useless for purposes of forecasting someone's GPA (i.e., $r_{XY} = 0$), you should not make any predictions in this situation.

When there is no relevant information on which to base a prediction, linear regression also will not forecast any differences on the criterion. Instead, it "predicts" that each person will be average. That is, when the correlation between the predictor and the criterion is zero, the linear regression formula becomes:

$$b_{YX} = .00\frac{s_Y}{s_X} = 0$$

$$a_{YX} = \overline{Y} - (.00)\overline{X} = \overline{Y}$$

$$Y' = b_{YX}X + a_{YX}$$

$$= (0)X + \overline{Y}$$

$$= \overline{Y}$$

Thus, scores on X are ignored, since they are irrelevant for purposes of predicting Y, and the mean of the criterion is predicted for everyone. Of course, no behavioral scientist uses linear regression unless the predictor and criterion are nontrivially correlated, but it is desirable to understand this "worst of all possible worlds" in order to follow the logic of linear regression.

2. When all scores are expressed as z scores, the predicted z score on Y is equal to r multiplied by the z score on X.

It can be shown algebraically that[1]

$$z'_Y = r_{XY}z_X$$
Formula 10.4

where

z'_Y = predicted z value on Y

z_X = actual z value on X

This equation should help you in understanding linear regression. It shows that the predicted score (z'_Y) will be less extreme (i.e., closer to its mean) than the score from which the prediction is made (z_X), because z_X is multiplied by a fraction (r_{XY}). This illustrates the statement, made previously, about regression toward the mean of Y. The equation also shows once again that if r_{XY} is equal to zero, all predicted z'_Y values will equal the mean of Y (they will equal zero, which is the mean of z scores). This incidentally shows that the mean is a least-squares measure—that is, the sum of squared deviations of the values in the sample from it is a minimum. Finally, the equation indicates that, when dealing with z scores, the regression line passes through the origin of the graph (0,0), because if $z_X = 0$ (the mean of the X scores expressed as z scores), then $z'_Y = 0$ (the mean of the Y scores expressed as z scores). When graphing the original scores, the regression line will pass through the point where the two means meet $(\overline{X}, \overline{Y})$.

Although Formula 10.4 looks refreshingly simple, it is not in general convenient for calculating predicted scores. To use it for this purpose, you would first have to transform X to a z value, then compute the value of z'_Y, and then transform z'_Y to a raw score equivalent, Y'. Most of the time, it will be easier to use the raw score regression equation.

3. The closer the correlation between X and Y is to zero, the greater is the amount of prediction error.

It should be emphasized that while linear regression *minimizes* the sum of squared errors in prediction, this sum may still be prohibitively large. If the correlation between the predictor and the criterion is numerically small, such as $+.07$, linear regression will make a substantial amount of prediction error because the relationship between the two variables is so weak. This implies that a correlation near zero is likely to be useless for practical prediction purposes, even if it is statistically significant (as could happen with a very large sample). The *sign* of the correlation coefficient, however, is *not* related to prediction error. A correlation of (say) $+.55$ and one of $-.55$ are equally good for prediction purposes, because the *strength* of the relationship between the predictor and the criterion is the same.

4. Transforming either X or Y or both by a linear transformation will not affect the linear correlation between them.

---

[1]The standard deviation of both z_X and z_Y is equal to 1. Therefore, when dealing with z scores, $b_{YX} = r(1/1) = r$. Because the mean of both z_X and z_Y is equal to zero, $a_{YX} = 0$. Thus, for z scores, $Y' = rX + 0$, so $z_{Y'} = r_{XY}z_X$.

Suppose that the correlation between the high temperature for the day in a small town, as measured in degrees Fahrenheit, and the total weight of ice cream eaten that day by the people in that town, as measured in pounds, is equal to .4. If we wished to publish this result in a European journal, and its editors insisted that we convert our temperature measurements to degrees Celsius and our weights to kilograms, the Pearson r would not be affected by these transformations ($°C = .556 \times °F - 17.778$; wt. in kg $= .4 \times$ wt. in lbs.), because they are *linear transformations* (only multiplication, division, addition, and/or subtraction by constants are involved). Linearly transforming an entire set of raw scores will not change the z score for any individual, and the Pearson r depends only on the pairing of the z scores for the two variables and not the raw scores. Of course, a z score is itself just a linear transformation of a raw score, so the correlation between the raw scores on some variable and their corresponding z scores will always be perfect (i.e., $r = +1.0$).

A Technical Note: Formulas for Predicting X From Y

Because the assignment of X and Y to the two variables in a linear regression problem is usually up to the researcher, you can usually assign the Y designation to the criterion and X to the predictor and use the formulas given previously. If you should then wish to make predictions in the other direction (e.g., because you want to entertain the opposite causal theory), you can simply *change the designations* (relabel X as Y and Y as X) and use the same formulas. Note that it *is* necessary to recompute a new linear regression equation if you wish to predict in the other direction (unless $r = \pm 1$).

For purposes of reference, we note briefly the linear regression procedure for predicting scores on X from scores on Y. The equation is

$$X' = b_{XY}Y + a_{XY},$$

where

$$X' = \text{predicted score on } X$$

$$b_{XY} = r_{XY}\frac{\sigma_X}{\sigma_Y} = r_{XY}\frac{s_X}{s_Y}$$

$$a_{XY} = \overline{X} - b_{XY}\overline{Y}$$

This procedure minimizes $\sum(X - X')^2$, the sum of squared errors, when predicting X. While $r_{XY} = r_{YX}$, b_{XY} (the b value or slope for predicting X from Y) does *not* equal b_{YX} (the b value or slope for predicting Y from X), nor does $a_{XY} = a_{YX}$. In fact, the regression line for predicting X is not the same as the regression line for predicting Y unless the correlation between X and Y is perfect (numerically equal to 1), *and $\sigma_X = \sigma_Y$, and $\overline{X} = \overline{Y}$.*

Measuring Prediction Error: The Standard Error of Estimate

We have seen that when predicting scores on Y, the amount of squared error made for a given individual is equal to $(Y - Y')^2$. The *average* squared error for the entire sample can be obtained by summing the squared errors and dividing by N. Such a measure of error, the *variance of errors*, is in terms of squared units. As was the case with the standard deviation (SD) (Chapter 3), a measure in terms of actual score units can be obtained by taking the positive square root. This gives a useful measure of prediction error that is called the **standard error of estimate**, symbolized by σ_{est}:

$$\sigma_{est} = \sqrt{\frac{\sum (Y - Y')^2}{N}}$$

In practice, the standard error of estimate (which is also the SD of the residuals) can more easily be obtained by the following formula, which can be proved to be equivalent to the one above by algebraic manipulation:

$$\sigma_{est} = \sigma_Y \sqrt{1 - r_{XY}^2} \qquad \text{Formula 10.5}$$

Note that if $r = \pm 1$, there is no error ($\sigma_{est} = 0$); if $r = 0$, the standard error of estimate reaches its maximum possible value, which is the ordinary SD of Y, or σ_Y.

The standard error of estimate of Y may be thought of as the variability of Y about the regression line for a particular X value, averaged over all values of X. This is illustrated in Figure 10.3. In Panel A of Figure 10.3, the variability of the Y scores within each X value is relatively

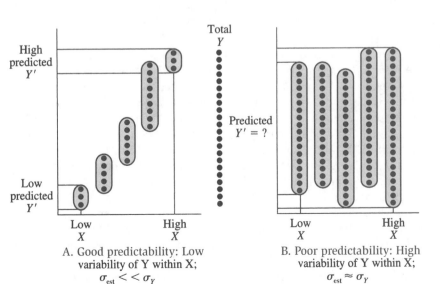

A. Good predictability: Low
variability of Y within X;
$\sigma_{est} << \sigma_Y$

B. Poor predictability: High
variability of Y within X;
$\sigma_{est} \approx \sigma_Y$

Figure 10.3

Relationship Between the Standard Error of Estimate (σ_{est}), the Standard Deviation of $Y(\sigma_Y)$, and the Accuracy of Prediction

low, because the scores within each X value cluster closely together. You can see that Y takes on a relatively narrow range of values for any given X. By contrast, the total variability of Y (for all X combined), which is given by σ_Y, is relatively large. Thus, σ_{est} is *small compared to* σ_Y; the standard error of estimate is always considerably smaller than the SD of Y, whenever the correlation is fairly high. On the one hand, in Figure 10.3A, the correlation between X and Y is fairly close to 1.0. This is good for purposes of prediction, since an individual with a low score on X is likely to have a low score on Y, whereas an individual with a high score on X is likely to have a high score on Y.

Figure 10.3B, on the other hand, illustrates a situation in which prediction will be poor. The average variability within each X value is about equal to the total variability of Y; that is, the standard error of estimate (σ_{est}) is *nearly equal to* the SD of $Y(\sigma_Y)$ whenever the correlation is very small. In Figure 10.3B, the correlation is actually close to zero. In this instance, therefore, knowing an individual's X score will *not* permit you to make a good prediction as to what his Y score will be. As a whole, Figure 10.3 shows that prediction will be good to the extent that for any given X, Y shows relatively little variability.

The Proportion of Variance Accounted for by a Correlation

By solving Formula 10.5 for the square of the correlation coefficient, we can obtain a useful expression that relates the magnitude of the squared correlation to the difference between the variance of errors and the total variance, in terms of a proportion.

$$r_{XY}^2 = 1 - \frac{\sigma_{est}^2}{\sigma_Y^2}$$

$$= \frac{\sigma_Y^2 - \sigma_{est}^2}{\sigma_Y^2}$$

Thus, the *squared* correlation coefficient shows *by what proportion the variability* (specifically, the variance) *in predicting Y has been reduced by knowing X*. If, on one hand, this reduction has been great (as in Figure 10.3A), σ_{est}^2 will be small compared to σ_Y^2, and r^2 will be large. If, on the other hand, little reduction has been achieved (as in Figure 10.3B), σ_{est}^2 will be about equal to σ_Y^2, and r^2 will be close to zero. In the example involving GPA and SAT scores, r^2 is equal to $(.65)^2$, or .42. So in that example, 42% of the variance of the GPAs is said to be *explained by* the SAT scores. That is considered a rather high proportion of variance to be explained in one variable by a totally separate variable in behavioral research; clearly a fairly good job has been done of identifying a (linear) relationship between two variables that are not ostensibly measuring the same thing. Note that the expression *is explained by* does not mean *is caused by*, even though it sounds as if it should. Instead, it means that some of the variance in the Y variable is explained *by its relationship with* the *X* variable; unless random assignment has been conducted, the nature of that relationship cannot be deduced from the correlation.

Estimated Standard Error From a Sample

The standard error of estimate computed from Formula 10.5 is a good descriptive statistic, which is appropriate when you are dealing with an entire population. (You may have inferred this from the fact that we used the Greek letter σ.) When you wish to draw inferences about the standard error of estimate in a population *from the data in a random sample*, you could correct for bias by using the following formula:

$$s_{est} = \sqrt{\frac{\sum (Y - Y')^2}{N - 2}}$$

Note that whereas s_Y is based on $N - 1$ degrees of freedom, s_{est}, like the Pearson r, is based on $N - 2$ degrees of freedom (*df*) (with the ordinary variance, you lose one *df* for the sample mean; with the variance around a regression line, you lose one *df* for the slope and another *df* for the *Y*-intercept that, together, define that regression line). However, this formula is clearly not convenient for calculation. Fortunately, you can greatly simplify the calculations by basing your formula on the Pearson r, as follows:

$$s_{est} = s_Y \sqrt{\frac{N - 1}{N - 2} \left(1 - r_{xy}^2\right)},\qquad \text{Formula 10.6}$$

where s_Y is the unbiased standard deviation of your *Y* scores.

The Connection Between Correlation and the *t* Test

Now that you have learned the concept of regression, it is possible to show you that you do not really need to know the procedure for testing a difference of two independent sample means (as shown in Chapter 7). Instead, you can treat the two-sample comparison as a form of correlation. That is, you can compute the correlation between a two-valued (i.e., *categorical*) variable and a continuous variable. It can be useful to think of the two-sample *t* test as a special case of correlation, as we demonstrate in the next section. Nonetheless, the two-sample *t* test is a commonly used procedure in the behavioral sciences, so it was certainly not a waste of time for you to have learned all about it in Chapter 7.

Let us return to the problem of predicting weight from height (as depicted in Figure 10.2). This time, suppose that your data set contains five men and five women. By a strange coincidence, all of the women are the same height (i.e., 64 inches) and all of the men are the same height as each other (i.e., 69 inches). There is still variability in weight for each group, as you can see in the scatterplot in Figure 10.4. The data for Figure 10.4 are

Figure 10.4

A Scatter Plot in Which One of the Variables Has Only Two Values

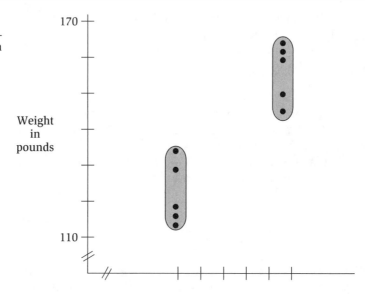

Table 10.1 Height and Weight Data for Figure 10.1

Height (in.) X	z_X	Weight (lbs.) Y	z_Y	$z_X z_Y$	
64	−1	116	−1.31	+1.31	
64	−1	118	−1.20	+1.20	$\overline{X}_1 = 123.8$
64	−1	120	−1.10	+1.10	$\sigma_1 = 8.635$
64	−1	125	−0.83	+0.83	$s_1 = 9.654$
64	−1	140	−0.03	+0.03	
69	+1	145	+0.24	+0.24	
69	+1	150	+0.51	+0.51	$\overline{X}_2 = 157.2$
69	+1	162	+1.15	+1.15	$\sigma_2 = 8.134$
69	+1	164	+1.26	+1.26	$s_2 = 9.094$
69	+1	165	+1.31	+1.31	

$$\sum X = 665 \quad \sum z_X = 0 \quad \sum Y = 1405 \quad \sum z_Y = 0 \quad \sum z_X z_Y = +8.94$$

$$\overline{X} = 66.5 \qquad\qquad \overline{Y} = 140.5 \qquad\qquad r = \frac{\sum z_X z_Y}{N}$$

$$\sigma_X = 2.5 \qquad\qquad \sigma_Y = 18.69 \qquad\qquad = \frac{8.94}{10} = .894$$

shown, and the Pearson r is calculated for the height/weight relationship (using the z-product method) in Table 10.1.

It should not be surprising that the linear correlation is high ($r = .894$) for these data (note the similarity between Figure 10.4 and Figure 10.3A), even though the X variable has only two values in this case.

What *is* surprising is that the correlation would be exactly the same if the X values were simply 1 for all women and 2 for all men. In fact, *any* two different values for X would yield the same magnitude for the

Pearson r. (However, the r would have a negative sign if women were assigned the higher of the two X values.) This phenomenon becomes much less surprising when you look carefully at the calculation of r in terms of z scores (see Table 10.1). It is easy to show that whenever you convert a set of only two different numbers to z scores, the z score for the smaller number will be -1 and the z score for the larger one will be $+1$, regardless of which two numbers you are working with.

The Point-Biserial Correlation Coefficient

In our height/weight example, all of the women have one height and all of the men have another (i.e., height and *gender* are perfectly correlated). Therefore, the correlation between height and weight is also the correlation between *gender* and weight. You can correlate any variable with gender (as long as you have measured your dependent variable on at least some individuals of each gender) by arbitrarily assigning an X value to each gender (e.g., 1 and 2) and then correlating these X values with your continuous variable as the Y value for each individual. For instance, suppose you correlate gender with height. After assigning the X value of 1 to females and 2 to males, you will be measuring the tendency for height to be higher whenever the gender value (1 versus 2) is higher.

The type of correlation just described is usually called a **point-biserial correlation**, symbolized as r_{pb}, because one of the variables being correlated has only two levels, which are assigned arbitrary values. The main problem with r_{pb} is that its sign will change if you reverse the assignment of the X values (e.g., r_{pb} for gender with height will become negative if males are assigned a value that is *lower* than the one assigned to the females). Therefore, we routinely ignore the sign of r_{pb} and look at the means of the two groups to determine the direction of the relationship.

When squared, r_{pb} is interpreted in the same way as any squared correlation coefficient. Note that any time you can calculate an r_{pb}, you can also compute a t value to compare the two group means instead. The information you get from the r_{pb} complements the information you get from the t value, as we will now demonstrate for the gender/weight example.

The Relationship Between r_{pb} and the t Test

In the rightmost column of Table 10.1 we included the means and the biased and unbiased standard deviations for weight separately for each height (i.e., gender). Using the simplified t formula for equal sample sizes (Formula 7.15), we can easily calculate t for comparing the mean weights of the two groups:

$$t = \frac{\overline{X}_1 - \overline{X}_2}{\sqrt{\dfrac{s_1^2 + s_2^2}{n}}} = \frac{123.8 - 157.2}{\sqrt{\dfrac{93.2 + 82.7}{5}}} = \frac{-33.4}{\sqrt{35.18}} = \frac{-33.4}{5.93} = -5.63$$

This t value shows that the difference in weight between the two genders is statistically significant. Recall that the r_{pb} between height and weight (and therefore in this example, between gender and weight) was high—in fact, it was .894. However, even such a large r should be tested for significance, which we will do by using the t formula found in the footnote on page 237 in Chapter 9, substituting r_{pb} for r. (We could look up the critical value in Table C in the Appendix, but we want to make a point about the t value.)

$$t = \frac{r_{pb}\sqrt{N-2}}{\sqrt{1 - r_{pb}^2}}$$

$$t = \frac{.894\sqrt{8}}{\sqrt{1 - .8}} \qquad \text{Formula 10.7}$$

$$t = \frac{2.5286}{.4472}$$

$$t = 5.65,$$

where N represents the total number of men and women, which is also the number of pairs on which r_{pb} was calculated.

The slight difference in magnitude between these two t values is due entirely to rounding off intermediate terms (e.g., the variance of each group). The sign of the t value can be ignored in each case. The point is that when you test r_{pb} for significance, you are testing the relationship between a (two-valued) independent variable and a continuous dependent variable, which is equivalent to testing the difference of the means of the dependent variable for the two values of the independent variable using a t test for two independent samples.

The Relationship Between r_{pb} and g (Effect Size)

Recall that in Chapter 7 we introduced a measure of the relative separation of two sample means, called g. The ordinary (pooled-variance) two-sample t test can be viewed as a test of the significance of g, where

$$t = g\sqrt{\frac{N_1 N_2}{N_1 + N_2}}$$

In fact, both r_{pb} and g are alternative measures of effect size. We already solved the preceding formula for g to create Formula 7.12, which enables you to calculate g from a published t value (if you know the sample sizes):

$$g = t\sqrt{\frac{N_1 + N_2}{N_1 N_2}} \qquad \text{Formula 7.12}$$

Similarly, you can modify the formula for testing the significance of r_{pb} so that you can also calculate r_{pb} from a published t value:

$$r_{pb} = \sqrt{\frac{t^2}{t^2 + df}},$$ Formula 10.8

where $df = N - 2$ (N is the *total* $N = N_1 + N_2$). If in the formula for r_{pb} you substitute the expression for t in terms of g, N_1, and N_2, you will get a formula (if you are really good with algebra) that relates r_{pb} directly to g (with an adjustment for sample size, df/N, that is only noticeable with small samples) and demonstrates how closely these two effect-size measures are related.

$$r_{pb} = \sqrt{\frac{g^2}{g^2 + 4(df/N)}}$$ Formula 10.9

For the data in Table 10.1, g equals $t\sqrt{(10/25)} = 5.65(.632) = 3.57$—a very large value for an effect size. (We could also have calculated this value by dividing the difference between the male and female means by the square root of the pooled variance.) Of course, we should expect a large g from already knowing that r_{pb} is extremely large (i.e., close to 1.0). We demonstrate next that, although Formula 10.9 looks pretty strange, it does indeed produce the correct value for r_{pb}:

$$r_{pb} = \sqrt{\frac{3.57^2}{3.57^2 + 4(8/10)}} = \sqrt{\frac{12.75}{12.75 + 3.2}} = \sqrt{\frac{12.75}{12.75 + 3.2}} = \sqrt{.8} = .894$$

Given these two choices for measuring effect size, the question is this: Under what circumstances would r_{pb} be preferred, and when would g be considered more desirable? As you will see in the next chapter, g is the preferred effect-size measure for power analysis. Also, g has a straightforward interpretation when dealing with roughly symmetric, bell-shape curves; it gives you a clear sense of the degree to which the scores in one group overlap with the scores of the other group. This aspect of g is described further in the next chapter as well.

The Proportion of Variance Accounted for by a Grouping Variable

The advantage of r_{pb} is that squaring r_{pb}, as with any correlation coefficient, gives the proportion of variance in one of your variables that is *accounted* for by the other. In the two-group case, you will, of course, always want to look at the proportion of variance in your dependent variable that is accounted for by your grouping variable, rather than the other way around. As an example, we first compute the proportion of variance accounted for directly in the data of Table 10.1. First, we find the total variance in weight by squaring the (biased) standard deviation at the bottom of the

Weight column in Table 10.1: $\sigma_y^2 = 349.25$. The variance in weight that is *not* explained by gender is the average (a weighted average if the ns are not equal) of the variances *within* the two genders. Therefore, we square and average the σ's of the two groups to obtain the unexplained variance: $(8.635^2 + 8.134^2)/2 = 140.725/2 = 70.36$. Now we can find the explained variance (i.e., the *variance accounted for*) by subtracting the unexplained variance (which is the same as σ_{est}^2) from the total:

$$\sigma_{explained}^2 = \sigma_{total}^2 - \sigma_{unexplained}^2 = 349.25 - 70.36 = 278.89$$

The proportion of the total variance in weight that is accounted for is therefore $278.89/349.25 = .799$, or approximately 80%. Note that r_{pb}^2 equals $.894^2 = .799$. This shows that we did not have to go through the trouble of dividing variances; squaring the point-biserial r gives us the proportion of variance accounted for. Even when a large t value is obtained that easily reaches statistical significance, it is possible that very little variance is being accounted for. This consideration is true of all procedures in inferential statistics. Statistical significance does *not* imply a *large* relationship or effect; it just suggests that the effect in the population is *unlikely to be zero.* A t value does *not* offer a solution to this problem, because it does not provide a ready measure of how large the relationship is (the effect size). So it is desirable to convert values of t obtained from the procedures in Chapter 7 into point-biserial correlation coefficients (or g's) and to report *both* t (with its p value) and r_{pb}. A glance at the formula for r_{pb} in terms of t and df reveals that any particular t that is obtained with large samples (hence, many df) is less impressive (i.e., it will be associated with a smaller r_{pb}) than the same t value obtained with smaller samples.

As an illustration, consider once again the caffeine study discussed in Chapter 7. It was found that caffeine did have a positive association with heart rates; a statistically significant value of t was obtained. The question remains, however, as to *how strong* is the relationship between the presence or absence of that dosage of caffeine and test scores. Recalling that $t = 2.91$ and $df = (22 + 20 - 2) = 40$, we have

$$r_{pb} = \sqrt{\frac{(2.91)^2}{(2.91)^2 + 40}}$$

$$= \sqrt{\frac{8.47}{48.47}}$$

$$= \sqrt{.175}$$

$$= .42$$

Thus, there is a rather strong relationship between the presence or absence of caffeine and test scores; $r_{pb}^2 = (.42)^2$, so 17% of the variance in test scores is explained by whether or not caffeine is present. You therefore know that caffeine is an important factor that accounts for differences among people on this test, though it is far from the only one—83% of the variance in test scores is still not accounted for. If it could be assumed that caffeine has no harmful side effects, a cautious recommendation that students take caffeine before a mathematics examination would be justified.

Suppose instead that, using a very large sample, the statistically significant t had yielded a value of r_{pb} of .10. Here, only $(.10)^2$ or 1% of the variance in test scores is explained by the presence or absence of caffeine. You are therefore warned that this experimental finding, while statistically significant, is probably not of much practical value. You certainly would *not* recommend that caffeine actually be used, for the probable effect on test scores would be too small to matter. (The possibility does exist, however, that such a finding might be of theoretical importance in understanding brain functioning.)

Estimating the Proportion of Variance Accounted for in the Population

As we have seen, squaring r_{pb} produces a useful descriptive statistic. However, r_{pb}^2 tends to *over*estimate the proportion of variance that would be accounted for in the data for the entire population from which you drew your samples. Fortunately, the formula for r_{pb}^2 can easily be adjusted to remove nearly all of its *bias*.

It would be reasonable to expect that calculating r_{pb}^2 for the entire population would produce a quantity referred to as ρ_{pb}^2. However, the proportion of variance accounted for in the *population* is usually referred to as ω^2 (the lowercase Greek letter omega, squared). To create a nearly unbiased estimate of ω^2, we need only square Formula 10.8 for r_{pb} and modify it slightly, as shown:

$$\text{est. } \omega^2 = \frac{t^2 - 1}{t^2 + df + 1} \qquad \text{Formula 10.10}$$

If we apply this formula to the caffeine study, we see that whereas 17.47% of the heart rate variance is accounted for by the presence of caffeine in the sample data, our best guess about the percent of variance that would be accounted for in the *population* is a bit less: 15.1%.

$$\text{est. } \omega^2 = \frac{2.91^2 - 1}{2.91^2 + 40 + 1} = \frac{7.468}{8.468 + 41} = \frac{7.468}{49.468} = .151$$

Note that when t is less than 1 it does not make sense to use Formula 10.10, because variances cannot be negative. However, t values less than 1 are so far from being statistically significant that it would generally be safer to assume that no (i.e., zero) variance is being accounted for in the population than to try to estimate that quantity.

The Relationship Between ω^2 and d^2

As just mentioned, if you were to calculate r_{pb}^2 on an entire population, you would refer to the result as ω^2. And, as we explained in Chapter 7, calculating the effect-size measure g for an entire population results in a quantity that we will be referring to as $\mathbf{d}$, the lowercase letter d printed in boldface. Note that although g is a slightly biased estimator of $\mathbf{d}$, the bias is so small for fairly large sample sizes that you rarely see g being corrected when it is used to estimate $\mathbf{d}$. We have a great deal to say about $\mathbf{d}$ when we discuss power in the next chapter.

Just as there is a simple relationship between r_{pb} and g for the data in your samples, there is a correspondingly simple relationship between ω^2 and $\mathbf{d}^2$ in the population. To express this relationship as a formula, all that needs to be done is to square both sides of the equation relating r_{pb} to g, drop out the df/N term (there is no distinction between df and N when you are dealing with an entire population), and change the notation:

$$\omega^2 = \frac{\mathbf{d}^2}{\mathbf{d}^2 + 4} \qquad \text{Formula 10.11}$$

For example, when $\mathbf{d}$ is 2 (i.e., the means of the two populations are 2 standard deviations apart), the proportion of variance accounted for is .5 [i.e., $4/(4+4)$]. That ω^2 equals .5 tells us that the average variance within the populations is only half as large as the variance measured across the two populations. If the gender difference in height in an entire population were such that $\mathbf{d} = 2$, then you would know that the variance in height for all humans is twice as large as the variance measured separately for each gender. You can use the formula to verify the following examples for yourself: $\omega^2 = .2$ when $\mathbf{d} = 1$; $\omega^2 = .8$ when $\mathbf{d} = 4$.

Publishing Effect-Size Estimates

As we mentioned in Chapter 7, supplementing the results of a t test by reporting a corresponding confidence interval is especially helpful when you are dealing with familiar units (inches, kilograms, IQ points). When you are not, it is highly recommended to report a measure of effect size. Sometimes the quantity that we are calling g is used for this purpose, but it is more likely to be referred to as d, or Cohen's d (often without using boldface), even though it has been calculated from sample data and has not been corrected for bias. Sometimes researchers use a correlational measure, such as r_{pb} or r_{pb}^2, to represent effect size in the two-group case, but in our experience, the correlational measures are much more likely to be used in multi-group situations, such as those described in Chapter 12.

Summary

To the extent that two continuous variables exhibit a linear relationship, we can use the value on one variable to predict a person's value on the other variable. The closer the points on a scatterplot of the two variables fall on a single straight (regression) line, the more accurate will be the predictions. However, the concept and mechanics of linear regression can also be useful for understanding the relationship between a continuous variable and a dichotomous (two-valued) variable.

Linear Regression

When the goal is to obtain the predicted score Y', given a raw score for X, the formula to use is:

$$Y' = b_{YX}X + a_{YX}$$ Formula 10.1

where

$$b_{YX} = r_{XY}\frac{\sigma_Y}{\sigma_X} = r_{XY}\frac{s_Y}{s_X}$$ Formula 10.2

$$a_{YX} = \overline{Y} - b_{YX}\overline{X}$$ Formula 10.3

The standard error of estimate for predicting Y from X, a measure of error in the prediction process, is equal to

$$\sigma_{est} = \sqrt{\frac{\sum (Y - Y')^2}{N}} = \sigma_Y\sqrt{1 - r_{XY}^2}$$ Formula 10.5

This measure is a descriptive statistic. If you wish to estimate the standard error of estimate in a population from sample data, use the following formula:

$$s_{est} = s_Y\sqrt{\frac{N-1}{N-2}\left(1 - r_{xy}^2\right)}$$ Formula 10.6

Points to Remember

1. The foregoing regression equations minimize the sum of squared errors in prediction, $\sum(Y - Y')^2$.
2. The closer r is to zero, the greater the errors in prediction. If $r = \pm1$, $\sigma_{est} = 0$ (prediction is perfect). If $r = 0$, σ_{est} equals its maximum possible value σ_Y (prediction is useless).
3. If r is not statistically significant, linear regression should probably *not* be used.
4. The regression line always passes through the point $\overline{X}, \overline{Y}$.

5. The foregoing procedure is used only for purposes of predicting scores on Y *from* X (Y is the criterion and X is the predictor). Different formulas are needed to predict scores on X, and the simplest procedure in such cases is to change the designations (relabel X as Y and Y as X) so that the foregoing procedure may be used.

The Connection Between Correlation and the *t* Test

An r_{pb} is calculated like any other Pearson r, except that the two X values may be assigned arbitrarily to two distinct groups. Therefore, the sign of the correlation is usually ignored.

Testing the Point-Biserial Correlation Coefficient for Significance

The magnitude of r_{pb} can be tested for significance with a t test, like any other Pearson r:

$$t = \frac{r_{pb}\sqrt{N-2}}{\sqrt{1 - r_{pb}^2}} \qquad \text{Formula 10.7}$$

where N is the total number of pairs, which equals the total number of cases in the two groups $= n_1 + n_2$.

Converting Significant Values of t to r_{pb}

When a statistically significant value of t in a test of the difference between two means is obtained, it is often helpful to convert it to r_{pb} so as to determine the *strength* of the relationship. This is readily done as follows:

$$r_{pb} = \sqrt{\frac{t^2}{t^2 + df}} \qquad \text{Formula 10.8}$$

where

$$df = N_1 + N_2 - 2$$

Comparing r_{pb} to Another Measure of Effect Size, g

Both r_{pb} and g are alternative measures of the strength of the relationship between a dichotomous grouping variable and a continuous dependent variable. You can compute r_{pb} directly from g with the following formula:

$$r_{pb} = \sqrt{\frac{g^2}{g^2 + 4(df/N)}} \qquad \text{Formula 10.9}$$

Estimating the Proportion of Variance Accounted for in the Population

Squaring r_{pb} gives you the proportion of variance accounted for in your data, but this is a *biased* estimate of that proportion in the population, which is called ω^2. A nearly unbiased estimate of ω^2 is given by the following formula, based on the t value from the corresponding pooled-variance t test comparing the means of the two groups:

$$\text{est. } \omega^2 = \frac{t^2 - 1}{t^2 + df + 1} \qquad \text{Formula 10.10}$$

The relationship between ω^2 and Cohen's **d** for the population, two alternative measures of the population effect size, is a simple one, as shown in the following formula:

$$\omega^2 = \frac{\mathbf{d}^2}{\mathbf{d}^2 + 4} \qquad \text{Formula 10.11}$$

Exercises

1. Use the data and your results from Exercise 1 in Chapter 9 to compute the linear regression equation for predicting the sophomore average (Y) from the number of cuts (C). What sophomore average would be predicted for a student who cut class eight times during the semester in question?

2. (a) Use the data and your results from Exercise 1 in Chapter 9 to compute the linear regression equation for predicting the sophomore average (Y) from the test score (X). (Advanced exercise: Compute the linear regression equation for predicting the test score [X] from the sophomore average [Y].) (b) Use the linear regression equation you calculated in part (a) to compute the predicted (Y') sophomore average for each particular student. Then compute the error (or residual, $Y - Y'$) for each student and the squared error as well. (c) Using the results of part (b), compute the standard error of the estimate for predicting Y from X (i.e., the test score). Verify that this value (σ_{est}) is indeed equal to the value you would calculate by using Formula 10.5.

3. Compute the linear regression equation for predicting Y from X for each of the data sets in Exercise 3 in Chapter 9. What proportion of the variance in Y is accounted for by X in each data set? For each data set, use the appropriate formula to calculate the *unbiased* standard error of the estimate (s_{est}).

4. Use the t value you calculated for Exercise 1 in Chapter 7 to find the point-biserial r that corresponds to the difference in means between Turck and Kirk Halls. Then use the appropriate t formula to test the r_{pb} you just computed for significance. How does this t value compare with the original t value you calculated for Exercise 1 in Chapter 7?

5. An industrial psychologist obtains scores on a job-selection test from 41 men and 31 women, with the following results (see Exercise 4 in Chapter 7): men, $M = 48.75$ ($SD = 9.0$); women, $M = 46.07$ ($SD = 10.0$). First, calculate g for these data. Then use the appropriate

formula to calculate r_{pb} directly from g. What proportion of variance in these data is accounted for by gender?

6. The following data come from Exercise 5 in Chapter 7. Calculate r_{pb} for these data by assigning an X value of 0 to Group 1 and an X value of 1 to Group 2. What proportion of the variance in the scores is accounted for by group membership?

Group 1	Group 2
62	46
54	53
59	50
56	52
59	54

7. Convert each of the following statistically significant values of t, obtained from the t test for the difference between two independent means, to r_{pb}.

t	N_1	N_2
2.11	12	8
2.75	12	8
6.00	12	8
2.11	19	23
2.75	19	23
6.00	19	23
2.11	51	51
2.75	51	51
6.00	51	51

8. Another industrial psychologist asks a group of 9 assembly-line workers and 11 workers not on an assembly line (but doing similar work) to indicate how much they like their jobs on a 9-point scale ($9 =$ like, $1 =$ dislike). The results are as follows:

Assembly-line workers:	4	4	4	2	1	5	3	4	3		
Other workers:	6	5	7	5	3	7	6	8	7	3	3

(a) Test the null hypothesis that there is no relationship between the assembly line variable and job satisfaction by computing r_{pb} and then using Table C to find the critical value. What should the psychologist decide? (b) Calculate the corresponding t value using Formula 10.7, and then compute an estimate of omega squared (ω^2) by using Formula 10.10. Does it look like there is a fairly large effect of job type on job satisfaction in the population?

Thought Questions

1. In a research study using a sample of 30 participants, the Pearson r correlation between X and Y is .09 and is *not* statistically significant. Should linear regression be used to predict scores on Y given scores on X? Why or why not?

2. When using linear regression, does the researcher want the standard error of estimate to be small or large? Why? (a) If the standard error of estimate is large, what does this imply about the variability of scores on Y for any given value of X? Why does this make predicting scores on Y from scores on X less accurate? (b) If the standard error of estimate is small, what does this imply about the variability of scores on Y for any given value of X? Why does this make predicting scores on Y from scores on X more accurate?

3. Explain why each of the following statements is true: (a) The data from any research study that uses the t test for the difference between two independent sample means can also be analyzed by computing a point-biserial correlation coefficient. (b) Any researcher using the t test for the difference between two independent sample means should also compute a point-biserial correlation coefficient (or other measure of effect size) for the same data. (c) When computing a point-biserial correlation coefficient, it does not matter what two numbers you assign to the dichotomous variable.

4. (a) How do the variables in a research study that uses the ordinary Pearson r correlation coefficient differ from the variables in a study that uses the point-biserial correlation coefficient? (b) Is the procedure for computing a point-biserial correlation coefficient different from the procedure for computing a Pearson r correlation coefficient? Why or why not? (c) Is the procedure for testing a Pearson r correlation coefficient for statistical significance different from the procedure for testing a point-biserial correlation coefficient for statistical significance? Why or why not? (d) In what way is the meaning of a squared point-biserial correlation coefficient the same as the meaning of any other squared Pearson r correlation coefficient?

5. When using the Pearson r correlation coefficient (and virtually all other statistical procedures), it is important to pay attention to the sign of a coefficient (plus or minus). Why, then, do we ignore the sign when interpreting a point-biserial correlation coefficient?

Computer Exercises

1. Use your statistical package to perform a linear regression predicting the statistics quiz score from the math background quiz score. Write out the formula for the raw-score regression line. What statistics quiz score would be predicted for a student who obtained a score of 20 on the math background quiz? A score of 40?

2. Perform a linear regression to predict the statistics quiz score from the student's self-reported math phobia level, and write out the raw-score regression formula. Use a scatter plot to help you interpret this result. Repeat the linear regression and scatter plot using math phobia to predict pre-quiz anxiety. (Advanced exercise: Redo these two regressions for just the psychology majors in Ihno's class.)

3. Use your statistical package to compute the Pearson r between gender and baseline anxiety for Ihno's students; calculate the t value for testing r, using Formula 10.7, and compare it to the t value you obtained for Computer Exercise 1 of Chapter 7.

4. Repeat Exercise 1 for baseline heart rate (compare to Chapter 7, Computer Exercise 2). How can you interpret the sign of the correlation for this and the previous exercise?

5. Create a new variable whose value is 1 for psychology majors and 2 for all other majors. Compute Pearson's r between this new variable and the math background quiz score. Interpret both the sign and the magnitude of this correlation.

Bridge to SPSS

SPSS handles regression analyses completely separately from correlation. Moreover, to perform simple linear regression (i.e., just one predictor with one criterion), SPSS employs the same module that it uses for multiple regression. Fortunately, it is easy to use that module for simple, bivariate linear regression and to interpret the output.

Linear Regression

To compute any linear regression in SPSS, select **Regression** from the Analyze menu, and then choose **Linear . . . .** In the dialog box that opens, move the variable that *you want to predict* to the area labeled "Dependent:" (there is room for only one variable in this space). Then move the variable that you want to use as your *predictor* to the area labeled "Independent(s):"; this space can accommodate more than one variable, in case you want to perform multiple regression. The various Options, Plots, and Statistics you can request deal mainly with evaluating the assumptions (such as the linearity of the relation between the two variables) that underlie the use of linear regression and are especially useful when performing multiple regression. [For simple linear regression, the default selection for Method (i.e., "Enter") is used.] The space labeled **Selection Variable:** allows you to perform your regression on a particular subgroup of cases defined by values on some other variable not involved in the regression. For example, to perform your regression on participants of one gender only, move your gender variable to "Selection Variable," which will activate the **Rule . . .** button. Clicking on the **Rule** button will allow you to specify the numeric code (i.e., value) for the gender you want to select.

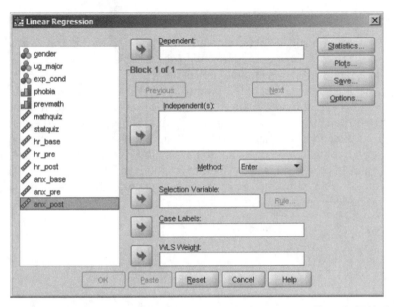

Source: Reprint courtesy of International Business Machines Corporation, © SPSS, Inc., an IBM company. SPSS was incorporated by IBM in October 2009.

The default output for linear regression consists of four boxes. In simple (one-predictor) regression, the first box contains the one (and only) independent variable (IV), under "Variables Entered," and the dependent variable (DV) is indicated below the box. The second box (Model Summary) provides the Pearson r between the IV and the DV, and some related statistics (an uppercase R is used, because with more than one predictor this value is the coefficient of *multiple* correlation). The third box (ANOVA) provides a significance test for the Pearson r, in terms of an F ratio—a statistic that will be described in Chapter 12. Finally, it is the fourth box (Coefficients) that provides you with the slope and intercept for the least-squares regression line, though the labels do not make this clear. Under the first column, headed "Model," the term "(Constant)" refers to the Y-intercept of the regression line. The second column, headed "B" (under the larger heading of Unstandardized Coefficients), gives you the value for the Y-intercept of the raw-score equation (next to Constant) and the value for the slope (next to the name of your IV). These values are divided by the ones in the next column ("Std. Error") to create t values for testing both the intercept and the slope for significance. You will rarely be interested in the significance test for the intercept, and the t value for the slope is exactly the same as the one you would get from the t formula for testing r. In fact, squaring this t value will give you the F value in the ANOVA box, and the "Sig." value in the ANOVA box will always be the same as the Sig. for your IV in the Coefficients box, when you are using only one IV (i.e., predictor).

Point-Biserial Correlation

There is nothing special about computing a point-biserial correlation with SPSS; as long as a variable is not a *string* variable, it can be selected in the Bivariate Correlations dialog box as described in the previous chapter. And, as long as the variable contains at least two different values in the data sheet, it will produce a correlation coefficient when selected along with any other variable that meets the same criterion. Whether the magnitude of that correlation will be meaningful depends on the nature of the variables involved. In particular, if one of the variables has only two values, representing two distinct groups, and the other variable is measured on a continuous scale, the resulting correlation coefficient (r_{pb}) should be interpretable.

Chapter 11
Introduction to Power Analysis

PREVIEW

Introduction

What is the power of a statistical test? How is it related to a Type II error? What are the practical consequences of making a Type II error?

Concepts of Power Analysis

How is the power of a statistical test related to the criterion of significance? To the size of the sample?

What is the population effect size, and how is it related to the power of a statistical test?

How large must the sample size be in order to use the procedures described in this chapter?

The Significance Test of the Mean of a Single Population

What are the procedures for determining the power of statistical tests about the mean of a single population?

What are the procedures for determining the sample size required to have a specified power?

The Significance Test of the Proportion of a Single Population

What are the procedures for determining the power of statistical tests about the proportion of a single population?

What are the procedures for determining the sample size required to have a specified power?

The Significance Test of a Pearson *r*

What are the procedures for determining the power of statistical tests about the Pearson *r*?

What are the procedures for determining the sample size required to have a specified power?

Testing the Difference Between Independent Means

What are the procedures for determining the power of statistical tests about the difference between two means, using independent samples?

(continued)

PREVIEW (*continued*)

What are the procedures for determining the sample size required to have a specified power?

Testing the Difference Between the Means of Two Matched Populations

What are the procedures for determining the power of a matched-pairs *t* test? How do they differ from the procedures for independent samples?

How can the sample size be determined for a given level of power?

Choosing a Value for d for a Power Analysis Involving Independent Means

How can you estimate the value of **d** from previously published results?

How can extreme possible values of **d** be used to make decisions about what sample sizes to use?

Using Power Analysis Concepts to Interpret the Results of Null Hypothesis Tests

Why does a lack of statistical significance with small samples tell you little about whether the null hypothesis is true?

Why should you be more impressed when statistically significant results are attained with smaller samples?

Why should you be extra cautious when interpreting the results of a significance test involving very large samples?

How can Type II errors actually be useful in some circumstances?

Summary

Exercises

Thought Questions

Computer Exercises

Bridge to SPSS

Introduction

Thus far, this text has been chiefly concerned with procedures for controlling the rate of Type I errors (incorrect rejections of the null hypothesis). This reflects a long-term emphasis among both behavioral researchers and statisticians. However, in hypothesis testing, there is a second important type of error to consider. You also run the risk that even if H_0 is false, you may fail to reject it. Incorrectly retaining a null hypothesis is called a *Type II error*. Of the cases in which the null hypothesis is *not* true, the proportion for which H_0 is nonetheless retained is the (conditional) probability of a Type II error, symbolized by β. The complement of this probability, $1 - \beta$, is the probability of getting a significant result when H_0 is false, and it is called the *power* of the statistical test.

To truly understand null hypothesis testing, you must also understand the factors that affect the rate of Type II errors and therefore statistical power.

When behavioral scientists test a null hypothesis, they almost always want to reject it; therefore, they want the power of the statistical test to be high rather than low. That is, they hope that there is a good chance that the statistical test will indicate that H_0 can be rejected. Despite its importance, this topic has received less emphasis in introductory statistical textbooks than it deserves. The unfortunate result of the ignorance about power is that research may be done in which, unknown to the investigator, power is low (and therefore the probability of a Type II error is high), a false null hypothesis is not rejected (i.e., a Type II error is actually made), and much time and effort are wasted. Worse, a promising line of research may be prematurely and mistakenly abandoned because the investigators do not know that they should have relatively little confidence concerning their failure to reject H_0.

This chapter deals first with the concepts involved in power analysis. Then methods are presented for accomplishing the two major forms of power analysis that can be applied to the null hypothesis tests discussed thus far in this text.

Concepts of Power Analysis

The material in this section, because it holds generally for a variety of statistical tests, is abstract and requires careful reading. In ensuing sections, these ideas will be incorporated into concrete procedures for power and sample size analysis of five types of hypothesis tests. There are four major factors involved in power analysis:

1. *The significance criterion, α.* This, of course, is the familiar criterion for rejecting the null hypothesis. It equals the probability of a Type I error given that H_0 is true (usually .05). A little thought should convince you that the more stringent (the smaller) this criterion, other things being equal, the harder it is to reject H_0 even when it is *not* true, and therefore power is reduced.

2. *The sample size, N.* Whatever else the accuracy of a sample statistic may depend upon, it *always* depends on the size of the sample for which it has been determined. Thus, all the standard errors you have encountered in this book contain some function of N in the denominator. It follows that, other things being equal, error decreases and power increases as N increases.

3. *The population "effect" size, d.* Effect size is a critical concept for understanding power, and a very general one that applies to many

statistical tests. When a null hypothesis about a population is false, it is false to some degree. (In other words, H_0 might be very wrong, or somewhat wrong, or only slightly wrong.) The parameter **d**, as described in Chapter 7, is a standardized measure of the *degree* to which the null hypothesis is false, or how large the "effect" is in the population. Within the framework of hypothesis testing, **d** can be looked on as a *specific* value that is an alternative to H_0. Specific alternative hypotheses, in contrast to such universal alternative hypotheses as $H_A: \mu_1 - \mu_2 \neq 0$ or $H_A: \rho \neq 0$, are what make power analyses possible. We will consider **d** in detail in subsequent sections.

Other things being equal, power increases as **d**, the degree to which H_0 is false increases. That is, you are more likely to reject a false H_0 if H_0 is very false. Given that power is a function of both **d** and N, it is generally true that the larger the **d**, the smaller the N that is required for significance to be obtained.

4. ***Power, or*** $1 - \beta$. The fourth parameter is power, the probability of rejecting H_0 at the given significance criterion when H_0 is not true. It is equal to the complement of the probability of a Type II error. That is, power $= 1 - \beta$.

These four factors are mathematically related in such a way that any one of them is an exact function of the other three. We deal with the two most useful ones:

1. *Power determination.* Given that a statistical test is performed with a specified α and N, if you can specify (or at least estimate) the population state of affairs, **d**, the power of the statistical test can be determined.

2. *N determination.* For a given population state of affairs, **d**, if a statistical test using α is desired to have some specified level of power (say .80), the necessary sample size, N, can be determined.

One final foundational concept that will prove useful in statistical power analysis is δ (lowercase delta), where

$$\delta = \mathbf{d} \times f(N)$$

That is, δ is equal to **d** times a function of N. Thus, δ combines the population effect size and the sample size into a single index. The table from which power is read (Table D in the Appendix) is entered using δ. As you will see, δ can be thought of as the expected value of your test statistic (e.g., t value), and therefore, the larger δ is, the more likely it is that your test statistic will beat the critical value and become statistically significant. So, the larger δ is, the more power you have.

In the sections that follow, the general system described above for analyses of power determination and sample size determination will be implemented for five different statistical tests:

1. Tests of hypotheses about the mean of a single population (Chapter 6).

2. Tests of hypotheses about the proportion of a single population (Chapter 6).

3. Tests of the significance of a Pearson correlation coefficient (Chapter 9).

4. Tests of the difference between the means of two independent populations (Chapter 7).

5. Tests of the difference between the means of two matched populations (Chapter 7).

The procedures to be described are approximate, and are not very accurate except for fairly large samples (N at least 25 or 30). This is because the system we will be describing is based on the normal curve, which is only a good approximation to the t distribution once N is fairly large.

The Significance Test of the Mean of a Single Population

In Chapter 5, we introduced null hypothesis testing in an example involving the math SAT. The value of 500 was known to be the mean of the population, and the issue was whether the mean of individually tested students differed from that value. Thus, the null hypothesis is H_0: $\mu = \mu_0 = 500$.

The alternative hypothesis stated in Chapter 5 was merely that H_A: $\mu \neq 500$. However, power analysis is impossible unless a *specific H_A* is stated.

Power Determination

For the purposes of power analysis, let us assume that you suspect (or are interested in the possibility) that the population mean of individually tested participants is 25 points higher than 500, so that H_A: $\mu = 525$. Assume further that, to be cautious, a two-tailed .05 decision rule is to be used and that the sample size you have available is $N = 164$. Finally, assume that you know that the population standard deviation (σ) for the math SAT is 100. The power determination question can then be formulated as follows: If we perform a test at $\alpha = .05$ of H_0: $\mu = 500$ using a random sample of $N = 164$, and in fact μ is 525, what is the probability that we will get a significant result and hence reject H_0?

The size of the effect postulated in the population, which is 25 points in *raw score* terms, must be expressed as a **d** value to accomplish the power analysis. For a test of the mean of a single population, **d** is expressed essentially as a z score:

$$\mathbf{d} = \frac{\mu_1 - \mu_0}{\sigma}$$

In the present example,

$$\mathbf{d} = \frac{525 - 500}{100} = \frac{25}{100} = .25$$

Note that this is *not* a statement about *sample* results. It expresses, as an alternative hypothesis, the *population* state of affairs. That is, μ_1 is postulated to be $.25\sigma$ away from μ_0, the value specified by H_0. Note also that the sign of $\mathbf{d}$ is ignored; an effect size of $-.25$ (i.e., $\mu_1 = -475$) would lead to the same results for power.

Having obtained the measure of effect size, the next step is to obtain δ. In the previous section, we pointed out that $\delta = \mathbf{d} \times f(N)$. For the test of the mean of a single population, the specific function of N required is $\sqrt{N}$, so that

$$\delta = \mathbf{d}\sqrt{N} \qquad\qquad \text{Formula 11.1}$$

In the present example,

$$\delta = .25\sqrt{164} = 3.2$$

Entering Table D in the Appendix with $\delta = 3.2$ and $\alpha = .05$, the power is found to be .89. Thus, if the mean of the population of individually tested participants is 25 points away from 500, the probability of rejecting H_0 in this situation is .89 (or the probability of a Type II error is .11). If the mean of the population of individually tested participants is more than 25 points away from 500, the power will be greater than .89. Conversely, if the population mean is less than 25 points away from 500, the power will be less than .89.

It is important to understand that power analysis is based entirely on population values, whether we know them or whether we are just hypothesizing about them. The above analysis could well take place before the data were gathered to determine what the power would be under the specified α, $\mathbf{d}$, and N. Or it could take place after an experiment was completed to determine the power the statistical test most likely *had*, given α, $\mathbf{d}$, and N, using your own experimental results to estimate $\mathbf{d}$, as we will explain shortly.

If the power for a reasonably postulated $\mathbf{d}$ were equal to a low value like .2 or .3, and the results of the experiment turned out not to be statistically significant, the nonsignificant result would hardly be surprising, since the *a priori* probability of obtaining significance was so small (and the probability of a Type II error was so high). However, a power of .90 associated with a nonsignificant result tends to suggest that the actual $\mathbf{d}$ is not likely to be as large as postulated.

In order to compute $\mathbf{d}$ in the above example, it was necessary to posit a specific value of μ_1 (525) and also to know σ (100). This can often be difficult when the unit is not a familiar one. (For example, extensive a priori data may not be available for a new psychological test.) For such situations, it is useful to specify conventional values corresponding to "small," "medium," and "large" values of **d**, which, although arbitrary, are reasonable and widely accepted (in much the same way as the .05 decision rule). For the test of the mean of a single population, the values suggested by J. Cohen (1988) are:

$$small: \mathbf{d} = .20$$

$$medium: \mathbf{d} = .50$$

$$large: \mathbf{d} = .80$$

If you are unable to posit specific values of μ_1 or σ, you can select the value of **d** corresponding to how large you believe the effect size in the population to be. However, do *not* use the above conventional values if you can specify **d** values that are appropriate to the specific problem or field of research in which the statistical test occurs, for conventional values are only reasonable approximations. As you get to know a substantive research area, the need for reliance on these conventions should diminish. Later in this chapter, we discuss how previously published research results can help you to estimate **d** for your study.

To clarify the general logic of power analysis, let us reconsider the preceding problem in terms of the concepts introduced in Chapter 5. The null hypothesis states that $\mu_0 = 500$ and the standard error of the mean is equal to 7.81 ($\sigma/\sqrt{N}$ is equal to 100/12.81), so the sampling distribution of means postulated by H_0 can be illustrated by the graph shown at the *top* in Figure 11.1. Assume that the true value of μ is equal to 525, for which the sampling distribution of means is as shown by the graph at the *bottom* in Figure 11.1. How likely is it that you will retain the incorrect μ_0 of 500?

Because we are using the normal curve as an approximation to the appropriate t distribution, the critical value (z_0) is equal to ± 1.96. If a sample mean is obtained that (when expressed as a z value) is numerically less than 1.96, the incorrect H_0 will be retained. This z_0 value can readily be converted to a critical value of the sample mean:

$$z_0 = \frac{\overline{X} - \mu_0}{s_{\overline{X}}}$$

$$1.96 = \frac{\overline{X} - 500}{7.81}$$

$$\overline{X} = (1.96)(7.81) + 500$$

$$\overline{X} = 515.31$$

The incorrect H_0 will be rejected if the sample mean is greater than 515.31. To see how likely this is to occur when the population mean is actually equal to 525, consider only the bottom curve in Figure 11.1, and

Figure 11.1

Sampling Distribution of Means ($N = 164$) Assuming $\mu_0 = 500$ and $\mu_1 = 525$

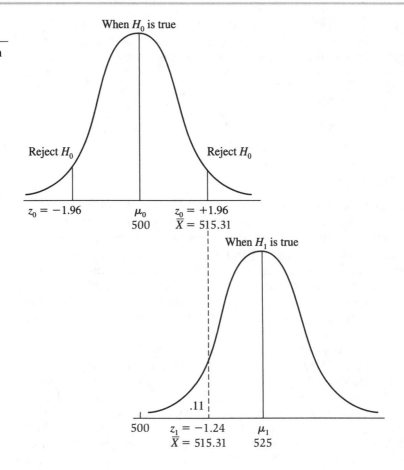

convert the mean value of 515.31 to a z value:

$$z_1 = \frac{\overline{X} - \mu_1}{\sigma_{\overline{X}}}$$

$$z_1 = \frac{515.31 - 525}{7.81} = \frac{9.69}{7.81} = -1.24$$

The percent of the area under the normal curve to the right of this z value can be found by using Table A: At $z = -1.24$, it is about 89% (39.25% + 50.00%). Therefore, when $\mu = 525$, about 89% of the sample means which one can obtain would be greater than 515.31 and thus significant. So the probability of rejecting H_0 when $\mu = 525$, and hence the power of this test, is .89. Of course, it was much easier to find the power for this problem by calculating δ and then looking up the power in Table D. However, we would like you to know how the values in Table D arise. Because the test is two-tailed and the analysis symmetrical, the preceding steps would lead to the same conclusion if the true μ were equal to 475,

25 points *below* H_0. Thus, we can conclude that, under these conditions, if $\mu = 525$ *or* 475, the probability of rejecting H_0 ($\mu_0 = 500$) is .89.

If the null hypothesis is so wrong that there is virtually no chance of a Type II error (i.e., if the effect size is extremely large), power will be virtually perfect (approaching 1.0). This does *not* indicate that the research is necessarily good, for the researcher may be testing a proposition so obviously wrong that the research would be pointless. (For example, the null hypothesis might be that the mean IQ of college graduates is 68!) If, however, the null hypothesis is only slightly wrong (the researcher is studying a small-size effect), a large sample size will be needed in order for the research to have acceptable power.

Sample Size Determination

We now turn to what is arguably the main purpose of statistical power analysis, sample size determination. Here, α, **d**, and the desired power are specified, and you wish to determine the necessary sample size. This form of analysis is particularly useful in experimental planning, because it provides the only rational method for making the crucially important decision about the size of N.

First, we must consider the concept of "desired power." Your first inclination might be to set power very high, such as .99 or .999. But, as your intuition might suggest, the quest for near certainty is likely to result in the requirement of a very large N, usually far beyond your resources. This is similar to the drawback of choosing a very small significance criterion, such as .0001: Although a Type I error is very unlikely with such a criterion, you are also very unlikely to obtain statistical significance unless the effect size and/or sample size is unrealistically large. Therefore, just as it is prudent to seek less than certainty in minimizing Type I errors by being content with a significance criterion such as .05 or .01, a prudent power value is also in order insofar as Type II errors are concerned.

Although a researcher is free to set any power value that makes sense to her, we suggest the value .80 (which makes the probability of a Type II error equal to .20) when a conventional standard is desired. Why is this suggested value larger than the customary .05 value for the probability of a Type I error? In most instances in science, it is seen as less desirable to mistakenly reject a true H_0 (which leads to falsely positive, and possibly even embarrassing, claims) than to mistakenly fail to reject H_0 (which leads only to the failure to find something and no claim at all: "The evidence is insufficient to warrant the conclusion that...."). The bottom line is that, if desired power was conventionally set at .95 (making $\beta = .05$), most studies would demand larger samples than most investigators could muster. We repeat, however, that the .80 value should be used only as a general standard, with investigators quite free to make their own decision based on the availability of participants, the cost of running the study, and other pertinent factors.

Let us return to the individual SAT test study, but now with a different purpose. Instead of assuming that N is to be 164, suppose that you are now interested in the following question: "If I test at $\alpha = .05$ the null hypothesis that $\mu = 500$ when in fact $\mu = 525$ or 475 (and $\sigma = 100$), how large must N be for me to have a .80 probability of rejecting H_0 (i.e., to have power = .80)?" To answer this question, the first step is to obtain two values: d, determined by the same methods as in the preceding section and equal to $(\mu_1 - \mu_0)/\sigma$ or .25 in this case, and the desired power, specified as .80. Next, δ is obtained by entering Table E in the Appendix in the row for desired power = .80 and the column for α (two-tailed) = .05; δ is found to be 2.80. (You could find the power value of .80 in the body of Table D and then see that it corresponds to a δ of 2.8, but Table D won't always contain the nice even values of power that you will usually want to look up, so we created Table E as a convenience.) Finally, for this test of the mean of a single population, N is found as follows:

$$N = \left(\frac{\delta}{d}\right)^2 \qquad \qquad \text{Formula 11.2}$$

In the present example,

$$N = \left(\frac{2.80}{.25}\right)^2$$

$$= (11.2)^2$$

$$= 125$$

To have power = .80 in the present situation, the sample must have 125 cases in it. Note that this is consistent with the previous result where we saw that, other things (d, α) being equal, $N = 164$ resulted in power = .89. To illustrate the consequences of demanding very high power, consider what happens in this problem if desired power is set at .999. From Table E in the Appendix, $\delta = 5.05$. Substituting,

$$N = \left(\frac{\delta}{d}\right)^2 = \left(\frac{5.05}{.25}\right)^2 = (20.2)^2 = 408$$

In this problem, to go from .80 to .999 power requires increasing N from 125 to 408. This is more than most psychological researchers can easily manage. Of course, if data are easily obtained (e.g., a brief online survey), or if the cost of making a Type II error is great, no objection can be raised about such a high power demand.

The Significance Test of the Proportion of a Single Population

The structure of the power analysis procedures remains the same as before; only the details need to be adjusted when dealing with proportions. The null hypothesis in question is that the population proportion, π, is equal to some specified value. That is, H_0: $\pi = \pi_0$. H_0 is tested against some specific alternative, H_A: $\pi = \pi_1$.

Power Determination

Let us return to the worried politician in Chapter 6, who wants to forecast the results of an upcoming two-person election by obtaining a random sample of $N = 400$ voters and testing the null hypothesis that the proportion favoring him is $\pi_0 = .50$. He thinks that he is separated from his opponent by about .08. That is, he expects the vote to be .54 to .46 or .46 to .54. (His expectations are stated in both directions because a two-tailed significance test is intended.) The question can be summarized as follows: If a statistical test is performed at $\alpha = .05$ of H_0: $\pi = .50$ against the specific alternative H_A: $\pi = .54$ (or .46) with $N = 400$, what is the power of this statistical test?

For the test of a proportion from a single population, the effect size, **d**, and δ are defined as follows:

$$\mathbf{d} = \frac{\pi_1 - \pi_0}{\sqrt{\pi_0(1 - \pi_0)}}$$

$$\delta = \mathbf{d}\sqrt{N}$$

For the data of this problem,

$$\mathbf{d} = \frac{.54 - .50}{\sqrt{.50(1 - .50)}}$$

$$= \frac{.04}{.50}$$

$$= .08$$

$$\delta = .08\sqrt{400}$$

$$= 1.60$$

Entering Table D with $\delta = 1.60$ and $\alpha = .05$, the power is found to be .36. So our worried politician has something else to worry about: As he has planned the study, he has only about one chance in three of coming to a positive conclusion (rejecting the null hypothesis that $\pi = .50$) if the race is as close as he thinks (H_A: $\pi = .54$ or .46). If the poll had already been conducted as described and the results were not statistically significant, he should consider the results inconclusive. Even if π is as far from .50 as .54 or .46, the probability of a Type II error (β) is .64.

Sample Size Determination

Let us now invert the problem to one of determining N, given the same **d** = .08, $\alpha = .05$ and specifying the desired power as .80. The formula for

N for the test of a proportion from a single population, like the previous formula for δ, is the same as in the case of the mean of a single population:

$$N = \left(\frac{\delta}{d}\right)^2$$

The value of δ for the joint specification of power $= .80$, and α (two-tailed) $= .05$ is found from Table E (again) to be 2.80. Therefore,

$$N = \left(\frac{2.80}{.08}\right)^2$$

$$= (35)^2$$

$$= 1,225$$

This sample size is considerably larger than the $N = 400$ that yielded a power of .36 under these conditions. It is hardly a coincidence that in surveys conducted both for political polling and for market and advertising research, sample sizes typically run about 1,000 to 1,500.

If conventional values for effect size for this test are needed, the conventional **d** values for correlation (see next section) can be used: small, .10; medium, .30; large, .50.

The Significance Test of a Pearson r

Recall from Chapter 9 that for testing Pearson's r, the null hypothesis is usually H_0: $\rho = 0$. For the purpose of power analysis, the alternative hypothesis is that the population value is some *specific* value other than zero: H_A: $\rho = \rho_1$. For example, you might be testing an r for significance when expecting that the population value is .30. In this case, H_A: $\rho = .30$. (Again, for two-tailed tests, the value is taken as either .30 or $-.30$.)

Power Determination

When dealing with a Pearson r, you do not need a formula to define the effect size, because r is already in the form of an effect-size measure; the value for **d** is simply the value of ρ specified by H_A (.30 in this example). To find δ, the appropriate function of N to be combined with **d** is $\sqrt{(N-1)}$.

$$\delta = \mathbf{d}\sqrt{N-1} = \rho_1\sqrt{N-1} \qquad \text{Formula 11.3}$$

Let us consider again the study in Chapter 9 in which we measured the degree of linear relationship between GPA and SAT scores in a random sample of 25 college students. Suppose we had planned a two-tailed statistical test with $\alpha = .01$, and we had expected the population ρ to be .43; thus $\rho_1 = .43$, whereas H_0: $\rho = 0$. What is the power of this test? We can go directly to

$$\delta = .43\sqrt{25 - 1} = 2.10$$

Entering Table D for $\delta = 2.10$ and $\alpha = .01$, power is found to be .32. One chance in three of finding significance seems hardly worth the effort. We may then reconsider the stringency of our significance criterion and check $\alpha = .05$; the power of .56 with this more lenient criterion may still be disappointing. If so, we could plan to increase our sample size (as shown in the next section). However, if ρ was actually equal to the obtained sample r of .65 (see Table 9.2), δ would be about 3.2, with $N = 25$, and power would be as high as .73, even for $\alpha = .01$.

If the investigator has difficulty in formulating an alternative-hypothetical value for ρ_1, the following conventional values are offered (J. Cohen, 1988): small, .10; medium, .30; large, .50. The value of .50 may not seem "large," but over most of the range of behavioral science where correlation is used, correlations between different variables do not often get much larger than that.

Sample Size Determination

Returning to the SAT/GPA study, we can ask what N is necessary for a test at α (two-tailed) $= .05$, assuming $\mathbf{d} = \rho_1 = .30$, in order to have power of (let us say) .75. The value of N is just one more than for the other two one-sample tests previously described:

$$N = \left(\frac{\delta}{\mathbf{d}}\right)^2 + 1 = \left(\frac{\delta}{\rho_1}\right)^2 + 1 \qquad \text{Formula 11.4}$$

δ is found from Table E for power $= .75$, $\alpha = .05$, to be 2.63, so

$$N = \left(\frac{2.63}{.30}\right)^2 + 1$$

$$= (8.77)^2 + 1$$

$$= 78$$

To have a .75 chance (i.e., three-to-one odds) of finding r to be significant if $\rho_1 = .30$ (or $-.30$), the researcher needs a sample of 78 cases.

Testing the Difference Between Independent Means

The next significance test whose power analysis we consider is the test of the difference between the means of two independently drawn random samples. This is probably the most frequently performed test in the behavioral sciences, so we will go into a good deal of detail for this case.

As stated in Chapter 7, the null hypothesis most frequently tested is H_0: $\mu_1 - \mu_2 = 0$ (often written as $\mu_1 = \mu_2$). For power analysis, a *specific* alternative hypothesis is needed. We will write this as H_A: $\mu_1 - \mu_2 = \theta$ (theta), where θ is the difference between the means expressed in *raw* units. To obtain **d**, the standard measure of effect size, this difference must be standardized. This is done using the standard deviation of the population, σ (which is a single value since we assume that $\sigma_1 = \sigma_2$ for the two populations). Thus, the value of **d** in this instance is conceptually the same as for the test of a single population mean, namely

$$\mathbf{d} = \frac{\text{alternative-hypothetical } \mu_1 - \mu_2}{\sigma} = \frac{\theta}{\sigma}$$

Thus the effect size in the two-group case can be looked upon as the difference in means expressed in units of σ. Again, the direction of the difference (the sign of θ) is ignored in two-tailed tests.

This device of "standardizing" the difference between two means is generally useful, and not only for purposes of power analysis. Frequently in behavioral science, there is no sure sense of how large one unit of a raw score really is. How large *is* a point? Well, they come in different sizes: An IQ point comes about 15 to the standard deviation (σ_{IQ}), while an SAT point is much smaller, coming 100 to the standard deviation (σ_{SAT}). By always using σ as the unit of measurement, we achieve comparability from one measure to another, as was the case with *z* scores.

This device helps us with regard to other related problems. One occurs whenever we have not had much experience with a measure (e.g., a new test of attention), and we have little if any basis for estimating the population σ, which the foregoing formula for **d** requires. Paradoxically enough, we can use this σ as our unit, despite the fact that it is unknown, by thinking directly in terms of **d**. Thus, a **d** of .25 indicates a difference between two population means (whose exact value we do not know) equal to .25σ (whose exact value we also do not know). It is as if our ignorance cancels out, and in a most useful sense **d** = .25 is always the same size difference whether we are talking about IQ, height, socioeconomic status, or a brand-new measure of "oedipal intensity."

How large *is* a **d** of .25, or any other? Here, as before, it is possible (and sometimes necessary) to appeal to some conventions, and they are the same as in the test of the mean of a single population: small, .20; medium, .50; large, .80. In this framework, a **d** of .25 would be characterized as a "smallish" difference. To gain a more concrete feeling with respect to the size of **d**, it may help to think about **d** in terms of the overlap of the two distributions involved. When **d** is 2.0, the mean of one population is two SDs away from the mean of the other; only a little more than 2% of the population with the lower mean, for instance, will extend above the mean of the "higher" population. When **d** is merely "large" (see Figure 11.2A), about 21% of the lower population exceeds the mean of the higher population, and when **d** is "small," more than 42% of the lower

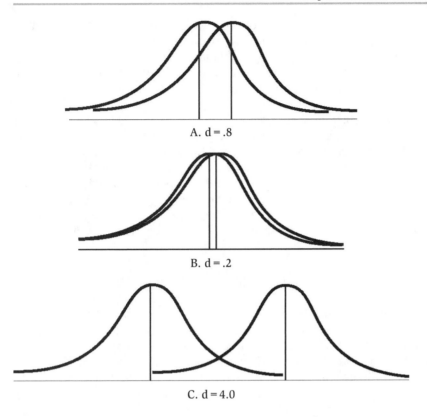

Figure 11.2

Overlap of Populations as a Function of Effect Size

A. d = .8

B. d = .2

C. d = 4.0

population is above the mean of the higher one (see Figure 11.2B). By contrast, with a **d** of 4.0, there would be so little overlap between the two distributions that relatively few scores from the lower population would surpass *any* of the scores from the higher population (see Figure 11.2C).

Power Determination

For the comparison of two means, the value of δ is equal to

$$\delta = \mathbf{d}\sqrt{\frac{n}{2}} \qquad \text{Formula 11.5}$$

where

n = size of *each* of the two samples (thus $2n$ cases are needed in all)

Compare this formula to Formula 7.10A for finding t in terms of g (the effect size in your samples) and n (reproduced here):

$$t = g\sqrt{\frac{n}{2}} \qquad \text{Formula 7.10A}$$

Over many exact replications of a particular experiment, the values of g will average out (approximately) to $\mathbf{d}$, the effect size in the population. And the t's for these replications should, in the long run, average out to (approximately) δ (delta), which can be thought of as the *expected t value* for an experiment with a particular value for $\mathbf{d}$ and a fixed size of n for each of the two samples.

As an illustration, consider the caffeine study in Chapter 7 (revised to make it a true experiment). Given two groups, each with $n = 40$ cases, one of which is given a dose of caffeine and the other a placebo, we will test at $\alpha = .05$ (two-tailed) the difference between their means on a mathematics test following the treatment. If between the populations there is a mean difference of medium size, operationally defined as $\mathbf{d} = .50$, what is the power of the test? With $\mathbf{d}$ given on the basis of convention, there is no need to compute it and hence no need to estimate μ_1, μ_2, or σ. Thus, given a fixed n, all we need to calculate is:

$$\delta = .50\sqrt{\frac{40}{2}} = 2.24$$

Entering Table D in the column for $\alpha = .05$, we find that for $\delta = 2.2$ power $= .59$ and for $\delta = 2.3$ power $= .63$. Given that 2.24 is about halfway between 2.2 and 2.3, it is reasonable to say that our power is about halfway between .59 and .63, or approximately .61. Thus, for medium differences (as defined here) and samples of 40 cases each, we have only a .61 probability of rejecting H_0 for a two-tailed test using $\alpha = .05$.

Ordinarily, in research where variables are to be manipulated, such as the caffeine experiment described here, it is possible to arrange the experiment so that the total available pool of participants is divided equally among the groups. This division is usually optimal. But it is not always possible or desirable to have equal sample sizes. For example, it would be a mistake to reduce the larger of two available samples of convenience to make it equal to the smaller. Instead, to determine power when $N_1 \neq N_2$, we can use the same device we employed in Chapter 7; we can compute the *harmonic mean* of the two Ns and then use this obtained value for n in the formula for δ. As an example, consider a psychiatric hospital study where there are resources to place a random sample of 50 newly admitted schizophrenic patients into a special experimental treatment program. After 1 month, their progress is compared with a control group of 150 cases receiving regular treatment for the same period. It is planned to rate each patient on an improvement scale 30 days following admission and to test for the significance of the difference in means for rated improvement, using a two-tailed test where $\alpha = .05$. If it is anticipated that $\mathbf{d} = .40$ (between "small" and "medium"), what is the power of the test?

Because $N_1 \neq N_2$, first compute:

$$\overline{X}_{\text{harmonic}} = \frac{2N_1N_2}{N_1 + N_2} = \frac{2(50)(150)}{50 + 150} = 75$$

Then enter this value as n in the formula for δ:

$$\delta = .40\sqrt{\frac{75}{2}} = 2.45$$

Interpolating between the values for $\delta = 2.4$ and $\delta = 2.5$ in Table D in the $\alpha = .05$ column yields power $= .69$ (i.e., midway between .67 and .71).

Note that a total of $N_1 + N_2 = 200$ cases will be studied. But since $N_1 \neq N_2$, the resulting power is the same as if two samples of 75 cases each, or 150 cases, were to be studied. There is a smaller effective n, and hence less power, when the sample sizes are not equal. Equal sample sizes usually yield the optimal level of power for a given total N. Were it possible to divide the total of 200 cases into two equal samples of 100, δ would then equal $.40 \sqrt{(100/2)} = .40 \times 7.07 = 2.83$, and the resulting power at $\alpha = .05$ obtained from Table D by interpolation is about .81.

Sample Size Determination

The sample size needed for *each* independent sample when two means are to be compared can be found for specified values of α, **d**, and the desired power, as was shown for the other statistical tests in this chapter. The combination of α and power is expressed as δ by looking in Table E, and the values for δ and **d** are substituted in the equation appropriate for this statistical test, which is:

$$n = 2\left(\frac{\delta}{\mathbf{d}}\right)^2 \qquad\qquad \text{Formula 11.6}$$

For example, it was found in the caffeine experiment that for $\alpha = .05$ and $\mathbf{d} = .50$, the plan to use samples of $n = 40$ each resulted in power $= .61$. If power $= .90$ is desired, what n per sample is needed?

For a two-tailed test where $\alpha = .05$ and power $= .90$, Table E yields $\delta = 3.24$. Substituting these values in Formula 11.6, we obtain:

$$n = 2\left(\frac{3.24}{.50}\right)^2$$

$$= 84 \text{ cases in each group, or 168 cases in all}$$

Again we see that large desired power values demand large sample sizes. Were the more modest power of .80 specified, δ would equal 2.80 (Table E) and n would equal $2(2.80/.50)^2$, or about 63, a substantially smaller number.

Testing the Difference Between the Means of Two Matched Populations

The last significance test whose power analysis we will consider is the test of the difference between *dependent* or *correlated* means—that is, the test that is applied to the data of a matched-pairs design. The formulas and procedures for power analysis in this case differ from the preceding one (i.e., the difference between two independent means) by the inclusion of one additional term that depends on the degree to which the two sets of scores are matched in the population, as expressed by the correlation coefficient ρ.

Power Determination

Given that **d** is defined as in the case of two independent means, the value of δ for a matched (or repeated-measures) design is given by:

$$\delta = \mathbf{d}\sqrt{\frac{1}{1-\rho}}\sqrt{\frac{n}{2}} \qquad \text{Formula 11.7A}$$

where ρ is the correlation between the two sets of scores in the population. Note that as ρ gets closer to 1.0, the denominator of the first term gets smaller, making the first term larger. When ρ is .75, the term based on ρ becomes 2.0, and δ therefore becomes twice as large as it would be for an otherwise similar experiment without matching. The power boost from this degree of matching is substantial; it is equivalent to the boost you would get by quadrupling your sample sizes. It is instructive to express Formula 11.7A in terms of Formula 11.5:

$$\delta_{\text{matched}} = \delta_{\text{independent}}\sqrt{1/(1-\rho)} \qquad \text{Formula 11.7B}$$

where $\delta_{\text{independent}}$ is given by Formula 11.5.

You can see from Formula 11.7B that a ρ of zero would leave $\delta_{\text{independent}}$ unchanged—that is, δ_{matched} would equal $\delta_{\text{independent}}$ in that case. Conversely, a ρ close to +1 would cause δ_{matched} to be much larger than $\delta_{\text{independent}}$. A negative ρ, which is unlikely when you are making an effort to match participants, would actually *reduce* your δ and therefore your power. To illustrate, let us return to the before-after heart rate comparison as shown in Table 7.2 of Chapter 7. Suppose that you expect a large effect size (**d** = .8), and a population correlation (ρ) of .5, for the 10 participants in the study. You plan to perform a two-tailed matched-pairs t test at the .05 level. Given these values,

$$\delta = .8\sqrt{\frac{1}{1-.5}}\sqrt{\frac{10}{2}} = .8\sqrt{2}\sqrt{5} = (.8)(1.414)(2.236) = 2.53$$

From Table D, we can see that a δ of 2.53 corresponds to a power of about .72 for a two-tailed significance test using .05 for alpha. This is a barely adequate level of power for conducting an experiment, and if a lower value of **d** or ρ were expected, the sample size would have to be increased to maintain even this minimal level of power.

Sample Size Determination

The formula for finding the sample size required for a given level of power, with values specified for **d** and ρ, is the same as the one for independent samples multiplied by a factor of $(1 - \rho)$. So if you expect a matching correlation of .9 in the population, you will only need one-tenth the number of participants $(1 - .9)$ to achieve the level of power that would result with no matching at all.

For the heart rate comparison, suppose you want power to be .8 for a .05, two-tailed test ($\delta = 2.8$, from Table D), and you expect a medium effect size (**d** = .5) and a ρ of only .3. The number of pairs of scores that would be required is given by the following formula:

$$n = 2(1 - \rho) \left(\frac{\delta}{\mathbf{d}}\right)^2 \qquad \text{Formula 11.8}$$

For this example,

$$n = 2(1 - .3) \left(\frac{2.8}{.5}\right)^2 = 1.4(31.36) = 43.9$$

Therefore, 44 participants would each have to be measured twice in order to attain the desired level of power.

Choosing a Value for d for a Power Analysis Involving Independent Means

Students often feel uneasy when they first discover that power analysis is only as accurate as your estimate of **d.** Unless you are replicating an experiment for which you already have the results, it is not obvious how you can make a reasonable guess about the **d** that corresponds to your new experiment. Let us now consider the relatively simple case in which you *are* contemplating the replication of a published result.

Estimating d From Previous Research

Suppose you read a journal article reporting that a group of participants listening to music composed by Mozart produced significantly higher scores on a test of spatial ability than a control group who listened to popular (e.g., "soft rock") music. Further suppose that the chief result was reported as "$t(34) = 2.4, p < .05$." If you know that the two groups were the same size, then you know that n was 18 ($2n - 2 = 34$), and you can then find g from t and n by using Formula 7.10B:

$$g = t\sqrt{\frac{2}{n}} = 2.4\sqrt{\frac{2}{18}} = 2.4\left(\frac{1}{3}\right) = .8$$

If you were to replicate this study exactly, it would be reasonable to use g from the previous study as the estimated **d** for your new study when calculating power for different possible sample sizes. Even if you planned to use a different spatial ability measure whose mean and standard deviation were quite different from those in the previous study, it would not be unreasonable to suppose that **d** (which is in standardized units) would be fairly similar for both studies.

At what point is your new study so different from a previously published study that you can no longer use g from the previous study as an estimate of **d** for your new study? This is a judgment call that requires a thorough knowledge of your research domain. It is the same kind of judgment that underlies the increasingly popular statistical procedure known as *meta-analysis*. In meta-analysis, the gs for any number of similar studies are averaged together, with greater weight being given to studies with larger samples, to arrive at an improved estimate of **d.** This (weighted) average g can then be tested for significance using the combined N of all the studies involved. This method creates one large "meta" study, which greatly increases power relative to any one individual study, and thus makes a Type II error much less likely.

If the two samples are not equal in size in a previous study but you are given both N_1 and N_2, you can still calculate g from t by using the unequal-N formula for g (based on the harmonic mean) given in Chapter 7, and reproduced here:

$$g = t\sqrt{\frac{N_1 + N_2}{N_1 N_2}}$$ Formula 7.12

Suppose that the Ns for the Mozart study were as follows: $N_1 = 30$ and $N_2 = 6$ (degrees of freedom [df] is still 34). In order for t to be 2.4, g would have to be:

$$g = 2.4\sqrt{\frac{36}{180}} = 2.4\sqrt{\frac{1}{5}} = 1.07$$

We showed earlier that as your two Ns diverge, your power decreases. Here we are showing a related principle: When your Ns are unequal, you need a larger effect size to have the same power you would have had with the same total N, but equal sample sizes.

Trying Extreme Values for d

One possible approach to sample-size determination begins with deciding on the smallest effect size for which you would like to have adequate power. For instance, suppose you feel that for your experiment there would be little point to having an adequate level of power (say, .7) for an effect size of only .1. This constraint corresponds to a size for each sample of

$$n = 2\left(\frac{\delta}{d}\right)^2 = 2\left(\frac{2.48}{.1}\right)^2 = 2(24.8)^2 = 2(615) = 1230$$

Thus, you would not consider running your experiment with more than about 1,200 participants in each group, because that would give you adequate power for an effect size too small to be of interest.

Conversely, you can begin by deciding on the largest value that is reasonably possible for your effect size. Suppose you think it unlikely that **d** is greater than 1.0. Again using the value of .7 for barely adequate power (which corresponds to a δ of 2.48 for a .05, two-tailed test), your target sample size would be:

$$n = 2\left(\frac{2.48}{1}\right)^2 = 2(6.15) = 12.3$$

This calculation tells you that there would be little point to running your experiment with *fewer* than 13 participants per group, because in that case you would expect your power to be less than adequate (i.e., below .7).

Using Power Analysis Concepts to Interpret the Results of Null Hypothesis Tests

Whether you ever perform a power analysis before running an experiment, it is important to understand the factors that affect the power of a statistical test. This can help you to interpret the results of null hypothesis tests correctly and avoid some serious misconceptions.

Lack of Statistical Significance Does Not Imply That the Null Hypothesis Is Likely to Be True

The smaller your samples (all else being equal), the less power you will have to detect a given effect size in the population. In many common situations, power is surprisingly low. For instance, if your two-group experiment involves 32 participants in each group, your power will be only about .5 whenever you test medium-size effects at the .05 level. Here's the calculation that demonstrates that:

$$\delta = .5\sqrt{\frac{32}{2}} = .5(4) = 2.0$$

Looking up δ in Table D, you can see that you will reject H_0 (correctly) 52% of the time, but you will retain H_0 (and therefore commit a Type II error) nearly half of the time. So when you see a study involving small samples and H_0 is *not* rejected, you should be aware that H_0 could easily be false, nonetheless. Unfortunately, even when the true effect size is considerably more than zero, there is a good chance that the null hypothesis will not be rejected if the samples are small. All that a lack of statistical significance can suggest is that the true effect size is not likely to be extremely large.

Statistical Significance Is More Impressive When the Samples Are Smaller

For a given value of t, the *smaller* n is, the larger g has to be. And a larger g for your samples suggests a larger **d** in the population, which is more impressive than a smaller effect size. (For any particular set of experimental results, g could accidentally be much larger or much smaller than the **d** of which it is just an estimate, but on the average, a large g implies a large **d**.) By itself a large t value only suggests that H_0 is not very likely to be true, but a large t obtained with a small n tells you that g is fairly large and that **d** therefore is not likely to be even near zero. Although it may be counterintuitive, significant results are more impressive when obtained with *small* rather than large samples, because it is so rare for the results from small samples to attain statistical significance unless the effect size in the population is fairly large.

Large Samples Tend to Produce More Accurate Results But Can Lead to Misleading Conclusions

The larger your samples, the more accurate is g as an estimate of **d**. Because it is the magnitude of **d** that you would really like to know (not just whether it is unlikely to be zero, which is all you can conclude from null hypothesis testing [NHT]), larger samples are always more informative. However, there is usually some economic cost that comes with increasing your sample size (e.g., paying participants, paying research assistants), and the additional information may not be worth the cost. Moreover, very large samples make it easy to obtain statistically significant t values even when g (and probably **d**) is rather small. So you should not be overly impressed with statistically significant results that are obtained from large samples; in such cases you need to pay extra attention to effect-size estimates.

Also, remember that using repeated measures or matched samples can be similar to using larger samples without matching, in terms of attaining statistical significance with experimental treatments that are quite weak in their effects. Note that *statistical* significance is less likely to imply *practical* significance when the samples are very large or the correlation between matched sets of scores is very high.

The Null Hypothesis Testing Controversy Revisited

As we mentioned in the appendix of Chapter 5, there is much confusion concerning what null hypothesis testing does and does not tell you about the state of affairs in a population, and there has been much debate in the literature on this topic, especially in recent years. (We repeat our suggestion here that a good way to learn more about these issues is by reading *Beyond Significance Testing* [Kline, 2004], and if you skipped the appendix to Chapter 5, it would be a good idea to read that appendix before reading this section.) However, even though there does seem to be some increased reporting of confidence intervals and effect-size estimates, NHT, with its reporting of p values and decisions about H_0 still dominates the results sections of articles published in many branches of behavioral science research.

There is one major advantage of NHT that would be difficult to achieve with any new system: the widespread agreement on the .05 level as the largest, routinely acceptable value for alpha. This fixed criterion of significance, coupled with the usual constraints on sample sizes (behavioral researchers rarely employ very large samples), tends to make it likely that *statistically* significant results will be associated with effect sizes that are large enough to be interesting. Conversely, whereas NHT screens out 95% of studies in which the null hypothesis is actually true (i.e., with $\alpha = .05$, 95% of the null experiments will fail to attain statistical significance), it also screens out about 93% of very small effect sizes (e.g., **d** $\leq$ .1) when using small samples (e.g., about 30 participants in each of the two groups being compared). (As we pointed out in the appendix to Chapter 5, if the null hypothesis was true for the majority of studies conducted in a particular area of research, screening out 95% of them would not be very helpful; the absolute number of Type I errors committed could still get rather large. If there is reason to expect that the null hypothesis is often true in a research domain, studies in that domain should be required to use a smaller value for alpha.)

Technically, failing to reject H_0 when **d** is anything more than zero is a Type II error, but given all of the small effects that behavioral researchers may explore, many of these Type II errors save us the trouble of dealing with effects too small to be practical or even worthy of further exploration. For example, consider the "Mozart effect": the finding that listening to music composed by Mozart improves performance on a spatial ability test (Rauscher, Shaw, & Ky, 1993). It is not really interesting if Mozart's music produces an extremely tiny, temporary effect on spatial ability (especially when compared to popular music, as in the original study). Did anyone think that listening to Mozart's music was likely to reduce spatial ability? And would anyone be surprised if the music of other classical composers also produced such an effect? So, in many cases, especially when dealing with purely exploratory studies, for which the true effect size might easily be quite small, some Type II errors can actually be helpful.

However, (effect) size isn't everything. Sometimes even a tiny effect can be very interesting indeed, especially if it represents a phenomenon that was thought to be impossible (e.g., learning to control directly and voluntarily the function of your kidneys). It is often important to look carefully at estimates of effect size when a result is statistically significant, but it is also important to consider the theoretical significance of a study. When you are dealing with a tiny but important effect, it may indeed be worth the expense of gathering the large samples you will need to obtain adequate power, unless, of course, you can achieve a large power gain with matching or repeated measures.

Summary

Power is the *probability of getting a significant result* in a statistical test for which H_0 is *not* true. Power is equal to $1 - \beta$, where $\beta =$ the probability of a Type II error.

The Importance of Power

If power is not known, a researcher may waste a great deal of time by conducting an experiment that has little chance to produce significance even if H_0 is false. Worse, she may abandon a promising line of research because she does not know that she should have relatively little confidence concerning her failure to reject H_0 (i.e., the probability of a Type II error is large).

The Four Major Parameters of Power Analysis

1. *The significance criterion*, α. A Type II error is more likely as α gets smaller because you fail to reject H_0 more often. Thus, power decreases as α decreases.

2. *The sample size*, N. Larger samples yield better estimates of population parameters and make it more likely that you will reject H_0 when it is correct to do so. Thus, power increases as N increases.

3. *The population "effect" size*, **d**. You are less likely to fail to reject a false H_0 if H_0 is "very wrong"—that is, if there is a large effect size in the population. Thus, power increases as **d** increases.

4. Power, $1 - \beta$.

Any one of these four parameters can be determined mathematically from the other three.

The General Procedures for the Two Most Common Forms of Power Analysis

1. Power determination.
   (a) Compute or posit the value of **d**.
   (b) Compute δ (delta), which combines the N that you are considering and **d**.
   (c) Obtain power from the appropriate table, according to your desired α.

2. Sample size determination.
   (a) Specify desired power. (If a conventional value is needed, we recommend .80 for most purposes.)
   (b) Compute or posit the value of **d**.
   (c) Obtain δ from the appropriate table, according to your desired α.
   (d) Compute N.

If you have no basis for estimating **d**, or the population values from which **d** is computed, you can use the appropriate conventional values of **d**, as devised by J. Cohen (1988), for the statistical test in question.

The Specific Formulas for d, δ, and N

These depend on the statistical test that is being performed. (Note: All of the procedures given here are approximate and are accurate only for fairly large samples [n is at least 25 or 30].)

1. The test of the mean of a single population:

    (a) $\mathbf{d} = \dfrac{\mu_1 - \mu_0}{\sigma}$,

    where

    μ_0 = value of μ specified by H_0
    μ_1 = value of μ specified by H_A (a *specific* H_A is always
    necessary in power analysis)
    σ = population standard deviation

    (b) $\delta = \mathbf{d}\sqrt{N}$ Formula 11.1

    (c) $N = \left(\dfrac{\delta}{d}\right)^2$ Formula 11.2

    (d) Conventional values of **d**: small, .20; medium, .50; large, .80

2. The test of the proportion of a single population:

    (a) $\mathbf{d} = \dfrac{\pi_1 - \pi_0}{\sqrt{\pi_0(1 - \pi_0)}}$

    where

    π_0 = value of π specified by H_0
    π_1 = value of π specified by H_A

    (b) $\delta = \mathbf{d}\sqrt{N}$

    (c) $N = \left(\dfrac{\delta}{\mathbf{d}}\right)^2$

    (d) Conventional values of **d**: small, .10; medium, .30; large, .50

3. The significance test of a Pearson r (includes r_{pb})

    (a) $\mathbf{d} = \rho_1$, the value specified by H_A

    (b) $\delta = \mathbf{d}\sqrt{(N-1)}$ Formula 11.3

    (c) $N = \left(\dfrac{\delta}{\rho_1}\right)^2 + 1$ Formula 11.4

    (d) Conventional values of **d**: small, .10; medium, .30; large, .50

4. The test of the difference between independent means

    (a) $\mathbf{d} = \dfrac{\theta}{\sigma}$

where

$$\theta = \text{value of } \mu_1 - \mu_2 \text{ specified by } H_A$$
$$\sigma = \text{population standard deviation (a single value}$$
$$\text{because it is assumed that } \sigma_1 = \sigma_2)$$

(b) $\delta = \mathbf{d}\sqrt{\dfrac{n}{2}}$ Formula 11.5

where

n is the size of *each* sample (thus, $2n$ cases have been used in the experiment)

If the sample sizes are unequal, use the harmonic mean:

$$n = \frac{2N_1 N_2}{N_1 + N_2}$$ Formula 7.11

(c) $n = 2\left(\dfrac{\delta}{\mathbf{d}}\right)^2$ Formula 11.6

where

n is the size of *each* sample (so $2n$ cases will be needed in all)

(d) Conventional values of $\mathbf{d}$: small, .20; medium, .50; large, .80

5. The test of the difference between *dependent* (i.e., correlated) means

(a) $\mathbf{d} = \dfrac{\theta}{\sigma}$ where θ is the difference of the population means according to the null hypothesis

(b) $\delta = \mathbf{d}\sqrt{\dfrac{1}{1-\rho}}\sqrt{\dfrac{n}{2}}$ Formula 11.7A

where ρ represents the linear correlation of the two sets of scores in the population

(c) $n = 2(1-\rho)\left(\dfrac{\delta}{\mathbf{d}}\right)^2$ Formula 11.8

6. Estimating $\mathbf{d}$ from published research

You can calculate g from a published t value if you are given the two sample sizes:

$$g = t\sqrt{\frac{N_1 + N_2}{N_1 N_2}}$$ Formula 7.12

If the sample sizes are equal, this formula reduces to

$$g = t\sqrt{\frac{2}{n}}$$ Formula 7.10B

where n is the size of each of the two samples.

Exercises

1. Suppose that the students at Bigbrain University are planning to test whether the mean math SAT score for their school is higher than the national average (μ) of 500 (assume that $\sigma = 100$).

(a) If they believe that their mean is 520, and they plan to sample 25 students, what is the power of their statistical test at the .05 level, two-tailed? What would the power be for a one-tailed test? Explain why power is higher for the one-tailed test.

(b) Recalculate the one- and two-tailed power values in part (a) assuming that the Bigbrain students expect their average to be 50 points higher than the national average. Explain why these power values are higher than the ones you calculated in part (a).

(c) Redo part (a) assuming that a sample of 100 Bigbrain students is being planned. Explain why these power values are higher than the ones you calculated in part (a).

(d) Given the expected effect size in part (a), what sample size would be needed to obtain a power of .8 for a two-tailed .05 test? For a two-tailed .01 test?

(e) Repeat part (d) given the expected effect size in part (b).

2. Calculate the power for the tests you conducted for Turck and Kirk Halls in Exercise 1 of Chapter 6. (Use the t values you calculated for that exercise as the values for δ in your power calculation.)

3. (a) A politician needs 50% or more of the vote to win an election. To find out how his campaign is going, he plans to obtain a random sample of 81 voters and see how many plan to vote for him. He is willing to posit a specific alternative hypothesis of 60% (or 40%) and wishes to use the .01 criterion of significance. Compute the power of the statistical test. How would you evaluate this research plan?

(b) Suppose the politician decides to switch to the .05 criterion of significance (but that the other values are not changed). Will this improve the power of the statistical test to a satisfactory level?

(c) The politician finally resigns himself to doing more work and obtaining a larger sample. He wants power to be .75. How large a sample does he need (using the .05 criterion)?

4. (a) A personality theorist expects that two particular traits have a linear correlation on the order of .40 in the population she plans to sample. She wishes to test the null hypothesis that the correlation between the two traits is exactly zero, using the .05 criterion of significance and a random sample of 65 subjects. Is the power of this statistical test satisfactory? Explain.

(b) How large a sample would the theorist in part (a) need to obtain power $= .9$ with alpha set at .01 for a two-tailed test? For a one-tailed test?

5. If the sample r you calculated in Exercise 2 of Chapter 9 was equal to ρ for the population, how large a sample would you need to obtain power $= .7$ for a two-tailed test at the .05 level?

6. (a) Calculate g for the comparison of the means of Turck and Kirk Halls (if you did not already calculate that value for Exercise 1 of Chapter 7). Use g as your estimate of **d**, and compute the sample

sizes you would need for power = .75, for a .05 two-tailed test, comparing the two dormitories.

   (b) Given the sizes of the samples from Turck and Kirk Halls, how large would **d** have to be to obtain power = .85, for a .01, two-tailed test?

7. (a) Calculate g from the pooled-variance t value you computed to solve Exercise 2 in Chapter 7. Use that value for g as your estimate of **d**, and compute the sample sizes you would need for power = .9, for a .05 two-tailed test, assuming that you plan to use two equal-size samples to compare Turck and Dupre Halls.

   (b) Given the sizes of the samples in Exercise 2 of Chapter 7, how large would **d** have to be to obtain power = .8, for a .05, two-tailed test?

8. Calculate the missing values in the following table, assuming that you are comparing two independent, equal-size samples with a two-tailed t test. (Note: Small = .2, Medium = .5, Large = .8.)

Proposed n in each sample	Effect size	Power $\alpha = .05$	Power $\alpha = .01$	n in *each* sample needed for power of .85 if: $\alpha = .05$	$\alpha = .01$
30	Small	————	————		
100	Small	————	————	————	————
30	Medium	————	————		
100	Medium	————	————	————	————
30	Large	————	————		
100	Large	————	————	————	————

9. Suppose that you plan to match students between Turck and Kirk Halls so that the population correlation corresponds to .4. Given the **d** you found in part (b) of Exercise 6 and the sizes of the samples from Turck and Kirk Halls, how much power would you have for a two-tailed matched-pairs t test at the .01 level?

10. Recalculate the required sample sizes for part (a) of Exercise 7 if the two populations are matched with $\rho = .6$.

11. (a) Calculate the power your test would have in Exercise 7 of Chapter 7 if the two sets of scores were not correlated at all in the population (use g for those data as **d** in your power calculation).

    (b) Calculate the power your test would have in Exercise 7 of Chapter 7 if the two sets of scores had a population correlation of $\rho = .5$ (again, use g for those data as **d** in your power calculation).

Thought Questions

1. What is the power of a statistical test? Why is it important when planning a research study?

2. "Using the .05 criterion of significance, the probability of a Type I error is .05. Using the .001 criterion of significance, the probability of a Type I error is .001 (much smaller). Therefore, researchers should always use the .001 criterion of significance." Use the concept of statistical power to explain why the last sentence in the quotation is not a good idea.

3. A researcher argues as follows: "I performed a correlational study with a very large sample. Because my sample was so large, I obtained a correlation of $r = .07$ that was statistically significant. But this correlation is too small to be of any practical value, as there is very little (linear) relationship between the two variables that I studied. I therefore warn other researchers *not* to use large samples so as to avoid getting such misleading results." (a) Use the concept of statistical power to explain why the last sentence in the preceding quotation is not entirely true. (b) What is the advantage of obtaining the largest sample that a researcher can afford?

4. In the following table, decide which of the numbered statements belongs in each box:

Sample size	You retained H_0	You rejected H_0
Very small		
Very large		

1. You are studying an effect that is likely to be quite large.
2. Caution is indicated because you are studying an effect that may be quite small.
3. Power is likely to be so low, and the probability of a Type II error so large, that no conclusions of any kind should be drawn.
4. Power is likely to be high, so it may well be that H_0 is (approximately) true.

Computer Exercises

1. Suppose that Ihno is planning to compare the men with the women in her class. Use the noncentral t distribution function in your statistical package to answer the following questions. Assume that alpha is .05 and that each test is two-tailed.

   (a) Use the t value you computed for the gender difference in baseline anxiety (first computer exercise of Chapter 7) as your value for delta (δ) to determine the power of that test.

   (b) If the population effect size for another dependent variable (DV) was only .3, how much power would Ihno have for that gender comparison?

   (c) If Ihno had equal-size groups of men and women, how large would each have to be to attain power = .8, given the effect size in part (b)?

   (d) Repeat part (b) for $\mathbf{d} = .7$.

2. Solve this problem using the same methods and assumptions that you used for Exercise 1.

(a) Use the t value you computed to compare the students in the "impossible to solve" condition with those in the "easy to solve" condition in terms of postquiz heart rates (see Computer Exercise 3 of Chapter 7) as your value for δ (delta) to determine the power of that test.

(b) Had the population effect size for this DV been medium in size ($\mathbf{d} = .5$), how many students would Ihno have needed to have in each condition to attain power $= .7$?

Bridge to SPSS

In this chapter, we simplified power analysis by using the normal distribution as an approximation of the t distribution; that is why we needed only two brief tables (Tables D and E) to complete our analyses. Unfortunately, as the samples you are dealing with get smaller, the normal approximation becomes less accurate. In fact, the distribution we really need for power analysis when comparing the means of two small samples is not the family of t distributions but an even more complex family known as the **noncentral t distributions**. A noncentral t distribution (NCTD), unlike the ordinary null hypothesis distribution for a two-sample t test, does not have zero at its center. For power analysis we use an NCTD that is centered on δ (delta). Note that there is a different NCTD for each possible combination of δ and degrees of freedom (df). There are printed tables and graphs that can deal with this complexity (see J. Cohen, 1988), but you can use SPSS to get an even more accurate value with little effort. (You can also find various "power calculator" programs on the Web.)

To find the power that corresponds to a particular combination of δ and df, first look up the critical t value that corresponds to your df and desired alpha. Then open a new data sheet and type the value of δ into the first cell. Name the first column something like "delta." Next, click on **Compute** from the Transform menu, and in the dialog box that opens type a name like **Power** in the target variable box. In the Numeric Expression box, type $1 - \text{NCDF.T}$ (t_{crit}, **df, delta**), but in place of t_{crit} type the actual critical value you looked up and in place of df type the appropriate number (note that the commas between numbers in the parentheses are necessary). For "delta," type whatever variable name you assigned to the first column of your data sheet.

For example, suppose that you have two samples available, and each has 10 participants (so $df = 18$). For a .05, two-tailed test, the critical t is 2.101. If you expect $\mathbf{d}$ to be .8 (or just want to check what your power would be *if* $\mathbf{d}$ was large), $\delta = .8\sqrt{5} = 1.79$. This is the value you would type into the first cell of your data sheet. If you named your first data column "delta," then you would type the following expression in the appropriate space in the Compute dialog box: $1 - \text{NCDF.T}$ (**2.101, 18,**

delta), and then click **OK**. (If instead of typing in this expression you select it from the Function list in the Compute dialog box, you will get NCDF.T (q, df, nc), where "q" must be replaced by the critical value, "df" by df, and "nc" by the name of your first column. Do not forget to precede the expression by **1** followed by a minus sign, unless you want to get beta instead of power.)

A new column will appear in your data sheet bearing whatever name you typed in as the Target Variable, and it will contain the power value for your test—for this example, it is .40 (you can get an even more accurate value by requesting 3 or 4 under Decimals in Variable View). Note that if you use Table D to look up power for a delta of 1.79, you will see that power is listed as .44 for 1.8 and .40 for 1.7

(Table D is using 1.96 as the critical value instead of the more accurate value of 2.101, and it is using the normal distribution instead of the appropriate noncentral t distribution.)

Suppose, however, that you are not starting out with fixed sample sizes but are trying to determine what sample size to use for a particular value of **d** and a desired level of power. First, calculate your needed sample size with the formula given in this chapter. Then you can use trial and error with the SPSS expression described above to arrive at a more accurate answer. For instance, if you want power to be .8 (for a .05, two-tailed test) for an effect size of 1.0, δ (from Table E) is 2.8, and the calculated n is $2(2.8/1.0)^2 = 2(7.84) = 15.68$. Now you can plan to use 16 participants per group, giving you a df of 30, which corresponds to a critical t of 2.042. However, if you insert these values into the SPSS expression above, you will find that the power is .77, not .8. The normal approximation contained in Table E is overly optimistic. So you might next try $n = 18(df = 34)$, which gives you a critical t of 2.03. With **d** still at 1.0, delta equals $1.0\sqrt{9} = 3.0$, and SPSS will return a value for power of .83. This time we made n a bit too large. If you try $n = 17$, you will see that this sample size yields the desired level of power (approximately) for an effect size of 1.0.

Part III
Analysis of Variance Methods

Chapter 12   One-Way Analysis of Variance

Chapter 13   Multiple Comparisons

Chapter 14   Introduction to Factorial Design: Two-Way Analysis of Variance

Chapter 15   Repeated-Measures ANOVA

Chapter 12
One-Way Analysis of Variance

PREVIEW

Introduction

We wish to draw inferences about the differences among more than two population means. Why is it a poor idea to perform numerous t tests between the various pairs of means?

What is the experimentwise error rate?

In what way is one-way analysis of variance similar to the t test for the difference between two means? How does it differ?

The General Logic of ANOVA

If we wish to draw inferences about population means; why are we analyzing variances?

What is the within-group (or error) variance estimate? What is the between-group variance estimate?

What is the F ratio?

Computational Procedures

What are the procedures for drawing inferences about any number of population means by computing a one-way analysis of variance?

What are sums of squares? Mean squares?

Testing the F Ratio for Statistical Significance

What is the correct statistical model to use for testing an ANOVA?

How do we test the F ratio for statistical significance?

Calculating the One-Way ANOVA From Means and Standard Deviations

How can you calculate the F ratio for an ANOVA if you do not have the raw data but only a table of means, standard deviations, and sample sizes? Why might you need to do this?

Comparing the One-Way ANOVA With the t Test

What is the relationship between the t value and the F ratio in the two-group case?

What is the relationship between the pooled variance of the t test and MS_W in ANOVA?

(continued)

PREVIEW (*continued*)

A Simplified ANOVA Formula for Equal Sample Sizes

How does the equal-n formula show that the magnitude of the F ratio depends on the variance of the sample means, the variance within the samples, and the size of the samples?

Effect Size for the One-Way ANOVA

How can the formula for F be separated into a measure of effect size and a measure of sample size?

Why is it desirable to convert a statistically significant value of F into a correlational measure that shows the strength of the relationship between the independent and dependent variable? How is this done? And how can this measure be corrected for bias?

Some Comments on the Use of ANOVA

What assumptions underlie the use of one-way analysis of variance?

What format should you use to report your results?

What more specific tests may follow a significant ANOVA?

A Nonparametric Alternative to the One-Way ANOVA: The Kruskal-Wallis H Test

What are the procedures for testing the hypothesis that three or more independent samples of ranked data come from populations with equal locations?

What is the power efficiency of the Kruskal-Wallis H test?

When should the Kruskal-Wallis H test be used in place of the one-way analysis of variance?

How do we convert a significant result to a measure of strength of relationship?

Summary

Exercises

Thought Questions

Computer Exercises

Bridge to SPSS

Appendix: Proof That the Total Sum of Squares Is Equal to the Sum of the Between-Group and the Within-Group Sum of Squares

Introduction

Chapter 7 provided techniques for testing the significance of the difference between two means. These techniques enable you to determine the effect of a single independent variable (e.g., the presence or absence of a particular dosage of caffeine) on the mean of a dependent variable (e.g., mathematics test scores) when there are *two* samples of interest, such as an experimental group and a control group.

Suppose that you would like to determine whether *different dosages* of caffeine affect performance on a test of manual dexterity. As before, there is one independent variable (amount of caffeine), but this time you wish to include the following *five* conditions:

Sample 1: very large dose of caffeine

Sample 2: large dose of caffeine

Sample 3: moderate dose of caffeine

Sample 4: small dose of caffeine

Sample 5: placebo (no caffeine)

As usual, you would like the probability of a Type I error in this experiment to be .05 or less. Therefore, it would *not* be correct to perform 10 separate t tests for the difference between two means (i.e., first test H_0: $\mu_1 = \mu_2$; then test H_0: $\mu_1 = \mu_3$; etc.) and then compare each obtained t value to the appropriate critical t value for $\alpha = .05$.

The more statistical tests you perform, the more likely it is that some will be statistically significant purely by chance. When $\alpha = .05$, the probability that one t test will yield statistical significance when H_0 actually is true is .05. This is the probability of committing a Type I error. However, if you run 20 t tests when H_0 is always true, an average of 1 of them ($.05 \times 20 = 1.0$) will be statistically significant just on the basis of chance, so it is likely that you will commit at least one Type I error somewhere along the line. Similarly, if you run 10 separate t tests in order to test the null hypothesis for every possible pair of different caffeine dosages, the probability that you will commit at least one Type I error is clearly *greater* than the desired .05. (It can be shown that this probability is closer to .3.) The greater the number of sample means among which you perform pairwise significance tests, the more likely you are to make at least one Type I error. In statistical terminology, the rate of occurrence of *any* Type I errors over a *series* of individual but related statistical tests is called the **experimentwise error rate, α_{EW}**.

Fortunately, there is a procedure for testing differences among three or more means for statistical significance simultaneously, which overcomes this difficulty. This procedure is the *analysis of variance,* abbreviated as ANOVA. ANOVA can also be used with just two samples, in which case it yields equivalent results to the procedures given in Chapter 7. The null hypothesis tested by ANOVA is that the means of the populations from which the samples were randomly drawn are *all* equal. For example, the null hypothesis in the caffeine experiment is:

$$H_0: \mu_1 = \mu_2 = \mu_3 = \mu_4 = \mu_5$$

The alternative hypothesis merely states that H_0 taken as a whole is *not* true. There are many ways in which it may be false: It may be that $\mu_1 \neq \mu_2$, or that $\mu_3 \neq \mu_5$, or both, or that all five population means are unequal, or only two are equal, and so forth. The rejection of the ANOVA H_0 tells us only that *some* inequality exists. In the next chapter, we will describe separate procedures for testing pairwise mean differences following an ANOVA. Such procedures enable us to add greater specificity to the meaning of rejecting the ANOVA H_0.

The caffeine experiment is an example in which both the independent (amount of caffeine) and dependent (score on a test of manual dexterity) variables are measured quantitatively. More commonly, the independent variable in an ANOVA has qualitative levels (e.g., persuasive arguments are attributed either to a fellow student, a faculty member, or a member of the school administration), and that is the type of ANOVA on which this chapter is based. The type of ANOVA in which the independent variable (often called the **factor**) has quantitative levels is described only briefly near the end of the chapter.

The General Logic of ANOVA

It may seem paradoxical to test a null hypothesis about *means* by testing *variances,* so the general logic of ANOVA will be discussed before proceeding to the computational procedures. The ANOVA procedure is based on a mathematical proof that the sample data can be made to yield two independent estimates of the population variance:

1. **Within-group (or "error") variance estimate.** This estimate is based on how different each of the scores in a given sample (or group) is from other scores in the same group.

2. **Between-group variance estimate.** This estimate is based on how different the *means* of the various samples (or *groups*) are from one another, as well as on the sizes of those groups.

If the samples all come from the same normally distributed population (or from normally distributed populations with equal means and variances), it can be proved mathematically that the between-group variance estimate and the within-group variance estimate will be about equal to each other and equal to the common population variance (σ^2). The larger the between-group variance estimate is in comparison to the within-group variance estimate, the more likely it is that the samples do *not* come from populations with equal means.

Table 12.1   Two Versions of the Music Experiment (Hypothetical Data)

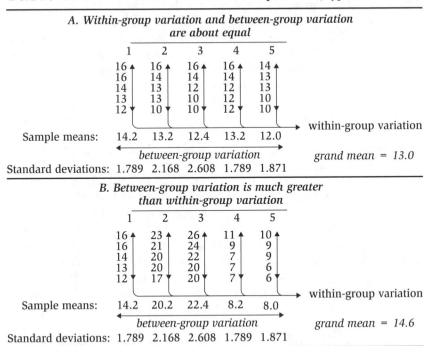

A. Within-group variation and between-group variation are about equal

	1	2	3	4	5
	16	16	16	16	14
	16	14	14	14	13
	14	13	12	12	13
	13	13	10	12	10
	12	10	10	12	10

within-group variation

Sample means: 14.2   13.2   12.4   13.2   12.0

between-group variation   grand mean = 13.0

Standard deviations: 1.789 2.168 2.608 1.789 1.871

B. Between-group variation is much greater than within-group variation

	1	2	3	4	5
	16	23	26	11	10
	16	21	24	9	9
	14	20	22	7	9
	13	20	20	7	6
	12	17	20	7	6

within-group variation

Sample means: 14.2   20.2   22.4   8.2   8.0

between-group variation   grand mean = 14.6

Standard deviations: 1.789 2.168 2.608 1.789 1.871

As an illustration, consider the hypothetical data in Table 12.1A. There are five groups, each of which listened to music by a different classical composer while completing a spatial ability test. Group 1 listened to Mozart, Group 2 to Chopin, and so on. Each group contains five people, so there are 25 participants in all, and the entries in the table represent the score of each person on the spatial ability test. There is some between-group variation and some within-group variation. The means of the five groups may differ because the composer of the music does have an effect on test scores or merely because they are affected by the presence of sampling error (i.e., the accident of which cases happened to be in each sample), or for both reasons. Whether to retain or reject the null hypothesis that the samples all come from the same population is decided by applying ANOVA procedures to the data. Inspection of Table 12.1A suggests that the between-group variation and within-group variation are about equal, as would be expected if H_0 is true.

What if the composer of the music *does* have an effect on spatial ability, at least temporarily? Suppose that one particular composer (e.g., Mozart) causes a real increase in test scores. Ideally, this implies that music by Mozart produces about the same helpful effect on all of the participants in the Mozart group. If that's true, the variability *within* that group will barely be affected, because adding a constant to all scores or subtracting a constant from all scores does *not* change the variance or standard deviation. Thus, the overall within-group variance estimate based on all the groups will also be little affected. The mean of the Mozart group, however, can be expected to be higher than the mean of the other groups. Therefore, the *between*-group variance estimate will increase. Similarly, if several different classical composers have different effects on test scores (e.g., some composers increase test scores more than others), the within-group variance estimate will not necessarily increase, but the between-group variance estimate will certainly get larger. The greater the differences among the group means, the larger will be the between-group variance estimate.

As an illustration, consider the data in Table 12.1B. Imagine that the groups in this version of the experiment heard very different *types* of music (e.g., bluegrass, jazz, classical, New Age, and heavy metal). (In reality, these data were obtained from the data in Table 12.1A as follows: Scores in Group 1 were not changed; 7 was added to each score in Group 2; 10 was added to each score in Group 3; 5 was subtracted from each score in Group 4; and 4 was subtracted from each score in Group 5.) The variance of each of the groups in Table 12.1B, and hence the within-group variance estimate, is equal to that of Table 12.1A. However, the between-group variance estimate is much greater in the case of Table 12.1B. Thus it is more likely that the five samples of scores in Table 12.1B do *not* come from the same population.

To clarify further the meaning of between-group variation and within-group variation, consider the score of the first person (let's call him Bill) in Group 1 of Table 12.1A, which is equal to 16. The total deviation of Bill's score from the grand mean is 3.0 (i.e., $16.0 - 13.0$). However, Bill's score also deviates by 1.8 points from the mean of his group ($16.0 - 14.2 = 1.8$). This part of his deviation is "error" in the sense that it cannot be explained by the composer variable, because all people in Bill's group (Group 1) listened to the same music. It simply reflects the basic person-to-person variance of the spatial ability scores.

The difference between the mean of Group 1 and the grand mean ($14.2 - 13.0$) is equal to 1.2 points. This part reflects the amount of Bill's deviation that can be explained by the composer he was listening to (Mozart). Of course, the within-group variation of 1.8 and the between-group variation of 1.2 sum to 3.0, the total variation of Bill's score from the grand mean. The three deviation scores involving just this one person are:

1. Total deviation = 3.0
2. Within-group (from own group) deviation (*error*) = 1.8
3. Between-group (from own group to grand mean) deviation = 1.2

The total variance of the spatial ability scores, the within-group variance estimate, and the between-group variance estimate are a function of the magnitude of these deviations, respectively, across everyone in the experiment. As you may recall, variances are computed by squaring all the deviations from the mean first, then summing them, and then dividing by the appropriate number of degrees of freedom (df). However, for some purposes it is easier to put off dividing by the dfs and deal instead with just the sums of the squared deviations (the SS's for short). For instance, it is useful that the total sum of squared deviations from the grand mean (the total sum of squares, or SS_T) is equal to the sum of the between-group sum of squares (SS_{bet}) and the within-group sum of squares (SS_W). (The proof is given in the appendix at the end of this chapter.) This does not hold true for the variances.

It is important to understand that the between-group variance estimate is influenced by *both* the effects of the different types of music (if any) *and* error variance. (The sample means will tend to vary because the individuals scores tend to vary, even if the independent variable is *not* having any effect.) Actually, there are two distinct sources of error variance; thus, the group means will be affected by not only the experimental treatment, but by individual differences in spatial ability as well as the error variance of the scores used to measure spatial ability. The within-group variance estimate, however, reflects solely the error variance (which includes both individual differences and measurement error). The effect due solely to the different types of music can therefore be isolated by computing the following F ratio:

$$F = \frac{\text{treatment variance} + \text{error variance}}{\text{error variance}}$$

$$= \frac{\text{between-group variance estimate}}{\text{within-group variance estimate}}$$

If H_0 is true, there is no treatment variance. The between-group and within-group variance estimates will therefore be approximately equal on average, so that F will usually be near 1.0. The more F is greater than 1.0, the more sure you can be that music type does have an effect on test scores. You reject H_0 when F is so large as to have a probability of .05 or less of occurring if H_0 is true.

Values of F less than 1.0 would indicate that H_0 should be retained, because the between-group variance estimate is smaller than the within-group variance estimate. Since the value of F expected if H_0 is true is about 1.0, one might conceive of a *significantly small* value of F (e.g., 0.2). There would be no obvious explanation for such a result other than chance or perhaps failure of one of the assumptions underlying the F test. Thus, you would retain H_0 in such instances, but if your F ratio was extremely tiny, you might check the possibility that some systematic factor like nonrandom sampling has crept in.

Computational Procedures

Although we do not expect that you will be using these formulas to calculate ANOVAs on research data you collect in the future, we feel that calculating a few ANOVAs by hand will give you a deeper appreciation of both the numerator and denominator of an ANOVA F ratio than you could ever get by clicking on the menu of a statistical program and then inspecting the results.

Sums of Squares

The first step in the calculation of any ANOVA is to compute the **sum of squares between groups** (symbolized by SS_{Bet}), **the sum of squares within groups** (symbolized by SS_W), and the **total sum of squares** (symbolized by SS_T). As we hope you recall, *a sum of squares* (SS) is just the numerator of the variance formula, as defined in Chapter 3.

1. ***Total sum of squares (SS_T).*** The definition formula for the total sum of squares is:

$$SS_T = \sum (X - \overline{X}_G)^2 \qquad \text{Formula 12.1A}$$

where

$\overline{X}_G = $ grand mean of all observations in the experiment
$\sum = $ summation across all *observations*

In Table 12.1A, for example,

$$SS_T = (16 - 13)^2 + (16 - 13)^2 + (14 - 13)^2$$
$$+ \ldots + (13 - 13)^2 + (10 - 13)^2$$
$$+ (10 - 13)^2$$
$$= 3^2 + 3^2 + 1^2 + \ldots + 0^2 + (-3)^2 + (-3)^2$$
$$= 100$$

As is the case with any variance (see Chapter 3), however, it is also possible to compute SS_T by using a shortcut computing formula:

$$SS_T = \sum X^2 - N_T \overline{X}_G^2 \qquad \text{Formula 12.1B}$$

where

$N_T = $ total number of observations in the experiment

For the data in Table 12.1A,

$$\sum X^2 = 16^2 + 16^2 + 14^2 + \ldots 13^2 + 10^2 + 10^2$$
$$= 4,325$$
$$N_T \overline{X}_G^2 = 25(13)^2 = 25 \times 169 = 4,225$$
$$SS_T = 4,325 - 4,225 = 100$$

[**Note: Calculator method for SS_T.** The computational formula just given is traditional; it comes from a time before handheld calculators were readily available. These days, it is quite possible that you are using a calculator that allows you to enter a set of numbers, and then select the sum of squares (SS) from a menu. However, even if your calculator does not have that function (or you cannot find it), it is likely that it is easy to obtain the unbiased standard deviation (s) from your calculator by pressing one or two keys, after you have entered a set of numbers. (Calculators often indicate the *un*biased standard deviation (SD) with a symbol created by adding the subscript "N-1" to either s or σ, like this: s_{N-1} or σ_{N-1}.) Let us assume that you have entered all 25 scores from Table 12.1A, for instance. To obtain SS_T from the unbiased SD of these numbers, first square the SD to get the unbiased variance, and then multiply this variance by N−1 (hence, the symbol on the calculator) — that is, multiply by 1 less than the number of scores you entered into your calculator to get the unbiased SD.]

2. **Sum of squares between groups (SS_{Bet}).** The definition formula for the sum of squares between groups is

$$SS_{Bet} = \sum_{i=1}^{k} N_i (\overline{X}_i - \overline{X}_G)^2 \qquad \text{Formula 12.2A}$$

where

N_i = number of scores in group i
$\overline{X}_i$ = mean of group i
$\overline{X}_G$ = grand mean
k = the number of groups
$\sum_{i=1}^{k}$ = summation across all the *groups* (*not* the subjects)

As we have seen, the between-groups sum of squares is based on the differences between the mean of each group and the grand mean. The multiplication by N_i in the formula ensures that the squared difference of the group mean from the grand mean is effectively counted once for each person in the group. (Samples need not be of equal size.)
In Table 12.1A,

$$SS_{Bet} = 5(14.2 - 13.0)^2 + 5(13.2 - 13.0)^2$$
$$+ 5(12.4 - 13.0)^2 + 5(13.2 - 13.0)^2 + 5(12.0 - 13.0)^2$$
$$= 5(1.2)^2 + 5(.2)^2 + 5(-.6)^2 + 5(.2)^2 + 5(-1.0)^2$$
$$= 14.4$$

When all of the samples are the same size, the formula for SS_{Bet} can be simplified to:

$$SS_{Bet} = n \sum_{i=1}^{k} (\overline{X}_i - \overline{X}_G)^2 \qquad \text{Formula 12.2B}$$

where

$$n = \text{number of scores in } each \text{ of the } k \text{ groups}$$

This is the same as finding the SS for the k sample means and then multiplying it by the common sample size.

3. **Sum of squares within groups (SS_W).** The definition formula for the SS within groups is:

$$SS_W = \sum^{n_1} (X - \overline{X}_1)^2 + \sum^{n_2} (X - \overline{X}_2)^2 + \cdots + \sum^{n_k} (X - \overline{X}_k)^2 \quad \text{Formula 12.3}$$

where

$$\overline{X}_1 = \text{mean of first group, } \overline{X}_2 = \text{mean of second group, and so on}$$
$$\sum = \text{summation across the } n_i \text{ cases of the group in question}$$
$$\text{(i.e., the } i\text{th group)}$$

This is the same as calculating the SS separately for the scores in each group and then adding all of these SS's together.

In Table 12.1A,

$$SS_W = (16 - 14.2)^2 + (16 - 14.2)^2 + (14 - 14.2)^2 + (13 - 14.2)^2$$
$$+ (12 - 14.2)^2 + (16 - 13.2)^2 + (14 - 13.2)^2 + (13 - 13.2)^2$$
$$+ \cdots + (10 - 12.0)^2 + (10 - 12.0)^2$$
$$= 85.6$$

That is, the difference between each score and the mean of the group containing the score is squared. (In this example, there is a total of 25 squared differences, but we are showing only the first 8 and the last 2.) Once this has been done for every score, the results are summed. This is the most tedious of the three sums of squares to compute, and it is possible to save a lot of work by making use of the fact that

$$SS_T = SS_{Bet} + SS_W \qquad \text{Formula 12.4}$$

That is, the sum of squares between groups and the sum of squares within groups must add up to the total sum of squares. (See the Appendix at the end of this chapter.) Therefore, the within-group sum of squares can readily be computed as follows:

$$SS_W = SS_T - SS_{Bet} = 100 - 14.4 = 85.6$$

You should be careful in using this shortcut, however, because it provides no check on computational errors. If SS_W is found directly, the foregoing formula can be used as a check on the accuracy in computation. (In a later section, we will show you how to skip the calculation of SS_W and instead calculate MS_W directly from the standard deviations of your groups.)

Mean Squares

Next, SS_{Bet} and SS_W are each divided by the appropriate degrees of freedom. The values thus obtained are called *mean squares* and are estimates of the population variance. The degrees of freedom between groups (symbolized by df_{Bet}) are equal to:

$$df_{Bet} = k - 1 \qquad \text{Formula 12.5}$$

where

> k = number of groups

The degrees of freedom within groups (symbolized by df_W) are equal to:

$$df_W = N_T - k \qquad \text{Formula 12.6}$$

where

> N_T = total number of observations

This is equivalent to obtaining the degrees of freedom for each group separately $(N_i - 1)$ and then adding the degrees of freedom across all groups. The *total df*, helpful as a check on the calculations of df, is equal to $N_T - 1$.

In Table 12.1A, $df_{Bet} = (5 - 1) = 4$; $df_W = (25 - 5) = 20$. The total $df = N_T - 1 = 24$, which is in fact equal to $4 + 20$.

The mean squares between groups (symbolized by MS_{Bet}) and the mean squares within groups (symbolized by MS_W) are equal to:

$$MS_{Bet} = \frac{SS_{Bet}}{df_B} \qquad \text{Formula 12.7}$$

$$MS_W = \frac{SS_W}{df_W} \qquad \text{Formula 12.8}$$

Thus, for Table 12.1A,

$$MS_{Bet} = \frac{14.4}{4}$$

$$= 3.60$$

$$MS_W = \frac{85.6}{20}$$

$$= 4.28$$

For Table 12.1B, MS_W is the same, but $MS_{Bet} = 884.4/4 = 221.1$. (We suggest that you calculate MS_{Bet} for Table 12.1B, using Formula 12.2B, as a check on your comprehension of this chapter thus far.)

Testing the F Ratio for Statistical Significance

Before we calculate and test our F ratio for significance, let us review the ANOVA procedure in terms of the three-step method of null hypothesis testing introduced in Chapter 7.

Step 1: State the null and alternative hypotheses and the significance criterion, α: Because we are dealing with five distinct populations (corresponding either to five different composers or five types of music), the null hypothesis is stated in terms of the equality of those five means: $H_0: \mu_1 = \mu_2 = \mu_3 = \mu_4 = \mu_5$. The only easy way to state the alternative hypothesis is as follows: H_A: not $(\mu_1 = \mu_2 = \mu_3 = \mu_4 = \mu_5)$. As usual, we will set alpha at the maximum value ordinarily allowed: $\alpha = .05$.

Step 2: Calculate the appropriate test statistic: Having computed the mean squares (MS), it is easy to compute the F ratio (we are pursuing two examples at once, so we will calculate both F ratios), as follows:

$$F = \frac{MS_{Bet}}{MS_W} \qquad \text{Formula 12.9}$$

For Table 12.1A,

$$F = \frac{3.60}{4.28} = .84$$

For Table 12.1B,

$$F = \frac{221.1}{4.28} = 51.66$$

Step 3: Find the critical value and make a statistical decision with respect to your null hypothesis: As noted earlier, we encounter a new statistical model when we wish to test the ANOVA H_0 for statistical significance: the F *distributions*. Here again, the correct model (i.e., the null hypothesis distribution) enables us to determine the probability of obtaining the results observed in the samples if H_0 is true.

Just as there are different t distributions for different degrees of freedom, so are there different F distributions for all combinations of different df_{Bet} and df_W. Although the exact shape of an F distribution depends on df_{Bet} *and* df_W, all of the F distributions used in psychological research are positively skewed. Two are illustrated in Figure 12.1.

To obtain the minimum value of F needed to reject H_0, you can refer to Table F in the Appendix of this book. Check the *column* corresponding to df_{Bet} (the degrees of freedom in the *numerator* of the F ratio) and the *row* corresponding to df_W (the degrees of freedom in the *denominator* of

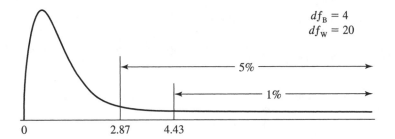

Figure 12.1

**F Distributions
for $df_{Bet} = 4$ and
$df_W = 20$, and for
$df_{Bet} = 6$ and $df_W = 6$**

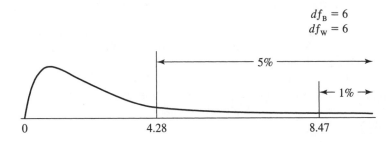

the F ratio). The critical F values for 4 df (numerator) and 20 df (denominator) are as follows:

			df-numerator				
		1	2	3	4	5	...
	1						
	2						
	3						
df-denominator	...						
	20				2.87		
					4.43		
	...						

The critical values for 20 df (numerator) and 4 df (denominator) are *not* the same; be sure to enter the table in the proper place. The smaller of the two values is the .05 criterion; the larger (in boldface) is the .01 criterion. In the case of Table 12.1A, the obtained value of 0.84 is less than the critical value of 2.87. Therefore, using $\alpha = .05$, you retain H_0 and conclude that there is not sufficient reason to believe that there are any differences among the five population means. (Because the computed value of F is less than 1.0, you could have reached this conclusion without bothering to consult the table in this instance; because an ANOVA is essentially a one-tailed test, an F ratio of 1.0 or less can never be statistically significant.)

For the experiment shown in Table 12.1B, the calculated F value of 51.66 easily exceeds the critical value for the .05 level (2.87) and even the .01 level (4.43). We present these statistically significant results in the form of a summary table.

Table 12.2   Summary of the One-Way ANOVA of the Second Music Experiment (Table 12.1B)

Source of variation	SS	df	MS	F	p
Between groups	884.4	4	221.1	51.66	<.01
Within groups (error)	85.6	20	4.28		
Total	970.0	24			

The ANOVA Summary Table

It is customary to summarize the results of an analysis of variance in a table such as the one shown in Table 12.2. Note that the between-groups source of variation is listed first and that the value of F (and sometimes p as well) is entered at the extreme right of the between-groups row. The denominator of the F ratio (i.e., MS_W for this type of ANOVA) is often called the *error term*, for reasons already explained under "The General Logic of ANOVA."

Calculating the One-Way ANOVA From Means and Standard Deviations

Traditionally, when statistics texts describe the calculation of a t test, they do so in terms of the means, standard deviations, and sample sizes of the two groups. However, when these same texts describe the calculation of an ANOVA, the emphasis is usually placed on proceeding directly from the raw data (i.e., individual scores) to the SS components of the ANOVA, without stopping to calculate the SD or variance of each separate group. (That is the approach we have taken in this chapter thus far.) There is certainly some computational efficiency to this approach, but in the age of handheld calculators and statistical computer programs, computational efficiency is no longer an important advantage. From a pedagogical standpoint, there is much understanding to be gained by describing the calculation of an ANOVA from the means and SDs, in a way that is parallel to the usual calculation of the t test. Moreover, it is not inconceivable that you may someday want to calculate an ANOVA from a published table of the means, SDs, and ns for a study for which the F ratio you are most interested in is not presented. Therefore, in this section, we will start with the type of data summary table that is often published for the results of an experiment and show you how to calculate the ANOVA from those data.

A particularly convenient table to use as an example for this section is the one that summarized the data for the caffeine experiment in Chapter 7, which is reproduced here as Table 12.3.

Before we can use Formula 12.2A for SS_{Bet}, we need to calculate the grand mean for these data. If the two groups were the same size, $\overline{X}_G$ would

Table 12.3 Data From the Caffeine Experiment of Chapter 7

	Caffeine Group	Control Group
X	81	68
s	12.0	16.8
N	22	20

be the simple average of the two group means, which is 74.5 in this case. However, when the ns are not equal, as in Table 12.3, a weighted average of the two means must be used. The grand mean for these data is:

$$\overline{X}_G = \frac{22(81) + 20(68)}{22 + 20} = \frac{3142}{42} = 74.8$$

Now we can calculate SS_{Bet}:

$$SS_{Bet} = n_1(\overline{X}_1 - \overline{X}_G)^2 + n_2(\overline{X}_2 - \overline{X}_G)^2$$

$$= 22(81 - 74.8)^2 + 20(68 - 74.8)^2 = 845.68 + 924.8 = 1770.48$$

To find SS_W when given SDs but not the raw data, you must first square each s to obtain the variance and then multiply each s^2 by its df. (Recall that $s^2 = SS/df$, so $SS = s^2 df$, where $df = N - 1$ for that group.) In this example, $SS_{W-caffeine} = 21(12)^2 = 3024$, and $SS_{W-control} = 19(16.8)^2 = 5362.56$. Therefore, $SS_W = 3024 + 5362.56 = 8386.6$.

Next, we calculate the two MSs for the ANOVA by dividing each SS by the appropriate df term: $df_{Bet} = k - 1 = 2 - 1 = 1$; $df_W = N_T - k = 42 - 2 = 40$. Therefore, $MS_{Bet} = SS_{Bet}/1 = 1770.48$, and $MS_W = 8386.6/40 = 209.66$. Finally, we calculate the F ratio: $MS_{Bet}/MS_W = 1770.48/209.66 = 8.44$.

Comparing the One-Way ANOVA With the t Test

When you compare the means of only two groups, you have a choice. You can test the difference of the means with a t test or a one-way ANOVA. Although both procedures lead to the same p value, it is instructive to see how closely connected these two seemingly diverse statistical methods are. That is why we chose a two-group example for our calculation in the previous section. If you take the t value calculated for these same data in Chapter 7 (2.91) and square it, you will get (within rounding error) the F ratio just calculated for those data. In fact, F always equals t^2 in the two-group case. This also holds true for the corresponding critical values. The critical t that we found in Chapter 7 for this example was 2.02, and the critical F for the corresponding ANOVA is $F_{.05}$ (1, 40), which is 4.08, which equals 2.02^2.

Comparing the t and F calculations for the same data reveals another important connection. Consider once again the calculation of the standard error of the difference for the t test of these data in Chapter 7:

$$s_{\overline{X}_1 - \overline{X}_2} = \sqrt{209.664 \left(\frac{1}{22} + \frac{1}{20} \right)}$$

Note that the value for s^2_{pooled} in this formula is 209.664, which rounds off to the value we calculated for the denominator of the F ratio, MS_W. Indeed, MS_W is just a new label for the pooled variance when more than two groups are involved; it is a weighted average of the variances of all the groups in an ANOVA. When you add the SS's from all the groups to create SS_W and then divide by the sum of the dfs from all the groups (i.e., df_W), what you are actually finding is the weighted average of the variances, also known as the pooled variance.

A Simplified ANOVA Formula for Equal Sample Sizes

When all of the samples are the same size in a one-way ANOVA, the F ratio formula can be reduced to a simple expression that is easy to understand as well as to use. If we divide the expression for SS_{Bet} when the ns are equal (shown previously) by df_{Bet}, we get

$$MS_{\text{Bet}} = \frac{n \sum (\overline{X}_i - \overline{X}_G)^2}{df_{\text{Bet}}} = n \frac{\sum (\overline{X}_i - \overline{X}_G)^2}{df_{\text{Bet}}}$$

Notice that the part of this formula that is multiplied by n is really a formula for the variance of the sample *means,* so we can simplify the formula to $n s^2_{\overline{X}}$. When all the ns are equal, MS_W has a simple form as well; it is just the ordinary average of the sample variances. So

$$MS_W = \frac{\sum s^2_i}{k}$$

Putting the two halves of the F ratio together, we come up with a convenient formula for the (fairly common) case when all the samples are the same size:

$$F = \frac{n s^2_{\overline{X}}}{\dfrac{\sum s^2_i}{k}} \qquad \text{Formula 12.10}$$

From this formula we can see at a glance that the magnitude of F depends entirely on three important factors: how far apart the sample means are from each other (the larger the spread, the larger is $s^2_{\overline{X}}$); how large the samples are (n is the size of *each* sample); and how much individuals vary from each other within each group. Because all of the

ns are equal in Table 12.1, we can illustrate the use of this simplified formula by applying it to the music/spatial ability data. We begin by finding the (unbiased) variance of the five sample means in Table 12.1B. For 14.2, 20.2, 22.4, 8.2, and 8.0, $s^2_{\overline{X}} = 44.22$.[1] MS_{Bet} equals $n\, s^2_{\overline{X}}$, so $MS_{Bet} = (5)(44.22) = 221.1$. (Note that this value agrees with the entry for MS_{Bet} in Table 12.2.)

Next, we find MS_W by squaring the (unbiased) s's for the five groups and averaging them. (The s's are the same in both the A and B sections of Table 12.1.) MS_W equals $(1.789^2 + 2.168^2 + 2.608^2 + 1.789^2 + 1.871^2)/5 = 21.4/5 = 4.28$. (Again, this value agrees with Table 12.2.) Dividing MS_{Bet} by MS_W yields the same F ratio that we calculated previously with the more tedious raw-score formula.

Effect Size for the One-Way ANOVA

Just as we were able to write a t formula in terms of the effect size in the samples (g) and the size of the sample (n), we can begin with the equal-n formula for F and separate it into an effect size term and a sample size term. If we define f^2 as $s^2_{\overline{X}}/MS_W$, then the one-way ANOVA formula can be written as $F = nf^2$.

If we do not square it, f is an effect size measure comparable to g for the two-sample t test. (In fact, in the two-group case, f is equal to g divided by the square root of 2.) Just as g is an estimate of **d** in the population, f can be viewed as an estimate of a corresponding population quantity that J. Cohen (1988) referred to as **f** (a lower-case f in **boldface**). Although estimates of **f** are sometimes used as the basis of a power analysis for one-way ANOVA, they are not routinely reported as effect-size measures in journal articles. The commonly reported measures of effect size for ANOVA are correlational measures related to the square of the point-biserial r in the two-group case.

The analysis of variance procedure begins (at least conceptually) by dividing SS_{total} into two components: SS_{Bet} and SS_W. These components can be thought of, in regression terms, as the variability explained and unexplained, respectively. Therefore, dividing SS_{Bet} by SS_T gives the proportion of variance explained in your dependent variable by the ANOVA factor. Although this proportion comes from sample data, it is most commonly referred to as η^2 (eta squared) and can be found from the following formula:

$$\eta^2 = \frac{SS_{Bet}}{SS_T} \qquad\qquad \text{Formula 12.11A}$$

In the two-group case, η^2 will always be exactly equal to r^2_{pb}.

---

[1] What makes this formula so easy to use is the ready availability of scientific or statistical calculators that give you the unbiased standard deviation at the touch of a button after the scores are entered. This SD is then squared to obtain the (unbiased) variance.

And just as r_{pb}^2 can be calculated from a t value without access to the raw data, η^2 can be calculated from your F ratio by the following formula:

$$\eta^2 = \frac{df_{Bet}F}{df_{Bet}F + df_W} \qquad \text{Formula 12.11B}$$

For example, the F ratio for testing the group differences in Table 12.1B was 51.66, with $df_{Bet} = 4$ and $df_W = 20$. Such a large F ratio associated with moderate sample sizes tells us that a large proportion of variance has been accounted for. We can confirm this by using Formula 12.11B:

$$\eta^2 = \frac{4(51.66)}{4(51.66) + 20} = \frac{206.64}{226.64} = .91$$

Such a large value for η^2 will not often occur in behavioral research, unless you are performing something like a manipulation check (e.g., did the participants who were moved to tears by watching a sad movie clip report more sadness than those participants who were laughing at a comedy clip?). Note that you will get the same value for η^2 if you divide SS_{Bet} by SS_T, as given in Table 12.2: $\eta^2 = 884.4/970 = .91$.

Interpreting the Size of Eta Squared

Clearly, .9 is a very large value for η^2, given that the largest possible value is 1.0, but what is less obvious is that a value of .25—that is, one-fourth of the total variation in the dependent variable (DV) accounted for by the independent variable (IV)—is considered large in psychological research. The square root of η^2 can be interpreted as a correlation coefficient, and a correlation of .5 (the square root of .25) is considered large, except in obvious cases like test-retest reliability. What then is considered small? A correlation of only .1 is considered small, and therefore a value of η^2 of .01 (i.e., only 1% of the variance accounted for) is also considered small. Effect sizes smaller than that are rarely interesting unless they represent something thought not to be possible at all. Because a correlation of .3 is considered to be of medium size, an η^2 of .09 or, rounding off, about 10% is considered to be a moderately large effect size.

Another way to think about effect size is that it is inversely related to the amount of overlap among the population distributions being sampled, while being completely unrelated to the size of the samples. By itself, η^2 just describes the overlap of the scores among your different samples, but it is also your best basis for guessing about the overlap among the corresponding populations, after correcting for its bias (see next section). A very large effect size suggests, for instance, that rather few scores in the group with the lowest mean will be as high as even just the middle of the group with the highest mean. Conversely, a very small effect size suggests a great deal of overlap from group to group. It is critical to remember, however, that even when there's a great deal of overlap among the populations and this is reflected in your samples, it is still possible to obtain a large F ratio with a correspondingly small p value, if the samples are very large. A small p value does suggest that the population effect size is not zero, but, by itself, even a very tiny p value does not tell you anything about the size of the effect in the population or even in your samples. That is why it is so important to supplement your test statistic (e.g., t or F) with an effect size measure that takes the sample sizes into consideration. Simply deciding whether you think the population effect size is zero or not, which is all that you are doing when you decide whether to reject the null hypothesis, is not very informative.

Unbiased Estimate of the Amount of Variance Accounted for in the Population (Omega Squared)

Just as in the two-group case, the proportion of variance accounted for in the population is designated by ω^2. And, like r_{pb}^2, η^2 is a biased (over)estimate of ω^2. More than one way has been recommended to correct this bias, but the simplest correction is to subtract 1 from the calculated F ratio before using Formula 12.11B for η^2, as follows:

$$\text{est. } \omega^2 = \frac{df_{\text{Bet}}(F-1)}{df_{\text{Bet}}(F-1) + df_{\text{W}}} \qquad \text{Formula 12.12}$$

One advantage of this correction formula is that you can see at a glance that it is pointless to estimate ω^2 if your F ratio is less than 1.0 (ω^2 cannot be negative). Whenever F is less than 1, the separation between the sample means is *less* than you would expect from sampling error, so the data are suggesting that the effect in the population, and therefore ω^2, is zero.

Some Comments on the Use of ANOVA

The general considerations we included in Chapter 7 under the heading "The t Test for Two Sample Means" apply equally well to the ANOVA, with minor modifications, as described next.

Underlying Assumptions

The procedures discussed in this chapter assume that observations are *independent* both within and between all of the samples. The value of any observation should *not* be related in any way to that of any other observation, as would be the case if all of the samples in your ANOVA were truly selected at random from an infinite, or at least very large, population. (For experimental studies, the usual procedure is to employ random assignment to all conditions in the study from one large convenience sample, in the manner discussed for the two-sample t test in Chapter 7.) It is also assumed that the populations are normally distributed. Fortunately, ANOVA is fairly robust with regard to the latter assumption, and will yield accurate results even if the population distributions depart considerably from normality (unless you also have small sample sizes or the distributions for different groups are skewed oppositely).

In addition, the use of MS_W as the error term requires that you assume that all of the populations have the same amount of (within-group) variance. As in the case of the t test, homogeneity of variance (HOV) can be tested, and if it looks like you cannot assume HOV, an adjusted form of ANOVA (see B. H. Cohen, 2008) can be performed. However, when researchers are dealing with sample sizes and variances that both vary a great deal or small samples that are very skewed, they are more likely to apply either an appropriate data transformation or a nonparametric test, such as the *Kruskal-Wallis* test, described at the end of this chapter.

Publishing Your Results

In behavioral research journals, the syntax for reporting an F ratio is as follows (as applied to the results presented in Table 12.2): "The different types of music produced large differences in spatial ability and yielded a significant one-way ANOVA on the group means, $F(4,20) = 51.66, p < .01$, est. $\omega^2 = .89$." Note that df_{Bet} and df_W are always given, in that order, in parentheses after F. However, p may be given exactly (except when four or more zeroes are required to the right of the decimal point), or in terms of an even smaller alpha (e.g., $p < .001$), if applicable. As was pointed out in previous chapters, statistical significance (even at an unusually small alpha level) does not necessarily imply a strong relationship between the IV and DV. It is therefore desirable, and becoming increasingly common, to report a distance measure of effect size (e.g., g of f) or strength of relationship measure (e.g., estimated ω^2) in addition to the test of significance. (Instead of estimated ω^2, η^2 is often reported without correction although in the example given here, F is so large that it made little difference; η^2 was .91, while est. ω^2 was .89.) However, effect-size measures of any type are generally not reported if the results fail to reach significance at the .05 level.

Following Up on a Significant ANOVA

An investigator is rarely satisfied with knowing that a set of three or more population means is not equal, yet this is all that the rejection of the ANOVA null hypothesis signifies when k is greater than 2. Instead, the researcher would usually like to conclude that certain particular population means are larger (or smaller) than others. Therefore, it is usually necessary to make more specific comparisons among the k means. Depending on the structure and purpose of the experiment, these *multiple comparisons* may take many forms and are subject to many considerations.

Sometimes the investigator wishes to make all $k(k-1)/2$ of the possible pairwise mean comparisons. At other times, only some of the possible comparisons are of interest (e.g., when several experimental groups are each to be compared with a single control group). Another important issue is whether a given comparison was planned in advance of the research (*a priori*) or was suggested by seeing the actual results (*post hoc*).

The area of multiple comparisons is a rather complex one, which is why we devote the entire next chapter to it.

ANOVA When the Independent Variable Has Quantitative Levels

In the type of ANOVA we have been presenting in this chapter, the dependent variable has been measured on an interval or ratio scale (ANOVA for ordinal, or ranked, DVs are discussed a little later in this chapter), and the independent variable has categorical levels, often in the form of qualitatively different experimental treatments. However, it is possible, and sometimes very desirable, for the levels of the ANOVA factor to be in the form of different amounts of the same treatment—for example, different dosages of a drug (usually including zero, in the form of a placebo); different numbers of letters in an anagram to be solved; different numbers of repetitions of words in a list to be recalled. When the factor has such levels, the ANOVA procedure of this chapter does not capitalize on an important potential source of regularity in the data: The DV, on average, may increase linearly, or in some other regular way, as a function of the level (i.e., amount) of the factor. For instance, if performance on a task (the DV) improves to a greater degree according to the amount of caffeine participants are given (the IV), the data are said to exhibit an increasing (possibly linear) trend. Even if the performance starts to decline for the largest doses, producing a simple curve (often referred to as a quadratic trend), a modified ANOVA procedure that is sensitive to such trends can produce considerably larger F ratios (and therefore more power) than the ordinary one-way ANOVA. The greater the number of levels the IV has, the greater is the potential advantage of an ANOVA based on trends, as compared to the ANOVA described in this chapter. The error term of a trend-based ANOVA is the same as the MS_W described in this chapter, but the MS_{Bet} is calculated differently, and generally more efficiently, for each possible trend. Because trends in the data fall under the general heading of *multiple comparisons*, they are dealt with, albeit briefly, in the next chapter.

Computational Practice for the One-Way ANOVA: Three Unequal-Sized Groups

Suppose that the dean of a small college wishes to survey student attitudes about participating in determining college curricula and requirements. She circulates a five-item questionnaire in which students respond to each item on a Likert scale that goes from 1 (no interest in student participation) to 5 (very interested). Therefore, total scores on this questionnaire can range from 5 to 25. Although the students do not give their names, they do provide such demographic items as their college major, year in school, and gender.

Table 12.4   ANOVA of Attitudes of Students From Three Areas of Study at a Small College to Student Participation in Determining College Curricula

| Areas of study | | | |
Natural sciences	Social sciences	Humanities	
15	17	6	$F = \dfrac{85.10}{16.74} = 5.08$
18	22	9	
12	5	12	
12	15	11	
9	12	11	
10	20	8	
12	14	13	
20	15	14	
	20	7	
	21		

Looking only at the data she has collected so far for seniors, the dean notices that student attitudes seem to differ according to their principal areas of study. She decides to arrange the scores of the seniors according to whether they are majoring in a natural science, a social science, or one of the humanities. The (hypothetical) data, broken down by these three areas, are shown in Table 12.4. We leave it as an exercise for the reader to calculate the SS components using Formulas 12.2A and 12.3, and therefore present the results of the ANOVA in Table 12.4 only in terms of the MSs and F ratio. Because the critical F at the .05 level for 2 and 24 df is 2.064, the null hypothesis for these data ($\mu_1 = \mu_2 = \mu_3$) can be rejected, and measures of effect size should be calculated. For this example, the estimate of ω^2 comes out to .254, which, according to the guidelines described in a preceding section, is considered large. For additional practice, we suggest that you use both Formula 12.11A and Formula 12.11B to calculate eta squared from the data in Table 12.4 in order to demonstrate that (a) both formulas yield the same value for η^2 and (b) the value for η^2 is somewhat larger than the value for ω^2.

A Nonparametric Alternative to the One-Way ANOVA: The Kruskal-Wallis H Test

Anytime you are dealing with more than two groups but it seems more appropriate to perform the rank-sum test than a t test to compare any two of the groups, you can compare all of your groups simultaneously with a distribution-free test based on ranks, called the **Kruskal-Wallis (K-W) H test**. The K-W H test is an extension of the rank-sum test (described in Chapter 8) to the multigroup case, just as the one-way ANOVA is an extension of the t test. As you might guess, when k (the number of groups) is equal to 2, the rank-sum test and the Kruskal-Wallis H test yield the same p values. Moreover, the K-W H test resembles the one-way ANOVA in several important ways. However, because statistics based on ranks are simple functions of N, the computation of the H statistic is much more basic than is the computation of F. In fact, H is a function of just the sum of squares between groups (SS_{Bet}), except that SS_{Bet} is computed on the ranks instead of the scores.

To illustrate the calculation of the H statistic, we have applied the K-W H test to the data in Table 12.4. The ranks for the data are shown next to the original scores for each group in Table 12.5. Those ranks were obtained by taking the total of ($N =$)27 observations and ranking them together from the lowest score of all (rank $= 1$) to the highest score among all three groups (rank $= 27$); then we placed those ranks next to their corresponding scores, organized into $k = 3$ groups, as in the original table (i.e., Table 12.4). Tied scores were assigned mean ranks in the usual manner. For example, there are two scores of 9 (one from natural sciences and one from humanities) that should occupy ranks 5 and 6, so each has been assigned the rank of 5.5 (the mean of 5 and 6). The next highest score, 10 (which is not tied), therefore received a rank of 7.

The sum of the ranks for each of the three groups (using the symbol T_i to represent the total of the ranks for any one group) is shown in Table 12.5: $T_1 = 113.5$; $T_2 = 189.5$; and $T_3 = 75$. (To guard against errors in ranking or summing, the sum of all T values should be verified as equal to $\sum R$ or $N_T[N_T + 1]/2$, as shown at the bottom of the table.) The next

Table 12.5 The Kruskal-Wallis H Test for $k = 3$ Independent Samples

Natural sciences (Group 1)		Social sciences (Group 2)		Humanities (Group 3)	
X	R	X	R	X	R
15	19	17	21	6	2
18	22	22	27	9	5.5
12	12	5	1	12	12
12	12	15	19	11	8.5
9	5.5	12	12	11	8.5
10	7	20	24	8	4
12	12	14	16.5	13	15
20	24	15	19	14	16.5
		20	24	7	3
		21	26		
$T_1 = 113.5$		$T_2 = 189.5$		$T_3 = 75$	
$N_1 = 8$		$N_{10} = 10$		$N_3 = 9$	

$$N_T = N_1 + N_2 + N_3 = 27$$
$$\sum R = N_T(N_T + 1)/2 = (27)(28)/2 = 378$$
$$= T_1 + T_2 + T_3 = 113.5 + 189.5 + 75 = 378$$

step is to compute the sum of squares between groups, SS_{Bet}, for the ranks; the following formula is particularly convenient in that it is based on the sum of the ranks for each group:

$$SS_{Bet} = \frac{T_1^2}{N_1} + \frac{T_2^2}{N_2} + \cdots + \frac{T_k^2}{N_k} - \frac{N_T(N_T + 1)^2}{4} \qquad \text{Formula 12.13}$$

Substituting the T and N values from Table 12.5 yields:

$$SS_{Bet} = \frac{(113.5)^2}{8} + \frac{(189.5)^2}{10} + \frac{(75)^2}{9} - \frac{27(28)^2}{4}$$

$$= 5826.31 - 5292.00$$

$$= 534.31$$

The final step is to compute the Kruskal-Wallis H statistic:

$$H = \frac{12 SS_{Bet}}{N_T(N_T + 1)} \qquad \text{Formula 12.14}$$

The value of 12 in the numerator is a constant, and it arises from the fact that the variance of a full set of N untied ranks is equal to $(N + 1)^2/12$. In our example,

$$H = \frac{(12)(534.31)}{(27)(28)} = 8.48$$

Under the null hypothesis that the locations of the k populations are identical, H follows, approximately, a distribution known as the chi-square (symbolized as χ^2) distribution with $k - 1$ degrees of freedom. Thus, the computed H value of 8.48 can be compared to a critical value found in Table H of the Appendix. The critical value in Table H that corresponds to the .05 criterion of significance for 2 df is 5.99. Because 8.48 is larger than 5.99, you can reject the null hypothesis that the three populations have equal locations. The chi-square distribution is discussed in some detail in Chapter 17, in which it becomes the main tool for null hypothesis testing with categorical data.

Like the normal approximation for the rank-sum test, the chi-square approximation used to test H for statistical significance is a good one unless the size of any group is very small. If there are no more than three groups, each group should have at least five cases in it; otherwise the Kruskal-Wallis H test should not be used. With more than three groups, as few as two cases in a group are sufficient. The existence of tied ranks tends to make the H test conservative (smaller and less likely to yield statistical significance), but this tendency is slight unless ties are very long and numerous. If necessary, it is possible to correct for ties and to perform this test for very small samples using special tables (see Siegel & Castellan [1988]). Finally, as compared to the analogous parametric F test in a one-way ANOVA, the H test has a power efficiency ranging from 90% for small samples to 95% for large samples.

A Measure of the Strength of the Relationship: η^2_{RI}

A measure of the strength of the relationship between membership in one of the k groups and rank on the dependent variable may be obtained by computing a form of eta squared. This is the same index that was used to measure effect size for the one-way ANOVA, but it is now applied to the ranks rather than the original scores. Just as η^2 for the scores was a function of F and the degrees of freedom, so η^2_R may be found from H, k, and N_T:

$$\eta^2_R = \frac{H - k + 1}{N_T - k} \qquad \text{Formula 12.15}$$

where

$k = $ number of groups
$N_T = $ total number of observations

For example, the ranked attitude scores in Table 12.5 yielded an H of 8.48. Therefore, for these data,

$$\eta^2_R = \frac{(8.48 - 3) + 1}{27 - 3} = \frac{6.48}{24} = .27$$

For the continuous score data in Table 12.4, η^2 was equal to .298 (i.e., $SS_{Bet}/SS_T = 170.21/572$)—a very similar (and rather large) value. This similarity will usually be the case, with the nonparametric eta squared usually being a bit smaller. However, sometimes a few outliers so increase the error variance in a one-way ANOVA that the nonparametric eta squared is actually larger, and the K-W H test may attain significance when the ANOVA does not. (Just as the statistical significance of η^2 is tested by the F ratio, so the significance of η^2_R is tested by H. So, as with the other measures of strength of relationship that we have discussed, there is no need to conduct an additional significance test for η^2_R.)

Summary

Analysis of variance (ANOVA) permits null hypotheses to be tested that involve the means of three or more samples (groups). One-way ANOVA deals with one independent variable made up of membership in one of k groups or levels. Total variance is partitioned into two sources: *between-group variance* and *within-group (error) variance.* These are compared by using the F ratio to determine whether the independent variable can be said to have an effect on the dependent variable. A significant F ratio in ANOVA indicates that it is reasonable to decide that not all k population means are equal. Follow-up procedures can be used to specify which pairs of means differ significantly, as detailed in the next chapter.

Meaning of Symbols

Symbol	General meaning
k	Number of groups (or the last group)
N_T	Total number of observations
N_i	Number of observations in group i
$\overline{X}_G$	Grand mean
$\overline{X}_i$	Mean of group i
X_i	A score in group i

Definition and Computing Formulas

1. Total sum of squares

$$\text{Definition: } SS_T = \sum (X - \overline{X}_G)^2 \qquad \text{Formula 12.1A}$$

$$\text{Computing formula: } SS_T = \sum X^2 - N_T \overline{X}_G^2 \qquad \text{Formula 12.1B}$$

2. Between-groups sum of squares

$$\text{Definition: } SS_{\text{Bet}} = \sum_{i=1}^{k} N_i (\overline{X}_i - \overline{X}_G)^2 \qquad \text{Formula 12.2A}$$

$$\text{For equal } ns \text{ only: } SS_{\text{Bet}} = n \sum_{t=1}^{k} (\overline{X}_i - \overline{X}_G)^2 \qquad \text{Formula 12.2B}$$

where n is the size of *each* sample

3. Within-groups sum of squares

Definition:

$$SS_W = \sum^{n_1} (X - \overline{X}_1)^2 + \sum^{n_2} (X - \overline{X}_2)^2 + \cdots + \sum^{n_k} (X - \overline{X}_k)^2$$

$$\text{Formula 12.3}$$

Shortcut computing formula: $SS_W = SS_T - SS_{\text{Bet}}$

Steps in One-Way Analysis of Variance

1. Compute SS_T, SS_{Bet}, and SS_W.
2. Compute the degrees of freedom:

$$df_{\text{Bet}} = k - 1 \qquad \text{Formula 12.5}$$

$$df_W = N - k \qquad \text{Formula 12.6}$$

3. Compute the two mean squares (*MS*s):

$$MS_{Bet} = \frac{SS_{Bet}}{df_{Bet}}$$
Formula 12.7

$$MS_W = \frac{SS_W}{df_W}$$
Formula 12.8

If all of the *n*s are equal:

$$MS_{Bet} = ns_{\overline{X}}^2$$
(Top of Formula 12.10)

where $s_{\overline{X}}^2$ is the unbiased variance of the sample means, and

$$MS_W = \frac{\sum s_i^2}{k}$$
(Bottom of Formula 12.10)

where s_i^2 is the unbiased variance within group *i*.

4. Compute the *F* ratio:

$$F = \frac{MS_{Bet}}{MS_W}$$
Formula 12.9

5. Obtain the (.05 or .01) critical value from the *F* table ($dfs = k - 1, N - k$) and test for significance. If the computed *F* is equal to or greater than the tabled *F*, reject H_0 (that all population means are equal) in favor of H_A (that H_0 is not true). Otherwise, retain H_0.

6. Especially if *F is statistically significant*, a corresponding effect-size measure should be computed. The most commonly used strength-of-relationship measure is the proportion of variance accounted for as determined by the following formula:

$$\eta^2 = \frac{SS_{Bet}}{SS_T}$$
Formula 12.11A

Eta squared can also be calculated from the *F* ratio using this formula:

$$\eta^2 = \frac{df_{Bet}F}{df_{Bet}F + df_W}$$
Formula 12.11B

A less biased estimate of the variance accounted for in the population requires the following adjustment:

$$\eta^2 = \frac{df_{Bet}(F - 1)}{df_{Bet}(F - 1) + df_W}$$
Formula 12.12

The Kruskal-Wallis *H* Test

1. Parametric analog: *F* test of one-way ANOVA
   Power efficiency: Approximately 90%–95%

2. Computational procedures: Rank *all* scores from 1 (smallest) to N (largest), ignoring which group they are in. In case of ties, follow the usual procedure of assigning the mean of the ranks in question to each of the tied scores. Then find the sum of ranks separately for each group, and compute the sum of squares between groups (SS_{Bet}) for the ranks, using the following simple formula, which was especially designed for ranked data:

$$SS_{Bet} = \frac{T_1^2}{N_1} + \frac{T_2^2}{N_2} + \cdots + \frac{T_k^2}{N_k} - \frac{N_T(N_T + 1)^2}{4} \qquad \text{Formula 12.13}$$

where

T_1 = sum of ranks in Group 1
T_2 = sum of ranks in Group 2
T_k = sum of ranks in Group k
N_1 = number of observations in Group 1
N_2 = number of observations in Group 2
N_k = number of observations in Group k
k = number of groups
N_T = total number of observations

Once SS_{Bet} has been obtained, compute

$$H = \frac{12 SS_{Bet}}{N_T(N_T + 1)} \qquad \text{Formula 12.14}$$

The value of H is then referred to the χ^2 table (Table H) with $k - 1$ degrees of freedom. If H exceeds the tabled value, reject the null hypothesis that all populations have equal locations. Otherwise retain H_0. Do *not* use this procedure if there are only two or three groups *and* any group has fewer than five cases.

3. Measure of strength of relationship: If H is statistically significant, a measure of the strength of relationship between group membership and rank on the dependent variable may be obtained by computing eta squared as applied to ranks (η_R^2):

$$\eta_R^2 = \frac{H - k + 1}{N_T - k} \qquad \text{Formula 12.15}$$

where

k = number of groups
N_T = total number of observations

Exercises

1. Following are two separate (hypothetical) sets of data that are some-what exaggerated to help clarify the procedures underlying analysis of variance. In each case, the experimenter is interested in conditions that affect the number of errors made by participants on a simple clerical task that must be performed quickly. Group 1 listens to upbeat dance music while performing the tasks; Group 2 listens to soothing, New Age music; and Group 3 listens to white noise (e.g., the steady hum of a machine in the background).

	Experiment 1			**Experiment 2**		
	Group 1	**Group 2**	**Group 3**	**Group 1**	**Group 2**	**Group 3**
	1	8	6	4	10	10
	3	7	5	0	0	0
	2	5	3	5	9	8
	1	4	3	0	1	1
	3	6	3	1	10	1
$\overline{X}$	2	6	4	2	6	4

(a) By inspection, in which case would you guess that the difference among groups is more likely to be statistically significant? Why?

(b) Carry out the analysis of variance for Experiment 1. Are the results significant at the .05 level? Calculate eta squared.

(c) Carry out the analysis of variance for Experiment 2. Are these results significant at the .05 level? Calculate eta squared.

(d) Briefly describe why the F ratio and eta squared statistics differ dramatically for the two experiments even though the sample means (i.e., 2, 6, and 4) are the same in both cases.

(e) Calculate an unbiased estimate of ω^2 for whichever experiment is significant.

2. Using the means and standard deviations you have already calculated for the data from the four dormitories (i.e., Turck, Dirk, Dupre, and Doty Halls), perform an analysis of variance to decide whether you can reject the null hypothesis that the four samples come from populations with identical means. Calculate eta squared for this comparison, and comment on the proportion of variance accounted for by the different dormitories.

3. For each of the following two experiments, calculate the means and variances for each group first, and then use those statistics to perform the ANOVA.

(a) Can you reject the null hypothesis for Experiment 1? Display your results in an ANOVA summary table, and state the significance of your F ratio in a sentence, using the proper format. Include the value for eta squared.

Experiment 1		
Group 1	**Group 2**	**Group 3**
17	15	9
12	11	21
3	4	3
10	26	7
1	18	20
14	23	
5		

(b) Can you reject the null hypothesis for Experiment 2? Display your results in an ANOVA summary table, and state the significance of your F ratio in a sentence, using the proper format. Include an estimate of omega squared.

Experiment 2		
Group 1	**Group 2**	**Group 3**
1	4	26
10	17	21
3	11	15
12	20	9
3	14	23
5	18	
7		

4. Calculate the one-way ANOVA and determine its statistical significance for the following data:

	Group				
	1	**2**	**3**	**4**	**5**
$\overline{X}$	23	30	34	29	26
s	6.5	7.2	7.0	5.8	6.0
N	12	15	14	12	15

5. For each of the two (separate) experiments that follow, perform the Kruskal-Wallis H test. If an experiment yields statistically significant results, compute the appropriate eta squared.

(a) Experiment 1			(b) Experiment 2		
Group 1	Group 2	Group 3	Group 1	Group 2	Group 3
36	43	26	36	33	43
8	33	28	33	6	36
33	6	19	22	26	28
14	11	36	14	19	38
26	22	46	28	28	43
43	24	9	11	8	46
28	28	31	26	30	42
35	36	38	31	9	48
42	40		35	24	
30			36		
48			40		

6. The following data table comes from Exercise 4 in Chapter 8, in which a psychology professor used three different methods of instruction in three small classes. In Chapter 8 you were asked to compare each pair of groups with the nonparametric rank-sum test. This time we would like you to: (a) test the null hypothesis that all three methods of instruction have the same effect on examination scores, using the Kruskal-Wallis H test, and compute η_R^2; (b) repeat the analysis by computing the ordinary one-way ANOVA and η^2; (c) compare the results of parts a and b.

Group 1	Group 2	Group 3
94	60	86
97	97	42
100	96	61
72	57	73
99	93	40
96	90	63
98	92	87
97		65
		67

7. Consider the following hypothetical results, as published in a hypothetical journal: "The participants had been divided equally among three experimental conditions—negative feedback, positive feedback, and no feedback—and the mean scores for the three groups at the end of the study were 11.1, 14.7, and 12.4, respectively. Moreover, the group differences were found to be statistically significant, $F(2, 57) = 3.69$, $p < .05$." (a) Find the value of η^2 for these data. How would you describe the size of this effect? (b) Estimate ω^2 for the population represented by these groups.

Thought Questions

1. A researcher wishes to test the hypothesis that the means of five populations are different. Why would it be a bad idea to test the researcher's hypothesis by computing 10 separate t tests (first test population 1 versus population 2, then test population 1 versus population 3, then test population 1 versus population 4, etc.)?

2. If there are only two groups (i.e., the researcher wishes to test the hypothesis that the means of two populations are different), will a one-way ANOVA yield the same results as the t test for two independent sample means? Explain.

3. If the results of a one-way ANOVA are statistically significant, why is it desirable to compute a measure of effect size?

4. Give an example of when the Kruskal-Wallis H test should be used instead of an ordinary one-way ANOVA.

Computer Exercises

1. Perform one-way ANOVAs to test whether the different quiz conditions (last question is easy, moderate, difficult, or impossible) had a significant effect on postquiz anxiety and postquiz heart rate. Request descriptive statistics and draw a graph of the sample means, with the levels of the independent variable on the horizontal axis. Use the sample means to explain the results of your ANOVA.

2. Using college major as the independent variable, perform one-way ANOVAs to test for significant differences in both the math background quiz and the statistics quiz. Request descriptive statistics and a homogeneity of variance (HOV) test. Use the sample means to explain the results of each ANOVA. Do the standard deviations of the samples seem consistent with the results of the HOV test in each case?

3. Create a grouping variable from the number of math courses taken (Group 1 = none; Group 2 = one or two; Group 3 = three or more), and perform one-way ANOVAs on both the math background quiz and the statistics quiz. In each case, explain your results in terms of the means of the three groups.

4. Repeat Exercise 2 using the Kruskal-Wallis H test, and compare these results to the corresponding ANOVA results.

Bridge to SPSS

There are two ways to perform a one-way ANOVA in SPSS: by selecting **One-Way ANOVA** from the Analyze/Compare Means menu or by selecting **Univariate** from the Analyze/General Linear Model (GLM) menu. The

latter method, because it allows for a variety of complex ANOVA procedures, lacks some of the useful features found in the more specific One-Way
ANOVA subprogram. So, we describe the Compare Means method here
and postpone a description of the GLM method until Chapter 14.

One advantage of the One-Way ANOVA dialog box not shared by its
GLM counterpart is that you can move a large number of variables into the
Dependent List (but, of course, only one IV into the Factor slot), and after
you click **OK**, separate one-way ANOVAs will be performed for each DV in
the list. You do not have to specify the levels of your factor; every different
value of your factor variable will be assumed to indicate a different group
of cases. The results of each one-way ANOVA are presented in a summary
table much like the one in Table 12.2, except that the exact p value is
displayed under the heading "Sig." Unlike the t test procedure, descriptive
statistics and homogeneity of variance tests are not reported automatically
for a one-way ANOVA; they must be requested by checking the appropriate
choices in the Options box. In addition to **Options**, there are two other
buttons along the bottom of the One-Way ANOVA dialog box: **Contrasts**
and **Post Hoc**. We will describe the function of these buttons in the next
chapter.

The Kruskal-Wallis *H* Test

As we mentioned in Chapter 8, SPSS provides continuity for long-term
users through its "Legacy Dialogs." If you are using one of the latest
versions of SPSS, we recommend using the Legacy Dialogs for your
nonparametric tests.

From the Analyze/Nonparametric Tests/Legacy Dialogs menu, select
K Independent Samples . . . . It is the first (and default) choice in the dialog
box under Test Type that you will want to use, and it is appropriately
labeled **Kruskal–Wallis H**. The main difference between this dialog box
(titled **Tests for Several Independent Samples**) and the one for two
independent samples (see Chapter 8) is that you are asked to "Define
Range" after inserting the Grouping Variable, instead of to "Define
Groups." You must enter integers to define the minimum and maximum
values of interest for your Grouping Variable. Those integers entered, and
all integer values between them, will each define a different group in the
analysis. If your grouping variable contains the integers from 1 to 5, and
you want to perform the Kruskal-Wallis H test only on Groups 2, 3, and 5,
you can enter **2** as the minimum of the range and **5** as the maximum, but
you will then have to use Select Cases to exclude cases that have a value of
4 on the grouping variable. (For example, click the **If** button in the Select
Cases box, and then type in **group ~ 4**, because "~" means "not equal.")

The Kruskal-Wallis procedure creates two boxes of output, the first
of which contains the size and mean rank for each group. The second
box contains only the H statistic, the formula for which was given earlier
in this chapter, along with its df (one less than the number of groups
being compared) and its approximate p value, labeled **Asymp. Sig**. The

H statistic is actually labeled **Chi-Square** in the output box, because that is the distribution from which the (asymptotic) p value is obtained. (Note that for a small N, it may be desirable to find the exact p value for H, but for larger N, the chi-square distribution with $df = k - 1$ serves as a good approximation).

The relation between the Kruskal-Wallis and the rank-sum tests is perfectly analogous to the relation between the one-way ANOVA and the independent-samples t test. If you run the Kruskal-Wallis H test on just two groups, the chi-square value you will obtain is just the square of the z score produced by the rank-sum test for the same two groups. And, of course, the p value will be the same for both tests.

Appendix: Proof That the Total Sum of Squares Is Equal to the Sum of the Between-Group and the Within-Group Sum of Squares

We begin with the mathematical statement that the total deviation of any score from the grand mean is equal to the sum of two parts: the score's deviation from the mean of its own group plus the deviation of the mean of its group from the grand mean:

$$X - \overline{X}_G = (X - \overline{X}_i) + (\overline{X}_i - \overline{X}_G)$$

Squaring both sides of the equation and summing over *all* people yields:

$$\sum (X - \overline{X}_G)^2 = \sum (X - \overline{X}_i)^2 + \sum (\overline{X}_i - \overline{X}_G)^2 + 2 \sum (X - \overline{X}_i)(\overline{X}_i - \overline{X}_G)$$

For any one group, $(\overline{X}_i - \overline{X}_G)$ is a constant, and the sum of deviations about the group mean must equal zero. The last term is therefore always equal to zero, leaving

$$\sum (X - \overline{X}_G)^2 = \sum (X - \overline{X}_i)^2 + \sum (\overline{X}_i - \overline{X}_G)^2$$

For ANOVA purposes, the sums of squares are then divided by the appropriate degrees of freedom to yield estimates of the population variance, which are then compared by the F ratio.

Chapter 13
Multiple Comparisons

PREVIEW

Introduction

What is the purpose of pairwise multiple comparisons?

Fisher's Protected t Tests and the Least Significant Difference (LSD)

How is the error term used by Fisher's protected t tests an improvement over the one used by the ordinary t test for comparing two independent means? How can these tests be simplified when all of the samples are the same size?

Tukey's Honestly Significant Difference (HSD)

What do Fisher's protected t tests "protect" against, and under what conditions does that protection break down?

How does Tukey's HSD test use the studentized range statistic to provide greater protection against Type I errors than Fisher's protected t tests?

What is meant by the statement that the HSD test is overly "conservative" when dealing with a three-group study?

How can you use HSD when your samples differ slightly in size?

Other Multiple Comparison Procedures

Why did the Newman-Keuls test become so popular for multiple comparisons, and why has its use decreased in recent years?

How does the Fisher-Hayter test combine elements of both the LSD and HSD tests to optimize power while remaining acceptably conservative?

Planned and Complex Comparisons

How does the Bonferroni correction provide greater power when you are planning to test a small subset of the comparisons that are possible? Why is the Bonferroni test overly conservative if you want to test all of the possible pairwise comparisons?

What is a complex comparison, and how can it lead to greater power if you predict the pattern of sample means correctly?

(continued)

PREVIEW (*continued*)

Nonparametric Multiple Comparisons: The Protected Rank-Sum Test

What is the appropriate way to follow up a significant Kruskal-Wallis *H* test with pairwise comparisons?

Under what conditions would a Bonferroni correction be recommended?

Summary

Exercises

Thought Questions

Computer Exercises

Bridge to SPSS

Introduction

To introduce the need for *multiple comparisons*, we now return to the analysis of variance (ANOVA) we presented for computational practice in Table 12.4 of the previous chapter. For that ANOVA, the dean was able to reject the null hypothesis and conclude that attitudes toward student participation in campus governance differ depending on whether seniors at her college are majoring in a natural science, a social science, or one of the humanities. However, it is hard to imagine that anyone would be satisfied with that general conclusion and not want to probe further for more specific conclusions. For instance, do all three groups differ significantly from each other, or is it perhaps the case that the natural science majors differ significantly from each of the other two groups, but that the difference between social science and humanities majors is not significant? It is important to understand that rejecting the null hypothesis in a three-group experiment does *not* automatically allow you to conclude that all three population means are different from each other (i.e., $\mu_1 \neq \mu_2 \neq \mu_3$). There are three other possibilities that are consistent with rejecting the null hypothesis: $\mu_1 = \mu_2 \neq \mu_3$; $\mu_1 \neq \mu_2 = \mu_3$; and $\mu_1 \neq \mu_3 = \mu_2$. To decide which of the four possibilities (including $\mu_1 \neq \mu_2 \neq \mu_3$) is true requires what are called, in this context, *pairwise* multiple comparisons. Pairwise comparisons can be performed with the ordinary two-sample *t* tests you learned about in Chapter 7, but they can be slightly improved, as you will see next. We reproduced Table 12.4 here as Table 13.1, and added means and standard deviations, to help us illustrate the procedure for performing pairwise comparisons on those data.

Now, you might be thinking: If I must follow my ANOVA with *t* tests anyway, why can I not just skip the ANOVA and proceed directly to the

Table 13.1   ANOVA of Attitudes of Students From Three Areas of Study at a Small College to Student Participation in Determining College Curricula

Areas of study			
Natural sciences	Social sciences	Humanities	
15	17	6	$F = \dfrac{85.10}{16.74} = 5.08$
18	22	9	
12	5	12	
12	15	11	
9	12	11	
10	20	8	
12	14	13	
20	15	14	
	20	7	
	21		
$\overline{X}_1 = 13.5$	$\overline{X}_2 = 16.1$	$\overline{X}_3 = 10.11$	
$S_1 = 3.85$	$s_2 = 5.13$	$S_3 = 2.76$	
$N_1 = 8$	$N_2 = 10$	$N_3 = 9$	$N_T = 27$

t tests? This is not a silly question to ask in the three-group case, when there are only three pairwise comparisons to perform (e.g., natural versus social sciences, and each of these versus humanities); the problem with performing multiple *t* tests is not obvious in this simple case. However, suppose that the dean has collected enough data for her to conduct a one-way ANOVA on the means from *eight* different college majors. As mentioned in the previous chapter, the number of possible pairwise comparisons is given by the formula $k(k-1)/2$, so in the eight-group case there would be $(8 \times 7)/2 = 28$ *t* tests to perform. If you were to use .05 (i.e., 1 in 20) as your alpha, the chances would be better than 50% of obtaining at least one Type I error even if all eight of the corresponding population means were exactly the same. In fact, the *experimentwise* alpha (α_{EW}) in this case would be at least .6. The advantage of performing an ANOVA at the .05 level first is that it will screen out about 95% of those experiments in which all of the population means are equal, and follow-up *t* tests will be performed only on the 5% that accidentally reach significance. For this reason, Fisher, who was the first to formalize the ANOVA procedure back in the 1920s, devised the following **protected *t* test** procedure.

Fisher's Protected *t* Tests and the Least Significant Difference (LSD)

According to Fisher's original recommendation, if *and only if* an ANOVA *F* test has resulted in the rejection of the overall null hypothesis that all *k* means are equal, any (or all) of the paired means may be compared by *t* tests using the usual (.05) decision rule for each pair. If it is reasonable to assume homogeneity of variance (HOV) among all of the populations represented in the ANOVA, these follow-up t tests can be slightly improved relative to ordinary two-group t tests. An ordinary t test between any $\overline{X}_i$ and $\overline{X}_j$ (where the subscript i represents any one of the samples in the ANOVA, and the subscript j represents any *other* sample) would be based on only the N_i and N_j observations involved, and it would only have degrees of freedom $(df) = N_i + N_j - 2$. However, by making the HOV assumption, you can take advantage of the more stable estimate of the population variance provided by the ANOVA's MS_W, which is based on $df_W = N_T - k$. Specifically, you can use MS_W (sometimes referred to as the *omnibus* error term) in place of the pooled variance in each of your (protected) follow-up t tests, and therefore you can base your critical t value on the df_W from the ANOVA. Because df_W in a multigroup study will always be larger than the df for just two groups, the critical t value will be lower for these follow-up t tests, giving them a better chance at statistical significance (i.e., more power) than ordinary t tests (unless the sample sizes are so large that your critical t values are close to critical z's even for an ordinary t test). Note that by requiring the ANOVA F to be significant, we protect the follow-up t tests from the large experimentwise Type I error rate that would otherwise occur. At the same time, these t tests are more powerful in detecting real population mean differences, if HOV can be assumed, because then they are based on more df.

Next, we illustrate the protected t procedure using the results of the ANOVA on student attitudes, as shown in Table 13.1. Because the F test for the ANOVA was indeed significant at $\alpha = .05$, we are allowed to proceed to compare the three pairs of means by t tests. The null hypothesis for any pair of means, $\overline{X}_i$ and $\overline{X}_j$, can be tested by

$$t = \frac{\overline{X}_i - \overline{X}_j}{\sqrt{MS_W \left(\dfrac{1}{N_i} + \dfrac{1}{N_j} \right)}} \qquad \text{Formula 13.1}$$

Here, df for the critical t equals $N_T - k$, and MS_W is taken from the one-way ANOVA results (the denominator of the F ratio given in Table 13.1). Note that Formula 13.1 is just the ordinary formula for the two-group t test, with MS_W serving as the pooled-variance estimate.

Table 13.2 uses the means, group sizes, and MS_W of Table 13.1 to illustrate the computation of these t's. For $df = 24$, the critical value for t at $\alpha = .05$ (two-tailed) is 2.064. Only the difference between the means of Groups 2 and 3 leads to a t value that is larger than 2.064, so only this pairwise difference can be declared significant. We can now get more specific in our rejection of the overall ANOVA null hypothesis; rather than merely stating that it is not the case that all three population means are equal to each other, we can assert that, in particular, $\mu_2 \neq \mu_3$. At the same time, we have to retain the null hypotheses that $\mu_1 = \mu_2$ and $\mu_1 = \mu_3$.

When all groups are of the same size, $N_i = N_j$, and therefore the denominator of the foregoing t test becomes a constant for all the pairwise

Table 13.2 Protected t Tests Among the Three Mean Attitude Scores Following a Significant ANOVA F

Means	$\overline{X}_1 = 13.50$ $N_1 = 8$	$\overline{X}_2 = 16.10$ $N_2 = 10$	$\overline{X}_3 = 10.11$ $N_3 = 9$

$$MS_w = 16.74$$

$\overline{X}_1$ versus $\overline{X}_2$:
$$t = \frac{13.50 - 16.10}{\sqrt{16.74\left(\frac{1}{8} + \frac{1}{10}\right)}} = \frac{-2.60}{1.94} = -1.34$$

$\overline{X}_1$ versus $\overline{X}_3$:
$$t = \frac{13.50 - 10.11}{\sqrt{16.74\left(\frac{1}{8} + \frac{1}{9}\right)}} = \frac{-3.39}{1.99} = 1.70$$

$\overline{X}_2$ versus $\overline{X}_3$:
$$t = \frac{16.10 - 10.11}{\sqrt{16.74\left(\frac{1}{10} + \frac{1}{9}\right)}} = \frac{-5.99}{1.88} = 3.19$$

df for t's $= df_w = N_T - k = 24$

comparisons. It then becomes possible to greatly simplify the protected t test procedure. There must be some difference between the two means that is just large enough so that when it is divided by the (constant) denominator, it yields a t value exactly equal to the critical t needed for significance at a given alpha level. This particular difference between the means is called the **Least Significant Difference (LSD)**. When it is inserted into the t formula given previously, we get

$$t_{crit} = \frac{LSD}{\sqrt{MS_W\left(\frac{2}{n}\right)}} = \frac{LSD}{\sqrt{\frac{2MS_W}{n}}}$$

where n is the size of each sample.

Solving for LSD, we obtain the following easy-to-use formula:

$$LSD = t_{crit}\sqrt{\frac{2MS_W}{n}} \qquad \text{Formula 13.2}$$

The value of t_{crit} is chosen for $df = N_T - k$ and the two-tailed α of the decision rule. Assume that all of the sample sizes were 9 ($= n$) in the preceding example, and the usual $\alpha = .05$ decision rule is to be used. Then the df would still be 24 (i.e., $27 - 3$), and the critical t value would still be equal to 2.064. If we assume that MS_W is still 16.74, the size of LSD would be:

$$LSD = 2.052\sqrt{16.74\left(\frac{2}{9}\right)} = 2.052(1.93) = 3.96$$

Finding LSD saves you the work of performing all of the follow-up t tests. Instead, you need only look at the amount of difference for each pair of means. In this example, all pairs of means differing by at least about 4 attitude scale points would be significantly different at $\alpha = .05$ (two-tailed). Looking at the numerators of the t tests in Table 13.2, we see differences of -2.6, -3.39, and -5.99; only the last of these—the difference between Groups 2 and 3—is larger in magnitude than LSD, so that is the only difference that would attain significance according to the LSD test. Of course, these conclusions are consistent with the conclusions of the individual t tests (in the equal-n condition, the conclusions would have to always be consistent).

Although the protected t procedure provides good control and balance of Type I and Type II errors when you are dealing with only three population means, the protection afforded by requiring F to be significant drops unacceptably as k increases. Some other procedure should be used (which will be described shortly) when k is more than 3, especially when strict control of the experimentwise Type I error rate is desired. Also, it is possible (though highly unlikely) to find F significant and none of the pairwise t's significant, in which case the proper conclusion is that the k means are not all equal but the data do not justify any further specification (*not* that all paired means are equal, which would be a contradiction). Much more often, one of the t tests is significant when the ANOVA is not, which is why requiring a significant ANOVA before performing the t tests makes a real difference in reducing Type I errors.

Confidence Intervals for the Protected t Test

In the previous section, we tested the null hypothesis for each pair of means using three protected t tests. An alternative procedure would be to calculate three confidence intervals (CIs), as discussed in Chapters 6 and 7. This has the advantage of specifying all reasonably likely values of the difference between the two population means in each comparison.

To use the CI procedure for the protected t test, the ANOVA F test must have resulted in the rejection of the overall null hypothesis that all k means are equal. As we saw in Chapter 7, the CI for the difference between two population means is given by Formula 7.7, reproduced here:

$$\left[(\overline{X}_1 - \overline{X}_2) - t_{\text{crit}} s_{\overline{X}_1 - \overline{X}_2}\right] \leq \mu_1 - \mu_2 \leq \left[(\overline{X}_1 - \overline{X}_2) + t_{\text{crit}} s_{\overline{X}_1 - \overline{X}_2}\right]$$

Formula 7.7

The critical value of t for a 95% CI is the same as for the corresponding .05, two-tailed t test, which is 2.064 in this example. For each comparison, the standard error of the difference is equal to $\sqrt{MS_W(1/N_i + 1/N_j)}$. Since $MS_W = 16.74$, $N_1 = 8$, $N_2 = 10$, and $N_3 = 9$, the three standard errors of the difference that we need are:

1. Group 1 versus Group 2: $\sqrt{16.74(1/8 + 1/10)} = 1.94$

2. Group 1 versus Group 3: $\sqrt{16.74(1/8 + 1/9)} = 1.99$

3. Group 2 versus Group 3: $\sqrt{16.74(1/10 + 1/9)} = 1.88$

Therefore, the three 95% CIs are:

1. Group 1 versus Group 2:

$$-2.60 - (2.064)(1.94) \leq \mu_1 - \mu_2 \leq -2.60 + (2.064)(1.94)$$

$$-6.60 \leq \mu_1 - \mu_2 \leq 1.40$$

2. Group 1 versus Group 3:

$$3.39 - (2.064)(1.99) \leq \mu_1 - \mu_3 \leq 3.39 + (2.064)(1.99)$$

$$-0.72 \leq \mu_1 - \mu_3 \leq 7.50$$

3. Group 2 versus Group 3:

$$5.99 - (2.064)(1.88) \leq \mu_2 - \mu_3 \leq 5.99 + (2.064)(1.88)$$

$$2.11 \leq \mu_2 - \mu_3 \leq 9.87$$

As would be expected from the results in Table 13.2, only for the comparison between Groups 2 and 3 does zero fall outside the confidence interval. Here again, CIs provide us with important additional information about the probable difference between the population means in each comparison.

Tukey's Honestly Significant Difference (HSD)

The problem with using Fisher's procedure when you are dealing with more than three groups is that you are "protected" only in experiments for which the *complete* null hypothesis is true (e.g., for four groups, H_0: $\mu_1 = \mu_2 = \mu_3 = \mu_4$). As the number of groups increases, there is an increasing number of ways that the null hypothesis can be *partially* true.

For five groups, a worst-case scenario for Fisher's procedure would be an experiment for which $\mu_1 = \mu_2 = \mu_3 = \mu_4 \neq \mu_5$. Perhaps four antidepressant drugs are being tested against each other and against a placebo, and the drugs have identical effects, all of which exceed the placebo effect. If the ANOVA involving the five means reaches statistical significance (this would not be surprising, given the difference of the placebo from the drugs), then, according to Fisher, it is acceptable to test each of the six possible pairs of drugs for significance, in addition to testing each drug against the placebo. But in this example, all of the drug-to-drug comparisons are "null." If any accidentally reach significance, you have committed a Type I error within the experiment, even though you were correct to reject the (complete) null hypothesis of the ANOVA. The more "null" pairwise comparisons you are permitted to perform, the larger the experimentwise alpha becomes for your study.

We cannot know how many "partial-null" experiments are being conducted (or how "partial" they are), but the more that are tested, the more often α_{EW} will rise above .05. J. W. Tukey (the same statistician who brought us the stemplot) understood this problem and was able to find a distribution that could keep α_{EW} below .05, regardless of how many groups are involved in the study and how complete the null hypothesis might be. This distribution is known as the *studentized range.*

The Studentized Range Statistic

Tukey recognized that when you draw, say, five samples from the same population and compare the smallest sample mean to the largest, the difference is likely to be considerably larger than if you had only drawn two sample means and compared them. Therefore, his **studentized range statistic** (symbolized by q) grows appropriately larger as the total number of samples becomes larger. Also, the statistic is "studentized," like the t distributions, in that it gets smaller as the size of each sample gets larger, although it changes very little after the size of the samples rises above 40 or so.

It is not unreasonable to think of q as a t statistic that has been adjusted for the total number of groups being compared. We can see the extent of this adjustment by looking at Table G in the Appendix, which is a table of the critical values of the studentized range statistic for alpha = .05, two-tailed. An excerpt of this table is reprinted here as Table 13.3.

Notice that the value of q increases as you move to the right in any of the rows in Table 13.3. However, by the time you are dealing with six groups, adding another group or two does not have nearly the impact on q that it does when you are dealing with only two or three groups.

Although increasing the size of the groups (i.e., going down the columns in Table 13.3) decreases the size of q, these decreases get smaller as the samples become large (as is the case with t). It may seem odd that q is larger than t even for only two groups (e.g., at infinity, q for two groups equals 2.77, while the critical t equals 1.96). It should seem odd, because this is not an actual adjustment in the test statistic but rather an artifact of how Tukey decided to present his table and his formula, as we show next.

Using Tukey's HSD Formula

Tukey's original formula merely substituted q_{crit} for t_{crit} in Fisher's formula and called the minimal difference for significance the **Honestly Significant**

Table 13.3   Selected Critical Values of Tukey's Studentized Range Statistic

df_W	Number of groups						
	2	3	4	5	6	7	8
. . .	. . .	. . .	. . .	. . .	. . .	. . .	. . .
4	3.93	5.04	5.76	6.29	6.71	7.05	7.35
. . .	. . .	. . .	. . .	. . .	. . .	. . .	. . .
8	3.26	4.04	4.53	4.89	5.17	5.40	5.60
. . .	. . .	. . .	. . .	. . .	. . .	. . .	. . .
12	3.08	3.77	4.20	4.51	4.75	4.95	5.12
. . .	. . .	. . .	. . .	. . .	. . .	. . .	. . .
16	3.00	3.65	4.05	4.33	4.56	4.74	4.90
. . .	. . .	. . .	. . .	. . .	. . .	. . .	. . .
40	2.86	3.44	3.79	4.04	4.23	4.39	4.52
. . .	. . .	. . .	. . .	. . .	. . .	. . .	. . .
∞	2.77	3.31	3.63	3.86	4.03	4.17	4.29

Difference (HSD):

$$HSD = q'_{crit}\sqrt{\frac{2MS_W}{n}}$$

where q'_{crit} refers to a value from Tukey's original q table. However, Tukey decided to simplify his formula.

We can imagine that he first separated it, like this,

$$HSD = q'_{crit}\sqrt{2}\sqrt{\frac{MS_W}{n}},$$

and then multiplied his original q' values by the square root of 2 to obtain critical values of q. The resulting formula is:

$$HSD = q_{crit}\sqrt{\frac{MS_W}{n}} \qquad \text{Formula 13.3}$$

where q_{crit} is a value from Table G and equals $\sqrt{2}$ times q'_{crit}. Because the first column of Table G is for two groups, and therefore requires no adjustment from the critical t value, it actually consists of the .05, two-tailed critical values of t, each multiplied by the square root of 2 (e.g., $2.77 = 1.96\sqrt{2}$). Unfortunately, dropping the number 2 from the formula for LSD to create HSD, originally intended just to simplify its calculation (at a time before there were handheld calculators and personal computers) serves these days only to confuse students of statistics, who may think that the formulas for LSD and HSD are more different than they actually are. Let us see what happens when we apply Tukey's formula to the data in Table 13.1.

For three groups and $df = 24$, the critical q from Table G is 3.53. For the purpose of comparison with LSD, we will once again use 9 for the common n. Therefore,

$$\text{HSD} = 3.53\sqrt{\frac{16.74}{9}} = 3.53(1.364) = 4.81$$

Note that HSD, which equals 4.81, is considerably larger than LSD, which equals 3.96. This leads to larger CIs for Tukey's than Fisher's test, as we demonstrate next.

Confidence Intervals for Tukey's HSD Test

It could hardly be any easier to find confidence intervals for the difference of any two population means represented by samples in your study, after you have calculated HSD, because HSD is already designed to tell you the difference between two means that is just on the borderline of significance. The formula for the CI for any two means in your study, according to Tukey's test, is:

$$\mu_i - \mu_j = \overline{X}_i - \overline{X}_i \pm \text{HSD} \qquad \text{Formula 13.4}$$

For example, the CI for the difference between the social sciences and the humanities, as represented by Groups 2 and 3, respectively, in Table 13.1 is:

$$\mu_i - \mu_j = 5.99 \pm 4.81,$$

so the 95% CI extends from +1.18 to +10.80.

Note that this CI is wider than the one we found for these same two groups based on Fisher's procedure (+2.13 to +9.85). This will always be the case when there are more than two groups in the study, because Tukey's test uses a larger critical value.

Of course, the percentage of the CI depends on the alpha you used to look up the q value that you used to calculate HSD. If you found q from our Table G, which is only for $\alpha = .05$, then Formula 13.4 will give you 95% CIs. We have not included q values for $\alpha = .01$, because Tukey's test is already so conservative with $\alpha = .05$, but that is what you would need to construct 99% CIs that correspond to Tukey's test.

Tukey's HSD for Unequal Sample Sizes: The Harmonic Mean

Both the LSD and HSD formulas assume that all of the samples have the same size (n). If your sample sizes differ only slightly, as when equal groups were planned but a few data points have been lost, it is acceptable to calculate the harmonic mean of your actual sample sizes and use that value as n in the formula for LSD or HSD. As a crude approximation, we have been using the arithmetic mean of the samples sizes in Table 13.1 (i.e., 9) to calculate LSD and HSD. However, it is more accurate to use the harmonic mean. In Chapter 7, we presented a formula (7.11) for the harmonic mean of two numbers; the harmonic mean of any number of sample sizes can be expressed as follows:

$$n_h = \frac{k}{\sum \dfrac{1}{n_i}}$$

Formula 13.5

For the sample sizes in our present example, the harmonic mean (n_h) is:

$$n_h = \frac{3}{\dfrac{1}{8} + \dfrac{1}{9} + \dfrac{1}{10}} = \frac{3}{.33611} = 8.93$$

As you can see, with small differences among your sample sizes, the harmonic mean does not differ much from the arithmetic mean, but the harmonic mean is always more accurate in these cases, and it becomes increasingly discrepant from the arithmetic mean when your numbers are more spread out proportionally. However, note that when your sample sizes differ considerably, Tukey's HSD test loses its accuracy and is therefore not recommended.

Comparing HSD to LSD

Although HSD (4.81) is considerably larger than LSD (3.96), our pairwise conclusions do not change. The difference between Group 2 and Group 3, which is 5.99, is still statistically significant. Given that HSD can never be smaller than LSD, you cannot have a difference that exceeds HSD but not LSD. However, the reverse is certainly possible (e.g., a mean difference in this example of 4.2 would be significant by the LSD but not the HSD procedure). Although both procedures usually lead to the same set of conclusions, there is no doubt that Tukey's HSD is the more *conservative* of the two, which means that it does a better job of controlling Type I errors than Fisher's LSD. In fact, HSD keeps α_{EW} below .05 for any number of groups, which makes Tukey's test *overly* conservative, especially in the case of three groups, for which Fisher's procedure maintains α_{EW} appropriately at the value used to look up the critical t. Therefore, Fisher's protected t tests should be used whenever you are dealing with only three groups, and the LSD formula can be used in particular whenever the samples are the same size or nearly so. Fisher's system is too *liberal*, however, when dealing with more than three groups: The larger the number of groups, the more Fisher's procedure allows α_{EW} to increase.

Follow-Up Tests for Published Results

The results of the ANOVA performed on the data in Table 13.1, if published in a journal that follows the guidelines of the *APA Publication Manual* (APA, 2010), would be expressed something like this: "The mean attitudes toward student participation in campus governance were found to differ among students majoring in a natural science ($M = 13.5$), a social science ($M = 16.1$), or one of the humanities ($M = 10.11$), and this difference attained statistical significance, $F(2, 24) = 5.08$, $p < .05$." Sometimes an effect-size measure is included, and less often the error term (i.e., denominator of the F ratio) is also given. Suppose, however, that the error term is *not* given, and the authors do not report the results of follow-up tests at all (unlikely) or report the p values associated with pairwise comparisons according to Tukey's procedure without reporting the size of HSD (fairly likely). Do you have enough information to perform Fisher's protected t tests instead? You do, as long as you know the size of each sample ($ns = 8$, 10, and 9, respectively, for this example). Then you could calculate SS_{Bet} using Formula 12.2A, and divide it by df_{Bet} to obtain MS_{Bet}, which was 85.1. Because you know that F equals MS_{Bet}/MS_W, and you were given F in the report (5.08), and you calculated MS_{Bet}, you can find MS_W with a little algebra: $MS_W = 85.1/5.08 = 16.75$ (which is within rounding error of the MS_W we obtained from the raw data). Once you have MS_W, you can perform your own follow-up t tests; for instance, in the three-group case, you could use the more powerful, and perfectly acceptable Fisher procedure if, say, the follow-up tests were given according to Tukey's procedure. For more than three groups, Fisher's protected t tests are not considered acceptable, but there are other follow-up procedures that are not only acceptable but more *powerful* than Tukey's test (because they are less conservative). We describe one of these alternatives in the next section.

Other Multiple Comparison Procedures

Although Tukey's HSD test is acceptable for any number of groups (as long as they are all about the same size), it is more conservative and therefore less powerful than is desirable (i.e., it is less likely to detect small effects than it could be). This realization has led many statisticians to devise alternative (and sometimes highly complex) multiple comparison procedures designed to keep α_{EW} at a predetermined rate while maximizing power. One such test, which uses the studentized range statistic in a way that makes it more powerful than HSD, is called the Newman-Keuls (N-K) test. This test was the most popular multiple comparisons method in the behavioral sciences a few decades ago, but its use has declined sharply in recent years. This decline is due to the results of computer simulation studies that have demonstrated that the N-K test was not keeping α_{EW} fixed, as was previously thought. Rather, the N-K test was gaining most of its extra power by letting α_{EW} increase as the number of groups increased. Although the N-K test is not as liberal as LSD when many groups are involved, it is no longer considered acceptably conservative.

In the past 20 years or so, a number of multiple comparison procedures have been shown to keep α_{EW} at the desired level without being overly conservative. Unfortunately, most of these methods are unreasonably tedious to calculate by hand, and only some of them have been

Table 13.4   Means for the Music Experiment Data in Table 12.1B

Bluegrass	Jazz	Classical	New Age	Heavy metal
14.2	20.2	22.4	8.2	8.0

included in major statistical software packages. However, there is one pro-cedure that combines elements of both Fisher's and Tukey's approaches to create a test that is not only more powerful than HSD *and* acceptably conservative but is easy to use as well. This test, proposed by Hayter (1986), is known as the *Fisher-Hayter* (F-H) test or the *modified* LSD test.

The Fisher-Hayter (Modified LSD) Test

In keeping with Fisher's approach, the F-H test typically begins with a one-way ANOVA. If the null hypothesis of the ANOVA cannot be rejected, the test does not proceed. If the ANOVA is significant (usually at the .05 level), HSD is calculated. However, the critical value of q that is used is the one that corresponds to $k - 1$ (rather than k) groups.

To illustrate the use of the F-H test, let us return to the example in the previous chapter, in which different types of music differentially affected performance on a spatial ability test (Table 12.1B). The means for each music type are shown in Table 13.4.

Recall that the size of each sample (n) is 5 and that the value for MS_{Bet}, as calculated in the previous chapter, is 221.1. However, for the purposes of this example, we will ignore the standard deviations from the original data and just assume that MS_W equals 62 for the one-way ANOVA. Therefore, the F ratio for this version of the music-type example is $221.1/62 = 3.57$. The critical value for F at the .05 level with degrees of freedom equal to 4 and 20 is 2.87, so the null hypothesis of the ANOVA can be rejected; even with this larger error term, we can conclude that the population means for the five music conditions are not all equal to each other. This allows us to proceed to the next step of the F-H test. The critical q for 4 (i.e., $k - 1$) groups and $df_W = 20$ is 3.96, so

$$HSD = 3.96\sqrt{\frac{62}{5}} = 3.96(3.52) = 13.94$$

Table 13.5, which illustrates the differences between pairs of means, makes it easy to see which music conditions differ significantly. According to the F-H test, classical music differs significantly from both New Age and heavy metal. In both cases, the difference of sample means is greater than 13.94. No other differences are statistically significant.

By comparison, Tukey's method requires that the critical q be based on k (i.e., 5) groups. For this example, Tukey's HSD is equal to $4.23(3.52) = 14.9$. Thus, Tukey's method would not find any pair of conditions to differ significantly, as no differences are greater than 14.9. It should be clear from

Table 13.5 Difference Between Each Pair of Means in Table 13.4

	Jazz	Classical	New Age	Heavy metal
Bluegrass	6.0	8.2	6.0	6.2
Jazz		2.2	12.0	12.2
Classical			14.2	14.4
New Age				0.2

this example that the F-H test is more powerful than Tukey's HSD. The original LSD test is more powerful still, as you can see from the following calculation:

$$\text{LSD} = 2.086\sqrt{\frac{124}{5}} = 2.086(4.98) = 10.4$$

According to Fisher's LSD test, jazz also differs significantly from New Age and heavy metal. However, this test is widely considered to be too liberal for use with more than three groups and should therefore not be used in the situation represented by this example.

Which Multiple Comparison Test Should I Use?

Our recommendation is clear. For multiple pairwise comparisons, use Fisher's protected t tests (LSD, if all ns are equal) when dealing with only three groups, and use the F-H test with more than three groups. However, when presenting your results to researchers who are unfamiliar with the (relatively) new F-H test, you may have to resort to the more conservative but much more widely known (and respected) Tukey HSD test.

If you are dealing with more than three samples and their sizes differ considerably, it is not legitimate to use any of the tests mentioned above. You may have to use an even more conservative general-purpose comparison test, like the Bonferroni or Scheffé tests described in the next section.

Planned and Complex Comparisons

Whenever we have used the expression *multiple comparisons*, we were referring only to **post hoc pairwise comparisons**. The Latin term *post hoc* means "after the fact." In this context, it implies that no decision was made about which particular t tests to compute before looking at the data or performing the ANOVA. If you inspect your sample means and then test the difference between the largest and the smallest, you need the same α_{EW} protection that you would if you had conducted all of the possible t tests. Selecting specific pairs of means for comparison based on your theoretical research questions *before* seeing your actual data can give you a boost in power much like the added power that you can derive from planning a one- rather than two-tailed test. You can get "credit" for predicting the statistical significance of a few particular **planned comparisons**.

The Bonferroni Correction

If you want to keep α_{EW} at .05, say, you should not use .05 as your alpha for each of the possible pairwise comparisons (the alpha for any one comparison can be symbolized as α_{pc}, for alpha per comparison). But if you plan on testing relatively few of the possible comparisons, you do not need to increase your critical value as much as you would for Tukey's HSD. The simplest and most common procedure for finding the appropriate alpha for each of several planned (also called "a priori") comparisons is based on a formula for the maximum accumulation of probabilities, derived by the Italian mathematician Carlo Bonferroni in the 1930s. Applied to the problem of multiple comparisons, Bonferroni's "inequality" can be stated as follows: $c \times \alpha_{pc} \leq \alpha_{EW}$, where c is the number of comparisons being performed.

For example, if you use an alpha of .01 for each of five null comparisons, the chance that one or more of the five tests will turn out to be statistically significant (i.e., α_{EW}) will not be greater than $c \times \alpha_{pc} = 5 \times .01 = .05$. This fact leads to a simple rule for adjusting alpha for each comparison, based on the number of comparisons planned and the experimentwise value for alpha that you do not want to exceed. The formula for the *Bonferroni correction* (or "adjustment") is

$$\alpha_{pc} = \frac{\alpha_{EW}}{c} \qquad \text{Formula 13.6}$$

To illustrate the use of the Bonferroni correction, let us return to the example mentioned at the beginning of the HSD section—that is, the study of four similar drugs and a placebo. If you plan to test each drug against the placebo, but you do not plan to compare one drug to another, you are planning 4 comparisons out of a total of 10 (i.e., $5 \times 4/2$). To keep α_{EW} from rising above .05, you should use the following alpha for each of the 4 drug-to-placebo comparisons: $\alpha_{pc} = .05/4 = .0125$.

Before the ready availability of statistical software, special tables were needed to find critical t values corresponding to the various possible values of α_{pc}. If you are using statistical software to conduct your planned t tests, you will get an exact p value for each of your comparisons (the two-tailed p value is usually the default option). For this example, any t test producing a p value less than .0125 would be declared significant, but H_0 would not be rejected whenever p was .0125 or larger.

For the purpose of comparison with other procedures, note that the critical t for $df_W = 20$ and $\alpha_{pc} = .0125$ equals 2.744. This is a rather drastic increase over the critical t for the .05 level, which equals 2.086. The Bonferroni correction is very conservative. That is, it tends to keep α_{EW} well below .05. But if you are planning relatively few comparisons, the Bonferroni test gives you more power than Tukey's HSD. You can see from Table G that q for five groups and $df_W = 20$ is 4.23. This is equivalent to a critical t of $4.23/\sqrt{2}$, which equals 2.99, and is even larger than the Bonferroni-corrected critical t of 2.744.

The Bonferroni correction is too conservative, however, to be used as a post hoc test when you are performing all of the possible t tests. In the five-group case, a total of 10 pairwise comparisons is possible. So α_{pc} would equal .005, which corresponds to a Bonferroni-corrected critical t ($df_W = 20$) of 3.15. This is even larger than the equivalent t for the HSD test (2.99), which is already a bit more conservative than is necessary. A reasonable compromise would be to use the Bonferroni correction to test a few planned pairwise comparisons (assuming you have a solid basis on which to plan those tests) and then use Tukey's HSD (basing q on the total number of groups) to test the rest of the pairs.

Complex Comparisons

Selecting a few pairs of conditions for planned tests is one way to increase power. A more sophisticated (and increasingly popular) way is to create a **complex comparison**, which involves more than two conditions in one test.

For example, if your study included a drug, an herbal remedy, and a placebo, you could subtract the average of the herbal remedy and placebo means from the drug mean to create a single difference, or *contrast*. This contrast can then be tested for significance as a planned comparison. Such planned contrasts allow you to get "credit" for correctly predicting the pattern, or relative spacing, of the means. If it turns out that the sample mean for the herbal remedy is much closer to the placebo mean than the drug mean, our contrast (the average of herbal and placebo versus drug) will be larger than if the herbal and drug means were close together and very different from the placebo. (Conversely, planning to average the drug and herbal means for comparison with the placebo would imply that you are predicting that the effect of the herbal remedy will be comparable to the drug and that both are clearly better than the placebo.) If the pattern of the sample means fits well with your prediction, a planned comparison can attain significance, legitimately, even when the ANOVA would not. With few planned comparisons, it is reasonable to test each at the .05 level. When testing more than a few such comparisons, a Bonferroni correction on alpha may be called for.

Although it is not commonly done, when trying to follow up the results of a significant one-way ANOVA, you could devise and test a complex comparison based on a pattern you have seen in your data. For such post hoc complex contrasts, the Scheffé test is widely recommended to keep α_{EW} under control. The Scheffé test is so conservative that when the ANOVA is not significant, you can be sure that you will not be able to create any comparison that will be found significant by Scheffé's test (see B. H. Cohen, 2008).

Trend Components

When the factor in your one-way ANOVA has quantitative levels, the types of complex comparisons you are likely to want to test are the simplest trends—usually just the linear and quadratic trends, and sometimes the cubic trend—rarely any more complex trend. The fact that the levels are quantitative automatically justifies the test of the linear trend as a planned comparison. The SS_{Bet} for the linear trend is based on how close the means for the levels come to being on a single straight line; the closer the means of the dependent variable (DV) come to exhibiting a linear trend, the more similar SS_{Bet} for the trend will be to the SS_{Bet} for the one-way ANOVA. The added power of testing the linear trend, as with any complex comparison, comes from the fact that the MS for the linear trend is found by dividing the SS for the linear trend by 1, whereas the SS_{Bet} for the ANOVA must be divided by one less than the number of levels of the factor. The greater the number of quantitative factor levels, the greater the potential power advantage of testing any one particular trend (or other complex comparison).

If the means of your factor levels tend to show one reversal in trend (e.g., the linear trend starts out steeply upward and then levels off or even begins to slope downward), testing your means for a quadratic trend may give you a larger F ratio (and therefore a better chance for statistical significance) than testing for a linear trend, though both may prove to be significant. Some extra justification is generally needed to test the quadratic trend as a planned comparison, but it often makes sense that the independent variable (IV) levels, if extended far enough, will eventually reach an optimum point, after which further increases will have decreasing effects on the DV. If the data tend to exhibit a second reversal, this will contribute to the amount of the cubic trend, and so on for higher trend components.

Nonparametric Multiple Comparisons: The Protected Rank-Sum Test

We have seen that when the overall (often called *omnibus*) F test in an analysis of variance is statistically significant and there are only three groups, it is then acceptable to perform the three possible (protected) t tests, each at the .05 level, in order to draw more specific conclusions about which of the population means can be considered different from which other ones. Similarly, if and only if your Kruskal-Wallis H is statistically significant for a three-group study, a method called the **protected rank-sum test** may be used to determine which pairs of populations differ significantly in location. As with the protected t test, you may perform the three possible pairwise rank-sum tests using an alpha of .05 for each, because the tests are protected against a larger experimentwise Type I error rate by the precondition that H be significant. Note that in the nonparametric case, there is no omnibus error term to use; completely separate (two-group) rank-sum tests, just like the ones described in Chapter 8, are performed. Also, note that there is no nonparametric version of Tukey's test. When k is larger than 3, a Bonferroni adjustment of the alpha for each follow-up rank-sum test is recommended.

To illustrate the use of rank-sum tests following a significant H test, we turn once again to the data in Table 13.1. Since H was statistically significant (see Chapter 12, in which H was found to be 8.48, $p < .05$), any or all of the three pairs of groups (1 versus 2, 1 versus 3, or 2 versus 3) may be compared by using the protected rank-sum test. In order to do so, however, *the scores must be reranked for each test* (rather than ranking all three groups together, as shown in Table 12.5). For example, if Groups 1 and 2 are being compared, the third group is ignored. The third score in Group 2 is ranked 1 (the lowest score), the fifth score in Group 1 is now ranked 2, the score right below this one is now ranked 3, and so on until the highest score in these two groups (i.e., the second score in Group 2) receives a rank of 18. Thus $N_1 = 8$, $N_2 = 10$, and $N_T = 18$ for this comparison. After reranking it is found that $T_1 = 59.5$ (and $T_2 = 111.5$), $T_E = (8)(19)/2 = 76$, and $\sigma_T = \sqrt{(8)(10)(19)/12} = 11.25$. Therefore, using the formula for the rank-sum test given previously, we obtain:

$$z = \frac{T_1 - T_E}{\sigma_T} = \frac{59.5 - 76}{11.25} = -1.47$$

This z value is not statistically significant. When Group 1 and Group 3 are compared, a nonsignificant z value (1.73) is also obtained. But when Group 2 and Group 3 are compared, a statistically significant z value of 2.69 results. Therefore, the conclusion is that the locations of these three populations are not the same because the location (or median) of Population 2 is greater than that of Population 3. However, the data do not warrant concluding that the location of Population 1 differs from either of the other two.

Summary

When the F ratio for a one-way ANOVA is statistically significant, it is likely that the researcher will want to run multiple comparisons on the data to determine which of the population means can be said to differ from one another. A general procedure for post hoc pairwise comparisons, which can be applied whether the sample sizes are equal or not even similar, is the Fisher protected t test. It is "protected" only if the null hypothesis for the one-way ANOVA can be rejected. Unfortunately, it is not adequately conservative when dealing with more than three groups.

Fisher's Protected t Tests

For any (or every) pair of groups, compute as follows:

$$t = \frac{\overline{X}_i - \overline{X}_j}{\sqrt{MS_W \left(\dfrac{1}{N_i} + \dfrac{1}{N_j} \right)}}, \qquad \text{Formula 13.1}$$

$$df = N_T - k$$

where

$$\overline{X}_i = \text{mean of group } i$$
$$\overline{X}_j = \text{mean of group } j$$
$$MS_W = \text{within-groups mean square}$$
$$N_i = \text{number of observations in group } i$$
$$N_j = \text{number of observations in group } j$$

If all of the sample sizes are equal, Fisher's procedure can be simplified by calculating LSD. Any pair of means that differs by more than LSD can be said to differ significantly. The formula is

$$\text{LSD} = t_{\text{crit}} \sqrt{\frac{2MS_W}{n}} \qquad \text{Formula 13.2}$$

where n is the size of *each* sample and t_{crit} is two-tailed and is based on df_W and the alpha used to test the one-way ANOVA. Fisher's procedure is not recommended for following up an ANOVA that involves more than three groups, because it allows α_{EW} to increase as k increases, for $k > 3$.

Tukey's HSD Test

This test is appropriate for any number of samples, as long as the samples are all the same size, or nearly so. (In the latter case, the harmonic mean of the sample sizes is used as n; see Formula 13.5.) It is not necessary to perform a one-way ANOVA before applying this test, but Tukey's test will rarely find a pair of means to differ significantly when the ANOVA would not be significant. The difference between each pair of means is compared to

$$\text{HSD} = q_{\text{crit}} \sqrt{\frac{MS_W}{n}} \qquad \text{Formula 13.3}$$

where n is the size of each sample and q_{crit} is a value from Table G, based on k groups and df_W. The HSD test is more conservative than is desirable, but it is simpler and better known than most alternative multiple comparison procedures. You can obtain a confidence interval for the difference between any two population means represented in your study by using the following formula, based on Tukey's test:

$$\mu_i - \mu_j = \overline{X}_i - \overline{X}_j \pm \text{HSD} \qquad \text{Formula 13.4}$$

The Fisher-Hayter (or Modified LSD) Test

This test requires that the one-way ANOVA be statistically significant before proceeding. The difference between each pair of means is compared to HSD, as calculated previously, except that q_{crit} is based on $k - 1$, rather than k, groups. Although this test is acceptably conservative and more powerful than Tukey's test, it is not yet well known.

The Bonferroni Correction

If a relatively small number of comparisons are planned in advance, each one can be tested using the following value for alpha:

$$\alpha_{pc} = \frac{\alpha_{EW}}{c} \qquad \text{Formula 13.6}$$

where c is the number of planned comparisons and α_{EW} is the largest acceptable value for the experimentwise alpha. This test is too conservative to be used as a post hoc test—for example, to test all possible pairwise comparisons following an ANOVA.

Exercises

1. Calculate LSD for the two experiments in Exercise 1 of the previous chapter. For which experiment is the calculation of LSD justified? Determine which pairs of means differ significantly in the experiment for which the calculation of LSD is justified.

2. Calculate protected t tests to compare all possible pairs of the four dormitories (e.g., Turck, Kirk, etc.), using the error term for Exercise 2 of the previous chapter. Which pairs differ significantly at the .05 level? Give two reasons why it would not be appropriate to calculate LSD for the data from the four dormitories.

3. Calculate both LSD and HSD for the two experiments in Exercise 3 of the previous chapter, using the harmonic mean of the three sample sizes as your value for n. What conclusions can you draw for each experiment? Use your values for LSD and HSD to compare the relative statistical power of these two procedures.

4. For your convenience, the data from Exercise 4 from the previous chapter are reprinted in the following table:

	Group				
	1	2	3	4	5
X	23	30	34	29	26
s	6.5	7.2	7.0	5.8	6.0
N	12	15	14	12	15

   (a) Using the harmonic mean of all the sample sizes as your value for n, calculate HSD for these data, and determine which pairs of groups differ significantly.

   (b) Recalculate HSD according to the rules of the Fisher-Hayter test. Would the use of the F-H test be justified in this case? Assuming the F-H test is justified, what conclusions can be drawn from this test? Use the values for HSD in this part and part (a) to compare the power of Tukey's test with the modified LSD test.

Table 13.4 Means for the Music Experiment Data in Table 12.1B

Bluegrass	Jazz	Classical	New Age	Heavy metal
14.2	20.2	22.4	8.2	8.0

5. A study using five samples finds that the mean of each sample is as follows: Sample 1 = 6.7; Sample 2 = 14.2; Sample 3 = 13.8; Sample 4 = 10.4; Sample 5 = 15.8. Suppose that HSD (with q based on $\alpha = .05$) for this study is 5.3. (a) Which population means should be regarded as different from each other at the .05 level? (b) Find the 95% CIs for comparing Sample 5 to each of the others.

6. For this exercise, we will use Table 13.4, reprinted here, for the sample means. This time, however, imagine that the size of each sample (n) is 7 and that you do not know MS_W. Fortunately, you are given the results of the ANOVA: $F(4, 30) = 5.53$.

   (a) Find the error term for the ANOVA and use it to calculate Tukey's HSD.

   (b) Which types of music differ significantly from which other types, according to Tukey's HSD test?

7. In Exercise 7 of the previous chapter, the means for the negative feedback, positive feedback, and no feedback groups were $\overline{X}_{neg} = 11.1$, $\overline{X}_{pos} = 14.7$, and $\overline{X}_{no} = 12.4$, and the F ratio for the one-way ANOVA was equal to 3.69. Given that the ANOVA was significant at the .05 level and that there were 20 participants in each group: (a) Find the value of LSD for this study. (b) Which pair(s) of means differ significantly, according to the LSD test?

Thought Questions

1. An F test from an ANOVA using five samples is statistically significant. The researcher now wishes to determine which pairs of the five population means differ significantly from each other. Why are multiple comparisons procedures necessary rather than just performing all of the possible t tests?

2. If a multiple comparisons procedure involves the use of t tests, why is it that a researcher cannot skip the ANOVA and just do these t tests?

3. (a) When should you use Tukey's HSD test rather than Fisher's protected t tests? (b) When should you use Fisher's protected t tests rather than Tukey's HSD test?

4. What are the advantages of using the Fisher-Hayter modified LSD test? When should this test be used?

5. (a) What is the difference between post hoc comparisons and a priori comparisons? (b) What advantage results from using a priori comparisons?

6. Give an example of when the Bonferroni correction should be used.

Computer Exercises

1. Redo the one-way ANOVAs requested in Computer Exercise 1 of the previous chapter, selecting both LSD and Tukey from the list of post hoc tests in each case. For postquiz anxiety, which pairs of quiz conditions (last question easy, moderate, difficult, or impossible) differ significantly from each other, according to each multiple comparison procedure (MCP)? Answer this question again for postquiz heart rate. Use Table G in your text, and your own calculations, to perform the Fisher-Hayter test for each dependent variable, and state the conclusions for this test. Compare the three MCPs with respect to power, using the results you found in this exercise to illustrate the differences.

2. Redo the one-way ANOVAs requested in Computer Exercise 2 of the previous chapter, selecting both Tukey and Bonferroni from the list of post hoc tests in each case. What is the problem with using HSD to make comparisons between groups in this exercise? Use the results for this exercise to compare the power of Tukey and Bonferroni for testing all possible pairs of means.

3. Redo the one-way ANOVAs requested in Computer Exercise 3 of the previous chapter, selecting LSD as your MCP. Also, use your statistical software to perform ordinary t tests for each pair of math groups for each dependent variable. Explain the differences between the LSD test and ordinary t tests as applied to the data in this exercise.

4. (a) Use the Kruskal-Wallis procedure to test whether the different quiz conditions (last question easy, moderate, difficult, or impossible) had a significant effect on postquiz anxiety scores. Regardless of the significance of your test, perform all of the possible pairwise comparisons as rank-sum tests. Which of these pairwise tests would be significant after a Bonferroni adjustment of your alpha for each comparison?

(b) Repeat part (a) for the postquiz heart rates.

Bridge to SPSS

Whether you use the Analyze/Compare Means or the Analyze/General Linear Model menu to perform your one-way ANOVA, you can obtain the same selection of multiple-comparison procedures by clicking on the **Post Hoc...** button from the initial dialog box. If you choose to assume that all of the population variances are equal (you can request a homogeneity of variance test under Options, to help you decide), there are 14 choices for multiple comparisons, only a few of which we have discussed in this chapter. The choice labeled "Tukey" corresponds to the HSD test we have described; "Tukey's-b" refers to a less-used modification that we did not discuss. "S-N-K" refers to the Newman-Keuls test, which we discussed briefly and did not recommend. (The "S" in S-N-K stands for Student and is sometimes added to the name as a reminder that this test is based on the "studentized" range statistic.)

For each post hoc test selected, SPSS will give you an appropriately adjusted and interpretable p value for each possible pairwise comparison, assuming that your goal is to keep the experimentwise alpha at .05. For instance, if you choose "Tukey," your output will not present you with the size of HSD. Rather, t tests will be performed for each possible pair of levels of your factor, and the exact p level will be given for each, adjusted according to the studentized range statistic. As an example, if the difference between a pair of means is exactly equal to HSD, its p value (labeled "Sig.") will be given as .05, because it is just on the borderline of significance for Tukey's test. For LSD, no adjustment is made to the p values, so it is up to you to note whether the ANOVA is significant and to decide whether to use LSD if dealing with more than three groups (not recommended). For a pair of means that yields a p value of .05 for "Tukey," the p value for LSD will be smaller (i.e., more "significant"), because the latter is not adjusted.

If Bonferroni is selected, the p value from the LSD test is simply multiplied by the total number of possible pairwise comparisons. For example, if there are four conditions in your one-way ANOVA (and therefore six possible pairs), and the p value for comparing a particular pair by the LSD test is .01, the Bonferroni p for that pair will be given as $6 \times .01 = .06$, and therefore that pair will not differ significantly at the .05 level, when using the Bonferroni correction. (Note that this method yields the same conclusions as dividing .05 by 6 to get a Bonferroni-adjusted alpha of .00833. Because .01 is not less than .00833, a pair associated with that p value will not differ significantly when the Bonferroni procedure is used.) The other post hoc choices are beyond the level of this text, but they are rarely used, anyway.

Both the Analyze/Compare Means/One-Way ANOVA and the Analyze/General Linear Model/Univariate dialog boxes contain a **Contrasts** button, but only the former allows you to create your own customized combination of means to test a complex comparison. However, a discussion of how to choose the "coefficients" needed to create a particular contrast is beyond the scope of this text (see B. H. Cohen, 2008).

Chapter 14
Introduction to Factorial Design: Two-Way Analysis of Variance

PREVIEW

Introduction

When should you use a factorial design instead of a one-way analysis of variance? In what way are these two procedures similar? What are some of the important differences between them?

What is meant by the interaction between two variables?

Computational Procedures

What are the procedures for computing a two-way (factorial) analysis of variance?

Why do we calculate the sums of squares for the main effects before the SS for the interaction?

How do we test the F ratios for statistical significance?

What are the multiple comparison procedures in two-way analysis of variance?

What is meant by the term *familywise alpha*, and how does it differ from experimentwise alpha?

The Meaning of Interaction

What is meant by a zero interaction versus some interaction between two variables?

What are the two major types of interaction for a 2×2 factorial design?

Why are we cautious about interpreting the results of the main effects when the interaction is significant?

Following Up a Significant Interaction

What are simple main effects, and when is it appropriate to test them?

How can tests of simple main effects lead to more specific conclusions from a two-way ANOVA?

How do you follow up a significant simple main effect that involves three or more levels of a factor?

PREVIEW (*continued*)

Measuring Effect Size in a Factorial ANOVA

How does a partial eta squared differ from an ordinary eta squared? When would each be preferred?

Summary

Exercises

Thought Questions

Computer Exercises

Bridge to SPSS

Introduction

The one-way analysis of variance presented in Chapter 12 is used to investigate the relationship of a *single* independent variable to a dependent variable, where the independent variable has two or more levels (i.e., groups). For example, the music experiment in Chapter 12 dealt with the effect of five different types of music (five levels of the independent variable) on performance on a spatial ability test (the dependent variable).

The **factorial design** is used to study the relationship of *two or more* independent variables (called *factors*) to a dependent variable, where each factor has two or more levels. Suppose you are interested in the relationship between four different dosages of caffeine (four levels: large, moderate, small, zero) and sex (two levels: male and female) to scores on a test of manual dexterity. There are several hypotheses of interest: Different dosages of caffeine may affect test scores differently; males and females may differ in test performance; certain caffeine dosages may affect test scores more for one sex than for the other. These hypotheses may be evaluated in a single statistical framework by using a factorial design. This example would be called a "two-way" analysis of variance, because there are two independent variables. It could also be labeled as a 4×2 factorial design, because there are four levels of the first independent variable and two levels of the second independent variable. Each combination of levels of the two factors is called a **cell**, so there are eight possible cells in a 4×2 factorial design. If all of the possible cells are tested in a study, the design is said to be *completely crossed*. When we refer to a factorial design, we always mean a completely-crossed factorial design. (It is rare to see a factorial design with any empty cells, because that situation greatly complicates the analysis.)

Figure 14.1

Partitioning of Variation in a Two-Way Factorial Design

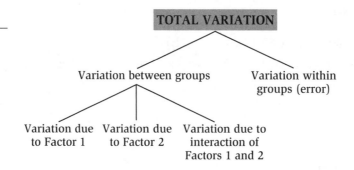

The logic of the factorial design begins with the logic of the more simple one-way design. The total sum of squares is partitioned into within-group (error) sum of squares and between-group sum of squares. In the factorial design, however, the between-group sum of squares (which could just as well be called the between-cells *SS*) is itself partitioned into several parts: variation due to the first factor, variation due to the second factor, and variation due to the joint effects of the two factors, called the **interaction**. (See Figure 14.1.) One example of an interaction effect would be if a particular dosage of caffeine improved test scores for males but *not* for females, while other dosages had the same effect on test scores for both sexes. (The interaction, a particularly important feature of factorial design, is discussed in detail later in this chapter.)

It can be shown algebraically that the total sum of squares is equal to the sum of these various parts: (a) the within-group (error) sum of squares, (b) the sum of squares due to Factor 1, (c) the sum of squares due to Factor 2, and (d) the sum of squares due to the interaction of Factors 1 and 2. Thus a factorial design makes it possible to break down the total variability into *several* meaningful parts. That is, it permits several possible explanations as to why people are different on the dependent variable. As was pointed out in earlier chapters, explaining variation—why people differ from one another—is the *raison d'être* of the behavioral scientist.

Computational Procedures

The outline of the raw-score computational procedure for the two-way factorial design is as follows:

1. (a) Compute SS_T.
   (b) Compute SS_{Bet}.
   (c) Subtract SS_{Bet} from SS_T to obtain SS_W (error).
   (d) Compute SS_1 (the SS_{Bet} just for Factor 1).
   (e) Compute SS_2 (the SS_{Bet} just for Factor 2).
   (f) Subtract SS_1 and SS_2 from SS_{Bet} to obtain the sum of squares for the interaction of Factors 1 and 2 (called SS_{inter} or $SS_{1 \times 2}$).

2. Convert the sums of squares in steps (c), (d), (e), and (f) to mean squares by dividing each one by the appropriate number of degrees of freedom.

3. (a) Test the *main effect* for Factor 1 (MS_1) for statistical significance by computing the appropriate F ratio (i.e., divide MS_1 by MS_W).
   (b) Test the main effect for Factor 2 (MS_2) for statistical significance by computing the F ratio, as in (a).
   (c) Test the interaction of the two factors ($MS_{1\times2}$) for statistical significance by computing the F ratio, as in (a) and (b).

The two-way factorial design permits you to test three null hypotheses—one concerning the effect of Factor 1, one concerning the effect of Factor 2, and one concerning the *joint effect* of Factor 1 and Factor 2—in a single statistical framework. The separate effects of Factors 1 and 2 are referred to as the **main effects** of those factors.

As an illustration, consider the hypothetical results for the music experiment shown in Table 14.1. There are five observations in each *cell*; for example, the scores of 16, 16, 14, 13, and 12 are the test scores of five participants with no musical training who completed a spatial ability test while listening to Mozart. Just as in the one-way design, the within-group variance estimate is based on the variability *within* each of the eight cells. Variation due to the composer factor is reflected by the variability across the four *column* means, while variation due to the musical background factor is reflected by the variability (i.e., difference) of the two *row* means (row and column means are both referred to as *marginal means*). (Note that the data for the participants with no musical training in Table 14.1 come from Table 12.1A, after deleting Group 4.)

Table 14.1   Scores on a 20-Item Spatial Ability Test as a Function of Classical Composer and Musical Background (4 × 2 Factorial Design)

	Musical composer (Factor 1)				
	Mozart	Chopin	Bach	Beethoven	Row means
No musical training	16 16 $\overline{X} = 14.2$ 14 13 $s = 1.79$ 12	16 14 $\overline{X} = 13.2$ 13 13 $s = 2.17$ 10	16 14 $\overline{X} = 12.4$ 12 10 $s = 2.61$ 10	14 13 $\overline{X} = 12.0$ 13 10 $s = 1.87$ 10	12.95
Musical background (Factor 2)					
Professional musician	16 18 $\overline{X} = 17.4$ 20 15 $s = 1.95$ 18	17 10 $\overline{X} = 13.2$ 13 12 $s = 2.95$ 14	14 14 $\overline{X} = 12.2$ 11 10 $s = 1.79$ 12	16 10 $\overline{X} = 12.8$ 13 14 $s = 2.39$ 11	13.90
Column means	15.8	13.2	12.3	12.4	Grand mean $= \overline{X}_G$ $= 13.425$

Sums of Squares

1. **Total sum of squares (SS_T).** The total SS is computed in the same way as in Chapter 12, using Formula 12.1B, repeated here:

$$SS_T = \sum X^2 - N_T \overline{X}_G^2, \qquad \text{Formula 12.1B}$$

where

N_T = total number of observations
$\sum$ = summation across all observations

In Table 14.1,

$$\sum X^2 = 16^2 + 16^2 + 14^2 + \cdots + 13^2 + 14^2 + 11^2$$

$$= 7{,}467$$

$$N_T \overline{X}_G^2 = 40(13.425)^2 = 7{,}209.2$$

$$SS_T = 7{,}467 - 7{,}209.2$$

$$= 257.8$$

(See the note on using your calculator to obtain SS_T in the corresponding part of Chapter 12.)

2. **Sum of squares between groups (SS_{Bet}).** We can ignore for a moment the fact that this is a factorial design, treat the data in Table 14.1 as coming from eight groups, and find SS_{Bet} as in Chapter 12. Because this is a *balanced* analysis of variance (ANOVA) design[1] (i.e., all of the groups, or cells, are the same size), we could use the equal-N version of the SS_{Bet} formula (Formula 12.2B), but to further reduce computational effort, we use an even more convenient version of that formula as shown here:

$$SS_{Bet} = n \sum_{i=1}^{k} \overline{X}_i^2 - N_T \overline{X}_G^2 \qquad \text{Formula 14.1}$$

where n is the size of *each* cell, and k is the number of cells.
For the data in Table 14.1, $k = 8$ and $n = 5$. Therefore,

$$n \sum_{i=1}^{k} \overline{X}_i^2 = 5(14.2^2 + 13.2^2 + 12.4^2 + 12.0^2 + 17.4^2 + 13.2^2 + 12.2^2 + 12.8^2)$$

$$= 5(1{,}463.32)$$

$$= 7{,}316.6$$

---

[1]The calculation of factorial ANOVAs that are *not* balanced is a rather complex topic, which is beyond the scope of an introductory statistics text.

We have already calculated $N_T\overline{X}_G^2$ as part of the formula for SS_T, so

$$SS_{bet} = 7,316.6 - 7,209.2 = 107.4$$

3. **Sum of squares within groups (error) (SS_W).** The within-groups SS may be found by Formula 12.3 or, more easily, by subtraction as shown in Chapter 12 and here:

$$SS_W = SS_T - SS_{Bet}$$
$$= 257.8 - 107.4$$
$$= 150.4$$

Later we will divide SS_W by df_W to obtain the usual denominator of our F ratios, MS_W. However, MS_W can be found directly from the unbiased standard deviations (SDs) given in Table 14.1. You may recall from Chapter 12 that in the equal-n one-way ANOVA, MS_W is the average of all the group variances. Similarly, in a balanced factorial design, MS_W is just the average of the *cell* variances. If you square all of the s's in Table 14.1, sum them, and then divide by 8, you will get 4.7061. This agrees, within rounding error, with SS_W/df_W, as you will soon see.

Computing MS_W directly from the SDs can act as a check on the accuracy of your other calculations, but it has a more important function. If for any reason you need to calculate a factorial ANOVA from a table of means and SDs, and you do *not* have the individual scores, you will not be able to calculate SS_T directly. Therefore, you will not have the option of finding SS_W by subtraction. But that's not a problem, because you can always square and average the SDs to find MS_W directly—provided, of course, that the SDs have been reported, and you are dealing with a balanced design.

Before we proceed to divide SS_{Bet} into smaller, more specific pieces, some additional notation will help to prevent confusion. Let us arbitrarily define Factor 1 as the *column factor* and represent the number of columns by c. Similarly, we will define Factor 2 as the *row factor* and use r to represent the number of rows. Thus, the number of cells in a two-way design can be written as rc, and the total N (N_T) therefore equals rcn. (For the design in Table 14.1, $N_T = rcn = 2 \times 4 \times 5 = 40$.)

4. **Sum of squares for Factor 1 (SS_1).** We have defined the column factor as Factor 1. In this example, the columns vary by musical composer. The SS for the composer factor, *which ignores differences in musical background*, is computed using a slight variation of Formula 12.2B:

$$SS_1 = rn\sum_{i=1}^{c}\overline{X}_i^2 - N_T\overline{X}_G^2 \qquad \text{Formula 14.2A}$$

where $\overline{X}_i$ is the mean of any *column* and rn is the number of scores in any column (i.e., the number of rows times the size of each cell), which replaces n in Formula 12.2B.

If composer has a substantial effect on test scores (ignoring musical background), the means of the *columns* of Table 14.1 should show considerable variability. The value of $N_T \overline{X}_G^2$ has already been found to be equal to 7,209.2. Then,

$$SS_1 = 10(15.8^2 + 13.2^2 + 12.3^2 + 12.4^2) - 7{,}209.2$$

$$= 7{,}289.3 - 7{,}209.2$$

$$= 80.1$$

5. **Sum of squares for Factor 2 (SS_2).** In this example, musical background is the row factor and hence Factor 2. The SS for the background factor, *which ignores differences in musical composer,* is computed by the same formula used for SS_1, except for changing rn to cn:

$$SS_2 = cn \sum_{i=1}^{r} \overline{X}_i^2 - N_T \overline{X}_G^2 \qquad \text{Formula 14.2B}$$

where $\overline{X}_i$ is the mean of any row and cn is the number of scores in any row (i.e., the number of columns times the size of each cell). If musical background has an effect on test scores (ignoring composer), the means of the rows of Table 14.1 should differ at least somewhat.

$$SS_2 = 20(12.95^2 + 13.90^2) - 7{,}209.2$$

$$= 7{,}218.2 - 7{,}209.2$$

$$= 9.0$$

6. **Sum of squares for interaction ($SS_{1\times2}$).** The interaction SS is part of the variability of the eight cells and is obtained by subtraction:

$$SS_{1\times2} = SS_{\text{Bet}} - SS_1 - SS_2 \qquad \text{Formula 14.3}$$

For the data in Table 14.1,

$$SS_{1\times2} = 107.4 - 80.1 - 9.0$$

$$= 18.3$$

Mean Squares

The next step is to convert each sum of squares to an estimate of the population variance, or mean square. This is done by dividing by the

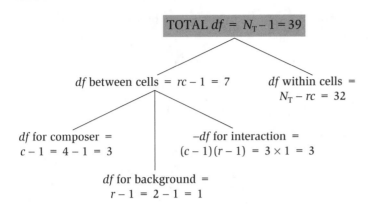

Figure 14.2

Partitioning of Degrees of Freedom in the Music Experiment

appropriate degrees of freedom (df), as shown in the following table. The way that the df are partitioned in a two-way ANOVA is illustrated in Figure 14.2.

Source	Degrees of freedom	Computation for Table 14.1
Total	$N_T - 1$	$df_T = 40 - 1 = 39$
Within groups	$N_T - k$	$df_W = 40 - 8 = 32$
Between groups	$k - 1$	$df_{Bet} = 8 - 1 = 7$
Factor 1	c (i.e., number of levels of factor 1) $- 1$	$df_1 = 4 - 1 = 3$
Factor 2	r (i.e., number of levels of factor 2) $- 1$	$df_2 = 2 - 1 = 1$
Interaction	$df_1 \times df_2$ (i.e., $[r-1] \times c - 1]$)	$df_{1\times2} = 3 \times 1 = 3$

Note: N_T = total number of observations
    k = number of cells = rc

The first three values in the preceding table are the same as in the case of the one-way design (Chapter 12). The total df equal $N_T - 1$, or one less than the total number of observations. The within-group df is equal to $N_T - k$, where k equals the number of cells (or groups). This is equivalent to obtaining the df for each cell (one less than the number of observations in the cell, or 4 in this example) and summing over all cells ($4 \times 8 = 32$). The between-group df equals one less than the number of cells (i.e., $rc - 1$).

It is also necessary, however, to partition the between-group df in the same way as the between-group variance is partitioned. The df for Factor 1 is one less than the number of levels of Factor 1. In this example Factor 1 has four levels (the four different composers), so the df are $4 - 1 = 3$. Similarly, the df for Factor 2, musical background, are $2 - 1 = 1$. The df for the interaction of composer and background are found by *multiplying* the df for each factor ($3 \times 1 = 3$).

The mean squares (*MSs*) are then found by dividing each *SS*, as usual, by the corresponding *df*:

Mean square within groups (i.e., cells):

$$MS_W = \frac{SS_W}{df_W} = \frac{150.4}{32} = 4.70$$

Mean square for composer:

$$MS_1 = \frac{SS_1}{df_1} = \frac{80.1}{3} = 26.7$$

Mean square for background:

$$MS_2 = \frac{SS_2}{df_2} = \frac{9.0}{1} = 9.0$$

Mean square for interaction:

$$MS_{1\times2} = \frac{SS_{1\times2}}{df_{1\times2}} = \frac{18.3}{3} = 6.1$$

F Ratios and Tests of Significance

As with the one-way analysis of variance, the appropriate statistical model to use with factorial designs is the *F* distribution. The first null hypothesis to be tested is that regardless of which of the four classical composers they listen to, the populations will have equal means. The mean square for the composer factor is divided by the mean square within, yielding the following *F* ratio:

$$F = \frac{MS_1}{MS_W} = \frac{26.7}{4.70} = 5.68$$

The critical value from the *F* table for 3 *df* in the numerator and 32 *df* in the denominator and $\alpha = .05$ is 2.90. Since the computed *F* of 5.68 is greater than this value, you reject H_0 and conclude that the participants in the four composer conditions do *not* come from populations with equal means—that is, different musical composers *do* have an effect on spatial ability test scores.

The second null hypothesis to be tested is that the musicians and novices come from populations with equal means for spatial ability (we refer to the participants who lack musical training as *novices*, for convenience). The mean square for the background factor is divided by the mean square within, yielding the following *F* ratio:

$$F = \frac{MS_2}{MS_W} = \frac{9.0}{4.70} = 1.915$$

The critical value from the F table for 1 df in the numerator and 32 df in the denominator and $\alpha = .05$ is 4.15. (Note that the critical values for the various F tests differ if the dfs differ, because they come from different F distributions.) The computed value of 1.915 is less than the critical value, so you retain H_0 and conclude that there is not sufficient reason to believe that musical training is associated with differences in spatial ability.

The third null hypothesis to be tested is that the interaction effect is zero:

$$F = \frac{MS_{1\times2}}{MS_W} = \frac{6.1}{4.70} = 1.30$$

This computed value of F is less than the critical value obtained from the F table of 2.90 for 3 and 32 df and $\alpha = .05$. So you retain H_0 and conclude that there is not sufficient reason to reject the null hypothesis of no interaction effect.

ANOVA Summary Table

The results of the foregoing analysis of variance are summarized in Table 14.2. Note that the factors are identified by name for the convenience of the reader. Also, as was the case with the one-way analysis of variance, within-group variation (error) is listed last. No F value is listed for error because error is used as the denominator of the various F ratios and is not itself the subject of a statistical test.

Multiple Comparisons Following a Factorial ANOVA

We saw in Chapter 13 how we could specify the meaning of a significant F ratio by means of a multiple comparison procedure. In a two-way factorial design, there are potentially three F tests that may require further specification as to which means differ from which others, and the same types of procedures may be followed.

When the F for interaction is *not* significant, it is meaningful to follow up each of the independent variables (factors) as if it were from a one-way ANOVA. If the F for a factor is *not* significant, there is nothing to follow up. Doing so is not only unnecessary but improper, because the resulting tests would not be protected. Of course, if a significant factor has only two

Table 14.2 Summary of Two-Way ANOVA of Music Experiment

Source	SS	df	MS	F
Composer	80.1	3	26.7	5.68
Music background	9.0	1	9.0	1.92
Composer × background	18.3	3	6.1	1.30
Error (i.e., within cells)	150.4	32	4.7	

levels, there is nothing to follow up. There is only one difference, so it must be significant. But a significant F for a factor of three or more levels requires specification just as in the one-way design.

In the foregoing example, the interaction F is not significant but the F for composer is. So you may proceed to perform follow-up tests among the column means corresponding to the four different classical composers. Table 14.1 gives these as 15.8, 13.2, 12.3, and 12.4. All of the levels have the same $N_i = rn = 10$, and more than three levels are being compared, so Tukey's Honestly Significant Difference (HSD) test is recommended. Here, Formula 13.3 has been modified to show the appropriate "n":

$$\text{HSD} = q\sqrt{\frac{MS_W}{rn}},$$

where q (from Table G) is based on four groups (i.e., columns), df_W is from the ANOVA, and rn is the number of scores in each group (i.e., column).

Filling in the relevant values in the formula, we find that

$$\text{HSD} = 3.84\sqrt{\frac{4.70}{10}} = 3.84\,(.686) = 2.63$$

Thus, two column means must differ by at least 2.63 points on the spatial ability test to be declared statistically significant at the .05 level. By this criterion, the mean for the Mozart condition (15.8) is significantly larger than the means for both the Bach (12.3) and Beethoven (12.4) conditions [and very nearly significantly larger than the Chopin mean (13.2)], thus further refining the "Mozart effect" we first mentioned in Chapter 12. There are no significant differences among the other three composers. (The Fisher-Hayter, or modified Least Significant Difference (LSD), test can be used instead of Tukey's test, as described in the previous chapter. In this example, the Fisher-Hayter test would find the Mozart-Chopin difference to be significant, in addition to all the significant differences found by Tukey's test.)

Alternatively, a confidence interval (CI) may be established for each pairwise comparison, using Formula 13.4:

$$\mu_i - \mu_j = \overline{X}_1 - \overline{X}_2 \pm \text{HSD}$$

Thus, the 95% CI for the difference between Column 1 (Mozart) and Column 3 (Bach) is

$$[(15.8 - 12.3) - 2.63)] \leq \mu_1 - \mu_3 \leq [(15.8 - 12.3) + 2.63)]$$

$$+.87 \leq \mu_1 - \mu_3 \leq +6.13$$

The value of zero falls outside (below) this interval, indicating that this comparison is statistically significant. In addition, the CI specifies all reasonably likely values of the difference between the two population means. Other CIs for the composer factor may be obtained in a similar fashion.

Familywise Alpha

The second factor in the music experiment, music background, was not significant in this example, so no follow-up tests would be justified. It should also be noted that even if the music background factor *were* significant, no follow-up tests would be possible, because the factor has only two levels. It is when both main effects in a two-way ANOVA are significant and both have more than two levels that an interesting question arises as to how to perform multiple comparisons for *both* factors, and still keep the experimentwise alpha (α_{EW}) at .05. Suppose, for instance, that music background had three levels and led to a significant F ratio. Because there are only three levels, it would be appropriate to use the LSD test to make comparisons among them. However, if the .05 level is used to find the critical t for the LSD test and the .05 level is used again to find the critical q for Tukey's HSD test on the other factor, are we not using the .05 level *twice* to follow-up on the *same* experiment? And would not that raise α_{EW} above .05? The answer is yes! But rather than try to protect α_{EW}, the traditional approach is to invoke a related concept called the **familywise alpha** (α_{FW}) and direct our efforts toward controlling α_{FW}.

It is important to note that it is entirely acceptable to test each of the three F ratios in a two-way ANOVA at the .05 level without using a Bonferroni correction or any other adjustment for multiple tests within the same experiment. That is because all three of the F ratios are automatically considered planned comparisons in a two-way ANOVA. Moreover, the set of post hoc comparisons that would be needed to follow up on any one of these F ratios is thought of as representing a separate *family* of tests, and it is considered acceptable to perform all of the tests in such a family if the corresponding F ratio is significant at the traditional .05 level. For a set of three possible post hoc comparisons, the significance of the F ratio is considered adequate protection to perform all three tests using $\alpha = .05$ for each (e.g., the LSD test). If the set of possible comparisons is greater than three, you would need a procedure like Tukey's HSD to keep the alpha for the whole family of tests (i.e., α_{FW}) down to .05. Thus, if all three F ratios in a two-way ANOVA are significant at the .05 level, you are permitted to perform three sets of post hoc tests, as long as you keep the overall (i.e., familywise) alpha for each set to the .05 level. However, when the F ratio for the interaction of the two factors is significant, you may lose your interest in comparing column or row means.

When the F for interaction *is* significant, it indicates that the factors operate *jointly.* Under these circumstances, our interest may be drawn to differences between *cells*—that is, specific combinations of the two factors. In the previous example, the F for interaction was not significant, so the focus was on the two main effects. But an alternative set of results for this experiment, illustrating a large interaction, is posited in Table 14.3B. The way follow-up tests are conducted for a two-way ANOVA is quite different when the interaction of the factors is found to be statistically significant. We describe procedures for further specifying

Table 14.3 Cell Means Illustrating Some Interaction and Zero Interaction

Music background	Classical composer				Row means
	Mozart	Chopin	Bach	Beethoven	
A. Cell means from Table 14.1 (some interaction)					
Novices	14.2	13.2	12.4	12.0	12.95
Musicians	17.4	13.2	12.2	12.8	13.90
$\overline{X}_{musician} - \overline{X}_{novice}$	3.2	0.0	−.2	.8	.95
B. Cell means illustrating zero interaction					
Novices	14.2	13.2	12.4	12.0	12.95
Musician	12.6	11.6	10.8	10.4	11.35
$\overline{X}_{musician} - \overline{X}_{novice}$	1.6	1.6	1.6	1.6	1.60

a significant interaction after we discuss several ways to interpret the meaning of an interaction.

The Meaning of Interaction

Interaction refers to the *joint* effect of two or more factors on the dependent variable. As an illustration, consider once again the music experiment. The interaction effect of composer and music background refers to the unique effect of particular combinations of levels of the two factors, such as the musicians listening to Mozart or the novices listening to Bach, and *not* to the sum of the separate effects of the two factors. The interaction is the joint effect *over and above* the sum of the separate effects.

Comparing Zero to Some Interaction

The interaction in the music experiment is highlighted in Table 14.3A, which displays the cell means from Table 14.1, along with the differences between the two background groups for each composer. The fact that these differences (3.2, 0, −.2, .8) are not all the same tells you that the amount of interaction is not zero. If, however, the professional musicians always scored exactly the same number of points higher (or lower) in spatial ability than the musical novices (say 1.6 points higher, as in Table 14.3B), regardless of the classical composer being listened to, the interaction would indeed be equal to zero. Also, note that a zero amount of interaction implies that the difference between mean test scores for any two composers would be the same for both musicians and novices. (See Table 14.3B.) If the mean differences for each composer were considerably different from one another, there could be a significant interaction effect; the composer factor would affect test scores differently for participants with different musical backgrounds. (Cell means that produce a significant interaction effect are shown in Table 14.4.) The interaction effect for the data in Table 14.3A was found to be *not* significant, so the differences among the observed mean differences of 3.2, 0, −.2, and .8 are likely enough to have occurred

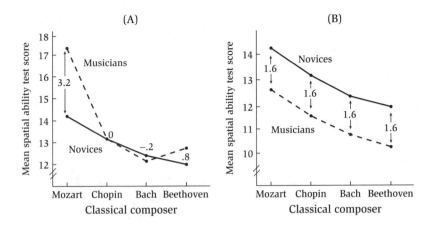

Figure 14.3

Graphic Representation of the Data in Table 14.3

by chance (random sampling error) that there is *not* sufficient reason to believe that there is an interaction effect in the population from which the samples in this experiment were drawn.

A graphic illustration of the examples in Table 14.3 is shown in Figure 14.3. When the interaction effect is zero (Figure 14.3B), the line connecting the points corresponding to the cell means for musicians follows the same pattern as the corresponding line for novices. That is, the two lines are parallel, which means that the distance between the two lines is the same at all points. When there is some amount of interaction (Figure 14.3A), musical background differences are different from one composer to another. From Figure 14.3A, you can see that whereas musicians produced the higher means while listening to Mozart and Beethoven, novices had the higher mean during the Bach condition.

Different Types of Interactions

The (main) effects of the two factors in a two-way ANOVA are independent of each other. That is, either one could be significant while the other is not. Indeed, one factor could have a very large effect while the other has none at all. Or both effects, or neither effect, could be significant.

The size of the interaction in a two-way ANOVA is completely independent of the sizes of the main effects. Both main effects could be very large, while the amount of interaction is zero. Or there could be a large interaction with no main effects at all. Different relative amounts and directions of the two main effects can combine with different amounts of interaction to produce a variety of different patterns when the cell means are graphed, as illustrated in Figure 14.4.

In order to categorize two major types of cell-mean patterns, we will deal with an example of the simplest two-way ANOVA design: the 2×2 ANOVA. That is, each factor has only two levels. The first factor is sex, and the two levels are male and female. The second factor is drug type: The pill that is given at the beginning of the experiment contains caffeine

Figure 14.4

Two Kinds of Interaction Patterns for Caffeine and Sex on Test Scores (2 × 2 Factorial Design)

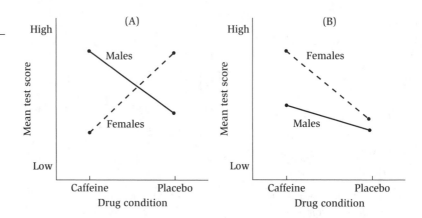

for half of the males and half of the females, but only sugar (i.e., it is a placebo) for the other half of the participants. The dependent variable is the score each participant obtains on a test of manual dexterity. For this experiment, two different kinds of interaction are shown in Figure 14.4.

In Figure 14.4A, women obtain higher average dexterity scores than men in the placebo condition. But when caffeine is administered, it is the men who achieve higher scores. This "reversal" effect leads to a large amount of interaction while virtually obliterating the main effects (e.g., when you average the men and women together for each drug condition, you get about the same mean for caffeine as you do for placebo). This pattern is often referred to as a *disordinal interaction,* because the effect of one factor changes its direction (order) depending on the levels of the other factor. For example, the gender difference changes its direction from the placebo to the caffeine condition.

There is a good deal of interaction in Figure 14.4B (the two lines are far from being parallel), but this time there is no reversal. Because the order of the effect for one factor does not change with different levels of the other factor (e.g., the gender difference favors females in both drug conditions), this pattern is called an *ordinal interaction.* With this pattern, it is not uncommon to find that both main effects are significant, as well as the interaction.

Notice that a large interaction can cause the main effects to be misleading. You could easily get a significant gender effect for the data depicted in Figure 14.4B, but it would be due almost entirely to the gender difference that is produced by the caffeine condition. Similarly, if you attained a significant drug effect for these data, it would be due mostly to the effect of caffeine on females, as there is not much of a caffeine/placebo difference for the males. The main effects are even more misleading in Figure 14.4A. Reporting that both main effects were small and not significant would seem to suggest that caffeine is no different from a placebo in its effect on manual dexterity and that there are no gender differences. However, a quick look at Figure 14.4A shows that this is not the case. A large interaction, especially one that is statistically significant, is an indication that you should *not* focus your follow-up tests on the main effects (e.g., comparing pairs of row or column means), whether they are significant or not. Following up a significant interaction usually involves tests that are more specific; such comparison procedures are described in the next section.

Following Up a Significant Interaction

A common approach to further specifying the source of a significant interaction is to test what are called **simple main effects**. A simple main effect is the effect of one factor at only one level of the other factor. This is easier to understand in terms of a graph of cell means. For example, in Figure 14.4A, each line is a simple main effect. The line that represents the men is the main effect of drug *only for the men*; hence it is a *simple main effect*. The same is true for the line representing the women. In addition, the cell means for the men and the women who were given caffeine represent the (simple) main effect of gender *only for the caffeine condition*. Similarly, there is a simple main effect for gender differences just for the placebo condition. You could highlight the simple main effects of gender by regraphing the cell means of Figure 14.4A so that the two genders would be specified along the horizontal axis. Then each line would represent the simple main effect of gender for one of the drug conditions.

Significant Interactions in a 2 × 2 ANOVA

In the 2 × 2 case, testing the simple main effects is just like testing cell-to-cell comparisons, and you can proceed by using Fisher's protected t test procedure. The cell-to-cell tests are protected if the F ratio for the interaction attains significance, as would be likely for the data shown in Figure 14.4A. However, not all of the possible cell-to-cell comparisons represent simple main effects. Of the six possible pairs of cells (i.e., 4 × 3/2), two pairs make little sense to test. If you were to compare men taking caffeine with women taking the placebo, or vice versa, and obtain a significant difference, you could not say which of the two factors (sex or drug versus placebo) is responsible, or whether both are. However, it would be meaningful to compare either the two sexes separately for both the placebo and caffeine conditions or the two drug conditions for each gender. Given a balanced two-way design, you could use the LSD formula to test either pair of differences of cell means:

$$LSD = t_{crit}\sqrt{\frac{2MS_W}{n}},$$

where n is the size of each cell. However, if you want to test all four of the meaningful pairwise comparisons, the more conservative approach would be to use Tukey's HSD.

In Figure 14.4A, it looks like all four of the simple main effects could easily be significant. However, the situation would likely be different for the pattern represented in Figure 14.4B. Again, the interaction could turn out to be significant. But whereas you could expect the simple main effect of drug condition to be significant for women, the relative flatness of the line representing men suggests that this simple main effect might fail to attain significance. Similarly, it looks like the simple main effect of sex could easily be significant for the caffeine but not the placebo condition.

The results you can obtain from testing simple main effects provide a more nuanced and specific story concerning the effects of your two factors, a story that can have practical implications. For example, if the simple effects of drug in Figure 14.4A were significant for both genders (albeit in different directions), the clear recommendation would be that a cup of coffee or two could improve performance for male workers but that females should avoid any source of caffeine before starting skilled manual work. However, the results in Figure 14.4B seem to suggest that females can benefit from caffeine, whereas the results for males are less clear. Moreover, this figure suggests a general female superiority in the skill being tested, which may only become noticeable, however, when both genders ingest caffeine before performing the task.

In general, the larger the interaction, the more the simple main effects differ from each other. A statistically significant interaction implies that the simple main effects differ from each other significantly. Specifying the source of a significant interaction becomes more complicated when one or both factors have more than two levels, because there are more options. The most common approach is to test simple main effects as an intermediate step before proceeding to cell-to-cell comparisons, as we describe next.

Significant Interactions Involving Multilevel Factors

For an example involving a significant interaction with a factor that has more than two levels, we will return to the music experiment, with one modification. We subtracted 2 points from each of the five participants who lacked musical training and listened to Mozart. MS_W is unaffected, but the numerator MSs have changed, yielding the following F ratios for the data shown in Table 14.4: $F_{composer}(3, 32) = 2.84, p = .053$; $F_{background}(1, 32) = 4.47, p < .05$; $F_{interaction}(3, 32) = 3.42, p < .05$. Although the F ratio for composer is so close to being statistically significant that it would be tempting to apply pairwise comparisons to the composer (column) means, the significant two-way interaction suggests that tests of simple main effects may be more legitimate and informative. For example, to test the simple main effect of composer *just for the musicians,* you can perform a one-way ANOVA on the four cell means for the musicians, ignoring the cell means of the novices in finding MS_{Bet}, and then use MS_W from the original ("omnibus") two-way ANOVA as your error term. Given the equal

Table 14.4   Cell Means for the Music Experiment, With One Cell Modified to Produce a Significant Interaction

Music background	Classical composer				Row mean
	Mozart	Chopin	Bach	Beethoven	
Novice	12.2	13.2	12.4	12.0	12.45
Musician	17.4	13.2	12.2	12.8	13.90
$\overline{X}_{\text{musician}} - \overline{X}_{\text{novice}}$	5.2	0.0	−.2	.8	1.45

cell sizes, we can use the following simplified formula from Chapter 12:

$$MS_{\text{bet}} = ns_{\overline{X}}^2 = 5 \times \text{variance of } (17.4, 13.2, 12.3, 12.8) = 5(5.614) = 28.07$$

Therefore, $F_{\text{composer (for musicians)}} = 28.07/4.7 = 5.97$, which substantially exceeds the critical value for $F_{.05}(3, 32) = 2.90$. (Note that our error df is df_W from the two-way ANOVA, because we are using MS_W from the two-way ANOVA as our error term.) Because we did not change any of the cell means for the musicians, this simple main effect would have been the same, and therefore statistically significant, for the data in Table 14.1. However, the interaction was not even close to significance before we changed one of the cell means for the novices, so we would not have been justified in testing simple main effects in the original data. Our follow-up tests would not have had the "protection" of having obtained a significant interaction.

Now that we know that the choice of musical composer affects the spatial ability (at least temporarily) of musicians, we still want to clarify this result further by conducting follow-up tests for each possible pair of composers. For this purpose, an appropriate multiple comparison procedure is Tukey's HSD test. In fact, we can use the same formula and the same values we used earlier to test pairs of column means, but with one important change:

$$\text{HSD} = q_{\text{crit}}\sqrt{\frac{MS_W}{n}} = 3.84\sqrt{\frac{4.7}{5}} = 3.84\,(.97) = 3.72$$

Note that when we were comparing column means, we used rn (number of rows times size of each cell) as the number of subjects per group. In this latest test, we are comparing cell means, so it is appropriate to use just n as the number per group. The HSD is higher than it was for the column means (smaller groups can vary more easily by chance), but the Mozart condition is nonetheless significantly higher than the other three conditions, and none of the other composers differs significantly from each other. The test of the simple main effect of composer for novices is nowhere near statistical significance $(F < 1)$, so no pairwise tests would be conducted among those cells.

Given the significant interaction in Table 14.4, there is another way that simple main effects could be tested. We would be justified in comparing the musicians to the novices for each composer. Because these simple main effects involve only two levels each, they are the same as cell-to-cell comparisons and would yield the same results whether conducted as one-way ANOVAs or t tests. As the number of levels increases for each factor, so does the number of possible follow-up tests. At some point, it becomes helpful if the researcher can plan to test just some of the comparisons, and use the appropriate Bonferroni correction.

Measuring Effect Size in a Factorial ANOVA

In Chapter 12, we presented two very different formulas for finding the most common measure of effect size for a one-way ANOVA, eta squared (η^2), which is the proportion of variance in the dependent variable accounted for by the independent variable. The two different formulas, which always yield the same answer in a one-way ANOVA, are:

$$\eta^2 = \frac{SS_{\text{Bet}}}{SS_{\text{Total}}} \qquad \text{Formula 12.11A}$$

and

$$\eta^2 = \frac{df_{\text{Bet}}F}{df_{\text{Bet}}F + df_W} \qquad \text{Formula 12.11B}$$

If applied to any one of the three effects in a two-way ANOVA (i.e., the two main effects and the interaction), however, the two formulas will give different answers—sometimes *very* different answers. In order to apply Formula 12.11A to just one effect in a two-way ANOVA, the notation has to be modified slightly, as follows:

$$\eta^2_{\text{ord}} = \frac{SS_{\text{effect}}}{SS_{\text{Total}}} \qquad \text{Formula 14.4}$$

For example, if you want to measure the effect size corresponding to the composer variable, the SS for that effect (from Table 14.2) is 80.1; dividing that value by the SS_T for the two-way ANOVA (the first SS we calculated in this chapter, 257.8) gives you what is called **ordinary η^2** (abbreviated as η^2_{ord} in Formula 14.3), which equals $80.1/257.8 = .311$—a large effect size, but nonetheless an underestimate, as we demonstrate next.

Unfortunately, a serious problem arises with ordinary η^2 when both factors involve experimental manipulations. Imagine that the music background factor was really a music training factor and that participants had been assigned to either intensive musical training or a control group. Because the denominator of η^2_{ord} contains SS_T, which includes the between-group SS's for *both* factors (along with other components), the more effective the music training, the larger SS_T would get (because the SS for music training would get larger)—and the larger SS_T gets, the smaller η^2_{ord}

for the composer factor gets. (The same thing happens to the effect size of Music Training as the composer effect increases, of course.)

The measure we usually want in a two-way ANOVA, especially when both factors involve experimental manipulations (rather than individual differences that are selected for), compares the SS for an effect just to that same effect combined with the amount of error, and not to a denominator inflated by the inclusion of variation from the other factor (or the interaction). Therefore, this measure is called a *partial eta squared* (η_p^2) and can be found by the following formula:

$$\eta_p^2 = \frac{SS_{\text{eff}}}{SS_{\text{eff}} + SS_{\text{error}}} \qquad \text{Formula 14.5A}$$

Applied to the composer effect, η_p^2 equals $80.1/(80.1 + 150.4)$, where the 150.4 is the SS for error from Table 14.2; therefore, $\eta_p^2 = 80.1/230.5 = .348$. Note that this proportion is larger than ordinary η^2; η_p^2 can never be smaller than η_{ord}^2 and can be a good deal larger, depending on the size of the SS's for the other factor and the interaction.

However, we need to point out that when the second factor is selected for, such as music background (participants already had a certain degree of background at the outset of the study, and that amount was not altered by the experimenter), the ordinary η^2, when applied to the experimental (i.e., composer) factor, does make some sense. Because the experimenter did not create the variation due to different music backgrounds, and such variation is likely to exist in any future experiment, it is not necessary to remove the SS for music background (or its interaction with the composer factor) from the bottom of the eta-squared proportion. In terms of reporting an effect size that will be useful for the next researcher, an argument can be made for using η_{ord}^2 in such situations. Nonetheless, partial η^2 has become so popular as an effect-size measure for factorial ANOVAs that we doubt that the ordinary η^2 is often reported, even when appropriate.

Although Formula 14.4A is easy enough to use when you have all of the SS's from your two-way ANOVA calculations, it can be even more convenient to obtain η_p^2 directly from your F ratios, as shown in Formula 12.11B. In fact, you have no choice but to use the F ratio and the appropriate dfs when you are trying to measure the effect size from results that were already published and did not include any effect-size measures. Using the F ratios gives you partial η^2's automatically, because the denominators of the F ratios are based on the error term only and do not include variation from other factors. Therefore, we just need to change the notation in Formula 12.11B to create a formula that yields the partial eta squared for a factorial ANOVA:

$$\eta_p^2 = \frac{df_{\text{eff}}F_{\text{eff}}}{df_{\text{eff}}F_{\text{eff}} + df_{\text{W}}} \qquad \text{Formula 14.5B}$$

where df_{eff} and F_{eff} are the df and F ratio, respectively, for any one effect in a factorial ANOVA.

Summary

A two-way ANOVA is so named because *two* independent variables are being combined. The statistical analysis of a two-way factorial design makes possible a significance test (using the *F* ratio) of the effect of *each* independent variable and of the effect of the *interaction* of the two variables—that is, the *joint* effect of the two variables over and above the separate effects of each one. Interaction is an important concept for behavioral science research.

Sums of Squares for a Balanced (i.e., Equal-*n*) Design

1. Total sum of squares (SS_T)

   $$\text{Computing formula: } SS_T = \sum X^2 - N_T \overline{X}_G^2 \qquad \text{Formula 12.1B}$$

   where $\overline{X}_G$ is the grand mean

2. Between-groups sum of squares (SS_{Bet})

   $$\text{Computing formula: } SS_{Bet} = n \sum_{i=1}^{k} \overline{X}_i^2 - N_T \overline{X}_G^2 \qquad \text{Formula 14.1}$$

   where
   $$k = \text{number of groups (i.e., cells)},$$
   $$n = \text{the number of scores in each cell},$$
   $$\overline{X}_i = \text{any of the cell means}$$

3. Within-groups sum of squares (SS_W)

   $$\text{Shortcut computing formula: } SS_W = SS_T - SS_{Bet}$$

4. Sum of squares for Factor 1, the "column" factor (SS_1):

   $$\text{Computing formula: } SS_1 = rn \sum_{i=1}^{c} \overline{X}_i^2 - N_T \overline{X}_G^2 \qquad \text{Formula 14.2A}$$

   where
   $$r = \text{number of rows in the data table},$$
   $$c = \text{number of columns},$$
   $$\overline{X}_i = \text{any of the } column \text{ means}$$

5. Sum of squares for Factor 2, the "row" factor (SS_2):

   $$\text{Computing formula: } SS_2 = cn \sum_{i=1}^{r} \overline{X}_i^2 - N_T \overline{X}_G^2 \qquad \text{Formula 14.2B}$$

   where
   r, c, and n are defined as before, and $\overline{X}_i$ can be any of the *row* means

6. Sum of squares for interaction ($SS_{1 \times 2}$):

Computing formula: $SS_{1 \times 2} = SS_{\text{Bet}} - SS_1 - SS_2$ Formula 14.3

Degrees of Freedom

Total degrees of freedom:

$$df_{\text{T}} = N_{\text{T}} - 1$$

where

N_{T} = total number of observations

Degrees of freedom within groups:

$$df_{\text{W}} = N_{\text{T}} - k$$

where

k = number of cells

Degrees of freedom for the column factor (Factor 1):

$$df_1 = c - 1$$

where

c = number of columns

Degrees of freedom for the row factor (Factor 2):

$$df_2 = r - 1$$

where

r = number of rows

Degrees of freedom for interaction:

$$df_{1 \times 2} = df_1 \times df_2 = (c - 1)(r - 1)$$

Also, note that $k = r \times c$ and $N_{\text{T}} = r \times c \times n$.

Mean Squares

Mean square within groups:

$$MS_{\text{W}} = \frac{SS_{\text{W}}}{df_{\text{W}}}$$

Mean square for Factor 1:

$$MS_1 = \frac{SS_1}{df_1}$$

Mean square for Factor 2:

$$MS_2 = \frac{SS_2}{df_2}$$

Mean square for interaction:

$$MS_{1\times2} = \frac{SS_{1\times2}}{df_{1\times2}}$$

F Ratios and Tests of Significance

Main effect of Factor 1:

$$F_1 = \frac{MS_1}{MS_W}$$

Main effect of Factor 2:

$$F_2 = \frac{MS_2}{MS_W}$$

Effect of interaction:

$$F_{1\times2} = \frac{MS_{1\times2}}{MS_W}$$

Each computed F value is compared to the critical value from the F table for the degrees of freedom associated with the numerator and denominator *of that test*. If the computed F is less than the critical F, H_0 is retained; otherwise, H_0 is rejected in favor of H_A (i.e., the effect is labeled as statistically significant).

Types of Interactions

A graph of the cell means for a two-way ANOVA allows you to see at a glance whether there is very little interaction (the lines on the graph are nearly parallel to each other) or a good deal of interaction. However, even an interaction that looks large (the lines sharply converge or diverge) could fail to attain statistical significance. If the *direction* of one factor's effect changes at different levels of the other factor, the interaction is said to be *disordinal.* If the lines converge or diverge while sloping in the same direction, the interaction is an *ordinal* one. A large interaction, especially a disordinal one, can lead to misleading main effects.

Follow-Up Tests (Multiple Comparisons) for a Two-Way ANOVA

1. **If the interaction is *not* significant:** In this case, the focus is on the main effects of each factor. If the F ratio for a factor is statistically significant and that factor has more than two levels, pairwise comparisons among the column or row means may be conducted to

ascertain which levels differ from which others. Fisher's protected *t* tests are acceptable when the factor has only three levels, whereas Tukey's test (or the modified LSD test) is recommended when there are four or more levels. Remember that when column or row means are being compared, the value for *n* in the basic LSD or HSD formula should be the number of scores in each column (i.e., *rn*) or each row (i.e., *cn*), as appropriate.

2. **If the interaction *is* significant:** In this case, the focus usually turns to the *simple main effects*—that is, the effects of one factor at *each level* of the other factor. If the *F* ratio for a simple main effect is significant and more than two levels are involved, cell-to-cell comparisons may be conducted to further specify the effect. LSD can be used when there are only three levels, and HSD can be used for more than three levels, where *n* in these formulas is the size of each cell.

3. It is considered acceptable to ignore the experimentwise alpha (α_{EW}) and instead use procedures to keep the overall alpha at .05 for the *family* of comparisons that are used to follow-up each significant *F* ratio, thus keeping the familywise alpha (α_{EW}) at .05.

Measuring Effect Size in a Factorial ANOVA

Especially when the levels of both factors in a two-way ANOVA have been created/manipulated by the researcher, the preferred measure of effect size for each of the three effects is the **partial eta squared** (η_p^2), given by the following formula:

$$\eta_p^2 = \frac{SS_{eff}}{SS_{eff} + SS_{error}} \qquad \text{Formula 14.5A}$$

The exact same values can be obtained conveniently from the *F* ratios corresponding to each effect, by using the following formula, instead:

$$\eta_p^2 = \frac{df_{eff}F_{eff}}{df_{eff}F_{eff} + df_W} \qquad \text{Formula 14.5B}$$

If you are measuring the effect size of an experimental factor when the other factor is a grouping (i.e., preexisting) factor, like gender, it may be more appropriate to use the formula for **ordinary eta squared:**

$$\eta_{ord}^2 = \frac{SS_{effect}}{SS_{Total}} \qquad \text{Formula 14.4}$$

Exercises

1. The following table contains the statistics quiz scores for 18 students as a function of their phobia level and gender.

	Low phobia	Moderate phobia	High phobia
Males	5	8	5
	4	5	6
	4	7	9
Females	3	7	4
	4	5	9
	2	6	7

(a) Compute the two-way ANOVA for these data, and present your results in the form of an ANOVA summary table (see Table 14.2).

(b) Conduct the appropriate follow-up tests to determine which phobic levels differ significantly from other levels. Are these follow-up tests justified by your results in part (a)? Explain.

2. An industrial psychologist wishes to determine the effects of satisfaction with pay and satisfaction with job security on overall job satisfaction. He obtains measures of each variable for a total group of 20 employees, and the results are shown in the following table. (Cell entries represent overall job satisfaction, where 7 = very satisfied and 1 = very dissatisfied.)

	Satisfaction with pay	
Satisfaction with job security	High	Low
High	7	3
	7	1
	6	2
	4	2
	6	2
Low	1	2
	2	1
	5	3
	2	1
	2	1

(a) Perform a two-way ANOVA on these data. Using an alpha of .05, what can the psychologist conclude?

(b) Compute partial eta squared for each of the main effects. Comment on the size of each effect.

(c) Graph the cell means for these data. What type of interaction do you see: ordinal or disordinal?

(d) Test all of the simple main effects. What specific conclusions can you draw from these tests?

3. Suppose that a 2 × 2 factorial design is conducted to determine the effects of caffeine and sex on scores on a 20-item English test. The cell means are given in the following table.

Sex	Caffeine factor	
	Caffeine	**Placebo**
Males	$\overline{X} = 17.3$	$\overline{X} = 12.0$
Females	$\overline{X} = 12.3$	$\overline{X} = 16.4$

(a) Given that $n = 7$ and $MS_W = 2.0$, compute the appropriate F ratios, and test each for significance at the .05 level.

(b) Graph the cell means for these data. What type of interaction do you see: ordinal or disordinal?

(c) Test all of the simple main effects. What specific conclusions can you draw from these tests?

4. For each of the following experiments, perform a two-way ANOVA and then the follow-up tests that are appropriate for your results. Use a graph of the cell means to explain the results you obtained.

(a) Experiment 1

	Factor 1		
Factor 2	**1**	**2**	**3**
1	8	14	1
	17	10	7
	2	3	15
2	18	6	3
	10	2	3
	19	2	7
3	5	16	4
	17	15	16
	6	9	1

(b) Experiment 2

	Factor 1		
Factor 2	**1**	**2**	**3**
1	2	17	8
	3	14	10
	1	15	7
2	4	18	6
	2	16	5
	3	17	9
3	3	19	10
	2	15	6
	1	16	7

(c) Experiment 3

Factor 2	Factor 1		
	1	2	3
1	18	8	2
	16	10	3
	17	7	1
2	4	19	6
	2	15	5
	3	16	9
3	10	3	17
	6	2	14
	7	1	15

Thought Questions

1. (a) What is a factorial design? (b) What is the difference in purpose between a two-way ANOVA and a one-way ANOVA?

2. Complete the following table by stating what sums of squares, mean squares, and F tests are computed in *both* one-way ANOVA and two-way ANOVA, and what sums of squares, mean squares, and F tests are computed in a two-way ANOVA but *not* in a one-way ANOVA.

	Computed in *both* one-way and two-way ANOVA	Computed in two-way ANOVA but *not* in one-way ANOVA
Sums of squares		
Mean squares		
F tests		

3. A researcher conducts a two-way ANOVA. One factor is sex: male or female. The other factor is drug level: whether participants receive a pill designed to treat obsessive-compulsive disorder or a placebo that looks and tastes the same but contains no medicine. Describe some of the interactions that might occur in this experiment.

4. What is the difference between a disordinal interaction and an ordinal interaction?

5. Give an example of how a large interaction in a two-way ANOVA could cause the main effects to be misleading.

6. (a) What is a simple main effect? (b) When should a researcher test simple main effects, and what procedure should the researcher use?

Computer Exercises

1. Using college major and sex as your independent variables, perform a two-way ANOVA on the math background quiz. Request descriptive statistics. Use the cell means to explain your results. (Advanced exercise: Redo the two-way ANOVA without the psychology majors.)

2. Redo Exercise 1, replacing the college-major factor with the grouping variable you created in Computer Exercise 3 of Chapter 12 (from the number of math courses taken).

3. Create a grouping variable based on an approximate "median split" of the phobia scores so that one group contains the students with the 55 lowest phobia scores, and the other has the 45 highest phobia scores. Then perform a two-way ANOVA on postquiz heart rate, using the new phobia grouping variable and the quiz conditions (last question easy, moderate, difficult, or impossible) as your two factors.

    (a) Request a graph of the cell means, and refer to the graph to explain the results of the two-way ANOVA.

    (b) Test all of the possible pairs of levels for the quiz-condition factor.

4. Redo the two-way ANOVA in Exercise 3 using postquiz anxiety as your dependent variable.

    (a) Request a graph of the cell means, and refer to the graph to explain the results of the two-way ANOVA.

    (b) Regardless of your ANOVA results, test the simple main effect of quiz condition for each phobic group, and test all of the possible pairwise (cell-to-cell) comparisons for each of those simple main effects.

Bridge to SPSS

To perform a two-way ANOVA in SPSS, select "Univariate" from the Analyze/General Linear Model menu. Then move your two independent variables into the Fixed Factor(s) space (we will not be discussing Random Factors in this text, but they are rarely used anyway) and your dependent variable to its appropriately labeled space. If you want to create a plot of the cell means (and you probably will), click on the **Plots** button. If one factor has more levels than the other, the graph will look neater if you move that factor to the Horizontal Axis space and the factor with fewer levels to Separate Lines. Do not forget to click the **Add** button before you click on **Continue**.

   If you have a factor with more than two levels and you know you will want to see pairwise comparisons among its levels (e.g., you expect the main effect of that factor to be significant), click on **Post Hoc** and, after moving over the factor(s) of interest, check the appropriate post hoc test (e.g., LSD for a three-level factor; Tukey for more than three levels). Under Options, you will likely want to check Descriptive statistics, in order to get the mean, SD, and n for each cell. However, for a balanced design, there is little reason to request Homogeneity tests, because it is routine to ignore all but the most extreme differences in cell variances if all the ns are the same. The other options are quite advanced, but we will describe one more of them briefly at the end of this section.

The easiest way to compute simple main effects in SPSS is to use Split File on one of the factors and perform a one-way ANOVA with the other factor. The only problem with this approach is that each one-way ANOVA will use its own error term rather than the within-cell error term from the original two-way ANOVA. To correct this, you could calculate your own F ratios by dividing the numerator MSs from the one-way ANOVAs by MS_W from the two-way ANOVA (and then looking up critical values in Table F to make a decision about each null hypothesis). There is a way to get SPSS to print out these F ratios automatically, but it requires modifying a command in a Syntax Window, so it is not necessarily an easier procedure.

Similar to Compare Means/One-Way ANOVA, General Linear Model (GLM)/Univariate produces an ANOVA summary table as its main output. However, the summary table created by the latter procedure contains several extra rows, which are labeled in a way that can easily be confusing. So we will describe the SPSS output for a two-way ANOVA row by row, using Table 14.5, which contains the analysis of the data in Table 14.1, as our example. The first row is labeled "Corrected Model." The SS in this row corresponds to what we have been calling SS_{Bet}—the between-group SS that you get when you treat all the cells of the two-way design as the groups of a one-way ANOVA. (This quantity was calculated in Step 2 of the Sums of Squares calculations near the beginning of this chapter.) The SS in the row labeled "Intercept" is equal to $N_T \times \overline{X}_G^2$; this quantity is sometimes called the "correction factor" (CF) in computational ANOVA

Table 14.5 Tests of Between-Subjects Effects

Dependent Variable: Score

Source	Type III sum of squares	df	Mean square	F	Sig.
Corrected model	107.375[a]	7	15.339	3.264	.010
Intercept	7,209.225	1	7,209.225	1,533.878	.000
Composer	80.075	3	26.692	5.679	.003
Background	9.025	1	9.025	1.920	.175
Composer × Background	18.275	3	6.092	1.296	.293
Error	150.400	32	4.700		
Total	7,467.000	40			
Corrected total	257.775	39			

[a]R Squared = .417 (Adjusted R Squared = .289)

formulas, because it is the quantity that gets subtracted in the formulas for SS_{Bet} and SS_T. (The CF, which rounds off to 7,209.2, was the amount subtracted in Steps 1, 2, 4, and 5 of the SS calculations.) The test of the Intercept is really a test of the grand mean against a null hypothesis of zero, so it usually leads to a very large F and is rarely of any interest.

The next three rows represent the main effects of your two factors and their interaction, and are clearly labeled in terms of the variable names you assigned to your factors. (The sum of the SS's in these three rows equals the SS for the "Corrected Model" in a balanced design.) The following row, labeled "Error," contains what we have been referring to as SS_W, df_W, and MS_W. The row labeled "Total" is the sum of the Corrected Model, Intercept, and Error, and will generally be of no interest to you (because it contains the Intercept), but the last row, "Corrected Total," contains the sum of the SS's for the Corrected Model (i.e., SS_{Bet}) and for Error (i.e., SS_W) and is therefore equal to what we have been calling SS_T.

Finally, we describe one more statistic available from Options. First, note that under the two-way ANOVA summary table, you will see a value for R Squared. This is the same as the statistic more commonly referred to as eta squared (η^2) in the context of one-way ANOVA. It is equal to the SS for the Corrected Model divided by the SS for the Corrected Total—in other words, it is SS_{Bet}/SS_T. (The adjusted R squared is the unbiased estimate of omega squared, as described in Chapter 12.) This tells you the proportion of variance accounted for by the cell means, but for a two-way ANOVA you are more likely to be interested in the variance proportions for each factor separately, as well as for the interaction. By default, SPSS gives you the *partial* eta-squared values when you select "Estimates of effect size" under Options. Ordinary eta-squared values are not obtainable for a factorial ANOVA in SPSS, so if you decide that ordinary η^2 is appropriate for a particular effect, you would have to calculate η^2_{ord} yourself, by dividing the SS for that effect by the SS for the Corrected Total, as in Formula 14.4.

Chapter 15
Repeated-Measures ANOVA

PREVIEW

Introduction

How can the advantage of the matched-pairs t test be extended to more than two conditions?

Calculating the One-Way RM ANOVA

How can the formulas for a two-way ANOVA be used to compute a one-way repeated-measures (RM) ANOVA?

How does the critical value for a one-way RM ANOVA compare to the critical value for the corresponding independent-samples ANOVA?

Rationale for the RM ANOVA Error Term

Why does it make sense to use the subject by treatment interaction as the error term for the RM ANOVA? How does this interaction compare to the variance of the difference scores when the RM ANOVA has only two levels?

Assumptions and Other Considerations Involving the RM ANOVA

How are the usual ANOVA assumptions modified in the case of RM ANOVA? What is the sphericity assumption, and why is it important?

What precautions are recommended when conducting pairwise comparisons following a significant RM ANOVA?

How does repeated measures or matching subjects affect the power and effect size of an ANOVA?

The RM Versus RB Design: An Introduction to the Issues of Experimental Design

Under what conditions is the RM design highly recommended, and when is it problematic?

When is it advantageous to add an individual-difference factor to an ordinary one-way ANOVA?

What are the advantages and disadvantages of the treatment-by-block and the randomized-blocks (RB) design?

PREVIEW (*continued*)

The Two-Way Mixed Design

What steps must be added to the two-way ANOVA procedure to obtain the two different error terms needed to compute a two-way mixed-design ANOVA?

What additional assumption is needed for the two-way mixed ANOVA as compared to the one-way RM ANOVA?

When a one-way RM ANOVA involves counterbalancing, why is it important to transform it to a mixed design by including order as a between-groups factor?

Summary

Exercises

Thought Questions

Computer Exercises

Bridge to SPSS

Introduction

In Chapter 7 we demonstrated the advantage of matching subjects into pairs or measuring the same subject twice as compared to giving two different treatments (or conditions) to two independent samples. Our goal in this chapter is to show how analysis of variance (ANOVA) can be used to extend the same advantage to a situation in which the independent variable (IV) has three or more levels. The procedure we describe in this chapter is commonly called the **repeated-measures (RM) ANOVA**, but it can be applied equally well to an experimental design in which subjects are matched across several conditions. The latter design is referred to as a **randomized-blocks (RB) design**; when there are only two conditions, it is identical to the matched-pairs design discussed in Chapter 7.

The trick that made it easy to compute a matched-pairs *t* test was to first calculate a difference score for each pair and then compute a one-sample *t* test to compare these difference scores to the mean for the null hypothesis (namely, zero). There is also a simple trick to calculating an RM ANOVA; it makes use of the two-way ANOVA formulas presented in the previous chapter. We discuss the calculation procedure first and then explain why it makes sense that the RM ANOVA is computed this way.

Calculating the One-Way RM ANOVA

To demonstrate the power of the RM ANOVA, we will take a set of data for which we have already computed an independent-samples

Table 15.1 **Music Experiment Data From Table 12.1A Presented as Repeated Measures**

Subject number	Mozart	Chopin	Bach	Schubert	Beethoven	Subject $\overline{X}$
1	16	16	16	16	14	15.6
2	16	14	14	14	13	14.2
3	14	13	12	12	13	12.8
4	13	13	10	12	10	11.6
5	12	10	10	12	10	10.8
Column $\overline{X}$	14.2	13.2	12.4	13.2	12.0	13.0

ANOVA and show how much larger the F ratio would be if the same data were analyzed according to a RM design. For our example, we will use the data from Table 12.1, for which the F ratio was quite small ($F = 3.60/4.28 = .84$). These data are reprinted in Table 15.1.

Note that if each row of data contains five scores *from the same person* (each obtained while he or she listened to a different one of the five classical composers included in this experiment), it is meaningful to calculate the means for the rows, as well as the columns, in the data set. The row means are therefore subject means. To view the data in Table 15.1 as coming from a two-way factorial design, you have to view the *second* factor (composer is the first factor) as the "subject" factor. Each particular subject is automatically at a different level of the subject factor by virtue of being a different person. Let us now apply the procedure of the previous chapter to begin the computation of a two-way ANOVA for the data in Table 15.1.

The first step, as in any ANOVA in which you have all of the raw data, is to calculate the total sum of squares (SS_T). The same formula is used in both the one- and two-way ANOVAs, and in fact, SS_T was already calculated for these data in Chapter 12:

$$SS_T = \sum X^2 - N_T \overline{X}_G^2 = 4{,}325 - 25\,(13.0)^2 = 4{,}325 - 4{,}225 = 100$$

In an ordinary two-way ANOVA, the next step would be to calculate $SS_{\text{between-cells}}$. However, when dealing with a one-way RM ANOVA design, there is only one score per cell (i.e., $n = 1$), so $SS_{\text{between-cells}}$ is the same as SS_T (i.e., there is no SS_W component). As it turns out, this is not a problem; it simply saves us a step. Therefore, we can proceed to calculate SS_1 and SS_2 for the main effects of the two-way ANOVA. However, we can relabel these components as $SS_{\text{treatment}}$ (or SS_{treat}, for short) and SS_{subject} (or SS_{sub}, for short), respectively, keeping in mind that the usual way to view the data from an RM ANOVA is with the subjects in the different rows and the treatments in the different columns. Using the formulas from the previous chapter (keeping in mind that in this application $n = 1$) and relabeling appropriately, we obtain

$$SS_{treat} = r \sum \overline{X}_i^2 - N_T \overline{X}_G^2$$

$$= 5 \left(14.2^2 + 13.2^2 + 12.4^2 + 13.2^2 + 12.0^2\right) - 4{,}225$$

$$= 5 \left(201.64 + 174.24 + 153.76 + 174.24 + 144\right) - 4{,}225$$

$$= 5 \left(847.88\right) - 4{,}225 = 4{,}239.4 - 4{,}225 = 14.4$$

$$SS_{sub} = c \sum \overline{X}_j^2 - N_T \overline{X}_G^2$$

$$= 5 \left(15.6^2 + 14.2^2 + 12.8^2 + 11.6^2 + 10.8^2\right) - 4{,}225$$

$$= 5 \left(860.04\right) - 4{,}225 = 4{,}300.2 - 4{,}225 = 75.2.$$

(The index j is used to represent the means for the latter summation, as a reminder that these means are different from the ones in the previous summation. The j means are found across rows or subjects rather than columns or treatments.)

When applied to the one-way RM ANOVA, r (the number of rows) always equals the number of different subjects (or blocks), and c (the number of columns) always equals the number of levels of the IV. Also note that SS_{treat} agrees with the value that was calculated in Chapter 12 (albeit by a more tedious version of the same formula), when it was called just SS_{Bet}. The SS for the interaction, which in this case is the interaction of the subject factor with the different treatment levels, is found by subtraction, as it was in Formula 14.3. However, although this SS is based on an interaction, it will be used as the basis of our error term, so we will label it SS_{error} for simplicity.

$$SS_{error} = SS_T - SS_{treat} - SS_{sub} = 100 - 14.4 - 75.2 = 10.4$$

The total df $(rc - 1)$ break down into three components in this design:

$$df_{treat} = c - 1; \ df_{sub} = r - 1; \ \text{and} \ df_{error} = (c - 1)(r - 1)$$

Thus,

$$MS_{treat} = \frac{SS_{treat}}{df_{treat}} = \frac{14.4}{4} = 3.6 \ (\text{compare to } MS_{bet} \text{ in Chapter 12})$$

$$\text{and} \quad MS_{error} = \frac{SS_{error}}{df_{error}} = \frac{10.4}{16} = .65$$

We will not bother to calculate MS_{sub} because it is not used in this design, for reasons that will be described shortly. Instead, it is MS_{error} that is used as the denominator of the F ratio. Therefore,

$$F_{treat} = \frac{MS_{treat}}{MS_{error}} = \frac{3.6}{.65} = 5.54$$

The Critical F for the RM ANOVA

The appropriate critical F at the .05 level is $F_{.05}$ $(df_{treat}, df_{error}) = F_{.05}$ $(4, 16) = 3.01$. In fact, our calculated F is significant even at the .01 level, because $F_{treat} = 5.54 > F_{.01}$ $(4, 16) = 4.77$. Notice how much larger the F for the RM ANOVA is (5.54) compared to the F for the independent-samples ANOVA calculated on the same data (.84). This difference is not due to the numerators of the two F ratios, which are the same (MS_{treat} and MS_{bet} are based on the same column means). It is due to the difference in the denominators. Recall that the error term in the Chapter 12 ANOVA was based on SS_W, which was equal to 85.6. It is not a coincidence that the sum of SS_{error} and SS_{sub} in the RM ANOVA (i.e., $10.4 + 75.2$) also equals 85.6. In fact, put another way, it will always be true that $SS_{error} = SS_W - SS_{sub}$. Why does it make sense to use the subject by treatment interaction as the error term for the RM ANOVA instead of MS_W, or even MS_{sub}? We answer this question in the section after the next one.

SS_{error} is almost always smaller than SS_W (it can never be larger), which works to the advantage of the RM ANOVA. It is also true that df_{error} will *always* be smaller than df_W (16 versus 20, for this example), which means that the critical value for the RM ANOVA will always be *larger* than the critical value for the corresponding independent-samples ANOVA. This will make it more difficult to reject H_0, so the loss in degrees of freedom and corresponding increase in the critical value is clearly a disadvantage of the RM ANOVA. In practice, however, it is usually more than compensated for by the increase in the calculated F ratio. You may recall an analogous situation involving the matched-pairs t test. The connections between the RM ANOVA and the matched-pairs t test will become more obvious next when we apply both statistical procedures to the same data set that has only two treatment levels.

Comparing the Matched-Pairs t Test With the One-Way RM ANOVA for Two Conditions

To make the comparison with the matched-pairs t test, let us look at only the last (i.e., rightmost) two composers in Figure 15.1. The difference scores (i.e., Schubert–Beethoven) for the five subjects are 2, 1, −1, 2, and 2. The amount of subject by treatment interaction for the last two composers is directly related to the variability of these difference scores. If all the difference scores were the same, the variability of the difference scores would be zero, and so would MS_{error}, because the lines on the graph for the last two composers would all be parallel to each other. The mean for the Schubert–Beethoven differences is $\Sigma D/N = 6/5 = 1.2$, and the (unbiased) standard deviation (SD) is 1.304. The matched t value for these two composers is therefore $1.2/(1.304/\sqrt{5} = 1.2/.583 = 2.06$, which is not significant with only 4 degrees of freedom. It can be instructive to compare this result to the RM ANOVA for just the last two composers.

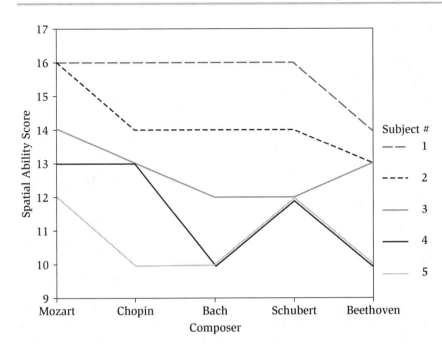

Figure 15.1

Graph of Data in Table 15.1

As an exercise, the reader should verify that, based on the data in Table 15.2.

$$SS_T = 30.4; \ SS_{sub} = 23.4; \ SS_{treat} = 3.6; \ \text{and} \ SS_{error} = 3.4$$

$$MS_{treat} = \frac{3.6}{1} = 3.6; \ MS_{error} = \frac{3.4}{4} = .85; \ F_{RM} = \frac{3.6}{.85} = 4.235$$

As in the case of independent samples, squaring the matched t value yields the same value (within rounding error) as calculating the RM ANOVA on the same data: matched $t^2 = 2.06^2 = 4.24 = F_{RM}$. There is a simple relationship between the variance of the difference scores for two matched sets of scores (for the data in Table 15.2, s_D^2 is $1.304^2 = 1.7$) and MS_{error} for the same data. The latter value is .85, which is exactly half of s_D^2, as will always be the case.

Table 15.2   Data From Table 15.1 for Schubert and Beethoven Only

Subject number	Schubert	Beethoven	Subject $\overline{X}$
1	16	14	15.0
2	14	13	13.5
3	12	13	12.5
4	12	10	11.0
5	12	10	11.0
Column $\overline{X}$	13.2	12.0	12.6

Rationale for the RM ANOVA Error Term

Now let us return to the question of why it makes sense to use the subject by treatment interaction as the error term for the RM ANOVA. First, note that in the two-condition case, MS_{error} is very closely related to the variance of the difference scores, as we just demonstrated, so the rationale for using the interaction as the error term for the simplest RM ANOVA is exactly the same as the rationale for using s_D^2 as the basis of the error term in the matched t test. Both MS_{error} and s_D^2 are measures of how closely subjects follow the same pattern over the different levels of the treatment, and therefore both can be thought of as indices of the reliability of the difference in treatment effects. However, the subject by treatment interaction has the advantage that it can be quantified over any number of treatments, and not just two. The amount of interaction for a multilevel study can be inspected by creating a graph of the data from an RM ANOVA, as you would for the cell means of a two-way ANOVA, except that in the RM case, the cell means are really just the individual scores. That is how we created the graph in Figure 15.1.

If all of the subjects in Figure 15.1 were to exhibit almost exactly the same profile over all of the treatment levels, the lines would be nearly parallel, and the amount of subject by treatment interaction for the RM ANOVA would be quite small. As MS_{error} decreases, the F ratio for the RM ANOVA increases, appropriately reflecting the increasing reliability of the treatment effects across the different subjects. Of course, with several repeated levels, the interaction for one pair of conditions can be much larger or smaller than for another pair. The size of MS_{error} is an average of the different pieces of the interaction, and therefore the use of the subject by treatment interaction as the error term of the overall analysis requires making a homogeneity assumption, as we explain in the next section.

Assumptions and Other Considerations Involving the RM ANOVA

The RM ANOVA makes the usual three assumptions demanded by inferential parametric statistics:

1. The dependent variable has been measured on an interval or ratio scale.
2. The dependent variable follows a normal distribution in each population.
3. The observations are all mutually independent *within each sample.*

This last assumption has had to be modified, because the key element of an RM ANOVA is that the scores are *not* independent *across* samples. In fact, you are hoping that there is a fairly high positive correlation between the scores for every pair of samples.

Moreover, several statistical procedures, such as the pooled-variance *t* test and the ordinary independent-samples ANOVA (as presented in Chapter 12), require the assumption of homogeneity of variance. The one-way RM ANOVA described in this chapter also requires an appropriate homogeneity assumption, as described next.

The Sphericity Assumption

In the one-way independent-samples ANOVA, MS_W is found by computing a weighted average of all of the sample variances. However, averaging all of the sample variances to create a single-error term leads to a straightforward statistical test only if you can assume that the variances of the populations represented by those samples are all the same. As we mentioned in Chapter 12, the homogeneity of variance (HOV) assumption can be tested for a one-way ANOVA, and if the HOV test is significant (indicating heterogeneity of variance) *and* the samples differ considerably in size, statisticians recommend that the ordinary one-way ANOVA procedure not be used.

Similarly, the error term in the RM ANOVA is based on an average of the variances *of the difference scores* for every different pair of levels of the RM factor. (In the case of five composers, there are 10 different pairs for which the variance of the difference scores can be calculated: 1 versus 2, 1 versus 3, 1 versus 4, 1 versus 5, 2 versus 3, etc.) The assumption that these variances of difference scores are all equal in the population is commonly referred to as the **sphericity assumption**. We could have referred to the error term of the RM ANOVA as MS_{inter}, based on the analogy with the two-way ANOVA, or as the $MS_{residual}$ (for reasons we will not discuss here), but the least confusing label is, undoubtedly, MS_{error}. The latter term will help us to avoid confusion when we discuss the two-way mixed-design ANOVA, in which there is an interaction between the two independent variables, as well as an interaction between the subjects and one of the independent variables.

Although a test of the sphericity assumption has been devised by Mauchly (1940), it is rarely used to make decisions about RM ANOVAs. However, because a lack of population sphericity generally leads to a higher Type I error rate than the alpha used to look up the critical value, it is becoming increasingly common to adjust the degrees of freedom downward in order to increase the critical value and make the test more conservative. The most popular *df* adjustment is the one devised by Greenhouse and Geisser (1959), but it is best left to statistical software that will also give you the corresponding adjusted *p* value.

Without statistical software, you can easily test your RM ANOVA by assuming the worst-case scenario (i.e., maximum violation of sphericity). Just use *df* of 1 for the numerator and $r - 1$ for the denominator to find the worst-case critical value. On one hand, if your calculated *F* exceeds this conservative criterion, you can declare your results statistically significant without worrying that your Type I error rate might be higher than you think it is. On the other hand, if your RM ANOVA is not significant using the usual (unadjusted) critical F, you cannot be making a Type I error at all, because you cannot reject the null hypothesis. (There is no adjustment that lowers your critical value to give you more power.) If your calculated F falls between the unadjusted and the worst-case critical F values, we advise the use of statistical software.

Returning to our example, in which the calculated F (5.54) was greater than the ordinary critical F (3.01), the worst-case critical F would be $F_{.05}(1, 4) = 7.71$. Because the calculated F does not exceed the maximally adjusted critical F, you would need to obtain a more exact adjustment of your critical F from statistical software before you could decide whether to reject the null hypothesis.

Follow-Up Tests

Due to concerns about sphericity, some statisticians favor abandoning the RM ANOVA entirely in favor of a multivariate approach, but that topic is well beyond the scope of an introductory text. However, even those who want to retain the RM ANOVA approach in general may be concerned about the effects of a lack of sphericity on the multiple comparisons that follow a significant ANOVA to locate the significant results more specifically.

In our example involving the music of five different composers, the overall RM ANOVA was statistically significant. To determine which pairs of composers differ significantly, we could compute Tukey's Honestly Significant Difference (HSD), substituting MS_{error} for MS_W in the formula given in Chapter 13. However, suppose that the subject by treatment interaction involving just Mozart and Chopin is considerably larger than it is for any other pair of composers. Using Tukey's HSD essentially compares those two composers with an error term that has been reduced by averaging in the much smaller interactions involving other pairs of composers.

Unless it is clear that the variability of the difference scores is quite similar for every pair of conditions in your RM ANOVA, the recommended (cautious) approach to follow-up tests is to use an error term based only on the conditions being compared. When conducting pairwise comparisons, this amounts to performing separate matched-pairs t tests for each pair of levels of your RM factor. When dealing with five RM levels, as in our music example, there are a total of 10 matched t tests to conduct. Because of the danger of an increased experimentwise alpha when conducting so many individual follow-up tests, it is often recommended that the researcher use a Bonferroni adjustment to determine the alpha for each comparison (see Chapter 13). In the music example, this would mean testing each pair of composers at the .005 level (i.e., .05/10).

Power and Effect Size

In Chapter 9 we showed how the power of a matched-pairs t test increases as the correlation between the two sets of scores increases. Similarly, the RM ANOVA gains power as the correlation between each pair of conditions increases. (If the correlations are not similar from one pair of factor levels to another, this is an indication that the RM ANOVA may not be appropriate for that data set.) As the correlations increase, the subject by treatment interaction—the error term of the RM ANOVA—decreases, so the F ratio tends to get larger, thus increasing power. Thus, when applicable, repeated measures or matching participants can serve as an economical alternative to increasing your sample size in order to increase power. Generally, the highest correlations (i.e., the best matching) are obtained when measuring the same participant at all levels of the RM factor, but this experimental approach can have its drawbacks, which we will point out in the next section.

The effect size in your RM ANOVA data can be measured as eta squared by applying Formula 12.11B to your obtained F ratio. This is what is typically done, but note that measuring η^2 in this way can be misleading. A large F ratio that arises from modest sample sizes will be associated with a large proportion of variance accounted for, but bear in mind that highly consistent responses across participants can enlarge an F ratio just as easily as a larger separation in sample means. Therefore, a large η^2 does not tell you whether your effect is large in a practical sense (i.e., the different RM levels produce markedly different average magnitudes of subject responses) or merely consistent (i.e., the levels do not make a large difference on average, but each subject exhibits, almost exactly, the same small changes). Moreover, when predicting the effect size in a future, similar experiment, you have to take into consideration whether the same degree of matching can be expected in a replication. It is not difficult to adjust your η^2 measure to indicate the effect size you would have without the benefit of matching (see B. H. Cohen, 2008), but this is not commonly done, so we will not add confusion to this matter by showing you how to do that.

The RM Versus RB Design: An Introduction to the Issues of Experimental Design

You may recall from Chapter 7 that the same matched-pairs t test formula is used whether the two measurements come from the same person or two participants who were matched together. The matched-subjects version of the RM design is referred to as the *RB* design, for reasons we will soon make clear.

Problems With the RM Design

As we just pointed out, the power of the RM ANOVA increases as the correlations between pairs of treatments increase. Generally, the highest correlations (i.e., the best matching) are obtained when measuring the same subject under all of the conditions. Although a RM design works well when the different conditions can be randomly mixed together (e.g., when five different types of words are mixed together in one long list to be memorized), this design can be problematic when the conditions must be presented successively.

For example, the only reasonable way to conduct the music experiment in terms of repeated measures would be to test a particular subject's spatial ability only once for each composer. However, if the same order of composers were used for each subject, you would not be able to separate practice and/or fatigue effects (i.e., simple order effects) from the specific effects of each composer's music (e.g., think about the difference in spatial ability measured for the composer who is always presented first, as compared to the one who is always presented last). A possible solution is counterbalancing, as described near the end of Chapter 7. But the problems inherent in this approach increase rapidly with the number of conditions.

In the case of five conditions, **complete counterbalancing** is not feasible. It would require 120 subjects ($5 \times 4 \times 3 \times 2 \times 1 = 120$) just to have one subject assigned to each possible order. Fortunately, a form of counterbalancing can be achieved using the same number of orders as there are conditions, according to a design called the **Latin square**. However, any form of counterbalancing leaves your experimental design susceptible to complex carryover effects—that is, the effect of a particular composer could depend on which composer had been presented just before. Carryover effects can sometimes be avoided simply by allowing enough time or by inserting a distracting task between each pair of conditions. When serious carryover effects cannot be avoided (as described in Chapter 7), a design that involves the matching of participants on some relevant variable should be considered, as described next.

Advantages and Disadvantages of Alternatives to the RM Design

When appropriate, the repeated-measures design is the most economical way to increase the power of an ANOVA test. It increases power by essentially increasing the effect size you are dealing with, which avoids the expense of increasing the size of the samples. Theoretically, the effect size of an ANOVA could be increased by producing greater differences among the factor levels (as by increasing the strength of your experimental manipulations). However, this approach is often not feasible or desirable (or even ethical, if a very strong manipulation could become harmful). The alternative is to increase power by reducing variability (i.e., the denominator of any standardized measure of effect size), and the RM ANOVA does this by focusing on the *consistency* of subjects' responses (as represented by SS_{error}), while ignoring the subjects' overall differences on the dependent variable (as represented by SS_{sub}).

There are simpler (albeit less effective) ways to reduce the error term of an ANOVA (and therefore increase power). We discuss three of these designs in this section.

Adding a Grouping Factor to a One-Way Independent-Samples ANOVA

Suppose that you are studying three methods for increasing vocabulary size in children by assigning a different method to each of three separate groups. After 6 months of applying these methods to your samples, your results could come out as depicted in Figure 15.2A. Notice that the subject-to-subject variability is large compared to any average differences among the groups. You then realize that your groups are mixed with respect to gender and that vocabulary size may differ by gender, especially for the age group you are studying. By adding gender as a second between-groups factor, thus creating a two-way ANOVA, it is proper to calculate MS_W separately for each *cell* of the two-way design.

Looking at Figure 15.2B, you can see that the average of the six within-*cell* MS_W's is much smaller than the average of the three within-group MS_W's ignoring gender. This greatly reduces the denominator of the F ratio you will use to test the effect of the different methods. (The numerator of that F ratio would *not* change, because the means of the three methods would remain the same.) Adding a grouping factor based on preexisting individual differences (e.g., gender) allows you to convert *within-group* variability to *between-cell* variability.

Of course, we created an unusually dramatic example to illustrate this point. Adding a grouping factor to your ANOVA is not likely to have such a large effect. But as long as you can identify a preexisting individual-difference factor that is relevant to your dependent variable, it can be worth

Figure 15.2

Reduction in Error Variance as a Result of Adding a Relevant Grouping Factor to an ANOVA

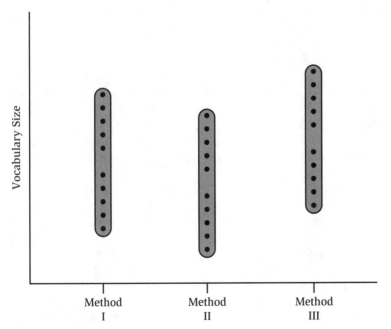

A. Large Within-Group Variability Due Partly to Gender Differences in Each Method Group

(continued)

Figure 15.2

(*continued*)

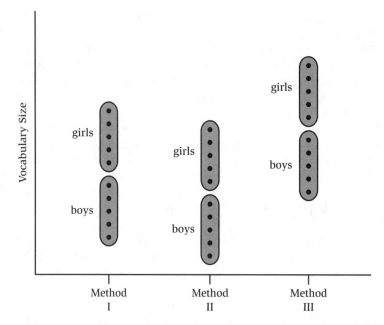

B. Reduced Within-Group Variability as a Result of Adding Gender as a Factor

adding it to your ANOVA design. Moreover, you gain the opportunity to test whether the grouping variable interacts with your treatment factor (e.g., are the differences among the methods the same for both genders?).

The Treatment-by-Block Design

In the preceding example, the added factor (i.e., gender) was a categorical one. However, it is also quite possible to find an individual-difference factor that is related to your dependent variable and is at least crudely quantitative. In the case of children at a particular school, it should not be difficult to use existing information to classify the students into several levels of scholastic ability that can be expected to translate, on average, into differences in vocabulary size.

For convenience, you will want to make sure that the number of students included in each scholastic group (called a *block* in this context) is some multiple of the number of levels of your treatment factor. For example, if you are comparing three methods of instruction, you will want the number of children in each scholastic block to be some multiple of 3. Then, separately for each block, you would be able to assign, at random, exactly one third of the students to each of the three methods.

The data can be collected and then analyzed as they would be for any two-way ANOVA. Of course, the main effect of the blocking factor will not yield any new information, because you chose that factor for its obvious relationship to your dependent variable. However, the test of the main effect of the method factor should become more accurate due to the reduction in the error term (as occurred when adding gender in the previous example), and the interaction could show whether the relative superiority of one or another method depends on the initial level of the student.

The Randomized-Blocks (RB) Design

The most precise—and potentially the most powerful—form of the treatment by block design is the one in which the size of the block is equal to the number of different treatment conditions. If testing three vocabulary-enhancing methods, students would be matched into groups of three so that, within each block, the three students would be as similar as possible on whichever relevant criteria were available. The term *randomized-blocks design* usually refers to this special case of the treatment by block design, in which there is only one subject in each block/treatment combination (i.e., cell) and therefore no way to calculate MS_W. The data are analyzed as though the different subjects in a particular block were really different measurements of the same subject. The data can be arranged as in Table 15.1 (with block number replacing subject number) and then analyzed using the RM ANOVA procedure described earlier in this chapter. When the treatment factor has only two levels, the RB design becomes the matched-pairs design discussed in Chapter 7.

The responses of the subjects in the same block are generally not as similar as would be the responses of the same subject, and the RB design lacks the economy of measuring the same subject multiple times. But the RB design has the desirable feature of usually increasing power, while completely eliminating the possibility of carryover effects as well as the need for counterbalancing. Unfortunately, the RB design is difficult to arrange if your subjects are not all known at the beginning of the study. For instance, if patients are being randomly assigned to one of three treatment methods as they arrive at a clinic seeking help (and meet the screening criteria of the study), they can be classified as belonging to one of several crudely defined blocks (in terms of gender, age, duration and intensity of symptoms, etc.), but they cannot be matched closely to patients who have not yet sought help at that clinic. When precise matching over your entire subject pool is not possible, it may still be helpful to create blocks along the way, in preparation for a treatment-by-block ANOVA.

The Two-Way Mixed Design

Now that you have learned how to conduct a one-way RM ANOVA as well as a two-way ANOVA, you have the tools you will need to analyze one of the most useful experimental designs in behavioral research: the two-way mixed design. There are a number of common situations that lead to this design. For example, subjects are assigned to one of two therapy conditions or to a control group, and they are then measured at the beginning of the experiment, at the midpoint, and again at the end. Or subjects are selected for being either high or low in visual imagery ability, and each is asked to memorize several lists of words that differ in how concrete the words are. Or subjects must read and respond to some opinions that they are told have been written by students and others that ostensibly come from professors. For half of these subjects, the person conducting their experimental session is obviously a student, whereas for the other half, the experimenter is clearly a professor. Each of the three two-way factorial designs just described is best designed, and then analyzed, as a mixed-design ANOVA, in which one independent variable is a between-groups factor and the other is a *within-subjects* (i.e., RM) factor.

Calculating the Mixed-Design ANOVA

Just as we illustrated the calculation of the one-way RM ANOVA by taking a previous example of a one-way ANOVA and recasting it in terms of repeated measures, we will create a mixed design by taking the two-way ANOVA example from the previous chapter and imagining that the participants were matched across the four musical composers. (The analysis is the same whether the participants had been matched in blocks of four and then randomly assigned to the different composers or each participant was measured four times, once for each composer.) The matching makes it meaningful to add subject means to Table 14.1, as shown in Table 15.3. Recall that the first five subjects have no musical training, whereas the second five are professional musicians. (In case you are wondering why Schubert does not appear in Table 15.3, recall that we dropped him when we introduced two-way ANOVA, in order to simplify the analysis. Sorry, Schubert fans.)

When computing a two-way mixed ANOVA by hand, there are several reasonable ways to proceed. One instructive approach is to first calculate the numerators of the three F ratios, which we already did in the previous chapter. (Matching does not affect any of the numerators.) As a reminder,

Table 15.3 Music Experiment Data From Table 14.1 Presented as Repeated Measures

Subject number	Mozart	Chopin	Bach	Beethoven	Subject $\overline{X}$
1	16	16	16	14	15.5
2	16	14	14	13	14.25
3	14	13	12	13	13.0
4	13	13	10	10	11.5
5	12	10	10	10	10.5
6	16	17	14	16	15.75
7	18	10	14	10	13.0
8	20	13	11	13	14.25
9	15	12	10	14	12.75
10	18	14	12	11	13.75

Table 15.4   Cell Means by Composer and Subject Group for the Data in Table 15.3

Music background	Mozart	Chopin	Bach	Beethoven	Row mean
No training	14.2	13.2	12.4	12.0	12.95
Professional	17.4	13.2	12.2	12.8	13.90
Column means	15.8	13.2	12.3	12.4	13.425

we display a table of the cell means for this example (see Table 15.4), and briefly review the calculations of the numerator MSs.

$$SS_{\text{between-cell}} = 107.4; \quad SS_{\text{composer}} = 80.1; \quad SS_{\text{background}} = 9.0;$$

$$SS_{\text{inter}} = 107.4 - 80.1 - 9.0 = 18.3;$$

$$MS_{\text{composer}} = \frac{80.1}{3} = 26.7; \quad MS_{\text{background}} = \frac{9.0}{1} = 9.0; \quad MS_{\text{inter}} = \frac{18.3}{3} = 6.1.$$

It is when we calculate the denominators of our F ratios that we must account for the fact that the participants are now matched across composers.

In the mixed-design ANOVA, the F ratio for the main effect of the between-groups factor can be calculated separately from the rest of the design. You can simply perform an ordinary one-way ANOVA on the subject means in Table 15.3, completely ignoring the particular scores on which these means are based, except that you need to multiply your SS components by the number of scores that contribute to each subject mean (in this example, 4):

$$SS_T = \sum X^2 - N_T \overline{X}_G^2$$

$$= \left(15.5^2 + 14.25^2 + \cdots + 12.75^2 + 13.75^2\right) - 10\,(13.425)^2$$

$$= 1{,}826.56 - 1{,}802.31 = 24.25.$$

After multiplying by 4,

$$SS_T = 4 \times 24.25 = 97$$

SS_{bet} for this one-way between-groups ANOVA is based on the means of the two groups of subjects (the row means in Table 15.4). It was already calculated as $SS_{\text{background}}$, which is equal to 9.0 (because, to save effort, we are taking $SS_{\text{background}}$ from the original two-way ANOVA, it should *not* be multiplied by 4).

Then

$$SS_W = SS_T - SS_{\text{bet}} = 97 - 9 = 88$$

$$MS_W = \frac{SS_W}{df_W} = \frac{88}{(10 - 2)} = \frac{88}{8} = 11.0$$

and

$$MS_{background} = \frac{SS_{background}}{1} = \frac{9}{1} = 9.0$$

Therefore,

$$F_{background} = \frac{9.0}{11.0} = .82$$

Given that F for the between-groups factor is less than 1, it cannot be statistically significant. Note that, although we can refer to $SS_{background}$ and $SS_{composer}$ in this example, more generally, we will refer to the SS for the effect of the between-groups factor as SS_{groups} and the SS for the repeated-measures factor as SS_{RM}.

Before we complete the analysis of our example of a two-way mixed-design ANOVA, we think it is important, as with any complex design, to show how the total degrees of freedom are partitioned into the different components of the analysis. To reduce the potential for confusion, we will use symbols for this design in a way that is as consistent as possible with the use of those symbols in previous chapters, as well as the earlier part of this chapter. First, we will use k to represent the number of different levels of the between-groups factor, because that is consistent with our use of k to represent the number of different groups in a one-way ANOVA. Next, we will use the letter r to represent the number of subjects (or blocks) in each group. This only makes sense for a balanced design, in which all of the groups have the same number of subjects, but that is the only type of mixed design we will consider in this text. Therefore, the total number of subjects (or blocks) in a balanced mixed design can be expressed as kr. However, it is critical to note that this is not the total number of observations or scores in the analysis, because each subject contributes a score for each level of the repeated-measures (also called *within-subjects*) factor. We will continue to use the letter c (think columns or conditions) to represent the number of levels of the RM factor, so the total number of observations, N_T, is equal to krc. For our example in Table 15.3, you can see that the total number of scores is $(2)(5)(4) = 40$. The total df is just one less than N_T, which leads to the following formula:

$$df_{total} = krc - 1 \qquad \text{Formula 15.1}$$

Given the symbols we just defined, the following formulas for df components should be obvious:

$$df_{groups} = k - 1 \qquad \text{Formula 15.2}$$

$$df_{RM} = c - 1 \qquad \text{Formula 15.3}$$

$$df_{inter} = df_{groups} \times df_{RM} = (k-1)(c-1) \qquad \text{Formula 15.4}$$

These are the degrees of freedom for the numerators of the three F ratios in a two-way mixed design. Note that df_{groups} could be called $df_{between\text{-}groups}$, but we prefer the shorter version. For the present example, there are two between-group levels (no training, professional training), so $k = 2$, five subjects per group, so $r = 5$, and four repeated (or matched) conditions, so $c = 4$. Therefore, $df_{total} = 39$, $df_{groups} = 1$, $df_{RM} = 3$, and $df_{inter} = 3$.

The degrees of freedom for the denominators (i.e., error terms) of the three F ratios are not so obvious but should make sense after we have described how to calculate the SS's for the two error terms. We have already described the calculation of SS_W in terms of computing a one-way ANOVA on the subject means, so we just need to change the notation a bit to incorporate this part of the analysis into the larger picture. To be consistent with the one-way RM ANOVA, the SS based on the subject means (e.g., there are 10 of them in Table 15.3) should be called SS_{sub}, rather than SS_{total}. The SS based on the group means (there are two, in the present example) can be called SS_{groups}, in which case, $SS_W = SS_{sub} - SS_{groups}$.

All that remains is to calculate the error term for the within-subjects part of the ANOVA. Both the main effect of the RM factor and the interaction of the two factors use the same error term, which is based on the amount of subject by (RM) treatment interaction in each group. One straightforward way to obtain this error term is to subtract the SS_W just calculated for the between-groups factor from the $SS_{within-cell}$ from the original (i.e., unmatched) two-way ANOVA. $SS_{within-cell}$, which was just labeled SS_W in the previous chapter (when there was only one error term to talk about), was found to be 150.4. As in the one-way RM ANOVA, we will label the SS for the within-subject error term simply as SS_{error}. So $SS_{error} = SS_{within-cell} - SS_W = 150.4 - 88 = 62.4$. The degrees of freedom can be subtracted in the same way: $df_{error} = df_{within-cell} - df_W = 32 - 8 = 24$ ($df_{within-cell}$ is the same as df_W in the previous chapter). Therefore, $MS_{error} = 62.4/24 = 2.6$.

Let us look at how we can determine the degrees of freedom for the two error terms by formulas, using the symbols we have just defined for the numerator dfs. First, $df_{within-cell}$ is defined as in any two-way ANOVA, as the total number of observations minus the number of cells. Using our current notation:

$$df_{within-cell} = krc - kc = kc(r - 1)$$

Then, df_W, for the between-groups error term, is defined *not* in terms of total observations but rather in terms of the total number of different subjects (or blocks), which is kr. One df is lost for each group, so:

$$df_W = kr - k = k(r - 1) \qquad \text{Formula 15.5}$$

Finally, because df_{error} equals $df_{within-cell}$ minus df_W, df_{error} equals $kc\,(r - 1) - k\,(r - 1)$, which equals $(kc - k)(r - 1)$. This leads to our last df formula for this design:

$$df_{error} = k\,(c - 1)(r - 1) \qquad \text{Formula 15.6}$$

For the present example, $df_W = 2(5 - 1) = 2 \times 4 = 8$, and $df_{error} = 2(4 - 1)(5 - 1) = 2 \times 3 \times 4 = 24$.

Finally, we can find the F ratios for the RM factor (composer) and the interaction of the two factors from the previously computed numerator MSs and the just-calculated error term:

$$F_{composer} = \frac{MS_{composer}}{MS_{error}} = \frac{26.7}{2.6} = 10.3$$

$$F_{inter} = \frac{MS_{inter}}{MS_{error}} = \frac{6.1}{2.6} = 2.35$$

The critical value for both of these F ratios is $F_{.05}\,(3, 24) = 3.01$. Therefore, the statistical conclusions from Chapter 14 have not changed: The main effect of composer is significant at the .05 level, and the interaction effect is not. However, it is important to note that the F's for these two effects have nearly doubled, because the error term based on the matching of subjects (MS_{error}) is only a bit more than half as large as the original two-way ANOVA error term (2.6 versus 4.7). This will often be the case when subjects are matched or repeatedly measured.

The results of the mixed-design ANOVA just computed can be neatly summarized in a table much like the one for an independent-groups two-way ANOVA (see Table 14.2), except that now there are two error terms included (see Table 15.5). Note that the total SS and total df in Table 15.5 are the same as in Table 14.2, because we were working here with the same 40 data points as were contained in Table 14.1.

Assumptions

In addition to all of the assumptions of the RM ANOVA, including sphericity, the mixed-design ANOVA also requires you to assume that the amount of interaction (in the population) between any two treatment levels is the same for each subgroup (i.e., level of the between-groups factor) in the design. This is called **multi-sample sphericity**. For example, when there are only two repeated measurements (e.g., before and after some intervention) and two different groups (e.g., drug and placebo), the usual

Table 15.5   **Summary of Two-Way Mixed-Design ANOVA of Music Experiment**

Source	SS	df	MS	F
Music background	9.0	1	9.0	.82
Error (within-group)	88.0	8	11.0	
Composer	80.1	3	26.7	10.3
Composer × background	18.3	3	6.1	2.35
Error (subject × composer)	62.4	24	2.6	
Total	257.8	39		

sphericity assumption does not apply (there is only one pair of treatment levels), but the 2 × 2 mixed-design ANOVA assumes that the amount of before–after interaction is the same for the placebo subjects as it is for those given the real drug. There is a test for multi-sample sphericity, but it is well beyond the scope of an introductory text.

Just as in the one-way RM ANOVA, you can retest the F ratio for the RM factor of a mixed-design ANOVA against a worst-case critical F: $F[1, k(r-1)]$. For this example, the worst-case F_{crit} is $F(1, 8)$, which equals 5.32, for an .05 test. Because $F_{composer}$ for this example is 10.3, which is larger than 5.32, you can reject the null hypothesis at the .05 level without having to worry about whether your data meet the sphericity assumption. The F ratio for the interaction of the two factors also requires the sphericity assumption, because it uses the same error term as F_{RM}; the worst-case F_{crit} for the interaction is $F[(k-1), k(r-1)]$, which in this example is again $F(1, 8)$, because k is only 2. However, in this example, F_{inter} was not significant even when assuming sphericity (i.e., using the ordinary dfs), so there's no need to retest it. It will fail to be significant regardless of what is assumed about sphericity.

Follow-Up Tests

If the interaction in a mixed design fails to approach significance, you can turn your attention to the main effects. Post hoc comparisons for a significant between-groups factor can use the MS_W error term from the original mixed-design ANOVA, unless there is a strong reason to be concerned about homogeneity of variance among the different groups. (This is one reason it is a good idea to have the same number of participants or blocks at each level of the between-group factor.) Following up a significant RM main effect evokes the same concern as expressed previously for the one-way design. Unless you can be quite confident in assuming sphericity in the population, it is recommended that each pair of levels of the RM factor be compared with an error term based on only those two levels.

If the interaction in a mixed design *is* significant, the follow-up procedures are the same as for an independent-samples two-way ANOVA with a significant interaction (as described in the previous chapter), except for the error terms. The simplest and most conservative approach is not to use either error term from the original mixed-design ANOVA but rather to base the error terms for your follow-up tests on only the data involved in those tests. For example, if, based on a significant interaction, you were to test the simple main effect of composer just for the group with no musical training, the recommendation is to use for your error term the subject by treatment interaction for only the untrained participants rather than MS_{error} from the mixed-design ANOVA. Similarly, if comparing musicians to untrained participants only for the Mozart condition, base MS_W on the Mozart data only, instead of using MS_W from the original design.

The Before–After Case

A very common form of mixed-design ANOVA is one in which the RM factor is time, and it has only two levels (e.g., the dependent variable is measured at the beginning and end of some experimental treatment). Perhaps half the participants receive some new form of therapy, while the other half of them receive sham therapy. In such a case, there would be little interest in the *main* effect of time, because this effect would involve averaging the real with the sham therapy participants. Similarly, the main effect of the group would not be of interest, because it would involve an average of the before scores (when no group difference is expected) with the after scores. The chief interest in this design is the group by time interaction. It is likely that you would want the before–after difference to be much larger in magnitude for the real, as compared to the sham, therapy recipients.

You do not need to conduct a mixed-design ANOVA to assess the amount of interaction in the design just described. If you calculate the before–after difference for each participant and then compute the ordinary (independent-samples) one-way ANOVA on these difference scores, the *F* ratio you obtain will be exactly the same as the *F* ratio for the interaction effect of the mixed-design ANOVA. When there are only two groups in the study, you also have the option of conducting an independent-samples *t* test on the difference scores. Of course, the *p* value for the *t* test will be the same as for the *F* ratio from the corresponding ANOVA. If there are more than two levels of the between-groups factor, you can still compute a one-way ANOVA on the difference scores, and this *F* ratio will be the same as the *F* ratio for the interaction in the corresponding mixed-design ANOVA.

The One-Way RM ANOVA With Counterbalancing

The cautions described in this subsection apply to mixed designs in which the RM factor literally involves repeated measures, and not just the matching of subjects into blocks. By now it should be clear that if you are going to present the same participants with two or more conditions, one after another, you should not present these different conditions in the same order to all participants. What is less obvious is that even though simple order (e.g., practice) effects will be eliminated from the numerator of your *F* ratio by counterbalancing, order effects will increase the size of your denominator (i.e., error term) unless you add order as a between-groups factor to your analysis. Consider the simplest case: Participants perform the same task under two different distraction conditions. If the performance of most participants is enhanced a bit by practice on whichever condition they receive second, this will cause participants receiving one order of the conditions to differ somewhat in the relative effects of the two conditions from participants receiving the conditions in the reverse order.

For instance, if the individual participants are graphed as in Figure 15.1, the lines representing participants receiving one of the orders will tend to slant a bit differently between the two conditions when compared to the lines of participants receiving the other order. Thus a simple order effect would cause the lines to be less parallel. This translates to a larger amount of subject by condition interaction, which forms the basis of the error term in an RM ANOVA. The solution to this problem involves creating a mixed design in which participants receiving different orders of the conditions are considered to be in different groups—that is, they are at different levels of a between-groups factor that we will refer to as *order*. If a mixed-design ANOVA is then computed, the subject by treatment interaction will be measured separately for each order group and then averaged. Participants from different levels of the order factor are separated in the analysis and therefore cannot interact with each other.

When adding order to create a mixed design, the amount of interaction caused by the simple order effects appears in the *SS* for the interaction of the two factors (order and the RM factor), rather than in the subject by treatment interaction. This reduces the error term when testing the main effect of the RM factor. A significant interaction between order and treatment just affirms that you have sizable order effects. A main effect of order, however, is worrisome, because there is no good reason for participants from one order group to be performing better *overall* than the participants in another order group. This result suggests that you may have asymmetric carryover effects and need to look more closely at your data. As discussed earlier, a randomized-blocks design would eliminate the possibility of such carryover effects, while providing much of the increased power associated with the RM design. A mixed design with one between-groups factor is analyzed in the same way, of course, whether the second factor is based on repeated measures or randomized blocks.

Summary

The repeated-measures (RM) ANOVA extends the advantages of the matched-pairs *t* test to studies in which more than two treatments or conditions are being compared. The significance test for the RM ANOVA uses the interaction of subjects with treatments as its error term and is therefore able to ignore overall subject-to-subject differences on the dependent variable. When the RM ANOVA is not feasible (e.g., comparing three methods for teaching young children to read), much of the power of the RM ANOVA can be gained by matching subjects into blocks and then randomly assigning the members of the blocks to the different levels of the independent variable. This is called the randomized-blocks (RB) design. When each block contains the same number of subjects as there are different conditions, the data are analyzed in the same way as the RM ANOVA.

In the two-way mixed-design ANOVA, there is matching or repeated measures for one of the factors but not the other. This necessitates the calculation of two separate error terms. One of these, MS_W, is based on the subject means within each group and is used as the denominator for testing the main effect of the between-groups factor. The other, MS_{error}, is based on the subject by treatment interaction within each group and is used as the denominator for testing the main effect of the RM factor, as well as its interaction with the between-groups factor. One important application of the mixed-design ANOVA involves the one-way RM design with counterbalancing. Adding order as a between-groups factor takes variability away from the error term of an RM ANOVA and puts it in the numerator of a new F ratio, which tests the interaction of the order by treatment effect.

One-Way RM ANOVA

The computational procedure outlined next can be applied in exactly the same way to data from either an RM or an RB design. The formulas for the SS components are the same as those for a two-way ANOVA, in which $n = 1$ (there is only one score in each cell).

1. Sums of Squares
1. Total sum of squares (SS_T)

$$\text{Computing formula: } SS_T = \sum X^2 - N_T \overline{X}_G^2$$

where
$$\overline{X}_G = \text{(grand) mean of all of the scores}$$

2. Between-treatments sum of squares (SS_{treat})

$$\text{Computing formula: } SS_{treat} = r \sum \overline{X}_i^2 - N_T \overline{X}_G^2$$

where
$$r = \text{number of different subjects or blocks}$$
$$\overline{X}_i s = \text{means of the different treatments}$$

3. Between-subjects sum of squares (SS_{sub})

$$\text{Computing formula: } SS_{sub} = c \sum \overline{X}_j^2 - N_T \overline{X}_G^2$$

where
$$c = \text{number of different treatments or conditions}$$
$$\overline{X}_j s = \text{means of the different subjects or blocks}$$

4. Interaction (i.e., error) sum of squares (SS_{error})

$$\text{Computing formula: } SS_{error} = SS_T - SS_{treat} - SS_{sub}$$

2. Degrees of Freedom
Total degrees of freedom:

$$df_T = N_T - 1 = rc - 1$$

Degrees of freedom between treatments:

$$df_{treat} = c - 1$$

Degrees of freedom between subjects:

$$df_{sub} = r - 1$$

Degrees of freedom for (subject by treatment) interaction:

$$df_{error} = (c - 1)(r - 1)$$

3. Mean Squares

Mean square between treatments:

$$MS_{treat} = \frac{SS_{treat}}{df_{treat}}$$

Mean square for interaction:

$$MS_{error} = \frac{SS_{error}}{df_{error}}$$

4. F Ratio

$$F_{RM} \text{ (i.e., } F_{treat}) = \frac{MS_{treat}}{MS_{error}}$$

$$df = (c - 1), (c - 1)(r - 1)$$

5. The Sphericity Assumption

An important assumption that applies when an RM ANOVA has more than two levels is that the variability of the difference scores for any pair of conditions is the same as it is for any other pair of conditions in the population. A significant F ratio can be retested without assuming *sphericity* in the population by comparing it to a worst-case critical F based on 1 and $r - 1$ df. Because a lack of population sphericity tends only to increase the F ratio when the null hypothesis is true, there is no need to retest an RM ANOVA that does not attain significance. However, if the F from an RM ANOVA is significant with the usual critical F, but not with the conservatively adjusted (worst-case F_{crit}), it is recommended that statistical software be used to adjust the critical F more precisely.

6. Alternative Experimental Designs

Carryover effects can invalidate the results from an RM ANOVA conducted on an RM design. In such cases, the RB design may be preferable. Consult Table 15.6 for several error-reducing alternatives to the RM design.

Table 15.6 Recommended Experimental Designs That Reduce the Error Term of a One-Way ANOVA in Various Experimental Situations

Experimental situation	Recommended experimental design
1. You have several different conditions, but trials of each can be mixed together randomly.	Repeated-measures ANOVA (each participant experiences all of the conditions)
2. You have several conditions that must be presented in order, but the effects of one condition are *not* likely to carry over into the next one.	Repeated-measures ANOVA with counterbalancing (equal number of participants receive the conditions in different orders)
3. You have several conditions that must be presented in order, but the effects of one condition *are* likely to carry over into the next, and you have a basis for matching participants into blocks.	Randomized-blocks ANOVA (match k participants in each block, where k is the number of different conditions, and then assign the members of each block randomly to the different conditions)
4. You have several conditions that must be presented in order, and the effects of one condition are likely to carry over into the next. You have a basis for matching participants but do not have all of your participants at the outset of the experiment.	Treatment-by-blocks (two-way) ANOVA (categorize participants as belonging to one or another level of some relevant blocking factor, and make sure that the same number of participants from each block is assigned to each condition)
5. You have several conditions that must be presented in order, and the effects of one condition are likely to carry over into the next. It is *not* feasible to match your participants, but you can categorize your participants into groups that differ on your dependent variable.	Two-way ANOVA with grouping factor (start with a one-way independent-samples ANOVA and then add the grouping factor to create a two-way ANOVA, thereby reducing the error term for your factor of interest)

Two-Way Mixed-Design ANOVA

There are several ways to begin the partitioning of the SS total from a mixed design, but all result in the same final SS components. Probably the easiest way to begin the analysis is by following the procedure for an ordinary two-way ANOVA, as shown next.

1. Sums of Squares

1. Create a table of the cell means, and find the row and column means. Then calculate $SS_{between-cell}$, the SS for each of the two factors, and the SS for their interaction as described in Chapter 14. We can label the SS for the between-groups factor as $SS_{bet-groups}$, or just SS_{groups} and the SS for the repeated-measures factor as SS_{RM}; their interaction will be labeled SS_{inter}. Also, as in Chapter 14, calculate SS_T, and subtract $SS_{between-cell}$ to get what we have been calling $SS_{within-cell}$.

2. Calculate the between-subjects sum of squares (SS_{sub}), based on the subject means, as shown for the one-way RM ANOVA (i.e., ignore the fact that subjects belong to one group or another). Subtract SS_{groups} from SS_{sub} to get SS_W for the mixed design.

3. Subtract SS_W from $SS_{within-cell}$ to obtain SS_{error}.

2. Degrees of Freedom

Total degrees of freedom:

$$df_T = N_T - 1 = krc - 1 \qquad \text{Formula 15.1}$$

where k is the number of groups (i.e., levels of the between-groups factor), r is the number of subjects in each of the groups (we are considering only balanced designs), and c is the number of levels of the RM factor.

Numerator degrees of freedom:

$$df_{group} = k - 1 \qquad \text{Formula 15.2}$$

$$df_{RM} = c - 1 \qquad \text{Formula 15.3}$$

$$df_{inter} = (k - 1)(c - 1) \qquad \text{Formula 15.4}$$

Denominator degrees of freedom:

$$df_w = k(r - 1) \qquad \text{Formula 15.5}$$

$$df_{error} = k(c - 1)(r - 1) \qquad \text{Formula 15.6}$$

3. Mean Squares

Numerator mean squares:

$$MS_{groups} = \frac{SS_{groups}}{df_{groups}}; \quad MS_{RM} = \frac{SS_{RM}}{df_{RM}}; \quad MS_{inter} = \frac{SS_{inter}}{df_{inter}}$$

Denominator mean squares:

$$MS_W = \frac{SS_W}{df_W}; \quad MS_{error} = \frac{SS_{error}}{df_{error}}$$

4. F Ratios

$$F_{groups} = \frac{MS_{groups}}{MS_W}; \quad F_{RM} = \frac{MS_{RM}}{MS_{error}}; \quad F_{inter} = \frac{MS_{inter}}{MS_{error}}$$

5. Additional Assumption

The mixed-design ANOVA requires all of the assumptions of the RM ANOVA, including sphericity, but in addition, it must be assumed that the variability of the difference scores for any pair of conditions is the same in each population that is represented by a different level of the between-groups factor.

Common Situations for Which the Two-Way Mixed Design Is Useful

1. *Measuring two or more independent groups over several points in time.* The simplest version of this situation, the before–after design, usually requires only a one-way ANOVA on the difference scores to yield all the information of interest. However, when more than two points in time are involved, a mixed-design ANOVA is called for.

2. *A one-way repeated-measures ANOVA with counterbalancing.* A mixed-design ANOVA is created by adding order (of treatments) as a between-groups factor to reduce the error term.

3. *Adding a grouping factor to a one-way repeated-measures or randomized-blocks ANOVA.* Each participant serves in several conditions, or participants are matched in blocks, but each participant is also categorized as belonging to one level or another of a preexisting individual-differences factor (e.g., psychiatric diagnosis).

4. *One experimental factor has levels that are easily repeated, but the other does not.* For example, the RM factor might involve several versions of the same task, while the levels of the between-groups factor consist of different general mind-sets for approaching the tasks (e.g., your performance on each of these tasks reflects your overall level of intelligence versus some individuals perform better on some versions of the task according to their individual skills and aptitudes).

Exercises

1. Redo Exercise 7 from Chapter 7 as a one-way RM ANOVA. What is the relationship between the F ratio you calculated for this exercise and the t value you calculated for that exercise?

2. The following group means come from Exercise 4 in Chapter 12. Compute the one-way RM ANOVA for these data, assuming that there are a total of 15 blocks of (matched) participants and that $SS_{error} = 5,040$. Is the F ratio significant at the .05 level, based on the unadjusted df (i.e., assuming sphericity)? Would this F ratio be significant at the .05 level, given the worst-case adjustment of the df (i.e., assuming a maximum violation of sphericity)?

	Group				
	1	2	3	4	5
$\overline{X}$	23	30	34	29	26

3. The following data come from an experiment in which each participant has been measured under three different levels of distraction (the DV is the number of errors committed on a clerical task during a 5-minute period). Compute the one-way RM ANOVA for these data. Is the F ratio significant at the .01 level, assuming sphericity? Would this F ratio be significant at the .05 level, assuming a total lack of sphericity?

Sub. No.	Mild	Moderate	Strong
1	1	3	3
2	0	0	1
3	3	2	4
4	0	2	2
5	2	3	2
6	1	1	0
7	1	1	3
8	2	4	5
9	1	2	4
10	0	3	6
11	4	4	5
12	2	1	6

4. Suppose that, prior to performing the clerical tasks in the experiment of Exercise 3, the first six participants took pills they thought to be caffeine but that were actually placebos; the remaining six participants ingested real caffeine pills.

   (a) Reanalyze the data in Exercise 3 as a mixed-design ANOVA, adding drug condition (placebo versus caffeine) as the between-groups variable. Test each F ratio for significance at the .05 level.

   (b) Compare the SS components you found as part of your analysis in part (a) to the SS components you found in Exercise 3. Which SS components are the same, and which combinations of SSs in part (a) add up to one of the SS components in Exercise 3?

   (c) Compute separate one-way RM ANOVAs for the placebo and the caffeine participants, and test these simple main effects for significance at the .05 level. How do these tests relate to your analysis in part (a)?

   (d) If this design was completely counterbalanced for each of the two drug groups, how many participants would have been assigned to each possible treatment order within each group?

5. Suppose that participants are asked to memorize a list of words that range from very abstract to very concrete. The number of words recalled of each type for each participant are shown in the following table.

Participant number	Very abstract	Mildly abstract	Mildly concrete	Very concrete
1	2	5	11	14
2	0	8	4	11
3	7	9	13	20
4	3	12	10	15
5	3	7	8	6
6	2	6	6	9
7	5	8	7	7
8	4	9	5	8

(a) Compute the one-way RM ANOVA for these data. Test the F ratio for significance at the .05 level. How many pairwise comparisons could be tested if your ANOVA was significant? What alpha would you use to test each of these comparisons, if you used a Bonferroni adjustment to keep the experimentwise alpha at .05?

(b) Reanalyze the data as a mixed-design ANOVA, assuming that the first four participants were selected for their high scores on a spatial ability test, whereas the second group of four participants were chosen for their poor performance in spatial ability. Test each F ratio for significance at the .05 level.

(c) Graph the cell means of the two-way mixed-design ANOVA, as described in part (b). Explain how the pattern of the cell means is consistent with the results you obtained in part (b).

Thought Questions

1. (a) What advantage does repeated-measures ANOVA have over ANOVA without repeated measures (where every score is derived from a different participant)? (b) Why might a researcher decide *not* to use repeated-measures ANOVA in spite of this advantage, and what alternatives would be considered?

2. What is the sphericity assumption in behavioral science research? Give an example of when it might be violated.

3. Give an example for which each of the following is appropriate: (a) Repeated-measures ANOVA. (b) The randomized blocks design. (c) The two-way mixed design. (d) The before-and-after form of the two-way mixed design. (e) One-way repeated-measures design with counterbalancing.

Computer Exercises

1. Perform an RM ANOVA to test for a significant change in anxiety level in all subjects over time (baseline, prequiz, and postquiz). Regardless of whether or not the ANOVA is significant, follow it with

matched *t* tests (or two-level RM ANOVAs) for each pair of levels of the time factor.

2. Redo Exercise 1 for heart rate.

3. Add gender to the analysis in Exercise 1, and compute the mixed-design ANOVA. Request a plot of the cell means, and explain your ANOVA results in terms of the pattern in your graph. Regardless of whether the interaction is significant, follow the mixed-design ANOVA with separate one-way RM ANOVAs (i.e., simple main effects) for each gender.

4. Add the experimental factor (i.e., difficulty of the 11th quiz question) to the analysis in Exercise 1, and compute the mixed-design ANOVA. Request a plot of the cell means, and explain your ANOVA results in terms of the pattern in your graph. Follow the mixed-design ANOVA with separate one-way ANOVAs for each measurement period (i.e., baseline, prequiz, and postquiz).

5. Redo Exercise 4 using heart rate as the dependent variable instead of anxiety.

Bridge to SPSS

There is a fundamental difference between the ways in which data are entered for a repeated-measures design and for an independent-groups design. When the same subjects are measured at all the levels of your IV, there is no *one* column in your spreadsheet that contains your DV. Each level of your factor is represented by another column (i.e., variable) in your spreadsheet. You will have to tell SPSS which columns in your spreadsheet are the levels of your RM factor. If you are using an RB design, a single row does not literally represent one subject, but it does represent one *block,* which is treated as though it contained repeated measures of the same subject.

To perform an RM ANOVA in SPSS, select **Repeated Measures** from the **Analyze/General Linear Model** menu. The dialog box that opens will ask you to create a name for your RM factor. For example, if your matched blocks of subjects were randomly assigned across three methods for teaching reading, your three columns of final reading scores might be labeled: phonics, holistic, and traditional. In that case, it would be appropriate to type **method** in the space for Within-Subject Factor Name, and then type **3** for Number of Levels and click **Add**, followed by **Define**. This action opens the main dialog box for Repeated Measures, where you are required to move three names (in this example) from the usual list of variables on the left to slots for the three levels of your RM factor on the right in a space labeled Within-Subjects Variables. You have the usual **Options**, **Plots**, and **Contrasts** available, but **Post Hoc** is only for any Between-Subjects Factors you specify. We will discuss that possibility when we get to the Mixed-Design ANOVA.

One-Way RM ANOVA Output

Much of the work required to interpret the default SPSS output for RM ANOVA consists of knowing which information you can safely ignore. After a box that just lists the variables that serve as the levels of your RM factor, you will see a box of data labeled **Multivariate Tests**. This box offers an alternative statistical solution to the RM ANOVA, which makes no assumptions concerning sphericity; ignore it if you have decided to perform an RM ANOVA (or learn more about the multivariate approach to RM data in a more advanced statistics text). The next box contains **Mauchly's Test of Sphericity**; if the **Sig.** for this test is less than .05, take note. This knowledge could affect your interpretation of the following box: **Tests of Within-Subjects Effects**. SPSS always presents four variations of the RM ANOVA in this box, whether you want to see them or not. The first variation, labeled **Sphericity Assumed**, is the ordinary RM ANOVA result, as described in this chapter. The next two rows of this box contain the results of two different formulas for reducing both the numerator and denominator df to accommodate possible violations of the sphericity assumption. The first of these, known as the **Greenhouse-Geisser (G-G) correction**, is by far the more conservative and more popular of the two; the Huynh-Feldt (H-F) correction is rarely used.

The fourth variation, "Lower-bound" epsilon, uses what we referred to as the worst-case df adjustment earlier in this chapter. There is no need to use this overly conservative adjustment if the G-G solution is available. If your data seem very consistent with the sphericity assumption, it is reasonable to report the p value from the row labeled Sphericity Assumed. (The p values change from row to row, but the calculated F values do not.) However, if Mauchly's W test is significant (i.e., Sig. $<.05$), it is recommended that you report the p value according to the G-G correction, along with its (usually fractional) adjusted df.

The next output box, **Tests of Within-Subjects Contrasts**, makes sense only if the levels of your RM factor are quantitative rather than qualitative. For example, you are measuring the time it takes your participants to solve anagrams (the letters of common words have been rearranged) of different lengths; anagrams containing five, six, seven, or eight letters each are presented in a random order. In this case, it may well be of interest to test the linear trend in your data to answer the question: To what extent does the average time to solve an anagram increase as a linear function of the number of letters, and is this trend statistically significant? All of the possible higher-order trends (e.g., quadratic: To what extent do the means tend to increase at first and then decrease at higher levels of the factor, or vice versa?) are automatically tested as well, and this output box is presented even if your RM factor has qualitative levels (e.g., participants perform a task while listening to four different types of music), in which case the results in this box are meaningless, as they are based on the arbitrary order in which you list the different levels (e.g., types of music) in the RM ANOVA dialog box.

The final box is generally ignored if you are conducting a one-way RM ANOVA rather than a mixed-design ANOVA. If there are only RM factors, this box, **Tests of Between-Subjects Effects**, contains only a test of the intercept for your data. This is just a one-sample test to determine whether the grand mean of all your data is significantly greater than zero. If negative numbers are not possible in your data, the F ratio in this box will be surprisingly large, but of no practical interest.

Mixed-Design ANOVA

Requesting an analysis of a mixed-design ANOVA in SPSS begins the same way as for the one-way RM ANOVA. However, after you have defined the levels of your RM factor in the Repeated Measures dialog box, you can move one or more between-group factors (e.g., gender, order) into the space labeled **Between-Subjects Factors**. If you then click the **Post Hoc** button, you will see a list of those between-group variables under the heading **Factor(s)**. Moving one or more of those factors to the right will make available all of the choices for post hoc tests. Unfortunately, pairwise comparisons for your RM levels cannot be requested from this box. However, it is easy enough to request matched-pairs t tests for each pair of RM levels and to use the Bonferroni adjustment to lower the alpha for each pairwise test.

The output box that was the most relevant to us for the RM design contains an additional analysis for the mixed design. In the **Tests of Within-Subjects Effects** box, the analysis for the interaction of the two factors is inserted between the RM factor and the error term; the latter is used as the denominator for both the RM main effect and the interaction. The **Tests of Between-Subjects Effects** box, which contains only a seldom-needed test of the intercept for a purely RM ANOVA, includes a test of the main effect of the between-groups factor in a two-way mixed design.

Part IV
Nonparametric Statistics for Categorical Data

Chapter 16   **Probability of Discrete Events and the Binomial Distribution**

Chapter 17   **Chi-Square Tests**

Chapter 16
Probability of Discrete Events and the Binomial Distribution

PREVIEW

Introduction

What are dichotomous data, and how do they arise?

What does the distribution for dichotomous data look like?

Probability

How do we define the probability of a given event?

What is meant by the odds against a given event?

How do we compute the probability that either of two events will occur?

How do we compute the probability that one event and then another event will occur?

The Binomial Distribution

How can we use the laws of probability to construct a binomial distribution?

How can we use the binomial distribution to test a null hypothesis involving events with two possible outcomes?

How can we use the normal distribution as an approximation to the binomial distribution?

The Sign Test for Matched Samples

How can we use the binomial distribution as an alternative to the matched-pairs *t* test?

Under what conditions might you prefer the sign test to the matched-pairs *t* test?

Summary

Exercises

Thought Questions

Computer Exercises

Bridge to SPSS

Introduction

In the analysis of variance, as well as in the t test, the dependent variable (DV) is measured on a precise, quantitative (i.e., interval or ratio) scale. However, there are many possible DVs in behavioral research that cannot be measured precisely (at least at the present time). For example, if we want to test some new form of imagery exercise that is designed to increase creativity, we may be able to assemble a panel of judges that can reliably determine whether one work of art or writing is more creative than another, without being able to accurately quantify the *amount* of creativity separately for each work. Indeed, they may not even be able to rank the amounts by which pairs of works differ in creativity, thus ruling out the possibility of using Wilcoxon's matched-pairs test (see Chapter 8).

In another example, a behavioral outcome may have only two possible levels to begin with. For example, an (unknowing) participant may either return the wallet he or she found on the street (where the experimenter left it) or not. The independent variable (IV) in this study might also consist of just a few categories, such as the approximate economic level (wealthy, middle class, or disadvantaged) of the neighborhood that corresponds to the wallet owner's address.

When both the IVs and DVs in a study can only be categorized, the statistical methods discussed in previous chapters are not appropriate. Methods for dealing with purely categorical data, which, like the ordinal tests of Chapter 8, are referred to as *nonparametric statistics*, will be described in this chapter and the next. We begin by considering the simplest possible situation in which you would use a nonparametric test: You are observing an outcome that is **dichotomous**—it can fall into only one of two possible categories.

Dichotomous Data

If you want to make a statistical decision based on how many outcomes fall into one or another of two categories, you need an appropriate model to represent the distribution of frequencies that occur when the null hypothesis is true. However, when the outcome is dichotomous, the distribution corresponding to the null hypothesis will not be a smooth mathematical curve like the t or F distributions. It will tend to have a rather boxy shape, which is known as the *binomial* distribution. For a small number of outcomes, it is not difficult to determine the entire binomial distribution exactly. However, to fully understand how this is done, you will need to learn the basic rules of probability as they apply to discrete (i.e., countable) events, rather than smooth distributions based on infinite populations of precise measurements, such as those discussed in Chapter 4.

Flipping a coin, which can land only as heads or tails, is the example that we will use to introduce the laws of probability. An *unbiased* coin is one that is just as likely to land heads as it is to land tails.

Probability

After defining probability and odds, we cover the rules of probability.

Definition of Probability

The **probability (P)** of a given event can be defined by the following fraction:

$$P(\text{event}) = \frac{\text{number of ways the specified event can occur}}{\text{total number of equally likely possible events}} \qquad \text{Formula 16.1}$$

For example, if an unbiased coin is flipped and you wish to determine the probability that heads will come up, the solution is

$$P(\text{H}) = \frac{1}{2} = \frac{1 \text{ head}}{2 \text{ possible events: head or tail}}$$

Similarly, the probability of tails coming up is also 1/2. Decimals are often used to express probabilities, so we can also write $P(\text{H})$ (that is, the probability of obtaining a head on one toss of the coin), or $P(\text{T})$, as .50. These numbers express the fact that if the coin is fair, in the long run heads will occur half the time and tails will occur half the time.

To provide some further illustrations, let us assume that you have a standard 52-card deck of playing cards (any jokers or other special cards have been removed). The 52 cards are divided into four suits (spades, hearts, diamonds, and clubs), each of which contains 13 cards (2 through 10, jack, queen, king, and ace). The deck is thoroughly shuffled, and one card is drawn. The probability that it is the king of diamonds is 1/52 (or .019); there is only one way for that event to occur (only one king of diamonds) and 52 possible equally likely events (cards that could be drawn). In fact, the probability of drawing any one specific card from the deck is 1/52. The probability of drawing a 9 is 4/52 or 1/13 (or .077), since there are four ways for this event to occur (9 of spades, 9 of hearts, 9 of diamonds, and 9 of clubs) out of the total possible 52 events. If we define a *spot card* as anything below a 10, the probability of drawing a spot card in clubs is 8/52, or 2/13 (or .15), for there are eight specific equally likely events (the 2, 3, 4, 5, 6, 7, 8, and 9 of clubs) in the 52-card deck that fall under the category of this event.

Probability cannot be less than 0 or greater than 1. If an event has a probability of 1, that means that it must happen. The probability of drawing either a red or a black card from a standard deck is 1.00, if you draw a card at all, because all of the cards in the deck are either red or black (i.e., $P = 52/52 = 1.00$). The probability of drawing a purple card with yellow polka dots is zero ($P = 0/52 = 0$).

Odds

The *odds against an event* are defined as the ratio of the number of unfavorable outcomes to the number of favorable outcomes, all outcomes being equally likely. See, for example, the following table.

Outcome	Total events (T)	Number of ways of obtaining the event (W)	Number of ways of not obtaining the event (T – W)	Probability of event (W/T)	Odds against event (T – W to W)
King of diamonds	52	1	51	1/52	51 to 1
A nine	52	4	48	4/52 or 1/13	48 to 4 or 12 to 1
Spot card in clubs	52	8	44	8/52 or 2/13	44 to 8 or 11 to 2 (5½ to 1)

If the odds against your winning a game are (say) 12 to 1, you need to collect 12 times your wager when you win for the game to be fair. If you stand to win more than 12 times your bet, it is to your advantage to play the game. If you collect less than 12 times your bet when you win, you should refuse to play because you can expect to lose money in the long run; this is true of any game at a gambling casino, for instance.

The Probability of *A* or *B*

The probability of *either of two events* taking place is computed by using the following formula:

$$P(A \text{ or } B) = P(A) + P(B) - P(A \text{ and } B)$$ Formula 16.2

Example: Suppose that you will win a prize if you draw *either* a king *or* a club from a standard 52-card deck in a single try. The probability of winning is equal to

$$P(\text{king}) + P(\text{club}) - P(\text{king and club})$$

$$= 4/52 + 13/52 - 1/52$$

$$= 16/52 (or .31)$$

To verify these calculations, let us tackle the problem the long way. There are the usual 52 total possible events, and the number of favorable events may be counted as follows:

King (4 favorable events)	Club (13 favorable events)
king of spades	ace of clubs
king of hearts	*king of clubs*
king of diamonds	queen of clubs
king of clubs	jack of clubs
	ten of clubs
	nine of clubs
	eight of clubs
	seven of clubs
	six of clubs
	five of clubs
	four of clubs
	three of clubs
	two of clubs

There appear to be 17 favorable events: 13 clubs and 4 kings. But the king of clubs has been counted twice, and there is only one king of clubs in the deck. Therefore, the probability of king *and* club (1/52) must be subtracted, and the resulting probability (16/52) shows that there are 16 separate and distinct favorable events (cards) out of the total of 52 in the deck.

If events A and B cannot happen simultaneously (in mathematical terminology, they *are* **mutually exclusive**), then $P(A$ and $B) = 0$. For example, the probability of drawing a king or a queen from the deck is equal to $4/52 + 4/52 - 0/52 = 8/52$. The events are mutually exclusive because no card in the deck is *both* a king and a queen.

The Probability of *A* and Then *B*

Suppose that a card is drawn from a standard deck, looked at, and replaced in the deck. The deck is shuffled thoroughly, and a second card is drawn. We wish to know the probability of obtaining a king on the first draw *and then* the ace of spades on the second draw. In this situation, the two draws are *independent*—that is, what happens on the first draw does not affect the probabilities on the second draw (because of the replacement and shuffling). The probability of both A *and* B occurring is given by this formula:

$$P(A \text{ and then } B) = P(A) \times P(B) \qquad \text{Formula 16.3}$$

In the present example, the answer is

$$P(\text{king and then ace of spades}) = P(\text{king}) \times P(\text{ace of spades})$$

$$= 4/52 \times 1/52$$

$$= 4/2704 \text{ (}or\text{ .0015)}$$

Conditional Probability

If the card drawn on the first try is *not* returned to the deck, the probability becomes $4/52 \times 1/51$ (or 4/2652). Under this procedure, only 51 cards remain in the deck after the first draw, and the probability of success on the second draw is therefore 1/51.

Drawing two cards from a deck *without* replacement results in two events that are *not* independent. That is, the probability of the second card drawn is changed by the first draw. In statistical language, the probability of the second event is *conditional* on the outcome of the first event. For example, the probability of the second card being a club is certainly less if the first card drawn happens to also be a club.

Alpha is another example of a *conditional probability*. Alpha is the probability of rejecting the null hypothesis *under the condition* that the null hypothesis is true. With alpha fixed at .05, we know that 5% of all experiments *for which the null hypothesis is actually true* will be statistically significant and therefore Type I errors, but we do *not* know what percentage of *all* experiments will be statistically significant at the .05 level.

To create a binomial distribution, as we are about to do, all of the events involved must be independent of all of the others. Therefore, we will not deal further with conditional probabilities in this chapter.

The Binomial Distribution

Using only the simple rules of probability we have just described, we can now explain how the binomial distribution arises and how it can be used.

Constructing the Binomial Distribution for $N = 2$

To return to the coin-tossing example, the probability of obtaining a head on each of two consecutive flips of a coin is $P(\text{H}) \times P(\text{H})$, which is equal to $1/2 \times 1/2$ or 1/4. This can be verified by listing all possible outcomes of two flips of the coin:

First flip	Second flip	Overall result	Probability
H	H	2 heads	1/4 (or .25)
H	T	1 head, 1 tail	1/4
T	H	1 head, 1 tail	1/4
T	T	2 tails	1/4

Of the four possible outcomes (all of equal probability), only one yields two heads, so, using Formula 16.1, this probability is 1/4. Similarly, the probability of two tails is 1/4, and the probability of obtaining one head and one tail irrespective of order is 2/4 or 1/2. Since the events are independent (i.e., the results of the first flip do not affect the probabilities on the second flip), the probabilities are exactly the same if we flip two coins once. Notice also that the sum of the probabilities of the four possible outcomes is equal to 1.0.

The shape of a binomial distribution depends on two values: N, the number of events; and P, the probability of one of the two categories for each event. For coin tossing, the two categories are heads (H) and tails (T), and P is the probability of one of these. For a fair coin, P equals .5 for both heads and tails. This will *not* be the case for a biased coin, which will be more likely to fall heads up or tails up. In the general case, we choose one category to focus on and refer to it as X. Then we say that P is the probability of the X category occurring on any one event. (For flips of a coin, it is customary to choose heads as the X category.) The probability of the other category (in this case, tails) is sometimes labeled Q. But when there are only two categories, it is simpler to refer to the probability of the other category as $1 - P$, because P plus Q (the sums of the probabilities of the two possible outcomes) must equal 1.

To construct a graph of a binomial distribution, place all of the possible values for X along the horizontal axis. The height of the bar for each value of X depends on the relative frequency of that value occurring. For $N = 2$, there are three possible values for X: 0 (no heads), 1 head, and 2 heads. From the preceding table and discussion, it should be easy to imagine the binomial distribution for $N = 2$ and $P = .5$. It would consist of three bars: The bars over 0 and 2 would reach a height of .25, while the bar in the middle ($X = 1$) would reach .5.

It is particularly easy to construct a binomial distribution when P (and therefore Q) equals .5. In that case, all of the possible sequences of the two categories have the same probability (e.g., HTTT is no more or less likely than THTH), and the task becomes one of counting how many sequences contain a particular number of Xs (e.g., heads). If, instead, X represents drawing a club from a standard deck of cards (with replacement), P equals .25. If we use Y to represent a card that is not a club ($Q = .75$), then a sequence like $XYYY$ is *more* likely than a sequence like $YXYX$, not because of the order but because one has more Ys (which are 3 times more likely) than the other. When $P = Q = .5$, the binomial distribution is conveniently symmetric, as you will see in the next section. Fortunately, $P = .5$ is often a reasonable value for the null hypothesis when dealing with dichotomous events, so the kind of binomial distribution that we will construct next has many uses.

Constructing the Binomial Distribution for $N = 6$ ($P = .5$)

If you toss a coin six times, the number of possible different sequences is $2 \times 2 \times 2 \times 2 \times 2 \times 2$ (or 2^6), which equals 64. When $P = .5$, the probability is the same for all 64 sequences, so $p = 1/64$ for each sequence. However, the probability for a particular value of X (e.g., 5) depends on how many of the 64 sequences have that value for X (e.g., how many sequences contain exactly five heads). So how many sequences have exactly five heads? Let us count the ways, which are labeled A through F in the following table:

	Possible outcomes					
	Flip 1	Flip 2	Flip 3	Flip 4	Flip 5	Flip 6
A	H	H	H	H	H	T
B	H	H	H	H	T	H
C	H	H	H	T	H	H
D	H	H	T	H	H	H
E	H	T	H	H	H	H
F	T	H	H	H	H	H

As you can see, there are six different sequences that contain exactly five heads. Using the "or" rule of probability, the probability that you will get five heads from a fair coin that is flipped six times is equal to

$$P(A \text{ or } B \text{ or } C \text{ or } D \text{ or } E \text{ or } F)$$

Since these events are mutually exclusive, this equals $1/64 + 1/64 + 1/64 + 1/64 + 1/64 + 1/64 = 6/64$, or .094.

Using the same procedures, we can compute the probability of any number of heads if a coin is flipped six times. However, writing out all of the possible sequences can be quite tedious,[1] so we will just present the end product in the following table:

Number of heads	Probability
0	$1/64 = .016$
1	$6/64 = .094$
2	$15/64 = .234$
3	$20/64 = .312$
4	$15/64 = .234$
5	$6/64 = .094$
6	$1/64 = .016$
	$64/64 = 1.000$

Testing Null Hypotheses With the Binomial Distribution

The binomial distribution shown can be used to test some simple null hypotheses. Suppose a friend claims that he can taste the difference between two popular brands of root beer, and you decide to test his claim.

---

[1]Mathematics makes use of special techniques, called *permutations* and *combinations,* to speed the calculation of the number of sequences for each X. However, we do not need such fancy methods for the purposes of this chapter.

You present the two brands of root beer in identical cups, and he has to tell you which cup contains which brand. Suppose your friend answers correctly six times in a row. What should you decide?

The appropriate null hypothesis is that your friend was just guessing, in which case P equals .5 for each test. Because being correct six times out of six tests is represented by only one sequence out of 64, the p value is .016. If you want to be conservative and perform a two-tailed test (your friend being *wrong* six times in a row would also suggest that he does detect some difference), the p value would be .032. In either case, using the .05 decision rule, you would reject the null hypothesis and conclude that your friend has a greater than .5 chance of being correct on each trial.

If your friend was correct on only five of the six trials, the one-tailed p value would be .11. This is not significant at the .05 level, even for a one-tailed test. Notice that to get the p value in this case, you must add the probabilities of both one wrong, or .094, and zero wrong, or .016. Because zero wrong is farther out in the tail of the binomial distribution, it contributes to the possibility of committing a Type I error.

If your friend is correct on 10 out of 12 repetitions of the taste test, you need the binomial distribution with $N = 12, P = .5$, to find his p value. This distribution is shown in Figure 16.1. (You cannot read this accurately from the graph, but for $X = 10$, the one-tailed $p = .0161 + .0029 + .0002 = .0192$. So H_0 is rejected at the .05 level with either a one- or a two-tailed test.) We show the distribution for $N = 12$ so you can see its resemblance to the normal distribution. As N increases, the binomial distribution becomes smoother and resembles the normal distribution more closely. (Theoretically, the two distributions become identical when N is infinitely large.) When P is higher or lower than .5, the binomial distribution is skewed. The farther P is from .5, the larger N needs to be before the binomial begins to resemble the normal distribution.

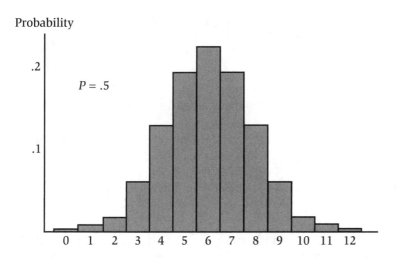

Probability

.2

$P = .5$

.1

0 1 2 3 4 5 6 7 8 9 10 11 12

Figure 16.1

Binomial Distribution for $N = 12, P = .5$

Using the Normal Distribution as an Approximation

It is not common to find tables of the binomial distribution for N greater than 20. Fortunately, if P is .5 (or even just close to .5), the resemblance to the normal distribution becomes so close with $N > 20$ that accurate results can be obtained by calculating a z score and referring it to a table of the standard normal distribution (like Table A in the Appendix).

It should be evident that the mean of a binomial distribution is NP (e.g., for $N = 12$ and $P = .5$, the mean is 6). It is not at all obvious, but the standard deviation (SD) for a binomial distribution is $\sqrt{NPQ}$. This leads to the following z score formula that can be applied to the binomial distribution when N is fairly large:

$$z = \frac{X - NP}{\sqrt{NPQ}}$$ Formula 16.4

For the example in which your friend identified the root beer brands correctly 10 out of 12 times, the z score would be

$$z = \frac{10 - 6}{\sqrt{12\,(.5)\,(.5)}} = \frac{4}{\sqrt{3}} = 2.31$$

We can see from Table A that the p value corresponding to a z score of 2.31 is .0104. Although this p value leads to the same conclusion with respect to H_0 that we reached by calculating p exactly for the binomial distribution (.0192), it is noticeably different. With $P = .5$, N needs to be at least about 20 before the normal approximation to the binomial distribution becomes sufficiently accurate to use in null hypothesis testing (NHT).

The Formula for Proportions

Rather than dealing with the actual number of trials on which your friend was correct (i.e., X) or the number correct expected by chance (NP), it may be more convenient to deal with the *proportion* of trials on which your friend was correct (i.e., X/N) and the proportion expected by chance (i.e., $NP/N = P$). Because we obtained the proportions by dividing by N, we also have to divide the SD of the binomial distribution by N to get the SD of the proportions:

$$\frac{\sqrt{NPQ}}{N} = \frac{\sqrt{NPQ}}{\sqrt{N^2}} = \sqrt{\frac{NPQ}{N^2}} = \sqrt{\frac{PQ}{N}}$$

Therefore, the z score for proportions is given by the following formula:

$$z = \frac{\dfrac{X}{N} - P}{\sqrt{\dfrac{PQ}{N}}}$$

This formula should seem familiar. To see why, let us change the notation. We will use a lowercase p to represent X/N, the proportion you observed in your sample. (For the example of 10 correct trials out of 12, $p = 10/12 = .833$.) Instead of using an uppercase P to represent the proportion under the null hypothesis, we will use the (lowercase) Greek letter pi (π), because this is the proportion of X in the entire population. Finally, because Q equals $1 - P$, it can now be written as $1 - \pi$. Using the modified notation, the previous formula can be written as

$$z = \frac{p - \pi}{\sqrt{\dfrac{\pi(1 - \pi)}{N}}} \qquad \text{Formula 6.5}$$

This is the formula we called the z score for proportions in Chapter 6. If we apply this version of the formula to the root beer taste test example, it yields the same z score:

$$z = \frac{.833 - .5}{\sqrt{\dfrac{.5(1 - .5)}{12}}} = \frac{.333}{\sqrt{.02083}} = \frac{.333}{.1443} = 2.31$$

You can also obtain a confidence interval for your friend's taste test proportion by using Formula 6.6.

Applications of the Binomial Test

The use of z scores in conjunction with the normal distribution yields only an approximation to the exact p value you would get from the binomial distribution. As we mentioned in Chapter 6, this approximation is not sufficiently accurate for null hypothesis testing when *either* $N\pi$ or $N(1 - \pi)$ is less than 5.

    In Chapter 6, we applied the z-score proportion formula to the results of an election poll. This test can also be applied to experimental situations more central to behavioral research. For example, a developmental researcher may want to test whether 10-month-old infants spend more time looking at photographs of adult faces rated as attractive by other adults than faces rated as relatively unattractive. By exposing the infants to equal numbers of attractive and unattractive faces and measuring their gaze time for each type of face, each infant can be categorized as preferring attractive faces or preferring unattractive faces. (It is not likely that an infant will spend *exactly* the same amount of time looking at both types of faces, but it would be reasonable to delete from the data set any infant who exhibited very little preference.) The proportion of infants out of, say, 20 or more who prefer attractive faces can be tested against the null hypothesis of $\pi = .5$ using the preceding formula. (You can demonstrate for yourself that 15 out of 20 infants preferring attractive faces would allow rejection of H_0 at the .05 level with a two-tailed test.)

    You can also test null hypotheses for which π is not .5. Imagine an observational study in which you find that out of 50 leading architects, 12 are left-handed. (There is some evidence that left-handers on the average have greater spatial ability than right-handers, because of the way the left and right sides of their brains are organized.) In this case, π is not .5. It is the actual proportion of left-handers in the population, which is closer to .15. The observed proportion is $p = 12/50 = .24$, and z is therefore as follows:

$$z = \frac{.24 - .15}{\sqrt{\dfrac{.15\,(.85)}{50}}} = \frac{.09}{.0505} = 1.78$$

This result would be significant at the .05 level only if a one-tailed test could be justified (which is not likely). Note that because $N\pi = 50 \times .15 = 7.5$, which is greater than 5, and $N(1 - \pi)$ is also greater than 5, the use of the normal approximation would be considered reasonably accurate in this case.

Simplified Formula for $P = .5$

In many common experimental situations, the null hypothesis will involve equal probabilities for the two alternatives. For this null hypothesis ($P = Q = .5$), the z-score formula that we started out with, $z = (X - NP)/\sqrt{NPQ}$, can be simplified to

$$z = (2X - N)/\sqrt{N} \qquad \text{Formula 16.5}$$

where X is the number of events that fall in (either) one of the two categories.

We will have the opportunity to use this specialized version of the z score formula in the next section.

The Sign Test for Matched Samples

A particularly useful application of the binomial distribution is to serve as the null hypothesis distribution for a simple nonparametric alternative to the matched t test. At the beginning of this chapter, we mentioned the example of testing a new form of imagery exercise that is designed to increase creativity. Suppose that we match young art students into pairs based primarily on the creativity they have already shown in their paintings. (The matching will not be precise, of course, but even an approximate matching can be quite helpful.) The members of each pair are assigned randomly to either the imagery training condition or a control condition that provides some plausible but ineffective version of the training. At the end of the training period, each art student produces a painting. A panel of art instructors is asked to determine, for each pair of participants, whose painting exhibited the greater amount of creativity. Let us further suppose that, of the 30 pairs of participants in the study, the experimental participant is judged to be more creative in 18 cases, the control participant is found to be more creative in 10 cases, and no determination is made in 2 cases (each of these two comparisons is judged a tie). The simplest approach is to delete the two ties from the analysis and use 28 as N in the z score for proportions.

Because we do not have actual measurements of creativity, we cannot calculate difference scores and compute a matched-pairs t test. We will further assume that it would not be reasonable to ask the judges to compare the creativity difference for one pair to the creativity differences of other pairs, so the Wilcoxon matched-pairs test (see Chapter 8) is not a viable alternative. However, we can, at least, count how many of the creativity differences are positive and how many are negative. (We will define a difference as positive when the experimental participant is judged as more creative than his or her pair in the control condition.) The appropriate null hypothesis in such situations is that there will be equal numbers of positive and negative differences in the population (i.e., P, or π, $= .5$). We can use the binomial distribution to decide whether it is reasonable to reject the hypothesis that the signs of the difference scores in the population are just as likely to be positive as negative, and this is called **the sign test for matched samples**. Given that H_0 for the sign test is always that $P = .5$, as long as N is at least about 15 or 20, we can use Formula 16.5, and look up our p value in Table A in the Appendix. For this example, X is 18, so

$$z = \frac{2X - N}{\sqrt{N}} = \frac{36 - 28}{\sqrt{28}} = \frac{8}{5.29} = 1.51$$

From Table A, the one-tailed p value corresponding to this z score is .0655. Even with a one-tailed test, this z score would not allow rejection of the null hypothesis at the .05 level: There is not sufficient reason to believe that the imagery exercise increases creativity.

The sign test is particularly appropriate when you cannot make quantitative measurements, but you can determine the direction in which a variable changes (e.g., mental health has improved, stayed the same, or worsened). However, as we noted in Chapter 8, there are times when a nonparametric test is preferred even when the dependent variable has been measured precisely and a matched t test can be computed. Although the matched t test is quite robust with respect to its assumption concerning normal distributions, when you are dealing with fairly small samples and the distribution of the difference scores bears little resemblance to a bell-shape curve (e.g., a few of the differences are far from the others, or the difference scores form two distinct clumps), a nonparametric, distribution-free test is recommended. If the pairwise differences can be rank ordered, then the Wilcoxon matched-pairs test is much preferred to the sign test, as it usually has considerably more power than a sign test performed on the same data. When applied to quantitative data, the sign test makes absolutely no use of the amounts of the differences, which is why it usually has much less power to detect a true population effect than a matched t test, or even the Wilcoxon test, applied to the same data. Nonetheless, if nearly all the differences are in the same direction, you may obtain statistical significance with the sign test, regardless of how the difference scores are distributed, or even if they cannot be compared to each other at all.

Summary

The rules of probability for discrete events can be described in terms of counting the number of events that fall into one category or another. When a fixed number of dichotomous events are counted in terms of how many events fell into either one of the two possible categories, it is easy to construct a binomial distribution, which can then be used to draw statistical inferences.

Probability

Definition:

$$P = \frac{\text{number of ways the specified event can occur}}{\text{total number of equally likely possible events}} \qquad \text{Formula 16.1}$$

Odds against an event = the number of unfavorable events divided by the number of favorable events

Additive law:

$$P(A \text{ or } B) = P(A) + P(B) - P(A \text{ and } B) \qquad \text{Formula 16.2}$$

Multiplicative law:

If A and B are independent events:

$$P(A \text{ and then } B) = P(A) \times P(B) \qquad \text{Formula 16.3}$$

Using the Normal Distribution as an Approximation to the Binomial Distribution

First, calculate

$$z = \frac{X - NP}{\sqrt{NPQ}} \qquad \text{Formula 16.4}$$

where
N = total number of events,
X = number of events that fall into the category whose probability is P,
$Q = 1 - P$.

Then look up the p value for that z score in Table A. (Double this value for a two-tailed test.)
  If $P = Q = .5$, the formula can be simplified to

$$z = \frac{2X - N}{\sqrt{N}} \qquad \text{Formula 16.5}$$

If we divide all of the terms of Formula 16.4 by N (and change our notation), we obtain the same z-score formula for proportions that we used in Chapter 6:

$$z = \frac{p - \pi}{\sqrt{\dfrac{\pi(1 - \pi)}{N}}}$$

Formula 6.5

The Sign Test for Matched Samples

For each matched pair of participants, determine the *sign* of the difference between them, using some arbitrary but consistent rule (e.g., if the participant in the experimental condition performs better than the paired participant in the control group, the difference is positive). If your dependent variable has been measured precisely, you can calculate the difference as you would for a matched-pairs t test, but for this test you would note only the sign (positive or negative) of the difference score. Then apply one of the preceding formulas, wherein N is the number of pairs (after subtracting any pairs with zero differences). Generally, the null hypothesis will be such that $P = Q = .5$.

Exercises

1. In the following problems, cards are drawn from a standard 52-card deck. Before a second draw, the first card drawn is replaced and the deck is thoroughly shuffled. Compute each of the following probabilities.

   (a) The probability of drawing a 10 on the first draw.
   (b) The probability of drawing either a deuce, a 3, a 4, a 5, a heart, or a diamond on the first draw.
   (c) The probability of drawing the ace of spades twice in a row.
   (d) The probability of drawing either a jack, a 10, a 7 of clubs, or a spade on the first draw *and then* drawing either the ace of diamonds or 9 of hearts on the second draw.
   (e) Recompute the probabilities asked for in parts (c) and (d) assuming that the first card drawn is *not* replaced.

2. The following questions refer to the throw of one fair, six-sided die.

   (a) What is the probability of obtaining an odd number on one throw?
   (b) What is the probability of obtaining seven odd numbers in seven throws?

3. One hundred slips of paper bearing the numbers from 1 to 100, inclusive, are placed in a large hat and thoroughly mixed. What is the probability of drawing

   (a) The number 17?
   (b) The number 92?

(c) Either a 2 or a 4?

(d) A number from 7 to 11, inclusive?

(e) A number in the 20s?

(f) An even number?

(g) An even number, and then a number from 3 to 19, inclusive? (The number drawn first is replaced prior to the second draw.)

(h) A number from 96 to 100, inclusive, or a number from 70 to 97, inclusive?

4. Slips of paper are placed in a large hat and thoroughly mixed. Ten slips bear the number 1, 20 slips bear the number 2, 30 slips bear the number 3, and 5 slips bear the number 4. What is the probability of drawing

(a) A 1?

(b) A 2?

(c) A 3?

(d) A 4?

(e) A 1 or a 4?

(f) A 1 or a 2 or a 3 or a 4?

(g) A 5?

(h) A 2 and then a 3? (The number drawn first is replaced prior to the second draw.)

5. Imagine that you want to test whether a particular coin is biased or fair by flipping the coin four times and counting the number of times it comes up heads.

(a) How many different sequences can be produced by flipping the coin four times? How many different values can X (the number of heads) take on?

(b) Graph the binomial distribution for $N = 4$ and $P = .5$ so that the height of each bar represents the probability that corresponds to each value of X.

(c) If the coin were to land on tails four times in a row, could you reject the null hypothesis that the coin is fair? Explain.

6. Apply the sign test to the data from Exercise 8 in Chapter 7, using one of the normal approximation formulas. Explain the difference in results between this exercise and the one in Chapter 7.

7. Suppose that after 6 months of a new form of treatment for chronic schizophrenia, 18 patients exhibited some improvement, 4 did not change, and 6 patients actually got worse.

(a) Using the sign test, can you reject the null hypothesis (that the new treatment has no effect) at the .05 level? (Show the z score and p value that you used to answer this question.)

(b) A more conservative way to conduct the binomial test is to assign half of the tied cases arbitrarily to each category (one pair is discarded if there is an odd number of ties). Redo part (a) after applying this approach to tied cases.

8. At a small rural college, incoming students are arranged into 320 *pairs* by the administration based on their high school credentials. (The students do not know this). One member of each pair is chosen randomly to participate in an enriched orientation program. At the end of the first semester, it is found that 55% of enriched-program students are getting higher grades than the (control) students they have been matched with. Can you reject the null hypothesis at the .05 level with a two-tailed test? With a one-tailed test? Explain the basis for your statistical decisions.

Thought Questions

1. Give an example of a psychological research study where the variables can be expressed only as categories, and not in any quantitative way.

2. You want to determine if a coin is biased in favor of falling heads up or tails up. (a) You flip the coin three times and obtain three heads. What should you decide? (b) Why is the informal experiment in part (a) badly designed? (c) Which error is more likely to result from the experiment in part (a), Type I or Type II? (d) Suppose you flip the coin six times and obtain six heads. What should you decide? (e) What distribution is used to reach a decision in part (a) and part (d)?

3. When should the normal distribution be used as an approximation to the binomial distribution?

4. A researcher wishes to determine if a particular form of psychotherapy will improve the mental health of patients who suffer from depression. If the researcher cannot obtain a quantitative measure of mental health but can conclude whether it has improved, stayed the same, or become worse for each patient, what application of the binomial distribution should the researcher use?

Computer Exercises

1. For Ihno's data, perform a binomial test on the gender variable, with $P = .5$. Can you reject the null hypothesis that Ihno's statistics class is a random sample from a population in which both genders are equally represented? Use the binomial test to compare the proportion of women in the class against the null hypothesis of $P = .55$. Can you reject the null hypothesis in this case?

2. Redo the binomial test on gender (with $P = .5$, only) separately for each college major.

3. In this exercise you will be testing the (two-valued) grouping variable you created from a median split of the phobia scores for the computer exercises in Chapter 14. Perform a binomial test for $P = .5$ separately for each gender. Explain the relationship between the tests of the two genders.

4. If you have not already done this for a previous exercise, create a variable that is the difference between baseline and prequiz heart rate. Then recode this new variable so that negative difference scores are assigned a numeric score of 1, positive difference scores are assigned a score of 2, and zero differences are assigned as missing. Perform a binomial test on this new variable with $P = .5$. Compare the p value from this test with the p value you obtained for the matched-pairs t test on the same two variables in Chapter 7. Explain the relationship between these two alternative tests of the same difference scores.

5. If your software has the capability, request a sign test of the baseline versus the prequiz heart rates, and compare the results to those from the binomial test in the previous exercise.

6. Repeat Exercise 5 for the baseline and prequiz anxiety scores. (If your software does not have the sign test, repeat Exercise 4 for the anxiety variable.)

Bridge to SPSS

SPSS has a number of options for creating and deriving probabilities from a binomial distribution, and it makes some arbitrary choices without informing you. So you will need to read this section carefully. Note that the procedures we discuss in this section have been moved to the "Legacy Dialogs" section of the Nonparametric Tests menu in the most recent versions of SPSS.

The Binomial Test

If one of your variables has only two different numerical values, you can perform a binomial test on that variable by selecting **Binomial** from the (Legacy Dialogs of the) Analyze/Nonparametric Tests menu. Only numeric variables will appear in the list on the left side of the dialog box, from which they can be moved to the Test Variable List. The default value for the Test Proportion is .5, but it can be changed to any value between .001 and .999. For instance, suppose you have a variable called "prefhand" with string values of "right," "left," and "ambi." If you want to test whether you have a significantly greater proportion of left-handed people in your study than in the larger population, you can type your best estimate of the relevant population proportion in the Test Proportion box. However, before you can run the binomial test, you will first have to recode the words *right* and *left* into two different numbers, and replace the *ambi*s with missing values. Under the list of variables, there is a Define Dichotomy choice, and if you use the default setting, **Get from data**, SPSS will *not* run the binomial test on any variable in the test list for which it reads three or more different values. However, there is another way to run the binomial test. If your test variable is numeric and multivalued, you can select **Cut point** to define your dichotomy, and then type in a value. SPSS will base the binomial test on the number of cases that fall below versus above the cut point on your test variable.

Assuming that the Test Proportion is left unchanged at the default value of .5, the basic output box for the binomial test gives you the N and the proportion for each of the two categories, and a *two-tailed p* value. If your total N is 25 or less, the p value you will get is labeled **Exact Sig. (2-tailed)**, and it is based on adding the exact binomial probabilities for your value of X (the number out of N that fall in the first of your two groups) and all possible values for X that are more extreme than yours, in either tail. If your N is greater than 25, the p value you will get is labeled **Asymp. Sig. (2-tailed)**, and it is based on calculating a z score corresponding to your value for X and doubling the area beyond that z score. (*Asymp.* is short for *asymptotic*—a term that is meant to remind you that the normal approximation to the binomial distribution does not become perfect until N reaches infinity.) To improve the approximation when N is considerably less than infinite, SPSS uses a correction for continuity in its calculation of the z score for a binomial distribution; the magnitude of the numerator of the z score is reduced by .5 before it is divided by the denominator. If you want a one-tailed p value, you will have to simply divide the two-tailed value that SPSS gives you in half.

If you change the Test Proportion to a value other than .5, you will be dealing with a binomial distribution that is not symmetrical, and you will no longer get two-tailed p values for your binomial test. In such cases, SPSS will give you a one-tailed p value and label it as such. Note that when P is not set to .5, it matters that SPSS automatically compares the proportion in the first group (defined as the group associated with the *lower* numerical value) to your test proportion. For example, if lefties are coded with a *higher* value than righties, your test proportion should be based on the population proportion of right-handed people in the population (e.g., .8). Otherwise, SPSS will compare the proportion of righties in your data (say, .7) with the population proportion of lefties that you typed in (e.g., .2) and will not give you the p value that you want.

Also note that SPSS always gives you the p value for the *tail* of the binomial distribution—that is, the portion of the binomial distribution that begins at your actual proportion and heads away from the test proportion. SPSS assumes that you would not want to know the p value if you picked the wrong tail. Of course, you can always subtract the one-tailed Sig. value that SPSS gives you from 1.0 to get the other portion of the binomial distribution.

The Sign Test

You could perform a sign test that compares two variables measured on the same cases (e.g., a "before" and an "after" variable) by computing a new variable that is the difference of the first two and then performing a binomial test on the difference scores using zero as the cut point. Fortunately, SPSS makes this procedure even easier by including the sign test as one of the choices in the dialog box that opens when you select **2 Related Samples** from the Analyze/Nonparametric Tests menu. Just select *two* variables from the list at the left of the dialog box, as you would for a matched-pairs *t* test, and move the *pair* over to the Test Pair(s) List. Then, under Test Type, click on the check box for **Sign**. When you click **OK**, SPSS will perform a binomial test by comparing the proportion of positive (or negative—the results are the same) difference scores (zero differences are excluded) to a test proportion (i.e., null hypothesis) of .5. The other two test choices are the Wilcoxon and McNemar tests. The first of these is the Wilcoxon matched-pairs test that we described in Chapter 8.

Chapter 17
Chi-Square Tests

PREVIEW

Chi Square and Goodness of Fit: One-Variable Problems

What are the procedures for testing the hypothesis that more than two population frequencies are distributed in a specified way?

What is the observed frequency? The expected frequency? The chi-square statistic?

What is the correct statistical model to use with frequency data?

How do we test chi square for statistical significance?

How does the chi-square test compare to the binomial test in the two-category case?

When should chi square not be used?

Chi Square as a Test of Independence: Two-Variable Problems

What are the procedures for testing the significance of the relationship between two variables when data are expressed in terms of frequencies?

How do we compute chi square from a 2×2 table?

Measures of Strength of Association in Two-Variable Tables

Why is it desirable to convert a statistically significant value of chi square into a measure that shows the strength of the relationship between the two variables?

What are the two most common categorical measures of strength of relationship? When should each of these measures be used?

Summary

Exercises

Thought Questions

Computer Exercises

Bridge to SPSS

Chi Square and the Goodness of Fit: One-Variable Problems

Consider the following problem:

A publisher introduces three titles for a new literary magazine for women—*Today, Choice,* and *New Alternatives.* She wonders whether these titles will be equally popular among female consumers. To test the hypothesis of equal preference, she obtains a random sample of 177 women and asks them which *one* of the three titles they like best. She finds that 65 women prefer *Today,* 60 prefer *Choice,* and 52 prefer *New Alternatives.* Are these results sufficient reason to reject the null hypothesis that equal numbers of women *in the population* prefer each of the three titles? Or are these results likely to occur as a result of sampling error if the preferences in the population are in fact equal, in which case the null hypothesis of equality in the population should be retained?

In the previous chapter, you saw how to test null hypotheses when events are constrained to only two possible categories. In this chapter, you will learn how to deal with data that consist of the number of objects (usually persons) falling in any one of a number of categories. That is, the data are in terms of empirically observed *frequencies* for *more than two* categories that can then be compared to frequencies expected on the basis of some hypothesis.

The data for the example just given consist of frequencies or head counts—that is, *how many* prefer a particular alternative—and the objective is to decide whether it is reasonable to conclude that the corresponding population frequencies are distributed in a specified way. Thus, in the example, the publisher now knows how many women in the sample prefer each title to the other two. However, what she would like to know is whether it is reasonable to conclude that the population from which her sample was randomly drawn is equally divided with regard to preference for the three titles.

Testing hypotheses about frequency data that fall in more than two category-sets is similar in strategy to the tests we performed on dichotomous data in the previous chapter. However, to find probabilities associated with observed frequencies involving three or more outcomes for each event, we cannot use the binomial distribution. With three categories, we would need a trinomial distribution. In the general case of any number of possible categories, the appropriate statistical model would be the *multinomial distribution.*

Just as the normal distribution can be used to approximate the more exact results from the binomial distribution, a convenient statistic can be calculated from multicategory frequency data. The distribution of this statistic can be reasonably approximated by what is known as the **chi-square distribution**. (An exception does occur if you are dealing with very small frequencies, a problem we discuss later in this chapter.) This statistic is named after the distribution it tends to follow, so it is called the **chi-square statistic** and is symbolized by the lowercase Greek letter chi (pronounced *kie* to rhyme with *pie*) squared: χ^2.

Because we may be dealing with any number of categories, we can no longer use X to represent the frequency of one category and $N - X$ as the number in the other category. Instead, we will need to keep track of the **observed frequency (f_o)** in each category. Similarly, rather than dealing with a single value that is expected for X according to the null hypothesis (i.e., NP), each category will have its own **expected frequency (f_e)**. The chi-square statistic is based on the discrepancy between the observed and expected frequency for each category, as expressed in the following formula:

$$\chi^2 = \sum \frac{(f_o - f_e)^2}{f_e} \qquad \text{Formula 17.1}$$

where

f_o = observed frequency
f_e = expected (null-hypothetical) frequency
$\sum$ is taken over all the categories

If the differences between the observed frequencies and the expected frequencies are small, χ^2 will be small. The greater the difference between the observed frequencies and those expected under the null hypothesis, the larger χ^2 will be. If the differences between the observed and expected values are so large collectively as to occur by chance only .05 or less of the time when the null hypothesis is true, the null hypothesis is rejected.

The problem given at the beginning of this chapter is concerned with differences in choice among different categories (or levels) of a *single* variable, so the appropriate statistical analysis is often referred to as a **one-way chi-square test**. In that example, the one variable is magazine title preference, and each respondent selects one of three possible choices.

To analyze such a problem, the first step is to set up a table with the three alternatives and tabulate the observed frequencies. (See Table 17.1.) Next, the expected frequencies must be stated before χ^2 can be determined. The null hypothesis states that the three titles are equally preferred, so *if* it is true, you would expect the sample of 177 women to be equally divided among the three categories. Thus, the expected frequencies under the null hypothesis are 177/3, or 59, 59, and 59. (Note that the sum of the expected frequencies must be equal to the sum of the observed frequencies.) Is it likely or unlikely that observed frequencies of 65, 60, and 52 would occur if the population frequencies are exactly equal? In other words, are the observed frequencies of 65, 60, and 52 significantly different from the expected frequencies of 59, 59, and 59? To answer this question, χ^2 has been computed in Table 17.1. Note that *each* value of $(f_o - f_e)^2$ is divided by its own expected frequency. (All the expected frequencies happen to be equal in this particular problem, but this will not always be true as it depends on the particular null hypothesis.) The resulting three values are then summed to obtain χ^2, which is equal to 1.46.

In order to test the significance of χ^2 using a specified criterion of significance, the obtained value is referred to Table H in the Appendix with the appropriate degrees of freedom (df). Note that in this table,

Table 17.1 Chi-Square Test for Literary Title Choices

Title	Observed frequency (f_o)	Expected frequency (f_e)	$f_o - f_e$	$(f_o - f_e)^2$	$\dfrac{(f_o - f_e)^2}{f_e}$
Today	65	59	6	36	.610
Choice	60	59	1	1	.017
New Alternatives	52	59	−7	49	.831

$$\chi^2 = \sum \frac{(f_o - f_e)^2}{f_e} = 1.458$$

Figure 17.1

Chi-Square Distribution for $df = 1$ and $df = 6$

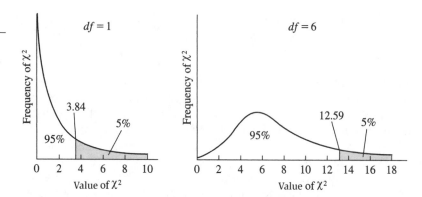

there is a different value of χ^2 for every df. Chi square, like t, yields a family of curves, with the shape of a particular curve depending on the df. (See Figure 17.1.) For the χ^2 distributions, however, the df is based on the number of *categories,* rather than on the sample size as in the case of the t distributions. In the one-variable case, the df are equal to $k - 1$, where k is equal to the number of categories of the variable. Thus, in the present problem, $df = 3 - 1 = 2$. For χ^2 to be significant at the .05 level, therefore, the obtained value must be equal to or greater than 5.99. Since the obtained value is only 1.46, the null hypothesis is retained; there is not sufficient reason to reject the null hypothesis that the frequencies in the population are equal. Therefore, we have an insufficient basis for concluding that any particular title or titles is (are) preferred.

Expected Frequencies From a Preexisting Population

In experimental applications, the null hypothesis for a one-way chi-square test is, most commonly, that all of the expected frequencies are equal. However, if you are dealing with preexisting groups in the population, this need not be the case. Suppose it is claimed that a local newspaper has a political slant, and as proof of this claim, it is offered that its readership does not reflect the political composition of the area it serves. For instance, if a survey of 210 readers found that 120 were registered Democrats,

60 were registered Republicans, and 30 were Independents, the expected frequencies to test against would not necessarily be 70 (i.e., 210/3) for each category. If the null hypothesis is that the readership *does* reflect the political affiliations of the community, it would make sense to derive the expected frequencies from voter registration records for that community. For example, the voter registration percentages might turn out to be: 40% Democrat, 35% Republican, and 25% Independents. In that case, the expected frequencies you would want to use for your one-way chi-square test would be: 84 for Democrats (i.e., .4 × 210), 73.5 for Republicans (i.e., .35 × 210), and 52.5 for Independents (i.e., .25 × 210), which sum to 210. You can see from the survey results that the newspaper does indeed have more Democratic and Independent readers and fewer Republican ones than you would expect from the proportions of political affiliations in that community. However, performing the chi-square test would allow you to determine whether the observed discrepancies are large enough to safely reject the null hypothesis and declare that the newspaper's readership is not a simple reflection of its community's political affiliations.

The preceding example demonstrates why the one-way chi-square test is often called a **goodness-of-fit** test: In that example, we were testing the fit between the political affiliations of the newspaper's readership and the political affiliations of the community served by that newspaper. In such cases, it is likely that the purpose of the test would be to reject the null hypothesis and declare a *lack of fit*. However, the one-way chi-square can just as easily be used to test the fit between the proportions of particular responses in your data and the specific proportions that can be predicted from a theory you want to test. In this type of example, the expected frequencies are not coming from a null hypothesis but rather from an alternative hypothesis based on your theory. Therefore, you do not want to reject the hypothesis being tested; instead, you would be hoping for a very small value of the χ^2 statistic (ideally, close to zero) that would demonstrate a good fit between your data and your predictions.

As an example of a case in which you would be hoping for the χ^2 value to be as far from statistical significance as possible, imagine that you are observing whether participants choose to sit on the right, on the left, or in the middle, when offered a choice of three chairs facing a small stage. Suppose that your theory predicts that people who are "purely" right handed will choose the left seat; those who are "purely" left handed will choose the right seat; and all others will choose to sit in the middle. In this example, the expected frequencies would again depend on proportions in the population from which your participants are drawn—specifically, the proportions of people who are purely right handed, purely left handed, or somewhere between. If these proportions were known to be .6, .1, and .3, respectively, and you plan to record the seating choice for 60 different participants, your expected frequencies would be: 36 (i.e., .6 × 60) for the right chair; 6 (i.e., .1 × 60) for the left chair; and 18 (i.e., .3 × 60) for the middle chair. If the actual preferences were to come out roughly equal for the three chairs (about 20 participants choosing each), you would not be happy at all. Even if the chi-square test were to fall short of statistical significance, the fact that the χ^2 statistic would not be very small in this case would be discouraging and should cause you to rethink your theory concerning the connection between handedness and seat preference.

The Relationship Between the Binomial Test and the Chi-Square Test With Two Categories

Based on comments that some of her students have made, Ihno believes that statistics students in general do not want their final examinations to be cumulative (i.e., encompassing all of the material from the beginning to the end of the course). Rather, the students seem to want the final exam to cover only the second half of the course. She decides to use her own class as though it were a random sample of all statistics students, and she asks her students to turn in anonymous notes stating whether they want the final exam to be cumulative or not. Of the 75 students who hand in notes, Ihno finds that 15 students are in favor of cumulative final exams and 60 students are against them. If the null hypothesis is that the population of statistics students is equally divided on this issue, the expected frequencies are $75/2 = 37.5$ for each category. (f_e's frequently come out to fractional values, even though it is not possible for half a student to vote one way or the other.) The computation of the chi-square statistic for this problem is shown in Table 17.2.

Because the calculated chi-square statistic, 27, is larger than the critical value of 3.84 from Table H for $2 - 1 = 1$ df using the .05 criterion of significance, the null hypothesis is rejected; it is *not* reasonable to assume that the student population is evenly divided on this issue. By inspecting the f_o, it may be concluded that a majority is opposed to final examinations that are cumulative. The χ^2 value of 27 would have been significant even if we used an alpha of .001 (e.g., we are performing 50 such tests and use the Bonferroni correction to adjust the alpha for each test), because 27 exceeds $\chi^2_{.001}(1) = 10.83$.

Because the situation just described involves only two categories (for and against), the null hypothesis can also be tested by using the binomial distribution. Given that $P = .5$ and N is rather large, we can use

Table 17.2 Chi-Square Test for Attitude Toward Cumulative Final Examinations

Attitude	f_o	f_e	$f_o - f_e$	$(f_o - f_e)^2$	$\dfrac{(f_o - f_e)^2}{f_e}$
For	15	37.5	−22.5	506.25	13.5
Against	60	37.5	22.5	506.25	13.5
	75	75.0			

$$\chi^2 = \sum \frac{(f_o - f_e)^2}{f_e} = 27$$

Formula 16.5 from the previous chapter to create a z score:

$$z = \frac{2X - N}{\sqrt{N}} = \frac{2\,(60) - 75}{\sqrt{75}} = \frac{45}{8.66} = 5.196$$

If you square this z score, you will get 27, which is the value we calculated for chi square. (If in this formula you used 15, the number of students who voted "for," instead of 60, the z score would have the same magnitude but the opposite sign, which would yield the same p value and make no difference at all after squaring.) Squaring the normal distribution yields a chi-square distribution with 1 degree of freedom. For example, the .05 critical value for $\chi^2(1)$ is 3.84, which equals 1.96 squared.

Some Precautions Involving the Use of χ^2

The χ^2 tests just described can be validly performed only when the observations are *independent*. That is, no response should be related to or dependent upon any other response. For example, it would be incorrect to apply χ^2 with $N = 100$ to the true-false responses of five schizophrenic patients to 20 questionnaire items. The 100 responses are not independent of each other, because the 20 responses given by each patient must be assumed to be mutually related. This assumption of independence is also critical to the validity of the binomial test.

Second, any case, participant, and so on must fall in *one and only one* category. Thus, in the problem involving the preference for magazine titles, each participant was asked to choose the one title she most preferred.

Third, the computations must be based on all the cases in the sample. In the previous example, a category of "for" as well as "against" had to be included so that χ^2 would be based on the total frequency of 75, the total size of the sample. As a check, the sum of the observed frequencies *must* be equal to the sum of the expected frequencies.

One final precaution is concerned with the size of the expected frequencies. Like the z-score formula for the binomial test, chi square is actually an approximate test for obtaining the probability values for the observed frequencies (i.e., the probability of getting the observed frequencies if the null hypothesis is true). This test is based on the expectation that within *any category*, sample frequencies are normally distributed about the population or expected value. Since frequencies cannot be negative, the distribution cannot be normal when the *expected* population values are *close to zero*. The sample frequencies cannot be much below the expected frequency, while they can be much above it—an asymmetric distribution.

Under certain conditions, therefore, you should *not* compute χ^2. For 1 df, all of the *expected* frequencies should be at least 5; this is consistent with the rule for the binomial test—that both NP and $N(1 - P)$ must be at least 5. For 2 df, all expected frequencies should exceed 2. With 3 or more df, if all expected frequencies but one are greater than or equal to 5, and if the one that is not is at least equal to 1, χ^2 is still a good approximation.

In general, the greater the df, the more lenient the requirement for minimum expected frequencies.

Chi Square as a Test of Independence: Two-Variable Problems

In the preceding section, χ^2 was used to test some a priori hypothesis about expected frequencies—that is, a hypothesis about f_e values formulated prior to the experiment—which involved frequency data concerning a single variable. Chi square can also be used, however, to test the significance of *the relationship between two variables when data are expressed in terms of frequencies of joint occurrence.*

Suppose you want to find out if students majoring in psychology differ in their career preferences from students majoring in economics. If the two variables of major and career choice are *not* related (are *independent*), you would expect the proportion of psychology majors who prefer, say, an academic to an applied career to be the same as the proportion of economics majors who prefer academia. A numerical example in which the proportions are equal for the two majors is shown in Table 17.3. Here, in contrast to one-variable problems, no a priori expected frequencies are involved. You are dealing with the relationship between two variables, each of which may have any number of categories or levels. (In this example, each variable has two levels.) The null hypothesis is that the two variables are independent, which (as you will see) implies a set of expected frequencies. Because there are two variables being jointly tested, the appropriate analysis is usually called a **two-way chi-square test**.

As an illustration of the psychology/economics example just mentioned, in which major is *not* independent of career choice, suppose you have a random sample of 108 psychology majors and a random sample of 72 economics majors. You ask each individual to state which of the two types of careers he or she prefers. With two categories of career type and two undergraduate majors, there are four possible combined categories, or *cells*: econ-applied; econ-academic; psych-applied; psych-academic. The entire analysis is shown in Table 17.4.

As you can see from the main entries in the top half of Table 17.4, 45 econ majors preferred applied careers, 55 psych majors preferred applied careers, 27 econ majors preferred academia, and 53 psych majors preferred academia. The total for the first column (called the *marginal frequency* for that column) indicates that the sample contains 72 (i.e., $45 + 27$) economics majors. The marginal frequency for the second column shows that the sample contains 108 psychology majors. Similarly, the row marginal frequencies indicate that 100 students across both majors preferred an applied career while 80 preferred academia. The total sample size, N, is equal to 180.

The null hypothesis is stated in terms of the independence of the two variables, undergraduate major and career preference.

H_0: major and career preference are independent (*not* related)

H_A: major and career preference *are* related

Table 17.3 Hypothetical Illustration of Perfectly Independent Relationship Between Major and Career Preference, Using Frequency Data

		Undergraduate major		Total
		Economics	Psychology	students
Career preference	Applied	40	60	100
	Academic	32	48	80
	Total	72 +	108 =	180

55.56% of the econ majors (40/72) prefer applied careers; 44.44% (32/72) prefer academia.

55.56% of the psych majors (60/108) prefer applied careers; 44.44% (48/108) prefer academia.

40.00% of the students who prefer applied careers are econ majors (40/100); 60.00% (60/100) are psych majors.

40.00% of the students who prefer academia are econ majors (32/80); 60.00% (48/80) are psych majors.

Thus, there is no relationship between major and career preference.

The expected frequencies, as shown in parentheses in the top half of Table 17.4, are the same as the frequencies used in Table 17.3 to illustrate the independence of the two variables, because independence is what is expected under the null hypothesis for the two-way chi-square test. The procedure for computing the expected frequencies can be summarized as follows: For any cell, the expected value is equal to the product of the two marginal frequencies common to the cell (the row total times the column total) divided by the total N. That is,

$$f_e = \frac{(\text{row total})(\text{column total})}{N} \qquad \text{Formula 17.2}$$

For example, in Table 17.4, the expected frequency for the econ-applied cell is equal to

$$\frac{(100)(72)}{180} = 40$$

Precisely 72/180, or 40.00%, of the sample are economics majors, and 100/180, or 55.56%, of the sample prefer applied careers. So 40.00% of 55.56%, or 22.22%, of the 180 cases, or $(72/180)(100/180)(180) = 40$ of them, would be expected to be economics majors preferring applied careers if there were no relationship between major and career preference in the sample. The other f_e values may be found by simply using Formula 17.2 in each case, based on the same rationale.

The computation of χ^2 is shown in the bottom half of Table 17.4. The resulting value of 2.34 is tested for statistical significance by referring to Table H in the Appendix with the proper df. For a two-variable problem, the df are equal to

$$df = (r-1)(c-1) \qquad \text{Formula 17.3}$$

where
$r = $ number of rows
$c = $ number of columns

Table 17.4 Table of Frequencies Relating Undergraduate Major to Career Preference (Hypothetical Data)*

		Undergraduate major		Total students
		Economics	Psychology	
Career preference	Applied	45 (40)	55 (60)	100
	Academic	27 (32)	53 (48)	80
	Total	72 +	108 =	180

Calculations				
f_o	f_e	$f_o - f_e$	$(f_o - f_e)^2$	$\dfrac{(f_o - f_e)^2}{f_e}$
45	40	5	25	.625
55	60	−5	25	.417
27	32	−5	25	.781
53	48	5	25	.521
				$\chi^2 = 2.344$

*Within each cell, f_e is in parentheses.

For the 2 × 2 table, the degrees of freedom are equal to $(2-1)(2-1)$ $= 1$. The reason why there is 1 df in a 2 × 2 table is as follows: Consider the expected frequency of 40 for the econ-applied cell. Having computed this value, the expected frequency for the psych-applied cell is fixed (not free to vary). This is because the total of the expected frequencies in the first row of the table, like the total of the observed frequencies, must add up to 100—the marginal frequency for that row. Thus, the expected frequency for the psych-applied cell is equal to

$$100 - 40 = 60$$

Similarly, the expected values in the first column must add up to the marginal frequency of 72. Having computed the expected value of 40 for the econ-applied cell, the expected frequency for the econ-academic cell is fixed; it must be

$$72 - 40 = 32$$

Finally, the expected frequency for the psych-academic cell is equal to

$$108 - 60 \text{ (or } 80 - 32) = 48$$

Thus, once any one f_e is known, all the others are automatically determined. In other words, only one f_e is free to vary; the values of the others depend on its value. Therefore, the 2 × 2 table has only 1 df.

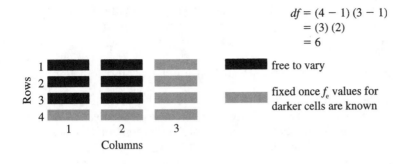

$$df = (4 - 1)(3 - 1)$$
$$= (3)(2)$$
$$= 6$$

Figure 17.2

Illustration of Degrees of Freedom for a 4 × 3 Table

In a larger table, all but one of the f_e values in a given row or column are free to vary. Once they are specified, the last one is fixed by virtue of the fact that the expected frequencies must add up to the marginal frequency. An illustration of the df for a 4 × 3 table is shown in Figure 17.2.

Returning to the problem in Table 17.4, the minimum value of χ^2 required to reject H_0 for $df = 1$ and $\alpha = .05$ is 3.84. Because the obtained value of 2.34 is less than the tabled value, you retain the null hypothesis and conclude that there is not sufficient reason to believe that the variables of undergraduate major and career preference are related.

Computing Formula for 2 × 2 Tables

For a 2 × 2 table, the following formula for χ^2 is equivalent to the one given previously and requires somewhat less work computationally:

Observed frequencies:

A	B
C	D

$$\chi^2 = \frac{N(AD - BC)^2}{(A+B)(C+D)(A+C)(B+D)}$$

Formula 17.4

As an illustration, consider the following 2 × 2 table:

50	70	120
19	41	60
69	111	180 = N

$$\chi^2 = \frac{180(50 \times 41 - 70 \times 19)^2}{(120)(60)(69)(111)}$$

$$= \frac{(180)(720)^2}{(120)(60)(69)(111)}$$

$$= 1.692$$

We leave it as an exercise for the reader to apply the 2×2 shortcut formula to the data in Table 17.4 and verify that it yields the same chi-square value as the longer method shown in that table.

Two-Way Chi-Square Example With Multiple Levels for Both Variables

The chi-square statistical procedure discussed in this section can be used for two-variable problems with any number of levels for each variable. To illustrate, consider a new environmental treatment that is designed to improve the general mental health of all inpatient psychiatric patients and facilitate the effectiveness of whatever other treatments they are receiving. (The environmental treatment could involve redecorating the ward in cheerful colors, playing soothing music, or even releasing pleasant aromas.) Suppose that this environmental manipulation is implemented in a large psychiatric facility in which 300 patients reside: 138 have been diagnosed with schizophrenia, 88 with bipolar disorder, 42 with major depressive disorder, and 32 with borderline personality disorder. After 3 months of living in the new environment, each patient is assessed by the hospital staff as having either improved, remained the same, or worsened with respect to his or her state of mental health. The (hypothetical) data for this experiment, along with the calculations needed to obtain the chi-square statistic, are displayed in Table 17.5.

As in the 2×2 chi-square design, the expected frequency for a given cell is obtained by multiplying the row total for the cell by the column total and dividing by the total N. For example, f_e for the Schizophrenic/No change cell is:

$$\frac{(200)(138)}{300} = 92.0$$

The computed value of χ^2 of 27.55 (see bottom of Table 17.5) exceeds the tabled value for $(r-1)(c-1) = (3-1)(4-1)$ or 6 df of 12.59 at the .05 level of significance. Though you might have expected amounts of improvement to be independent of diagnosis, the analysis indicates that you should reject H_0 and conclude that psychiatric diagnosis and response to the new environment are related.

Note that if you ignore the middle row of the data ("No change"), you could perform a sign test on the row totals to determine whether, across all diagnoses, patients were more likely to improve than to worsen. You could also perform sign tests for each diagnosis separately, but if you perform a two-way (4×2) chi-square test (without the middle row), you accomplish something that the sign test cannot do. You are testing the differences in the proportions of improvement among the four diagnoses against the null hypothesis that all four proportions are equal to each other (not that they are equal to .5). Adding the middle category of "No change" complicates the interpretation of the results, but it also gives you additional data and greater power to detect differences among the diagnostic groups.

If you perform smaller chi-square tests for follow-up purposes, you should use the Bonferroni correction. That is, the alpha you use for each of these tests should be .05 divided by the number of follow-up tests you plan to conduct.

Table 17.5 Table of Frequencies Relating Treatment Response to Psychiatric Diagnosis

Response	Psychiatric diagnosis				Row total
	Schizophrenic	Bipolar	Depressed	Borderline	
Improved	36	8	14	2	60
No change	84	72	18	26	200
Worse	18	8	10	4	40
Column Total	138	88	42	32	300

Calculations				
f_o	f_e	$f_o - f_e$	$(f_o - f_e)^2$	$\dfrac{(f_o - f_e)^2}{f_e}$
36	27.60	8.40	70.56	2.56
8	17.60	−9.60	92.16	5.24
14	8.40	5.60	31.36	3.73
2	6.40	−4.40	19.36	3.02
84	92.00	−8.00	64.00	.70
72	58.67	13.33	177.69	3.03
18	28.00	−10.00	100.00	3.57
26	21.33	4.67	21.81	1.02
18	18.40	−0.40	.16	0.01
8	11.73	−3.73	13.91	1.19
10	5.60	4.40	19.36	3.46
4	4.27	−0.27	.07	.02
				$\chi^2 = 27.55$

One important application of the chi-square test is as an alternative to a parametric test when your quantitative data have a very unusual distribution. (For example, the data have multiple modes or extreme outliers on one or both ends of the distribution.) For the psychiatric environment experiment just described, the researcher may have collected clinical ratings for each patient at the beginning and end of the 3-month period, with plans to perform a one-way analysis of variance (ANOVA) to compare the patient groups on the difference scores. However, the difference scores may be distributed so strangely that the researcher feels more comfortable simply categorizing those differences as exhibiting some improvement, some decline, or virtually no change at all. Considerable statistical power can be lost when converting precise measurements to just a few categories, but this conversion is justified (and even encouraged) if your data seriously violate the assumptions that underlie the planned parametric test. By just ignoring such violations, it is quite possible that you would be committing a higher rate of Type I errors than the alpha you are using would indicate.

Measures of Strength of Association in Two-Variable Tables

The χ^2 test of independence allows you to make decisions about *whether* there is a relationship between two variables, using frequency data. Thus, if H_0 is rejected, you can conclude that there *is* a statistically significant relationship between the two variables. As we have pointed out frequently in this text, however, statistical significance does not indicate the *strength* of the relationship; a significant result suggests only that the relationship in the population is unlikely to be zero. Here again, it is desirable to have a measure of the strength of the relationship—that is, an index of the degree of correlation. We next discuss such a measure.

The Phi Coefficient (ϕ) for 2 x 2 Tables

Recall that the chi-square statistic was not statistically significant for the relationship between undergraduate major and type of career preference. Suppose, however, that the researcher, undeterred, collects data for twice as many students, and the results come out proportionally the same as they did in Table 17.4. That is, the frequency in every individual cell is doubled as well. The data for these 360 students are shown in Table 17.6.

Using Formula 17.4 (for 2 × 2 tables), we find that not only have N and all of the observed frequencies doubled, but the value for χ^2 is also exactly twice as large as it was in Table 17.4. This new value for χ^2 is now statistically significant: $4.688 > 3.84$. Does it seem reasonable that increasing N, without changing the proportions, should turn a nonsignificant result into one that *is* significant?

Just like t or F, χ^2 depends on sample size; it tells you about statistical significance but says nothing about the size of the effect. To resolve this

Table 17.6 **Table of Frequencies Relating Undergrad Major to Career Preference**

		Undergraduate major		
		Economics	Psychology	Total students
Career preference	Applied	90	110	200
	Academic	54	106	160
	Total	144	216	360 $= N$

$$\chi^2 = \frac{360\,[(90 \times 106) - (110 \times 54)]^2}{200 \times 160 \times 144 \times 216}$$

$$= \frac{4,665,600.000}{995,328,000}$$

$$= 4.688$$

shortcoming, you need a measure of the strength of the relationship between two dichotomous variables that depends only on the proportions and does not change just because every frequency is, for instance, doubled. Such a measure does exist, and it is easy to calculate. For a 2 × 2 table, χ^2 can be converted to a correlation coefficient called the **phi coefficient** (symbolized by ϕ) by the following formula:

$$\phi = \sqrt{\frac{\chi^2}{N}} \qquad\qquad \text{Formula 17.5}$$

Thus, for the data in Table 17.6,

$$\phi = \sqrt{\frac{4.688}{360}}$$

$$= \sqrt{.013}$$

$$= .114$$

If you compare Table 17.4 to Table 17.6, you will see that N gets doubled (from 180 to 360), but so does χ^2 (from 2.344 to 4.688). Because 4.688/360 equals 2.344/180, the ratio under the square root sign in the formula for ϕ does not change (it remains .013), and therefore ϕ is also .114 for the original data in Table 17.4.

The ϕ is interpreted as a Pearson r. In fact, it *is* a Pearson r; you would get the same answer of .114 if you assigned scores of 1 and 2 to major (e.g., 1 = economics, 2 = psychology) and to career preference (1 = prefers academia, 2 = prefers an applied career) and then computed the correlation between the two variables using one of the usual formulas for the Pearson r given in Chapter 9. Thus the absolute value of ϕ varies between 0 and 1. The larger the value of ϕ, the stronger is the relationship between the two variables. When the assignment of score values is arbitrary (as it is in the present case; it would be just as acceptable to score 2 for economics majors and 1 for psychology majors), the sign of ϕ is irrelevant, and ϕ is therefore reported without sign. Just as with the point-biserial r, you must look at the data to determine the direction of the findings (which, in our example, is that the proportion of economics majors who prefer applied to academic careers is greater than that proportion for psychology majors).

In the present example, you would conclude from the value of ϕ that the relationship between major and career preference in the population, while likely to be greater than zero, is also likely to be fairly weak. In other words, there are likely to be numerous exceptions to the conclusion. This is evidenced, for instance, by the 54 out of 144 economics majors who expressed a preference for an academic career (see Table 17.6). The phi coefficient sums up this information conveniently in a readily interpretable correlation.

Note that there is no need to carry out a special significance test for ϕ. It has already been done with χ^2. In fact, the χ^2 test on a 2 × 2 table can just as well be viewed as testing the null hypothesis that the population ϕ value equals zero. When χ^2 is sufficiently large, this hypothesis is rejected, which then suggests that there is some degree of relationship other than zero.

Cramér's Phi Coefficient (ϕ_C)

When one (or both) of the two categorical variables whose relationship you are exploring has more than two levels, you cannot simply assign arbitrary numbers to their levels and calculate a Pearson r. The magnitude of the r will depend on how you assign the arbitrary numbers to the levels of any variable with more than two categories, so it will be uninterpretable. However, there is a strength-of-relationship index that is closely related to the phi coefficient and can be used with tables larger than 2×2. It is known as **Cramér's ϕ**, sometimes symbolized as ϕ_C. It is applicable to any $r \times c$ contingency table, and always varies between 0 and 1 regardless of the size of the table. It is simply

$$\text{Cramér's } \phi = \sqrt{\frac{\chi^2}{N(k-1)}} \qquad \text{Formula 17.6}$$

where

$$k = \text{smaller of } r \text{ or } c \text{ (or, when } r = c, k = r = c)$$

For the example in Table 17.5, which is a 3×4 table,

$$\phi_C = \sqrt{\frac{27.55}{300\,(3-1)}}$$

$$= \sqrt{.0459}$$

$$= .214$$

This degree of relationship is somewhere between small and moderate in size. For ϕ_C, like ordinary ϕ, and other correlational measures of effect size, a value of .1 is considered to be small, .3 is considered to be of medium size, and .5 is large.

Summary

Chi-square tests are designed to be used with *frequency* data.

$$\chi^2 = \sum \frac{(f_o - f_e)^2}{f_e} \qquad \text{Formula 17.1}$$

where

$f_o = $ observed frequency
$f_e = $ expected frequency

One-Variable Problems

$$df = k - 1$$

where

k = number of categories of the variable

Expected frequencies are readily determined from the null hypothesis. For example, if H_0 specifies that people in the population are equally divided among the k categories, f_e for each category is equal to N/k (where N = number of people in the sample).

Two-Variable Problems: Test of Association

$$df = (r - 1)(c - 1)$$ Formula 17.3

where

r = number of rows
c = number of columns

For a cell in a given row and column, the expected frequency is equal to

$$f_e = \frac{(\text{row total})(\text{column total})}{N}$$ Formula 17.2

For a 2 × 2 table, the following formula for χ^2 is equivalent to determining expected frequencies and using the usual chi-square formula, but does so in one step and therefore requires somewhat less work computationally:

$$\begin{array}{|c|c|} \hline A & B \\ \hline C & D \\ \hline \end{array} \quad \chi^2 = \frac{N(AD - BC)^2}{(A + B)(C + D)(A + C)(B + D)}$$

Formula 17.4

Measures of Strength of Association in Two-Variable Tables

For 2 × 2 tables, compute the phi coefficient:

$$\phi = \sqrt{\frac{\chi^2}{N}}$$ Formula 17.5

ϕ is interpreted like any other Pearson r.
    For *larger tables,* compute Cramér's ϕ:

$$\text{Cramérs } \phi = \sqrt{\frac{\chi^2}{N(k - 1)}}$$ Formula 17.6

where

$$k = \text{the } \textit{smaller} \text{ of } r \text{ (number of rows) or } c \text{ (number of columns);}$$
$$k = \text{either one if } r = c$$

These two effect-size measures are statistically significant if χ^2 is statistically significant. For both ϕ and ϕ_c, the following are the conventional guidelines: .1 is small; .3 is moderate; and .5 is large.

Some Precautions on the Use of χ^2

χ^2 should be used only when the observations are independent—that is, when no observation is related to or dependent on any other observation. The significance test of χ^2 is not sufficiently accurate when either of the following conditions applies:

(a) $df = 1$, and any *expected* frequency is less than 5.

(b) $df = 2$, and any *expected* frequency is less than 3.

Exercises

1. Out of 100 psychiatric patients given a new form of treatment, 60 improved, while 40 got worse.

   (a) Use a chi-square test to decide whether you can reject the null hypothesis that the treatment is totally ineffective (i.e., that patients are equally likely to improve or get worse).

   (b) Redo the significance test in part (a) using the z score formula (i.e., normal approximation) for the binomial test. Explain the relationship between the z score you calculated in this part and the χ^2 value you calculated in part (a).

2. A developmental researcher has observed that in a random sample of 60 toddlers, 27 preferred blue toys, 19 preferred red toys, and 14 preferred green toys. Perform a chi-square test of the null hypothesis that, in the entire population of toddlers, the preference for these three colors is equally divided.

3. Repeat the previous exercise, except that this time there are 79 toddlers choosing among toys that come in a total of four different colors. The number of toddlers preferring each color is as follows:

   (a) 21 chose red, 14 chose blue, 26 chose yellow, 18 chose green.

   (b) The same toddlers were tested a year later with the following results: 28 chose red, 20 chose blue, 9 chose yellow, 22 chose green.

4. At Bigbrain University, the typical grade distribution is A, 15%; B, 25%; C, 45%; D, 10%; F, 5%. The grades given by two professors

are shown here. For each one (separately), test the null hypothesis that the professor is a typical grader, using a one-variable chi-square analysis.

(a) Professor 1						(b) Professor 2				
A	B	C	D	F		A	B	C	D	F
f_o 7	13	22	4	6		13	12	8	3	3

5. A psychologist wants to test the hypothesis that college women will do better on a particular type of problem-solving task than will college men. He obtains the following results:

Sex	Result on problem-solving task	
	Succeed	Fail
Male	12	18
Female	10	10

(a) Test the null hypothesis that sex and success on the problem-solving task are independent. Does this mean the same as a statement about whether the percent success differs between males and females?

(b) Calculate the phi coefficient for these data. Does it look like the psychologist is dealing with a small, medium, or large effect?

6. A bond issue is to be put before the voters in a forthcoming election. An opinion poll company obtains a random sample of 200 registered voters and asks them what party they belong to and how they intend to vote on the bond issue. The results are as follows:

Political party	Prospective vote on bond issue		
	Yes	No	Undecided
Democratic	20	30	10
Republican	30	30	20
Independent	10	40	10

(a) Test the null hypothesis that political party and prospective vote on the bond issue are independent. What is your conclusion?

(b) Calculate Cramér's ϕ for these data. Does it look like there's a strong association between party affiliation and attitude toward this particular bond issue?

7. Suppose that students majoring in the natural sciences, social sciences, and humanities were asked whether they were in favor of

having greater student participation in academic decisions at their college. The data from the survey appear in the following table.

	Natural sciences	Social sciences	Humanities
In favor	20	18	16
Neutral	8	8	30
Against	6	19	18

(a) Compute the two-way chi-square test for these data. Can you reject the null hypothesis that students' attitudes on this question are not at all related to their academic areas? What critical value did you use to make your decision?

(b) Calculate the appropriate measure for the strength of relationship between the two variables, regardless of your decision in part (a). How strong does the relationship appear to be?

8. Repeat the previous exercise with the data in the following table. Note that the marginal frequencies have not changed, so you do not have to recompute the expected frequencies.

	Natural sciences	Social sciences	Humanities
In favor	11	17	26
Neutral	10	15	21
Against	13	13	17

(a) Now can you reject the null hypothesis that students' attitudes on this question are not at all related to their academic areas?

(b) Calculate the appropriate measure for the strength of relationship between the two variables, regardless of your decision in part (a). How strong does the relationship appear to be?

Thought Questions

1. A researcher wants to test the null hypothesis that three types of television programming are preferred equally by college students. She obtains a sample of 139 college students and finds that 57 prefer sitcoms, 44 prefer sports, and 38 prefer reality shows. What statistical procedure should be used to test this null hypothesis? Why?

2. The same researcher wants to test the relationship between gender differences and preference for the three television shows. For the data in Question 1, she finds the following: Of the 57 students who prefer sitcoms, 29 are female and 28 are male. Of the 44 who prefer sports, 9 are female and 35 are male. Of the 38 who prefer reality shows, 30 are female and 8 are male. What statistical procedure should be used to test this null hypothesis? Why?

3. Suppose that the same researcher asks the 139 students to vote yes or no as to whether they like each of the three types of television shows and obtains the following results: for sitcoms, 92 yes and 47 no; for sports, 61 yes and 78 no; for reality shows, 74 yes and 65 no. What type of chi-square analysis should be used to analyze these data, if any? What assumption of chi-square tests is being violated in this example? Explain.

4. (a) When using chi square for a two-variable problem, why is it desirable to compute either the ϕ or Cramér's ϕ when statistically significant results are obtained? (b) When should each of the coefficients in part (a) be used?

Computer Exercises

1. (a) Perform a one-way chi-square test to determine whether you can reject the null hypothesis that, at Ihno's university, there are the same number of students majoring in each of the five areas represented in Ihno's class, if you assume that her students represent a random sample with respect to major area.

   (b) Perform the test in part (a) separately for both the males and the females in Ihno's class.

2. Suppose that Ihno obtains registration information from her university and finds that the numbers of undergraduates who have declared each of the five majors are as follows: psychology, 400; pre-med, 310; biology, 270; sociology, 140; economics, 240. Can you reject the null hypothesis that Ihno's statistics class is a random sample from the undergraduate population of her university?

3. Conduct a two-way chi-square analysis of Ihno's data to test the null hypothesis that the proportion of females is the same for each of the five represented majors in the entire university population. Request a statistic to describe the strength of the relationship between gender and major.

4. Conduct a two-way chi-square analysis of Ihno's data to test the null hypothesis that the (two-valued) grouping variable you previously created from a median split of the phobia scores is independent of gender. Request the phi coefficient for this relationship. Use your software to compute the correlation directly between the high/low phobia variable and gender, and compare this value to the phi coefficient.

5. Create a grouping variable that equals 1 if a student has taken no more than one college math course prior to registering for statistics and 2 if the student has taken two or more math courses. Test whether taking more than one prior math course is independent of a student's major. Request a statistic to describe the strength of the relationship between these two variables.

Bridge to SPSS

The Analyze menu selection that SPSS uses to access one-way chi-square tests bears no resemblance to the menu selection that leads to a two-way chi-square test. It is not obvious why this is so, but both types of the test are easily obtained, as described next.

One-Way Chi-Square Tests

If one of your variables has been coded with at least two different numerical values, you can perform a one-way chi-square test on that variable by selecting **Chi-Square** from the (Legacy Dialogs of the) Analyze/ Nonparametric Tests menu. The chi-square test dialog box is similar to the one for the binomial test, but by necessity there are two major differences. First, replacing the Define Dichotomy choice is the selection of the Expected Range. As in the Define Dichotomy choice, the default setting is **Get from data**. In the chi-square test, this setting means that the number of categories for your one-way chi-square test (i.e., k) will be determined by the number of different values that SPSS reads for a variable that you selected (i.e., moved to the Test Variable list). The values of your test variable can be numeric codes that have been arbitrarily assigned to your categories (e.g., 1 = African American; 2 = European American; 3 = Asian American). However, the values can be real integer quantities, such as the number of children in a family. If there are quite a few possible values and you want to set some limits to avoid extreme values that occur quite infrequently, you can accomplish that by selecting **Use specified range** instead of **Get from data** and entering both upper and lower limits.

The second major difference from the binomial test is that Test Proportion is replaced by Expected Values. The default choice is **All categories equal**, and in the two-category case, this is equivalent to the binomial test's default Test Proportion of .5. This choice is often appropriate for experimental null hypotheses in which you want to see if some categorical distinction makes a difference to, or is even noticed by, your participants— for example, are people who find a wallet on the street (placed by a hidden experimental observer) more likely to return the wallet if it appears that the owner is poor, middle class, or wealthy? The other choice for Expected Values is to actually type in your expected frequencies for all of the possible values of your test variable. You must add your f_e's to the Values box starting with the category with the lowest numerical value and working your way up to the highest. For example, if you have coded right-handers as 1, left-handers as 2, and truly ambidextrous persons as 3, and the corresponding population proportions are 80%, 15%, and 5%, and your total N is 60, you would enter the following expected values in this order: 48, 9, and 3 (i.e., $.8 \times 60$, $.15 \times 60$, and $.05 \times 60$).

The basic output from the chi-square test consists of two boxes: one containing the observed and expected frequencies for each category (plus the residual, which is just $f_o - f_e$), and one containing the chi-square statistic. In addition to printing the value for χ^2 and its degrees of freedom $(k - 1)$, the latter box contains the p value for your test. This p value is labeled as **Asymp. Sig.** (asymptotic significance) to remind you that this is the area in the tail of the chi-square distribution that is beyond your computed χ^2 value. As the label implies, **Asymp. Sig.** is not an exact value from the appropriate multinomial distribution but an approximation analogous to the normal approximation to the binomial distribution. That is why SPSS tells you, under this box, how many cells have f_e's less than 5. The chi-square approximation is not very accurate when several cells have f_e's less than 5 (or any cells have f_e's less than 1 or 2).

Two-Way Chi-Square Tests

Surprisingly, the Chi-Square Test dialog box from the Analyze/Non-parametric Tests menu does not accommodate the two-way chi-square test. Even more surprising, perhaps, is that the two-way test is accessed from the Analyze/Descriptive Statistics menu; choose **Crosstabs** (short for *cross-tabulations*) from that list. The descriptive function of **Crosstabs** is that it produces a matrix of rows and columns that makes it easy to see the joint frequencies of two categorical variables—that is, how frequently each possible combination of levels of the two variables is represented in the data set. For example, if you were to move *gender* to the Row space and *major* to the Column space and then click **OK**, you would get a matrix with two rows (one for each gender) and five columns (one for each of the five majors represented in Ihno's class). In each of the 10 cells of the matrix would be the number of students who fell into the two particular categories represented by that cell (e.g., female psychology majors). To test the null hypothesis that the two variables are independent of each other (i.e., not associated at all), click on the **Statistics** button.

   The first choice (upper-left corner) in the **Crosstabs: Statistics** dialog box is **Chi-square**. This selection will give you the two-way chi-square statistic discussed in this chapter (it is called *Pearson chi-square*, after its originator, Karl Pearson), and its p value, which is labeled **Asymp. Sig.** for reasons we have already explained in the context of the one-way chi-square test. (We cannot explain why it is also labeled as 2-sided, as this does not make sense in this context and therefore appears to be a labeling error on the part of SPSS.) Two alternative statistics are included in the output box, but they are not needed for the simple cases we have been describing in this chapter and will not be explained here. When both of your variables are dichotomous, two other statistics are added to the output box. The one labeled **Continuity Correction** is the same as the chi-square statistic but made somewhat smaller by an adjustment analogous to the one described for SPSS's binomial test, when N is greater than 25. The other, **Fisher's Exact Test**, is based on the multinomial distribution rather than a chi-square approximation. (It is analogous to SPSS's binomial test when N is 25 or less.)

To obtain a measure of effect size from the Crosstabs: Statistics dialog box, you will want to check the second choice under **Nominal**, which is labeled **Phi and Cramér's V**. Phi is the phi coefficient as described in this chapter, and Cramér's V is what we have been calling Cramér's ϕ. SPSS does not allow you to request only one of these statistics; you must request both or neither, even though they will yield identical results, unless *both* of your variables have more than two categories. In the latter case (i.e., when the two measures diverge), you should use Cramér's V, rather than Phi, as your measure of effect size.

Appendix

Statistical Tables

Answer Key

Data from Ihno's Experiment

Statistical Tables

Table A Percent area under the normal curve between the mean and z

z	.00	.01	.02	.03	.04	.05	.06	.07	.08	.09
0.0	00.00	00.40	00.80	01.20	01.60	01.99	02.39	02.79	03.19	03.59
0.1	03.98	04.38	04.78	05.17	05.57	05.96	06.36	06.75	07.14	07.53
0.2	07.93	08.32	08.71	09.10	09.48	09.87	10.26	10.64	11.03	11.41
0.3	11.79	12.17	12.55	12.93	13.31	13.68	14.06	14.43	14.80	15.17
0.4	15.54	15.91	16.28	16.64	17.00	17.36	17.72	18.08	18.44	18.79
0.5	19.15	19.50	19.85	20.19	20.54	20.88	21.23	21.57	21.90	22.24
0.6	22.57	22.91	23.24	23.57	23.89	24.22	24.54	24.86	25.17	25.49
0.7	25.80	26.11	26.42	26.73	27.04	27.34	27.64	27.94	28.23	28.52
0.8	28.81	29.10	29.39	29.67	29.95	30.23	30.51	30.78	31.06	31.33
0.9	31.59	31.86	32.12	32.38	32.64	32.89	33.15	33.40	33.65	33.89
1.0	34.13	34.38	34.61	34.85	35.08	35.31	35.54	35.77	35.99	36.21
1.1	36.43	36.65	36.86	37.08	37.29	37.49	37.70	37.90	38.10	38.30
1.2	38.49	38.69	38.88	39.07	39.25	39.44	39.62	39.80	39.97	40.15
1.3	40.32	40.49	40.66	40.82	40.99	41.15	41.31	41.47	41.62	41.77
1.4	41.92	42.07	42.22	42.36	42.51	42.65	42.79	42.92	43.06	43.19
1.5	43.32	43.45	43.57	43.70	43.82	43.94	44.06	44.18	44.29	44.41
1.6	44.52	44.63	44.74	44.84	44.95	45.05	45.15	45.25	45.35	45.45
1.7	45.54	45.64	45.73	45.82	45.91	45.99	46.08	46.16	46.25	46.33
1.8	46.41	46.49	46.56	46.64	46.71	46.78	46.86	46.93	46.99	47.06
1.9	47.13	47.19	47.26	47.32	47.38	47.44	47.50	47.56	47.61	47.67
2.0	47.72	47.78	47.83	47.88	47.93	47.98	48.03	48.08	48.12	48.17
2.1	48.21	48.26	48.30	48.34	48.38	48.42	48.46	48.50	48.54	48.57
2.2	48.61	48.64	48.68	48.71	48.75	48.78	48.81	48.84	48.87	48.90
2.3	48.93	48.96	48.98	49.01	49.04	49.06	49.09	49.11	49.13	49.16
2.4	49.18	49.20	49.22	49.25	49.27	49.29	49.31	49.32	49.34	49.36
2.5	49.38	49.40	49.41	49.43	49.45	49.46	49.48	49.49	49.51	49.52
2.6	49.53	49.55	49.56	49.57	49.59	49.60	49.61	49.62	49.63	49.64
2.7	49.65	49.66	49.67	49.68	49.69	49.70	49.71	49.72	49.73	49.74
2.8	49.74	49.75	49.76	49.77	49.77	49.78	49.79	49.79	49.80	49.81
2.9	49.81	49.82	49.82	49.83	49.84	49.84	49.85	49.85	49.86	49.86
3.0	49.87									
3.5	49.98									
4.0	49.997									
5.0	49.99997									

Table B Critical values of *t*

	Level of significance for one-tailed test					
	.10	.05	.025	.01	.005	.0005
	Level of significance for two-tailed test					
df	.20	.10	.05	.02	.01	.001
1	3.078	6.314	12.706	31.821	63.657	636.619
2	1.886	2.920	4.303	6.965	9.925	31.598
3	1.638	2.343	3.182	4.541	5.841	12.941
4	1.533	2.132	2.776	3.747	4.604	8.610
5	1.476	2.015	2.571	3.365	4.032	6.859
6	1.440	1.943	2.447	3.143	3.707	5.959
7	1.415	1.895	2.365	2.998	3.449	5.405
8	1.397	1.860	2.306	2.896	3.355	5.041
9	1.383	1.833	2.262	2.821	3.250	4.781
10	1.372	1.812	2.228	2.764	3.169	4.587
11	1.363	1.796	2.201	2.718	3.106	4.437
12	1.356	1.782	2.179	2.681	3.055	4.318
13	1.350	1.771	2.160	2.650	3.012	4.221
14	1.345	1.761	2.145	2.624	2.977	4.140
15	1.341	1.753	2.131	2.602	2.947	4.073
16	1.337	1.746	2.120	2.583	2.921	4.015
17	1.333	1.740	2.110	2.567	2.898	3.965
18	1.330	1.734	2.101	2.552	2.878	3.922
19	1.328	1.729	2.093	2.539	2.861	3.883
20	1.325	1.725	2.086	2.528	2.845	3.850
21	1.323	1.721	2.080	2.518	2.831	3.819
22	1.321	1.717	2.074	2.508	2.819	3.792
23	1.319	1.714	2.069	2.500	2.807	3.767
24	1.318	1.711	2.064	2.492	2.797	3.745
25	1.316	1.708	2.060	2.485	2.787	3.725
26	1.315	1.706	2.056	2.479	2.779	3.707
27	1.314	1.703	2.052	2.473	2.771	3.690
28	1.313	1.701	2.048	2.467	2.763	3.674
29	1.311	1.699	2.045	2.462	2.756	3.659
30	1.310	1.697	2.042	2.457	2.750	3.646
40	1.303	1.684	2.021	2.423	2.704	3.551
60	1.296	1.671	2.000	2.390	2.660	3.460
120	1.289	1.658	1.980	2.358	2.617	3.373
∞	1.282	1.645	1.960	2.326	2.576	3.291

Table C Critical values of the Pearson r

df (= N − 2; N = number of pairs)	Level of significance for one-tailed test			
	.05	.025	.01	.005
	Level of significance for two-tailed test			
	.10	.05	.02	.01
1	.988	.997	.9995	.9999
2	.900	.950	.980	.990
3	.805	.878	.934	.959
4	.729	.811	.882	.917
5	.669	.754	.833	.874
6	.622	.707	.789	.834
7	.582	.666	.750	.798
8	.549	.632	.716	.765
9	.521	.602	.685	.735
10	.497	.576	.658	.708
11	.476	.553	.634	.684
12	.458	.532	.612	.661
13	.441	.514	.592	.641
14	.426	.497	.574	.623
15	.412	.482	.558	.606
16	.400	.468	.542	.590
17	.389	.456	.528	.575
18	.378	.444	.516	.561
19	.369	.433	.503	.549
20	.360	.423	.492	.537
21	.352	.413	.482	.526
22	.344	.404	.472	.515
23	.337	.396	.462	.505
24	.330	.388	.453	.496
25	.323	.381	.445	.487
26	.317	.374	.437	.479
27	.311	.367	.430	.471
28	.306	.361	.423	.463
29	.301	.355	.416	.456
30	.296	.349	.409	.449
35	.275	.325	.381	.418
40	.257	.304	.358	.393
45	.243	.288	.338	.372
50	.231	.273	.322	.354
60	.211	.250	.295	.325
70	.195	.232	.274	.302
80	.183	.217	.256	.283
90	.173	.205	.242	.267
100	.164	.195	.230	.254
200	.116	.138	.164	.181
500	.073	.088	.104	.115
1000	.052	.062	.073	.081

Table D   Power as a function of δ and significance criterion (α)

	One-tailed test (α)					One-tailed test (α)			
	.05	.025	.01	.005		.05	.025	.01	.005
	Two-tailed test (α)					Two-tailed test (α)			
δ	.10	.05	.02	.01	δ	.10	.05	.02	.01
0.0	.10[a]	.05[a]	.02	.01	2.5	.80	.71	.57	.47
0.1	.10[a]	.05[a]	.02	.01	2.6	.83	.74	.61	.51
0.2	.11[a]	.05	.02	.01	2.7	.85	.77	.65	.55
0.3	.12[a]	.06	.03	.01	2.8	.88	.80	.68	.59
0.4	.13[a]	.07	.03	.01	2.9	.90	.83	.72	.63
0.5	.14	.08	.03	.02	3.0	.91	.85	.75	.66
0.6	.16	.09	.04	.02	3.1	.93	.87	.78	.70
0.7	.18	.11	.05	.03	3.2	.94	.89	.81	.73
0.8	.21	.13	.06	.04	3.3	.96	.91	.83	.77
0.9	.23	.15	.08	.05	3.4	.96	.93	.86	.80
1.0	.26	.17	.09	.06	3.5	.97	.94	.88	.82
1.1	.30	.20	.11	.07	3.6	.97	.95	.90	.85
1.2	.33	.22	.13	.08	3.7	.98	.96	.92	.87
1.3	.37	.26	.15	.10	3.8	.98	.97	.93	.89
1.4	.40	.29	.18	.12	3.9	.99	.97	.94	.91
1.5	.44	.32	.20	.14	4.0	.99	.98	.95	.92
1.6	.48	.36	.23	.16	4.1	.99	.98	.96	.94
1.7	.52	.40	.27	.19	4.2	.99	.99	.97	.95
1.8	.56	.44	.30	.22	4.3	[b]	.99	.98	.96
1.9	.60	.48	.33	.25	4.4		.99	.98	.97
2.0	.64	.52	.37	.28	4.5		.99	.99	.97
2.1	.68	.56	.41	.32	4.6		[b]	.99	.98
2.2	.71	.59	.45	.35	4.7			.99	.98
2.3	.74	.63	.49	.39	4.8			.99	.99
2.4	.77	.67	.53	.43	4.9			.99	.99
					5.0			[b]	.99
					5.1				.99
					5.2				[b]

[a]Values inaccurate for *one-tailed* test by more than .01.
[b]The power at and below this point is greater than .995.

Table E δ as a function of significance criterion (α) and power

	One-tailed test (α)			
	.05	.025	.01	.005
	Two-tailed test (α)			
Power	.10	.05	.02	.01
.25	0.97	1.29	1.65	1.90
.50	1.64	1.96	2.33	2.58
.60	1.90	2.21	2.58	2.83
.67	2.08	2.39	2.76	3.01
.70	2.17	2.48	2.85	3.10
.75	2.32	2.63	3.00	3.25
.80	2.49	2.80	3.17	3.42
.85	2.68	3.00	3.36	3.61
.90	2.93	3.24	3.61	3.86
.95	3.29	3.60	3.97	4.22
.99	3.97	4.29	4.65	4.90
.999	4.37	5.05	5.42	5.67

Table F   Critical values of F ($\alpha = .05$ in standard type, $\alpha = .01$ in boldface)

n_2	n_1 degrees of freedom (for numerator mean square)											
	1	2	3	4	5	6	7	8	9	10	11	12
1	161	200	216	225	230	234	237	239	241	242	243	244
	4,052	**4,999**	**5,403**	**5,625**	**5,764**	**5,859**	**5,928**	**5,981**	**6,022**	**6,056**	**6,082**	**6,106**
2	18.51	19.00	19.16	19.25	19.30	19.33	19.36	19.37	19.38	19.39	19.40	19.41
	98.49	**99.00**	**99.17**	**99.25**	**99.30**	**99.33**	**99.34**	**99.36**	**99.38**	**99.40**	**99.41**	**99.42**
3	10.13	9.55	9.28	9.12	9.01	8.94	8.88	8.84	8.81	8.78	8.76	8.74
	34.12	**30.82**	**29.46**	**28.71**	**28.24**	**27.91**	**27.67**	**27.49**	**27.34**	**27.23**	**27.13**	**27.05**
4	7.71	6.94	6.59	6.39	6.26	6.16	6.09	6.04	6.00	5.96	5.93	5.91
	21.20	**18.00**	**16.69**	**15.98**	**15.52**	**15.21**	**14.98**	**14.80**	**14.66**	**14.54**	**14.45**	**14.37**
5	6.61	5.79	5.41	5.19	5.05	4.95	4.88	4.82	4.78	4.74	4.70	4.68
	16.26	**13.27**	**12.06**	**11.39**	**10.97**	**10.67**	**10.45**	**10.27**	**10.15**	**10.05**	**9.96**	**9.89**
6	5.99	5.14	4.76	4.53	4.39	4.28	4.21	4.15	4.10	4.06	4.03	4.00
	13.74	**10.92**	**9.78**	**9.15**	**8.75**	**8.47**	**8.26**	**8.10**	**7.98**	**7.87**	**7.79**	**7.72**
7	5.59	4.74	4.35	4.12	3.97	3.87	3.79	3.73	3.68	3.63	3.60	3.57
	12.25	**9.55**	**8.45**	**7.85**	**7.46**	**7.19**	**7.00**	**6.84**	**6.71**	**6.62**	**6.54**	**6.47**
8	5.32	4.46	4.07	3.84	3.69	3.58	3.50	3.44	3.39	3.34	3.31	3.28
	11.26	**8.65**	**7.59**	**7.01**	**6.63**	**6.37**	**6.19**	**6.03**	**5.91**	**5.82**	**5.74**	**5.67**
9	5.12	4.26	3.86	3.63	3.48	3.37	3.29	3.23	3.18	3.13	3.10	3.07
	10.56	**8.02**	**6.99**	**6.42**	**6.06**	**5.80**	**5.62**	**5.47**	**5.35**	**5.26**	**5.18**	**5.11**
10	4.96	4.10	3.71	3.48	3.33	3.22	3.14	3.07	3.02	2.97	2.94	2.91
	10.04	**7.56**	**6.55**	**5.99**	**5.64**	**5.39**	**5.21**	**5.06**	**4.95**	**4.85**	**4.78**	**4.71**
11	4.84	3.98	3.59	3.36	3.20	3.09	3.01	2.95	2.90	2.86	2.82	2.79
	9.65	**7.20**	**6.22**	**5.67**	**5.32**	**5.07**	**4.88**	**4.74**	**4.63**	**4.54**	**4.46**	**4.40**
12	4.75	3.88	3.49	3.26	3.11	3.00	2.92	2.85	2.80	2.76	2.72	2.69
	9.33	**6.93**	**5.95**	**5.41**	**5.06**	**4.82**	**4.65**	**4.50**	**4.39**	**4.30**	**4.22**	**4.16**
13	4.67	3.80	3.41	3.18	3.02	2.92	2.84	2.77	2.72	2.67	2.63	2.60
	9.07	**6.70**	**5.74**	**5.20**	**4.86**	**4.62**	**4.44**	**4.30**	**4.19**	**4.10**	**4.02**	**3.96**

Table F (*continued*)

				n_1 degrees of freedom (for numerator mean square)							
14	16	20	24	30	40	50	75	100	200	500	∞
245	246	247	248	259	251	252	253	253	254	254	254
6,142	6,169	6,208	6,234	6,258	6,286	6,302	6,323	6,334	6,352	6,361	6,366
19.42	19.43	19.44	19.45	19.46	19.47	19.47	19.48	19.49	19.49	19.50	19.50
99.43	99.44	99.45	99.46	99.47	99.48	99.48	99.49	99.49	99.49	99.50	99.50
8.71	8.69	8.66	8.64	8.62	8.60	8.58	8.57	8.56	8.54	8.54	8.53
26.92	26.83	26.69	26.60	26.50	26.41	26.35	26.27	26.23	26.18	26.14	26.12
5.87	5.84	5.80	5.77	5.74	5.71	5.70	5.68	5.66	5.65	5.64	5.63
14.24	14.15	14.02	13.93	13.83	13.74	13.69	13.61	13.57	13.52	13.48	13.46
4.64	4.60	4.56	4.53	4.50	4.46	4.44	4.42	4.40	4.38	4.37	4.36
9.77	9.68	9.55	9.47	9.38	9.29	9.24	9.17	9.13	9.07	9.04	9.02
3.96	3.92	3.87	3.84	3.81	3.77	3.75	3.72	3.71	3.69	3.68	3.67
7.60	7.52	7.39	7.31	7.23	7.14	7.09	7.02	6.99	6.94	6.90	6.88
3.52	3.49	3.44	3.41	3.38	3.34	3.32	3.29	3.28	3.25	3.24	3.23
6.35	6.27	6.15	6.07	5.98	5.90	5.85	5.78	5.75	5.70	5.67	5.65
3.23	3.20	3.15	3.12	3.08	3.05	3.03	3.00	2.98	2.96	2.94	2.93
5.56	5.48	5.36	5.28	5.20	5.11	5.06	5.00	4.96	4.91	4.88	4.86
3.02	2.98	2.93	2.90	2.86	2.82	2.80	2.77	2.76	2.73	2.72	2.71
5.00	4.92	4.80	4.73	4.64	4.56	4.51	4.45	4.41	4.36	4.33	4.31
2.86	2.82	2.77	2.74	2.70	2.67	2.64	2.61	2.59	2.56	2.55	2.54
4.60	4.52	4.41	4.33	4.25	4.17	4.12	4.05	4.01	3.96	3.93	3.91
2.74	2.70	2.65	2.61	2.57	2.53	2.50	2.47	2.45	2.42	2.41	2.40
4.29	4.21	4.10	4.02	3.94	3.86	3.80	3.74	3.70	3.66	3.62	3.60
2.64	2.60	2.54	2.50	2.46	2.42	2.40	2.36	2.35	2.32	2.31	2.30
4.05	3.98	3.86	3.78	3.70	3.61	3.56	3.49	3.46	3.41	3.38	3.36
2.55	2.51	2.46	2.42	2.38	2.34	2.32	2.28	2.26	2.24	2.22	2.21
3.85	3.78	3.67	3.59	3.51	3.42	3.37	3.30	3.27	3.21	3.18	3.16

(*continued*)

Table F (*continued*)

n_2	n_1 degrees of freedom (for numerator mean square)											
	1	2	3	4	5	6	7	8	9	10	11	12
14	4.60	3.74	3.34	3.11	2.96	2.85	2.77	2.70	2.65	2.60	2.56	2.53
	8.86	**6.51**	**5.56**	**5.03**	**4.69**	**4.46**	**4.28**	**4.14**	**4.03**	**3.94**	**3.86**	**3.80**
15	4.54	3.68	3.29	3.06	2.90	2.79	2.70	2.64	2.59	2.55	2.51	2.48
	8.68	**6.36**	**5.42**	**4.89**	**4.56**	**4.32**	**4.14**	**4.00**	**3.89**	**3.80**	**3.73**	**3.67**
16	4.49	3.63	3.24	3.01	2.85	2.74	2.66	2.59	2.54	2.49	2.45	2.42
	8.53	**6.23**	**5.29**	**4.77**	**4.44**	**4.20**	**4.03**	**3.89**	**3.78**	**3.69**	**3.61**	**3.55**
17	4.45	3.59	3.20	2.96	2.81	2.70	2.62	2.55	2.50	2.45	2.41	2.38
	8.40	**6.11**	**5.18**	**4.67**	**4.34**	**4.10**	**3.93**	**3.79**	**3.68**	**3.59**	**3.52**	**3.45**
18	4.41	3.55	3.16	2.93	2.77	2.66	2.58	2.51	2.46	2.41	2.37	2.34
	8.28	**6.01**	**5.09**	**4.58**	**4.25**	**4.01**	**3.85**	**3.71**	**3.60**	**3.51**	**3.44**	**3.37**
19	4.38	3.52	3.13	2.90	2.74	2.63	2.55	2.48	2.43	2.38	2.34	2.31
	8.18	**5.93**	**5.01**	**4.50**	**4.17**	**3.94**	**3.77**	**3.63**	**3.52**	**3.43**	**3.36**	**3.30**
20	4.35	3.49	3.10	2.87	2.71	2.60	2.52	2.45	2.40	2.35	2.31	2.28
	8.10	**5.85**	**4.94**	**4.43**	**4.10**	**3.87**	**3.71**	**3.56**	**3.45**	**3.37**	**3.30**	**3.23**
21	4.32	3.47	3.07	2.84	2.68	2.57	2.49	2.42	2.37	2.32	2.28	2.25
	8.02	**5.78**	**4.87**	**4.37**	**4.04**	**3.81**	**3.65**	**3.51**	**3.40**	**3.31**	**3.24**	**3.17**
22	4.30	3.44	3.05	2.82	2.66	2.55	2.47	2.40	2.35	2.30	2.26	2.23
	7.9	**5.72**	**4.82**	**4.31**	**3.99**	**3.76**	**3.59**	**3.45**	**3.35**	**3.26**	**3.18**	**3.12**
23	4.28	3.42	3.03	2.80	2.64	2.53	2.45	2.38	2.32	2.28	2.24	2.20
	7.88	**5.66**	**4.76**	**4.26**	**3.94**	**3.71**	**3.54**	**3.41**	**3.30**	**3.21**	**3.14**	**3.07**
24	4.26	3.40	3.01	2.78	2.62	2.51	2.43	2.36	2.30	2.26	2.22	2.18
	7.82	**5.61**	**4.72**	**4.22**	**3.90**	**3.67**	**3.50**	**3.36**	**3.25**	**3.17**	**3.09**	**3.03**
25	4.24	3.38	2.99	2.76	2.60	2.49	2.41	2.34	2.28	2.24	2.20	2.16
	7.77	**5.57**	**4.68**	**4.18**	**3.86**	**3.63**	**3.46**	**3.32**	**3.21**	**3.13**	**3.05**	**2.99**
26	4.22	3.37	2.98	2.74	2.59	2.47	2.39	2.32	2.27	2.22	2.18	2.15
	7.72	**5.53**	**4.64**	**4.14**	**3.82**	**3.59**	**3.42**	**3.29**	**3.17**	**3.09**	**3.02**	**2.96**

Table F (*continued*)

| \multicolumn{12}{c}{n_1 degrees of freedom (for numerator mean square)} |
14	16	20	24	30	40	50	75	100	200	500	∞
2.48	2.44	2.39	2.35	2.31	2.27	2.24	2.21	2.19	2.16	2.14	2.13
3.70	**3.62**	**3.51**	**3.43**	**3.34**	**3.26**	**3.21**	**3.14**	**3.11**	**3.06**	**3.02**	**3.00**
2.43	2.39	2.33	2.29	2.25	2.21	2.18	2.15	2.12	2.10	2.08	2.07
3.56	**3.48**	**3.36**	**3.29**	**3.20**	**3.12**	**3.07**	**3.00**	**2.97**	**2.92**	**2.89**	**2.87**
2.37	2.33	2.28	2.24	2.20	2.16	2.13	2.09	2.07	2.04	2.02	2.01
3.45	**3.37**	**3.25**	**3.18**	**3.10**	**3.01**	**2.96**	**2.89**	**2.86**	**2.80**	**2.77**	**2.75**
2.33	2.29	2.23	2.19	2.15	2.11	2.08	2.04	2.02	1.99	1.97	1.96
3.35	**3.27**	**3.16**	**3.08**	**3.00**	**2.92**	**2.86**	**2.79**	**2.76**	**2.70**	**2.67**	**2.65**
2.29	2.25	2.19	2.15	2.11	2.07	2.04	2.00	1.98	1.95	1.93	1.92
3.27	**3.19**	**3.07**	**3.00**	**2.91**	**2.83**	**2.78**	**2.71**	**2.68**	**2.62**	**2.59**	**2.57**
2.26	2.21	2.15	2.11	2.07	2.02	2.00	1.96	1.94	1.91	1.90	1.88
3.19	**3.12**	**3.00**	**2.92**	**2.84**	**2.76**	**2.70**	**2.63**	**2.60**	**2.54**	**2.51**	**2.49**
2.23	2.18	2.12	2.08	2.04	1.99	1.96	1.92	1.90	1.87	1.85	1.84
3.13	**3.05**	**2.94**	**2.86**	**2.77**	**2.69**	**2.63**	**2.56**	**2.53**	**2.47**	**2.44**	**2.42**
2.20	2.15	2.09	2.05	2.00	1.96	1.93	1.89	1.87	1.84	1.82	1.81
3.07	**2.99**	**2.88**	**2.80**	**2.72**	**2.63**	**2.58**	**2.51**	**2.47**	**2.42**	**2.38**	**2.36**
2.18	2.13	2.07	2.03	1.98	1.93	1.91	1.87	1.84	1.81	1.80	1.78
3.02	**2.94**	**2.83**	**2.75**	**2.67**	**2.58**	**2.53**	**2.46**	**2.42**	**2.37**	**2.33**	**2.31**
2.14	2.10	2.04	2.00	1.96	1.91	1.88	1.84	1.82	1.79	1.77	1.76
2.97	**2.89**	**2.78**	**2.70**	**2.62**	**2.53**	**2.48**	**2.41**	**2.37**	**2.32**	**2.28**	**2.26**
2.13	2.09	2.02	1.98	1.94	1.89	1.86	1.82	1.80	1.76	1.74	1.73
2.93	**2.85**	**2.74**	**2.66**	**2.58**	**2.49**	**2.44**	**2.36**	**2.33**	**2.27**	**2.23**	**2.21**
2.11	2.06	2.00	1.96	1.92	1.87	1.84	1.80	1.77	1.74	1.72	1.71
2.89	**2.81**	**2.70**	**2.62**	**2.54**	**2.45**	**2.40**	**2.32**	**2.29**	**2.23**	**2.19**	**2.17**
2.10	2.05	1.99	1.95	1.90	1.85	1.82	1.78	1.76	1.72	1.70	1.69
2.86	**2.77**	**2.66**	**2.58**	**2.50**	**2.41**	**2.36**	**2.28**	**2.25**	**2.19**	**2.15**	**2.13**

(*continued*)

Table F (*continued*)

n_2	\multicolumn{12}{c}{n_1 degrees of freedom (for numerator mean square)}
	1	2	3	4	5	6	7	8	9	10	11	12
27	4.21	3.35	2.96	2.73	2.57	2.46	2.37	2.30	2.25	2.20	2.16	2.13
	7.68	**5.49**	**4.60**	**4.11**	**3.79**	**3.56**	**3.39**	**3.26**	**3.14**	**3.06**	**2.98**	**2.93**
28	4.20	3.34	2.95	2.71	2.56	2.44	2.36	2.29	2.24	2.19	2.15	2.12
	7.64	**5.45**	**4.57**	**4.07**	**3.76**	**3.53**	**3.36**	**3.23**	**3.11**	**3.03**	**2.95**	**2.90**
29	4.18	3.33	2.93	2.70	2.54	2.43	2.35	2.28	2.22	2.18	2.14	2.10
	7.60	**5.42**	**4.54**	**4.04**	**3.73**	**3.50**	**3.33**	**3.20**	**3.08**	**3.00**	**2.92**	**2.87**
30	4.17	3.32	2.92	2.69	2.53	2.42	2.34	2.27	2.21	2.16	2.12	2.09
	7.56	**5.39**	**4.51**	**4.02**	**3.70**	**3.47**	**3.30**	**3.17**	**3.06**	**2.98**	**2.90**	**2.84**
32	4.15	3.30	2.90	2.67	2.51	2.40	2.32	2.25	2.19	2.14	2.10	2.07
	7.50	**5.34**	**4.46**	**3.97**	**3.66**	**3.42**	**3.25**	**3.12**	**3.01**	**2.94**	**2.86**	**2.80**
34	4.13	3.28	2.88	2.65	2.49	2.38	2.30	2.23	2.17	2.12	2.08	2.05
	7.44	**5.29**	**4.42**	**3.93**	**3.61**	**3.38**	**3.21**	**3.08**	**2.97**	**2.89**	**2.82**	**2.76**
36	4.11	3.26	2.86	2.63	2.48	2.36	2.28	2.21	2.15	2.10	2.06	2.03
	7.39	**5.25**	**4.38**	**3.89**	**3.58**	**3.35**	**3.18**	**3.04**	**3.04**	**2.86**	**2.78**	**2.72**
38	4.10	3.25	2.85	2.62	2.46	2.35	2.26	2.19	2.14	2.09	2.05	2.02
	7.35	**5.21**	**4.34**	**3.86**	**3.54**	**3.32**	**3.15**	**3.02**	**2.91**	**2.82**	**2.75**	**2.69**
40	4.08	3.23	2.84	2.61	2.45	2.34	2.25	2.18	2.12	2.07	2.04	2.00
	7.31	**5.18**	**4.31**	**3.83**	**3.51**	**3.29**	**3.12**	**2.99**	**2.88**	**2.80**	**2.73**	**2.66**
42	4.07	3.22	2.83	2.59	2.44	2.32	2.24	2.17	2.11	2.06	2.02	1.99
	7.27	**5.15**	**4.29**	**3.80**	**3.49**	**3.26**	**3.10**	**2.96**	**2.86**	**2.77**	**2.70**	**2.64**
44	4.06	3.21	2.82	2.58	2.43	2.31	2.23	2.16	2.10	2.05	2.01	1.98
	7.24	**5.12**	**4.26**	**3.78**	**3.46**	**3.24**	**3.07**	**2.94**	**2.84**	**2.75**	**2.68**	**2.62**
46	4.05	3.20	2.81	2.57	2.42	2.30	2.22	2.14	2.09	2.04	2.00	1.97
	7.21	**5.10**	**4.24**	**3.76**	**3.44**	**3.22**	**3.05**	**2.92**	**2.82**	**2.73**	**2.66**	**2.60**
48	4.04	3.19	2.80	2.56	2.41	2.30	2.21	2.14	2.08	2.03	1.99	1.96
	7.19	**5.08**	**4.22**	**3.74**	**3.42**	**3.20**	**3.04**	**2.90**	**2.80**	**2.71**	**2.64**	**2.58**

Table F (*continued*)

14	16	20	24	30	40	50	75	100	200	500	∞
2.08	2.03	1.97	1.93	1.88	1.84	1.80	1.76	1.74	1.71	1.68	1.67
2.83	**2.74**	**2.63**	**2.55**	**2.47**	**2.38**	**2.33**	**2.25**	**2.21**	**2.16**	**2.12**	**2.10**
2.06	2.02	1.96	1.91	1.87	1.81	1.78	1.75	1.72	1.69	1.67	1.65
2.80	**2.71**	**2.60**	**2.52**	**2.44**	**2.35**	**2.30**	**2.22**	**2.18**	**2.13**	**2.09**	**2.06**
2.05	2.00	1.94	1.90	1.85	1.80	1.77	1.73	1.71	1.68	1.65	1.64
2.77	**2.68**	**2.57**	**2.49**	**2.41**	**2.32**	**2.27**	**2.19**	**2.15**	**2.10**	**2.06**	**2.03**
2.04	1.99	1.93	1.89	1.84	1.79	1.76	1.72	1.69	1.66	1.64	1.62
2.74	**2.66**	**2.55**	**2.47**	**2.38**	**2.29**	**2.24**	**2.16**	**2.13**	**2.07**	**2.03**	**2.01**
2.02	1.97	1.91	1.86	1.82	1.76	1.74	1.69	1.67	1.64	1.61	1.59
2.70	**2.62**	**2.51**	**2.42**	**2.34**	**2.25**	**2.20**	**2.12**	**2.08**	**2.02**	**1.98**	**1.96**
2.00	1.95	1.89	1.84	1.80	1.74	1.71	1.67	1.64	1.61	1.59	1.57
2.66	**2.58**	**2.47**	**2.38**	**2.30**	**2.21**	**2.15**	**2.08**	**2.04**	**1.98**	**1.94**	**1.91**
1.98	1.93	1.87	1.82	1.78	1.72	1.69	1.65	1.62	1.59	1.56	1.55
2.62	**2.54**	**2.43**	**2.35**	**2.26**	**2.17**	**2.12**	**2.04**	**2.00**	**1.94**	**1.90**	**1.87**
1.96	1.92	1.85	1.80	1.76	1.71	1.67	1.63	1.60	1.57	1.54	1.53
2.59	**2.51**	**2.40**	**2.32**	**2.22**	**2.14**	**2.08**	**2.00**	**1.97**	**1.90**	**1.86**	**1.84**
1.95	1.90	1.84	1.79	1.74	1.69	1.66	1.61	1.59	1.55	1.53	1.51
2.56	**2.49**	**2.37**	**2.29**	**2.20**	**2.11**	**2.05**	**1.97**	**1.94**	**1.88**	**1.84**	**1.81**
1.91	1.89	1.82	1.78	1.73	1.68	1.64	1.60	1.57	1.54	1.51	1.49
2.54	**2.46**	**2.35**	**2.26**	**2.17**	**2.08**	**2.02**	**1.94**	**1.91**	**1.85**	**1.80**	**1.78**
1.92	1.88	1.81	1.76	1.72	1.66	1.63	1.58	1.56	1.52	1.50	1.48
2.52	**2.44**	**2.32**	**2.24**	**2.15**	**2.06**	**2.00**	**1.92**	**1.88**	**1.82**	**1.78**	**1.75**
1.91	1.87	1.80	1.75	1.71	1.65	1.62	1.57	1.54	1.51	1.48	1.46
2.50	**2.42**	**2.30**	**2.22**	**2.13**	**2.04**	**1.98**	**1.90**	**1.86**	**1.80**	**1.76**	**1.72**
1.90	1.86	1.79	1.74	1.70	1.64	1.61	1.56	1.53	1.50	1.47	1.45
2.48	**2.40**	**2.28**	**2.20**	**2.11**	**2.02**	**1.96**	**1.88**	**1.84**	**1.78**	**1.73**	**1.70**

n_1 degrees of freedom (for numerator mean square)

(*continued*)

Table F (*continued*)

n_2	\multicolumn{12}{c}{n_1 degrees of freedom (for numerator mean square)}
	1	2	3	4	5	6	7	8	9	10	11	12
50	4.03	3.18	2.79	2.56	2.40	2.29	2.20	2.13	2.07	2.02	1.98	1.95
	7.17	5.06	4.20	3.72	3.41	3.18	3.02	2.88	2.78	2.70	2.62	2.56
55	4.02	3.17	2.78	2.54	2.38	2.27	2.18	2.11	2.05	2.00	1.97	1.93
	7.12	5.01	4.16	3.68	3.37	3.15	2.98	2.85	2.75	2.66	2.59	2.53
60	4.00	3.15	2.76	2.52	2.37	2.25	2.17	2.10	2.04	1.99	1.95	1.92
	7.08	4.98	4.13	3.65	3.34	3.12	2.95	2.82	2.72	2.63	2.56	2.50
65	3.99	3.14	2.75	2.51	2.36	2.24	2.15	2.08	2.02	1.98	1.94	1.90
	7.04	4.95	4.10	3.62	3.31	3.09	2.93	2.79	2.70	2.61	2.54	2.47
70	3.98	3.13	2.74	2.50	2.35	2.23	2.14	2.07	2.01	1.97	1.93	1.89
	7.01	4.92	4.08	3.60	3.29	3.07	2.91	2.77	2.67	2.59	2.51	2.45
80	3.96	3.11	2.72	2.48	2.33	2.21	2.12	2.05	1.99	1.95	1.91	1.88
	6.96	4.88	4.04	3.56	3.25	3.04	2.87	2.74	2.64	2.55	2.48	2.41
100	3.94	3.09	2.70	2.46	2.30	2.19	2.10	2.03	1.97	1.92	1.88	1.85
	6.90	4.82	3.98	3.51	3.20	2.99	2.82	2.69	2.59	2.51	2.43	2.36
125	3.92	3.07	2.68	2.44	2.29	2.17	2.08	2.01	1.95	1.90	1.86	1.83
	6.84	4.78	3.94	3.47	3.17	2.95	2.79	2.65	2.56	2.47	2.40	2.33
150	3.91	3.06	2.57	2.43	2.27	2.16	2.07	2.00	1.94	1.89	1.85	1.82
	6.81	4.75	3.91	3.44	3.14	2.92	2.76	2.62	2.53	2.44	2.37	2.30
200	3.89	3.04	2.65	2.41	2.26	2.14	2.05	1.98	1.92	1.87	1.83	1.80
	6.76	4.71	3.88	3.41	3.11	2.90	2.73	2.60	2.50	2.41	2.34	2.28
400	3.86	3.02	2.62	2.39	2.23	2.12	2.03	1.96	1.90	1.85	1.81	1.78
	6.70	4.66	3.83	3.36	3.06	2.85	2.69	2.55	2.46	2.37	2.29	2.23
1000	3.85	3.00	2.61	2.38	2.22	2.10	2.02	1.95	1.89	1.84	1.80	1.76
	6.66	4.62	3.80	3.34	3.04	2.82	2.66	2.53	2.43	2.34	2.26	2.20
∞	3.84	2.99	2.60	2.37	2.21	2.09	2.01	1.94	1.88	1.83	1.79	1.75
	6.64	4.60	3.78	3.32	3.02	2.80	2.64	2.51	2.41	2.32	2.24	2.18

Table F   (*continued*)

				n_1 degrees of freedom (for numerator mean square)							
14	16	20	24	30	40	50	75	100	200	500	∞
1.90	1.85	1.78	1.74	1.69	1.63	1.60	1.55	1.52	1.48	1.46	1.44
2.46	**2.39**	**2.26**	**2.18**	**2.10**	**2.00**	**1.94**	**1.86**	**1.82**	**1.76**	**1.71**	**1.68**
1.88	1.83	1.76	1.72	1.67	1.61	1.58	1.52	1.50	1.46	1.43	1.41
2.43	**2.35**	**2.23**	**2.15**	**2.06**	**1.96**	**1.90**	**1.82**	**1.78**	**1.71**	**1.66**	**1.64**
1.86	1.81	1.75	1.70	1.65	1.59	1.56	1.50	1.48	1.44	1.41	1.39
2.40	**2.32**	**2.20**	**2.12**	**2.03**	**1.93**	**1.87**	**1.79**	**1.74**	**1.68**	**1.63**	**1.60**
1.84	1.80	1.73	1.68	1.63	1.57	1.54	1.49	1.46	1.42	1.39	1.37
2.37	**2.30**	**2.18**	**2.09**	**2.00**	**1.90**	**1.84**	**1.76**	**1.71**	**1.64**	**1.60**	**1.56**
1.84	1.79	1.72	1.67	1.62	1.56	1.53	1.47	1.45	1.40	1.37	1.35
2.35	**2.28**	**2.15**	**2.07**	**1.98**	**1.88**	**1.82**	**1.74**	**1.69**	**1.62**	**1.56**	**1.53**
1.82	1.77	1.70	1.65	1.60	1.54	1.51	1.45	1.42	1.38	1.35	1.32
2.32	**2.24**	**2.11**	**2.03**	**1.94**	**1.84**	**1.78**	**1.70**	**1.65**	**1.57**	**1.52**	**1.49**
1.79	1.75	1.68	1.63	1.57	1.51	1.48	1.42	1.39	1.34	1.30	1.28
2.26	**2.19**	**2.06**	**1.98**	**1.89**	**1.79**	**1.73**	**1.64**	**1.59**	**1.51**	**1.46**	**1.43**
1.77	1.72	1.65	1.60	1.55	1.49	1.45	1.39	1.36	1.31	1.27	1.25
2.23	**2.15**	**2.03**	**1.94**	**1.85**	**1.75**	**1.68**	**1.59**	**1.54**	**1.46**	**1.40**	**1.37**
1.76	1.71	1.64	1.59	1.54	1.47	1.44	1.37	1.34	1.29	1.25	1.22
2.20	**2.12**	**2.00**	**1.91**	**1.83**	**1.72**	**1.66**	**1.56**	**1.51**	**1.43**	**1.37**	**1.33**
1.74	1.69	1.62	1.57	1.52	1.45	1.42	1.35	1.32	1.26	1.22	1.19
2.17	**2.09**	**1.97**	**1.88**	**1.79**	**1.69**	**1.62**	**1.53**	**1.48**	**1.39**	**1.33**	**1.28**
1.72	1.67	1.60	1.54	1.49	1.42	1.38	1.32	1.28	1.22	1.16	1.13
2.12	**2.04**	**1.92**	**1.84**	**1.74**	**1.65**	**1.57**	**1.47**	**1.42**	**1.32**	**1.24**	**1.19**
1.70	1.65	1.58	1.53	1.47	1.41	1.36	1.30	1.26	1.19	1.13	1.08
2.09	**2.01**	**1.89**	**1.81**	**1.71**	**1.61**	**1.54**	**1.44**	**1.38**	**1.28**	**1.19**	**1.11**
1.69	1.64	1.57	1.52	1.46	1.40	1.35	1.28	1.24	1.17	1.11	1.00
2.07	**1.99**	**1.87**	**1.79**	**1.69**	**1.59**	**1.52**	**1.41**	**1.36**	**1.25**	**1.15**	**1.00**

Table G Critical values of the studentized range statistic (q) for $\alpha = .05$

df for error term	\multicolumn{19}{c}{Number of groups}

df for error term	2	3	4	5	6	7	8	9	10	11	12	13	14	15	16	17	18	19	20
1	17.97	26.98	32.82	37.08	40.41	43.12	45.40	47.36	49.07	50.59	51.96	53.20	54.33	55.36	56.32	57.22	58.04	58.83	59.56
2	6.08	8.33	9.80	10.88	11.74	12.44	13.03	13.54	13.99	14.39	14.75	15.08	15.38	15.65	15.91	16.14	16.37	16.57	16.77
3	4.50	5.91	6.82	7.50	8.04	8.48	8.85	9.18	9.46	9.72	9.95	10.15	10.35	10.52	10.69	10.84	10.98	11.11	11.24
4	3.93	5.04	5.76	6.29	6.71	7.05	7.35	7.60	7.83	8.03	8.21	8.37	8.52	8.66	8.79	8.91	9.03	9.13	9.23
5	3.64	4.60	5.22	5.67	6.03	6.33	6.58	6.80	6.99	7.17	7.32	7.47	7.60	7.72	7.83	7.93	8.03	8.12	8.21
6	3.46	4.34	4.90	5.30	5.63	5.90	6.12	6.32	6.49	6.65	6.79	6.92	7.03	7.14	7.24	7.34	7.43	7.51	7.59
7	3.34	4.16	4.68	5.06	5.36	5.61	5.82	6.00	6.16	6.30	6.43	6.55	6.66	6.76	6.85	6.94	7.02	7.10	7.17
8	3.26	4.04	4.53	4.89	5.17	5.40	5.60	5.77	5.92	6.05	6.18	6.29	6.39	6.48	6.57	6.65	6.73	6.80	6.87
9	3.20	3.95	4.41	4.76	5.02	5.24	5.43	5.59	5.74	5.87	5.98	6.09	6.19	6.28	6.36	6.44	6.51	6.58	6.64
10	3.15	3.88	4.33	4.65	4.91	5.12	5.30	5.46	5.60	5.72	5.83	5.93	6.03	6.11	6.19	6.27	6.34	6.40	6.47
11	3.11	3.82	4.26	4.57	4.82	5.03	5.20	5.35	5.49	5.61	5.71	5.81	5.90	5.98	6.06	6.13	6.20	6.27	6.33
12	3.08	3.77	4.20	4.51	4.75	4.95	5.12	5.27	5.39	5.51	5.61	5.71	5.80	5.88	5.95	6.02	6.09	6.15	6.21
13	3.06	3.73	4.15	4.45	4.69	4.88	5.05	5.19	5.32	5.43	5.53	5.63	5.71	5.79	5.86	5.93	5.99	6.05	6.11
14	3.03	3.70	4.11	4.41	4.64	4.83	4.99	5.13	5.25	5.36	5.46	5.55	5.64	5.71	5.79	5.85	5.91	5.97	6.03
15	3.01	3.67	4.08	4.37	4.59	4.78	4.94	5.08	5.20	5.31	5.40	5.49	5.57	5.65	5.72	5.78	5.85	5.90	5.96
16	3.00	3.65	4.05	4.33	4.56	4.74	4.90	5.03	5.15	5.26	5.35	5.44	5.52	5.59	5.66	5.73	5.79	5.84	5.90
17	2.98	3.63	4.02	4.30	4.52	4.70	4.86	4.99	5.11	5.21	5.31	5.39	5.47	5.54	5.61	5.67	5.73	5.79	5.84
18	2.97	3.61	4.00	4.28	4.49	4.67	4.82	4.96	5.07	5.17	5.27	5.35	5.43	5.50	5.57	5.63	5.69	5.74	5.79
19	2.96	3.59	3.98	4.25	4.47	4.65	4.79	4.92	5.04	5.14	5.23	5.31	5.39	5.46	5.53	5.59	5.65	5.70	5.75
20	2.95	3.58	3.96	4.23	4.45	4.62	4.77	4.90	5.01	5.11	5.20	5.28	5.36	5.43	5.49	5.55	5.61	5.66	5.71
24	2.92	3.53	3.90	4.17	4.37	4.54	4.68	4.81	4.92	5.01	5.10	5.18	5.25	5.32	5.38	5.44	5.49	5.55	5.59
30	2.89	3.49	3.85	4.10	4.30	4.46	4.60	4.72	4.82	4.92	5.00	5.08	5.15	5.21	5.27	5.33	5.38	5.43	5.47
40	2.86	3.44	3.79	4.04	4.23	4.39	4.52	4.63	4.73	4.82	4.90	4.98	5.04	5.11	5.16	5.22	5.27	5.31	5.36
60	2.83	3.40	3.74	3.98	4.16	4.31	4.44	4.55	4.65	4.73	4.81	4.88	4.94	5.00	5.06	5.11	5.15	5.20	5.24
120	2.80	3.36	3.68	3.92	4.10	4.24	4.36	4.47	4.56	4.64	4.71	4.78	4.84	4.90	4.95	5.00	5.04	5.09	5.13
∞	2.77	3.31	3.63	3.86	4.03	4.17	4.29	4.39	4.47	4.55	4.62	4.68	4.74	4.80	4.85	4.89	4.93	4.97	5.01

Source: Adapted from Biometrika Tables for Statisticians Vol. 1, 3rd ed., by E. Pearson and H. Hartley, Table 29. Copyright © 1966 University Press. Used with the permission of the Biometrika Trustees.

Table H Critical values of chi square

df	Level of significance					
	.20	.10	.05	.02	.01	.001
1	1.64	2.71	3.84	5.41	6.63	10.83
2	3.22	4.61	5.99	7.82	9.21	13.82
3	4.64	6.25	7.82	9.84	11.34	16.27
4	5.99	7.78	9.49	11.67	13.28	18.46
5	7.29	9.24	11.07	13.39	15.09	20.52
6	8.56	10.64	12.59	15.03	16.81	22.46
7	9.80	12.02	14.07	16.62	18.48	24.32
8	11.03	13.36	15.51	18.17	20.09	26.12
9	12.24	14.68	16.92	19.68	21.67	27.88
10	13.44	15.99	18.31	21.16	23.21	29.59
11	14.63	17.28	19.68	22.62	24.72	31.26
12	15.81	18.55	21.03	24.05	26.22	32.91
13	16.98	19.81	22.36	25.47	27.69	34.53
14	18.15	21.06	23.68	26.87	29.14	36.12
15	19.31	22.31	25.00	28.26	30.58	37.70
16	20.46	23.54	26.30	29.63	32.00	39.25
17	21.62	24.77	27.59	31.00	33.41	40.79
18	22.76	25.99	28.87	32.35	34.81	42.31
19	23.90	27.20	30.14	33.69	36.19	43.82
20	25.04	28.41	31.41	35.02	37.57	45.32
21	26.17	29.62	32.67	36.34	38.93	46.80
22	27.30	30.81	33.92	37.66	40.29	48.27
23	28.43	32.01	35.17	38.97	41.64	49.73
24	29.55	33.20	36.42	40.27	42.98	51.18
25	30.68	34.38	37.65	41.57	44.31	52.62
26	31.80	35.56	38.89	42.86	45.64	54.05
27	32.91	36.74	40.11	44.14	46.96	55.48
28	34.03	37.92	41.34	45.42	48.28	56.89
29	35.14	39.09	42.56	46.69	49.59	58.30
30	36.25	40.26	43.77	47.96	50.89	59.70

Table I Critical values of r_s (Spearman rank-order correlation coefficient)

No. of pairs (N)	Level of significance for one-tailed test			
	.05	.025	.01	.005
	Level of significance for two-tailed test			
	.10	.05	.02	.01
5	.900	1.000	1.000	—
6	.829	.886	.943	1.000
7	.714	.786	.893	.929
8	.643	.738	.833	.881
9	.600	.683	.783	.833
10	.564	.648	.746	.794
12	.506	.591	.712	.777
14	.456	.544	.645	.715
16	.425	.506	.601	.665
18	.399	.475	.564	.625
20	.377	.450	.534	.591
22	.359	.428	.508	.562
24	.343	.409	.485	.537
26	.329	.392	.465	.515
28	.317	.377	.448	.496
30	.306	.364	.432	.478

Source. G. E. Olds, *Ann. Math. Statistics* 9 (1938); 20 (1949). Reproduced by permission of the publisher.

Answers to Odd-Numbered Exercises

Chapter 1

1. (a) $\sum X = 195$ $\sum X^2 = 2{,}801$ $\left(\sum X\right)^2 = 38{,}025$
   (b) $\sum X = 138$ $\sum X^2 = 1{,}512$ $\left(\sum X\right)^2 = 19{,}044$
   (c) $\sum X = 70$ $\sum X^2 = 550$ $\left(\sum X\right)^2 = 4{,}900$
   (d) $\sum X = 55$ $\sum X^2 = 685$ $\left(\sum X\right)^2 = 3{,}025$

3. (a) $\sum X = 10$ $\left(\sum X\right)^2 = 100$ $\sum(X - Y) = -20$
   $\sum Y = 30$ $\left(\sum Y\right)^2 = 900$ $\sum X - \sum Y = -20$
   $\sum X^2 = 30$ $\left(\sum X + Y\right) = 40$ $\sum XY = 73$
   $\sum Y^2 = 206$ $\sum X + \sum Y = 40$ $\sum X \sum Y = 300$
   (b) $40 = 40$; $-20 = -20$; $73 \neq 300$; $30 \neq 100$
   (c) $\sum(X + k) = 10 + 20 = 30$; $\sum X + k = 10 + 4 = 14$; Sum of new
   scores $= 30$

5. Data set 3:
   $N = 14$
   $\sum X = 1{,}176$; $\sum X^2 = 100{,}288$; $\left(\sum X\right)^2 = 1{,}382{,}976$;
   $\sum XY = 96{,}426$; $\sum(X + Y) = 2{,}305$;
   $\sum Y = 1{,}129$; $\sum Y^2 = 93{,}343$; $\left(\sum Y\right)^2 = 1{,}274{,}641$;
   $\sum X \sum Y = 1{,}327{,}704$; $\sum(X - Y) = 47$

Chapter 2

1.

Score	Turck f	Turck cf	Kirk f	Kirk cf	Dupre f	Dupre cf
20	1	15	0	15		
19	0	14	0	15		
18	1	14	0	15		
17	2	13	1	15		
16	1	11	0	14		
15	1	10	0	14		
14	1	9	1	14		
13	2	8	0	13		
12	0	6	3	13		
11	2	6	2	10	1	10
10	1	4	0	8	1	9
9	1	3	1	8	2	8
8	0	2	2	7	0	6
7	0	2	2	5	1	6
6	1	2	1	3	1	5
5	1	1	0	2	2	4
4			0	2	2	2
3			1	2	0	0
2			0	1	0	0
1			1	1	0	0

3.

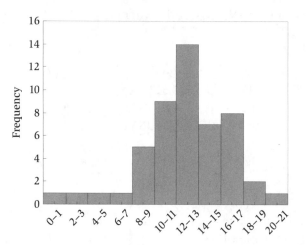

Approximately symmetrical, bimodal in shape.

5.

Stems (Intervals)	Leaves (Observations)
3–5	5
6–8	6
9–11	9 0 1 1
12–14	3 3 4
15–17	5 6 7 7
18–20	8 0

7. (a) The *cf* corresponding to a score of 8 is 2; PR = (2/15) × 100 = 13.33%, so the PR for 8 is about 13.
   (b) The *cf* for a score of 12 is 6; PR = (6/15) × 100 = 40%, so the PR for 12 is 40.

9. (a) The desired *cf* = (25/100) × 15 = 3.75, so the score at the 25th percentile is about 10.
   (b) The desired *cf* = (75/100) × 15 = 11.25, so the score at the 75th percentile is about 16.

Chapter 3

1. The means are: Turck Hall = 13.0; Kirk Hall = 9.2; Dupre Hall = 7.0; Doty Hall = 11.0

3. The mode for Kirk Hall is 12. (It has a frequency of 3, which is more than any other score in the distribution.)

5. Subtracting the mean from each score, we obtain: −3, −3, −2, −2, −1, 0, +2, +2, +3, +4. These deviations from the mean sum to zero.

7. First, obtain the sum of squares (*SS*) for a dorm, and then divide by N for σ^2, or $N - 1$ for s^2. The *SS* is found by first squaring the

sum of the scores and dividing it by N; then subtract that amount from the sum of the squared scores. For Turck Hall, $SS = 2{,}801 - (195^2/15) = 2{,}801 - 2{,}535 = 266$, so $\sigma^2 = 266/15 = 17.733$, $s^2 = 266/14 = 19$, $\sigma = \sqrt{17.733} = 4.21$, and $s = \sqrt{19} = 4.36$. For Kirk Hall, $\sigma^2 = 16.16$, $s^2 = 17.314$, $\sigma = 4.02$, and $s = 4.16$. For Dupre Hall, $\sigma^2 = 6.0$, $s^2 = 6.67$, $\sigma = 2.45$, and $s = 2.58$. For Doty Hall, $\sigma^2 = 16.0$, $s^2 = 20.0$, $\sigma = 4.0$, and $s = 4.47$.

9. (a) The SD will not be changed (but the mean will increase to 62.3). (b) The SD will not be changed (but the mean will decrease to 53.3). (c) The SD will become $9.6 \times 2 = 19.2$. (d) The SD will become $9.6/3 = 3.2$.

11. The interquartile range for Turck Hall is $16 - 10 = 6$; the SIQR $= 6/2 = 3$. For Kirk Hall, the interquartile range is about $11.5 - 6.5 = 5$; therefore the SIQR is about 2.5.

13. The MD for Doty Hall $= [|14 - 11| + |18 - 11| + |17 - 11| + |6 - 11| + |10 - 11|]/5 = (3 + 3 + 6 + 5 + 1)/5 = 18/5 = 3.6$. The MD is slightly smaller than σ for Doty Hall, which equals 4.0. An extreme score would affect σ more than MD, thus increasing the difference between the two measures.

Chapter 4

1.

	$\overline{X}$	σ	σ^2
(a)	14.8	4	16
(b)	4	4	16
(c)	25.6	12.8	163.84
(d)	2	1	1
(e)	7	2	4

3. Psychology z score $= -1.60$; English z score $= -1.00$. This student performed relatively better on the English test.

5.

S	z_x	z_y
1	+1.25	+0.65
2	−1.54	−1.85
3	+0.10	+0.50
4	−0.97	−0.36
5	+0.77	+1.28
6	+0.77	−0.13
7	+1.54	+0.81
8	−2.03	−2.39
9	+0.10	+0.34
10	+0.29	+0.26
11	−0.29	+0.81
12	+0.87	+0.81
13	−0.68	−0.44
14	−0.19	−0.28

7. $z = -0.90$, area between mean and $z = 31.59\%$; Answer $= 18.41\%$

9. $z = -2.25$ (area $= 48.78\%$); $z = -1.25$ (area $= 39.44\%$); Answer $= 9.34\%$

11. $z = +1.65$; Answer $= 665$

13. (a) $p = .184$; (b) $p = .376$; (c) $p = .093$; (d) $p = .050$

Chapter 5

1. (a) $\sigma_{\bar{X}} = 0.5$
   (b) $z = -1.60$, one-tailed $p = .0548$, two-tailed $p = .1096$
   (c) $p > .05$ for both one- and two-tailed tests, so retain H_0 in both cases
   (d) $z = +4.80$, reject H_0 at .05 and .01

3. (a) $z = +1.50 < +1.96$ (two-tailed z_{crit}), retain H_0; $z = +1.50 < +1.65$ (one-tailed z_{crit}), not significant for a one-tailed test either.
   (b) $z = +2.40 > +1.96$; reject H_0 for both the one- and two-tailed tests

5. (a) $z = (\bar{X} - \mu)/(\sigma/\sqrt{N})$; for Dupre Hall, $z = (7 - 10)/(5/\sqrt{10}) = -3/1.58 = -1.90$. Area beyond $z = -1.90$ is .0287, so the one-tailed p value $= .0287$, and the two-tailed p value $= 2 \times .0287 = .0574$
   (b) Reject H_0 at the .05 level for a one-tailed test, but not for a two-tailed test. Compared to Exercise 4, the difference between the sample mean and the population mean is the same in magnitude, though opposite in direction. This changes the sign of the z score for groups, but that by itself does not affect the size of the p values. The population standard deviation is also the same as in Exercise 4, but the sample size is smaller (10 instead of 15), which makes the standard error larger, which makes the z score smaller, which makes the p values larger.

7. (a) $z = (50 - 60)/(27.386/\sqrt{20}) = -10/6.124 = -1.633$. The one-tailed p value corresponding to this z score is about .0516, and the two-tailed p value is about .1032, so the data are consistent with the null hypothesis that the population mean is 60 ($p > .05$).
   (b) $z = (50 - 36)/(27.386/\sqrt{20}) = 14/6.124 = 2.286$. The two-tailed p value corresponding to this z score is about .022, so the data are not consistent with the null hypothesis that the population mean is 36, even with a two-tailed test ($p < .05$).

Chapter 6

1. (a) $s_{\bar{X}} = 1.125$; $t = -2.67$. Reject H_0 ($2.67 > t_{\text{crit}} = 2.145$)
   (b) $s_{\bar{X}} = 1.074$; $t = 1.12$. Retain H_0

3. (a) $s_{\bar{X}} = .63$; $t = -0.62$; $df = 8$. Retain H_0
   (b) $s_{\bar{X}} = .63$; $t = -6.17$; $df = 8$. Reject H_0

(c) $ts_{\bar{X}} = 1.45$; CI = 0.66 to 3.56. When the CI includes the null hypothesis mean, retain the null; when the null hypothesis mean falls outside of the CI, reject the null.

5. $z = (.6 - .5)/\sqrt{(.5)(.5)/100} = 2.0$; $p < .05$. Reject H_0; conclude that the electorate will support the new constitution.

Chapter 7

1. $s^2_{pooled} = 18.16$; $df = 28$; $t = 3.8/1.56 = 2.44$; reject H_0 at the .05 but not .01 level. This is a possible Type I error. On average, the scores for Turck Hall were higher ($M = 13.0$) than the scores for Kirk Hall ($M = 9.2$); this difference was found to be statistically significant, $t(28) = 2.44$, $p < .05$, $g = .89$.

   The 95% CI = 3.8 ± 2.048 (1.56), so it goes from .61 to 7.0. The 99% CI = 3.8 ± 2.763 (1.56), so it goes from $-.50$ to 8.1. Because zero is contained in the 99% CI, but not the 95% CI, we know that the difference of means is significant at the .05 but not the .01 level.

3. $t = 2.2/1.48 = 1.49$; one-tailed $t_{.05}$ (23) $= 1.714 > 1.49$, so t is not significant at the .05 or .01 levels (possible Type II error).

   The mean for Kirk Hall ($M = 9.2$) was higher than the mean for Dupre Hall ($M = 7.0$), but this trend did not attain significance at the .05 level, even for a one-tailed test, $t(23) = 1.49$, $p > .05$, $g = .61$. The 95% CI goes from $-.86$ to $+5.26$, and the 99% CI goes from (approx.) -2.0 to $+6.4$. The separate variance $t = 1.63$, which is slightly larger than the pooled-variances t value.

5. $s^2_1 = 9.49$; $s^2_2 = 10.00$; $s^2_{pooled} = 9.75$; $df = 8$; $t = 7/1.97 = 3.55$; $p < .05$. Reject H_0; ethnic groups differ in performance.

7. $\sum D = 10$; $\bar{D} = 1$; $s^2_D = 4.67$; $df = 9$; $t = 1.46$; $p > .05$. Retain H_0; there is not sufficient reason to conclude that the two techniques differ.

9. $\sum D = 47$; $\bar{D} = 3.36$; $s_D = 18.54$; $df = 13$; $t = 0.68$; $p > .05$. Retain H_0.

Chapter 8

1. (a) $\sum R = (19)(20)/2 = 190$; $T_1 = 63.5$; $T_2 = 126.5$. Based on Group 1, $T_E = 90$ and $\sigma_T = 12.25$, so $z = -26.5/12.25 = -2.16$; $p < .05$. Conclude that the new signal (Group 1) is superior.

   (b) $r_c = -.59$, indicating a strong relationship between group membership and reaction times, such that Group 1 reacts more quickly.

3. (a) Exp. 1: $\sum R = 378$; $T_1 = 159.5$; $T_2 = 218.5$. Based on Group 1, $T_E = 210$ and $\sigma_T = 20.49$, so $z = -50.5/20.49 = -2.46$; $p < .05$. Reject H_0.

   Exp. 2: $\sum R = 378$; $T_1 = 213.5$; $T_2 = 164.5$. Based on Group 1, $T_E = 210$ and $\sigma_T = 20.49$, so $z = +3.5/20.49 = 0.17$; $p > .05$. Retain H_0.

(b) Exp. 1: $r_G = -.56$. Exp. 2: no need to calculate r_G ($= .04$), because rank-sum test is not statistically significant.

5. (a) Exp. 5: $N = 14$; $z = (95.5 - 52.5)/\sqrt{29(52.5)/6} = 2.70, p < .05$; reject H_0. $r_c = .82$.

(b) Exp. 6: $N = 13$; $z = (33.5 - 45.5)/\sqrt{27(45.5)/6} = -0.84, p > .05$; retain H_0.

7. (a) $N = 10$; $z = (42.5 - 27.5)/\sqrt{21(27.5)/6} = 1.53, p > .05$; retain H_0.

(b) $r_c = 4(42.5 - 27.5)/10(11) = .55$

Chapter 9

1. (a) $\sum z_x z_y = 4.70$; $r_{xy} = +.67$. (This is a highly positive correlation, which tells us that there is a strong tendency for students who do well in the first semester to also do well in their sophomore year and that those who do poorly in the first semester tend to do poorly in their sophomore year.)

(b) $\sum CY = 61$; $\mu_c = 3$; $\sigma_c = 1.41$; $\mu_y = 3$; $\sigma_y = .60$; $r_{cy} = -.34, df = 5$, $p > .05$. Retain H_0; there is not sufficient reason to believe that the correlation is different from zero in the population.

(c) $\sum CX = 1{,}695$; $\mu_c = 3$; $\sigma_c = 1.41$; $\mu_x = 80$; $\sigma_x = 8.02$; $r_{cx} = .19$, $df = 5$, $p > .05$.
    Retain H_0; there is not sufficient reason to believe that the correlation is different from zero in the population.

3. (a) $\sum XY = 96{,}426$; $\overline{X} = 84$; $s_x = 10.76$; $\overline{Y} = 80.64$; $s_y = 13.29$; $r_{xy} = .855, df = 12, p < .01$. Reject H_0.

(b) $\sum z_x z_y = 11.98$; $r_{xy} = .855$. The same value, except for possible rounding error.

(c) $\sum XY = 94{,}502$; $\overline{X} = 84$; $s_x = 10.76$; $\overline{Y} = 80.64$; $s_y = 13.29$; $r_{xy} = -.18, df = 12, p < .05$. Retain H_0.

5. (a) $r_s = 1 - (6 \times 104)/2{,}730 = .77 > .648$ (critical r_s for $N = 10$ for a .05, two-tailed test); reject H_0. $r_s = .77 < r_{xy} = .855$. The Spearman correlation throws away some of the quantitative information in the data and is, therefore, often smaller (and has less power) than the corresponding Pearson r calculated on the raw data. However, for some data patterns, r_s will be higher than r. Also, the critical value for r_s will be higher than the corresponding critical value for r, although the difference becomes negligible when N is large.

(b) $r_s = 1 - (6 \times 586)/2{,}730 = |-.28| < .648$, so $p > .05$; retain H_0. This is a case in which r_s is actually larger in magnitude than the corresponding r_{xy}—that is, $|-.28| > |-.18|$.

Chapter 10

1. $b_{yc} = -.14$; $a_{yc} = 3.42$; $Y' = -.14C + 3.42$; $Y' = 2.3$

3. Data set 3: $b_{YX} = .86$ $(13.29/10.76) = 1.06$; $a_{YX} = 80.64 - 1.06$ $(84) = -8.4$; $Y' = 1.06X - 8.4$; $r_{xy}^2 = .86^2 = .74$; $s_{est} = 13.29\sqrt{(13/12)(1 - .74)} = 7.05$

Data set 3: X rearranged: $b_{YX} = -.18 \ (13.29/10.76) = -.22$; $a_{YX} = 80.64 - (-.22)(84) = 99.12$; $Y' = -.22X + 99.12$; $r^2_{xy} = -.18^2 = .0324$; $s_{est} = 13.29\sqrt{(13/12)(1 - .0324)} = 13.61$

5. The t value for these data $= 1.19$, so, using Formula 7.12, $g =$

$$1.19\sqrt{\frac{41 + 31}{41 \times 31}} = .28; \text{ using Formula 10.9, } r_{pb} = \sqrt{\frac{.28^2}{.28^2 + 4\left(\dfrac{70}{72}\right)}} =$$

$$\sqrt{\frac{.28^2}{.28^2 + 3.89}} = .141; \ r^2_{pb} = .141^2 = .02; \text{ only 2\% of the variance is accounted for.}$$

7.

t	N_1	N_2	r_{pb}
2.11	12	8	.445
2.75	12	8	.544
6.00	12	8	.816
2.11	19	23	.316
2.75	19	23	.399
6.00	19	23	.688
2.11	51	51	.206
2.75	51	51	.265
6.00	51	51	.514

Chapter 11

1. (a) $\mathbf{d} = 20/100 = .20$; $\delta = .20\sqrt{25} = 1.0$; for a two-tailed test, power $= .17$; for a one-tailed test, power $= .26$. Power is higher for the one-tailed test, because you are putting all your alpha in just one tail and therefore have a smaller critical value to beat.

  (b) $\mathbf{d} = 50/100 = .50$; $\delta = .50\sqrt{25} = 2.5$; power $= .71$ (two-tailed), or power $= .80$ (one-tailed). These power values are higher because the effect size increased from .20 to .50. As $\mathbf{d}$ increases, power increases.

  (c) $\delta = .20\sqrt{100} = 2.0$; power $= .52$ (two-tailed), or power $= .64$ (one-tailed). Larger samples yield higher values for delta (all else equal) and thus increase the likelihood of correctly rejecting H_0. So, power increases as N increases.

  (d) For .05, two-tailed: $N = (2.80/.20)^2 = 196$; for .01, two-tailed: $N = (3.40/.20)^2 = 289$.

  (e) For .05, two-tailed: $N = (2.80/.50)^2 = 31$; for .01, two-tailed: $N = (3.40/.50)^2 = 46$

3. (a) $\mathbf{d} = .10/\sqrt{(.5)(.5)} = .10/.50 = .20$; $\delta = .20\sqrt{81} = 1.8$; Power $= .22$. He is very unlikely to reject H_0 even when specified H_A is true, so the experimental plan is not good.

  (b) Power improves to .44, but he still has a better chance of failing to reject H_0 than rejecting it, when the specified H_A is true.

  (c) $N = (2.63/.20)^2 = 173$

5. $\rho = .52$; $N = (2.47/.52)^2 + 1 = 24$

7. (a) $n = 2(41)(31)/(41 + 31) = 35.31$; $g = \sqrt{2/35.31}\,(1.19) = .283$;
$n = 2(2.47/.283)^2 = 152$.
   (b) $\mathbf{d} = \sqrt{2/35.31}\,(2.8) = .67$

9. $\delta = \sqrt{1/.6}\sqrt{15/2}\,(1.32) = 4.66$; power $= .98$

11. (a) $g = \sqrt{2/10}\,(1.45) = .65$; $\delta = \sqrt{10/2}\,(.65) = .29$; power $= .06$
    (b) $\delta = \sqrt{1/.5}\sqrt{2/10}\,(.65) = 2.01$; power $= .52$

Chapter 12

1. (a) There appears to be less within-group variability in Experiment 1 and the between-group variability is equal, so the results of Experiment 1 are more likely to be statistically significant.
   (b) $\sum X^2 = 302$; $\overline{X}_G = 4$; $SS_T = 62$; $SS_{bet} = 40$; $SS_W = 22$; $MS_{bet} = 20$; $MS_W = 1.83$; $F(2, 12) = 10.93$, $p < .05$. Reject H_0; conclude that reward type affects performance. $\eta^2 = 40/62 = .65$.
   (c) $\sum X^2 = 490$; $\overline{X}_G = 4$; $SS_T = 250$; $SS_{bet} = 40$; $SS_W = 210$; $MS_{bet} = 20$; $MS_W = 17.5$; $F(2, 12) = 1.14$, $p > .05$. Retain H_0; there is not sufficient reason to conclude that reward type affects performance. $\eta^2 = 40/250 = .16$.
   (d) There is much more within-group (error) variation in Experiment 2, thus group differences comprise a smaller part of the total variance. In Experiment 1, most of the total variation is due to between-groups differences.
   (e) Est. $\omega^2 = 36.34/63.83 = .57$

3. (a) Experiment 1:

Source	SS	df	MS	F	p
Between-groups	173.36	2	86.68	1.63	> .05
Within-groups	797.70	15	53.18		
Total	971.06	17			

There is not sufficient evidence to reject the null hypothesis that the means of the three populations are equal, $F(2, 15) = 1.63$, $p > .05$, $\eta^2 = .217$.
   (b) Experiment 2:

Source	SS	df	MS	F	p
Between-groups	527.98	2	263.99	8.77	< .01
Within-groups	451.64	15	30.11		
Total	979.62	17			

The three population means are not all equal, $F(2, 15) = 8.77$, $p < .01$, est. $\omega^2 = .46$.

5. (a) Exp. 3: $\sum R = 406$; $df = 2$; $H = 12(40.99)/812 = 0.61$, $p > .05$ (not significant).

(b) Exp. 4: $H = 12(966.45)/812 = 14.28$, $p < .01$; reject H_0. $\eta^2 = 966.45/3745.25 = .258$. Group 1 versus 2, $z = 25/13.16 = 1.90$, $p > .05$ (not significant, but close). Group 2 versus 3, $z = 33.5/10.39 = 3.22$, $p < .01$. Group 1 versus 3, $z = 34.5/12.11 = 2.85$, $p < .01$.

7. (a) $\eta^2 = (2 \times 3.69)/[(2 \times 3.69) + 57] = 7.38/64.38 = .115$; this is a moderately large effect size.

   (b) $\omega^2 = (2 \times 2.69)/[2 \times 2.69) + 57] = .086$.

Chapter 13

1. Exp. 1: $\text{LSD} = 2.179\sqrt{3.66/5} = 1.82$; Exp. 2: $\text{LSD} = 2.179\sqrt{35/5} = 5.64$. LSD is justified only for Experiment 1 because H_0 is rejected in that case. All pairs of means differ significantly for Experiment 1.

3. Exp. 1: $\text{LSD} = 2.131\sqrt{106.36/5.89} = 9.06$; no pairs of means differ.
   $\text{HSD} = 3.67\sqrt{53.18/5.89} = 11.03$; no pairs of means differ.
   Exp. 2: $\text{LSD} = 2.131\sqrt{60.22/5.89} = 6.81$; Group 1 differs from Groups 2 and 3.
   $\text{HSD} = 3.67\sqrt{30.11/5.89} = 8.30$; Group 1 differs from Groups 2 and 3.
   LSD values are smaller than HSD, which increases the chance of finding a significant difference between pairs of means. LSD is generally more powerful than HSD.

5. (a) Sample 1 differs significantly from Samples 2, 3, and 5; also, Samples 4 and 5 differ significantly. (b) The 95% CI for Sample 5 is 15.8 ± 5.3, so it goes from 10.5 to 21.1 [Note that the means for Samples 1 and 4 do not fall within the CI for Sample 5, which is consistent with the results in part (a).]

7. (a) $MS_W = MS_{\text{Bet}}/F = 66.467/3.69 = 18.01$; $\text{LSD} = 2.0 \times \sqrt{(36.02/20)} = 2.68$. (b) Only the means for positive and negative feedback differ significantly according to the LSD test.

Chapter 14

1. (a)

Source	SS	df	MS	F	p
Phobia	32.44	2	16.22	6.34	< .05
Gender	2.00	1	2.00	.78	> .05
Phobia × Gender	1.33	2	.67	.26	> .05
Error	30.67	12	2.56		
Total	66.44	17			

(b) $\text{LSD} = 2.179\sqrt{5.12/6} = 2.01$. Therefore, the low-phobia group differs from the moderate- and high-phobia groups. The F value for phobia is statistically significant, so these follow-up tests comparing the marginal means of the phobia groups are justified.

3. (a) $MS_{caffeine} = 2.52$; $MS_W = 2.0$; $F_{caffeine}\,(1,24) = 1.26$, $p > .05$
$MS_{sex} = .63$; $MS_W = 2.0$; $F_{sex}\,(1,24) = .32$, $p > .05$
$MS_{inter} = 154.63$; $MS_W = 2.0$; $F_{inter}\,(1,24) = 77.32$, $p < .01$

(b) Graph shows a disordinal interaction.

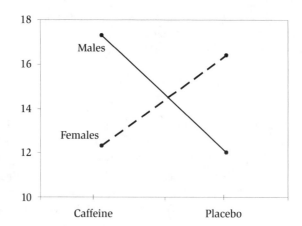

(c) The significant interaction justifies the testing of the four simple main effects. Thus, men given caffeine scored significantly higher than men given placebos, $t(24) = 7.01$, $p < .01$, whereas women with caffeine had lower scores than women given placebos, $t(24) = -5.42$, $p < .01$. Men with caffeine had higher scores than women with caffeine, $t(24) = 6.61$, $p < .01$, but men given placebos had lower scores than women given placebos, $t(24) = -5.82$, $p < .01$. In general, these results show that caffeine increases performance for men but decreases performance for women.

Chapter 15

1. $SS_{total} = 91.0$; $SS_{treat} = 5.0$; $SS_{sub} = 65$; $SS_{error} = 21.0$; $MS_{treat} = 5.0$; $MS_{error} = 2.33$; $F(1,9) = 2.14$, $p > .05$. Relationship is that $F = t^2$.

3. $SS_{total} = 100.0$; $SS_{treat} = 24.5$; $SS_{sub} = 46.1$; $SS_{error} = 29.4$; $MS_{treat} = 12.25$; $MS_{error} = 1.336$; $F(2,22) = 9.17$, $p > .01$, sphericity assumed. Adjusted $F_{.05}(1,11) = 4.84$; therefore, F is significant at the .05 level without assuming sphericity.

5. (a) $SS_{total} = 551.5$; $SS_{treat} = 260.5$; $SS_{sub} = 155.5$; $SS_{error} = 135.5$; $MS_{treat} = 86.83$; $MS_{error} = 6.45$; $F(3,21) = 13.46$, $p < .01$; $(4-1)/2 = 6$ pairwise comparisons; $\alpha_{pc} = .05/6 = .00833$.

(b) $SS_{groups} = 33.89$; $SS_W = 121.61$; $SS_{RM} = 260.5$; $SS_{inter} = 99.11$; $SS_{error} = 36.39$; $F_{ability} = 33.89/20.27 = 1.67$, $p > .05$; $F_{word} = 86.83/2.02 = 42.99$, $p < .01$; $F_{inter} = 33.04/2.02 = 16.36$, $p < .01$.

(c) Graph of cell means.

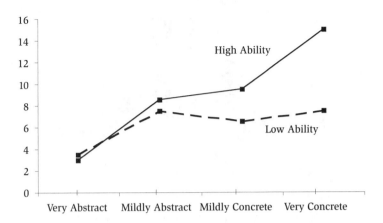

You can see from the graph that there is some interaction, as the lines increasingly diverge with greater concreteness. There is also a visible main effect for word concreteness, due chiefly to the high-ability participants. Also, the high-ability participants are somewhat higher than low-ability participants across word conditions, but the (usually) larger error term for the between-group test prevented this result from attaining significance.

Chapter 16

1. (a) $p = 4/52 = 1/13 = .077$
   (b) $p = 45/52 - 8/52 = 34/52 = .654$
   (c) $p(A \text{ and } B) = 1/52 \times 1/52 = .00037$
   (d) $p(A \text{ and } B) = 20/52 \times 2/52 = .0148$
   (e) $p(A \text{ and } B) = 1/52 \times 0 = 0$; $p(A \text{ and } B) = 20/52 \times 2/51 = .0151$

3. (a) $1/100 = .01$
   (b) $1/100 = .01$
   (c) $.01 + .01 = .02$
   (d) $5/100 = .05$
   (e) $10/100 = .10$
   (f) $50/100 = .50$
   (g) $.50 \times .17 = .085$
   (h) $.05 + .28 - .02 = .31$

5. (a) $2^4 = 16$; $4!/2! = 24/2 = 12$
   (b) Binomial distribution for $N = 4$ and $P = .5$

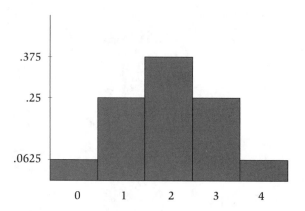

(c) From your answer to part b, it should be clear that the p for 4 tails (or 0 heads) is .0625. Even for a one-tailed test, $p > .05$, so you cannot reject the null hypothesis that the coin is fair (i.e., $P = .5$).

7. (a) $z = [18 - 28\,(.5)]/\sqrt{28\,(.5)\,(.5)} = 1.51, p = .0655$; retain H_0.

    (b) $z = [20 - 28\,(.5)]/\sqrt{28\,(.5)\,(.5)} = 2.27, p = .0116$; reject H_0.

Chapter 17

1. (a) $\chi^2 = 4.0$; $df = 1$; $p < .05$. Reject H_0; conclude that patients are more likely to improve with new treatment.

    (b) $z = [60 - 100\,(.5)]/\sqrt{100\,(.5)\,(.5)} = 2.0$; relationship is $z^2 = \chi^2$

3. (a) $\chi^2 = [(21 - 19.75)^2/19.75] + [(14 - 19.75)^2/19.75] + [(26 - 19.75)^2/19.75] + [(18 - 19.75)^2/19.75] = 3.89$. Retain H_0; $3.89 < \chi^2_{.05}\,(3) = 7.82$

    (b) $\chi^2 = 9.56$; $df = 3$, $p < .05$. Reject H_0; $9.56 > \chi^2_{.05}\,(3) = 7.82$

5. (a) $\chi^2 = [(12 - 13.2)^2/13.2] + [(10 - 8.8)^2/8.8] + [(18 - 16.8)^2/16.8] + [(10 - 11.2)^2/11.2] = .49$. Retain H_0; $.49 < \chi^2_{.05}\,(1) = 3.84$. This is equivalent to saying that the percent success is not significantly different between the sexes.

    (b) $\phi = \sqrt{.49/50} = .10$; small effect

7. (a) $\chi^2 = 18.84$; $df = 4$; $p < .01$. Reject H_0; $18.84 > \chi^2_{.01}\,(4) = 13.28$

    (b) $\phi_c = \sqrt{18.84/\,(143)\,(2)} = .26$; moderate relationship

Data from Ihno's Experiment

Sub_num	Gender	Major	Reason	Exp_cond	Coffee	Num_cups	Phobia	Prevmath	Mathquiz	Statquiz	Exp_sqz	Hr_base	Hr_pre	Hr_post	Anx_base	Anx_pre	Anx_post
1	1	1	3	1	1	0	1	3	43	6	7	71	68	65	17	22	20
2	1	1	2	1	0	0	1	4	49	9	11	73	75	68	17	19	16
3	1	1	1	1	0	0	4	1	26	8	8	69	76	72	19	14	15
4	1	1	1	1	0	0	4	0	29	7	8	72	73	78	19	13	16
5	1	1	1	1	0	1	10	1	31	6	6	71	83	74	26	30	25
6	1	1	1	2	1	1	4	1	20	7	6	70	71	76	12	15	19
7	1	1	1	2	0	0	4	2	13	3	4	71	70	66	12	16	17
8	1	1	3	2	1	2	4	1	23	7	7	77	87	84	17	19	22
9	1	1	1	2	0	0	4	1	38	8	7	73	72	67	20	14	17
10	1	1	1	2	1	2	5	0		7	6	78	76	74	20	24	19
11	1	1	1	2	0	1	5	1	29	8	10	74	72	73	21	25	22
12	1	1	1	2	0	0	4	0	32	8	7	73	74	74	32	35	33
13	1	1	1	2	0	1	7	0	18	1	3	73	76	78	19	23	20
14	1	1	3	3	0	2	4	1		5	4	72	83	77	18	27	28
15	1	1	1	4	1	3	3	1	21	8	6	72	74	68	21	27	22
16	1	1	1	4	1	0	8	0		3	1	76	76	79	14	18	21
17	1	1	1	4	0	0	4	1	37	8	7	68	67	74	15	19	18
18	1	1	1	4	1	3	5	1	37	7	4	77	78	73	39	39	40
19	1	1	3	4	1	2	0	3	32	10	9	74	74	75	20	12	18
20	1	2	1	2	1	1	4	1		7	7	74	75	73	15	11	20
21	1	2	2	2	1	2	4	0	25	7	6	74	84	77	19	27	23
22	1	2	1	3	1	0	3	1	22	4	3	73	71	79	18	13	19
23	1	2	1	3	0	2	4	1	35	8	7	71	74	76	18	22	25
24	1	2	2	2	1	2	0	3	47	8	7	75	75	71	23	28	24
25	1	2	2	3	1	2	1	3	41	6	6	76	73	72	18	24	26
26	1	2	2	4	0	0	1	4	26	7	6	71	76	75	14	10	18
27	1	2	2	4	1	2	0	6	39	8	8	74	79	79	17	12	16
28	1	2	3	1	1	3	4	2	21	7	8	78	79	73	18	13	16
29	1	2	1	1	0	0	3	2		7	9	70	63	66	18	12	14
30	1	2	3	1	1	0	5	1	22	4	7	73	78	69	21	14	17
31	1	3	1	1	1	1	9	1	21	8	8	75	83	73	18	21	23
32	1	3	1	3	1	3	3	0		7	6	78	76	84	24	27	25
33	1	3	1	4	1	2	4	1	26	8	7	76	74	81	17	26	15
34	1	3	2	1	1	1	1	1	20	8	9	76	69	71	17	25	19
35	1	3	2	1	0	0	2	1	30	6	9	69	69	64	22	16	18
36	1	3	2	2	1	1	0	0	40	8	9	77	79	74	21	14	19
37	1	3	2	4	1	2	3	1	35	8	7	78	73	78	19	12	17
38	1	3	3	1	0	0	2	0	10	7	8	74	72	72	15	21	16
39	1	3	3	2	0	1	8	1	35	6	5	71	70	75	20	27	22
40	1	3	3	4	0	0	4	1	44	6	4	67	67	73	12	19	17
41	1	3	3	4	0	0	4	1	26	7	5	77	78	78	21	15	15
42	1	4	2	1	0	0	0	1		9	11	71	72	67	20	23	21
43	1	4	2	2	1	0	3	1	15	3	4	76	79	71	19	21	17
44	1	4	2	4	0	0	2	1	42	7	7	69	70	64	13	24	22

(continued)

Data from Ihno's Experiment (*continued*)

Sub_num	Gender	Major	Reason	Exp_cond	Coffee	Num_cups	Phobia	Prevmath	Mathquiz	Statquiz	Exp_sqz	Hr_base	Hr_pre	Hr_post	Anx_base	Anx_pre	Anx_post
45	1	4	2	4	0	0	2	1	33	8	7	72	64	68	20	14	22
46	1	4	2	4	0	1	1	0	29	6	6	72	79	76	22	27	24
47	1	4	3	1	0	0	1	1	39	7	8	71	63	66	15	21	13
48	1	4	3	1	1	1	5	0	38	8	8	71	82	79	20	26	26
49	1	4	3	2	1	1	5	1		5	4	75	76	70	16	18	23
50	1	4	3	3	0	0	4	1	24	7	6	74	76	75	22	27	23
51	1	4	3	3	0	0	4	1		7	5	74	74	69	30	36	32
52	1	4	3	4	1	0	10	0	26	5	2	78	80	80	19	24	24
53	1	4	3	4	0	0	7	1	14	5	3	68	78	73	20	29	30
54	1	5	1	3	1	1	3	5	45	9	9	76	79	75	15	8	17
55	1	5	1	3	1	2	4	1	28	8	8	73	78	77	19	13	18
56	1	5	2	4	0	1	2	2	31	8	7	74	78	82	27	21	24
57	1	5	3	1	0	0	2	0		8	9	72	67	67	16	20	22
58	2	1	1	1	1	1	1	1	32	8	10	74	84	76	17	19	14
59	2	1	2	1	0	0	7	0	15	3	6	73	73	71	19	16	16
60	2	1	1	2	0	1	5	0	26	8	7	73	74	76	16	20	17
61	2	1	1	3	1	1	5	1	26	8	7	80	82	86	18	27	20
62	2	1	1	3	0	0	1	2	32	5	5	67	68	73	20	25	24
63	2	1	1	3	0	0	3	0	21	8	7	65	75	69	26	29	23
64	2	1	1	4	0	0	3	1	43	8	8	71	72	76	18	13	16
65	2	1	1	4	0	1	5	1		8	5	72	75	68	21	26	27
66	2	1	2	2	0	0	1	4	34	9	11	70	73	65	11	19	9
67	2	1	3	1	0	0	0	3	33	10	11	72	67	68	16	25	15
68	2	2	1	2	0	0	5	0	30	7	7	69	70	74	18	15	15
69	2	2	1	3	0	0	6	2	46	8	6	68	74	71	16	10	17
70	2	2	1	3	1	1	3	2		7	7	76	79	71	19	13	15
71	2	2	1	4	1	1	5	0	33	7	4	68	71	77	18	21	19
72	2	2	1	4	1	2	4	2	29	7	6	76	79	71	22	15	20
73	2	2	2	3	0	0	0	4	30	9	10	69	70	74	15	21	17
74	2	2	2	3	0	0	2	4	34	8	7	68	70	69	18	21	19
75	2	2	2	4	0	0	2	3	32	9	8	70	62	71	17	23	19
76	2	2	3	1	0	0	3	1	37	6	8	70	73	77	15	23	14
77	2	2	1	2	1	1	1	2		8	10	69	67	64	14	17	15
78	2	2	3	2	0	0	1	3	31	7	8	64	74	70	22	25	19
79	2	2	3	3	1	1	0	2	30	8	8	68	72	71	10	13	15
80	2	2	3	3	0	0	2	2	28	5	5	71	74	67	15	17	17
81	2	2	3	4	0	1	10	0	14	6	3	69	78	76	20	25	23
82	2	3	1	1	0	0	3	1	9	7	8	71	69	76	13	10	13
83	2	3	1	1	0	1	3	1	11	4	7	72	83	73	14	16	15
84	2	3	1	1	1	1	8	1	30	6	7	76	78	71	15	18	17
85	2	3	1	1	1	0	3	1	15	5	7	76	67	71	18	12	17
86	2	3	3	2	0	0	3	1	32	3	5	72	70	67	15	9	13
87	2	3	2	2	1	0	1	0	22	5	4	74	78	72	20	27	18
88	2	3	2	3	0	0	1	4		8	9	70	71	69	10	16	14
89	2	3	3	2	0	0	2	0	25	6	7	68	70	73	16	20	19
90	2	3	3	3	0	0	8	1	18	4	3	71	73	77	15	19	21
91	2	3	3	3	1	1	3	1	11	4	3	72	75	76	24	17	21
92	2	4	2	1	0	0	0	1	11	6	9	71	78	72	16	21	15
93	2	4	2	4	0	0	0	2	37	9	9	72	71	73	17	11	17
94	2	4	3	3	1	2	4	0	28	7	6	73	77	79	24	18	20

Data from Ihno's Experiment (*continued*)

Sub_num	Gender	Major	Reason	Exp_cond	Coffee	Num_cups	Phobia	Prevmath	Mathquiz	Statquiz	Exp_sqz	Hr_base	Hr_pre	Hr_post	Anx_base	Anx_pre	Anx_post
95	2	5	3	3	0	0	7	2		8	6	69	70	71	23	28	24
96	2	5	2	2	1	1	0	1	33	7	9	74	73	71	17	18	17
97	2	5	2	3	0	0	0	2	28	8	9	70	66	65	17	12	13
98	2	5	2	3	0	0	2	2	38	9	10	65	65	69	18	14	19
99	2	5	2	4	1	1	1	4	41	8	8	72	68	73	17	11	18
100	2	5	1	2	0	0	2	2	39	7	7	70	70	64	17	11	14

Key

Sub_num: arbitrary ID number for each participant.

Gender: 1 = Female; 2 = Male.

Major: 1 = Psychology; 2 = Pre-Med; 3 = Biology; 4 = Sociology; 5 = Economics.

Reason: 1 = Program requirement; 2 = Personal interest; 3 = Advisor recommendation.

Exp_cond: 1 = Easy; 2 = Moderate; 3 = Difficult; 4 = Impossible.

Coffee: 0 = not a regular coffee drinker; 1 = regularly drinks coffee.

Num_cups = number of cups of coffee drunk prior to the experiment on the same day.

Phobia: 0 = No phobia to 10 = Extreme phobia.

Prevmath = Number of math courses taken prior to statistics course.

Mathquiz = Score on Math Background Quiz (a blank for this value indicates that a student did not take the quiz).

Statquiz = Score on 10-question stats quiz given one week before the experiment.

Exp_sqz = Score on stats quiz given as part of the experiment (number correct, including the 11th question).

HR_base = Baseline heart rate (in beats per minute).

HR_pre = Prequiz heart rate.

HR_post = Postquiz heart rate.

Anx_base = Baseline anxiety score.

Anx_pre = Prequiz anxiety score.

Anx_post = Postquiz anxiety score.

Glossary of Terms

Absolute values Numerical values with the signs ignored; thus all absolute values are treated as positive.

Alpha The (conditional) probability of committing a Type I error (i.e., rejecting the null hypothesis when the null hypothesis is true).

Alternative hypothesis The hypothesis that states that the null hypothesis is *not true* and specifies some other value or set of values for the population parameter(s) in question.

Analysis of variance (ANOVA) Procedures for testing hypotheses about the equality of population means.

A *priori* (planned) comparison In analysis of variance, a significance test involving two or more group means that was planned before the results were in.

Area of rejection All numerical results of a statistical test that will cause the null hypothesis to be rejected.

Bar chart A graph in which the heights of the bars show how often each measure or range of measures was obtained. Spaces between adjacent bars are used to indicate that the data come from a discrete variable.

Beta The (conditional) probability of committing a Type II error (i.e., failing to reject the null hypothesis when the null hypothesis is *not* true).

Between-group variance In analysis of variance, variability based on differences among the means of the various groups.

Bimodal distribution A distribution that has two pronounced peaks when graphed as a frequency polygon.

Bivariate normal distribution A joint distribution of two variables, wherein scores on one variable are normally distributed for each score value of the other.

Bonferroni correction (or adjustment) A reduction in the alpha used for each of several planned comparisons based on dividing the desired experimentwise alpha by the number of tests planned.

Carryover effects In a repeated-measures design, it is the persistence of the effect of one condition that affects a participant's response to subsequent conditions; they can produce misleading results.

Central tendency The general location of a set of scores.

Chi square distribution This statistical model can be used to test hypotheses when data are in the form of frequencies.

Class interval One set of score values in a grouped frequency distribution.

Complex comparison (or contrast)   In analysis of variance, a significance test involving a weighted combination of three or more group means.

Confidence interval   A range of values within which a specified population parameter has a given probability of falling.

Confidence limits   The upper and lower end points of a confidence interval.

Constant   A numerical value that is exactly the same for all cases or subjects; the opposite of a *variable*.

Continuous variable   A variable for which it is theoretically possible for an intermediate value to occur between any specified pair of score values.

Control group   A group that does *not* receive the treatment whose effects are being investigated by the researcher. Used as a baseline against which to evaluate the performance of the experimental group.

Correlation coefficient   A measure of the extent to which scores on one variable are related to scores on a second variable.

Counterbalancing   In a repeated-measures design, it is a system of assigning different orders of the RM conditions to different participants, so that no one condition will benefit from order effects more than any other condition.

Cramér's phi   A measure of the strength of the relationship between two variables, both of which are categorical, and at least one of which has more than two levels.

Criterion   The variable being predicted in a linear regression analysis; a dependent variable.

Criterion of significance   A numerical value or decision rule that specifies when the null hypothesis is to be rejected.

Cumulative frequency distribution   A listing that shows how many times a given score or less was obtained.

d   The standardized difference between two population means (a measure of effect size).

Decile   One of nine transformed scores that divides the number of cases into 10 equal parts.

Degrees of freedom   The number of quantities that are free to vary when we estimate the value of a parameter from a statistic.

Delta   In power analysis, an index that combines the population effect size and the sample size.

Dependent variable   A variable that may or may not change with changes in one or more independent variables.

Descriptive statistics   Mathematical procedures for summarizing and describing the characteristics of a set of data.

Deviation score   The difference between a score and the mean of the set of scores of which it is a member.

Dichotomous variable   A variable with only two categories.

Discrete variable   A variable for which it is *not* theoretically possible for any value to occur between any specified pair of score values.

Distribution-free statistical test   A statistical test that does *not* require any assumptions about the shape of the distribution in the population.

Effect size   How large the phenomenon we wish to investigate is in the population; the extent to which the null hypothesis is false.

Error variance   In analysis of variance, differences among scores or group means that *cannot* be explained by the experimental treatment(s).

Eta squared   The proportion of variance accounted for in analysis of variance.

Experimental group   A group that receives the treatment whose effects are being investigated by the researcher.

Experimental (or empirical) sampling distribution   A distribution whose elements are statistics (e.g., sample means) obtained by drawing repeated samples from the population and computing that statistic for each sample.

Experimentwise error rate   The rate of occurrence of *any* (one or more) Type I errors when a *series* of individual statistical tests is conducted within the same study.

F distributions   The statistical model used to test hypotheses when the analysis involves the comparison of variance estimates.

Factorial design   A procedure used to study the relationship of two or more independent variables (factors) to a dependent variable.

Familywise error rate   The experimentwise error rate for a subset of the tests in an experiment, such that the subset can be viewed as a "family" of tests (e.g., pairwise comparisons for the main effect of one factor in a two-way factorial analysis of variance).

Frequency   The number of times a specified score or range of scores was obtained.

Frequency polygon   A graph showing how often each score or range of scores was obtained.

Glass rank biserial correlation   A measure of the strength of the relationship between membership in one of two independent samples and a set of ranked data.

Grouped frequency distribution   A listing of sets of two or more score values (class intervals) together with the number of times that scores in each class interval were obtained.

Histogram   A bar graph in which there is no space between adjacent bars (for use with continuous data).

Homogeneity of variance   In a *t* test or analysis of variance, equality of the variances for all treatment populations.

Hypothesis testing   Procedures for deciding whether to retain or reject the null hypothesis about one or more population parameters.

Independent events   Events whose occurrence or nonoccurrence is unrelated to the occurrence (or probability of occurrence) of specified other events.

Independent samples   Samples such that any element in one sample has no connection of any kind with any element in another sample.

Independent variable   A variable whose variation is studied with regard to its effect on another (dependent) variable.

Inferential statistics   Mathematical procedures for drawing inferences about characteristics of a population, based on what is observed in samples from that population.

Interaction   The joint effect of two or more independent variables on a dependent variable, over and above their separate (main) effects.

Interval estimate   A synonym for confidence interval.

J-curve   A distribution that looks like the letter J or its mirror image when graphed as a frequency polygon.

Kruskal-Wallis H test   A nonparametric procedure for testing hypotheses about differences among the locations of two or more independent populations, used when data are in the form of ranks.

Least squares regression line   The regression line that minimizes the sum of squared errors in prediction (the sum of squared deviations between the predicted scores and actual scores).

Linear regression   Procedure for determining the straight line that will enable us to predict scores on one variable (the criterion) from scores on another variable (the predictor), while minimizing the amount of (squared) error.

Lower real limit   The lower end point of a score or class interval when dealing with continuous data.

Marginal frequency   A column or row total in a two-way table of joint frequencies.

Matched-pairs rank biserial correlation   A measure of the strength of the relationship between membership in one of two matched samples and a set of ranked data.

Matched samples   Samples such that each element in one sample is paired with one element in the other sample(s).

Matched t test   Procedure for testing a hypothesis about the difference between two population means, using matched samples, or two measurements on each participant.

Mean (arithmetic)   A measure of the central tendency of a set of scores, obtained by summing all scores and dividing by the number of scores. When the term *mean* is used without a qualifier, it is the arithmetic mean that is meant.

Mean (Harmonic)   A measure of central tendency that is based on averaging the reciprocals of the scores and then taking the reciprocal of that average.

Mean square   In analysis of variance, an estimate of the population variance that is obtained by dividing a sum of squares by its associated degrees of freedom.

Median   The score in the middle of a distribution such that exactly half the scores are higher and exactly half the scores are equal or lower; the score corresponding to the 50th percentile.

Midpoint   The value halfway between the lower real limit and the upper real limit of a class interval.

Mode   The score that occurs most often in a frequency distribution.

Multiple comparisons   In analysis of variance, procedures for testing hypotheses about differences between specified pairs of means.

Mutually exclusive events   Events that cannot happen simultaneously.

Negatively skewed distribution   A distribution with some extremely low scores, resulting in a frequency polygon with a pronounced tail at the left.

Nonparametric statistical test   A statistical test that does not involve the estimation of any population parameters.

Normal distribution   A particular bell-shape, symmetric, and unimodal distribution defined by a specific mathematical equation.

Null hypothesis   The hypothesis that specifies the value of a population parameter or a difference between two or more population parameters (usually zero) and that is assumed to be true at the outset of the statistical analysis.

Odds against an event   The ratio of the number of unfavorable outcomes to the number of favorable outcomes.

One-tailed test of significance   A statistical test wherein the null hypothesis can be rejected only if results are in the direction predicted by the experimenter.

Order effects   In a repeated-measures design, simple order effects can be produced on later conditions from the practice or fatigue of having been involved in previous conditions. Simple order effects can be neutralized by counterbalancing, but carryover effects may not; see also carryover effects.

Parameter   A numerical quantity that summarizes some characteristic of a population.

Pearson *r*   A measure of the strength of the linear relationship between two variables, both of which are either continuous or dichotomous.

Percentile   A score at or below which a given percent of the cases fall.

Percentile rank   The percent of cases in a specific reference group that fall at or below a given score.

Phi coefficient   A measure of the strength of the relationship between two variables, both of which are dichotomous (that is, they have only two categories).

Point-biserial correlation coefficient   A measure of the strength of the relationship between one dichotomous and one continuous variable.

Point estimate   A single statistic used to estimate the value of the corresponding population parameter.

Pooled variance   In the significance test of the difference between two means, an estimate of the population variance (assumed to be the same for both populations) obtained from a weighted average of the sample variances.

Population   *All* of the cases in which a researcher is interested; a (usually very large) group of people, animals, objects, or responses that are alike in at least one respect.

Population variance estimate   An estimate of the variability in a population, obtained by dividing the sum of squared deviations from the sample mean by $N - 1$.

Positively skewed distribution   A distribution with some extremely high scores, resulting in a frequency polygon with a pronounced tail at the right.

Post hoc comparison   In analysis of variance, a significance test involving two or more group means that was not planned prior to obtaining the results.

Power efficiency of a nonparametric test   How many fewer cases, expressed as a percent, that are required by a parametric test to have the same power as the nonparametric test when the assumptions of the parametric test are met.

Power of a statistical test   The probability of obtaining a statistically significant result if the null hypothesis is actually false; the probability of rejecting a false null hypothesis.

Predicted score   In linear regression, the score on the criterion that is estimated for a case with a specified score on the predictor.

Predictor   In linear regression, the variable from which criterion scores are estimated; an independent variable.

Probability of an event   The number of ways the specified event can occur, divided by the total number of possible occurrences.

Protected t test   In analysis of variance, a procedure for conducting multiple comparisons between pairs of group means that requires the analysis of variance to be statistically significant before proceeding.

Quartile   One of three transformed scores that divide the number of cases into four equal parts.

Randomized-blocks design   This is an extension of the matched-pairs design to more than two conditions. Participants are matched in blocks according to the number of different levels of the factor, and then one member of each block is randomly assigned to each condition.

Random sample   A sample drawn in such a way that each element in the population has an equal chance of being included in the sample.

Range   The largest score minus the smallest score in a set of scores.

Rank   A measure that shows where a given case falls with respect to others in the group but gives no indication of the distance between the cases. Thus, ranks provide less information than do scores.

Rank-sum test   A nonparametric procedure for testing hypotheses about the difference in location between two populations; used when data are in the form of ranks.

Raw score   A score not subjected to any statistical transformations, such as the number correct on a test.

Rectangular distribution   A distribution wherein each score occurs with the same frequency.

Regular frequency distribution   A listing of every score value, from the lowest to the highest, together with the number of times that each score was obtained (its frequency).

Repeated-measures analysis of variance   Procedure for testing differences between two or more population means by measuring each participant under all of the conditions (i.e., levels) of the independent variable or by matching participants across two or more conditions; it is an extension of the matched (or RM) t test to any number of matched samples.

Restriction of range   Low variability, caused by the way in which the samples were defined, that will usually underestimate the correlation between two variables.

Robust statistical test   A statistical test that gives fairly accurate results even if the underlying assumptions are not met.

Sample   Any subgroup of cases drawn from a clearly specified population.

Sample size   The number of cases in a sample.

Sampling error   Differences between the value of a statistic observed in a sample and the corresponding population parameter (thus, error), caused by the accident of which cases happened to be included in the sample.

Scatter plot   A graph showing the relationship between two variables, wherein the score of each case on both variables is expressed as a point in two dimensions.

Sign test   A nonparametric method for testing hypotheses about differences in location between two matched populations that is based only on the directions of the differences between the members of the various pairs; it can be used as an alternative to the matched-pairs t test or the Wilcoxon test.

Significance test   A procedure for deciding whether to retain or reject a null hypothesis.

Simple main effect   In a two-way analysis of variance, it is the effect of one factor at only one level of the other factor.

Skewed distribution   A distribution with some extremely low scores (negatively skewed, skewed to the left) or some extremely high scores (positively skewed, skewed to the right), resulting in a frequency polygon with a pronounced tail in one direction.

Slope   In linear regression, the average rate of change in the criterion per unit increase in the predictor.

Spearman (rank-order) correlation coefficient   A measure of the strength of the relationship between two variables, both of which are in the form of ranks.

Sphericity   In an repeated-measures analysis of variance, the assumption that the variance of the difference scores is the same, in the population, for every possible pair of levels of the RM factor.

Standard deviation   A measure of the variability of the scores in a specified group, or how much the scores differ from one another; the positive square root of the variance.

Standard error   The standard deviation of some statistic in a sampling distribution (e.g., based on means rather than individual scores), which tells us how trustworthy the single statistic we have on hand is as an estimate of the corresponding parameter. Examples of parameters that are estimated include a population mean (*standard error of the mean*), a population proportion (*standard error of a proportion*), and the difference between two population means (*standard error of the difference*).

Standard error of estimate   In linear regression, a measure of the variability (average error) in prediction.

Standard scores   A synonym for z scores.

Statistic   A numerical quantity that summarizes some characteristic of a sample.

Statistical model   A summary of the probability of all possible events of a specified type (e.g., each possible value of a sample mean drawn at random from one population) under specified conditions (e.g., that the null hypothesis is true). Examples include the normal distribution, the t, the F, and the chi-square distributions.

Statistical significance   Occurs when the results of a statistical analysis indicate that the null hypothesis can be rejected.

Stem-and-leaf display   A pictorial description of a set of data that combines features of the frequency distribution and the histogram.

Summation sign   A mathematical symbol that represents the sum of a set of numbers.

Sum of squares   The sum of the squared deviations of observations from their mean.

Symmetric distribution   A distribution wherein one half is the mirror image of the other half.

t **distributions**   This statistical model can be used to test hypotheses about: the mean of one population when the population standard deviation is *not* known; the differences between the means of two populations (independent or matched samples); the significance of certain correlation coefficients; and certain multiple comparison procedures in the analysis of variance.

T **scores**   Transformed scores that have a mean of 50 and standard deviation of 10.

Theoretical sampling distribution   An estimate of an experimental sampling distribution that is determined mathematically (rather than by drawing repeated samples).

Transformed score   A score that has been altered mathematically to show its standing relative to a specified group.

Two-tailed test of significance   A statistical test of two population means wherein the null hypothesis may be rejected regardless of the direction of the results.

Type I error   Rejecting a null hypothesis that is actually true.

Type II error   Retaining a null hypothesis that is actually false.

Unimodal distribution   A distribution that has one pronounced peak when graphed as a frequency polygon.

Upper real limit   The upper endpoint of a score or class interval when dealing with continuous data.

Variability   The extent to which the scores in a specified group differ from one another, or how spread out or scattered the scores are.

Variable   Any characteristic that can take on different values.

Variance   A measure of the variability of the scores in a specified group, or how much the scores differ from one another; the square of the standard deviation.

Wilcoxon (matched-pairs) test   A nonparametric procedure for testing hypotheses about the difference between the locations of two matched populations, used when data are in the form of ranks.

Within-group variance   In analysis of variance, differences among the scores within the groups. Reflects variation that cannot be explained by the experimental treatment(s) (error variance).

Y-**intercept**   The point at which the regression line crosses the *Y*-axis.

z **scores**   Transformed scores that have a mean of 0 and standard deviation of 1.

References

American Psychological Association. (2010). *Publication manual of the American Psychological Association* (6th ed.). Washington, DC: Author.

Cohen, B. H. (2008). *Explaining psychological statistics* (3rd ed.). Hoboken, NJ: Wiley.

Cohen, J. (1988). *Statistical power analysis for the behavioral sciences* (2nd ed.). Hillsdale, NJ: Erlbaum.

Finch, S., & Cumming, G. (2009). Putting research in context: Understanding confidence intervals from one or more studies. *Journal of Pediatric Psychology, 34,* 903–916.

Greenhouse, S. W., & Geisser, S. (1959). On methods in the analysis of profile data. *Psychometrika, 24,* 95–112.

Hayter, A. J. (1986). The maximum familywise error rate of Fisher's least significant difference test. *Journal of the American Statistical Association, 81,* 1000–1004.

Kline, R. B. (2004). *Beyond significance testing: Reforming data analysis methods in behavioral research.* Washington, DC: American Psychological Association.

Leventhal L., & Huynh, C. L. (1996). Directional decisions for two-tailed tests: Power, error rates, and sample size. *Psychological Methods, 1,* 278–293.

Mauchly, J. W. (1940). Significance test for sphericity of a normal n-variate distribution. *Annals of Mathematical Statistics, 11,* 204–209.

Rauscher, F. H., Shaw, G. L., & Ky, K. N. (1993). Music and spatial task performance. *Nature, 365,* 611.

Siegel, S., & Castellan, N. J., Jr. (1988). *Nonparametric statistics for the behavioral sciences* (2nd ed.). New York, NY: McGraw-Hill.

Tukey, J. W. (1977). *Exploratory data analysis.* Reading, MA: Addison-Wesley.

Index

A

Abbreviations, xxi–xxiii
Absolute values, 67, 514
Alpha, 126, 129, 140, 442. *See also*
    Criterion of significance
  Cronbach's, 235
  defined, 514
  experimentwise, 317
  familywise, 383–384
Alternative hypothesis, 514
  in null hypothesis testing,
    125–127, 130, 131
  tested by ANOVA, 318
American Psychological
    Association, 151, 171
Analysis of variance (ANOVA):
  defined, 317, 514
  factorial design (two-way),
    373–395
    computational procedures,
      374–384
    defined, 373
    F ratios, 380–381
    interactions, 374, 378,
      384–390
    mean squares, 378–380
    measuring effect size in,
      390–391
    multiple comparisons
      following, 381–383
    sum of squares, 376–378
    summary table, 327–328,
      381
    testing simple main effects,
      387–390
  general logic of, 318–321
  and Kruskal-Wallis *H* test,
    336–339

multiple comparisons, 334–335,
    350–368
  Bonferroni correction,
    363–364
  choosing test for, 362
  complex comparisons,
    364–365
  Fisher-Hayter test, 361–362
  Fisher's protected *t* test,
    351–356
  need for, 350–351
  Newman-Keuls test, 360
  planned comparisons,
    362–364
  protected rank-sum test,
    365–366
  Tukey's Honestly Significant
    Difference, 356–360
  Tukey's studentized range
    statistic, 356, 357
in null hypothesis testing,
    317–318, 326
one-way:
  assumptions, 333–334
  calculating from means and
    standard deviations,
    328–329
  comparing with *t* test,
    329–330
  computational procedures,
    321–326
  effect size for, 331–333
  for equal sample sizes,
    330–331
  general logic of, 318–321
  Kruskal-Wallis *H* test
    alternative to, 336–339
  mean squares, 325–326
  in null hypothesis testing, 326
  publishing results of, 334

Analysis of variance (ANOVA)
(*continued*)
significance of F ratio,
326–328
summary table, 328
sum of squares, 322–325
for three unequal-sized
groups, 335–336
underlying assumptions for,
333–334
repeated-measures, 403–428
assumptions, 408–411,
420–421
one-way, 403–415
two-way mixed, 415–423
Apparent limits, 33
frequency distributions,
33–34
and histograms, 40
A priori comparisons, 335, 514
Area of rejection, 128, 514
Areas under the normal curve, 92,
95–101
defined, 28
between the mean and z, 483
numerical value of, 92
table of standard normal
distribution, 93–95
Arithmetic mean, 58, 199, 517
Assumption(s):
ANOVA:
one-way, 333–334
one-way RM, 408–411
two-way mixed RM,
420–421
homogeneity of variance, 175,
334
of normal distribution, 133
of random samples, 133
sphericity, 409–410
test for mean of a single
population, 132–133
Average, 58, 166. *See also*
Mean(s)
Average deviation, 67

B

Bar charts (bar graphs), 39, 40,
514
Behavioral research, 10
Bell-shaped curve, 91, *See also*
Normal distribution (normal
curve)
Beta, 129, 514
Between-cell variability (RM
ANOVA), 413–414
Between groups sum of squares:
factorial design, 376–377
one-way ANOVA, 322–324
Between-group variance, 318–321,
514
Beyond Significance Testing
(Kline), 302
Biased standard deviation, 69–72
Biased variance, 68
Bimodal distributions, 44, 514
Binomial distribution, 438,
442–448
as alternative to matched-pairs
t test, 448–450
applications of, 447–448
defined, 438
for $N = 2$, 442–443
for $N = 6$, 443–444
simplified formula for $P = .5$,
448
testing null hypothesis with,
444–445, 447–448
using normal distribution as
approximation, 446–447
Bivariate normal distribution, 514
Bivariate outliers, 233–234
Block, 414
Bonferroni, Carlo, 363
Bonferroni correction, 363–365
and chi-square test, 462, 469
defined, 514
factorial design, 390
multiple comparisons, 371
RM ANOVA, 410, 433

C

Carryover effects, 185, 514
Categorical data, 8–10, 39, 195, 338, 438
Categorical levels, 56, 335
Categorical variables, 24, 219, 265, 414, 472, 479
Causality/causation, 10–11, 229–232
Cells, 373
Central Limit Theorem, 118, 133
Central tendency, 55, 514, *See also* Measures of central tendency
Chi-square approximation, 338
Chi-square distribution, 338, 348, 458, 460, 463, 479
Chi-square statistic, 458, 497
Chi-square tests, 458–474
  and binomial test, 462–464
  Cramér's phi coefficient, 472
  as goodness-of-fit test, 461–462
  one-way, 458–460
  phi coefficient for 2×2 tables, 470–472
  two-way, 464–469
    with multiple levels for both variables, 468–469
    for 2×2 table, 467–468
Class interval, 31, 515
Cohen, Jacob, 177, 287, 305, 331
Cohen's **d,** 177, 275, 302, 305, 515
College Entrance Examination Boards scores, 90, 123
Combinations, 444n.1
Complete counterbalancing, 412
Completely crossed designs, 373
Complex comparisons, 364–365, 515
Computing formulas, 69–72
Conditional probability, 442
Confidence intervals:
  defined, 515
  for difference between two population means, 172–174
  for matched sample mean difference scores, 181

for mean of a single population, 148–150
  95%, 160
  99%, 160
  and null hypothesis tests, 150–152
  for protected t test, 354–355
  for Tukey's HSD test, 358
Confidence limits, 149, 151, 515
Constants, 7
  added to the mean, 59
  defined, 7, 515
Content validity, 235
Continuous data, graphing, 39–40
Continuous variables, 515
Contrast, 515
Control group, 10, 133, 515
Correlation, 219–222. *See also* Linear correlation
  and bivariate outliers, 233–234
  and causation, 229–232
  and nonlinear relationships, 233
  point-biserial, 267–272
  and restriction of range, 232
  two-sample t test as special case of, 265–271
Correlation coefficient. *See also* Pearson's r
  defined, 515
  Glass rank biserial, 204–205
  point-biserial, 267–272
  population, 236
  Spearman rank-order correlation coefficient, 239–242, 250, 498
  testing significance of, 236–238
Counterbalancing, 183–184
  complete, 412
  defined, 515
  one-way RM ANOVA with, 422–423
Covariance, 226
Cramér's phi, 472, 515
Criterion, 256, 515
Criterion of significance, 125–126
  defined, 515
  delta as function of power and, 487

Criterion of significance
   (*continued*)
   .01, 128, 129
   in power analysis, 283
   power as function of delta and,
     486
Criterion validity, 236
Critical region, 128
Critical values, 126–129, 237
   of chi square, 497
   of *F*, 488–495
   of Pearson *r*, 485
   of Spearman rank-order
     correlation coefficient, 498
   of studentized range statistic,
     496
   of *t*, 484
Cronbach's alpha, 235
Cumulative frequencies, 30
Cumulative frequency
   distributions, 30–31, 515
Curvilinear relationship, 233
Cutoff scores, 127

D

d, 515. *See also* Cohen's **d**
Deciles, 38, 515
Definition formulas, 69–72, 252
Degrees of freedom, 144–148, 515
   chi-square test, 459, 463, 467,
     479
   factorial design, 375, 379–381
   linear correlation, 237, 239, 241
   one-way ANOVA, 321, 325, 326,
     338
   repeated measures ANOVA,
     406, 409, 418, 419, 424, 427
   t tests, 151, 168, 176, 181
   2 × 2 tables, 144–148
Delta, 284, 290–299
   defined, 296, 515
   as function of significance
     criterion and power, 487
   power as function of
     significance criterion and, 486

Dependent variables, 10, 11
   categorical, 438
   defined, 10, 256, 515
   linear regression, 256
Descriptive statistics, 5–6
   areas under the normal curve,
     92–101
     numerical value of, 92
     table of standard normal
       distribution, 93–95
   defined, 516
   frequency distributions, 28–43
   measures of central tendency,
     54–61
     defined, 55
     mean, 58–61
     median, 56–58
     mode, 56
     purpose of, 54–56
   purpose of, 27–28
   transformed (standardized)
     scores, 82–90
     IQ and SAT scores, 90
     rules for changing mean
      and standard deviation,
      84–85
     T scores, 89
     z scores, 85–88
   variability, 66–73
     average, 66
     concept of, 62–65
     measures of, 61
     in psychology, 64
     range, 65–66
     in sports, 63–64
     standard deviation and
      variance, 66–73
     in statistical inference, 65
     testing, 62–63
Deviation(s):
   of all scores, 67
   from the mean, 60, 66–67
   mean (average), 67
   from the median, 67
   of a single score, 66–67
   squaring, 67–68
Deviation score, 67, 516

Dichotomous data, 438
Dichotomous variable, 516
Difference between locations:
  of two independent samples,
    199–205
  of two matched samples,
    205–210
Difference between two
    population means, 161–187
  confidence intervals, 172–174
  measuring effect size, 176–178
  power analysis, 293–299
  standard error of the difference,
    162–167
  t test for:
    matched samples, 178–184
    two independent sample
      means, 167–172, 175–176
Differential carry-over effects, 185
Directional errors, 139–140
Directional test, 132. *See also*
    One-tailed test of significance
Discrete data, 39, 47, 51
Discrete events, 438
Discrete values, 61
Discrete variables, 219, 516
Disordinal interaction, 386
Distribution(s):
  binomial, 438, 442–448
  chi-square, 458
  F, 326–327, 380–381
  frequency, *see* Frequency
    distributions
  J-curve, 44–45
  Monte Carlo, 116n.1
  multinomial, 458
  noncentral *t*, 310–311
  normal, *see* Normal distribution
    (normal curve)
  rectangular, 44
  sampling, 114–119, 163–165
  standard normal, 93–95
  t, 144–148, 310–311
  theoretical, 91
  z, 147–148
Distribution-free statistical tests,
  195, 196, 516

E

Effect size. *See also* Population
    effect size
  defined, 516
  in factorial design, 390–391
  measuring two independent
    samples, 176–178
  for one-way ANOVA, 331–333
  and point-biserial correlation,
    268–269
  publishing, 272
  repeated-measures ANOVA, 411
Empirical sampling distribution,
  516
Errors:
  directional, 139–140
  experimentwise error rate, 317
  familywise (alpha) error rate,
    383, 516
  standard error of estimate,
    263–265
  Type I, 126, 139, 140
  Type II, 129, 139–141
  variance of, 263
Error term (ANOVA), 328, 408
Error variance, 166, 318–321, 516
Estimate(s):
  between-group variance,
    318–321
  interval, 114, 148–152
  point, 114
  pooled, 166
  of population variance, 68
  standard error of, 263–265
  of standard error of the
    difference, 166–167
  within-group variance, 318–321
Eta squared, 331–333, 339, 516
  ordinary, 390, 395
  partial, 391, 395
Experimental group, 317, 334, 516
Experimental research, 10
Experimental (empirical) sampling
    distribution, 116, 516
Experimentwise error rate, 317,
  516

F

F, critical values of, 488–495
Face validity, 235
Factors, 318, 373
Factorial design (two-way
    ANOVA), 373–395
  computational procedures,
    374–384
  defined, 373, 516
  familywise alpha, 383–384
  F ratios, 380–381
  interactions, 384–390
    comparing zero to, 384–385
    defined, 374
    sum of squares for, 378
    types of, 385–387
  mean squares, 378–380
  measuring effect size in,
    390–391
  multiple comparisons following,
    381–383
  sum of squares, 376–378
  testing simple main effects,
    387–390
Familywise (alpha) error rate,
    383–384, 516
F distributions:
  defined, 516
  factorial design, 380–381
  finding critical values, 326–327
  one-way ANOVA, 326–327
Fisher, Sir Ronald, 126, 351
Fisher-Hayter test, 361–362
Fisher's protected t test, 351–356,
    359, 360, 362. *See also* Least
    Significant Difference
F ratio:
  defined, 321
  factorial design, 380–382
  one-way ANOVA:
    reporting, 334
    significance of, 326–328
    in two-group case, 329
  RM ANOVA, 406
Frequency(-ies), 516
  on bar charts, 39

  marginal, 464
  of a score, 29
Frequency distributions:
  bimodal, 44
  computational procedures,
    35–38
  cumulative, 30–31
  defined, 28
  experimental sampling
    distribution, 116
  graphic representations of,
    39–43
  grouped, 31–33, 37–38
  interpreting raw scores, 34
  J-curve, 44–45
  normal, 44, 90–93
  percentile and percentile rank,
    34–35
  percentile values, 38–39
  real and apparent limits,
    33–34
  rectangular, 44
  regular, 28–30
  shapes of, 43–45
  skewed, 44
  symmetric, 43, 94
  unimodal, 44
Frequency polygons, 40–42, 516

G

Galton, Sir Francis, 254
Glass rank biserial correlation,
    204–205, 516
Goodness-of-fit, 461–462
Grade point average (GPA), 59,
    222–224
Graduate Record Examination
    scores, 90
Grand mean, 117–119, 319–320,
    322–323, 328–329, 340, 375,
    392
Graphs:
  bar charts (bar graphs), 39, 40
  of frequency distributions,
    39–43

frequency polygons, 40–42
histograms, 39–41
stem-and-leaf displays, 42–43
Grouped frequency distributions,
    31–33, 37–38, 516

H

Harmonic mean, 58
    defined, 518
    for more than two numbers,
        177–179, 358–359
Histograms, 39–41, 516
Homogeneity of variance (HOV)
        assumption:
    ANOVA, 334
    defined, 517
    t test, 175
Honestly Significant Difference
        (HSD), 356–362, 382, 410
    confidence intervals for, 358
    for unequal sample sizes,
        358–359
    use of, 362
HOV assumption, *see* Homogeneity
    of variance assumption
HSD, *see* Honestly Significant
    Difference
Hypothesis testing, 124–132
    ANOVA in, 317–318, 326
    with binomial distribution,
        444–445, 447–448
    and confidence intervals,
        150–152
    consequences of possible
        decisions, 129–130
    controversy over, 139–141,
        302–303
    criterion of significance,
        125–126
    critical values, 126–129
    defined, 517
    formation of alternative
        hypothesis, 125
    one- vs. two-tailed tests of
        significance, 130–132

power analysis in, 282–283,
    301–303
p values in, 123
statement of null hypothesis,
    124–125
t distribution for, 145–146
Type II error in, 282–283

I

Independent events, 441
Independent samples, 517
    difference between locations of,
        199–205
    power analysis of difference
        between means, 293–297
Independent variables, 10–11
    in ANOVA, 318, 373
    categorical, 438
    defined, 10, 256, 517
    linear regression, 256
Inferential statistics. *See also*
        Statistical inference
    assumptions for test of mean of
        a single population, 132–133
    defined, 113, 517
    difference between locations:
        of two independent samples,
            199–205
        of two matched samples,
            205–210
    difference between two
        population means, 161–187
        confidence intervals, 172–174
        measuring effect size,
            176–178
        standard error of the
            difference, 162–167
        t test for matched samples,
            178–184
        t test for two sample means,
            167–172, 175–176
    goals of, 114
    interval estimation, 148–152
    null hypothesis testing, 124–132
    power analysis, 282–306

Inferential statistics (*continued*)
  sampling distributions,
    114–119
  standard error of the mean,
    119–121
  t distributions, 144–148
    degrees of freedom, 144–145
    null hypothesis testing with,
      145–146
    and z distribution, 147–148
  variability in, 65
  z score for sample means,
    122–124
Interactions (factorial design),
  384–390
  comparing zero to, 384–385
  defined, 374, 517
  sum of squares for, 378
  types of, 385–387
Interquartile range, 66. *See also*
  Semi-interquartile range
Interrater reliability, 235
Interval estimates, 114, 148–152,
  517
Interval scales, 9–10
Interval size, 31
IQ scores, 90, 102

J

J-curve, 44–45, 517
Joint effects, 374, 375, 384
Joint frequencies, 479
Joint occurrence, 464

K

Kruskal-Wallis H test, 334,
  336–339, 517

L

Latin square, 412
Least Significant Difference (LSD),
  353–354, 359, 387

Least-squares regression line, 258,
  517
Likert, Rensis, 6
Likert scale, 6, 17, 335
Limits:
  apparent, 33–34, 40
  confidence, 149, 151, 515
  real, 33–34, 40
Linear correlation, 219–244
  computing formulas for r,
    225–229
  defined, 222
  describing, 222–223
  interpreting magnitude of
    Pearson's r, 229–234
  Pearson's correlation coefficient,
    224–225
  and reliability, 234–235
  Spearman rank-order correlation
    coefficient, 239–242
  testing significance of
    correlation coefficient,
    236–238
  and validity, 235–236
  z score product formula for r,
    223–225
Linear interpolation, 37
Linear regression, 254–272
  computational procedures,
    256–260
  defined, 254, 517
  predicting behavior with,
    254–262
  predicting X from Y, 262
  properties of, 260–262
  regression line, 257
  standard error of estimate,
    263–265
  t test and correlation, 265–271
  variance accounted for in
    population, 271–272
Line graphs, 40–41
Lower real limit, 47, 517
LSD (Least Significant Difference),
  353–354, 359

M

Main effects (factorial design), 375, 385
  simple, 387–390, 521
Mann-Whitney *U* test, 200, 203
Marginal frequency, 464, 517
Matched-pairs (MP) design, 184.
  See also Matched samples
Matched-pairs rank biserial
  correlation, 209–210, 517
Matched samples:
  defined, 517
  difference between locations of,
    205–210
  matched-pairs design, 184
  power analysis of difference
    between means, 297–299
  repeated-measures design,
    183–184
  sign test for, 448–450
  t test for, 178–183
Matched *t* test, 178–183
  binomial distribution as
    alternative to, 448–450
  defined, 517
  and one-way RM ANOVA,
    406–407
Mean(s), 58–61. *See also* Sample
    means
  arithmetic, 58, 199, 517
  computation, 58–59
  defined, 517–518
  difference between two
    population means, 161–187
  grand, 117–119, 319–320,
    322–323, 328–329, 340, 375,
    392
  harmonic, 58, 68, 177–179,
    358–359, 518
  population, 58, 68
  properties, 59–61
  rules for changing, 84–85
  sample, 115
    population means vs., 162
    variability of distribution of,
      119

z scores for, 122–124,
    132–133, 143
  sampling distribution of the,
    116
  in skewed distributions, 57
  standard error of, 119–121
  symbols for, 171
  usage, 58, 61
  weighted, 59
Mean deviation, 67, 73
Mean squares:
  defined, 325, 518
  factorial design, 375, 378–380
  one-way ANOVA, 325–326, 341
Measurement scales, 7–10
  interval/ratio, 9–10
  nominal, 7–8
  ordinal, 8
Measures of central tendency:
  defined, 28, 55
  mean, 58–61
  median, 56–58
  mode, 56
  purpose of, 54–56
Measures of variability, 28
  mean deviation, 67
  range, 65–66
  standard deviation and
    variance, 66–73
  standard error of the mean, 122
Median, 38–39, 56–58
  defined, 56, 518
  deviation from, 67
  properties, 57–58
  sampling distribution of the,
    116
  usage, 58
Meta-analysis, 300
Midpoint of a class interval, 37,
    42, 518
Mixed design ANOVA, 415–423
  assumptions, 420–421
  before-after case, 421–422
  calculating, 416–420
  follow-up tests, 421
Modality, 44
Mode, 44, 56, 57, 518

Monte Carlo distribution, 116n.1
Mozart effect, 303
Multinomial distribution, 458
Multiple comparisons (ANOVA),
    334–335, 350–368
  Bonferroni correction, 363–364
  choosing test for, 362
  complex comparisons, 364–365
  defined, 518
  Fisher-Hayter test, 361–362
  Fisher's protected t test,
    351–356
  following factorial design,
    381–383
  need for, 350–351
  Newman-Keuls test, 360
  planned comparisons, 362–364
  protected rank-sum test,
    365–366
  Tukey's Honestly Significant
    Difference, 356–360
Multi-sample sphericity, 420
Mutually exclusive events, 441,
    518

N

Negatively correlated variables,
    220
Negatively skewed distributions,
    57, 518
Newman-Keuls test, 360
Nominal scales, 7–8
Noncentral t distributions,
    310–311
Nondirectional hypotheses, 125
Nonlinear relationships,
    correlation and, 233
Nonparametric (statistical) tests:
  binomial distribution, 438,
    442–448
    as alternative to
      matched-pairs t test,
      448–450
    applications of, 447–448
    simplified formula for $P = .5$,
      448

testing null hypothesis with,
    444–445, 447–448
  using normal distribution as
    approximation, 446–447
  chi-square tests, 458–474
    and binomial test, 462–464
    as goodness-of-fit test,
      461–462
    one-way, 458–460
    two-way, 464–469
  defined, 195, 438, 518
  Kruskal-Wallis H test, 334,
    336–339
  parametric tests vs., 195
  protected rank-sum test,
    365–366
  rank-sum test, 199–205
  Spearman rank-order correlation
    coefficient, 239–242, 250
  Wilcoxon matched-pairs signed
    ranks test, 205–210
Normal curve table, 93–95, 483
Normal distribution (normal
    curve), 44, 90–93
  approximating binomial
    distribution, 446
  areas under, 92, 95–101
    defined, 28
    between the mean and z,
      483
    table of standard normal
      distribution, 93–95
  assumption of, 133
  bivariate, 514
  Central Limit Theorem, 118
  characteristics of, 94–95
  defined, 91, 518
  parameters of, 93
  theoretical, 118
Null experiment, 126, 129
Null hypothesis. *See also*
    Hypothesis testing
  for correlation, 236
  defined, 518
  for one-sample t test, 124–125
  for one-way chi-square test,
    459, 460

rejecting, 171
retaining, 171
statement of, 124–125
tested by ANOVA, 317–318
for two-sample t test, 167–168
for two-way chi-square test, 464, 465
and Type I and II errors, 139–141

O

Observational research, 10
Odds, 440, 518
Omnibus error term, 352
One-tailed p value, 126, 127
One-tailed test of significance, 127, 130–132, 518
One-way analysis of variance:
   calculating from means and standard deviations, 328–329
   comparing with t test, 329–330
   computational procedures, 321–326
   effect size for, 331–333
   for equal sample sizes, 330–331
   general logic of, 318–321
   Kruskal-Wallis H test alternative to, 336–339
   mean squares, 325–326
   in null hypothesis testing, 326
   publishing results of, 334
   significance of F ratio, 326–328
   summary table, 328
   sum of squares, 322–325
   for three unequal-sized groups, 335–336
   underlying assumptions for, 333–334
One-way chi-square tests, 458–460
One-way repeated measures ANOVA, 403–415
   advantages and disadvantages of, 412–415
   assumptions, 408–411

   with counterbalancing, 422–423
   effect size, 411
   error term, 408
   follow-up tests, 410
   power, 410–411
   problems with, 411–412
   sphericity assumption, 409–410
Order effects, simple:
   defined, 518
   one-way RM ANOVA, 422–423
   two repeated measures, 184
Order of operations, 13
Ordinal data, graphing, 40
Ordinal interaction, 386
Ordinal scales, 7, 8
Ordinal tests, 195–197
Ordinary eta squared, 390, 395
Outliers, bivariate, 233–234

P

Pairwise comparisons, 317, 334, 350, 351, 356, 360, 362, 364, 388, 410
Pairwise rank-sum tests, 365
Parameters, 6–7, 195, 518
Parametric statistics, 93, 199
Parametric tests:
   chi-square test as alternative to, 469
   nonparametric tests vs., 195
   power efficiency of, 196
   reasons for using, 196
Pearson, Karl, 224, 479
Pearson's r, 224–225
   applying to ranks, 239–240
   computing formulas for, 225–229
   critical values of, 485
   defined, 518
   equivalence of formulas for, 251–252
   interpreting magnitude of, 229–234
   phi coefficient and, 471, 472
   raw-score formula for, 226

Pearson's r (*continued*)
and reliability, 234–235
testing significance of, 237–236
and validity, 235–236
z score product formula for,
223–225
PEMDAS (order of operations),
13
Percentile(s), 34–35
computing raw scores from,
36–37, 46–47
defined, 34, 518
for frequency distributions,
34–35, 38–39
for grouped frequency
distributions, 37–38
for raw scores, 35–36, 46
Percentile rank(s), 34–35
defined, 34, 518
for frequency distributions,
34–35
for grouped frequency
distributions, 37–38
for raw scores, 35–36
Permutations, 444n.1
Phi coefficient, 470–472, 519
Planned (a *priori*) comparisons,
362–364, 514
Point-biserial correlation
coefficient, 267–272
defined, 519
and effect size, 268–269
and the t test, 267–268
variance accounted for by
grouping variable, 269–271
variance accounted for in
population, 271–272
Point estimate, 114, 172, 519
Pooled variance, 166, 519
Pooled-variances t test, 169, 176
Population:
defined, 519
proportion of variance
accounted for in, 271–272
Population correlation coefficient,
236
Population effect size, 177

difference between means:
independent means, 294–297
of two matched populations,
298–299
estimating from previous
research, 299–300
power analysis, 283–284,
299–301
and sample size, 302
trying extreme values for,
300–301
Population mean(s), 58
confidence interval for,
144–147
difference between two,
161–187
confidence intervals,
172–174
independent means, 294–297
measuring effect size,
176–178
power analysis, 293–299
standard error of the
difference, 162–167
t test for, 167–172, 175–176,
178–184
sample means vs., 162
Population variance estimate, 68,
519
Positively correlated variables,
220
Positively skewed distributions,
57, 519
Post hoc comparisons, 335,
349–362, 519. *See also*
Pairwise comparisons
Power analysis, 282–306
concepts of, 283–285
difference between means:
independent means,
293–297
of two matched populations,
297–299
in interpreting null hypothesis
tests, 301–303
repeated-measures ANOVA,
410–411

significance:
    of mean of a single
        population, 285–290
    of Pearson r, 292–293
    of proportion of a single
        population, 290–292
    value for **d** with independent
        means, 299–301
Power efficiency, 196–197, 519
Power of a statistical test, 519
Power tables:
    delta as a function of
        significance criterion and, 487
    as function of delta and
        significance criterion, 486
Predicted score, 256–260, 519
Prediction. *See also* Linear
        regression
    errors in, 257
    standard error of estimate,
        263–265
Predictor, 256, 519
Probability, 99, 105, 439–442
    binomial distribution and,
        442–448
    conditional, 442
    defined, 439, 519
    of either of two events, 440–441
    odds, 440
    of two independent events, 441
Proportion(s), 152
    of single population,
        significance of, 290–292
    standard error of, 152–154
    of variance:
        accounted for by grouping
            variable, 269–271
        accounted for in population,
            271–272
    z score for, 152–153, 446–447
Protected rank-sum test, 365–366
Protected t test, 351–356
    confidence intervals for,
        354–355
    defined, 519
    problems with, 355–356
    use of, 359, 360, 362

Psychology, variability in, 64
p values, 123, 126
    exact, 148, 363, 447
    one-tailed, 126, 127
    two-tailed, 126–127

Q

Qualitative data:
    defined, 8
    quantitative data vs., 9–10
Quantitative data:
    defined, 8
    qualitative data vs., 9–10
Quartiles, 38, 519
Quasi-independent variables, 10

R

Random assignment, 162, 230
Randomized-blocks (RB) design,
        403, 411, 415, 520
Random samples:
    assumption of, 133
    defined, 116, 519
Range, 65–66
    defined, 65, 520
    interquartile, 66
    restriction of, 232
    semi-interquartile, 65–66
    studentized range statistic, 356,
        357, 496
Ranks:
    applying Pearson r to, 239–240
    dealing with data in the form of,
        197–198
    defined, 520
    Kruskal-Wallis H test, 336–339
    tied, 198–199, 241
Rank-sum test, 199–205
    defined, 520
    Glass rank biserial correlation
        coefficient, 204–205
    interpreting results of, 203–204
    steps in, 200–203

Ratio scales, 9–10
Raw scores:
  computed from percentiles,
    36–37, 46–47
  computing percentile ranks for,
    35–36, 46
  converting to IQ scores, 90
  converting to SAT scores, 90
  converting to T scores, 89
  converting to z scores, 86–87,
    223–224
  defined, 34, 520
  inferential statistics and,
    119–121
  interpreting, 34, 82–84
  linear regression, 261–262
  for Pearson r, 226
Real limits:
  defined, 33
  frequency distributions, 33–34
  on histograms, 40
  lower, 47, 517
  upper, 46, 522
Rectangular distributions, 44, 520
Regression line:
  "best-fit," 259
  defined, 254
  least-squares, 258
  predicting scores with, 256–257
Regular frequency distributions,
  28–30, 520
Regular frequency polygons,
  41–42
Reliability, Pearson's r and,
  234–235
Repeated-measures ANOVA,
  403–428
  defined, 520
  one-way, 403–415
    advantages and disadvantages
      of, 412–415
    assumptions, 408–411
    with counterbalancing,
      422–423
    effect size, 411
    error term, 408
    follow-up tests, 410

  power, 410–411
  problems with, 411–412
  sphericity assumption,
    409–410
  two-way mixed, 415–423
    assumptions, 420–421
    before-after case, 421–422
    calculating, 416–420
    follow-up tests, 421
Repeated-measures (RM) design,
  183–184, 411–412
Replications, 172
Research, behavioral, 10
Residual scores, 257
Restriction of range, 232, 520
Retest reliability, 235
RM (repeated-measures) design,
  183–184, 411–412
Robust statistics, 196, 242, 520

S

Sample(s):
  defined, 6, 520
  matched:
    defined, 517
    difference between locations
      of, 205–210
    matched-pairs design, 184
    repeated-measures design,
      183–184
    sign test for, 448–450
  random, 116
    assumption of, 133
    defined, 116, 519
Sample effect size, 177
Sample means, 115
  population means vs., 162
  standard error of the mean,
    119–121
  two, t test for, 167–172
  variability of distribution of, 119
  z scores for, 122–124, 132–133,
    143
Sample size:
  defined, 520

and interpreting statistical
   significance, 302
one-way ANOVA:
   for equal sample sizes,
      330–331
   for unequal-sized groups,
      335–336
power analysis, 283
   difference between
      independent means, 297
   difference between means of
      two matched populations,
      299
   significance of a Pearson r,
      293
   significance of proportion of a
      single population, 291–292
   significance test of mean of a
      single population, 289–290
unequal, Tukey's HSD for,
   358–359
Sample variance, 68
Sampling distribution(s), 114–119
   of differences between two
      means, 163–165
   experimental, 116
   of the mean, 116
   of means drawn from one
      population, 144
   of the median, 116
   theoretical, 117
Sampling error, 120, 126,
   162–163, 166, 174, 236, 319,
   333, 385, 458
SAT scores, see Scholastic
   Aptitude Test scores
Scatter plots, 220, 520
Scheffé test, 364
Scholastic Aptitude Test (SAT)
   scores, 90, 95–101, 123–124,
   222–228
Score values (bar charts), 39
Semi-interquartile range, 65–66
Separate-variances t test, 176
Signed-ranks test, see Wilcoxon
   matched-pairs signed ranks
   test

Significance. See also Hypothesis
   testing
   criterion of (see Criterion of
      significance)
   for an interaction in a factorial
      design, 387–390
   for the mean of a single
      population, 146
   for Pearson r, 236–237
   statistical vs. practical, 172
Significance tests:
   defined, 520
   one-tailed, 127, 130–132, 518
   two-tailed, 126–127, 130–132,
      522
Sign test:
   defined, 520
   for matched samples, 448–450
Simple main effects, 387–390, 521
Simple order effects, 185
Skewed distributions, 44, 57, 521
Slope, 220, 256, 259, 262, 265, 521
Spearman rank-order correlation
   coefficient, 239–242, 250,
   498, 521
Sphericity assumption, 409–410,
   420–421, 521
Split-half reliability, 235
Sports, variability in, 63–64
Spot card, 439
SPSS, 24
   ANOVA:
      factorial design, 399–401
      multiple comparisons, 371
      one-way, 346–347
      repeated measures, 431–433
   areas under normal distribution,
      107–108
   binomial test, 454–455
   chi-square test:
      one-way, 478–479
      two-way, 479–480
   frequency distributions, 50–52
   independent-samples t test,
      191–192
   Kruskal-Wallis H test, 347–348
   linear correlation, 249–250

SPSS (*continued*)

   linear regression, 278–280

   matched-pairs *t* test, 192–193

   measures of central tendency, 78–80

   one-sample *t* test, 158–159

   point-biserial correlation, 280

   power analysis, 310–311

   p values from normal distributions, 138–139

   rank-sum test, 216–217

   sign test for matched samples, 455–456

   Spearman rank-order correlation coefficient, 250

   using Syntax window, 250–251

   variability, 78–80

   Variable View spreadsheet, 24–25

   Wilcoxon (signed ranks) test, 217

   z scores, 106–107

Standard deviation, 68–69

   biased and unbiased, 69–72

   calculating one-way ANOVA from mean and, 328–329

   defined, 68, 521

   definitional and computing formulas for, 69–72

   properties, 72–73

   rules for changing, 84–85

Standard error:

   defined, 120, 521

   of the difference, 162–167

   of estimate, 263–265, 521

   of the mean, 119–121

   of a proportion, 152–154

   of *T*, 198, 207

Standardized scores, *see* Transformed scores

Standard normal distribution, 93–95

Standard scores, 521. *See also* *z* scores

Stanford-Binet test, 90

Statistic (term), 6, 521

Statistics:

   descriptive, 5–6, 27–28

   inferential, 6

   measurement scales, 7–10

   parametric, 93

   purpose of, 5–6

   reasons for studying, 4–5

   summation notation, 12–16

   variables, 10–11

Statistical inference, 113. *See also* Inferential statistics

   goals of inferential statistics, 114

   null hypothesis testing, 124–132

   sampling distributions, 114–119

   standard error of the mean, 119–121

   variability in, 65

   z score for sample means, 122–124

Statistical model, 521

Statistical significance, 126, 172, 237. *See also* Significance

   defined, 521

   of *F* ratio, 326–328

   and sample size, 302

   and truth of null hypothesis, 301

Statistical tests:

   parametric vs. nonparametric, 195

   power efficiency of, 196–197

Stem-and-leaf displays, 42–43, 521

Studentized range statistic, 356, 357, 496

Summary table (ANOVA), 327–328, 381

Summation notation, 12–16

Summation rules, 12–16

Summation sign, 12, 521

Sum of squares, 68

   defined, 68, 521

   errors in prediction, 258

   factorial design, 376–378

   one-way ANOVA, 322–325

Symbols, xxi–xxiii

Symmetric distributions, 43, 94, 522

Syntax window (SPSS), 250, 400

T

t, critical values of, 237, 484
t distributions, 144–148
  defined, 144, 522
  degrees of freedom, 144–145
  noncentral, 310–311
  null hypothesis testing with,
    145–146, 170
  and *z* distribution, 147–148
Test–retest reliability, 235
Theoretical distributions, 91
Theoretical sampling distributions,
  117, 522
Tied ranks, 198–199, 241
Total population, 92
Total sum of squares:
  factorial design, 376
  one-way ANOVA, 322–323,
    348
Transformed (standardized)
  scores, 82–84
  defined, 28, 522
  IQ scores, 90
  rules for changing mean
    and standard deviation,
    84–85
  SAT scores, 90
  T scores, 89, 522
  z scores, 85–88
Treatment-by-block design,
  414–415
T scores, 89, 522
t test:
  and correlation, 265–271
  interpreting results of,
    171–172
  for matched samples, *see*
    Matched *t* test
  and one-way ANOVA,
    329–330
  and point-biserial correlation,
    267–268
  pooled-variances, 169, 176
  reporting results of, 170–171
  separate-variances, 176

  for two sample means,
    167–172, 175–176
Tukey, J. W., 356
  Honestly Significant Difference,
    356–360, 362, 382–410
  stem-and-leaf display, 42
  studentized range statistic,
    356–357
Two-sample *t* test, 265–271
  point-biserial correlation
    coefficient, 267–269
  proportion of variance
    accounted for by grouping
    variable, 269–271
Two-tailed *p* value, 126–127
Two-tailed test of significance,
  126–127, 130–132, 522
Two-way ANOVA. *See* Factorial
  design (two-way ANOVA)
Two-way chi-square tests,
  464–469
  for 2 × 2 table, 467–468
  with multiple levels for both
    variables, 468–469
Two-way mixed design ANOVA,
  415–423
  assumptions, 420–421
  before-after case, 421–422
  calculating, 416–420
  follow-up tests, 421
Type I error, 139, 140
  defined, 126, 522
  experimentwise error rate, 317
Type II error, 129, 139–141
  defined, 522
  familywise error rate, 383–384,
    516
  and power analysis, 282–283

U

Unbiased standard deviation,
  69–72
Unbiased variance, 68
Unimodal distributions, 44, 522
Upper real limit, 46, 522

V

Validity:
   criterion, 236
   and Pearson's r, 235–236
Values:
   absolute, 67, 514
   critical, 126–129, 237
      of chi square, 497
      of F, 488–495
      of Pearson r, 485
      of Spearman rank-order
         correlation coefficient, 498
      of studentized range statistic,
         496
      of t, 484
Variability, 61, 62
   average, 66
   between-cell, 413–414
   concept of, 62–65
   defined, 56, 62, 522
   of distribution of sample means,
      119
   measures of, 28, 61
   in psychology, 64
   range, 65–66
   in sports, 63–64
   standard deviation and
      variance, 66–73
   standard error of the mean, 122
   in statistical inference, 65
   testing, 62–63
   within-group, 413
Variables:
   categorical, 265, 438
   continuous, 515
   correlation of, 219–222
   defined, 7, 516, 522
   dependent, 10, 11, 256, 515
   dichotomous, 516
   discrete, 516
   independent, 10–11, 256, 318,
      373, 438, 517
   negatively correlated, 220
   positively correlated, 220
   quasi-independent, 10

scales measuring vs.
      characteristics of, 8
Variance, 68. *See also* Analysis of
      variance (ANOVA)
   accounted for by a correlation,
      264–265
   accounted for by a grouping
      variable, 269–271
   accounted for in population,
      271–272
   between-group, 318–321, 514
   biased, 68
   defined, 68, 522
   error, 516
   of errors, 263
   homogeneity of variance
      assumption, 175, 334
   pooled, 166, 169, 176, 519
   population, 68
   proportion of, 269–272
   sample, 68
   unbiased, 68
   within-group, 318–321, 522

W

Wechsler Adult Intelligence Scale
   (WAIS), 90
Weighted mean (also weighted
   average), 59, 166
Wilcoxon matched-pairs signed
   ranks test, 205–210
   defined, 522
   matched-pairs rank biserial
      correlation, 209–210
   rationale and computational
      procedures, 205–209
   sign test, 209
Within-group (error) variance,
   318–321, 522
Within groups sum of squares:
   factorial design, 377
   one-way ANOVA, 322, 324–325
Within-group variability (RM
   ANOVA), 413

Y

Y- intercept, 256, 259, 522

Z

z distribution, *t* distribution and, 147–148
z scores (standard scores), 85–88
  advantages of, 85–86
  converting raw scores to, 86–87, 223–224

converting SAT scores to, 95–101
critical values, 127–129
defined, 522
disadvantages of, 88–89
and normal curve table, 93–95
and normal distribution, 90–91
for proportions, 446–447
for rank-sum test, 202
for sample means, 122–124, 132–133, 143
for signed-ranks test, 208
and shape of distribution, 90–91
z test, 143, 144